Instructor's Solutions Manual

for

Calculus for the Managerial, Life and Social Sciences

Seventh Edition

S. T. Tan
Stonehill College

THOMSON
BROOKS/COLE

Australia • Canada • Mexico • Singapore • Spain • United Kingdom • United States

CONTENTS

CHAPTER 5   EXPONENTIAL AND LOGARITHMIC FUNCTIONS

CHAPTER 6   INTEGRATION

CHAPTER 7   ADDITIONAL TOPICS IN INTEGRATION

CHAPTER 8   CALCULUS OF SEVERAL VARIABLES

CHAPTER 1

EXERCISES 1.1, page 9

1. The statement is false because -3 is greater than -20. (See the number line that follows).

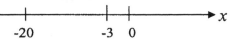

2. The statement is true because -5 is equal to -5.

3. The statement is false because 2/3 [which is equal to (4/6)] is less than 5/6.

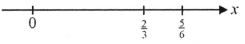

4. The statement is false because -5/6 (which is -10/12) is greater than -11/12.

5. The interval (3,6) is shown on the number line that follows. Note that this is an open interval indicated by (and).

6. The interval (-2,5] is shown on the number line that follows.

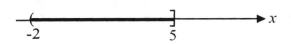

7. The interval [-1,4) is shown on the number line that follows. Note that this is a half-open interval indicated by [(closed) and) (open).

8. The closed interval [-6/5, -1/2] is shown on the number line that follows.

1 Preliminaries

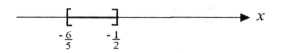

9. The infinite interval $(0,\infty)$ is shown on the number line that follows.

10. The infinite interval $(-\infty,5]$ is shown on the figure that follows.

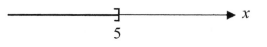

11. First, $2x + 4 < 8$

    Next, $2x < 4$ (Add -4 to each side of the inequality.)

    and $x < 2.$ (Multiply each side of the inequality by 1/2)

    We write this in interval notation as $(-\infty,2)$.

12. $-6 > 4 + 5x \Rightarrow -6 - 4 > 5x \Rightarrow -10 > 5x \Rightarrow -2 > x$ or $x < -2.$
    We write this in interval notation as $(-\infty,-2)$.

13. We are given the inequality $-4x \geq 20$.

    Then $x \leq -5.$ (Multiply both sides of the inequality by -1/4
                                  and reverse the sign of the inequality.)

    We write this in interval notation as $(-\infty,-5]$.

14. $-12 \leq -3x \Rightarrow 4 \geq x$, or $x \leq 4$. We write this in interval notation as $(-\infty,4]$.

15. We are given the inequality $-6 < x - 2 < 4$.

    First $-6 + 2 < x < 4 + 2$ (Add +2 to each member of the inequality.)

    and $-4 < x < 6,$

    so the solution set is the open interval $(-4,6)$.

16. We add -1 to each member of the given double inequality $0 \leq x + 1 \leq 4$ to obtain
$$-1 \leq x \leq 3,$$
    and the solution set is $[-1,3]$.

17. We want to find the values of x that satisfy the inequalities
$$x + 1 > 4 \text{ or } x + 2 < -1.$$
Adding -1 to both sides of the first inequality, we obtain
$$x + 1 - 1 > 4 - 1,$$
or $x > 3.$

Similarly, adding -2 to both sides of the second inequality, we obtain
$$x + 2 - 2 < -1 - 2,$$
or $x < -3$

Therefore, the solution set is $(-\infty, -3) \cup (3, \infty)$.

18. We want to find the values of x that satisfy the inequalities
$$x + 1 > 2 \text{ or } x - 1 < -2.$$
Solving these inequalities, we find that
$$x > 1 \text{ or } x < -1,$$
and the solution set is $(-\infty, -1) \cup (1, \infty)$.

19. We want to find the values of x that satisfy the inequalities
$$x + 3 > 1 \text{ and } x - 2 < 1.$$
Adding -3 to both sides of the first inequality, we obtain
$$x + 3 - 3 > 1 - 3,$$
or $x > -2.$

Similarly, adding 2 to each side of the second inequality, we obtain
$$x - 2 + 2 < 1 + 2, \text{ or } x < 3$$
Since both inequalities must be satisfied, the solution set is $(-2, 3)$.

20. We want to find the values of x that satisfy the inequalities
$$x - 4 \leq 1 \text{ and } x + 3 > 2.$$
Solving these inequalities, we find that $x \leq 5$ and $x > -1$, and the solution set is $(-1, 5]$.

21. $|-6 + 2| = 4.$
22. $4 + |-4| = 4 + 4 = 8.$

23. $\dfrac{|-12 + 4|}{|16 - 12|} = \dfrac{|-8|}{|4|} = 2.$
24. $\dfrac{|0.2 - 1.4|}{|1.6 - 2.4|} = \dfrac{|-1.2|}{|-0.8|} = 1.5$

25. $\sqrt{3}|-2| + 3|-\sqrt{3}| = \sqrt{3}(2) + 3\sqrt{3} = 5\sqrt{3}.$
26. $|-1| + |\sqrt{2}|-2| = 1 + 2\sqrt{2}.$

27. $|\pi - 1| + 2 = \pi - 1 + 2 = \pi + 1.$

28. $|\pi - 6| - 3 = 6 - \pi - 3 = 3 - \pi.$

29. $|\sqrt{2} - 1| + |3 - \sqrt{2}| = \sqrt{2} - 1 + 3 - \sqrt{2} = 2.$

30. $|2\sqrt{3} - 3| - |\sqrt{3} - 4| = 2\sqrt{3} - 3 - (4 - \sqrt{3}) = 3\sqrt{3} - 7$

31 False. If $a > b$, then $-a < -b$, $-a + b < -b + b$, and $b - a < 0$.

32. False. Let $a = -2$ and $b = -3$. Then $a/b = -2/-3 < 1$.

33. False. Let $a = -2$ and $b = -3$. Then $a^2 = 4$ and $b^2 = 9$, and $4 < 9$. Note that we only need to provide a counterexample to show that the statement is not always true.

34. False. Let $a = -2$ and $b = -3$. Then $1/a = -1/2$ and $1/b = -1/3$ and $-1/2 < -1/3$

35. True. There are three possible cases.

   Case 1 If $a > 0$, $b > 0$, then $a^3 > b^3$, since $a^3 - b^3 = (a - b)(a^2 + ab + b^2) > 0.$

   Case 2 If $a > 0$, $b < 0$, then $a^3 > 0$ and $b^3 < 0$ and it follows that $a^3 > b^3$

   Case 3 If $a < 0$ and $b < 0$, then $a^3 - b^3 = (a - b)(a^2 + ab + b^2) > 0$, and we see that $a^3 > b^3$. (Note that $(a - b) > 0$ and $ab > 0$.)

36. True. If $a > b$, then it follows that $-a < -b$ because an inequality symbol is reversed when both sides of the inequality are multiplied by a negative number.

37. False. Take $a = -2$, then $|-a| = |-(-2)| = |2| = 2 \neq a.$

38. True. If $b < 0$, then $b^2 > 0$, and $|b^2| = b^2$

39 True. If $a - 4 < 0$, then $|a - 4| = 4 - a = |4 - a|$. If $a - 4 > 0$, then
$$|4 - a| = a - 4 = |a - 4|.$$

40. False. Let $a = -2$, then $|a + 1| = |-2 + 1| = |-1| = 1 \neq |-2| + 1 = 3.$

1 Preliminaries   4

41. False. Take $a = 3$, $b = -1$. Then $|a + b| = |3 - 1| = 2 \neq |a| + |b| = 3 + 1 = 4$.

42. False. Take $a = 3$, $b = -1$. Then $|a - b| = 4 \neq |a| - |b| = 3 - (1) = 2$.

43. $27^{2/3} = (3^3)^{2/3} = 3^2 = 9$.

44. $8^{-4/3} = \left(\dfrac{1}{8^{4/3}}\right) = \dfrac{1}{2^4} = \dfrac{1}{16}$

45. $\left(\dfrac{1}{\sqrt{3}}\right)^0 = 1$. Recall that any number raised to the zero power is 1.

46. $(7^{1/2})^4 = 7^{4/2} = 7^2 = 49$

47. $\left[\left(\dfrac{1}{8}\right)^{1/3}\right]^{-2} = \left(\dfrac{1}{2}\right)^{-2} = (2^2) = 4$.

48. $\left[\left(-\dfrac{1}{3}\right)^2\right]^{-3} = \left(\dfrac{1}{9}\right)^{-3} = (9)^3 = 729$

49. $\left(\dfrac{7^{-5} \cdot 7^2}{7^{-2}}\right)^{-1} = (7^{-5+2+2})^{-1} = (7^{-1})^{-1} = 7^1 = 7$.

50. $\left(\dfrac{9}{16}\right)^{-1/2} = \left(\dfrac{16}{9}\right)^{1/2} = \dfrac{4}{3}$

51. $(125^{2/3})^{-1/2} = 125^{(2/3)(-1/2)} = 125^{-1/3} = \dfrac{1}{125^{1/3}} = \dfrac{1}{5}$

52. $\sqrt[3]{2^6} = (2^6)^{1/3} = 2^{6(1/3)} = 2^2 = 4$.

53. $\dfrac{\sqrt{32}}{\sqrt{8}} = \sqrt{\dfrac{32}{8}} = \sqrt{4} = 2$.

54. $\sqrt[3]{\dfrac{-8}{27}} = \dfrac{\sqrt[3]{-8}}{\sqrt[3]{27}} = -\dfrac{2}{3}$

55. $\dfrac{16^{5/8}16^{1/2}}{16^{7/8}} = 16^{(5/8+1/2-7/8)} = 16^{1/4} = 2.$

56. $\left(\dfrac{9^{-3} \cdot 9^5}{9^{-2}}\right)^{-1/2} = 9^{(-3+5+2)(-1/2)} = 9^{(4)(-1/2)} = \dfrac{1}{81}$

57 $16^{1/4} \cdot 8^{-1/3} = 2 \cdot \left(\dfrac{1}{8}\right)^{1/3} = 2 \cdot \dfrac{1}{2} = 1.$

58. $\dfrac{6^{2.5} \cdot 6^{-1.9}}{6^{-1.4}} = 6^{2.5-1.9-(-1.4)} = 6^{2.5-1.9+1.4} = 6^2 = 36.$
$6^{-1.4}$

59. True.

60. True. $3^2 \times 2^2 = (3 \times 2)^2 = 6^2 = 36.$

61. False. $x^3 \times 2x^2 = 2x^{3+2} = 2x^5 \neq 2x^6.$

62. False. $3^3 + 3 = 27 + 3 = 30 \neq 3^4$

63. False. $\dfrac{2^{4x}}{1^{3x}} = \dfrac{2^{4x}}{1} = 2^{4x}$

64. True. $(2^2 \times 3^2)^2 = (4 \times 9)^2 = (36)^2 = (6^2)^2 = 6^4.$

65. False. $\dfrac{1}{4^{-3}} = 4^3 = 64.$

66. True. $\dfrac{4^{3/2}}{2^4} = \dfrac{8}{16} = \dfrac{1}{2}$

67. False. $(1.2^{1/2})^{-1/2} = (1.2)^{-1/4} \neq 1.$

68. True. $5^{2/3} \times (25)^{2/3} = 5^{2/3}(5^2)^{2/3} = 5^{2/3} \times 5^{4/3} = 5^2 = 25$

69 $(xy)^{-2} = \dfrac{1}{(xy)^2}.$

70. $3s^{1/3} \cdot s^{-7/3} = 3s^{(1/3)-(7/3)} = 3s^{-6/3} = 3s^{-2} = \dfrac{3}{s^2}$

71 $\dfrac{x^{-1/3}}{x^{1/2}} = x^{(-1/3)-(1/2)} = x^{-5/6} = \dfrac{1}{x^{5/6}}.$

72. $\sqrt{x^{-1}}\ \sqrt{9x^{-3}} = x^{-1/2} \cdot 3x^{-3/2} = 3x^{(-1/2)+(-3/2)} = 3x^{-2} = \dfrac{3}{x^2}$

73. $12^0(s+t)^{-3} = 1 \cdot \dfrac{1}{(s+t)^3} = \dfrac{1}{(s+t)^3}.$

74. $(x-y)(x^{-1}+y^{-1}) = (x-y)\left(\dfrac{1}{x}+\dfrac{1}{y}\right) = (x-y)\left(\dfrac{y+x}{xy}\right) = \dfrac{(x-y)(x+y)}{xy} = \dfrac{x^2-y^2}{xy}$

75. $\dfrac{x^{7/3}}{x^{-2}} = x^{(7/3)+2} = x^{(7/3)+(6/3)} = x^{13/3}$

76. $(49x^{-2})^{-1/2} = (49)^{-1/2}\,x^{(-2)(-1/2)} = \dfrac{1}{7}x.$

77. $(x^2 y^{-3})(x^{-5}y^3) = (x^{2-5}y^{-3+3}) = x^{-3}y^0 = x^{-3} = \dfrac{1}{x^3}$

78. $\dfrac{5x^6 y^3}{2x^2 y^7} = \dfrac{5}{2}x^{6-2}y^{3-7} = \dfrac{5}{2}x^4 y^{-4} = \dfrac{5x^4}{2y^4}$

79. $\dfrac{x^{3/4}}{x^{-1/4}} = x^{(3/4)-(-1/4)} = x^{4/4} = x.$

80. $\left(\dfrac{x^3 y^2}{z^2}\right)^2 = \dfrac{x^{3(2)}y^{2(2)}}{z^{2(2)}} = \dfrac{x^6 y^4}{z^4}$

81. $\left(\dfrac{x^3}{-27y^{-6}}\right)^{-2/3} = x^{3(-2/3)}\left(-\dfrac{1}{27}\right)^{-2/3}y^{6(-2/3)} = x^{-2}\left(-\dfrac{1}{3}\right)^{-2}y^{-4} = \dfrac{9}{x^2 y^4}$

82. $\left(\dfrac{e^x}{e^{x-2}}\right)^{-1/2} = e^{[x-(x-2)](-1/2)} = e^{-1} = \dfrac{1}{e}.$

83. $\left(\dfrac{x^{-3}}{y^{-2}}\right)^2\left(\dfrac{y}{x}\right)^4 = \dfrac{x^{-3(2)}y^4}{y^{-2(2)}x^4} = \left(\dfrac{y^{4+4}}{x^{4+6}}\right) = \dfrac{y^8}{x^{10}}$

84. $\dfrac{(r^n)^4}{r^{5-2n}} = r^{4n-(5-2n)} = r^{4n+2n-5} = r^{6n-5}.$

85. $\sqrt[3]{x^{-2}}\ \sqrt{4x^5} = x^{-2/3}\cdot 4^{1/2}\cdot x^{5/2} = x^{-(2/3)+(5/2)}\cdot 2 = 2x^{11/6}$

86. $\sqrt{81x^6 y^{-4}} = (81)^{1/2}\cdot x^{6/2}\cdot y^{-4/2} = \dfrac{9x^3}{y^2}$

87. $-\sqrt[4]{16x^4 y^8} = -(16^{1/4}\cdot x^{4/4}\cdot y^{8/4}) = -2xy^2$

88. $\sqrt[3]{x^{3a+b}} = x^{(3a+b)(1/3)} = x^{a+(b/3)}$

89. $\sqrt[6]{64x^8 y^3} = (64)^{1/6}\cdot x^{8/6} y^{3/6} = 2x^{4/3} y^{1/2}$

90. $\sqrt[3]{27r^6}\cdot\sqrt{s^2 t^4} = (27)^{1/3}(r^6)^{1/3}(s^2)^{1/2}(t^4)^{1/2} = 3r^2 st^2.$

91. $2^{3/2} = (2)(2^{1/2}) = 2(1.414) = 2.828.$ 92. $8^{1/2} = (2^3)^{1/2} = 2^{3/2} = 2(2^{1/2}) = 2.828.$

93. $9^{3/4} = (3^2)^{3/4} = 3^{6/4} = 3^{3/2} = 3\ 3^{1/2} = 3(1\ 732) = 5\ 196.$

94. $6^{1/2} = (2\cdot 3)^{1/2} = 2^{1/2}\cdot 3^{1/2} = (1.414)(1.732) = 2.449$

95 $10^{3/2} = 10^{1/2}\cdot 10 = (3.162)(10) = 31.62.$

96. $1000^{3/2} = (10^3)^{3/2} = 10^{9/2} = 10^4\times 10^{1/2} = (10000)(3\ 162) = 31{,}620.$

97. $10^{2.5} = 10^2\cdot 10^{1/2} = 100(3\ 162) = 316.2.$

98. $(0.0001)^{-1/3} = (10^{-4})^{-1/3} = 10^{4/3} = 10\cdot 10^{1/3} = 10(2.154) = 21.54.$

99 $\dfrac{3}{2\sqrt{x}}\cdot\dfrac{\sqrt{x}}{\sqrt{x}} = \dfrac{3\sqrt{x}}{2x}.$

100. $\dfrac{3}{\sqrt{xy}}\cdot\dfrac{\sqrt{xy}}{\sqrt{xy}} = \dfrac{3\sqrt{xy}}{xy}$

101. $\dfrac{2y}{\sqrt{3y}}\cdot\dfrac{\sqrt{3y}}{\sqrt{3y}} = \dfrac{2y\sqrt{3y}}{3y} = \dfrac{2}{3}\sqrt{3y}$

102. $\dfrac{5x^2}{\sqrt{3x}}\cdot\dfrac{\sqrt{3x}}{\sqrt{3x}} = \dfrac{5x^2\sqrt{3x}}{3x} = \dfrac{5x}{3}\sqrt{3x}$

103 $\dfrac{1}{\sqrt[3]{x}}\cdot\dfrac{\sqrt[3]{x^2}}{\sqrt[3]{x^2}} = \dfrac{\sqrt[3]{x^2}}{\sqrt[3]{x^3}} = \dfrac{\sqrt[3]{x^2}}{x}.$

104. $\sqrt{\dfrac{2x}{y}} = \dfrac{\sqrt{2x}}{\sqrt{y}}\cdot\dfrac{\sqrt{y}}{\sqrt{y}} = \dfrac{\sqrt{2xy}}{y}$

105. $\dfrac{2\sqrt{x}}{3} \cdot \dfrac{\sqrt{x}}{\sqrt{x}} = \dfrac{2x}{3\sqrt{x}}.$

106. $\dfrac{\sqrt[3]{x}}{24} \cdot \dfrac{\sqrt[3]{x^2}}{\sqrt[3]{x^2}} = \dfrac{x}{24\sqrt[3]{x^2}}$

107. $\sqrt{\dfrac{2y}{x}} = \dfrac{\sqrt{2y}}{\sqrt{x}} \cdot \dfrac{\sqrt{2y}}{\sqrt{2y}} = \dfrac{2y}{\sqrt{2xy}}$

108. $\sqrt[3]{\dfrac{2x}{3y}} = \dfrac{\sqrt[3]{2x}}{\sqrt[3]{3y}} \cdot \dfrac{\sqrt[3]{(2x)^2}}{\sqrt[3]{(2x)^2}} = \dfrac{2x}{\sqrt[3]{12x^2y}}$

109 $\dfrac{\sqrt[3]{x^2z}}{y} \cdot \dfrac{\sqrt[3]{xz^2}}{\sqrt[3]{xz^2}} = \dfrac{\sqrt[3]{x^3z^3}}{y\sqrt[3]{xz^2}} = \dfrac{xz}{y\sqrt[3]{xz^2}}$

110. $\dfrac{\sqrt[3]{x^2y}}{2x} \cdot \dfrac{\sqrt[3]{xy^2}}{\sqrt[3]{xy^2}} = \dfrac{xy}{2x\sqrt[3]{xy^2}} = \dfrac{y}{2\sqrt[3]{xy^2}}$

111. If the car is driven in the city, then it can be expected to cover

$\qquad$ $(18.1)(20) = 362$ $\qquad$ (miles/gal · gal)

or 362 miles on a full tank. If the car is driven on the highway, then it can be expected to cover

$\qquad$ $(18.1)(27) = 488.7$ $\qquad$ (miles/gal · gal)

or 488.7 miles on a full tank. Thus, the driving range of the car may be described by the interval [362, 488.7].

112. $5(C - 25) \geq 1.75 + 2.5C \Rightarrow 5C - 125 \geq 1.75 + 2.5C \Rightarrow 5C - 2.5C \geq 1\,75 + 125$
$\qquad \Rightarrow 2.5C \geq 126.75 \Rightarrow C \geq 50.7$ Therefore, the minimum cost is \$50.70.

113. $\qquad 6(P - 2500) \leq 4(P + 2400)$
$\qquad 6P - 15000 \leq 4P + 9600$
$\qquad\qquad 2P \leq 24600$, or $P \leq 12300$.
$\qquad$ Therefore, the maximum profit is \$12,300.

114 a. We want to find a formula for converting Centigrade temperatures to Fahrenheit temperatures. Thus,

$$C = \tfrac{5}{9}(F - 32) = \tfrac{5}{9}F - \tfrac{160}{9}.$$

Therefore, $\qquad \tfrac{5}{9}F = C + \tfrac{160}{9}.$

$$5F = 9C + 160$$

or $\qquad\qquad F = \tfrac{9}{5}C + 32.$

Calculations for lower temperature range:
$\qquad F = \tfrac{9}{5}(-15) + 32 = 5$, or 5 degrees.

9

Calculations for upper temperature range:

$$F = \tfrac{9}{5}(-5) + 32 = 23, \quad \text{or } 23 \text{ degrees.}$$

Therefore, the temperature range is $5° < °F < 23°$.

b. Calculations for lower temperature range:

$$C = \tfrac{5}{9}(63-32) = \tfrac{155}{9} \approx 17.2, \quad \text{or } 17.2 \text{ degrees.}$$

Calculations for upper temperature range:

$$C = \tfrac{5}{9}(80-32) = \tfrac{5}{9}(48) \approx 26.7, \quad \text{or } 26.7 \text{ degrees.}$$

Therefore, the temperature range is $17.2° < °C < 26.7°$

115. Let x represent the salesman's monthly sales in dollars. Then

$$0.15(x - 12000) \geq 3000$$
$$15(x - 12000) \geq 300000$$
$$15x - 180000 \geq 300000$$
$$15x \geq 480000$$
$$x \geq 32000.$$

We conclude that the salesman must earn at least \$32,000 to reach his goal.

116. Let x represent the wholesale price of the car. Then

$$\frac{5600}{x} - 1 \geq 0.30 \quad (\tfrac{Selling\ price}{Wholesale\ price} - 1 \geq Markup)$$

$$\frac{5600}{x} \geq 1.30$$

$$1.3x \leq 5600$$

$$x \leq 4307.69$$

We conclude that the maximum wholesale price was \$4307.69

117. The rod is acceptable if $0.49 < x < 0.51$ or $-0.01 < x - 0.5 < 0.01$ This gives the required inequality $|x - 0.5| < 0.01$.

118. $|x - 0.1| \leq 0.01$ is equivalent to $-0.01 \leq x - 0.1 \leq 0.01$ or $0.09 \leq x \leq 0.11$. Therefore, the smallest diameter a ball bearing in the batch can have is 0.09 inch. The largest diameter is 0.11 inch.

119. We want to solve the inequality

$$-6x^2 + 30x - 10 \geq 14. \qquad \text{(Remember } x \text{ is expressed in thousands.)}$$

Adding -14 to both sides of this inequality, we have

$$-6x^2 + 30x - 10 - 14 \geq 14 - 14,$$

or

$$-6x^2 + 30x - 24 \geq 0.$$

Dividing both sides of the inequality by -6 (which reverses the sign of the inequality), we have $x^2 - 5x + 4 \leq 0$.

Factoring this last expression, we have $(x - 4)(x - 1) \leq 0$.

From the following sign diagram,

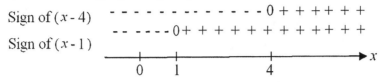

Sign of $(x - 4)$

Sign of $(x - 1)$

we see that x must lie between 1 and 4. (The inequality is only satisfied when the two factors have opposite signs.) Since x is expressed in thousands of units, we see that the manufacturer must produce between 1000 and 4000 units of the commodity.

120. a. $f(30000) = (2.8 \times 10^{11})(30000)^{-1.5} = 53{,}886$ or 53,886 families.
b. $f(60000) = (2.8 \times 10^{11})(60000)^{-1.5} = 19{,}052$ or 19,052 families.
c. $f(150{,}000) = (2.8 \times 10^{11})(150000)^{-1.5} = 4820$ or 4820 families.

121 False. Take $a = 1$, $b = 2$, and $c = 3$. Then $a < b$, but
$$a - c = 1 - 3 = -2 \not> 2 - 3 = -1 = b - c$$

122. True. $|b - a| = |(-1)(a - b)| = |-1||a - b| = |a - b|$

123 True. $|a - b| = |a + (-b)| \leq |a| + |-b| = |a| + |b|$.

124. False. Take $a = 3$ and $b = 1$. Then $\sqrt{a^2 - b^2} = \sqrt{9 - 1} = \sqrt{8} = 2\sqrt{2}$. But
$$|a| - |b| = 3 - 1 = 2.$$

EXERCISES 1.2, page 21

1 $(7x^2 - 2x + 5) + (2x^2 + 5x - 4) = 7x^2 - 2x + 5 + 2x^2 + 5x - 4$
$$= 9x^2 + 3x + 1.$$

2. $(3x^2 + 5xy + 2y) + (4 - 3xy - 2x^2) = 3x^2 + 5xy + 2y + 4 - 3xy - 2x^2$

11

$$= x^2 + 2xy + 2y + 4.$$

3. $(5y^2 - 2y + 1) - (y^2 - 3y - 7) = 5y^2 - 2y + 1 - y^2 + 3y + 7$
$$= 4y^2 + y + 8.$$

4. $3(2a - b) - 4(b - 2a) = 6a - 3b - 4b + 8a = 14a - 7b = 7(2a - b).$

5. $x - \{2x - [-x - (1 - x)]\} = x - \{2x - [-x - 1 + x]\}$
$$= x - \{2x + 1\}$$
$$= x - 2x - 1$$
$$= -x - 1$$

6. $3x^2 - \{x^2 + 1 - x[x - (2x - 1)]\} + 2$
$$= 3x^2 - \{x^2 + 1 - x[x - 2x + 1]\} + 2 \quad = 3x^2 - \{x^2 + 1 - x[-x + 1]\} + 2$$
$$= 3x^2 - \{x^2 + 1 + x^2 - x\} + 2 = 3x^2 - \{2x^2 - x + 1\} + 2$$
$$= x^2 - 1 + x + 2 = x^2 + x + 1.$$

7. $(\frac{1}{3} - 1 + e) - (-\frac{1}{3} - 1 + e^{-1}) = \frac{1}{3} - 1 + e + \frac{1}{3} + 1 - \frac{1}{e}$
$$= \frac{2}{3} + e - \frac{1}{e}$$
$$= \frac{3e^2 + 2e - 3}{3e}$$

8. $-\frac{3}{4}y - \frac{1}{4}x + 100 + \frac{1}{2}x + \frac{1}{4}y - 120 = -\frac{3}{4}y + \frac{1}{4}y - \frac{1}{4}x + \frac{1}{2}x + 100 - 120$
$$= -\frac{1}{2}y + \frac{1}{4}x - 20.$$

9. $3\sqrt{8} + 8 - 2\sqrt{y} + \frac{1}{2}\sqrt{x} - \frac{3}{4}\sqrt{y} = 3\sqrt{4 \cdot 2} + 8 + \frac{1}{2}\sqrt{x} - \frac{11}{4}\sqrt{y}$
$$= 6\sqrt{2} + 8 + \frac{1}{2}\sqrt{x} - \frac{11}{4}\sqrt{y}$$

10.
$$\frac{8}{9}x^2 + \frac{2}{3}x + \frac{16}{3}x^2 - \frac{16}{3}x - 2x + 2 = \frac{8x^2 + 6x + 48x^2 - 48x - 18x + 18}{9}$$

$$= \frac{56x^2 - 60x + 18}{9} = \frac{2(28x^2 - 30x + 9)}{9}$$

11 $(x + 8)(x - 2) = x(x - 2) + 8(x - 2) = x^2 - 2x + 8x - 16 = x^2 + 6x - 16.$

12. $(5x + 2)(3x - 4) = 5x(3x - 4) + 2(3x - 4) = 15x^2 - 20x + 6x - 8$
$$= 15x^2 - 14x - 8.$$

13. $(a + 5)^2 = (a + 5)(a + 5) = a(a + 5) + 5(a + 5) = a^2 + 5a + 5a + 25$
$$= a^2 + 10a + 25$$

14. $(3a - 4b)^2 = (3a - 4b)(3a - 4b) = 3a(3a - 4b) - 4b(3a - 4b)$
$$= 9a^2 - 12ab - 12ab + 16b^2 = 9a^2 - 24ab + 16b^2.$$

15 $(x + 2y)^2 = (x + 2y)(x + 2y) = x(x + 2y) + 2y(x + 2y)$
$$= x^2 + 2xy + 2yx + 4y^2 = x^2 + 4xy + 4y^2.$$

16. $(6 - 3x)^2 = (6 - 3x)(6 - 3x) = 6(6 - 3x) - 3x(6 - 3x)$
$$= 36 - 18x - 18x + 9x^2 = 36 - 36x + 9x^2.$$

17. $(2x + y)(2x - y) = 2x(2x - y) + y(2x - y) = 4x^2 - 2xy + 2xy - y^2$
$$= 4x^2 - y^2$$

18. $(3x + 2)(2 - 3x) = 3x(2 - 3x) + 2(2 - 3x) = 6x - 9x^2 + 4 - 6x$
$$= -9x^2 + 4.$$

19 $(x^2 - 1)(2x) - x^2(2x) = 2x^3 - 2x - 2x^3 = -2x.$

20. $(x^{1/2} + 1)(\frac{1}{2}x^{-1/2}) - (x^{1/2} - 1)(\frac{1}{2}x^{-1/2}) = \frac{1}{2}x^{-1/2}[(x^{1/2} + 1) - (x^{1/2} - 1)]$
$$= \frac{1}{2}x^{-1/2}(2) = \frac{1}{x^{1/2}} = \frac{1}{\sqrt{x}}$$

21 $2(t + \sqrt{t})^2 - 2t^2 = 2(t + \sqrt{t})(t + \sqrt{t}) - 2t^2$

$$= 2(t^2 + 2t\sqrt{t} + t) - 2t^2$$
$$= 2t^2 + 4t\sqrt{t} + 2t - 2t^2$$
$$= 4t\sqrt{t} + 2t = 2t(2\sqrt{t} + 1).$$

22. $2x^2 + (-x + 1)^2 = 2x^2 + (-x + 1)(-x + 1) = 2x^2 + x^2 - 2x + 1$
$$= 3x^2 - 2x + 1.$$

23. $4x^5 - 12x^4 - 6x^3 = 2x^3(2x^2 - 6x - 3).$

24. $4x^2y^2z - 2x^5y^2 + 6x^3y^2z^2 = 2x^2y^2(2z - x^3 + 3xz^2).$

25. $7a^4 - 42a^2b^2 + 49a^3b = 7a^2(a^2 + 7ab - 6b^2).$

26. $3x^{2/3} - 2x^{1/3} = x^{1/3}(3x^{1/3} - 2).$ 27. $e^{-x} - xe^{-x} = e^{-x}(1 - x).$

28. $2ye^{xy^2} + 2xy^3e^{xy^2} = 2ye^{xy^2}(1 + xy^2).$ 29. $2x^{-5/2} - \frac{3}{2}x^{-3/2} = \frac{1}{2}x^{-5/2}(4 - 3x).$

30. $\frac{1}{2}(\frac{2}{3}u^{3/2} - 2u^{1/2}) = \frac{1}{2} \cdot \frac{2}{3}u^{1/2}(u - 3) = \frac{1}{3}u^{1/2}(u - 3).$

31 $6ac + 3bc - 4ad - 2bd = 3c(2a + b) - 2d(2a + b) = (2a + b)(3c - 2d).$

32. $3x^3 - x^2 + 3x - 1 = x^2(3x - 1) + 1(3x - 1) = (x^2 + 1)(3x - 1).$

33 $4a^2 - b^2 = (2a + b)(2a - b).$ [Difference of two squares]

34. $12x^2 - 3y^2 = 3(4x^2 - y^2) = 3(2x + y)(2x - y).$

35 $10 - 14x - 12x^2 = -2(6x^2 + 7x - 5) = -2(3x + 5)(2x - 1).$

36. $x^2 - 2x - 15 = (x - 5)(x + 3).$

37 $3x^2 - 6x - 24 = 3(x^2 - 2x - 8) = 3(x - 4)(x + 2).$

38. $3x^2 - 4x - 4 = (3x + 2)(x - 2).$

39 $12x^2 - 2x - 30 = 2(6x^2 - x - 15) = 2(3x - 5)(2x + 3).$

40. $(x + y)^2 - 1 = (x + y - 1)(x + y + 1)$.

41. $9x^2 - 16y^2 = (3x)^2 - (4y)^2 = (3x - 4y)(3x + 4y)$.

42. $8a^2 - 2ab - 6b^2 = 2(4a^2 - ab - 3b^2) = 2(a - b)(4a + 3b)$.

43. $x^6 + 125 = (x^2)^3 + (5)^3 = (x^2 + 5)(x^4 - 5x^2 + 25)$.

44. $x^3 - 27 = x^3 - 3^3 = (x - 3)(x^2 + 3x + 9)$.

45. $(x^2 + y^2)x - xy(2y) = x^3 + xy^2 - 2xy^2 = x^3 - xy^2$

46. $2kr(R - r) - kr^2 = 2kRr - 2kr^2 - kr^2 = 2kRr - 3kr^2 = kr(2R - 3r)$.

47. $2(x - 1)(2x + 2)^3[4(x - 1) + (2x + 2)]$
$$= 2(x - 1)(2x + 2)^3[4x - 4 + 2x + 2]$$
$$= 2(x - 1)(2x + 2)^3[6x - 2]$$
$$= 4(x - 1)(3x - 1)(2x + 2)^3.$$

48. $5x^2(3x^2 + 1)^4(6x) + (3x^2 + 1)^5(2x) = (2x)(3x^2 + 1)^4[15x^2 + (3x^2 + 1)]$
$$= 2x(3x^2 + 1)^4(18x^2 + 1).$$

49. $4(x - 1)^2(2x + 2)^3(2) + (2x + 2)^4(2)(x - 1)$
$$= 2(x - 1)(2x + 2)^3[4(x - 1) + (2x + 2)] = 2(x - 1)(2x + 2)^3(6x - 2)$$
$$= 4(x - 1)(3x - 1)(2x + 2)^3.$$

50. $(x^2 + 1)(4x^3 - 3x^2 + 2x) - (x^4 - x^3 + x^2)(2x)$
$$= 4x^5 - 3x^4 + 2x^3 + 4x^3 - 3x^2 + 2x - 2x^5 + 2x^4 - 2x^3$$
$$= 2x^5 - x^4 + 4x^3 - 3x^2 + 2x.$$

51. $(x^2 + 2)^2[5(x^2 + 2)^2 - 3](2x) = (x^2 + 2)^2[5(x^4 + 4x^2 + 4) - 3](2x)$
$$= (2x)(x^2 + 2)^2(5x^4 + 20x^2 + 17).$$

52. $(x^2 - 4)(x^2 + 4)(2x + 8) - (x^2 + 8x - 4)(4x^3)$
$$= (x^4 - 16)(2x + 8) - 4x^5 - 32x^4 + 16x^3 = 2x^5 + 8x^4 - 32x - 128 - 4x^5 - 32x^4 + 16x^3$$
$$= -2x^5 - 24x^4 + 16x^3 - 32x - 128 = -2(x^5 + 12x^4 - 8x^3 + 16x + 64).$$

53. $x^2 + x - 12 = 0$, or $(x + 4)(x - 3) = 0$, so that $x = -4$ or $x = 3$ We conclude that the

15

roots are $x = -4$ and $x = 3$.

54. $3x^2 - x - 4 = 0$, or $(3x - 4)(x + 1) = 0$. Thus, $3x = 4$ or $x = -1$, and we conclude that the roots are $x = \frac{4}{3}$ and $x = -1$.

55. $4t^2 + 2t - 2 = (2t - 1)(2t + 2) = 0$. Thus, $t = 1/2$ and $t = -1$ are the roots.

56. $-6x^2 + x + 12 = (3x + 4)(-2x + 3) = 0$. Thus, $x = -4/3$ and $x = 3/2$ are the roots of the equation.

57. $\frac{1}{4}x^2 - x + 1 = (\frac{1}{2}x - 1)(\frac{1}{2}x - 1) = 0$. Thus $\frac{1}{2}x = 1$, and $x = 2$ is a double root of the equation.

58. $\frac{1}{2}a^2 + a - 12 = a^2 + 2a - 24 = (a + 6)(a - 4) = 0$. Thus, $a = -6$ and $a = 4$ are the roots of the equation.

59 Here we use the quadratic formula to solve the equation $4x^2 + 5x - 6 = 0$. Then, $a = 4$, $b = 5$, and $c = -6$. Therefore,

$$x = \frac{-b \pm \sqrt{b^2 - 4ac}}{2a} = \frac{-(5) \pm \sqrt{(5)^2 - 4(4)(-6)}}{2(4)} = \frac{-5 \pm \sqrt{121}}{8}$$
$$= \frac{-5 \pm 11}{8}$$

Thus, $x = -\frac{16}{8} = -2$ and $x = \frac{6}{8} = \frac{3}{4}$ are the roots of the equation.

60. Here we use the quadratic formula to solve the equation $3x^2 - 4x + 1 = 0$. Then, $a = 3$, $b = -4$, and $c = 1$. Therefore,

$$x = \frac{-b \pm \sqrt{b^2 - 4ac}}{2a} = \frac{-(-4) \pm \sqrt{(-4)^2 - 4(3)(1)}}{2(3)} = \frac{4 \pm \sqrt{4}}{6}.$$

Thus, $x = \frac{6}{6} = 1$ and $x = \frac{2}{6} = \frac{1}{3}$ are the roots of the equation.

61. We use the quadratic formula to solve the equation $8x^2 - 8x - 3 = 0$. Here $a = 8$, $b = -8$, and $c = -3$. Therefore,

$$x = \frac{-b \pm \sqrt{b^2 - 4ac}}{2a} = \frac{-(-8) \pm \sqrt{(-8)^2 - 4(8)(-3)}}{2(8)} = \frac{8 \pm \sqrt{160}}{16}$$

$$= \frac{8 \pm 4\sqrt{10}}{16} = \frac{2 \pm \sqrt{10}}{4}$$

Thus, $x = \frac{1}{2} + \frac{1}{4}\sqrt{10}$ and $x = \frac{1}{2} - \frac{1}{4}\sqrt{10}$ are the roots of the equation.

62. We use the quadratic formula to solve the equation $x^2 - 6x + 6 = 0$. Here, $a = 1$, $b = -6$, and $c = 6$. Therefore,

$$x = \frac{-b \pm \sqrt{b^2 - 4ac}}{2a} = \frac{-(-6) \pm \sqrt{(-6)^2 - 4(1)(6)}}{2(1)} = \frac{6 \pm 2\sqrt{3}}{2} = 3 \pm \sqrt{3}$$

Thus, the roots are $3 + \sqrt{3}$ and $3 - \sqrt{3}$.

63 We use the quadratic formula to solve $2x^2 + 4x - 3 = 0$. Here, $a = 2$, $b = 4$, and $c = -3$ Therefore

$$x = \frac{-b \pm \sqrt{b^2 - 4ac}}{2a} = \frac{-(4) \pm \sqrt{(4)^2 - 4(2)(-3)}}{2(2)} = \frac{-4 \pm \sqrt{40}}{4}$$

$$= \frac{-4 \pm 2\sqrt{10}}{4} = \frac{-2 \pm \sqrt{10}}{2}$$

Thus, $x = -1 + \frac{1}{2}\sqrt{10}$ and $x = -1 - \frac{1}{2}\sqrt{10}$ are the roots of the equation.

64. We use the quadratic formula to solve the equation $2x^2 + 7x - 15 = 0$. Then $a = 2$, $b = 7$, and $c = -15$.

Therefore, $x = \dfrac{-b \pm \sqrt{b^2 - 4ac}}{2a} = \dfrac{-(7) \pm \sqrt{(7)^2 - 4(2)(-15)}}{2(2)} = \dfrac{-7 \pm \sqrt{169}}{4}$

$$= \frac{-7 \pm 13}{4}.$$

We conclude that $x = \frac{3}{2}$ and $x = -5$ are the roots of the equation.

65 $\dfrac{x^2 + x - 2}{x^2 - 4} = \dfrac{(x + 2)(x - 1)}{(x + 2)(x - 2)} = \dfrac{x - 1}{x - 2}$

66. $\dfrac{2a^2 - 3ab - 9b^2}{2ab^2 + 3b^3} = \dfrac{(2a+3b)(a-3b)}{b^2(2a+3b)} = \dfrac{a-3b}{b^2}$.

67. $\dfrac{12t^2 + 12t + 3}{4t^2 - 1} = \dfrac{3(4t^2 + 4t + 1)}{4t^2 - 1} = \dfrac{3(2t+1)(2t+1)}{(2t+1)(2t-1)} = \dfrac{3(2t+1)}{2t-1}$

68. $\dfrac{x^3 + 2x^2 - 3x}{-2x^2 - x + 3} = \dfrac{x(x^2 + 2x - 3)}{-(2x^2 + x - 3)} = \dfrac{x(x+3)(x-1)}{-(2x+3)(x-1)} = -\dfrac{x(x+3)}{2x+3}$

69. $\dfrac{(4x-1)(3) - (3x+1)(4)}{(4x-1)^2} = \dfrac{12x - 3 - 12x - 4}{(4x-1)^2} = -\dfrac{7}{(4x-1)^2}$

70. $\dfrac{(1+x^2)^2(2) - 2x(2)(1+x^2)(2x)}{(1+x^2)^4} = \dfrac{(1+x^2)(2)(1+x^2 - 4x^2)}{(1+x^2)^4}$

$\qquad\qquad\qquad = \dfrac{(1+x^2)(2)(-3x^2 + 1)}{(1+x^2)^4} = \dfrac{2(1-3x^2)}{(1+x^2)^3}$

71. $\dfrac{2a^2 - 2b^2}{b-a} \cdot \dfrac{4a + 4b}{a^2 + 2ab + b^2} = \dfrac{2(a+b)(a-b)4(a+b)}{-(a-b)(a+b)(a+b)} = -8$.

72. $\dfrac{x^2 - 6x + 9}{x^2 - x - 6} \cdot \dfrac{3x + 6}{2x^2 - 7x + 3} = \dfrac{3(x-3)^2(x+2)}{(x-3)(x+2)(2x-1)(x-3)} = \dfrac{3}{2x-1}$

73. $\dfrac{3x^2 + 2x - 1}{2x + 6} \div \dfrac{x^2 - 1}{x^2 + 2x - 3} = \dfrac{(3x-1)(x+1)}{2(x+3)} \cdot \dfrac{(x+3)(x-1)}{(x+1)(x-1)} = \dfrac{3x-1}{2}$

74. $\dfrac{3x^2 - 4xy - 4y^2}{x^2 y} \div \dfrac{(2y-x)^2}{x^3 y} = \dfrac{(3x+2y)(x-2y)}{x^2 y} \cdot \dfrac{x^3 y}{(2y-x)(2y-x)} = \dfrac{x(3x+2y)}{x-2y}$.

75. $\dfrac{58}{3(3t+2)} + \dfrac{1}{3} = \dfrac{58 + 3t + 2}{3(3t+2)} = \dfrac{3t + 60}{3(3t+2)} = \dfrac{t + 20}{3t + 2}$

76. $\dfrac{a+1}{3a} + \dfrac{b-2}{5b} = \dfrac{5b(a+1) + 3a(b-2)}{15ab} = \dfrac{5ab + 5b + 3ab - 6a}{15ab} = \dfrac{-6a + 8ab + 5b}{15ab}$.

77. $\dfrac{2x}{2x-1} - \dfrac{3x}{2x+5} = \dfrac{2x(2x+5) - 3x(2x-1)}{(2x-1)(2x+5)} = \dfrac{4x^2 + 10x - 6x^2 + 3x}{(2x-1)(2x+5)}$

$$= \dfrac{-2x^2 + 13x}{(2x-1)(2x+5)} = -\dfrac{x(2x-13)}{(2x-1)(2x+5)}.$$

78. $\dfrac{-xe^x}{x+1} + e^x = \dfrac{-xe^x + (x+1)e^x}{x+1} = \dfrac{-xe^x + xe^x + e^x}{x+1} = \dfrac{e^x}{x+1}.$

79. $\dfrac{4}{x^2-9} - \dfrac{5}{x^2-6x+9} = \dfrac{4}{(x+3)(x-3)} - \dfrac{5}{(x-3)^2}$

$$= \dfrac{4(x-3) - 5(x+3)}{(x-3)^2(x+3)} = -\dfrac{x+27}{(x-3)^2(x+3)}$$

80. $\dfrac{x}{1-x} + \dfrac{2x+3}{x^2-1} = \dfrac{-x(x+1)+2x+3}{(x+1)(x-1)} = \dfrac{-x^2-x+2x+3}{x^2-1} = -\dfrac{x^2-x-3}{x^2-1}$

81 $\dfrac{1+\dfrac{1}{x}}{1-\dfrac{1}{x}} = \dfrac{\dfrac{x+1}{x}}{\dfrac{x-1}{x}} = \dfrac{x+1}{x} \cdot \dfrac{x}{x-1} = \dfrac{x+1}{x-1}$

82. $\dfrac{\dfrac{1}{x}+\dfrac{1}{y}}{1-\dfrac{1}{xy}} = \dfrac{\dfrac{x+y}{xy}}{\dfrac{xy-1}{xy}} = \dfrac{x+y}{xy} \cdot \dfrac{xy}{xy-1} = \dfrac{x+y}{xy-1}$

83 $\dfrac{4x^2}{2\sqrt{2x^2+7}} + \sqrt{2x^2+7} = \dfrac{4x^2 + 2\sqrt{2x^2+7}\sqrt{2x^2+7}}{2\sqrt{2x^2+7}} = \dfrac{4x^2 + 4x^2 + 14}{2\sqrt{2x^2+7}}$

$$= \dfrac{4x^2+7}{\sqrt{2x^2+7}}.$$

84. $6(2x+1)^2\sqrt{x^2+x}+\dfrac{(2x+1)^4}{2\sqrt{x^2+x}}=\dfrac{6(2x+1)^2\sqrt{x^2+x}\,(2)\sqrt{x^2+x}+(2x+1)^4}{2\sqrt{x^2+x}}$

$$=\dfrac{(2x+1)^2[12(x^2+x)+4x^2+4x+1]}{2\sqrt{x^2+x}}$$

$$=\dfrac{(2x+1)^2(16x^2+16x+1)}{2\sqrt{x^2+x}}$$

85. $\dfrac{2x(x+1)^{-1/2}-(x+1)^{1/2}}{x^2}=\dfrac{(x+1)^{-1/2}(2x-x-1)}{x^2}=\dfrac{(x+1)^{-1/2}(x-1)}{x^2}$

$$=\dfrac{x-1}{x^2\sqrt{x+1}}.$$

86. $\dfrac{(x^2+1)^{1/2}-2x^2(x^2+1)^{-1/2}}{1-x^2}=\dfrac{(x^2+1)^{-1/2}(x^2+1-2x^2)}{1-x^2}=\dfrac{(x^2+1)^{-1/2}(-x^2+1)}{1-x^2}$

$$=\dfrac{1}{\sqrt{x^2+1}}$$

87. $\dfrac{(2x+1)^{1/2}-(x+2)(2x+1)^{-1/2}}{2x+1}=\dfrac{(2x+1)^{-1/2}(2x+1-x-2)}{2x+1}$

$$=\dfrac{(2x+1)^{-1/2}(x-1)}{2x+1}=\dfrac{x-1}{(2x+1)^{3/2}}$$

88. $\dfrac{2(2x-3)^{1/3}-(x-1)(2x-3)^{-2/3}}{(2x-3)^{2/3}}=\dfrac{(2x-3)^{-2/3}[2(2x-3)-(x-1)]}{(2x-3)^{2/3}}$

$$=\dfrac{(2x-3)^{-2/3}(4x-6-x+1)}{(2x-3)^{2/3}}=\dfrac{3x-5}{(2x-3)^{4/3}}$$

89. $\dfrac{1}{\sqrt{3}-1}\cdot\dfrac{\sqrt{3}+1}{\sqrt{3}+1}=\dfrac{\sqrt{3}+1}{3-1}=\dfrac{\sqrt{3}+1}{2}.$

90. $\dfrac{1}{\sqrt{x}+5}\cdot\dfrac{\sqrt{x}-5}{\sqrt{x}-5}=\dfrac{\sqrt{x}-5}{x-25}.$

91. $\dfrac{1}{\sqrt{x}-\sqrt{y}}\cdot\dfrac{\sqrt{x}+\sqrt{y}}{\sqrt{x}+\sqrt{y}}=\dfrac{\sqrt{x}+\sqrt{y}}{x-y}$

92. $\dfrac{a}{1-\sqrt{a}}\cdot\dfrac{1+\sqrt{a}}{1+\sqrt{a}}=\dfrac{a(1+\sqrt{a})}{1-a}.$

93 $\dfrac{\sqrt{a}+\sqrt{b}}{\sqrt{a}-\sqrt{b}}\cdot\dfrac{\sqrt{a}+\sqrt{b}}{\sqrt{a}+\sqrt{b}}=\dfrac{(\sqrt{a}+\sqrt{b})^2}{a-b}.$

94. $\dfrac{2\sqrt{a}+\sqrt{b}}{2\sqrt{a}-\sqrt{b}}\cdot\dfrac{2\sqrt{a}+\sqrt{b}}{2\sqrt{a}+\sqrt{b}}=\dfrac{(2\sqrt{a}+\sqrt{b})^2}{4a-b}$

95. $\dfrac{\sqrt{x}}{3}\cdot\dfrac{\sqrt{x}}{\sqrt{x}}=\dfrac{x}{3\sqrt{x}}.$

96. $\dfrac{\sqrt[3]{y}}{x}\cdot\dfrac{\sqrt[3]{y^2}}{\sqrt[3]{y^2}}=\dfrac{y}{x\sqrt[3]{y^2}}$

97 $\dfrac{1-\sqrt{3}}{3}\cdot\dfrac{1+\sqrt{3}}{1+\sqrt{3}}=\dfrac{1^2-(\sqrt{3})^2}{3(1+\sqrt{3})}=-\dfrac{2}{3(1+\sqrt{3})}.$

98. $\dfrac{\sqrt{x}-1}{x}\cdot\dfrac{\sqrt{x}+1}{\sqrt{x}+1}=\dfrac{x-1}{x(\sqrt{x}+1)}.$

99 $\dfrac{1+\sqrt{x+2}}{\sqrt{x+2}}\cdot\dfrac{1-\sqrt{x+2}}{1-\sqrt{x+2}}=\dfrac{1-(x+2)}{\sqrt{x+2}(1-\sqrt{x+2})}=-\dfrac{x+1}{\sqrt{x+2}(1-\sqrt{x+2})}$

100. $\dfrac{\sqrt{x+3}-\sqrt{x}}{3}\cdot\dfrac{\sqrt{x+3}+\sqrt{x}}{\sqrt{x+3}+\sqrt{x}}=\dfrac{x+3-x}{3(\sqrt{x+3}+\sqrt{x})}=\dfrac{1}{\sqrt{x+3}+\sqrt{x}}$

101. True. The two real roots are $\dfrac{-b\pm\sqrt{b^2-4ac}}{2a}$

102. True. The two complex roots are $\dfrac{-b\pm\sqrt{4ac-b^2}\,\imath}{2a}.$

103. False. Take $a=2$, $b=3$, and $c=4$. Then
$$\dfrac{a}{b+c}=\dfrac{2}{3+4}=\dfrac{2}{7}.\ \text{But}\ \dfrac{a}{b}+\dfrac{a}{c}=\dfrac{2}{3}+\dfrac{3}{4}=\dfrac{8+9}{12}=\dfrac{17}{12}$$

104. True. Because $(a+b)(b-a)=b^2-a^2$

CONCEPT QUESTIONS, EXERCISES 1.3, page 28

1. a. $a < 0$ and $b > 0$;   b. $a < 0$ and $b < 0$ c. $a > 0$ and $b < 0$

2. a. $d = \sqrt{(x_2 - x_1)^2 + (y_2 - y_1)^2}$

   No. If we labeled $P_1(x_2, y_2)$ and $P_2(x_1, y_1)$, we obtain
   $$d = \sqrt{(x_1 - x_2)^2 + (y_2 - y_1)^2} = \sqrt{(x_2 - x_1) + (y_2 - y_1)^2}$$

EXERCISES 1.3, page 28

1. The coordinates of A are (3,3) and it is located in Quadrant I.

2. The coordinates of B are (-5,2) and it is located in Quadrant II.

3. The coordinates of C are (2,-2) and it is located in Quadrant IV.

4. The coordinates of D are (-2,5) and it is located in Quadrant II.

5. The coordinates of E are (-4,-6) and it is located in Quadrant III.

6. The coordinates of F are (8,-2) and it is located in Quadrant IV

7. A   8. (-5,4)   9. E, F, and G.   10. E   11. F   12. D

For Exercises 13-20, refer to the following figure.

13.(–2, 5) •

18.$(-\frac{5}{2}, \frac{3}{2})$•

14.(1.3)

15. (3, –1)

20.(1.2.-3.4)

16. (3.-4) 17. $(8, -\frac{7}{2})$

19. (4.5, –4.5)

21. Using the distance formula, we find that $\sqrt{(4-1)^2 + (7-3)^2} = \sqrt{3^2 + 4^2} = \sqrt{25} = 5$.

22. Using the distance formula, we find that
$$\sqrt{(4-1)^2 + (4-0)^2} = \sqrt{3^2 + 4^2} = \sqrt{25} = 5.$$

23. Using the distance formula, we find that
$$\sqrt{(4-(-1))^2 + (9-3)^2} = \sqrt{5^2 + 6^2} = \sqrt{25+36} = \sqrt{61}.$$

24. Using the distance formula, we find that
$$\sqrt{(10-(-2))^2 + (6-1)^2} = \sqrt{12^2 + 5^2} = \sqrt{144+25} = \sqrt{169} = 13.$$

25. The coordinates of the points have the form $(x,-6)$. Since the points are 10 units away from the origin, we have
$$(x-0)^2 + (-6-0)^2 = 10^2$$
$$x^2 = 64,$$
or $x = \pm 8$. Therefore, the required points are $(-8,-6)$ and $(8,-6)$.

26. The coordinates of the points have the form $(3,y)$. Since the points are 5 units away from the origin, we have $(3-0)^2 + (y-0)^2 = 5^2$, $y^2 = 16$, or $x = \pm 4$. Therefore, the required points are $(3,4)$ and $(3,-4)$.

27. The points are shown in the diagram that follows.

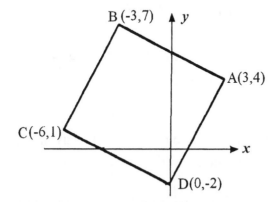

To show that the four sides are equal, we compute the following:
$$d(A,B) = \sqrt{(-3-3)^2 + (7-4)^2} = \sqrt{(-6)^2 + 3^2} = \sqrt{45}$$

23

$$d(B,C) = \sqrt{[(-6-(-3)]^2 +(1-7)^2} = \sqrt{(-3)^2 +(-6)^2} = \sqrt{45}$$

$$d(C,D) = \sqrt{[0-(-6)]^2 +[(-2)-1]^2} = \sqrt{(6)^2 +(-3)^2} = \sqrt{45}$$

$$d(A,D) = \sqrt{(0-3)^2 +(-2-4)^2} = \sqrt{(3)^2 +(-6)^2} = \sqrt{45}$$

Next, to show that $\triangle ABC$ is a right triangle, we show that it satisfies the Pythagorean Theorem. Thus,

$$d(A,C) = \sqrt{(-6-3)^2 +(1-4)^2} = \sqrt{(-9)^2 +(-3)^2} = \sqrt{90} = 3\sqrt{10}$$

and $[d(A,B)]^2 +[d(B,C)]^2 = 90 = [d(A,C)]^2$. Similarly, $d(B,D) = \sqrt{90} = 3\sqrt{10}$, so $\triangle BAD$ is a right triangle as well. It follows that $\angle B$ and $\angle D$ are right angles, and we conclude that $ADCB$ is a square

28. The triangle is shown in the figure that follows.

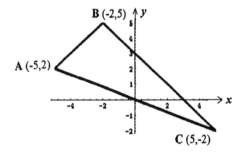

B (-2,5) \
A (-5,2) \
C (5,-2)

To prove that $\triangle ABC$ is a right triangle, we show that
$[d(A,C)]^2 =[d(A,B)]^2 +[d(B,C)]^2$ and the result will then follow from the Pythagorean Theorem. Now, $[d(A,C)]^2 = (-5-5)^2 +[2-(-2)]^2 = 100+16 = 116$
Next, we find

$$[d(A,B)]^2 +[d(B,C)]^2 =[-2-(-5)]^2 +(5-2)^2 +[5-(-2)]^2 +(-2-5)^2$$
$$= 9+9+49+49 = 116,$$

and the result follows.

29 The equation of the circle with radius 5 and center (2,-3) is given by
$$(x-2)^2 +[y-(-3)]^2 = 5^2 , \text{ or } (x-2)^2 +(y+3)^2 = 25.$$

30. The equation of the circle with radius 3 and center (-2,-4) is given by
$$[x-(-2)]^2 +(y+4)^2 = 9, \text{ or } (x+2)^2 +(y+4)^2 = 9$$

31. The equation of the circle with radius 5 and center (0, 0) is given by

$$(x-0)^2 + (y-0)^2 = 5^2, \text{ or } x^2 + y^2 = 25$$

32. The distance between the center of the circle and the point (2,3) on the circumference of the circle is given by $d = \sqrt{(3-0)^2 + (2-0)^2} = \sqrt{13}$.
Therefore $r = \sqrt{13}$ and the equation of the circle centered at the origin and passing through (2,3) is $x^2 + y^2 = 13$.

33 The distance between the points (5,2) and (2,-3) is given by
$$d = \sqrt{(5-2)^2 + (2-(-3))^2} = \sqrt{3^2 + 5^2} = \sqrt{34}$$
Therefore $r = \sqrt{34}$ and the equation of the circle passing through (5,2) and (2,-3) is
$$(x-2)^2 + [y-(-3)]^2 = 34, \text{ or } (x-2)^2 + (y+3)^2 = 34.$$

34. The equation of the circle with center $(-a, a)$ and radius $2a$ is given by
$$[x-(-a)]^2 + (y-a)^2 = (2a)^2, \text{ or } (x+a)^2 + (y-a)^2 = 4a^2$$

35. Referring to the diagram on page 29 of the text, we see that the distance from A to B is given by $d(A, B) = \sqrt{400^2 + 300^2} = \sqrt{250,000} = 500$. The distance from B to C is given by
$$d(B, C) = \sqrt{(-800-400)^2 + (800-300)^2} = \sqrt{(-1200)^2 + (500)^2}$$
$$= \sqrt{1,690,000} = 1300.$$
The distance from C to D is given by
$$d(C, D) = \sqrt{[-800-(-800)]^2 + (800-0)^2} = \sqrt{0 + 800^2} = 800.$$
The distance from D to A is given by
$$d(D, A) = \sqrt{[(-800)-0]^2 + (0-0)} = \sqrt{640000} = 800.$$
Therefore, the total distance covered on the tour, is
$$d(A, B) + d(B, C) + d(C, D) + d(D, A) = 500 + 1300 + 800 + 800$$
$$= 3400, \text{ or } 3400 \text{ miles.}$$

36. Suppose that the furniture store is located at the origin O so that your house is located at $A(20, -14)$.

1 Preliminaries

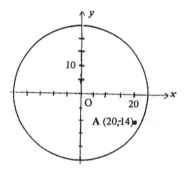

Since $d(O, A) = \sqrt{20^2 + (-14)^2} = \sqrt{596} \approx 24.4$, your house is located within a 25-mile radius of the store and you will not incur a delivery charge.

37 Referring to the following diagram,

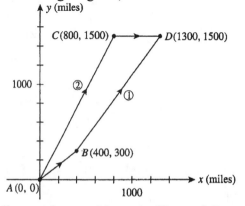

we see that the distance he would cover if he took Route (1) is given by

$$d(A,B) + d(B,D) = \sqrt{400^2 + 300^2} + \sqrt{(1300-400)^2 + (1500-300)^2}$$
$$= \sqrt{250,000} + \sqrt{2,250,000} = 500 + 1500 = 2000,$$

or 2000 miles. On the other hand, the distance he would cover if he took Route (2) is given by

$$d(A,C) + d(C,D) = \sqrt{800^2 + 1500^2} + \sqrt{(1300-800)^2}$$
$$= \sqrt{2,890,000} + \sqrt{250,000} = 1700 + 500 = 2200,$$

or 2200 miles. Comparing these results, we see that he should take Route (1).

38. Calculations to determine the cost of shipping by freight train:
       $(0.22)(2000)(100) = 44,000$ or $44,000.
     Calculations to determine the cost of shipping by truck:

$(0.21)(2200)(100) = 46,200$, or $46,200.

Comparing these results, we see that the automobiles should be shipped by freight train.   Net Savings: $46,200 - 44,000 = 2200$, or $2200.

39. Calculations to determine VHF requirements:
$$d = \sqrt{25^2 + 35^2} = \sqrt{625 + 1225} = \sqrt{1850} \approx 43.01.$$
Models B through D satisfy this requirement.

Calculations to determine UHF requirements:
$$d = \sqrt{20^2 + 32^2} = \sqrt{400 + 1024} = \sqrt{1424} = 37\ 74$$
Models C through D satisfy this requirement. Therefore, Model C will allow him to receive both channels at the least cost.

40. Length of cable required on land: $d(S, Q) = 10,000 - x$

Length of cable required under water·
$$d(Q, M) = \sqrt{(x^2 - 0) + (0 - 3000)^2} = \sqrt{x^2 + 3000^2}$$

Cost of laying cable: $1.5(10,000 - x) + 2.5\sqrt{x^2 + 3000^2}$

If $x = 2500$, then the total cost is given by
$$1.5(10000 - 2500) + 2.5\sqrt{2500^2 + 3000^2} \approx 21,012.80, \text{ or } \$21,012.80.$$
If $x = 3000$, then the total cost is given by
$$1.5(10000 - 3000) + 2.5\sqrt{3000^2 + 3000^2} \approx 21,106.60, \text{ or } \$21,106.60.$$

41. a. Let the position of ship A and ship B after t hours be $A(0, y)$ and $B(x, 0)$, respectively. Then $x = 30t$ and $y = 20t$. Therefore, the distance between the two ships is $D = \sqrt{(30t)^2 + (20t)^2} = \sqrt{900t^2 + 400t^2} = 10\sqrt{13}t.$

b. The required distance is obtained by letting $t = 2$ giving $D = 10\sqrt{13}(2)$ or approximately 72.11 miles.

42. a. Let the positions of ship A and ship B be $(0, y)$ and $(x, 0)$, respectively. Then $y = 25(t + \frac{1}{2})$ and $x = 20t$.   The distance D between the two ships is
$$D = \sqrt{(x - 0)^2 + (0 - y)^2} = \sqrt{x^2 + y^2} = \sqrt{400t^2 + 625(t + \frac{1}{2})^2} \quad (1)$$
b. The distance between the ships 2 hours after ship A has left port is obtained by letting $t = \frac{3}{2}$ in Equation (1) obtaining
$$D = \sqrt{400(\tfrac{3}{2})^2 + 625(\tfrac{3}{2} + \tfrac{1}{2})^2} = \sqrt{3400}, \text{ or approximately 58.31 miles.}$$

43 True. Plot the points.   44. True. Plot the points.

45 False. The distance between $P_1(a,b)$ and $P_3(kc,kd)$ is

$$d = \sqrt{(kc-a)^2 + (kd-b)^2}$$

$$\neq |k|D = |k|\sqrt{(c-a)^2 + (d-b)^2} = \sqrt{k^2(c-a)^2 + k^2(d-b)^2} = \sqrt{[k(c-a)]^2 + [k(d-b)]^2}$$

46. True. $kx^2 + ky^2 = a^2$; $x^2 + y^2 = \dfrac{a^2}{k} < a^2$ if $k > 1$. So the radius of the circle with

equation $kx^2 + ky^2 = a^2$ is a circle of radius smaller than a if $k > 1$ (and centered at the origin). Therefore, it lies inside the circle of radius a with equation $x^2 + y^2 = a^2$.

47 Referring to the figure in the text, we see that the distance between the two points is given by the length of the hypotenuse of the right triangle. That is,

$$d = \sqrt{(x_2 - x_1)^2 + (y_2 - y_1)^2}$$

48. $(x-h)^2 + (y-k)^2 = r^2$, $x^2 - 2xh + h^2 + y^2 - 2ky + k^2 = r^2$. This has the form

$$x^2 + y^2 + Cx + Dy + E = 0$$

where $c = -2h$, $D = -2k$, and $E = h^2 + k^2 - r^2$

1.4 CONCEPT QUESTIONS, page 40

1. The slope is $m = \dfrac{y_2 - y_1}{x_2 - x_1}$, where $P(x_1, y_1)$ and $P(x_2, y_2)$ are any two distinct points

on the nonvertical line. The slope of a vertical line is undefined.

2. a. $y - y_1 = m(x - x_1)$ b. $y = mx + b$
   c. $ax + by + c = 0$, where a and b are not both zero.

3. a. $m_1 = m_2$ b. $m_2 = -\dfrac{1}{m_1}$

EXERCISES 1.4, page 40

1. e   2. c   3. a   4. d   5. f   6. b

7. Referring to the figure shown in the text, we see that $m = \dfrac{2-0}{0-(-4)} = \dfrac{1}{2}$

8. Referring to the figure shown in the text, we see that $m = \dfrac{4-0}{0-2} = -2$

9 This is a vertical line, and hence its slope is undefined.

10. This is a horizontal line, and hence its slope is 0.

11 $m = \dfrac{y_2 - y_1}{x_2 - x_1} = \dfrac{8-3}{5-4} = 5.$

12. $m = \dfrac{y_2 - y_1}{x_2 - x_1} = \dfrac{8-5}{3-4} = \dfrac{3}{(-1)} = -3.$

13 $m = \dfrac{y_2 - y_1}{x_2 - x_1} = \dfrac{8-3}{4-(-2)} = \dfrac{5}{6}$

14. $m = \dfrac{y_2 - y_1}{x_2 - x_1} = \dfrac{-4-(-2)}{4-(-2)} = \dfrac{-2}{6} = -\dfrac{1}{3}$

15 $m = \dfrac{y_2 - y_1}{x_2 - x_1} = \dfrac{d-b}{c-a} \quad (a \neq c).$

16. $m = \dfrac{y_2 - y_1}{x_2 - x_1} = \dfrac{-b-(b-1)}{a+1-(-a+1)} = -\dfrac{-b-b+1}{a+1+a-1} = \dfrac{1-2b}{2a}$

17 Since the equation is in the slope-intercept form, we read off the slope $m = 4$.
   a. If x increases by 1 unit, then y increases by 4 units.
   b. If x decreases by 2 units, y decreases by $4(-2) = -8$ units.

18. Rewrite the given equation in slope-intercept form:
$$2x + 3y = 4, \quad 3y = 4 - 2x, \quad y = \tfrac{4}{3} - \tfrac{2}{3}x.$$
   a. Since $m = -2/3$, we conclude that the slope is negative.
   b. Since the slope is negative, y decreases as x increases in value.
   c. If x decreases by 2 units, then y increases by $-(2/3)(-2) = 4/3$ units.

19. The slope of the line through A and B is $\dfrac{-10-(-2)}{-3-1} = \dfrac{-8}{-4} = 2$.

   The slope of the line through C and D is $\dfrac{1-5}{-1-1} = \dfrac{-4}{-2} = 2$.

   Since the slopes of these two lines are equal, the lines are parallel.

20. The slope of the line through A and B is $\dfrac{-2-3}{2-2}$. Since this slope is undefined, we

see that the line is vertical. The slope of the line through C and D is $\dfrac{5-4}{-2-(-2)}$

Since this slope is undefined, we see that this line is also vertical. Furthermore, since the slopes of these two lines are equal, the lines are parallel.

21 The slope of the line through A and B is $\dfrac{2-5}{4-(-2)}=-\dfrac{3}{6}=-\dfrac{1}{2}$

The slope of the line through C and D is $\dfrac{6-(-2)}{3-(-1)}=\dfrac{8}{4}=2$ Since the slopes of these

two lines are the negative reciprocals of each other, the lines are perpendicular.

22. The slope of the line through A and B is $\dfrac{-2-0}{1-2}=\dfrac{-2}{-1}=2$.

The slope of the line through C and D is $\dfrac{4-2}{-8-4}=\dfrac{2}{-12}=-\dfrac{1}{6}$

Since the slopes of these two lines are not the negative reciprocals of each other, the lines are not perpendicular.

23 The slope of the line through the point $(1, a)$ and $(4,-2)$ is $m_1=\dfrac{-2-a}{4-1}$ and the

slope of the line through $(2,8)$ and $(-7, a+4)$ is $m_2=\dfrac{a+4-8}{-7-2}$ Since these two

lines are parallel, m_1 is equal to m_2. Therefore,

$$\dfrac{-2-a}{3}=\dfrac{a-4}{-9}$$
$$-9(-2-a)=3(a-4)$$
$$18+9a=3a-12$$
$$6a=-30 \quad \text{and} \quad a=-5$$

24. The slope of the line through the point $(a, 1)$ and $(5, 8)$ is $m_1=\dfrac{8-1}{5-a}$,

and the slope of the line through $(4, 9)$ and $(a+2,1)$ is $m_2=\dfrac{1-9}{a+2-4}$

Since these two lines are parallel, m_1 is equal to m_2. Therefore,

$$\dfrac{7}{5-a}=\dfrac{-8}{a-2},$$
$7(a-2)=-8(5-a)$, $7a-14=-40+8a$, and $a=26$.

25. An equation of a horizontal line is of the form $y = b$. In this case $b = -3$, so $y = -3$ is an equation of the line.

26. An equation of a vertical line is of the form $x = a$. In this case $a = 0$, so $x = 0$ is an equation of the line.

27 We use the point-slope form of an equation of a line with the point $(3, -4)$ and slope $m = 2$. Thus $y - y_1 = m(x - x_1)$,
and
$$y - (-4) = 2(x - 3)$$
$$y + 4 = 2x - 6$$
$$y = 2x - 10.$$

28. We use the point-slope form of an equation of a line with the point $(2,4)$ and slope $m = -1$. Thus $y - y_1 = m(x - x_1)$, and $y - 4 = -1(x - 2)$; $y - 4 = -x + 2$ and $y = -x + 6$.

29 Since the slope $m = 0$, we know that the line is a horizontal line of the form $y = b$. Since the line passes through $(-3,2)$, we see that $b = 2$, and an equation of the line is $y = 2$.

30. We use the point-slope form of an equation of a line with the point $(1,2)$ and slope $m = -1/2$. Thus $y - y_1 = m(x - x_1)$, and $y - 2 = -\frac{1}{2}(x - 1)$, $2y - 4 = -x + 1$; $2y = -x + 5$; and $y = -\frac{1}{2}x + \frac{5}{2}$.

31. We first compute the slope of the line joining the points $(2,4)$ and $(3,7)$. Thus,
$$m = \frac{7 - 4}{3 - 2} = 3$$
Using the point-slope form of an equation of a line with the point $(2,4)$ and slope $m = 3$, we find
$$y - 4 = 3(x - 2)$$
$$y = 3x - 2.$$

32. We first compute the slope of the line joining the points $(2,1)$ and $(2,5)$. Thus, $m = \frac{5-1}{2-2}$ Since this slope is undefined, we see that the line must be a vertical line of the form $x = a$. Since it passes through $(2,5)$, we see that $x = 2$ is the equation of the line.

1 Preliminaries

33. We first compute the slope of the line joining the points (1,2) and (–3,–2). Thus,

$$m = \frac{-2-2}{-3-1} = \frac{-4}{-4} = 1.$$

Using the point-slope form of an equation of a line with the point (1,2) and slope $m = 1$, we find

$$y - 2 = x - 1$$
$$y = x + 1.$$

34 We first compute the slope of the line joining the points (–1,–2) and (3,–4). Thus,

$$m = \frac{-4-(-2)}{3-(-1)} = \frac{-2}{4} = -\frac{1}{2}.$$

Using the point-slope form of an equation of a line with the point (–1,–2) and slope $m = -1/2$, we find $y-(-2) = -\frac{1}{2}[x-(-1)]$, $y+2 = -\frac{1}{2}(x+1)$; and $y = -\frac{1}{2}x - \frac{5}{2}$

35 We use the slope-intercept form of an equation of a line: $y = mx + b$. Since $m = 3$, and $b = 4$, the equation is $y = 3x + 4$

36. We use the slope-intercept form of an equation of a line: $y = mx + b$. Since $m = -2$, and $b = -1$, the equation is $y = -2x - 1$.

37 We use the slope-intercept form of an equation of a line: $y = mx + b$. Since $m = 0$, and $b = 5$, the equation is $y = 5$.

38. We use the slope-intercept form of an equation of a line: $y = mx + b$ Since $m = -1/2$, and $b = 3/4$, the equation is $y = -\frac{1}{2}x + \frac{3}{4}$.

39. We first write the given equation in the slope-intercept form:

$$x - 2y = 0$$
$$-2y = -x$$
$$y = \frac{1}{2}x$$

From this equation, we see that $m = 1/2$ and $b = 0$.

40. We write the equation in slope-intercept form: $y - 2 = 0$, $y = 2$.
From this equation, we see that $m = 0$ and $b = 2$.

41. We write the equation in slope-intercept form:

$$2x - 3y - 9 = 0$$

$$-3y = -2x + 9$$
$$y = \tfrac{2}{3}x - 3.$$

From this equation, we see that $m = 2/3$ and $b = -3$

42. We write the equation in slope-intercept form:
$$3x - 4y + 8 = 0$$
$$-4y = -3x - 8$$
$$y = \tfrac{3}{4}x + 2$$

From this equation, we see that $m = 3/4$ and $b = 2$.

43 We write the equation in slope-intercept form:
$$2x + 4y = 14$$
$$4y = -2x + 14$$
$$y = -\tfrac{2}{4}x + \tfrac{14}{4} = -\tfrac{1}{2}x + \tfrac{7}{2}$$

From this equation, we see that $m = -1/2$ and $b = 7/2$.

44. We write the equation in the slope-intercept form:
$$5x + 8y - 24 = 0$$
$$8y = -5x + 24$$
$$y = -\tfrac{5}{8}x + 3.$$

From this equation, we conclude that $m = -5/8$ and $b = 3$

45. We first write the equation $2x - 4y - 8 = 0$ in slope-intercept form:
$$2x - 4y - 8 = 0$$
$$4y = 2x - 8$$
$$y = \tfrac{1}{2}x - 2$$

Now the required line is parallel to this line, and hence has the same slope. Using the point-slope form of an equation of a line with $m = 1/2$ and the point $(-2, 2)$, we have
$$y - 2 = \tfrac{1}{2}[x - (-2)]$$
$$y = \tfrac{1}{2}x + 3.$$

46. We first write the equation $3x + 4y - 22 = 0$ in slope-intercept form:
$$3x + 4y - 22 = 0; \quad 4y = -3x + 22, \text{ and } y = -\tfrac{3}{4}x + \tfrac{22}{4}.$$

Now the required line is perpendicular to this line, and hence has slope 4/3 (the

negative reciprocal of $-3/4$). Using the point-slope form of an equation of a line with $m = 4/3$, and the point (2,4), we have
$$y - 4 = \tfrac{4}{3}(x - 2) \text{ and } y = \tfrac{4}{3}x + \tfrac{4}{3}$$

47 A line parallel to the x-axis has slope 0 and is of the form $y = b$ Since the line is 6 units below the axis, it passes through $(0,-6)$ and its equation is $y = -6$.

48. Since the required line is parallel to the line joining (2,4) and (4,7), it has slope $m = \dfrac{7-4}{4-2} = \dfrac{3}{2}$. We also know that the required line passes through (0,0) [the origin]. Using the point-slope form of an equation of a line, we find
$$y - 0 = \tfrac{3}{2}(x - 0), \text{ or } \quad y = \tfrac{3}{2}x$$

49 We use the point-slope form of an equation of a line to obtain
$$y - b = 0(x - a) \quad \text{or} \quad y = b.$$

50. Since the line is parallel to the x-axis, its slope is 0 and it has the form $y = b$ We know that the line passes through $(-3,4)$, so the required equation is $y = 4$.

51. Since the required line is parallel to the line joining $(-3,2)$ and (6,8), it has slope
$$m = \dfrac{8-2}{6-(-3)} = \dfrac{6}{9} = \dfrac{2}{3}.$$
We also know that the required line passes through $(-5,-4)$. Using the point-slope form of an equation of a line, we find
$$y - (-4) = \tfrac{2}{3}(x - (-5))$$
or $\qquad y = \tfrac{2}{3}x + \tfrac{10}{3} - 4;$ that is $\qquad y = \tfrac{2}{3}x - \tfrac{2}{3}$

52. Since the slope of the line is undefined, it has the form $x = a$. Furthermore, since the line passes through (a,b), the required equation is $x = a$.

53. Since the point $(-3,5)$ lies on the line $kx + 3y + 9 = 0$, it satisfies the equation. Substituting $x = -3$ and $y = 5$ into the equation gives
$$-3k + 15 + 9 = 0 , \text{ or } k = 8.$$

54 Since the point $(2,-3)$ lies on the line $-2x + ky + 10 = 0$, it satisfies the equation. Substituting $x = 2$ and $y = -3$ into the equation gives
$$-2(2) + (-3)k + 10 = 0; \; -4 - 3k + 10 = 0; \; -3k = -6, \text{ and } k = 2.$$

55 $3x - 2y + 6 = 0$

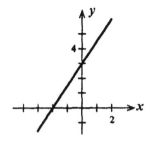

56. $2x - 5y + 10 = 0$

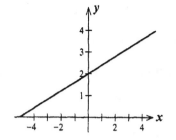

57 $x + 2y - 4 = 0$

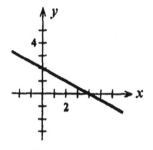

58. $2x + 3y - 15 = 0$

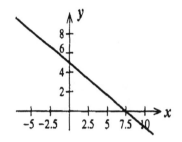

59 $y + 5 = 0$

60. $-2x - 8y + 24 = 0$

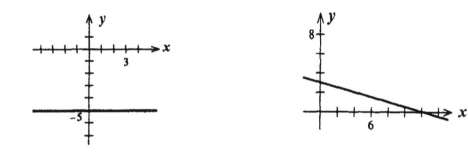

61. Since the line passes through the points $(a, 0)$ and $(0, b)$, its slope is
$m = \dfrac{b - 0}{0 - a} = -\dfrac{b}{a}$. Then, using the point-slope form of an equation of a line with the
point $(a, 0)$ we have

1 Preliminaries

$$y - 0 = -\frac{b}{a}(x - a)$$

$$y = -\frac{b}{a}x + b$$

which may be written in the form $\frac{b}{a}x + y = b$.

Multiplying this last equation by $1/b$, we have $\dfrac{x}{a} + \dfrac{y}{b} = 1$

62. Using the equation $\dfrac{x}{a} + \dfrac{y}{b} = 1$ with $a = 3$ and $b = 4$, we have $\dfrac{x}{3} + \dfrac{y}{4} = 1$ Then

$$4x + 3y = 12; \quad 3y = 12 - 4x, \quad y = -\frac{4}{3}x + 4$$

63. Using the equation $\dfrac{x}{a} + \dfrac{y}{b} = 1$ with $a = -2$ and $b = -4$, we have $-\dfrac{x}{2} - \dfrac{y}{4} = 1$

Then

$$-4x - 2y = 8$$
$$2y = -8 - 4x$$
$$y = -2x - 4.$$

64. Using the equation $\dfrac{x}{a} + \dfrac{y}{b} = 1$ with $a = -1/2$ and $b = 3/4$, we have

$$\frac{x}{-\frac{1}{2}} + \frac{y}{\frac{3}{4}} = 1; \quad \tfrac{3}{4}x - \tfrac{1}{2}y = \left(-\tfrac{1}{2}\right)\left(\tfrac{3}{4}\right); \quad -\tfrac{1}{2}y = -\tfrac{3}{4}x - \tfrac{3}{8};$$

$$y = 2\left(\tfrac{3}{4}x + \tfrac{3}{8}\right) = \tfrac{3}{2}x + \tfrac{3}{4}.$$

65. Using the equation $\dfrac{x}{a} + \dfrac{y}{b} = 1$ with $a = 4$ and $b = -1/2$, we have

$$\frac{x}{4} + \frac{y}{-\frac{1}{2}} = 1$$
$$-\tfrac{1}{4}x + 2y = -1$$
$$2y = \tfrac{1}{4}x - 1$$
$$y = \tfrac{1}{8}x - \tfrac{1}{2}$$

66. The slope of the line passing through A and B is $m = \dfrac{-2-7}{2-(-1)} = -\dfrac{9}{3} = -3$,

and the slope of the line passing through B and C is $m = \dfrac{-9-(-2)}{5-2} = -\dfrac{7}{3}$.

Since the slopes are not equal, the points do not lie on the same line.

67 The slope of the line passing through A and B is $m = \dfrac{7-1}{1-(-2)} = \dfrac{6}{3} = 2$,

and the slope of the line passing through B and C is $m = \dfrac{13-7}{4-1} = \dfrac{6}{3} = 2$

Since the slopes are equal, the points lie on the same line.

68. a.
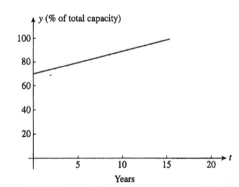

b. The slope is $\frac{9}{5}$. It represents the change in $°F$ per unit change in $°C$

c. The F-intercept of the line is 32. It corresponds to $0°C$ so it is the freezing point in $°F$

69 a.

b. The slope is 1.9467 and the y-intercept is 70.082.

c. The output is increasing at the rate of 1.9467%/yr; the output at the beginning of 1990 was 70.082%.

d. We solve the equation $1.9467t + 70.082 = 100$ giving $t = 15.37$. We conclude that the plants will be generating at maximum capacity shortly after 2005.

70. a. $y = 0.0765x$ b. $0.0765   c. $0.0765(35,000) = 2677.50$, or $2677.50.

71 a. $y = 0.55x$

b. Solving the equation $1100 = 0.55x$ for x, we have $x = \dfrac{1100}{0.55} = 2000$

72. a. Substituting $L = 80$ into the given equation, we have
$$W = 3.51(80) - 192 = 280.8 - 192 = 88.8, \text{ or } 88.8 \text{ British tons.}$$

b.

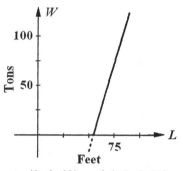

73 Using the points $(0, 0.68)$ and $(10, 0.80)$, we see that the slope of the required line

is $m = \dfrac{0.80 - 0.68}{10 - 0} = \dfrac{0.12}{10} = .012.$

Next, using the point-slope form of the equation of a line, we have
$$y - 0.68 = 0.012(t - 0)$$
or $y = 0.012t + 0.68.$

Therefore, when $t = 14$, we have $y = 0.012(14) + 0.68 = .848$, or 84.8%. That is, in 2004 women's wages are expected to be 84.8% of men's wages.

74. a. – b.

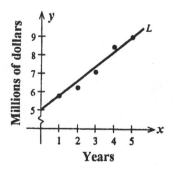

c. The slope of L is $m = \dfrac{9.0 - 5.8}{5 - 1} = \dfrac{3.2}{4} = 0.8$ Using the point-slope form of an

equation of a line, we have $y - 5.8 = 0.8(x - 1) = 0.8x - 0.8$, or $y = 0.8x + 5$.

d. Using the equation of part (c) with $x = 9$, we have
$$y = 0.8(9) + 5 = 12.2, \quad \text{or } \$12.2 \text{ million.}$$

75. a. – b.

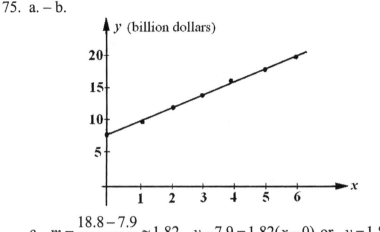

y (billion dollars)

c. $m = \dfrac{18.8 - 7.9}{6 - 0} \approx 1.82$, $y - 7.9 = 1.82(x - 0)$, or $y = 1.82x + 7.9$.

d. $y = 1.82(5) + 7.9 \approx 17$ or $\$17$ billion; This agrees with the actual data for that year.

76. a.

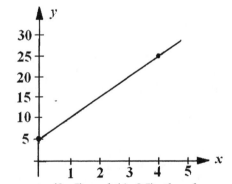

b. Using the points (0, 5) and (4, 25), the slope of the required line is
$$m = \dfrac{25 - 5}{4 - 0} = \dfrac{20}{4} = 5.$$

Next, using the point-slope form of an equation of a line, we have
$$y - 5 = 5(t - 0)$$

or $\qquad$ $y = 5t + 5$

c. When $x = 2$, $y = 5(2) + 5 = 15$, and we conclude that 15 percent of homes will have digital TV services at the beginning of 2001

77 True. The slope of the line is given by $-\dfrac{2}{4} = -\dfrac{1}{2}$

78. True. The slope of the line $Ax + By + C = 0$ is $-B/A$. (Write it in the slope-intercept form.) Similarly, the slope of the line $ax + by + c = 0$ is $-b/a$. They are parallel if and only if $-\dfrac{B}{A} = -\dfrac{b}{a}$, $Ab = aB$, or $Ab - aB = 0$.

79 False. Let the slope of L_1 be $m_1 > 0$. Then the slope of L_2 is $m_2 = -\dfrac{1}{m_1} < 0$.

80. True. the slope of the line $ax + by + c_1 = 0$ is $m_1 = -a/b$. The slope of the line $bx - ay + c_2 = 0$ is $m_2 = b/a$. Since $m_1 m_2 = -1$, the straight lines are indeed perpendicular.

81 True. Set $y = 0$ and we have $Ax + C = 0$ or $x = -C/A$ and this is where the line cuts the x-axis.

82. Yes. A straight line with slope zero ($m = 0$) is a horizontal line, whereas a straight line whose slope does not exist is a vertical line (m cannot be computed).

83 Writing each equation in the slope-intercept form, we have

$$y = -\frac{a_1}{b_1}x - \frac{c_1}{b_1} \quad (b_1 \ne 0) \quad \text{and} \quad y = -\frac{a_2}{b_2}x - \frac{c_2}{b_2} \quad (b_2 \ne 0)$$

Since two lines are parallel if and only if their slopes are equal, we see that the lines are parallel if and only if $-\dfrac{a_1}{b_1} = -\dfrac{a_2}{b_2}$, or $a_1 b_2 - b_1 a_2 = 0$.

84. The slope of L_1 is $m_1 = \dfrac{b - 0}{1 - 0} = b$ $\quad$ The slope of L_2 is $m_2 = \dfrac{c - 0}{1 - 0} = c$.

Applying the Pythagorean theorem to $\triangle OAC$ and $\triangle OCB$ gives
$$(OA)^2 = 1^2 + b^2 \quad \text{and} \quad (OB)^2 = 1^2 + c^2.$$
Adding these equations and applying the Pythagorean theorem to $\triangle OBA$ gives

$$(AB)^2 = (OA)^2 + (OB)^2 = 1^2 + b^2 + 1^2 + c^2 = 2 + b^2 + c^2$$

Also $(AB)^2 = (b - c)^2.$

Therefore, $(b - c)^2 = 2 + b^2 + c^2$

$$b^2 - 2bc + c^2 = 2 + b^2 + c^2$$
$$-2bc = 2, \; 1 = -bc.$$

Next, $m_1 m_2 = b \cdot c = bc = -1,$ as was to be shown.

CHAPTER 1, CONCEPT REVIEW, page 46

1 ordered; abscissa (x-coordinate); ordinate (y-coordinate)   2. a. x-, y-   b. Third

3 $\sqrt{(c-a)^2 + (d-b)^2}$ 4 $(x-a)^2 + (y-b)^2 = r^2$

5 a. $\dfrac{y_2 - y_1}{x_2 - x_1}$ b. Undefined   c. 0   d. Positive

6. $m_1 = m_2$; $m_1 = -\dfrac{1}{m_2}$

7 a. $y - y_1 = m(x - x_1)$;   point-slope form   b. $y = mx + b$; slope-intercept

8. a. $Ax + By + C = 0,$ where A and B are not both zero   b. $-\dfrac{a}{b}$

CHAPTER 1, REVIEW EXERCISES, page 47

1 Adding x to both sides yields $3 \le 3x + 9$ or $3x \ge -6,$ and $x \ge -2.$
We conclude that the solution set is $[-2, \infty)$.

2. $-2 \le 3x + 1 \le 7 \Rightarrow -3 \le 3x \le 6 \Rightarrow -1 \le x \le 2,$ and the solution set is $[-1,2]$.

3 The inequalities imply $x > 5$ or $x < -4$ So the solution set is
$(-\infty, -4) \cup (5, \infty)$.

4. $2x^2 > 50 \Rightarrow x^2 > 25 \Rightarrow x > 5$ and $x < -5$ and the solution set is $(-\infty, -5) \cup (5, \infty)$.

5 $|-5 + 7| + |-2| = |2| + |-2| = 2 + 2 = 4.$

6. $\left|\dfrac{5-12}{-4-3}\right| = \dfrac{|5-12|}{|-7|} = \dfrac{|-7|}{7} = \dfrac{7}{7} = 1.$ 7 $|2\pi - 6| - \pi = 2\pi - 6 - \pi = \pi - 6.$

8. $\left|\sqrt{3}-4\right|+\left|4-2\sqrt{3}\right|=(4-\sqrt{3})+(4-2\sqrt{3})=8-3\sqrt{3}$

9. $\left(\dfrac{9}{4}\right)^{3/2}=\dfrac{9^{3/2}}{4^{3/2}}=\dfrac{27}{8}$

10. $\dfrac{5^6}{5^4}=5^{6-4}=5^2=25.$

11. $(3 \quad 4)^{-2}=12^{-2}=\dfrac{1}{12^2}=\dfrac{1}{144}.$

12. $(-8)^{5/3}=[(-8^{1/3})]^5=(-2)^5=-32.$

13. $\dfrac{(3\ 2^{-3})(4\ 3^5)}{2\cdot 9^3}=\dfrac{3\cdot 2^{-3}\cdot 2^2\cdot 3^5}{2\cdot(3^2)^3}=\dfrac{2^{-1}\cdot 3^6}{2\ 3^6}=\dfrac{1}{4}.$

14. $\dfrac{3\sqrt[3]{54}}{\sqrt[3]{18}}=\dfrac{3\cdot(2\cdot 3^3)^{1/3}}{(2\cdot 3^2)^{1/3}}=\dfrac{3^2\cdot 2^{1/3}}{2^{1/3}\ 3^{2/3}}=3^{4/3}=3\ \sqrt[3]{3}.$

15. $\dfrac{4(x^2+y)^3}{x^2+y}=4(x^2+y)^2.$

16. $\dfrac{a^6 b^{-5}}{(a^3 b^{-2})^{-3}}=\dfrac{a^6 b^{-5}}{a^{-9}b^6}=\dfrac{a^{15}}{b^{11}}$

17. $\dfrac{\sqrt[4]{16x^5 yz}}{\sqrt[4]{81xyz^5}}=\dfrac{(2^4 x^5 yz)^{1/4}}{(3^4 xyz^5)^{1/4}}=\dfrac{2x^{5/4}y^{1/4}z^{1/4}}{3x^{1/4}y^{1/4}z^{5/4}}=\dfrac{2x}{3z}$

18. $(2x^3)(-3x^{-2})(\tfrac{1}{6}x^{-1/2})=-x^{1/2}$

19. $\left(\dfrac{3xy^2}{4x^3 y}\right)^{-2}\left(\dfrac{3xy^3}{2x^2}\right)^3=\left(\dfrac{3y}{4x^2}\right)^{-2}\left(\dfrac{3y^3}{2x}\right)^3=\left(\dfrac{4x^2}{3y}\right)^2\left(\dfrac{3y^3}{2x}\right)^3=\dfrac{(16x^4)(27y^9)}{(9y^2)(8x^3)}=6xy^7$

20. $\sqrt[3]{81x^5 y^{10}}\ \sqrt[3]{9xy^2}=\sqrt[3]{(3^4 x^5 y^{10})(3^2 xy^2)}=(3^6 x^6 y^{12})^{1/3}=3^2 x^2 y^4=9x^2 y^4.$

21. $-2\pi^2 r^3+100\pi r^2=-2\pi r^2(\pi r-50).$

22. $2v^3 w+2vw^3+2u^2 vw=2vw(v^2+w^2+u^2).$

23. $16-x^2=4^2-x^2=(4-x)(4+x).$

24. $12t^3-6t^2-18t=6t(2t^2-t-3)=6t(2t-3)(t+1).$

25. $8x^2+2x-3=(4x+3)(2x-1)=0$ and $x=-3/4$ and $x=1/2$ are the roots of the

equation.

26. $-6x^2 - 10x + 4 = 0$, $3x^2 + 5x - 2 = (3x - 1)(x + 2) = 0$ and so $x = -2$ or $x = 1/3$

27. $-x^3 - 2x^2 + 3x = -x(x^2 + 2x - 3) = -x(x + 3)(x - 1) = 0$ and the roots of the equation are $x = 0$, $x = -3$, and $x = 1$

28. $2x^4 + x^2 = 1$. Let $y = x^2$ and we can write the equation as
$$2y^2 + y - 1 = (2y - 1)(y + 1) = 0$$
giving $y = 1/2$ or $y = -1$ We reject the second root since $y = x^2$ must be nonnegative. Therefore, $x^2 = 1/2$ or $x = \pm 1/\sqrt{2} = \pm\sqrt{2}/2$.

29 Here we use the quadratic formula to solve the equation $x^2 - 2x - 5 = 0$. Then $a = 1$, $b = -2$, and $c = -5$ Thus,
$$x = \frac{-b \pm \sqrt{b^2 - 4ac}}{2a} = \frac{-(-2) \pm \sqrt{(-2)^2 - 4(1)(-5)}}{2(1)} = \frac{2 \pm \sqrt{24}}{2} = 1 \pm \sqrt{6}$$

30. Here we use the quadratic formula to solve the equation $2x^2 + 8x + 7 = 0$. Then $a = 2$, $b = 8$, and $c = 7$ So
$$x = \frac{-b \pm \sqrt{b^2 - 4ac}}{2a} = \frac{-(8) \pm \sqrt{(8)^2 - 4(2)(7)}}{4} = \frac{-8 \pm 2\sqrt{2}}{4} = -2 \pm \tfrac{1}{2}\sqrt{2}$$

31 $$\frac{(t+6)(60) - (60t + 180)}{(t+6)^2} = \frac{60t + 360 - 60t - 180}{(t+6)^2} = \frac{180}{(t+6)^2}$$

32. $$\frac{6x}{2(3x^2+2)} + \frac{1}{4(x+2)} = \frac{(6x)(2)(x+2) + (3x^2+2)}{4(3x^2+2)(x+2)} = \frac{12x^2 + 24x + 3x^2 + 2}{4(3x^2+2)(x+2)}$$
$$= \frac{15x^2 + 24x + 2}{4(3x^2+2)(x+2)}.$$

33. $$\frac{2}{3}\left(\frac{4x}{2x^2-1}\right) + 3\left(\frac{3}{3x-1}\right) = \frac{8x}{3(2x^2-1)} + \frac{9}{3x-1} = \frac{8x(3x-1) + 27(2x^2-1)}{3(2x^2-1)(3x-1)}$$
$$= \frac{78x^2 - 8x - 27}{3(2x^2-1)(3x-1)}.$$

1 Preliminaries

34. $$\frac{-2x}{\sqrt{x+1}}+4\sqrt{x+1}=\frac{-2x+4(x+1)}{\sqrt{x+1}}=\frac{2(x+2)}{\sqrt{x+1}}$$

35 $$\frac{\sqrt{x}-1}{x-1}=\frac{\sqrt{x}-1}{x-1}\cdot\frac{\sqrt{x}+1}{\sqrt{x}+1}=\frac{(\sqrt{x})^{2}-1}{(x-1)(\sqrt{x}+1)}=\frac{x-1}{(x-1)(\sqrt{x}+1)}=\frac{1}{\sqrt{x}+1}$$

36. $$\frac{\sqrt{x}-1}{2\sqrt{x}}=\frac{\sqrt{x}-1}{2\sqrt{x}}\cdot\frac{\sqrt{x}}{\sqrt{x}}=\frac{x-\sqrt{x}}{2x}$$

37 The distance is
$$d=\sqrt{[1-(-2)]^{2}+[-7-(-3)]^{2}}=\sqrt{3^{2}+(-4)^{2}}=\sqrt{9+16}=\sqrt{25}=5$$

38. The distance is
$$d=\sqrt{(-1/2-1/2)^{2}+(2\sqrt{3}-\sqrt{3})^{2}}=\sqrt{1+3}=\sqrt{4}=2$$

39 An equation is $x=-2$.   40. An equation is $y=4$.

41 The slope of L is $m=\dfrac{\frac{7}{2}-4}{3-(-2)}=-\dfrac{1}{10}$ and an equation of L is

$y-4=-\frac{1}{10}[x-(-2)]=-\frac{1}{10}x-\frac{1}{5}$, or $y=-\frac{1}{10}x+\frac{19}{5}$ The general form of this
equation is $x+10y-38=0$.

42. The line passes through the points $(-2, 4)$ and $(3, 0)$. So its slope is
$m=(4-0)/(-2-3)$ or $m=-4/5$. An equation is
$$y-0=-\tfrac{4}{5}(x-3)\quad\text{or}\quad y=-\tfrac{4}{5}x+\tfrac{12}{5}$$

43 Writing the given equation in the form $y=\frac{5}{2}x-3$, we see that the slope of the
given line is 5/2. So a required equation is $y-4=\frac{5}{2}(x+2)$ or $y=\frac{5}{2}x+9$
The general form of this equation is $5x-2y+18=0$.

44. Writing the given equation in the form $y=-\frac{4}{3}x+2$, we see that the slope of the
given line is –4/3. Therefore, the slope of the required line is 3/4 and an equation
of the line is $y-4=\frac{3}{4}(x+2)$ or $y=\frac{3}{4}x+\frac{11}{2}$

45 Rewriting the given equation in the slope-intercept form, we have $4y=-3x+8$

or $y = -\frac{3}{4}x + 2$ and conclude that the slope of the required line is –3/4. Using the point-slope form of the equation of a line with the point (2,3) and slope –3/4, we obtain $y - 3 = -\frac{3}{4}(x - 2)$, and so $y = -\frac{3}{4}x + \frac{6}{4} + 3 = -\frac{3}{4}x + \frac{9}{2}$ The general form of this equation is $3x + 4y - 18 = 0$.

46. The slope of the line joining the points $(-3,4)$ and $(2,1)$ is $m = \dfrac{1-4}{2-(-3)} = -\dfrac{3}{5}$

    Using the point-slope form of the equation of a line with the point $(-1,3)$ and slope $-3/5$, we have $y - 3 = -\frac{3}{5}[x - (-1)]$ Therefore, $y = -\frac{3}{5}(x + 1) + 3 = -\frac{3}{5}x + \frac{12}{5}$

47 The slope of the line passing through $(-2,-4)$ and $(1,5)$ is $m = \dfrac{5-(-4)}{1-(-2)} = \dfrac{9}{3} = 3$ So

    the required line is $y - (-2) = 3[x - (-3)]$ and $y + 2 = 3x + 9$, or $y = 3x + 7$.

48. Rewriting the given equation in the slope-intercept form $y = \frac{2}{3}x - 8$, we see that the slope of the line with this equation is 2/3. The slope of the required line is $-3/2$. Using the point-slope form of the equation of a line with the point $(-2, -4)$ and slope $-3/2$, we have $y - (-4) = -\frac{3}{2}[x - (-2)]$ or $y = -\frac{3}{2}x - 7$. The general form of this equation is $3x + 2y + 14 = 0$.

49. Setting $x = 0$ gives $y = -6$ as the y-intercept. Setting $y = 0$ gives $x = 8$ as the x-intercept. The graph of the equation $3x - 4y = 24$ follows:

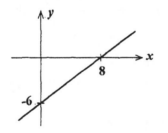

50. Using the point-slope form of an equation of a line, we have

    $y - 2 = -\dfrac{2}{3}(x - 3)$ or $y = -\dfrac{2}{3}x + 4$. If $y = 0$, then $x = 6$, and if $x = 0$, then $y = 4$. A

    A sketch of the line follows.

1 Preliminaries

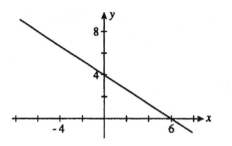

51. $2(1.5C + 80) \le 2(2.5C - 20) \Rightarrow 1.5C + 80 \le 2.5C - 20$, so $C \ge 100$ and the minimum cost is $100.

52. $3(2R - 320) \le 3R + 240$; $6R - 960 \le 3R + 240$; $3R \le 1200$ and $R \le 400$. We conclude that the maximum revenue is $400.

53 a.

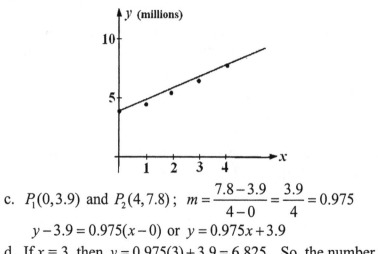

c. $P_1(0, 3.9)$ and $P_2(4, 7.8)$; $m = \dfrac{7.8 - 3.9}{4 - 0} = \dfrac{3.9}{4} = 0.975$

$y - 3.9 = 0.975(x - 0)$ or $y = 0.975x + 3.9$

d. If $x = 3$, then $y = 0.975(3) + 3.9 = 6.825$. So, the number of systems installed in 2005 ($x = 3$) is 6,825,000 which is close to the projection of 6.8 million.

CHAPTER 1, Before Moving On, page 48

1. a. $\left| \pi - 2\sqrt{3} \right| - \left| \sqrt{3} - \sqrt{2} \right| = -(\pi - 2\sqrt{3}) - (\sqrt{3} - \sqrt{2}) = \sqrt{3} + \sqrt{2} - \pi$

   b. $\left[\left(-\tfrac{1}{3} \right)^{-3} \right]^{1/3} = \left(-\tfrac{1}{3} \right)^{(-3)(\frac{1}{3})} = \left(-\tfrac{1}{3} \right)^{-1} = -3$.

2. a. $\sqrt[3]{64x^6} \cdot \sqrt{9y^2x^6} = (4x^2)(3yx^3) = 12x^5y$

b. $\left(\dfrac{a^{-3}}{b^{-4}}\right)^2 \left(\dfrac{b}{a}\right)^{-3} = \dfrac{a^{-6}}{b^{-8}} \cdot \dfrac{b^{-3}}{a^{-3}} = \dfrac{b^8}{a^6} \cdot \dfrac{a^3}{b^3} = \dfrac{b^5}{a^3}$

3 a. $\dfrac{2x}{3\sqrt{y}} \cdot \dfrac{\sqrt{y}}{\sqrt{y}} = \dfrac{2x\sqrt{y}}{3y}$ b. $-\dfrac{3x}{\sqrt{x+2}} + 3\sqrt{x+2} = \dfrac{x}{\sqrt{x}-4} \cdot \dfrac{\sqrt{x}+4}{\sqrt{x}+4} = \dfrac{x(\sqrt{x}+4)}{x-16}$

4. a. $\dfrac{(x^2+1)(\frac{1}{2}x^{-1/2}) - x^{1/2}(2x)}{(x^2+1)^2} = \dfrac{\frac{1}{2}x^{-1/2}[(x^2+1)-4x^2]}{(x^2+1)^2} = \dfrac{1-3x^2}{2x^{1/2}(x^2+1)^2}$

  b. $-\dfrac{3x+3(x+2)}{\sqrt{x+2}} = \dfrac{6}{\sqrt{x+2}} = \dfrac{6\sqrt{x+2}}{x+2}$

5 $\dfrac{\sqrt{x}+\sqrt{y}}{\sqrt{x}-\sqrt{y}} = \dfrac{\sqrt{x}+\sqrt{y}}{\sqrt{x}-\sqrt{y}} \cdot \dfrac{\sqrt{x}-\sqrt{y}}{\sqrt{x}-\sqrt{y}} = \dfrac{x-y}{(\sqrt{x}-\sqrt{y})^2}$

6. a. $12x^3 - 10x^2 - 12x = 2x(6x^2-5x-6) = 2x(2x-3)(3x+2)$
   b. $2bx - 2by + 3cx - 3cy = 2b(x-y) + 3c(x-y) = (2b+3c)(x-y)$

7 a. $12x^2 - 9x - 3 = 0$; $3(4x^2-3x-1) = 0$; $3(4x+1)(x-1) = 0$ so $x = -\frac{1}{4}$ or $x = 1$.
   b. $3x^2 - 5x + 1 = 0$ Using the quadratic equations, woth $a = 3$, $b = -5$, and $c = 1$, we
   have $x = \dfrac{-(-5) \pm \sqrt{25-12}}{2(3)} = \dfrac{5 \pm \sqrt{13}}{6}$

8. $d = \sqrt{[6-(-2)]^2 + (8-4)^2} = \sqrt{64+16} = \sqrt{80} = 4\sqrt{5}$

9. $m = \dfrac{5-(-2)}{4-(-1)} = \dfrac{7}{5}$; $y-(-2) = \dfrac{7}{5}(x-(-1))$; $y+2 = \dfrac{7}{5}x + \dfrac{7}{5}$ or $y = \dfrac{7}{5}x - \dfrac{3}{5}$

10. $m = -\dfrac{1}{3}$, $b = \dfrac{4}{3}$, $y = -\dfrac{1}{3}x + \dfrac{4}{3}$

Page 25

1 Let $P_1 = (2,6)$ and $P_2 = (-4,3)$. Then we have $x_1 = 2$, $y_1 = 6$, $x_2 = -4$, and $y_2 = 3$.

Using formula (1), we have $d = \sqrt{(-4-2)^2 + (3-6)^2} = \sqrt{36+9} = \sqrt{45} = 3\sqrt{5}$

as obtained in Example 1.

2. Let $P_1(x_1,y_1)$ and $P_2(x_2,y_2)$ be any two points in the plane. Then the result follows

from the equality $\sqrt{(x_2 - x_1)^2 + (y_2 - y_1)^2} = \sqrt{(x_1 - x_2)^2 + (y_1 - y_2)^2}$

Page 26

1 a. All points on and inside the circle with center (h, k) and radius r
   b. All points inside the circle with center (h, k) and radius r
   c. All points on and outside the cricle with center (h, k) and radius r
   d. All points outside the circle with center (h, k) and radius r

2. a. $y^2 = 4 - x^2$ and so $y = \pm\sqrt{4 - x^2}$

   b. (i) The upper semicircle with center at the origin and radius 2.
       (ii) The lower semicircle with center at the origin and radius 2.

Page 27

1. Let $P(x,y)$ be any point in the plane. Draw a line through P parallel to the y-axis and a line through P parallel to the x-axis (see figure).

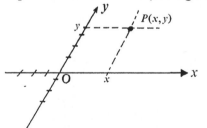

The x-coordinate of P is the number corresponding to the point on the x-axis at which the line through P hits the x-axis. Similarly y is the number that corresponds to the point on the y-axis at which the line parallel to the x-axis crosses the y-axis. To show the converse, reverse the process.

2. You can use the Pythagorean Theorem in the Cartesian coordinate system This simplifies the computations greatly.

Page 33

1 Refer to the accompanying figure. Observe that triangles $\Delta P_1Q_1P_2$ and $\Delta P_3Q_2P_4$

are similar. From this we conclude that $m = \dfrac{y_2 - y_1}{x_2 - x_1} = \dfrac{y_4 - y_3}{x_4 - x_3}$ Since P_3 and P_4 are

arbitrary, the conclusion follows.

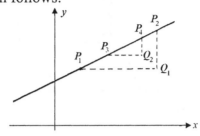

Page 38

1   We obtain a family of parallel lines each having slope m.
2.   We obtain a family of straight lines all of which pass through the point $(0,b)$.

Page 39

1.   In Example 11, we are told that the object is expected to appreciate in value at a
     given rate for the next five years, and the equation obtained in that example is
     based on this fact. Thus, the equation may not be used to predict the value of the
     object very much beyond five years from the date of purchase.

EXPLORING WITH TECHNOLOGY QUESTIONS

Page 37

1. The straight lines L_1 and L_2 are shown in the figure that follows.

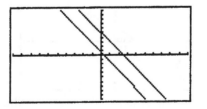

   a. L_1 and L_2 seem to be parallel to each other.
   b. Writing each equation in the slope-intercept form gives

$$y = -2x + 5 \quad \text{and} \quad y = -\tfrac{41}{20}x + \tfrac{11}{20}$$

from which we see that the slopes of L_1 and L_2 are -2 and $-41/20 = -2.05$, respectively This shows that L_1 and L_2 are not parallel to each other.

2. The straight lines L_1 and L_2 are shown in the following figure.

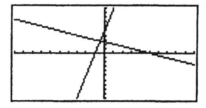

a. L_1 and L_2 seem to be perpendicular to each other.

b. The slopes of L_1 and L_2 are $m_1 = -1/2$ and $m_2 = 5$, respectively.

Since $m_1 = -\dfrac{1}{2} \neq -\dfrac{1}{5} = -\dfrac{1}{m_2}$, we see that L_1 and L_2 are not perpendicular to each

other.

Page 38

1. The straight lines with the given equations are shown in the figure that follows.

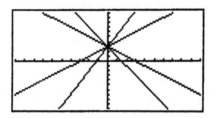

Changing the value of m in the equation $y = mx + b$ changes the slope of the line and thus rotates it.

2. The straight lines of interest are shown in the following figure.

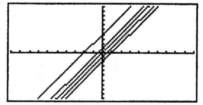

Changing the value of b in the equation $y = mx + b$ changes the y-intercept of the line and thus translates it (upwards if $b > 0$ and downwards if $b < 0$).

3 Changing both m and b in the equation $y = mx + b$ rotates as well as translates the line.

CHAPTER 2

CONCEPT QUESTIONS, EXERCISES 2.1, page 58

1. a. A function is a rule that associates with each element in a set A exactly one element in a set B

    b. The domain of a function f is the set of all elements x in the set such that $f(x)$ is an element in B The range of f is the set of all elements $f(x)$ whenever x is an element in its domain.

    c. An independent variable is a variable in the domain of a function f The dependent variable is $y = f(x)$.

2. a. The graph of a function f is the set of all ordered pairs (x, y) such that $y = f(x)$, x being an element in the domain of f

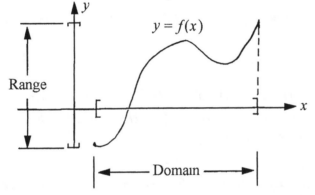

   b. Use the vertical line test to determine if every vertical line intersects the curve in at most one point. If so, then the curve is the graph of a function.

EXERCISES 2.1, page 58

1. $f(x) = 5x + 6$. Therefore $f(3) = 5(3) + 6 = 21,$ $f(-3) = 5(-3) + 6 = -9;$

    $f(a) = 5(a) + 6 = 5a + 6;$ $f(-a) = 5(-a) + 6 = -5a + 6;$ and

    $f(a + 3) = 5(a + 3) + 6 = 5a + 15 + 6 = 5a + 21$

2. $f(x) = 4x - 3$. Therefore, $f(4) = 4(4) - 3 = 16 - 3 = 13$; $f(\frac{1}{4}) = 4(\frac{1}{4}) - 3 = 1 - 3 = -2$

   $f(0) = 4(0) - 3 = -3$; $f(a) = 4(a) - 3 = 4a - 3$, $f(a + 1) = 4(a + 1) - 3 = 4a + 1$.

3. $g(x) = 3x^2 - 6x - 3$; $g(0) = 3(0) - 6(0) - 3 = -3$,

   $g(-1) = 3(-1)^2 - 6(-1) - 3 = 3 + 6 - 3 = 6$; $g(a) = 3(a)^2 - 6(a) - 3 = 3a^2 - 6a - 3$

   $g(x) = -x^2 + 2x$; $g(\sqrt{a}) = -(\sqrt{a})^2 + 2\sqrt{a} = -a + 2\sqrt{a}$

   $g(x + 1) = 3(x + 1)^2 - 6(x + 1) - 3 = 3(x^2 + 2x + 1) - 6x - 6 - 3$

   $\qquad\qquad = 3x^2 + 6x + 3 - 6x - 9 = 3x^2 - 6$.

4. $h(x) = x^3 - x^2 + x + 1$. $h(-5) = (-5)^3 - (-5)^2 + (-5) + 1 = -125 - 25 - 5 + 1 = -154$

   $h(0) = (0)^3 - (0)^2 + 0 + 1 = 1$; $h(a) = a^3 - (a)^2 + a + 1 = a^3 - a^2 + a + 1$

   $h(-a) = (-a)^3 - (-a)^2 + (-a) + 1 = -a^3 - a^2 - a + 1$.

5. $f(x) = 2x + 5$; $f(a + h) = 2(a + h) + 5 = 2a + 2h + 5$. $f(-a) = 2(-a) + 5 = -2a + 5$

   $f(a^2) = 2(a^2) + 5 = 2a^2 + 5$; $f(a - 2h) = 2(a - 2h) + 5 = 2a - 4h + 5$

   $f(2a - h) = 2(2a - h) + 5 = 4a - 2h + 5$

6. $g(x) = -x^2 + 2x$; $g(a + h) = -(a + h)^2 + 2(a + h) = -a^2 - 2ah - h^2 + 2a + 2h$

   $g(-a) = -(-a)^2 + 2(-a) = -a^2 - 2a = -a(a + 2)$

   $g(a) = -(a)^2 + 2(a) = -a^2 + 2a = -(a - 2)$

   $a + g(a) = a - a^2 + 2a = -a^2 + 3a = -a(a - 3)$

   $\dfrac{1}{g(a)} = \dfrac{1}{-a^2 + 2a} = -\dfrac{1}{a(a - 2)}$.

7. $s(t) = \dfrac{2t}{t^2 - 1}$ Therefore, $s(4) = \dfrac{2(4)}{(4)^2 - 1} = \dfrac{8}{15}$. $s(0) = \dfrac{2(0)}{0^2 - 1} = 0$

   $s(a) = \dfrac{2(a)}{a^2 - 1} = \dfrac{2a}{a^2 - 1}$; $s(2 + a) = \dfrac{2(2 + a)}{(2 + a)^2 - 1} = \dfrac{2(2 + a)}{a^2 + 4a + 4 - 1} = \dfrac{2(2 + a)}{a^2 + 4a + 3}$

$$s(t+1) = \frac{2(t+1)}{(t+1)^2 - 1} = \frac{2(t+1)}{t^2 + 2t + 1 - 1} = \frac{2(t+1)}{t(t+2)}.$$

8. $g(u) = (3u - 2)^{3/2}$ Therefore, $g(1) = (3(1) - 2)^{3/2} = (1)^{3/2} = 1$;

$g(6) = (3(6) - 2)^{3/2} = 16^{3/2} = 4^3 = 64$, $g(\frac{11}{3}) = [3(\frac{11}{3}) - 2]^{3/2} = (9)^{3/2} = 27$

$g(u + 1) = [3(u + 1) - 2]^{3/2} = (3u + 1)^{3/2}$

9 $f(t) = \dfrac{2t^2}{\sqrt{t-1}}$. Therefore, $f(2) = \dfrac{2(2^2)}{\sqrt{2-1}} = 8$; $f(a) = \dfrac{2a^2}{\sqrt{a-1}}$;

$f(x+1) = \dfrac{2(x+1)^2}{\sqrt{(x+1)-1}} = \dfrac{2(x+1)^2}{\sqrt{x}}$, $f(x-1) = \dfrac{2(x-1)^2}{\sqrt{(x-1)-1}} = \dfrac{2(x-1)^2}{\sqrt{x-2}}$

10. $f(x) = 2 + 2\sqrt{5-x}$ Therefore, $f(-4) = 2 + 2\sqrt{5-(-4)} = 2 + 2\sqrt{9} = 2 + 2(3) = 8$.

$f(1) = 2 + 2\sqrt{5-1} = 2 + 2\sqrt{4} = 2 + 4 = 6.$

$f(\frac{11}{4}) = 2 + 2(5 - \frac{11}{4})^{1/2} = 2 + 2(\frac{9}{4})^{1/2} = 2 + 2(\frac{3}{2}) = 5.$

$f(x+5) = 2 + 2\sqrt{5-(x+5)} = 2 + 2\sqrt{-x}$

11. Since $x = -2 \le 0$, we see that $f(-2) = (-2)^2 + 1 = 4 + 1 = 5$. Since $x = 0 \le 0$, we see that $f(0) = (0)^2 + 1 = 1$. Since $x = 1 > 0$, we see that $f(1) = \sqrt{1} = 1$.

12. Since $x = -2 < 2$, $g(-2) = -\frac{1}{2}(-2) + 1 = 1 + 1 = 2$. Since $x = 0 < 2$,

$g(0) = -\frac{1}{2}(0) + 1 = 0 + 1 = 1$. Since $x = 2 \ge 2$, $g(2) = \sqrt{2-2} = 0$.

Since $x = 4 \ge 2$, $g(4) = \sqrt{4-2} = \sqrt{2}$

13. Since $x = -1 < 1$, $f(-1) = -\frac{1}{2}(-1)^2 + 3 = \frac{5}{2}$. Since $x = 0 < 1$,

$f(0) = -\frac{1}{2}(0)^2 + 3 = 3.$ Since $x = 1 \geq 1$, $f(1) = 2(1^2) + 1 = 3.$

Since $x = 2 \geq 1, f(2) = 2(2^2) + 1 = 9.$

14. Since $x = 0 \leq 1$, $f(0) = 2 + \sqrt{1-0} = 2 + 1 = 3.$ Since $x = 1 \leq 1$,

$f(1) = 2 + \sqrt{1-1} = 2 + 0 = 2.$ Since $x = 2 > 1$, $f(2) = \frac{1}{1-2} = \frac{1}{-1} = -1.$

15 a. $f(0) = -2$ b. (i) $f(x) = 3$ when $x \approx 2$ (ii) $f(x) = 0$ when $x = 1$
   c. $[0,6]$ d. $[-2, 6]$

16. a. $f(7) = 3$ b. $x = 4$ and $x = 6$ c. $x = 2, 0$ d. $[-1, 9]$; $[-2, 6]$

17. $g(2) = \sqrt{2^2 - 1} = \sqrt{3}$ and the point $(2, \sqrt{3})$ lies on the graph of g.

18. $f(3) = \frac{3+1}{\sqrt{3^2+7}} + 2 = \frac{4}{\sqrt{16}} + 2 = \frac{4}{4} + 2 = 3.$ We conclude that the point $(3,3)$ lies on
   the graph of f.

19. $f(-2) = \frac{|-2-1|}{-2+1} = \frac{|-3|}{-1} = -3$ and the point $(-2,-3)$ does lie on the graph of f

20. $h(-3) = \frac{|-3+1|}{(-3)^3+1} = \frac{2}{-27+1} = -\frac{2}{26} = -\frac{1}{13}$, and the point $(-3, -\frac{1}{13})$ does lie on the
   graph of h.

21. Since $f(x)$ is a real number for any value of x, the domain of f is $(-\infty, \infty)$.

22. Since $f(x)$ is a real number for any value of x, the domain of f is $(-\infty, \infty)$.

23. $f(x)$ is not defined at $x = 0$ and so the domain of f is $(-\infty,0) \cup (0,\infty)$.

24. $g(x)$ is not defined at $x = 1$ and so the domain of g is $(-\infty,1) \cup (1,\infty)$.

25 $f(x)$ is a real number for all values of x. Note that $x^2 + 1 \geq 1$ for all x. Therefore, the domain of f is $(-\infty, \infty)$.

26. Since the square root of a number is defined for all real numbers greater than or equal to zero, we have $x - 5 \geq 0$ or $x \geq 5$, and the domain is $[5, \infty)$.

27. Since the square root of a number is defined for all real numbers greater than or equal to zero, we have $5 - x \geq 0$, or $-x \geq -5$ and so $x \leq 5$. (Recall that multiplying by -1 reverses the sign of an inequality.) Therefore, the domain of g is $(-\infty, 5]$.

28. Since $2x^2 + 3$ is always greater than zero, the domain of g is $(-\infty, \infty)$.

29. The denominator of f is zero when $x^2 - 1 = 0$ or $x = \pm 1$. Therefore, the domain of f is $(-\infty, -1) \cup (-1, 1) \cup (1, \infty)$.

30. The denominator of f is equal to zero when $x^2 + x - 2 = (x + 2)(x - 1) = 0$; that is, when $x = -2$ or $x = 1$. Therefore, the domain of f is $(-\infty, -2) \cup (-2, 1) \cup (1, \infty)$.

31. f is defined when $x + 3 \geq 0$, that is, when $x \geq -3$ Therefore, the domain of f is $[-3, \infty)$.

32. g is defined when $x - 1 \geq 0$; that is when $x \geq 1$. Therefore, the domain of f is $[1, \infty)$.

33 The numerator is defined when $1 - x \geq 0$, $-x \geq -1$ or $x \leq 1$. Furthermore, the denominator is zero when $x = \pm 2$. Therefore, the domain is the set of all real numbers in $(-\infty, -2) \cup (-2, 1]$.

34. The numerator is defined when $x - 1 \geq 0$, or $x \geq 1$, and the denominator is zero when $x \neq -2, 3$. So the domain is $[1, 3) \cup (3, \infty)$.

35. a. The domain of f is the set of all real numbers.
    b. $f(x) = x^2 - x - 6$. Therefore,
    $f(-3) = (-3)^2 - (-3) - 6 = 9 + 3 - 6 = 6$; $f(-2) = (-2)^2 - (-2) - 6 = 4 + 2 - 6 = 0$.
    $f(-1) = (-1)^2 - (-1) - 6 = 1 + 1 - 6 = -4$; $f(0) = (0)^2 - (0) - 6 = -6$.

$$f(2) = (2)^2 - 2 - 6 = 4 - 2 - 6 = -4; \quad f(3) = (3)^2 - 3 - 6 = 9 - 3 - 6 = 0.$$

c.

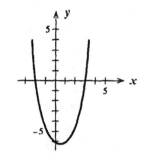

36. $f(x) = 2x^2 + x - 3$, a. Since $f(x)$ is a real number for all values of x, the domain of f is $(-\infty,\infty)$.

b.

x	-3	-2	-1	-1/2	0	1	2	3
y	12	3	-2	-3	-3	0	7	18

c.

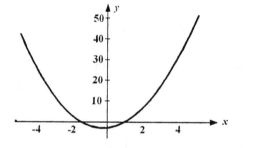

37 $f(x) = 2x^2 + 1$;

x	-3	-2	-1	0	1	2	3
f(x)	19	9	3	1	3	9	19

x	-3	-2	-1	0	1	2	3
$f(x)$	0	5	8	9	8	5	0

$(-\infty, \infty)$; $[1, \infty)$

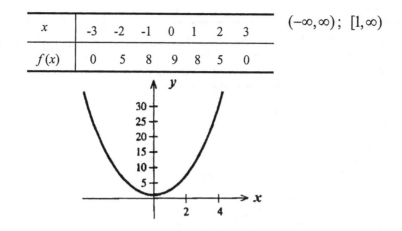

38. $f(x) = 9 - x^2$

$(-\infty, \infty)$; $(-\infty, 9]$

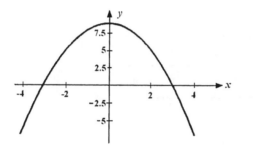

39 $f(x) = 2 + \sqrt{x}$

$[0, \infty)$; $[2, \infty)$

x	0	1	2	4	9	16
$f(x)$	2	3	3.41	4	5	6

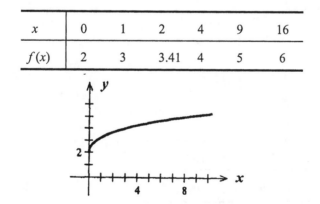

40. $g(x) = 4 - \sqrt{x}$

x	0	1	2	4	9	16
f(x)	4	3	2.6	2	1	0

$[0, \infty); (-\infty, 4]$

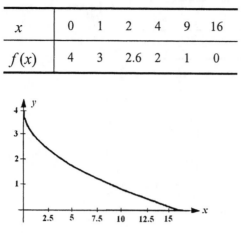

41. $f(x) = \sqrt{1 - x}$

x	0	-1	-3	-8	-15
f(x)	1	1.4	2	3	4

$(-\infty, 1]; [0, \infty)$

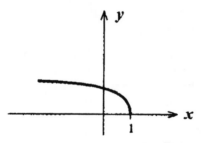

42. $f(x) = \sqrt{x - 1}$

x	1	3	5	10	17
f(x)	0	1.4	2	3	4

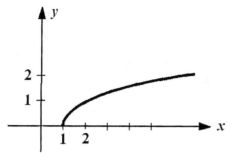

$(1,\infty); [0,\infty)$

43. $f(x) = |x| - 1$

x	-3	-2	-1	0	1	2	3
$f(x)$	2	1	0	-1	0	1	2

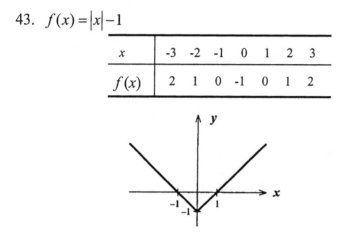

$(-\infty,\infty); [-1, \infty)$

44. $f(x) = |x| + 1$

x	-3	-2	-1	0	1	2	3
$f(x)$	4	3	2	1	2	3	4

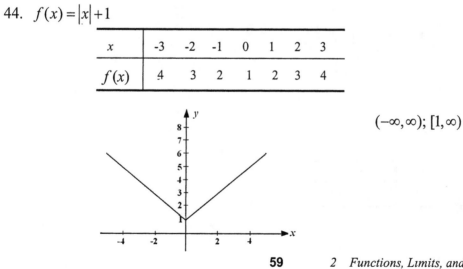

$(-\infty,\infty); [1, \infty)$

45. $f(x) = \begin{cases} x & \text{if } x < 0 \\ 2x+1 & \text{if } x \geq 0 \end{cases}$

x	-3	-2	-1	0	1	2	3
$f(x)$	-3	-2	-1	1	3	5	7

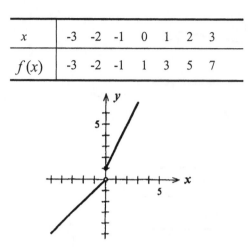

$(-\infty, \infty); (-\infty, 0) \cup [1, \infty)$

46. For $x < 2$, the graph of f is the half-line $y = 4 - x$.
    For $x \geq 2$, the graph of f is the half-line $y = 2x - 2$.

$(-\infty, \infty); [2, \infty)$

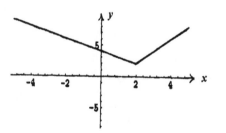

47. If $x \leq 1$, the graph of f is the half-line $y = -x + 1$. For $x > 1$, use the table

x	2	3	4
$f(x)$	3	8	15

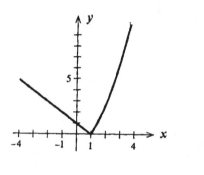

$(-\infty, \infty); [0, \infty)$

48. If $x < -1$ the graph of f is the half-line $y = -x - 1$. For $-1 \le x \le 1$, the graph consists of the line segment $y = 0$. For $x > 1$, the graph consists of the graph of the half-line $y = x + 1$.

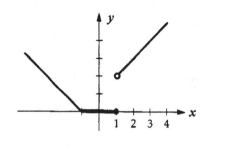

$(-\infty, \infty); [0, \infty)$

49. Each vertical line cuts the given graph at exactly one point, and so the graph represents y as a function of x.

50. Since the y-axis, which is a vertical line, intersects the graph at two points, the graph does not represent y as a function of x.

51. Since there is a vertical line that intersects the graph at three points, the graph does not represent y as a function of x.

52. Each vertical line intersects the graph of f at exactly one point, and so the graph represents y as a function of x.

53. Each vertical line intersects the graph of f at exactly one point, and so the graph represents y as a function of x.

54. The *y*-axis intersects the circle at *two* points and this shows that the circle is not the graph of a function of *x*.

55. Each vertical line intersects the graph of *f* at exactly one point, and so the graph represents *y* as a function of *x*.

56. A vertical line containing a line segment comprising the graph cuts it at infinitely many points and so the graph does not define *y* as a function of *x*.

57 The circumference of a circle with a 5-inch radius is given by
$$C(5) = 2\pi(5) = 10\pi, \text{ or } 10\pi \text{ inches.}$$

58. $V(2.1) = \frac{4}{3}\pi(2.1)^3 \approx 38.79, \qquad V(2) = \frac{4}{3}\pi(8) \approx 33.51$

$V(2.1) - V(2) = 38.79 - 33.51 = 5.28$ is the amount by which the volume of a sphere of radius 2.1 exceeds the volume of a sphere of radius 2.

59 $\frac{4}{3}(\pi)(2r)^3 = \frac{4}{3}\pi 8r^3 = 8(\frac{4}{3}\pi r^3)$. Therefore, the volume of the tumor is increased by a factor of 8.

60. Let r_1 = radius of the tumor before treatment and let r_2 = radius after treatment.
Then $\quad S(r_2) = 4\pi r_2^2 = \pi r_1^2, \ 4r_2^2 = r_1^2; \ r_1 = 2r_2 \text{ and } r_2 = \frac{1}{2}r_1$
and we conclude that the radius is 1/2 of its original size.

61. a. From $t = 0$ to $t = 5$, the graph for cassettes lies above that for CDs so from 1985 to 1990, sales of prerecorded cassettes were greater than that of CDs.
b. Sales of prerecorded CDs were greater than that of prerecorded cassettes from 1990 on.
c. The graphs intersect at the point with coordinates $x = 5$ and $y \approx 3.5$, and this tells us that the sales of the two formats were the same in 1990 with the level of sales at approximately $3.5 billion.

62. a. The slope of the straight line passing through (0, 0.61) and (10, 0.59) is
$$m = \frac{0.59 - 0.61}{10 - 0} = -0.002. \text{ Therefore, an equation of the straight line passing}$$

through the two points is $y - 0.61 = -0.002(t - 0)$ or $y = -0.002t + 0.61$.

Next, the slope of the straight line passing through $(10, 0.59)$ and $(20, 0.60)$ is

$m = \dfrac{0.60 - 0.59}{20 - 10} = 0.001$, and so an equation of the straight line passing through

the two points is $y - 0.59 = 0.001(t - 10)$ or $y = 0.001t + 0.58$. The slope of the

straight line passing through $(20, 0.60)$ and $(30, 0.66)$ is $m = \dfrac{0.66 - 0.60}{30 - 20} = 0.006$,

and so an equation of the straight line passing through the two points is

$y - 0.60 = 0.006(t - 20)$ or $y = 0.006t + 0.48$. The slope of the straight line passing

through $(30, 0.66)$ and $(40.0, 0.78)$ is $m = \dfrac{0.78 - 0.66}{40 - 30} = 0.012$, and so an equation

of the straight line passing through the two points is $y = 0.012t + 0.30$ Therefore,

the rule for f is

$$f(t) = \begin{cases} -0.002t + 0.61, & 0 \le t \le 10 \\ 0.001t + 0.58, & 10 < t \le 20 \\ 0.006t + 0.48 & 20 \le t \le 30 \\ 0.012t + 0.30 & 30 \le t \le 40 \end{cases}$$

b. The gender gap was expanding between 1960 and 1970 and shrinking between 1970 and 2000.

c. The gender gap was expanding at the rate of 0.002/yr between 1960 and 1970 and shrinking at the rate of 0.001/yr between 1970 and 1980, and shrinking at the rate of 0.006/yr between 1980 and 1990, and shrinking at the rate of 0.012/yr between 1990 and 2000.

63 a. The slope of the straight line passing through the points $(0, 0.58)$ and $(20, 0.95)$

is $m = \dfrac{0.95 - 0.58}{20 - 0} = 0.0185$, and so an equation of the straight line passing through

these two points is

$\qquad y - 0.58 = 0.0185(t - 0)$ or $y = 0.0185t + 0.58$

Next, the slope of the straight line passing through the points $(20, 0.95)$ and

$(30, 1.1)$ is $m = \dfrac{1.1 - 0.95}{30 - 20} = 0.015$, and so an equation of the straight line passing

through the two points is

$\qquad y - 0.95 = 0.015(t - 20)$ or $y = 0.015t + 0.65$

Therefore, the rule for f is

$$f(t) = \begin{cases} 0.0185t + 0.58 & 0 \le t \le 20 \\ 0.015t + 0.65 & 20 < t \le 30 \end{cases}$$

b. The ratios were changing at the rates of 0.0185/yr and 0.015/yr from 1960 through 1980, and from 1980 through 1990, respectively

c. The ratio was 1 when $t \approx 20.3$. This shows that the number of bachelor's degrees earned by women equaled the number earned by men for the first time around 1983

64 $C(0) = 6$, or 6 billion dollars; $C(50) = 0.75(50) + 6 = 43.5$, or 43.5 billion dollars.

$C(100) = 0.75(100) + 6 = 81$, or 81 billion dollars.

65 a. $T(x) = 0.06x$

 b. $T(200) = 0.06(200) = 12$, or \$12.00; $T(5.65) = 0.06(5.65) = 0.34$, or \$0.34.

66. $S(r) = 4\pi r^2$

67 The child should receive $D(4) = \frac{2}{25}(500)(4) = 160$, or 160 mg.

68. a. $I(x) = 1.053x$ b. $I(620) = 1.053(620) = 652.86$, or \$652.86.

69. a. Take $m = 7.5$ and $b = 20$, then $f(t) = 7.5t + 20$ $(0 \le t \le 6)$
 b. $f(6) = 7.5(6) + 20 = 65$, or 65 million households.

70. a. The daily cost of leasing from Ace is $C_1(x) = 30 + 0.45x$, while the daily cost of leasing from Acme is $C_2(x) = 25 + 0.50x$, where x is the number of miles driven.
 b.

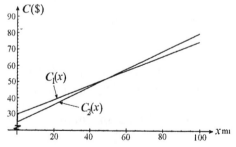

c. The costs will be the same when $C_1(x) = C_2(x)$, that is, when

c. The costs will be the same when $C_1(x) = C_2(x)$, that is, when

$$30 + 0.45x = 25 + 0.50x$$
$$-0.05x = -5, \text{ or } x = 100.$$

Since $\qquad C_1(70) = 30 + 0.45(70) = 61.5$

and $\qquad C_2(70) = 25 + 0.50(70) = 60,$

and the customer plans to drive less than 70 miles, she should rent from Acme.

71. a. The graph of the function is a straight line passing through $(0, 120,000)$ and $(10,0)$. Its slope is $m = \dfrac{0 - 120,000}{10 - 0} = -12,000$ The required equation is

$$V = -12,000n + 120,000.$$

b.

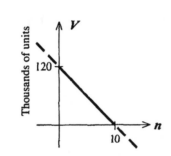

c. $V = -12,000(6) + 120,000 = 48,000$, or $48,000.

d. This is given by the slope, that is, $12,000 per year.

72. Here $V = -20,000n + 1,000,000.$

The book value in 2001 is given by $V = -20,000(15) + 1,000,000$, or $700,000.

The book value in 2005 is given by $V = -20,000(19) + 1,000,000$, or $620,000.

The book value in 2009 will be $V = -20,000(23) + 1,000,000$, or $540,000.

73. The domain of the function f is the set of all real positive numbers where $V \neq 0$, that is, $(0,\infty)$. The graph of f follows.

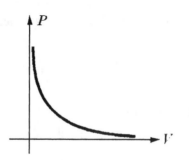

74. a. We require that $0.04 - r^2 \geq 0$ and $r \geq 0$. This is true if $0 \leq r \leq 0.2$. Therefore, the domain of v is $[0,0.2]$.
b. Compute
$v(0) = 1000[0.04 - (0)^2] = 1000(0.04) = 40.$
$v(0.1) = 1000[0.04 - (0.1)^2] = 1000(0.04 - .01) = 1000(0.03) = 30.$
$v(0.2) = 1000[0.04 - (0.2)^2] = 1000(0.04 - 0.04) = 0.$
c.

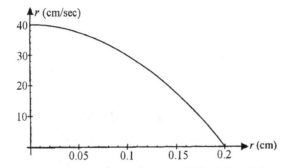

d. As the distance r increases, the velocity of the blood decreases.

75. a. $N(0) = 3.6$ or 3.6 million people;
$N(25) = 0.0031(25)^2 + 0.16(25) + 3.6 = 9.5375$, or approximately 9.5 million people.
b. $N(30) = 0.0031(30)^2 + 0.16(30) + 3.6 = 11.19$, or approximately 11.2 million people.

76. $N(t) = -t^3 + 6t^2 + 15t$. Between 8 A.M. and 9 A.M., the average worker can be expected to assemble
$$N(1) - N(0) = (-1 + 6 + 15) - 0 = 20,$$
or 20 walkie-talkies. Between 9 A.M. and 10 A.M., we can expect
$$N(2) - N(1) = [-2^3 + 6(2^2) + 15(2)] - (-1 + 6 + 15)$$

$$= 46 - 20 = 26,$$
or 26 walkie-talkies can be assembled by the average worker.

77 When the proportion of popular votes won by the Democratic presidential candidate is 0.60, the proportion of seats in the House of Representatives won by Democratic candidates is given by

$$s(0.6) = \frac{(0.6)^3}{(0.6)^3 + (1-0.6)^3} = \frac{0.216}{0.216 + 0.064} = \frac{0.216}{0.280} \approx 0.77$$

78. The percentage at age 65 that are expected to have Alzheimer's disease is given by
$$P(0) = 0.0726(0)^2 + 0.7902(0) + 4.9623 = 4.9623, \quad \text{or} \quad 4.96\%.$$
The percentage at age 90 that are expected to have Alzheimer's disease is given by
$$P(25) = 0.0726(25)^2 + 0.7902(25) + 4.9623 = 70.09, \quad \text{or} \quad 70.09\%.$$

79. $N(t) = -0.0014t^3 + 0.027t^2 - 0.008t + 4.1$
   a. $N(0) = 4.1$, or 4.1 million.
   b. $N(12) = -0.0014(12)^3 + 0.027(12)^2 - 0.008(12) + 4.1 = 5.4728$, or 5.47 million.

80. a. The domain of f is $(0,12]$.

$$f(x) = \begin{cases} 83 & \text{if } 2 < x \le 3 \\ 106 & \text{if } 3 < x \le 4 \\ 129 & \text{if } 4 < x \le 5 \\ 152 & \text{if } 5 < x \le 6 \\ 175 & \text{if } 6 < x \le 7 \\ 198 & \text{if } 7 < x \le 8 \\ 221 & \text{if } 8 < x \le 9 \\ 244 & \text{if } 9 < x \le 10 \\ 267 & \text{if } 10 < x \le 11 \\ 290 & \text{if } 11 < x \le 12 \end{cases}$$

b.

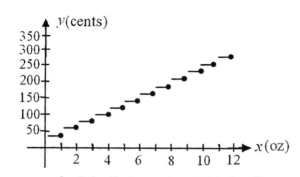

81. a. The amount of solids discharged in 1989 ($t = 0$) was 130 tons/day; in 1992 ($t = 3$), it was 100 tons/day; and in 1996 ($t = 7$), it was
$f(7) = 1.25(7)^2 - 26.25(7) + 162.5 = 40$, or 40 tons/day

b.

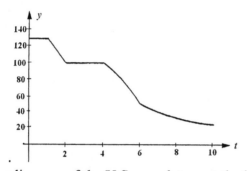

82. a. The median age of the U.S. population at the beginning of 1900 was $f(0) = 22.9$, or 22.9 years; at the beginning of 1950 was
$f(5) = -0.7(5)^2 + 7.2(5) + 11.5 = 30$, or 30 years; at the beginning of 1990 was
$f(9) = 2.6(9) + 9.4 = 32.8$, or 32.8 years.

b.

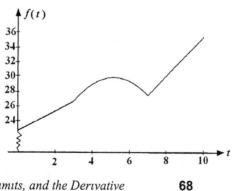

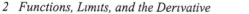

83 True, by definition of a function (page 50).

84. False. Take $f(x) = x^2$, $a = 1$, $b = -1$. Then $f(1) = 1 = f(-1)$, but $a \neq b$.

85 False. Let $f(x) = x^2$, then take $a = 1$, and $b = 2$. Then $f(a) = f(1) = 1$ and
    $f(b) = f(2) = 4$ and $f(a) + f(b) = 1 + 4 \neq f(a+b) = f(3) = 9$

86. False. It intersects the graph of a function in at most one point.

USING TECHNOLOGY EXERCISES 2.1, page 67

1.   2.

3   4.

5 a.   b.

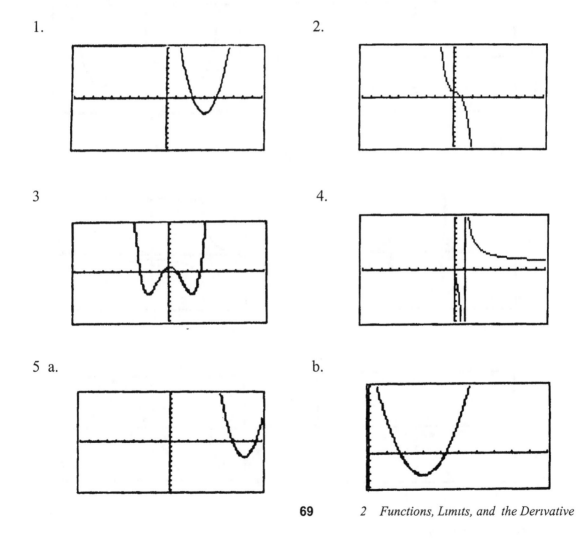

6 . a.

b.

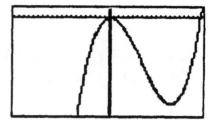

7. a.

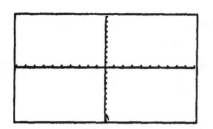

b.

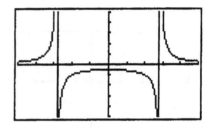

8. a.

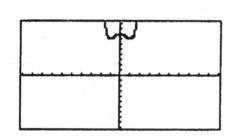

b.

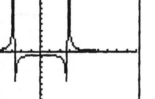

9 a.

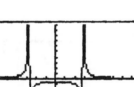

b.

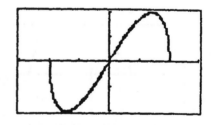

10. a 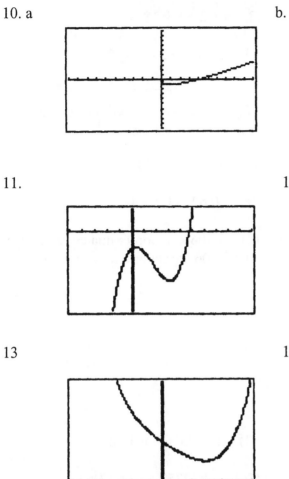 b.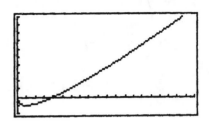

11.  12.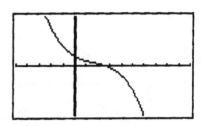

13 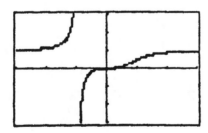 14.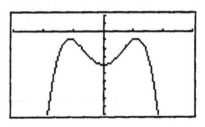

15 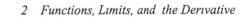 16.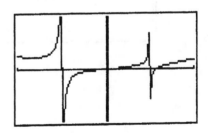

17. 18, $f(-1) = -3(-1)^3 + 5(-1)^2 - 2(-1) + 8 = 3 + 5 + 2 + 8 = 18.$

18. 13, $f(2) = 2(2)^4 - 3(2)^3 + 2(2)^2 + 2 - 5 = 32 - 24 + 8 + 2 - 5 = 13$

19. 2; $f(1) = \dfrac{(1)^4 - 3(1)^2}{1-2} = \dfrac{1-3}{-1} = 2.$

20. $f(2) = \dfrac{\sqrt{2^2 - 1}}{3(2) + 4} = \dfrac{\sqrt{3}}{10} \approx 0.1732.$

21. $f(2.145) \approx 18.5505$

22. $f(1.28) \approx 17.3850$

23. $f(2.41) \approx 4.1616$

24. $f(0.62) \approx 1\ 7214$

25. a.

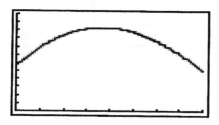

    b. $f(2) \approx 9\ 4066,$ or approximately 9 41%/yr
       $f(4) \approx 8.7062,$ or approximately 8.71 %/yr.

26. a.

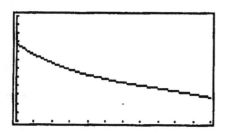

    b. $f(3) = 13.875061$ or 13.88%.

       $f(10) = 11.12257,$ or 11.12%.

27 a.

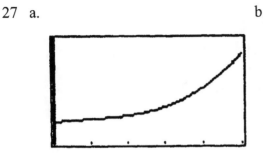

b. $f(6) = 44.7$;

$f(8) = 52.7$;

$f(11) = 129.2$.

28. a.

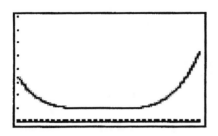

b. $f(18) = 3.3709$; $f(50) = 0.971$;
$f(80) = 4\ 4078$

2.2 CONCEPT QUESTIONS, page 73

1 a. $(f+g)(x) = f(x)+g(x)$, $(f-g)(x) = f(x)-g(x)$; $(fg)(x) = f(x)g(x)$, all
with domain $A \cap B$ $(f/g)(x) = \dfrac{f(x)}{g(x)}$, domain $A \cap B$ excluding $x \in A \cap B$ such
that $g(x) = 0$.

b. $(f+g)(2) = f(2)+g(2) = 3+(-2) = 1; (f-g)(2) = f(2)-g(2) = 3-(-2) = 5;$,
$(fg)(2) = f(2)g(2) = 3(-2) = -6; (f/g)(2) = \dfrac{f(2)}{g(2)} = \dfrac{3}{-2} = -\dfrac{3}{2}$

2. a. $(f \circ g)(x) = f[g(x)]$, domain is the set of all x in the domain of g such that $g(x)$
is in the domain of f $(g \circ f)(x) = g[f(x)]$, domain is the set of all x in the domain
of f such that $f(x)$ is in the domain of g

b. $(g \circ f)(2) = g[f(2)] = g(3) = 8$, We cannot conclude what $(f \circ g)(3)$ is because
$(f \circ g)(3) = f[g(3)] = f(8)$, and we don't know what $f(8)$ is.

1. $(f+g)(x) = f(x) + g(x) = (x^3 + 5) + (x^2 - 2) = x^3 + x^2 + 3$

2. $(f-g)(x) = f(x) - g(x) = (x^3 + 5) - (x^2 - 2) = x^3 - x^2 + 7$

3   $fg(x) = f(x)g(x) = (x^3 + 5)(x^2 - 2) = x^5 - 2x^3 + 5x^2 - 10.$

4. $gf(x) = g(x)f(x) = (x^2 - 2)(x^3 + 5) = x^5 - 2x^3 + 5x^2 - 10.$

5   $\dfrac{f}{g}(x) = \dfrac{f(x)}{g(x)} = \dfrac{x^3 + 5}{x^2 - 2}.$

6. $\dfrac{f-g}{h}(x) = \dfrac{f(x)-g(x)}{h(x)} = \dfrac{x^3 + 5 - (x^2 - 2)}{2x+4} = \dfrac{x^3 - x^2 + 7}{2x+4}$

7   $\dfrac{fg}{h}(x) = \dfrac{f(x)g(x)}{h(x)} = \dfrac{(x^3 + 5)(x^2 - 2)}{2x+4} = \dfrac{x^5 - 2x^3 + 5x^2 - 10}{2x+4}$

8. $fg\,h(x) = f(x)g(x)h(x) = (x^3 + 5)(x^2 - 2)(2x + 4)$
    $= (x^5 - 2x^3 + 5x^2 - 10)(2x + 4)$
    $= 2x^6 - 4x^4 + 10x^3 - 20x + 4x^5 - 8x^3 + 20x^2 - 40$
    $= 2x^6 + 4x^5 - 4x^4 + 2x^3 + 20x^2 - 20x - 40.$

9   $(f+g)(x) = f(x) + g(x) = x - 1 + \sqrt{x+1}.$

10. $(g-f)(x) = g(x) - f(x) = \sqrt{x+1} - (x-1) = \sqrt{x+1} - x + 1$

11 $(fg)(x) = f(x)g(x) = (x-1)\sqrt{x+1}$

12. $(gf)(x) = g(x)f(x) = \sqrt{x+1}(x-1)$

13 $\dfrac{g}{h}(x) = \dfrac{g(x)}{h(x)} = \dfrac{\sqrt{x+1}}{2x^3 - 1}.$ 14. $\dfrac{h}{g}(x) = \dfrac{h(x)}{g(x)} = \dfrac{2x^3 - 1}{\sqrt{x+1}}.$

15. $\dfrac{fg}{h}(x) = \dfrac{(x-1)(\sqrt{x}+1)}{2x^3-1}$

16. $\dfrac{fh}{g}(x) = \dfrac{(x-1)(2x^3-1)}{\sqrt{x}+1} = \dfrac{2x^4-2x^3-x+1}{\sqrt{x}+1}$

17. $\dfrac{f-h}{g}(x) = \dfrac{x-1-(2x^3-1)}{\sqrt{x}+1} = \dfrac{x-2x^3}{\sqrt{x}+1}$

18. $\dfrac{gh}{g-f}(x) = \dfrac{\sqrt{x+1}(2x^3-1)}{\sqrt{x+1}-(x-1)} = \dfrac{\sqrt{x+1}(2x^3-1)}{\sqrt{x+1}-x+1}$

19. $(f+g)(x) = x^2+5+\sqrt{x}-2 = x^2+\sqrt{x}+3.$

　　$(f-g)(x) = x^2+5-(\sqrt{x}-2) = x^2-\sqrt{x}+7$

　　$(fg)(x) = (x^2+5)(\sqrt{x}-2); \quad (\dfrac{f}{g})(x) = \dfrac{x^2+5}{\sqrt{x}-2}$

20. $(f+g)(x) = \sqrt{x-1}+x^3+1; \quad (f-g)(x) = \sqrt{x-1}-x^3-1$

　　$(fg)(x) = \sqrt{x-1}(x^3+1); \quad (\dfrac{f}{g})(x) = \dfrac{\sqrt{x-1}}{x^3+1}$

21. $(f+g)(x) = \sqrt{x+3}+\dfrac{1}{x-1} = \dfrac{(x-1)\sqrt{x+3}+1}{x-1}$

　　$(f-g)(x) = \sqrt{x+3}-\dfrac{1}{x-1} = \dfrac{(x-1)\sqrt{x+3}-1}{x-1}$

　　$(fg)(x) = \sqrt{x+3}\left(\dfrac{1}{x-1}\right) = \dfrac{\sqrt{x+3}}{x-1}. \quad (\dfrac{f}{g}) = \sqrt{x+3}(x-1).$

22. $(f+g)(x) = \dfrac{1}{x^2+1}+\dfrac{1}{x^2-1} = \dfrac{x^2-1+x^2+1}{(x^2+1)(x^2-1)} = \dfrac{2x^2}{(x^2+1)(x^2-1)}.$

$$(f-g)(x) = \frac{1}{x^2+1} - \frac{1}{x^2-1} = \frac{x^2-1-x^2-1}{(x^2+1)(x^2-1)} = -\frac{2}{(x^2+1)(x^2-1)}$$

$$(fg)(x) = \frac{1}{(x^2+1)(x^2-1)}, \quad \left(\frac{f}{g}\right)(x) = \frac{x^2-1}{x^2+1}$$

23 $$(f+g)(x) = \frac{x+1}{x-1} + \frac{x+2}{x-2} = \frac{(x+1)(x-2)+(x+2)(x-1)}{(x-1)(x-2)}$$

$$= \frac{x^2-x-2+x^2+x-2}{(x-1)(x-2)} = \frac{2x^2-4}{(x-1)(x-2)} = \frac{2(x^2-2)}{(x-1)(x-2)}$$

$$(f-g)(x) = \frac{x+1}{x-1} - \frac{x+2}{x-2} = \frac{(x+1)(x-2)-(x+2)(x-1)}{(x-1)(x-2)}$$

$$= \frac{x^2-x-2-x^2-x+2}{(x-1)(x-2)} = \frac{-2x}{(x-1)(x-2)}$$

$$(fg)(x) = \frac{(x+1)(x+2)}{(x-1)(x-2)}, \quad \left(\frac{f}{g}\right) = \frac{(x+1)(x-2)}{(x-1)(x+2)}$$

24 $$(f+g)(x) = x^2+1+\sqrt{x+1}; \quad (f-g)(x) = x^2+1-\sqrt{x+1}.$$

$$(fg)(x) = (x^2+1)\sqrt{x+1}; \quad \left(\frac{f}{g}\right)(x) = \frac{x^2+1}{\sqrt{x+1}}$$

25 $$(f \circ g)(x) = f(g(x)) = f(x^2) = (x^2)^2 + x^2 + 1 = x^4 + x^2 + 1.$$

$$(g \circ f)(x) = g(f(x)) = g(x^2+x+1) = (x^2+x+1)^2$$

26. $$(f \circ g)(x) = f(g(x)) = 3[g(x)]^2 + 2g(x) + 1$$

$$= 3(x+3)^2 + 2(x+3) + 1 = 3x^2 + 20x + 34.$$

$$(g \circ f)(x) = g(f(x)) = f(x) + 3 = 3x^2 + 2x + 1 + 3 = 3x^2 + 2x + 4.$$

27. $$(f \circ g)(x) = f(g(x)) = f(x^2-1) = \sqrt{x^2-1}+1$$

$$(g \circ f)(x) = g(f(x)) = g(\sqrt{x}+1) = (\sqrt{x}+1)^2 - 1 = x + 2\sqrt{x} + 1 - 1 = x + 2\sqrt{x}$$

28. $(f \circ g)(x) = f(g(x)) = 2\sqrt{g(x)} + 3 = 2\sqrt{x^2 + 1} + 3.$

$(g \circ f)(x) = g(f(x)) = [f(x)]^2 + 1 = (2\sqrt{x} + 3)^2 + 1 = 4x + 12\sqrt{x} + 10.$

29. $(f \circ g)(x) = f(g(x)) = f\left(\dfrac{1}{x}\right) = \dfrac{1}{x} \div \left(\dfrac{1}{x^2} + 1\right) = \dfrac{1}{x} \cdot \dfrac{x^2}{x^2 + 1} = \dfrac{x}{x^2 + 1}$

$(g \circ f)(x) = g(f(x)) = g\left(\dfrac{x}{x^2 + 1}\right) = \dfrac{x^2 + 1}{x}$

30. $(f \circ g)(x) = f(g(x)) = f\left(\dfrac{1}{x-1}\right) = \sqrt{\dfrac{x}{x-1}}.$

$(g \circ f)(x) = g(f(x)) = g(\sqrt{x+1}) = \dfrac{1}{\sqrt{x+1} - 1} \cdot \dfrac{\sqrt{x+1} + 1}{\sqrt{x+1} + 1} = \dfrac{\sqrt{x+1} + 1}{x}.$

31. $h(2) = g[f(2)]$. But $f(2) = 4 + 2 + 1 = 7$, so $h(2) = g(7) = 49.$

32. $h(2) = g[f(2)]$. But $f(2) = (2^2 - 1)^{1/3} = 3^{1/3}$, so
$h(2) = g(3^{1/3}) = 3(3^{1/3})^3 + 1 = 3(3) + 1 = 10.$

33. $h(2) = g[f(2)]$. But $f(2) = \dfrac{1}{2(2)+1} = \dfrac{1}{5}$, so $h(2) = g(\dfrac{1}{5}) = \dfrac{1}{\sqrt{5}} = \dfrac{\sqrt{5}}{5}$

34. $h(2) = g[f(2)]$. But $f(2) = \dfrac{1}{2-1} = 1$, so $g(1) = 1^2 + 1 = 2.$

35. $f(x) = 2x^3 + x^2 + 1, \; g(x) = x^5.$

36. $f(x) = 3x^2 - 4, \; g(x) = x^3.$

37. $f(x) = x^2 - 1, \; g(x) = \sqrt{x}$

38. $f(x) = (2x - 3), \; g(x) = x^{3/2}.$

39. $f(x) = x^2 - 1, \; g(x) = \dfrac{1}{x}.$

40. $f(x) = x^2 - 4, \; g(x) = \dfrac{1}{\sqrt{x}}$

41. $f(x) = 3x^2 + 2, \; g(x) = \dfrac{1}{x^{3/2}}$

42. $f(x) = \sqrt{2x+1}$, $g(x) = \dfrac{1}{x} + x$.

43 $f(a+h) - f(a) = [3(a+h)+4] - (3a+4) = 3a + 3h + 4 - 3a - 4 = 3h.$

44 $f(a+h) - f(a) = -\dfrac{1}{2}(a+h) + 3 - (-\dfrac{1}{2}a + 3) = -\dfrac{1}{2}a - \dfrac{1}{2}h + 3 + \dfrac{1}{2}a - 3 = -\dfrac{1}{2}h.$

45 $f(a+h) - f(a) = 4 - (a+h)^2 - (4 - a^2)$
$= 4 - a^2 - 2ah - h^2 - 4 + a^2 = -2ah - h^2 = -h(2a + h).$

46. $f(a+h) - f(a) = [(a+h)^2 - 2(a+h) + 1] - (a^2 - 2a + 1)$
$= a^2 + 2ah + h^2 - 2a - 2h + 1 - a^2 + 2a - 1 = h(2a + h - 2).$

47. $\dfrac{f(a+h) - f(a)}{h} = \dfrac{[(a+h)^2 + 1] - (a^2 + 1)}{h} = \dfrac{a^2 + 2ah + h^2 + 1 - a^2 - 1}{h} = \dfrac{2ah + h^2}{h}$
$= \dfrac{h(2a+h)}{h} = 2a + h.$

48. $\dfrac{f(a+h) - f(a)}{h} = \dfrac{[2(a+h)^2 - (a+h) + 1] - (2a^2 - a + 1)}{h}$

$\dfrac{2a^2 + 4ah + 2h^2 - a - h + 1 - 2a^2 + a - 1}{h} = \dfrac{4ah + 2h^2 - h}{h} = 4a + 2h - 1$

49 $\dfrac{f(a+h) - f(a)}{h} = \dfrac{[(a+h)^3 - (a+h)] - (a^3 - a)}{h}$
$= \dfrac{a^3 + 3a^2h + 3ah^2 + h^3 - a - h - a^3 + a}{h}$
$= \dfrac{3a^2h + 3ah^2 + h^3 - h}{h} = 3a^2 + 3ah + h^2 - 1$

50. $\dfrac{f(a+h)-f(a)}{h} = \dfrac{[2(a+h)^3 -(a+h)^2 +1]-(2a^3 -a^2 +1)}{h}$

$$= \dfrac{2a^3 +6a^2h+6ah^2 +2h^3 -a^2 -2ah-h^2 +1-2a^3 +a^2 -1}{h}$$

$$= \dfrac{6a^2h+6ah^2 +2h^3 -2ah-h^2}{h} = 6a^2 +6ah+2h^2 -2a-h$$

51 $\dfrac{f(a+h)-f(a)}{h} = \dfrac{\dfrac{1}{a+h}-\dfrac{1}{a}}{h} = \dfrac{\dfrac{a-(a+h)}{a(a+h)}}{h} = -\dfrac{1}{a(a+h)}$

52. $\dfrac{f(a+h)-f(a)}{h} = \dfrac{\sqrt{a+h}-\sqrt{a}}{h} \cdot \dfrac{(\sqrt{a+h})+\sqrt{a})}{(\sqrt{a+h}+\sqrt{a})} = \dfrac{(a+h)-a}{h(\sqrt{a+h}+\sqrt{a})} = \dfrac{1}{\sqrt{a+h}+\sqrt{a}}$

53 $F(t)$ represents the total revenue for the two restaurants at time t.

54. $F(t)$ represents the net rate of growth of the species of whales in year t.

55 $f(t)g(t)$ represents the (dollar) value of Nancy's holdings at time t.

56. $f(t)/g(t)$ represents the unit cost of the commodity at time t.

57. $g \circ f$ is the function giving the amount of carbon monoxide pollution at time t.

58. $f \circ g$ is the function giving the revenue at time t.

59. $C(x) = 0.6x + 12{,}100$.

60. a. $D(t) = (f - g)(t) = f(t) - g(t) = (1.54t^2 +7\ 1t +31.4) - (1.21t^2 +6t +14.5)$

$$= 0.33t^2 +1.1t +16.9$$

$D(4) = 0.33(4)^2 +1.1(4) +16.9 = 26.58$

and this gives the total number of email messages that are not spam messages per day as 26.6 billion.

b. $P(t) = (f/g)(t) = \dfrac{f(t)}{g(t)} = \dfrac{1.54t^2 + 7.1t + 31.4}{1.21t^2 + 6t + 14.5}$

$$P(4) = \dfrac{1.54(4)^2 + 7.1(4) + 31.4}{1.21(4)^2 + 6(4) + 14.5} \approx 1.459$$

and this says that the ratio of all email messages to spam messages is approximately 1.5.

61. a. $f(t) = 267; \; g(t) = 2t^2 + 46t + 733$

   b. $h(t) = (f+g)(t) = f(t) + g(t) = 267 + (2t^2 + 46t + 733) = 2t^2 + 46t + 1000$

   c. $h(13) = 2(13)^2 + 46(13) + 1000 = 1936$, or 1936 tons.

62. $C(x) = 0.000003x^3 - 0.03x^2 + 200x + 100{,}000$

   $C(2000) = 0.000003(2000)^3 - 0.03(2000)^2 + 200(2000) + 100{,}000$

   $= 404{,}000, \text{ or } \$404{,}000.$

63. a. $P(x) = R(x) - C(x)$

   $= -0.1x^2 + 500x - (0.000003x^3 - 0.03x^2 + 200x + 100{,}000)$

   $= -0.000003x^3 - 0.07x^2 + 300x - 100{,}000.$

   b. $P(1500) = -0.000003(1500)^3 - 0.07(1500)^2 + 300(1500) - 100{,}000$

   $= 182{,}375 \quad \text{or } \$182{,}375$

64. a. $C(x) = V(x) + 20000 = 0.000001x^3 - 0.01x^2 + 50x + 20000$

   $= 0.000001x^3 - 0.01x^2 + 50x + 20{,}000$

   b. $P(x) = R(x) - C(x) = -0.02x^2 + 150x - 0.000001x^3 + 0.01x^2 - 50x - 20{,}000$

   $= -0.000001x^3 - 0.01x^2 + 100x - 20{,}000$

   c. $P(2000) = -0.000001(2000)^3 - 0.01(2000)^2 + 100(2000) - 20{,}000$

   $= 132{,}000 \text{ or } \$132{,}000.$

65 a. The gap is

   $G(t) - C(t) = (3.5t^2 + 26.7t + 436.2) - (24.3t + 365)$

   $= 3.5t^2 + 2.4t + 71.2.$

   b. At the beginning of 1983, the gap was

   $G(0) = 3.5(0)^2 + 2.4(0) + 71.2 = 71.2, \text{ or } 71{,}200.$

   At the beginning of 1986, the gap was

$$G(3) = 3.5(3)^2 + 2.4(3) + 71.2 = 109.9, \text{ or } 109{,}900.$$

66. a.
$$N(r(t)) = \dfrac{7}{1 + 0.02\left(\dfrac{10t + 150}{t + 10}\right)^2}$$

   b.
$$N(r(0)) = \dfrac{7}{1 + 0.02\left(\dfrac{10(0) + 150}{0 + 10}\right)^2} = \dfrac{7}{1 + 0.02\left(\dfrac{150}{10}\right)^2} = \dfrac{7}{5.5} \approx 1.27,$$

   or 1.27 million units.

$$N(r(12)) = \dfrac{7}{1 + 0.02\left(\dfrac{120 + 150}{12 + 10}\right)^2} = \dfrac{7}{1 + 0.02\left(\dfrac{270}{22}\right)^2} = \dfrac{7}{4.01} \approx 1.74,$$

   or 1 74 million units.

$$N(r(18)) = \dfrac{7}{1 + 0.02\left(\dfrac{180 + 150}{18 + 10}\right)^2} = \dfrac{7}{1 + 0.02\left(\dfrac{330}{28}\right)^2} = \dfrac{7}{3.78} \approx 1.85,$$

   or 1.85 million units.

67. a. The occupancy rate at the beginning of January is
$$r(0) = \dfrac{10}{81}(0)^3 - \dfrac{10}{3}(0)^2 + \dfrac{200}{9}(0) + 55 = 55, \text{ or } 55 \text{ percent.}$$
$$r(5) = \dfrac{10}{81}(5)^3 - \dfrac{10}{3}(5)^2 + \dfrac{200}{9}(5) + 55 = 98.2, \text{ or } 98.2 \text{ percent.}$$

   b. The monthly revenue at the beginning of January is
$$R(55) = -\dfrac{3}{5000}(55)^3 + \dfrac{9}{50}(55)^2 = 444.68, \text{ or } \$444{,}700.$$
   The monthly revenue at the beginning of June is
$$R(98.2) = -\dfrac{3}{5000}(98.2)^3 + \dfrac{9}{50}(98.2)^2 = 1167.6, \text{ or } \$1{,}167{,}600.$$

68. $N(t) = 1.42(x(t)) = \dfrac{(1.42)(7)(t + 10)^2}{(t + 10)^2 + 2(t + 15)^2} = \dfrac{9.94(t + 10)^2}{(t + 10)^2 + 2(t + 15)^2}.$

   The number of jobs created 6 months from now will be

$$N(6) = \frac{9.94(16)^2}{(16)^2 + 2(21)^2} = 2.24, \text{ or } 2.24 \text{ million jobs.}$$

The number of jobs created 12 months from now will be

$$N(12) = \frac{9.94(22)^2}{(22)^2 + 2(27)^2} = 2.48, \text{ or } 2.48 \text{ million jobs.}$$

69. True. $(f+g)(x) = f(x) + g(x) = g(x) + f(x) = (g+f)(x)$.

70. False. Let $f(x) = x+2$ and $g(x) = \sqrt{x}$. Then $(g \circ f)(x) = \sqrt{x+2}$ is defined at $x = -1$ But $(f \circ g)(x) = \sqrt{x} + 2$ is not defined at $x = -1$.

71 False. Take $f(x) = \sqrt{x}$ and $g(x) = x+1$. Then $(g \circ f)(x) = \sqrt{x} + 1$, but $(f \circ g)(x) = \sqrt{x+1}$.

72. False. Take $f(x) = x+1$. Then $(f \circ f)(x) = f(f(x)) = x+2$. But $f^2(x) = [f(x)]^2 = (x+1)^2 = x^2 + 2x + 1$.

2.3 CONCEPT QUESTIONS, page 85

1. See page 77 (Answers will vary).

2. a. $P(x) = a_0 x^n + a_1 x^{n-1} + \cdots + a_n$ $(a_n \neq 0, n$ a positive integer
    Example: $P(x) = 4x^3 - 3x^2 + 2$

   b. $R(x) = \dfrac{P(x)}{Q(x)}$, where P and Q are polynomials with $Q(x) \neq 0$

    Example: $R(x) = \dfrac{3x^4 - 2x^2 + 1}{x^2 + 3x + 5}$

3 a. A demand function $p = D(x)$ gives the relationship between the unit price of a commodity, p, and the quantity, x, demanded. A supply function $p = S(x)$ gives the relationship between the unit price of a commodity, p, and the quantity, x, the supplier will make available in the market place. Market equilibrium occurs when

the quantity produced is equal to the quantity demanded. To find the market equilibrium, we solve the equations $p = D(x)$ and $p = S(x)$ simultaneously

EXERCISES 2.3, page 85

1. Yes. $2x + 3y = 6$ and so $y = -\frac{2}{3}x + 2$.
2. Yes. $4y = 2x + 7$ and so $y = \frac{1}{2}x + \frac{7}{4}$.

3. Yes. $2y = x + 4$ and so $y = \frac{1}{2}x + 2$.
4. Yes. $3y = 2x - 8$ and so $y = \frac{2}{3}x - \frac{8}{3}$

5. Yes. $4y = 2x + 9$ and so $y = \frac{1}{2}x + \frac{9}{4}$.
6. Yes. $6y = 3x + 7$ and so $y = \frac{1}{2}x + \frac{7}{6}$

7. No, because of the term x^2
8. No, because of the term $\sqrt{x}$.

9. f is a polynomial function in x of degree 6.

10. f is a rational function.

11. Expanding $G(x) = 2(x^2 - 3)^3$, we have $G(x) = 2x^6 - 18x^4 + 54x^2 - 54$, and we conclude that G is a polynomial function in x of degree 6.

12. We can write $H(x) = \dfrac{2}{x^3} + \dfrac{5}{x^2} + 6 = \dfrac{2 + 5x + 6x^3}{x^3}$

and conclude that H is a rational function.

13. f is neither a polynomial nor a rational function.

14. f is a rational function.

15. $f(0) = 2$ gives $f(0) = m(0) + b = b = 2$. Next, $f(3) = -1$ gives $f(3) = m(3) + b = -1$. Substituting $b = 2$ in this last equation, we have $3m + 2 = -1$, and $3m = -3$, or $m = -1$. So $m = -1$ and $b = 2$.

16. $f(2) = 4$ gives $f(2) = 2m + b = 4$. We also know that $m = -1$. Therefore, we find $2(-1) + b = 4$ and so $b = 6$.

17. a. $C(x) = 8x + 40,000$ b. $R(x) = 12x$
    c. $P(x) = R(x) - C(x) = 12x - (8x + 40,000) = 4x - 40,000.$
    d. $P(8000) = 4(8000) - 40,000 = -8000$, or a loss of $8000.
       $P(12,000) = 4(12,000) - 40,000 = 8000$, or a profit of $8000.

18. a. $C(x) = 14x + 100,000$ b. $R(x) = 12x$
    c. $P(x) = R(x) - C(x) = 20x - (14x + 100,000) = 6x - 100,000$
    d. $P(12,000) = 6(12,000) - 100,000 = -28,000$, or a loss of $28,000.
       $P(20,000) = 6(20,000) - 100,000 = 20,000$, or a profit of $20,000.

19 The individual's disposable income is $D = (1 - 0.28)60,000 = 43,200$, or $43,200.

20. The child should receive $D(0.4) = \dfrac{(0.4)(500)}{1.7} = 117.65$, or approximately 118 mg.

21 The child should receive $D(4) = \left(\dfrac{4+1}{24}\right)(500) = 104.17$, or 104 mg.

22. Two hours after starting work, the average worker will be assembling at the rate of
    $f(2) = -\frac{3}{2}(2)^2 + 6(2) + 10$, or 16 phones per hour.

23. $P(28) = -\frac{1}{8}(28)^2 + 7(28) + 30 = 128$, or $128,000.

24. $S(0) = 45.9$ or $45.9 billion
    $S(6) = 0.288(6)^2 + 3.03(6) + 45.9 = 74.448$ or $74.448 billion.

25 $S(6) = 0.73(6)^2 + 15.8(6) + 2.7 = 123.78$, or 123.78 million kw-hr.
    $S(8) = 0.73(8)^2 + 15.8(8) + 2.7 = 175.82$, or 175.82 million kw-hr.

26. $f(t) = 0.1714t^2 + 0.6657t + 0.7143$
    a. $f(0) = 0.7143$ or $714,300$.
    b. $f(5) = 0.1714(5)^2 + 0.6657(5) + 0.7143 = 8.3278$, or 8.33 million.

27 $N(0) = 0.7$, or 0.7 per 100 million vehicle miles driven.

$N(7) = 0.0336(7)^3 - 0.118(7)^2 + 0.215(7) + 0.7 = 7.9478$, or 7.95 per 100 million vehicle miles driven.

28. $N(0) = 648$ or 648,000

$N(1) = -35.8 + 202 + 87.7 + 648 \approx 902$ or 902,000

$N(2) = -35.8(2)^3 + 202(2)^2 + 87.8(2) + 648 = 1345.2$ or 1,345,200

$N(3) = -35.8(3)^3 + 202(3)^2 + 87.8(3) + 648 = 1762.8$ or 1,762,800

29 a. $N(0) = 0.32$ or 320,000

b. $N(4) = -0.0675(4)^4 + 0.5083(4)^3 - 0.893(4)^2 + 0.66(4) + 0.32 = 3.9232$ or 3,923,200.

30. a. $S(0) = 4.3(0 + 2)^{0.94} = 8.24967$, or approximately \$8.25 billion.

b. $S(6) = 4.3(6 + 2)^{0.94} = 30.365$, or approximately \$30.37 billion.

31 $N(5) = 0.0018425(10)^{2.5} \approx 0.58265$, or approximately 0.583 million.

$N(10) = 0.0018425(15)^{2.5} \approx 1.6056$, or approximately 1.606 million.

32. $A(0) = \dfrac{699}{1^{0.94}} = 699$ or \$699. $A(5) = \dfrac{699}{6^{0.94}} \approx 129\ 722$, or approximately \$130.

33 a.

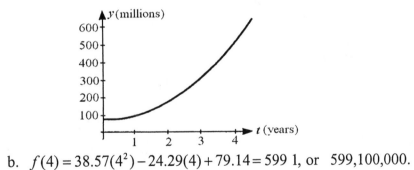

b. $f(4) = 38.57(4^2) - 24.29(4) + 79.14 = 599\ 1$, or 599,100,000.

34. a.

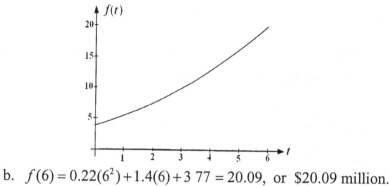

b. $f(6) = 0.22(6^2) + 1.4(6) + 3\ 77 = 20.09$, or $20.09 million.

35 a. The given data implies that $R(40) = 50$, that is,
$$\frac{100(40)}{b+40} = 50$$
$$50(b+40) = 4000, \quad \text{or} \quad b = 40.$$

Therefore, the required response function is $R(x) = \dfrac{100x}{40+x}$.

b. The response will be $R(60) = \dfrac{100(60)}{40+60} = 60$, or approximately 60 percent.

36. a.

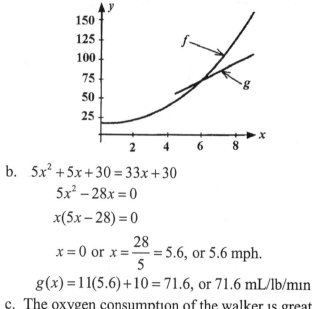

b. $5x^2 + 5x + 30 = 33x + 30$
$$5x^2 - 28x = 0$$
$$x(5x - 28) = 0$$
$$x = 0 \text{ or } x = \frac{28}{5} = 5.6, \text{ or 5.6 mph.}$$
$$g(x) = 11(5.6) + 10 = 71.6, \text{ or 71.6 mL/lb/min}$$

c. The oxygen consumption of the walker is greater than that of the runner.

37. a. $f(0) = 6.85$, $g(0) = 16.58$. Since $g(0) > f(0)$, we see that more film cameras were sold in 2001 ($t = 0$).

b. We solve the equation $f(t) = g(t)$, that is,

$$3.05t + 6.85 = -1.85t + 16.58$$

$$4.9t = 9\ 73$$

$$t = 1.99 \approx 2$$

So sales of digital cameras first exceed those of film cameras in approximately 2003

38. a. We are given that $T = aN + b$ where a and b are constants to be determined. The given conditions imply

$$70 = 120a + b$$

and $\qquad 80 = 160a + b$

Subtracting the first equation from the second gives $10 = 40a$, or $a = \frac{1}{4}$

Substituting this value of a into the first equation gives

$70 = 120(\frac{1}{4}) + b$, or $b = 40$. Therefore, $T = \frac{1}{4}N + 40$.

b. Solving the equation in (a) for N, we find

$$\tfrac{1}{4}N = T - 40, \quad \text{or} \quad N = f(t) = 4T - 160.$$

When $T = 102$, we find $N = 4(102) - 160 = 248$, or 248 times per minute.

39 The slope of the line is $m = \dfrac{S - C}{n}$.

Therefore, an equation of the line is $y - C = \dfrac{S - C}{n}(t - 0)$.

Letting $y = V(t)$, we have $V(t) = C - \dfrac{(C - S)}{n}t$.

40. Using the formula given in Problem 39, we have

$$V(2) = 100,000 - \frac{(100,000 - 30,000)}{5}(2) = 100,000 - \frac{70,000}{5}(2)$$

$$= 72,000, \text{ or } \$72,000.$$

41 The average U.S. credit card debt at the beginning of 1994 was

$$D(0) = 4.77(1+0)^{0.2676} = 4.77 \text{ or } \$4770.$$

At the beginning of 1996, it was $D(2) = 4.77(1+2)^{0.2676} = 6.400$
or $6400. At the beginning of 1999, it was
$$D(5) = 5.6423(5^{0.1818}) \approx 7.560 \text{ or } \$7560.$$

42. $P(0) = 4.6$ or 4.6%. $\quad P(15) = -0.01005(15)^2 + 0.945(15) - 3\ 4 \approx 8.51$, or 8.5%.
$P(30) = -0.01005(30)^2 + 0.945(30) - 3\ 4 \approx 15.905$ or 15.9%.

43 a. $A(0) = 16.4$, or $16.4 billion.
$A(1) = 16.4(1+1)^{0.1} \approx 17.58$, or $17.58 billion.
$A(2) = 16.4(2+1)^{0.1} \approx 18.30$, or $18.3 billion.
$A(3) = 16.4(3+1)^{0.1} \approx 18.84$, ot $18.84 billion.
$A(4) = 16.4(4+1)^{0.1} \approx 19.26$, or $19.26 billion.

The nutritional market has been growing over the years from 1999 through 2003
   b.

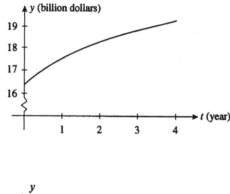

44. a.

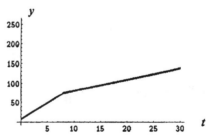

   b. $f(0) = 8.37(0) + 7\ 44 = 7\ 44$, or $7.44/kilo.
   $f(20) = 2.84(20) + 51.68 = 108.48$, or $108.48/kilo.

45 a.

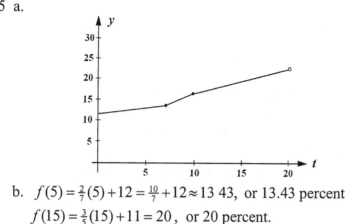

b. $f(5) = \frac{2}{7}(5) + 12 = \frac{10}{7} + 12 \approx 13\ 43$, or 13.43 percent

$f(15) = \frac{3}{5}(15) + 11 = 20$, or 20 percent.

46. a.

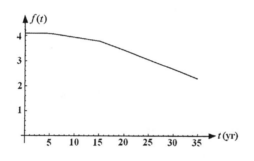

b. At the beginning of 2005, the ratio will be $f(10) = -0.03(10) + 4.25 = 3.95$

At the beginning of 2020, the ratio will be $f(25) = -0.075(25) + 4.925 = 3.05$

c. The ratio is constant from 1995 to 2000.

d. The decline of the ratio will be greatest from 2010 through 2030. It is given by

$$\frac{f(35) - f(15)}{35 - 15} = \frac{2.3 - 3.8}{20} = -0.075$$

47 $h(t) = f(t) - g(t) = \dfrac{110}{\frac{1}{2}t + 1} - 26(\frac{1}{4}t^2 - 1)^2 - 52.$

$h(0) = f(0) - g(0) = \dfrac{110}{\frac{1}{2}(0) + 1} - 26\left[\frac{1}{4}(0)^2 - 1\right]^2 - 52 = 110 - 26 - 52 = 32$, or \$32.

$$h(1) = f(1) - g(1) = \frac{110}{\frac{1}{2}(1)+1} - 26\left[\frac{1}{4}(1)^2 - 1\right]^2 - 52 = 6.71, \text{ or } \$6.71$$

$$h(2) = f(2) - g(2) = \frac{110}{\frac{1}{2}(2)+1} - 26\left[\frac{1}{4}(2)^2 - 1\right]^2 - 52 = 3, \text{ or } \$3$$

We conclude that the price gap was narrowing.

48. a. $f(0) = 5.6$ and $g(0) = 22.5$ Since $g(0) > f(0)$, we conclude that more VCRs were sold then DVDs in 2001.

b. We solve the equations $f(t) = g(t)$ over each of the subintervals.

$$5.6 + 5.6t = -9.6t + 22.5 \qquad 0 \le t \le 1$$
$$15.2t = 16.9$$
$$t \approx 1.11$$

This is outside the range for t, so we reject it.

$$5.6 + 5.6t = -0.5t + 13.4 \qquad 1 < t \le 2$$
$$6.1t = 7.8$$
$$t \approx 1.28$$

So sales of DVDs first exceeded those of VCRs at $t \approx 1.3$, or early 2002.

49 a. $P(0) = 59.8$; $P(1) = 58.9$; $P(2) = 59.2$; $P(3) = 60.7$; $P(4) = 61\ 7$

b.

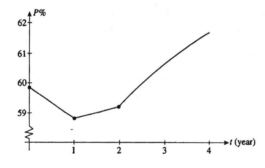

c. $P(3) = 60.7$, or 60.7%.

50. a.

t	0	1	2	3	4
$P(t)$	52.7	33 7	18.0	10.2	14.9

b.

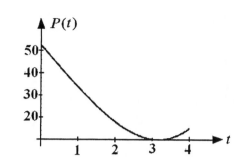

c. Greatest in the 1950s; smallest in the 1980s.

51. a.

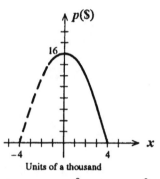

b. If $p = 7$, we have $7 = -x^2 + 16$, or $x^2 = 9$, so that $x = \pm 3$ Therefore, the quantity demanded when the unit price is \$7 is 3000 units.

52. a.

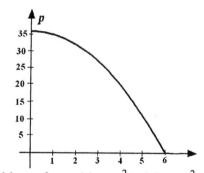

b. If $p = 11$, we have $11 = -x^2 + 36$, or $x^2 = 25$, so that $x = \pm 5$ Therefore, the quantity demanded when the unit price is \$11 is 5000 units.

53. a.

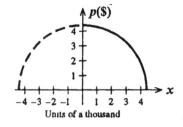

Units of a thousand

b. If $p = 3$, then $3 = \sqrt{18 - x^2}$, and $9 = 18 - x^2$, so that $x^2 = 9$ and $x = \pm 3$. Therefore, the quantity demanded when the unit price is $3 is 3000 units.

54. a.

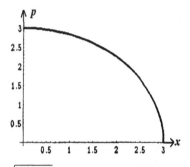

b. If $p = 2$, then $2 = \sqrt{9 - x^2}$, and $4 = 9 - x^2$, so that $x^2 = 5$ and and $x = \pm\sqrt{5}$, or $x = \pm 2.236$, Therefore, the quantity demanded when the unit price is $2 is 2236 units.

55 a.

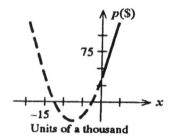

Units of a thousand

b. If $x = 2$, then $p = 2^2 + 16(2) + 40 = 76$, or $76.

56. a.

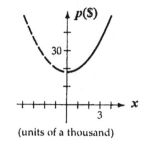

(units of a thousand)

b. If $x = 2$, then $p = 2(2)^2 + 18 = 26$, or \$26.

57 a.

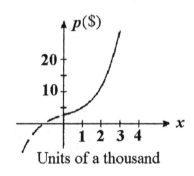

Units of a thousand

b. $p = 2^3 + 2(2) + 3 = 15$, or \$15

58. a.

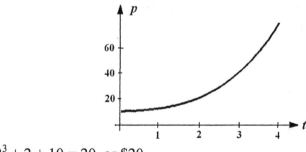

b. $p = 2^3 + 2 + 10 = 20$, or \$20.

59. The slope of L_2 is greater than that of L_1. This means that for each drop of a dollar in the price of a clock radio, the quantity demanded of model B clock radios is greater than that of model A clock radios.

60. The slope of L_2 is greater than that of L_1. This tells us that for each increase of a dollar in the price of a clock radio, more model A clock radios will be made available in the market place than model B clock radios.

61. Substituting $x = 10$ into the demand function, we have
$$p = \frac{30}{0.02(10)^2 + 1} = \frac{30}{3} = 10, \text{ or } p = \$10.$$

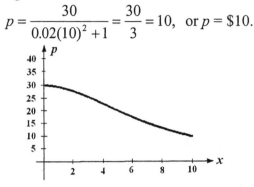

62. Substituting $x = 6$ and $p = 8$ into the given equation gives
$$8 = \sqrt{-36a + b}, \text{ or } -36a + b = 64.$$
Next, substituting $x = 8$ and $p = 6$ into the equation gives
$$6 = \sqrt{-64a + b}, \text{ or } -64a + b = 36.$$
Solving the system $\begin{cases} -36a + b = 64 \\ -64a + b = 36 \end{cases}$, for a and b, we find $a = 1$ and $b = 100$.

Therefore the demand equation is $p = \sqrt{-x^2 + 100}$. When the unit price is set at $\$7.50$, we have $7.5 = \sqrt{-x^2 + 100}$, or $56.25 = -x^2 + 100$ from which we deduce that $x = \pm 6.614$. So, the quantity demanded is 6614 units.

63

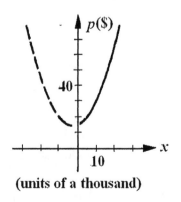

(units of a thousand)

If $x = 5$, then $p = 0.1(5)^2 + 0.5(5) + 15 = 20$, or \$20.

64. Substituting $x = 10,000$ and $p = 20$ into the given equation yields $20 = a\sqrt{10,000} + b = 100a + b$. Next, substituting $x = 62,500$ and $p = 35$ into the equation yields $35 = a\sqrt{62,500} + b = 250a + b$. Subtracting the first equation from the second yields $15 = 150a$, or $a = \frac{1}{10}$ Substituting this value of a into the first equation gives $b = 10$. Therefore, the required equation is $p = \frac{1}{10}\sqrt{x} + 10$. The graph of the supply function follows.

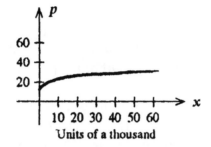

Substituting $x = 40,000$ into the supply equation yields
$$p = \frac{1}{10}\sqrt{40,000} + 10 = 30, \quad \text{or } \$30.$$

65. a. We solve the system of equations $p = cx + d$ and $p = ax + b$ Substituting the first equation in the second gives
$$cx + d = ax + b$$
$$(c - a)x = b - d$$
or
$$x = \frac{b - d}{c - a}.$$
Since $a < 0$ and $c > 0$, $c - a \neq 0$ and x is well-defined. Substituting this value of x into the second equation, we obtain
$$p = a\left(\frac{b - d}{c - a}\right) + b = \frac{ab - ad + bc - ab}{c - a} = \frac{bc - ad}{c - a}$$
Therefore, the equilibrium quantity is $\dfrac{b - d}{c - a}$ and the equilibrium price is $\dfrac{bc - ad}{c - a}$

b. If c is increased, the denominator in the expression for x increases and so x gets smaller. At the same time, the first term in the first equation for p decreases and so

p gets larger. This analysis shows that if the unit price for producing the product is increased then the equilibrium quantity decreases while the equilibrium price increases.

c. If b is decreased, the numerator of the expression for x decreases while the denominator stays the same. Therefore, x decreases. The expression for p also shows that p decreases. This analysis shows that if the (theoretical) upper bound for the unit price of a commodity is lowered, then both the equilibrium quantity and the equilibrium price drop.

66. We solve the system of equations $p = -x^2 - 2x + 100$ and $p = 8x + 25$ Thus, $-x^2 - 2x + 100 = 8x + 25$, or $x^2 + 10x - 75 = 0$. Factoring this equation, we have $(x + 15)(x - 5) = 0$, or $x = -15$ and $x = 5$ Rejecting the negative root, we have $x = 5$ and the corresponding value of p is $p = 8(5) + 25 = 65$. We conclude that the equilibrium quantity is 5000 and the equilibrium price is $65

67 We solve the equation $-2x^2 + 80 = 15x + 30$, or $2x^2 + 15x - 50 = 0$ for x. Thus, $(2x - 5)(x + 10) = 0$, or $x = 5/2$ or $x = -10$. Rejecting the negative root, we have $x = 5/2$. The corresponding value of p is $p = -2(\frac{5}{2})^2 + 80 = 67.5$. We conclude that the equilibrium quantity is 2500 and the equilibrium price is $67.50.

68. We solve the system $p = 60 - 2x^2$
    and $p = x^2 + 9x + 30.$
    Equating these two equations, we have
$$x^2 + 9x + 30 = 60 - 2x^2$$
$$3x^2 + 9x - 30 = 0$$
$$x^2 + 3x - 10 = 0$$
$$(x + 5)(x - 2) = 0$$
and $x = -5$ or $x = 2$. We take $x = 2$. The corresponding value of p is 5. Therefore, the equilibrium quantity is 2000 and the equilibrium price is $52.

69. Solving both equations for x, we have $x = -(11/3)p + 22$ and $x = 2p^2 + p - 10$. Equating these two equations, we have
$$-\tfrac{11}{3}p + 22 = 2p^2 + p - 10,$$
    or $-11p + 66 = 6p^2 + 3p - 30$
    and $6p^2 + 14p - 96 = 0.$
    Dividing this last equation by 2 and then factoring, we have
$$(3p + 16)(p - 3) = 0,$$

or $p = 3$. The corresponding value of x is $2(3)^2 + 3 - 10 = 11$. We conclude that the equilibrium quantity is 11,000 and the equilibrium price is $3.

70. Equating the two equations, we have

$$0.1x^2 + 2x + 20 = -0.1x^2 - x + 40$$
$$0.2x^2 + 3x - 20 = 0$$
$$2x^2 + 30x - 200 = 0$$
$$x^2 + 15x - 100 = 0$$
$$(x + 20)(x - 5) = 0,$$

and $x = -20$ or 5. Substituting $x = 5$ into the first equation gives

$$p = -0.1(25) - 5 + 40 = 32.5.$$

Therefore, the equilibrium quantity is 500 tents (x is measured in hundreds) and the equilibrium price is $32.50.

71 Equating the two equations, we have

$$144 - x^2 = 48 + \tfrac{1}{2}x^2$$
$$288 - 2x^2 = 96 + x^2$$
$$3x^2 = 192; \quad x^2 = 64,$$

or $x = \pm 8$. We take $x = 8$, and the corresponding value of p is $144 - 8^2 = 80$. We conclude that the equilibrium quantity is 8000 tires and the equilibrium price is $80.

72. Since there is 80 feet of fencing available,

$$2x + 2y = 80; \ x + y = 40 \text{ and } y = 40 - x.$$

Then the area of the garden is given by $f = xy = x(40 - x) = 40x - x^2$.
The domain of f is $[0, 40]$.

73. The area of Juanita's garden is 250 sq ft. Therefore $xy = 250$ and $y = \dfrac{250}{x}$.

The amount of fencing needed is given by $2x + 2y$.

Therefore, $f = 2x + 2\left(\dfrac{250}{x}\right) = 2x + \dfrac{500}{x}$. The domain of f is $x > 0$.

74. The volume of the box is given by the (area of the base) $\times$ the height of the box.

Thus, $V = f(x) = (15 - 2x)(8 - 2x)x$.

75. Since the volume of the box is given by
$$V = \text{(area of the base)} \times \text{the height of the box}$$
$$= x^2 y = 20,$$
we have $y = \dfrac{20}{x^2}$. Next, the amount of material used in constructing the box is given by the area of the base of the box, plus the area of the 4 sides, plus the area of the top of the box, or $x^2 + 4xy + x^2$. Then, the cost of constructing the box is given by $f(x) = 0.30x^2 + 0.40x \cdot \dfrac{20}{x^2} + .20x^2 = 0.5x^2 + \dfrac{8}{x}$

76. Since the perimeter of a circle is $2\pi r$, we know that the perimeter of the semicircle is πx. Next, the perimeter of the rectangular portion of the window is given by $2y + 2x$, so the perimeter of the Norman window is $\pi x + 2y + 2x$ and
$$\pi x + 2y + 2x = 28, \text{ or } y = \tfrac{1}{2}(28 - \pi x - 2x)$$
Since the area of the window is given by $2xy + \tfrac{1}{2}\pi x^2$, we see that
$$A = 2xy + \tfrac{1}{2}\pi x^2$$
Substituting the value of y found earlier, we see that
$$A = f(x) = x\left(28 - \pi x - 2x\right) + \tfrac{1}{2}\pi x^2$$
$$= \tfrac{1}{2}\pi x^2 + 28x - \pi x^2 - 2x^2$$
$$= 28x - \frac{\pi}{2}x^2 - 2x^2$$

77 The average yield of the apple orchard is 36 bushels/tree when the density is 22 trees/acre. Let x = the unit increase in tree density beyond 22. Then the yield of the apple orchard in bushels/acre is given by $(22 + x)(36 - 2x)$.

78. $xy = 50$ and so $y = \dfrac{50}{x}$. The area of the printed page is
$$A = (x-1)(y-2) = (x-1)(\tfrac{50}{x} - 2) = -2x + 52 - \tfrac{50}{x}$$
So the required function is $f(x) = -2x + 52 - \tfrac{50}{x}$. We must have $x > 0$, $x - 1 \geq 0$, and $\tfrac{50}{x} - 2 \geq 2$; The last inequality is solved as follows:

$\frac{50}{x} \geq 4; \quad \frac{x}{50} \leq \frac{1}{4}; \quad x \leq \frac{50}{4} = \frac{25}{2}.$ So the domain is $[1, \frac{25}{2}]$.

79 a. Let x denote the number of bottles sold beyond 10,000 bottles. Then
$$P(x) = (10,000 + x)(5 - 0.0002x)$$
$$= -0.0002x^2 + 3x + 50,000$$

b. He can expect a profit
$$P(6000) = -0.0002(6000^2) + 3(6000) + 50,000 = 60,800$$
or $60,800.

80 a. Let x denote the number of people beyond 20 who sign up for the cruise. Then the revenue is
$$R(x) = (20 + x)(600 - 4x) = -4x^2 + 520x + 12,000$$

b. $R(40) = -4(40^2) + 520(40) + 12000 = 26,400$, or 26,400 passengers.
       $R(60) = -4(60^2) + 520(60) + 12,000 = 28,800$ or 28,800 passengers.

81 False. $f(x) = 3x^{3/4} + x^{1/2} + 1$ is not a polynomial function. The powers in x must be nonnegative integers.

82. True. If $P(x)$ is a polynomial function, then $P(x) = \frac{P(x)}{1}$ and so it is a rational function. The converse if false. For example, $R(x) = \frac{x+1}{x-1}$ is a rational function that is not a polynomial.

83 False. $f(x) = x^{1/2}$ is not defined for negative values of x or $x = 0$.

84. False. A power function has the form x^r, where r is a real number.

USING TECHNOLOGY EXERCISES 2.3, page 94

1. (-3.0414, 0.1503); (3.0414, 7 4497)   2. (-5.3852, 9.8007); (5.3852, -4.2007)

3. (-2.3371, 2.4117); (6.0514, -2.5015)   4.   (-2.5863, -0.3585); (6.1863, -4.5694)

5.   (-1.0219, -6.3461); (1.2414, -1.5931), and (5 7805, 7.9391)

6.   (-0.0484, 2.0609); (2.0823, 2.8986) and (4.9661, 1 1405)

7   a.   b.   438 wall clocks; $40.92

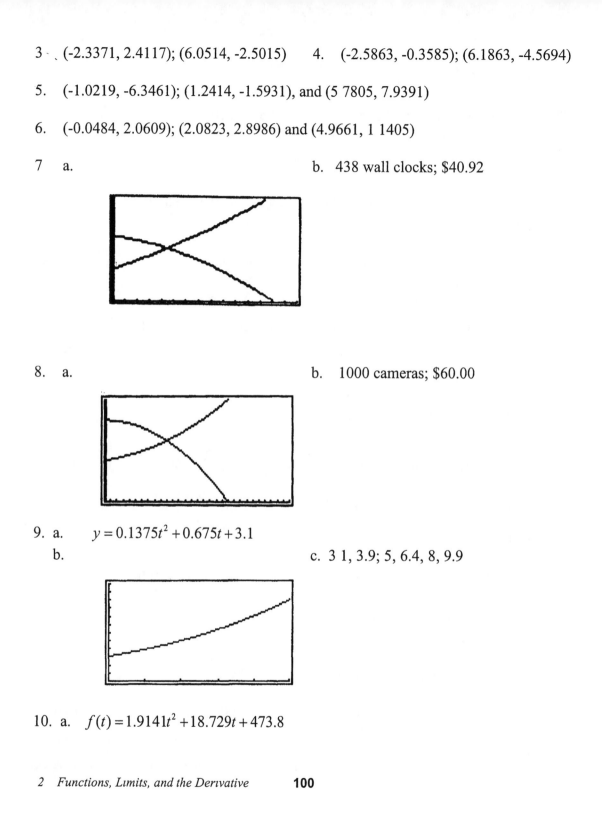

8.   a.   b.   1000 cameras; $60.00

9. a. $y = 0.1375t^2 + 0.675t + 3.1$
    b.   c. 3 1, 3.9; 5, 6.4, 8, 9.9

10. a. $f(t) = 1.91411t^2 + 18.729t + 473.8$

b.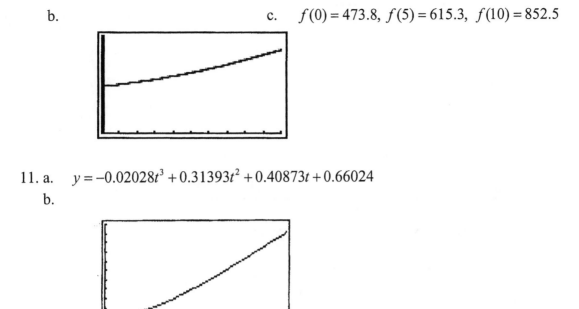

c. $f(0) = 473.8, \; f(5) = 615.3, \; f(10) = 852.5$

11. a. $y = -0.02028t^3 + 0.31393t^2 + 0.40873t + 0.66024$

b.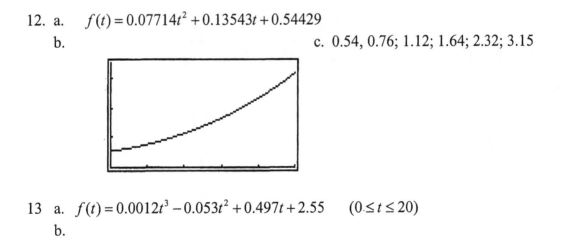

c. 0.66; 1.36; 2.57, 4.16; 6.02; 8.02; 10.03

12. a. $f(t) = 0.07714t^2 + 0.13543t + 0.54429$

b.

c. 0.54, 0.76; 1.12; 1.64; 2.32; 3.15

13 a. $f(t) = 0.0012t^3 - 0.053t^2 + 0.497t + 2.55 \qquad (0 \le t \le 20)$

b.

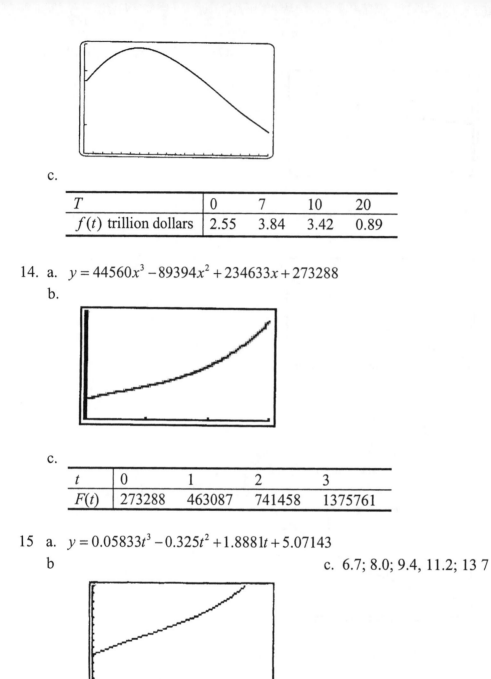

c.

T	0	7	10	20
$f(t)$ trillion dollars	2.55	3.84	3.42	0.89

14. a. $y = 44560x^3 - 89394x^2 + 234633x + 273288$

b.

c.

t	0	1	2	3
F(t)	273288	463087	741458	1375761

15 a. $y = 0.05833t^3 - 0.325t^2 + 1.8881t + 5.07143$

b

c. 6.7; 8.0; 9.4, 11.2; 13 7

16. a. $f(t) = 0.08333t^3 - 0.02857t^2 + 2.53095t + 2.40286$

b.   c. 2.4, 5.0; 8.0; 12.0; 17 4

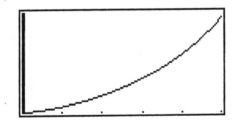

17 a. $y = 0.0125t^4 - 0.01389t^3 + 0.55417t^2 + 0.53294t + 4.95238$ $(0 \le t \le 5)$

b.   c. 5.0; 6.0; 8.3; 12.2; 18.3, 27.5

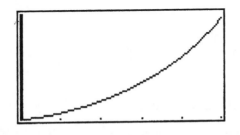

18. a. $f(t) = 0.09375t^4 - 0.6088t^3 + 3.94097t^2 + 1.77646t + 5.0496$

b.

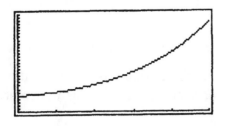

2.4 Concept Questions, page 111

1. The values of $f(x)$ can be made as close to 3 as we please by taking x sufficiently

close to $x = 2$.

2. a. Nothing. Whether $f(3)$ is defined or not does not depend on $\lim_{x \to 3} f(x)$

   b. Nothing. $\lim_{x \to 2} f(x)$ has nothing to do with the value of f at $x = 2$.

3 a. $\lim_{x \to 4} \sqrt{x}(2x^2 + 1) = \lim_{x \to 4} (\sqrt{x}) \lim_{x \to 4} (2x^2 + 1)$ (Rule 4)

   $$= \sqrt{4}\left[2(4)^2 + 1\right]$$ (Rules 1 and 3)

   $$= 66$$

   b. $\lim_{x \to 1} \left(\dfrac{2x^2 + x + 5}{x^4 + 1} \right) = \left(\lim_{x \to 1} \dfrac{2x^2 + x + 5}{x^4 + 1} \right)^{3/2}$ (Rule 1)

   $$= \left(\dfrac{2 + 1 + 5}{1 + 1} \right)^{3/2}$$ (Rules 2, 3, and 5)

   $$= 4^{3/2} = 8$$

4. A limit that has the form $\lim_{x \to a} \dfrac{f(x)}{g(x)} = \dfrac{"0"}{0}$. For example, $\lim_{x \to 3} \dfrac{x^2 - 9}{x - 3}$.

5 $\lim_{x \to \infty} f(x) = L$ means $f(x)$ can be made as close to L as we please by taking x sufficiently large. $\lim_{x \to -\infty} f(x) = M$ means $f(x)$ can be made as close to M as we please by taking x as large as please in absolute value but negative.

EXERCISES 2.4, page 111

1. $\lim_{x \to -2} f(x) = 3$.

2. $\lim_{x \to 1} f(x) = 2$.

3. $\lim_{x \to 3} f(x) = 3$.

4   $\lim_{x \to 1} f(x)$ does not exist. If we consider any value of x to the right of $x = 1$, we find that $f(x) = 3$ On the other hand, if we consider values of x to the left of $x = 1$, $f(x) \le 1.5$, so that $f(x)$ does not approach any one number as x approaches 1

5   $\lim_{x \to -2} f(x) = 3$.

6. $\lim_{x \to -2} f(x) = 3$.

7   The limit does not exist. If we consider any value of x to the right of $x = -2$, $f(x) \le 2$. If we consider values of x to the left of $x = -2$, $f(x) \ge -2$. Since $f(x)$ does not approach any one number as x approaches $x = -2$, we conclude that the limit

does not exist.

8. The limit does not exist.

9. $\lim_{x \to 2} (x^2 + 1) = 5.$

x	1.9	1.99	1.999	2.001	2.01	2.1
$f(x)$	4.61	4.9601	4.9960	5.004	5.0401	5.41

10. $\lim_{x \to 1} (2x^2 - 1) = 1.$

x	0.9	0.99	0.999	1.001	1.01	1.1
$f(x)$	0.62	0.9602	0.996002	1.004002	1.0402	1.42

11.

x	-0.1	-0.01	-0.001	0.001	0.01	0.1
$f(x)$	-1	-1	-1	1	1	1

The limit does not exist.

12.

x	0.9	0.99	0.999	1.001	1.01	1.1
$f(x)$	-1	-1	-1	1	1	1

The limit does not exist.

13.

x	0.9	0.99	0.999	1.001	1.01	1.1
$f(x)$	100	10,000	1,000,000	1,000,000	10,000	100

The limit does not exist.

14.

x	1.9	1.99	1.999	2.001	2.01	2.1
$f(x)$	-10	-100	-1000	1000	100	10

The limit does not exist.

15

x	0.9	0.99	0.999	1.001	1.01	1.1
$f(x)$	2.9	2.99	2.999	3.001	3.01	3.1

$$\lim_{x\to 1}\frac{x^2+x-2}{x-1}=3.$$

16.

x	0.9	0.99	0.999	1.001	1.01	1.1
$f(x)$	1	1	1	1	1	1

$$\lim_{x\to 1}\frac{x-1}{x-1}=1.$$

17

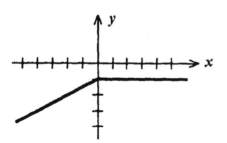

$$\lim_{x\to 0}f(x)=-1$$

18.

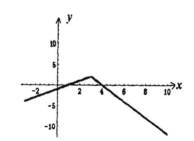

$$\lim_{x\to 3}f(x)=2$$

19.

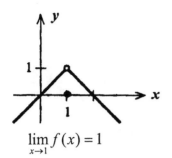

$$\lim_{x \to 1} f(x) = 1$$

20.

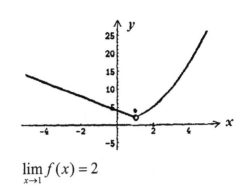

$$\lim_{x \to 1} f(x) = 2$$

21

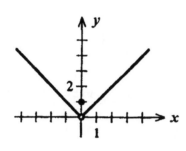

$$\lim_{x \to 0} f(x) = 0$$

22.

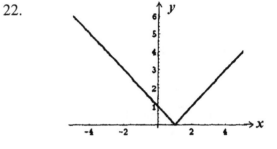

$$\lim_{x \to 1} f(x) = 0$$

23 $\lim_{x \to 2} 3 = 3$

24. $\lim_{x \to -2} -3 = -3$

25 $\lim_{x \to 3} x = 3$

26. $\lim_{x \to -2} -3x = -3(-2) = 6$

27. $\lim_{x \to 1} (1 - 2x^2) = 1 - 2(1)^2 = -1$

28. $\lim_{t \to 3} (4t^2 - 2t + 1) = 4(9) - 2(3) + 1 = 31.$

29. $\lim_{x \to 1} (2x^3 - 3x^2 + x + 2) = 2(1)^3 - 3(1)^2 + 1 + 2 = 2.$

30. $\lim_{x \to 0} (4x^5 - 20x^2 + 2x + 1) = 4(0)^5 - 20(0)^2 + 2(0) + 1 = 1.$

31. $\lim\limits_{s\to 0}(2s^2 - 1)(2s+4) = (-1)(4) = -4.$

32. $\lim\limits_{x\to 2}(x^2 + 1)(x^2 - 4) = (2^2 + 1)(2^2 - 4) = 0.$

33. $\lim\limits_{x\to 2}\dfrac{2x+1}{x+2} = \dfrac{2(2)+1}{2+2} = \dfrac{5}{4}$

34. $\lim\limits_{x\to 1}\dfrac{x^3 + 1}{2x^3 + 2} = \dfrac{1^3 + 1}{2(1^3) + 2} = \dfrac{2}{4} = \dfrac{1}{2}$

35. $\lim\limits_{x\to 2}\sqrt{x+2} = \sqrt{2+2} = 2.$

36. $\lim\limits_{x\to -2}\sqrt[3]{5x+2} = \sqrt[3]{5(-2)+2} = \sqrt[3]{-8} = -2.$

37. $\lim\limits_{x\to -3}\sqrt{2x^4 + x^2} = \sqrt{2(-3)^4 + (-3)^2} = \sqrt{162 + 9} = \sqrt{171} = 3\sqrt{19}$

38. $\lim\limits_{x\to 2}\sqrt{\dfrac{2x^3 + 4}{x^2 + 1}} = \sqrt{\dfrac{2(8)+4}{4+1}} = 2.$

39. $\lim\limits_{x\to -1}\dfrac{\sqrt{x^2 + 8}}{2x + 4} = \dfrac{\sqrt{(-1)^2 + 8}}{2(-1) + 4} = \dfrac{\sqrt{9}}{2} = \dfrac{3}{2}$

40. $\lim\limits_{x\to 3}\dfrac{x\sqrt{x^2 + 7}}{2x - \sqrt{2x+3}} = \dfrac{3\sqrt{3^2 + 7}}{2(3) - \sqrt{2(3)+3}} = \dfrac{12}{3} = 4.$

41. $\lim\limits_{x\to a}[f(x) - g(x)] = \lim\limits_{x\to a}f(x) - \lim\limits_{x\to a}g(x) = 3 - 4 = -1.$

42. $\lim\limits_{x\to a}2f(x) = 2(3) = 6.$

43. $\lim\limits_{x\to a}[2f(x) - 3g(x)] = \lim\limits_{x\to a}2f(x) - \lim\limits_{x\to a}3g(x) = 2(3) - 3(4) = -6.$

44. $\lim\limits_{x\to a}[f(x)g(x)] = \lim\limits_{x\to a}f(x)\,\lim\limits_{x\to a}g(x) = (3)(4) = 12.$

45. $\lim\limits_{x\to a}\sqrt{g(x)} = \lim\limits_{x\to a}\sqrt{4} = 2.$

46. $\lim\limits_{x \to a} \sqrt[3]{5f(x) + 3g(x)} = \sqrt[3]{5(3) + 3(4)} = \sqrt[3]{27} = 3.$

47. $\lim\limits_{x \to a} \dfrac{2f(x) - g(x)}{f(x)g(x)} = \dfrac{2(3) - (4)}{(3)(4)} = \dfrac{2}{12} = \dfrac{1}{6}$

48. $\lim\limits_{x \to a} \dfrac{g(x) - f(x)}{f(x) + \sqrt{g(x)}} = \dfrac{4 - 3}{3 + 2} = \dfrac{1}{5}$

49. $\lim\limits_{x \to 1} \dfrac{x^2 - 1}{x - 1} = \lim\limits_{x \to 1} \dfrac{(x - 1)(x + 1)}{x - 1} = \lim\limits_{x \to 1}(x + 1) = 1 + 1 = 2.$

50. $\lim\limits_{x \to -2} \dfrac{x^2 - 4}{x + 2} = \lim\limits_{x \to -2} \dfrac{(x - 2)(x + 2)}{x + 2} = \lim\limits_{x \to -2}(x - 2) = -2 - 2 = -4.$

51. $\lim\limits_{x \to 0} \dfrac{x^2 - x}{x} = \lim\limits_{x \to 0} \dfrac{x(x - 1)}{x} = \lim\limits_{x \to 0}(x - 1) = 0 - 1 = -1.$

52. $\lim\limits_{x \to 0} \dfrac{2x^2 - 3x}{x} = \lim\limits_{x \to 0} \dfrac{x(2x - 3)}{x} = \lim\limits_{x \to 0}(2x - 3) = -3.$

53. $\lim\limits_{x \to -5} \dfrac{x^2 - 25}{x + 5} = \lim\limits_{x \to -5} \dfrac{(x + 5)(x - 5)}{x + 5} = \lim\limits_{x \to -5}(x - 5) = -10.$

54. $\lim\limits_{b \to -3} \dfrac{b + 1}{b + 3}$ does not exist.

55. $\lim\limits_{x \to 1} \dfrac{x}{x - 1}$ does not exist.

56. $\lim\limits_{x \to 2} \dfrac{x + 2}{x - 2}$ does not exist.

57. $\lim\limits_{x \to -2} \dfrac{x^2 - x - 6}{x^2 + x - 2} = \lim\limits_{x \to -2} \dfrac{(x - 3)(x + 2)}{(x + 2)(x - 1)} = \lim\limits_{x \to -2} \dfrac{x - 3}{x - 1} = \dfrac{-2 - 3}{-2 - 1} = \dfrac{5}{3}$

58. $\lim\limits_{z \to 2} \dfrac{z^3 - 8}{z - 2} = \lim\limits_{z \to 2} \dfrac{(z - 2)(z^2 + 2z + 4)}{z - 2} = \lim\limits_{z \to 2}(z^2 + 2z + 4) = 2^2 + 2(2) + 4 = 12.$

59. $\lim\limits_{x\to1}\dfrac{\sqrt{x}-1}{x-1}=\lim\limits_{x\to1}\dfrac{\sqrt{x}-1}{x-1}\cdot\dfrac{\sqrt{x}+1}{\sqrt{x}+1}=\lim\limits_{x\to1}\dfrac{x-1}{(x-1)(\sqrt{x}+1)}=\lim\limits_{x\to1}\dfrac{1}{\sqrt{x}+1}=\dfrac{1}{2}$

60. $\lim\limits_{x\to4}\dfrac{x-4}{\sqrt{x}-2}=\lim\limits_{x\to4}\dfrac{x-4}{\sqrt{x}-2}\cdot\dfrac{\sqrt{x}+2}{\sqrt{x}+2}=\lim\limits_{x\to4}\sqrt{x}+2=2+2=4.$

61. $\lim\limits_{x\to1}\dfrac{x-1}{x^3+x^2-2x}=\lim\limits_{x\to1}\dfrac{x-1}{x(x-1)(x+2)}=\lim\limits_{x\to1}\dfrac{1}{x(x+2)}=\dfrac{1}{3}$

62. $\lim\limits_{x\to-2}\dfrac{4-x^2}{2x^2+x^3}=\lim\limits_{x\to-2}\dfrac{(2-x)(2+x)}{x^2(2+x)}=\lim\limits_{x\to-2}\dfrac{2-x}{x^2}=\dfrac{2-(-2)}{(-2)^2}=1.$

63. $\lim\limits_{x\to\infty}f(x)=\infty$ (does not exist) and $\lim\limits_{x\to-\infty}f(x)=\infty$ (does not exist).

64. $\lim\limits_{x\to\infty}f(x)=\infty$ (does not exist) and $\lim\limits_{x\to-\infty}f(x)=-\infty$ (does not exist).

65. $\lim\limits_{x\to\infty}f(x)=0$ and $\lim\limits_{x\to-\infty}f(x)=0.$

66. $\lim\limits_{x\to\infty}f(x)=1$ and $\lim\limits_{x\to-\infty}f(x)=1$

67. $\lim\limits_{x\to\infty}f(x)=-\infty$ (does not exist) and $\lim\limits_{x\to-\infty}f(x)=-\infty$ (does not exist).

68. $\lim\limits_{x\to\infty}f(x)=1$ and $\lim\limits_{x\to-\infty}f(x)=\infty$ (does not exist).

69.

x	1	10	100	1000
$f(x)$	0.5	0.009901	0.0001	0.000001

x	-1	-10	-100	-1000
$f(x)$	0.5	0.009901	0.0001	0.000001

$$\lim_{x\to\infty} f(x) = 0 \quad \text{and} \quad \lim_{x\to-\infty} f(x) = 0$$

70.

x	1	10	100	1000
$f(x)$	1	1.818	1.980	1.998

x	-5	-10	-100	-1000
$f(x)$	2.5	2.222	2.020	2.002

$$\lim_{x\to\infty} f(x) = \lim_{x\to-\infty} f(x) = 2$$

71.

x	1	5	10	100	1000
$f(x)$	12	360	2910	2.99×10^6	2.999×10^9

x	-1	-5	-10	-100	-1000
$f(x)$	6	-390	-3090	-3.01×10^6	-3.0×10^9

$\lim_{x\to\infty} f(x) = \infty$ (does not exist) and $\lim_{x\to-\infty} f(x) = -\infty$ (does not exist).

72.

x	1	10	100	-1	-10	-100
$f(x)$	1	1	1	-1	-1	-1

$\lim_{x\to\infty} f(x) = 1$ and $\lim_{x\to-\infty} f(x) = -1$.

73 $\lim_{x\to\infty} \dfrac{3x+2}{x-5} = \lim_{x\to\infty} \dfrac{3+\dfrac{2}{x}}{1-\dfrac{5}{x}} = \dfrac{3}{1} = 3.$

74. $\displaystyle\lim_{x\to-\infty}\frac{4x^2-1}{x+2}=\lim_{x\to-\infty}\frac{4x-\dfrac{1}{x}}{1+\dfrac{2}{x}}=-\infty$; that is, the limit does not exist.

75. $\displaystyle\lim_{x\to-\infty}\frac{3x^3+x^2+1}{x^3+1}=\lim_{x\to-\infty}\frac{3+\dfrac{1}{x}+\dfrac{1}{x^3}}{1+\dfrac{1}{x^3}}=3.$

76. $\displaystyle\lim_{x\to\infty}\frac{2x^2+3x+1}{x^4-x^2}=\lim_{x\to\infty}\frac{\dfrac{2}{x^2}+\dfrac{3}{x^3}+\dfrac{1}{x^4}}{1-\dfrac{1}{x^2}}=0.$

77. $\displaystyle\lim_{x\to-\infty}\frac{x^4+1}{x^3-1}=\lim_{x\to-\infty}\frac{x+\dfrac{1}{x^3}}{1-\dfrac{1}{x^3}}=-\infty$, that is, the limit does not exist.

78. $\displaystyle\lim_{x\to\infty}\frac{4x^4-3x^2+1}{2x^4+x^3+x^2+x+1}=\lim_{x\to\infty}\frac{4-\dfrac{3}{x^2}+\dfrac{1}{x^4}}{2+\dfrac{1}{x}+\dfrac{1}{x^2}+\dfrac{1}{x^3}+\dfrac{1}{x^4}}=2.$

79. $\displaystyle\lim_{x\to\infty}\frac{x^5-x^3+x-1}{x^6+2x^2+1}=\lim_{x\to\infty}\frac{\dfrac{1}{x}-\dfrac{1}{x^3}+\dfrac{1}{x^5}-\dfrac{1}{x^6}}{1+\dfrac{2}{x^4}+\dfrac{1}{x^6}}=0.$

80. $\displaystyle\lim_{x\to\infty}\frac{2x^2-1}{x^3+x^2+1}=\lim_{x\to\infty}\frac{\dfrac{2}{x}-\dfrac{1}{x^3}}{1+\dfrac{1}{x}+\dfrac{1}{x^3}}=0.$

81. a. The cost of removing 50 percent of the pollutant is

$$C(50)=\frac{0.5(50)}{100-50}=0.5\text{, or }\$500{,}000.$$

Similarly, we find that the cost of removing 60, 70, 80, 90, and 95 percent of the pollutants is $750,000; $1,166,667; $2,000,000, $4,500,000, and $9,500,000, respectively

b. $\lim\limits_{x \to 100} \dfrac{0.5x}{100-x} = \infty$, which means that the cost of removing the pollutant increases astronomically if we wish to remove almost all of the pollutant.

82. a. The number present initially is given by
$$P(0) = \frac{72}{9-0} = 8.$$

b. As t approaches 9 (remember that $0 < t < 9$), the denominator approaches 0 while the numerator remains constant at 72. Therefore, $P(t)$ gets larger and larger.
Thus $\lim\limits_{t \to 9} P(t) = \lim\limits_{t \to 9} \dfrac{72}{9-t} = \infty$

c.

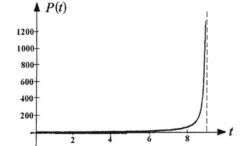

83 $\lim\limits_{x \to \infty} \overline{C}(x) = \lim\limits_{x \to \infty} 2.2 + \dfrac{2500}{x} = 2.2$, or $2.20 per DVD

In the long-run, the average cost of producing x DVDs will approach $2.20/disc.

84. $\lim\limits_{t \to \infty} C(t) = \lim\limits_{t \to \infty} \dfrac{0.2t}{t^2+1} = \lim\limits_{t \to \infty} \dfrac{\frac{0.2}{t}}{1 + \frac{1}{t^2}} = 0$, which says that the concentration of drug in

the bloodstream decreases to zero as time goes by

85 a. $T(1) = \dfrac{120}{1+4} = 24$, or $24 million. $T(2) = \dfrac{120(4)}{8} = 60$, $60 million.

$$T(3) = \frac{120(9)}{13} = 83.1, \text{ or } \$83\ 1 \text{ million.}$$

b. In the long run, the movie will gross

$$\lim_{x \to \infty} \frac{120x^2}{x^2 + 4} = \lim_{x \to \infty} \frac{120}{1 + \dfrac{4}{x^2}} = 120, \text{ or } \$120 \text{ million.}$$

86. a. The current population is $P(0) = \dfrac{200}{40} = 5, \text{ or } 5000.$

b. The population in the long run will be

$$\lim_{t \to \infty} \frac{25t^2 + 125t + 200}{t^2 + 5t + 40} = \lim_{t \to \infty} \frac{25 + \dfrac{125}{t} + \dfrac{200}{t^2}}{1 + \dfrac{5}{t} + \dfrac{40}{t^2}} = 25, \text{ or } 25{,}000.$$

87 a. The average cost of driving 5000 miles per year is

$$C(5) = \frac{2010}{5^{2.2}} + 17.80 = 76.07,$$

or 76.1 cents per mile. Similarly, we see that the average cost of driving 10,000 miles per year; 15,000 miles per year; 20,000 miles per year; and 25,000 miles per year is 30.5, 23; 20.6, and 19.5 cents per mile, respectively.

b.

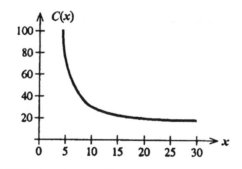

c. It approaches 17.80 cents per mile.

88. a. $R(I) = \dfrac{I}{1 + I^2}$ b. $\displaystyle \lim_{I \to \infty} R(I) = \lim_{I \to \infty} \frac{I}{1 + I^2} = 0$

I	1	2	3	4	5
$R(I)$	$\frac{1}{2}$	$\frac{2}{5}$	$\frac{3}{10}$	$\frac{4}{17}$	$\frac{5}{26}$

c

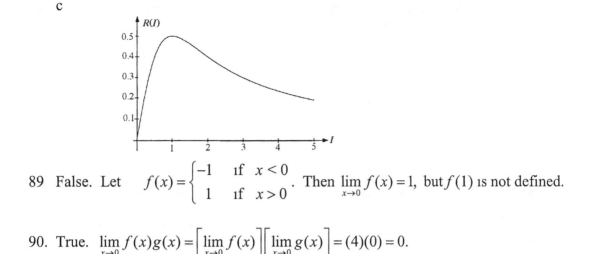

89 False. Let $f(x) = \begin{cases} -1 & \text{if } x < 0 \\ 1 & \text{if } x > 0 \end{cases}$. Then $\lim_{x \to 0} f(x) = 1$, but $f(1)$ is not defined.

90. True. $\lim_{x \to 0} f(x)g(x) = \left[\lim_{x \to 0} f(x)\right]\left[\lim_{x \to 0} g(x)\right] = (4)(0) = 0.$

91. True. Division by zero is not permitted.

92. False. Let $f(x) = (x-3)^2$ and $g(x) = x - 3$ Then $\lim_{x \to 3} f(x) = 0$ and $\lim_{x \to 3} g(x) = 0,$

but $\lim_{x \to 3} \dfrac{f(x)}{g(x)} = \lim_{x \to 3} \dfrac{(x-3)^2}{x-3} = \lim_{x \to 3} (x-3) = 0.$

93. True. Each limit in the sum exists. Therefore,

$$\lim_{x \to 2}\left(\frac{x}{x+1} + \frac{3}{x-1}\right) = \lim_{x \to 2} \frac{x}{x+1} + \lim_{x \to 2} \frac{3}{x-1} = \frac{2}{3} + \frac{3}{1} = \frac{11}{3}$$

94. False. Each of the limits $\lim_{x \to 1} \dfrac{2x}{x-1}$ and $\lim_{x \to 1} \dfrac{2}{x-1}$ do not exist.

95. $\lim_{x \to \infty} \dfrac{ax}{x+b} = \lim_{x \to \infty} \dfrac{a}{1 + \frac{b}{x}} = a.$ As the amount of substrate becomes very large, the initial

speed approaches the constant a moles per liter per second.

96. Consider the functions $f(x) = 1/x$ and $g(x) = -1/x$. Observe that

$\lim_{x \to 0} f(x)$ and $\lim_{x \to 0} g(x)$ do not exist, but $\lim_{x \to 0} [f(x) + g(x)] = \lim_{x \to 0} 0 = 0.$

This example does not contradict Theorem 1 because the hypothesis of Theorem 1 says that if $\lim_{x \to 0} f(x)$ and $\lim_{x \to 0} g(x)$ both exist, then the limit of the sum of f and g also exists. It does not say that if the former do not exist, then the latter might not exist.

97. Consider the functions $f(x) = \begin{cases} -1 & \text{if } x < 0 \\ 1 & \text{if } x \geq 0 \end{cases}$ and $g(x) = \begin{cases} 1 & \text{if } x < 0 \\ -1 & \text{if } x \geq 0 \end{cases}$

Then $\lim_{x \to 0} f(x)$ and $\lim_{x \to 0} g(x)$ do not exist, but $\lim_{x \to 0} [f(x)g(x)] = \lim_{x \to 0}(-1) = -1.$

This example does not contradict Theorem 1 because the hypothesis of Theorem 1 says that if $\lim_{x \to 0} f(x)$ and $\lim_{x \to 0} g(x)$ both exist, then the limit of the product of f and g also exists. It does not say that if the former do not exist, then the latter might not exist.

98. Take $f(x) = \dfrac{1}{x}$, $g(x) = \dfrac{1}{x^2}$, $a = 0$ Then $\lim_{x \to 0} f(x)$ and $\lim_{x \to 0} g(x)$ do not exist, but

$\lim_{x \to 0} \dfrac{f(x)}{g(x)} = \lim_{x \to 0} \dfrac{1}{x} \cdot \dfrac{x^2}{1} = \lim_{x \to 0} x = a$ exists. No, for a reason similar to that given in Exercise 96.

USING TECHNOLOGY EXERCISES 2.4, page 118

1 5   2. 11   3. 3   4. 0   5. $\dfrac{2}{3}$ 6. $\dfrac{10}{11}$ 7. $\dfrac{1}{2}$

8. 3   9. e^2, or 7.38906   10. ln 2, or 0.693147

11. From the graph we see that $f(x)$ does not approach any finite number as x approaches 3.

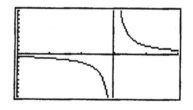

12. From the graph, we see that $f(x)$ does not approach any finite number as x approaches 2.

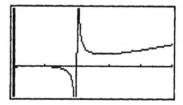

13 a.

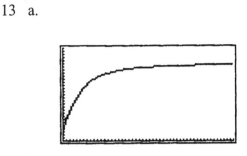

b. $\lim\limits_{t\to\infty}\dfrac{25t^2+125t+200}{t^2+5t+40}=25$, so in the long run the population will approach 25,000.

14. a.

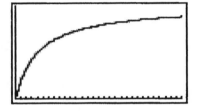

b. $\lim\limits_{t\to\infty}\dfrac{0.8t}{t+4.1}=\lim\limits_{t\to\infty}\dfrac{0.8}{1+\dfrac{4.1}{t}}=0.8$

2.5 CONCEPT QUESTIONS, page 127

1. $\lim\limits_{x\to3^-}f(x)=2$ means $f(x)$ can be made as close to 2 as we please by taking x sufficiently close to but to the left of $x=3$ $\lim\limits_{x\to3^+}f(x)=4$ means $f(x)$ can be made as close to 4 as we please by taking x sufficiently close to but to the right of $x=3$.

2. a. $\lim\limits_{x\to1}f(x)$ does not exist because the left- and right-hand limits at $x=1$ are different.

   b. Nothing, because the existence or value of f at $x=1$ does not depend on the existence (or non-existence) of the left-, right- or (two-sides)-limits of f

3 a. f is continuous at a if $\lim\limits_{x\to a}f(x)=f(a)$.

   b. f is continuous on an interval I if f is continuous at each point in I.

4. a. f is continuous because the flight path of the plane varies "continuously."

   b. f is continuous.

   c. f is discontinuous because the fare "jumps" after the cab has covered a certain distance or after a certain amount of time has elapsed.

d. f is discontinuous because the rates "jump" by a certain amount (up or down) when it is adjusted at certain times.

5 Refer to page 124. Answers will vary.

EXERCISES 2.5, page 127

1. $\lim_{x \to 2^-} f(x) = 3$, $\lim_{x \to 2^+} f(x) = 2$, $\lim_{x \to 2} f(x)$ does not exist.

2. $\lim_{x \to 3^-} f(x) = 3$, $\lim_{x \to 3^+} f(x) = 5$, $\lim_{x \to 3} f(x)$ does not exist.

3. $\lim_{x \to -1^-} f(x) = \infty$, $\lim_{x \to -1^+} f(x) = 2$. Therefore $\lim_{x \to -1} f(x)$ does not exist.

4. $\lim_{x \to 1^-} f(x) = 3$, $\lim_{x \to 1^+} f(x) = 3$, $\lim_{x \to 1} f(x) = 3$.

5   $\lim_{x \to 1^-} f(x) = 0$, $\lim_{x \to 1^+} f(x) = 2$, $\lim_{x \to 1} f(x)$ does not exist.

6. $\lim_{x \to 0^-} f(x) = 2$, $\lim_{x \to 0^+} f(x) = \infty$, $\lim_{x \to 0} f(x)$ does not exist.

7   $\lim_{x \to 0^-} f(x) = -2$, $\lim_{x \to 0^+} f(x) = 2$, $\lim_{x \to 0} f(x)$ does not exist.

8. $\lim_{x \to 0^-} f(x) = \lim_{x \to 0^+} f(x) = \lim_{x \to 0} f(x) = 2$.

9   True   10. True   11. True   12. True   13 False   14. True

15 True   16. True   17. False   18. True   19 True   20. False

21. $\lim_{x \to 1^+} (2x + 4) = 6$.

22. $\lim_{x \to 1^-} (3x - 4) = -1$.

23 $\lim_{x \to 2^-} \dfrac{x-3}{x+2} = \dfrac{2-3}{2+2} = -\dfrac{1}{4}$.

24. $\lim_{x \to 1^+} \dfrac{x+2}{x+1} = \dfrac{1+2}{1+1} = \dfrac{3}{2}$

25 $\lim_{x \to 0^+} \dfrac{1}{x}$ does not exist because $1/x \to \infty$ as $x \to 0$ from the right..

26. $\lim_{x \to 0^-} \dfrac{1}{x} = \infty$; that is, the limit does not exist.

26. $\lim\limits_{x \to 0^-} \dfrac{1}{x} = \infty$; that is, the limit does not exist.

27. $\lim\limits_{x \to 0^+} \dfrac{x-1}{x^2+1} = \dfrac{-1}{1} = -1.$

28. $\lim\limits_{x \to 2^+} \dfrac{x+1}{x^2-2x+3} = \dfrac{2+1}{4-4+3} = 1.$

29. $\lim\limits_{x \to 0^+} \sqrt{x} = \sqrt{\lim\limits_{x \to 0^+} x} = 0.$

30. $\lim\limits_{x \to 2^+} 2\sqrt{x-2} = 2 \cdot 0 = 0.$

31. $\lim\limits_{x \to -2^+} (2x + \sqrt{2+x}) = \lim\limits_{x \to -2^+} 2x + \lim\limits_{x \to -2^+} \sqrt{2+x} = -4 + 0 = -4.$

32. $\lim\limits_{x \to -5^+} x(1 + \sqrt{5+x}) = -5[1 + \sqrt{5 + (-5)}] = -5.$

33. $\lim\limits_{x \to 1^-} \dfrac{1+x}{1-x} = \infty$, that is, the limit does not exist.

34. $\lim\limits_{x \to 1^+} \dfrac{1+x}{1-x} = -\infty$

35. $\lim\limits_{x \to 2^-} \dfrac{x^2-4}{x-2} = \lim\limits_{x \to 2^-} \dfrac{(x+2)(x-2)}{x-2} = \lim\limits_{x \to 2^-} (x+2) = 4.$

36. $\lim\limits_{x \to -3^+} \dfrac{\sqrt{x+3}}{x^2+1} = \dfrac{0}{10} = 0.$

37. $\lim\limits_{x \to 0^+} f(x) = \lim\limits_{x \to 0^+} x^2 = 0,\ \lim\limits_{x \to 0^-} f(x) = \lim\limits_{x \to 0^-} 2x = 0$

38. $\lim\limits_{x \to 0^+} f(x) = \lim\limits_{x \to 0^+} (2x+3) = 3,\ \lim\limits_{x \to 0^-} f(x) = \lim\limits_{x \to 0^-} (-x+1) = 1.$

39. The function is discontinuous at $x = 0$. Conditions 2 and 3 are violated.

40. The function is not continuous because condition 3 for continuity is not satisfied.

41. The function is continuous everywhere.

42. The function is continuous everywhere.

43 The function is discontinuous at $x = 0$. Condition 3 is violated.

44 The function is not continuous at $x = -1$ because condition 3 for continuity is violated.

45 f is continuous for all values of x.　　　46. f is continuous for all values of x.

47 f is continuous for all values of x. Note that $x^2 + 1 \geq 1 > 0$.

48. f is continuous for all values of x. Note that $2x^2 + 1 \geq 1 > 0$.

49 f is discontinuous at $x = 1/2$, where the denominator is 0.

50. f is discontinuous at $x = 1$, where the denominator is 0.

51 Observe that $x^2 + x - 2 = (x + 2)(x - 1) = 0$ if $x = -2$ or $x = 1$. So, f is discontinuous at these values of x.

52. Observe that $x^2 + 2x - 3 = (x + 3)(x - 1) = 0$ if $x = -3$ or $x = 1$　So, f is discontinuous at these values of x.

53. f is continuous everywhere since all three conditions are satisfied.

54. f is continuous everywhere since all three conditions are satisfied.

55 f is continuous everywhere since all three conditions are satisfied.

56. f is not defined at $x = 1$ and is discontinuous there. It is continuous everywhere else.

57 Since the denominator $x^2 - 1 = (x - 1)(x + 1) = 0$ if $x = -1$ or 1, we see that f is discontinuous at these points.

58. The function f is not defined at $x = 1$ and $x = 2$. Therefore, f is discontinuous at $x = 1$ and $x = 2$.

59. Since $x^2 - 3x + 2 = (x - 2)(x - 1) = 0$ if $x = 1$ or 2, we see that the denominator is zero at these points and so f is discontinuous at these points.

60. The denominator of the function f is equal to zero when $x^2 - 2x = x(x - 2) = 0$; that is, when $x = 0$ or $x = 2$. Therefore, f is discontinuous at $x = 0$ and $x = 2$.

61. The function f is discontinuous at $x = 1, 2, 3, ..., 11$ because the limit of f does not exist at these points.

62. f is discontinuous at $t = 20$, 40, and 60. When $t = 0$, the inventory stands at 750 reams. The level drops to about 200 reams by the twentieth day at which time a new order of 500 reams arrives to replenish the supply. A similar interpretation holds for the other values of t.

63 Having made steady progress up to $x = x_1$, Michael's progress came to a standstill. Then at $x = x_2$ a sudden break-through occurs and he then continues to successfully complete the solution to the problem.

64. The total deposits of Franklin make a jump at each of these points as the deposits of the ailing institutions become a part of the total deposits of the parent company

65 Conditions 2 and 3 are not satisfied at each of these points.

66. The function P is discontinuous at $t = 12$, 16, and 28. At $t = 12$ and 16, the prime interest rate jumped from 10½ to 11% and from 11% to 11½, respectively· At $t = 18$, the prime interest rate jumped from 11½ back down to 11%.

67 The graph of f follows.

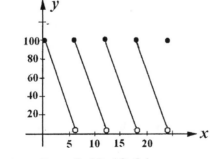

f is discontinuous at $x = 6, 12, 18, 24$.

68. The graph of f follows.

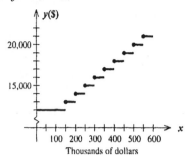

y($)

20,000

15,000

100 200 300 400 500 600
Thousands of dollars

f is discontinuous at $x = 150,000, 200,000, 250,000,.$ .6

69

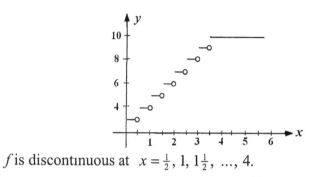

y

10

8

6

4

1 2 3 4 5 6

x

f is discontinuous at $x = \frac{1}{2}, 1, 1\frac{1}{2}, \ldots, 4.$

70. The graph of C follows.

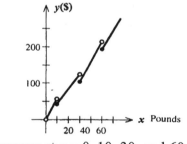

y($)

200

100

20 40 60

x Pounds

C is discontinuous at $x = 0, 10, 30,$ and $60.$

71. a. $\lim_{t \to 0^+} S(t) = \lim_{t \to 0^+} \frac{a}{t} + b = \infty$ As the time taken to excite the tissue is made smaller

and smaller, the strength of the electric current gets stronger and stronger.

2 Functions, Limits, and the Derivative   **122**

b. $\lim\limits_{t\to\infty}\dfrac{a}{t}+b=b$ As the time taken to excite the tissue is made larger and larger,

the strength of the electric current gets smaller and smaller and approaches b

72. a. $\lim\limits_{v\to u^+}\dfrac{aLv^3}{v-u}=\infty$ and this shows that, when the speed of the fish is very close to

that of the current, the energy expended by the fish will be enormous.

b. $\lim\limits_{v\to\infty}\dfrac{aLv^3}{v-u}=\infty$ and this says that if the speed of the fish increases greatly, so does

the amount of energy required to swim a distance of L ft.

73   We require that $f(1)=1+2=3=\lim\limits_{x\to1^+}kx^2=k$, or $k=3$.

74   Since $\lim\limits_{x\to-2}\dfrac{x^2-4}{x+2}=\lim\limits_{x\to-2}\dfrac{(x-2)(x+2)}{x+2}=\lim\limits_{x\to-2}(x-2)=-4,$
we define $f(-2)=k=-4$, that is, take $k=-4$.

75. a. Yes, because if $f+g$ were continuous at a, then $g=(f+g)-f$
would be continuous (the difference of two continuous functions is continuous),
and this would imply that g is continuous, a contradiction.
b. No. Consider the functions f and g defined by
$$f(x)=\begin{cases}-1 & \text{if } x<0 \\ 1 & \text{if } x\geq0\end{cases} \text{ and } g(x)=\begin{cases}1 & \text{if } x<0 \\ -1 & \text{if } x\geq0\end{cases}$$
Both f and g are discontinuous at $x=0$, but $f+g$ is continuous everywhere.

76. a. No. Consider the function $f(x)=0$ for all x in $(-\infty,\infty)$ and
$$g(x)=\begin{cases}1 & \text{if } x<0 \\ -1 & \text{if } x\geq0\end{cases}$$
b. No. Consider the functions f and g of Exercise 75b.

77 a. f is a polynomial of degree 2 and is therefore continuous everywhere, and in
particular in $[1,3]$.
b. $f(1)=3$ and $f(3)=-1$ and so f must have at least one zero in $(1,3)$.

78. a. f is a polynomial of degree 3 and so f is continuous everywhere.

b. $f(0) = 14$ and $f(1) = -23$ and so f has at least one zero in $(0,1)$.

79 f is a polynomial and is therefore continuous on $[-1,1]$.
$$f(-1) = (-1)^3 - 2(-1)^2 + 3(-1) + 2 = -1 - 2 - 3 + 2 = -4.$$
$$f(1) = 1 - 2 + 3 + 2 = 4.$$
Since $f(-1)$ and $f(1)$ have opposite signs, we see that f has at least one zero in $(-1,1)$.

80. f is continuous on $[14,16]$ and
$$f(14) = 2(14)^{5/3} - 5(14)^{4/3} \approx -6.06; \quad f(16) = 2(16)^{5/3} - 5(16)^{4/3} \approx 1.60,$$
and so f has at least one zero in $(14,16)$.

81. $f(0) = 6$ and $f(3) = 3$ and f is continuous on $[0,3]$. So the Intermediate Value Theorem guarantees that there is at least one value of x for which $f(x) = 4$. Solving $f(x) = x^2 - 4x + 6 = 4$, we find $x^2 - 4x + 2 = 0$. Using the quadratic formula, we find that $x = 2 \pm \sqrt{2}$ Since $2 \pm \sqrt{2}$ does not lie in $[0,3]$, we see that $x = 2 - \sqrt{2} \approx 0.59$.

82. Since $f(-1) = 3$ and $f(4) = 13$ and f is continuous on $[-1,4]$, the Intermediate Value Theorem guarantees that there is at least one value of x for which $f(x) = 7$ since $3 < 7 < 13$ Solving $f(x) = x^2 - x + 1 = 7$, we find $x^2 - x - 6 = (x - 3)(x + 2) = 0$, that is, $x = -2$, or 3 Since -2 does not lie in $[-1,4]$, the required solution is 3.

83. $x^5 + 2x - 7 = 0$

Step	Root of f(x) = 0 lies in
1	(1,2)
2	(1,1.5)
3	(1.25,1.5)
4	(1.25,1.375)
5	(1.3125,1.375)
6	(1.3125,1.34375)
7	(1.328125,1.34375)
8	(1.3359375,1.34375)
9	(1.33984375,1.34375)

We see that the required root is approximately 1.34.

84. $x^3 - x + 1 = 0$

Step	Root of f(x) = 0 lies in
1	$(-2,-1)$
2	$(-1.5,-1)$
3	$(-1.5,-1.25)$
4	$(-1.375,-1.25)$
5	$(-1.375,-1.3125)$
6	$(-1.34375,-1.3125)$
7	$(-1.328125,-1.3125)$
8	$(-1.328125,-1.3203125)$
9	$(-1.32421875,-1.3203125)$

We see that the required root is approximately -1.32.

85. a. $h(t) = 4 + 64(0) - 16(0) = 4$, and $h(2) = 4 + 64(2) - 16(4) = 68$.
    b. The function h is continuous on $[0,2]$. Furthermore, the number 32 lies between 4 and 68. Therefore, the Intermediate Value Theorem guarantees that there is at least one value of t such that $h(t) = 32$, that is, Joan must see the ball at least once during the time the ball is in the air.
    c. We solve

$$h(t) = 4 + 64t - 16t^2 = 32$$
$$16t^2 - 64t + 28 = 0$$
or
$$4t^2 - 16t + 7 = 0$$
$$(2t - 1)(2t - 7) = 0$$

giving $t = \frac{1}{2}$ or $t = \frac{7}{2}$. Joan sees the ball on its way up half a second after it was thrown and again $3\frac{1}{2}$ seconds later when it is on its way down.

86. a. $f(0) = 100\left(\dfrac{0+0+100}{0+0+100}\right) = 100$, $f(10) = 100\left(\dfrac{100+100+100}{100+200+100}\right) = \dfrac{30,000}{400} = 75$.
    b. Since 80 lies between 75 and 100 and f is continuous on $[75, 100]$, we conclude that there exists some t in $[0, 10]$ such that $f(t) = 80$.
    c. We solve $f(t) = 80$; that is,

$$100\left[\frac{t^2 + 10t + 100}{t^2 + 20t + 100}\right] = 80, \quad 5(t^2 + 10t + 100) = 4(t^2 + 20t + 100)$$

$$t^2 - 30t + 100 = 0, \ t = \frac{30 \pm \sqrt{900 - 400}}{2} = \frac{30 \pm \sqrt{500}}{2} = 3.82, \text{ or } 26.18.$$

Siince 26.18 lies outside the interval of interest, it is rejected. So, the oxygen content is at the 80% level 3.82 seconds after the organic waste has been dumped into the pond.

87 False. Take

$$f(x) = \begin{cases} -1 & \text{if } x < 2 \\ 4 & \text{if } x = 2 \\ 1 & \text{if } x > 2 \end{cases}$$

Then $f(2) = 4$ but $\lim_{x \to 2}$ does not exist.

88. False. Take $f(x) = \begin{cases} x+3 & \text{if } x \neq 0 \\ 1 & \text{if } x = 0 \end{cases}$. Then $\lim_{x \to 0} f(x) = 3$, but $f(0) = 1$.

89. False. Consider the function $f(x) = x^2 - 1$ on the interval [-2, 2]. Here, $f(-2) = f(2) = 3$, but f has zeros at $x = -1$ and $x = 1$.

90. False. If $\lim_{x \to a} f(x) = L$, then $\lim_{x \to a^-} f(x) = \lim_{x \to a^+} f(x) = L$ and so

$\lim_{x \to a^+} f(x) - \lim_{x \to a^-} f(x) = 0.$

91. False. Let $f(x) = \begin{cases} x & \text{if } x \neq 0 \\ 1 & \text{if } x = 0 \end{cases}$. Then $\lim_{x \to 0^+} f(x) = \lim_{x \to 0^-} f(x)$, but $f(0) = 1$.

92. False. Let $f(x) = x$ and let $g(x) = \begin{cases} x & \text{if } x \neq 1 \\ 2 & \text{if } x = 1 \end{cases}$ Then

$\lim_{x \to 1} f(x) = 1 = L$, $g(1) = 2 = M$, and $\lim_{x \to 1} g(x) = 1.$

$\lim_{x \to 1} f(x)g(x) = \left[\lim_{x \to 1} f(x) \right]\left[\lim_{x \to 1} g(x) \right] = (1)(1) = 1 \neq 2 = LM$

93 False. Take $f(x) = \begin{cases} \frac{1}{x} & \text{if } x \neq 0 \\ 0 & \text{if } x = 0 \end{cases}$. Then f is continuous for all $x \neq 0$ but

$\lim_{x \to 0} f(x)$ does not exist.

94. No. The Intermediate Value Theorem says that there is at least one number c in $[a, b]$ such that $f(c) = M$ if M is a number between $f(a)$ and $f(b)$

95 a. Both $g(x) = x$ and $h(x) = \sqrt{1-x^2}$ are continuous on $[-1,1]$ and so
   $f(x) = x - \sqrt{1-x^2}$ is continuous on $[-1,1]$.
   b. $f(-1) = -1$ and $f(1) = 1$ and so f has at least one zero in $(-1,1)$.
   c. Solving $f(x) = 0$, we have $x = \sqrt{1-x^2}$, $x^2 = 1-x^2$, $2x^2 = 1$, or $x = \frac{\pm\sqrt{2}}{2}$

96. a. f is a rational function whose denominator is never zero, and so it is continuous for all values of x.
   b. Since the numerator, x^2, is nonnegative and the denominator is $x^2 + 1 \geq 1$ for all values of x, we see that $f(x)$ is nonnegative for all values of x.
   c. $f(0) = \dfrac{0}{0+1} = \dfrac{0}{1} = 0$ and so f has a zero at $x = 0$. This does not contradict
   Theorem 4.

97 a. (i). Repeated use of Property 3 shows that $g(x) = x^n = x \cdot x \cdots x$ (n times) is a continuous function since $f(x) = x$ is continuous by Property 1
   (ii). Properties 1 and 5 combine to show that $c \cdot x^n$ is continuous using the results of (a).
   (iii). Each of the terms of $p(x) = a_0 x^n + a_1 x^{n-1} + \cdots + a_n$ is continuous and so Property 4 implies that p is continuous.
   b. Property 6 now shows that $R(x) = \dfrac{p(x)}{q(x)}$ is continuous if $q(a) \neq 0$ since p
   and q are continuous at $x = a$.

98. Consider the function f defined by
$$f(x) = \begin{cases} -1 & \text{if} \;\; -1 \leq x < 0 \\ 1 & \text{if} \;\;\;\; 0 \leq x < 1 \end{cases}.$$
   Then $f(-1) = -1$ and $f(1) = 1$. But, if we take the number $1/2$ which lies between $y = -1$ and $y = 1$, there is no value of x such that $f(x) = 1/2$.

1. $x = 0, 1$ 2. $x = -2, 1$ 3. $x = 2$ 4. $x = 0$ 5. $x = 0, \frac{1}{2}$

6. $x = -\frac{1}{2}, 3$ 7. $x = -\frac{1}{2}, 2$ 8. $x = -\frac{1}{3}, \frac{1}{2}$ 9. $x = -2, 1$ 10. $x = -1, 1$

11.

12.

13

14.

15.

16.

SECTION 2.6 CONCEPT QUESTIONS, page 147

1. a. $m = \dfrac{f(2+h) - f(2)}{h}$

    b. Slope of the tangent line is $\displaystyle\lim_{h \to 0} \dfrac{f(2+h) - f(2)}{h}$

2. a. Average rate of change is $\dfrac{f(2+h) - f(2)}{h}$

b. The instantaneous rate of change of f at 2 is $\lim\limits_{h \to 0} \dfrac{f(2+h) - f(2)}{h}$

c. The expression for the slope of the secant line is the same as that for the average rate of change. The expression for the slope of the tangent line is the same as that for the instantaneous rate of change.

3. a. It gives (i) the slope of the secant line passing through the points $(x, f(x))$ and $(x+h, f(x+h))$ and (ii) the average rate of change of f over the interval $[x, x+h]$.

   b. It gives (i) the slope of the tangent line to the graph of f at the point $(x, f(x))$ and (ii) the instantaneous rate of change of f at x.

4. If f is not continuous at a of if the graph of f has a kink at a.

EXERCISES 2.6, page 147

1   The rate of change of the average infant's weight when $t = 3$ is (7.5)/5, or 1.5 lb/month. The rate of change of the average infant's weight when $t = 18$ is (3.5)/6, or approximately 0.6 lb/month. The average rate of change over the infant's first year of life is (22.5 − 7.5)/(12), or 1.25 lb/month.

2.   The rate at which the wood grown is changing at the beginning of the 10th year is 4/12 or 1/3 cubic meters per hectare per year. At the beginning of the 30th year, it is 10/8 or 1.25 cubic meters per hectare per year.

3.   The rate of change of the percentage of households watching television at 4 P.M. is (12.3)/4, or approximately 3.1 percent per hour. The rate at 11 P.M. is (−42.3)/2 = −21.15; that is, it is dropping off at the rate of 21.15 percent per hour.

4.   The rate of change of the crop yield when the density is 200 aphids per bean stem is −500/300 or a decrease of approximately 1.7 kg/4000 sq meter per aphid per bean stem. The rate of change when the density is 800 aphids per bean stem is −150/300 or a decrease of approximately 0.5 kg/4000 sq meter per aphid per bean stem.

5.   a. Car A is travelling faster than Car B at t_1 because the slope of the tangent line to the graph of f is greater than the slope of the tangent line to the graph of g at t_1.

   b. Their speed is the same because the slope of the tangent lines are the same at t_2.

b. Their speed is the same because the slope of the tangent lines are the same at t_2.

c. Car B is travelling faster than Car A.

d. They have both covered the same distance and are once again side by side at t_3.

6. a. At t_1, the velocity of Car A is greater than that of Car B because $f(t_1) > g(t_1)$ but Car B has greater acceleration because the slope of the tangent line to the graph of g is increasing whereas the slope of the tangent line to f is decreasing as you move across t_1

b. Both cars have the same velocity at t_2, but the acceleration of Car B is greater than that of Car A because the slope of the tangent line to the graph of g is increasing, whereas the slope of the tangent line to the graph of f is decreasing as you move across t_2.

7. a. P_2 is decreasing faster at t_1 because the slope of the tangent line to the graph of g at t_1 is more negative than the slope of the tangent line to the graph of f at t_1.

b. P_1 is decreasing faster than P_2 at t_2.

c. Bactericide B is more effective in the short run, but bactericide A is more effective in the long run.

8. a. This occurs at $t = 0$.   b. This occurs at t_3.   c. This occurs at t_1.

d. This occurs at t_2 because the slope of the tangent line to the graph of f is greatest at the point $(t_2, f(t_2))$.

9. $f(x) = 13$

Step 1 $f(x+h) = 13$

Step 2 $f(x+h) - f(x) = 13 - 13 = 0$

Step 3 $\dfrac{f(x+h) - f(x)}{h} = \dfrac{0}{h} = 0$

Step 4 $f'(x) = \lim_{h \to 0} \dfrac{f(x+h) - f(x)}{h} = \lim_{h \to 0} 0 = 0$

10. $f(x) = -6$

Step 1 $f(x+h) = -6$

Step 2 $f(x+h) - f(x) = -6 - (-6) = 0$

Step 3 $\dfrac{f(x+h) - f(x)}{h} = \dfrac{0}{h} = 0$

Step 4 $f'(x) = \lim\limits_{h \to 0} \dfrac{f(x+h) - f(x)}{h} = \lim\limits_{h \to 0} 0 = 0$

11. $f(x) = 2x + 7$

Step 1 $f(x + h) = 2(x + h) + 7$

Step 2 $f(x + h) - f(x) = 2(x + h) + 7 - (2x + 7) = 2h$

Step 3 $\dfrac{f(x+h) - f(x)}{h} = \dfrac{2h}{h} = 2$

Step 4 $f'(x) = \lim\limits_{h \to 0} \dfrac{f(x+h) - f(x)}{h} = \lim\limits_{h \to 0} 2 = 2$

12. $f(x) = 8 - 4x$

Step 1 $f(x + h) = 8 - 4(x + h) = 8 - 4x - 4h$

Step 2 $f(x + h) - f(x) = (8 - 4x - 4h) - (8 - 4x) = -4h$

Step 3 $\dfrac{f(x+h) - f(x)}{h} = -\dfrac{4h}{h} = -4$

Step 4 $f'(x) = \lim\limits_{h \to 0} \dfrac{f(x+h) - f(x)}{h} = \lim\limits_{h \to 0} (-4) = -4.$

13 $f(x) = 3x^2$

Step 1 $f(x + h) = 3(x + h)^2 = 3x^2 + 6xh + 3h^2$

Step 2 $f(x + h) - f(x) = (3x^2 + 6xh + 3h^2) - 3x^2 = 6xh + 3h^2 = h(6x + 3h)$

Step 3 $\dfrac{f(x+h) - f(x)}{h} = \dfrac{h(6x + 3h)}{h} = 6x + 3h$

Step 4 $f'(x) = \lim\limits_{h \to 0} \dfrac{f(x+h) - f(x)}{h} = \lim\limits_{h \to 0} (6x + 3h) = 6x.$

14. $f(x) = -\frac{1}{2}x^2$

Step 1 $f(x + h) = -\frac{1}{2}(x + h)^2$

Step 2 $f(x + h) - f(x) = -\frac{1}{2}x^2 - xh - \frac{1}{2}h^2 + \frac{1}{2}x^2 = -h(x + \frac{1}{2}h)$

Step 3 $\dfrac{f(x+h) - f(x)}{h} = \dfrac{-h(x + \frac{1}{2}h)}{h} = -(x + \frac{1}{2}h).$

Step 4 $f'(x) = \lim\limits_{h \to 0} \dfrac{f(x+h) - f(x)}{h} = \lim\limits_{h \to 0} -(x + \frac{1}{2}h) = -x.$

15. $f(x) = -x^2 + 3x$

    Step 1 $f(x + h) = -(x + h)^2 + 3(x + h) = -x^2 - 2xh - h^2 + 3x + 3h$

    Step 2 $f(x + h) - f(x) = (-x^2 - 2xh - h^2 + 3x + 3h) - (-x^2 + 3x)$

$$= -2xh - h^2 + 3h = h(-2x - h + 3)$$

    Step 3 $\dfrac{f(x + h) - f(x)}{h} = \dfrac{h(-2x - h + 3)}{h} = -2x - h + 3$

    Step 4 $f'(x) = \lim\limits_{h \to 0} \dfrac{f(x + h) - f(x)}{h} = \lim\limits_{h \to 0} (-2x - h + 3) = -2x + 3.$

16. $f(x) = 2x^2 + 5x$

    Step 1 $f(x + h) = 2(x + h)^2 + 5(x + h) = 2x^2 + 4xh + 2h^2 + 5x + 5h$

    Step 2 $f(x + h) - f(x) = \quad 2x^2 + 4xh + 2h^2 + 5x + 5h - 2x^2 - 5x$

$$= \quad h(4x + 2h + 5)$$

    Step 3 $\dfrac{f(x + h) - f(x)}{h} = \dfrac{h(4x + 2h + 5)}{h} = 4x + 2h + 5$

    Step 4 $f'(x) = \lim\limits_{h \to 0} \dfrac{f(x + h) - f(x)}{h} = \lim\limits_{h \to 0} (4x + 2h + 5) = 4x + 5.$

17 $f(x) = 2x + 7$ Using the four-step process,

    Step 1 $f(x + h) = 2(x + h) + 7 = 2x + 2h + 7$

    Step 2 $f(x + h) - f(x) = 2x + 2h + 7 - 2x - 7 = 2h$

    Step 3 $\dfrac{f(x + h) - f(x)}{h} = \dfrac{2h}{h} = 2$

    Step 4 $f'(x) = \lim\limits_{h \to 0} \dfrac{f(x + h) - f(x)}{h} = \lim\limits_{h \to 0} 2 = 2$

    we find that $f'(x) = 2$. In particular, the slope at $x = 2$ is also 2. Therefore, a
required equation is $y - 11 = 2(x - 2)$ or $y = 2x + 7$

18. $f(x) = -3x + 4$. First, find $f'(x)$ using the four-step process. We obtain
$f'(x) = -3$. So the slope of the tangent line is $f''(-1) = -3$ and a desired equation
is $y - 7 = -3(x + 1)$ or $y = -3x + 4$.

19. $f(x) = 3x^2$. We first compute $f'(x) = 6x$ (see Problem 13). Since the slope of the

tangent line is $f'(1) = 6$, we use the point-slope form of the equation of a line and find that a required equation is $y - 3 = 6(x - 1)$, or $y = 6x - 3$

20. $f(x) = 3x - x^2$. Using the four-step process

Step 1 $f(x + h) = 3(x + h) - (x + h)^2 = 3x + 3h - x^2 - 2xh - h^2$

Step 2 $f(x + h) - f(x) = 3x + 3h - x^2 - 2xh - h^2 - 3x + x^2 = 3h - 2xh - h^2$
$$= h(3 - 2x - h)$$

Step 3 $\dfrac{f(x + h) - f(x)}{h} = \dfrac{h(3 - 2x - h)}{h} = 3 - 2x - h$

Step 4 $f'(x) = \lim\limits_{h \to 0} \dfrac{f(x + h) - f(x)}{h} = \lim\limits_{h \to 0} (3 - 2x - h) = 3 - 2x,$

we find that $f'(x) = 3 - 2x$. In particular, when $x = -2$, $f'(x) = 3 - 2(-2) = 7$
Using the point-slope form of an equation of a line, we find
$$y + 10 = 7(x + 2), \text{ or } y = 7x + 4.$$

21. $f(x) = -1/x$. We first compute $f'(x)$ using the four-step process.

Step 1 $f(x + h) = -\dfrac{1}{x + h}$

Step 2 $f(x + h) - f(x) = -\dfrac{1}{x + h} + \dfrac{1}{x} = \dfrac{-x + (x + h)}{x(x + h)} = \dfrac{h}{x(x + h)}$

Step 3 $\dfrac{f(x + h) - f(x)}{h} = \dfrac{\dfrac{h}{x(x + h)}}{h} = \dfrac{1}{x(x + h)}$

Step 4 $f'(x) = \lim\limits_{h \to 0} \dfrac{f(x + h) - f(x)}{h} = \lim\limits_{h \to 0} \dfrac{1}{x(x + h)} = \dfrac{1}{x^2}$

The slope of the tangent line is $f'(3) = 1/9$. Therefore, a required equation is
$$y - \left(-\tfrac{1}{3}\right) = \tfrac{1}{9}(x - 3) \quad \text{or} \quad y = \tfrac{1}{9}x - \tfrac{2}{3}$$

22. $f(x) = \dfrac{3}{2x}$ First use the four-step process to find $f'(x) = -\dfrac{3}{2x^2}$. (This is similar to Problem 21) The slope of the tangent line is $f'(1) = -\dfrac{3}{2}$ Therefore, a required

equation is $y - \tfrac{3}{2} = -\tfrac{3}{2}(x - 1)$ or $y = -\tfrac{3}{2}x + 3$.

23. a. $f(x) = 2x^2 + 1$. We use the four-step process.

Step 1 $f(x+h) = 2(x+h)^2 + 1 = 2x^2 + 4xh + 2h^2 + 1$

Step 2 $f(x+h) - f(x) = (2x^2 + 4xh + 2h^2 + 1) - (2x^2 + 1) = 4xh + 2h^2$
$$= h(4x + 2h)$$

Step 3 $\dfrac{f(x+h) - f(x)}{h} = \dfrac{h(4x+2h)}{h} = 4x + 2h$

Step 4 $f'(x) = \lim\limits_{h \to 0} \dfrac{f(x+h) - f(x)}{h} = \lim\limits_{h \to 0} (4x + 2h) = 4x$

b. The slope of the tangent line is $f'(1) = 4(1) = 4$. Therefore, an equation is $y - 3 = 4(x - 1)$ or $y = 4x - 1$.

c.

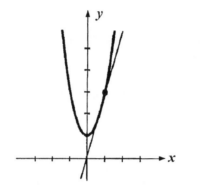

24. a. Using the four-step process, we find that $f'(x) = 2x + 6$.

b. At a point on the graph of f where the tangent line to the curve is horizontal, $f'(x) = 0$. Then $2x + 6 = 0$, or $x = -3$. Therefore, $y = f(-3) = (-3)^2 + 6(-3) = -9$. The required point is $(-3, -9)$.

c.

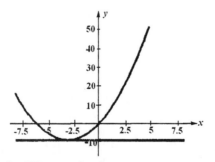

25. a. $f(x) = x^2 - 2x + 1$. We use the four-step process:

Step 1 $f(x + h) = (x+h)^2 - 2(x+h) + 1 = x^2 + 2xh + h^2 - 2x - 2h + 1$

Step 2 $f(x+h)-f(x) = (x^2+2xh+h^2-2x-2h+1)-(x^2-2x+1)\,]$
$$= 2xh+h^2-2h = h(2x+h-2)$$

Step 3 $\dfrac{f(x+h)-f(x)}{h} = \dfrac{h(2x+h-2)}{h} = 2x+h-2$

Step 4 $f'(x) = \lim\limits_{h\to 0}\dfrac{f(x+h)-f(x)}{h} = \lim\limits_{h\to 0}(2x+h-2) = 2x-2.$

b. At a point on the graph of f where the tangent line to the curve is horizontal, $f'(x)=0$ Then $2x-2=0$, or $x=1$. Since $f(1)=1-2+1=0$, we see that the required point is (1,0).

c.

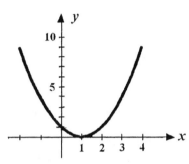

d. It is changing at the rate of 0 units per unit change in x.

26. a. We use the four-step process

Step 1 $f(x+h) = \dfrac{1}{(x+h)-1} = \dfrac{1}{x+h-1}$

Step 2 $f(x+h)-f(x) = \dfrac{1}{x+h-1} - \dfrac{1}{x-1}$
$$= \dfrac{x-1-(x+h-1)}{(x+h-1)(x-1)} = -\dfrac{h}{(x+h-1)(x-1)}$$

Step 3 $\dfrac{f(x+h)-f(x)}{h} = -\dfrac{1}{(x+h-1)(x-1)}$

Step 4 $f'(x) = \lim\limits_{h\to 0}\dfrac{f(x+h)-f(x)}{h} = \lim\limits_{h\to 0}\dfrac{1}{(x+h-1)(x-1)} = -\dfrac{1}{(x-1)^2}.$

b. The slope is $f'(-1)=-1/4$. So, an equation is

$$y-(-\tfrac{1}{2})=-\tfrac{1}{4}(x+1), \quad \text{or} \quad y=-\tfrac{1}{4}x-\tfrac{3}{4}$$

c.

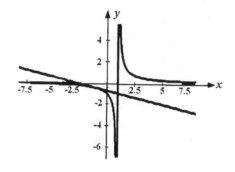

27 a. $f(x)=x^2+x$

$$\frac{f(3)-f(2)}{3-2}=\frac{(3^2+3)-(2^2+2)}{1}=6$$

$$\frac{f(2.5)-f(2)}{2.5-2}=\frac{(2.5^2+2.5)-(2^2+2)}{0.5}=5.5$$

$$\frac{f(2.1)-f(2)}{2.1-2}=\frac{(2.1^2+2.1)-(2^2+2)}{0.1}=5.1$$

b. We first compute $f'(x)$ using the four-step process.

Step 1 $f(x+h)=(x+h)^2+(x+h)=x^2+2xh+h^2+x+h$

Step 2 $f(x+h)-f(x)=(x^2+2xh+h^2+x+h)-(x^2+x)\,]$
$$=2xh+h^2+h=h(2x+h+1)$$

Step 3 $\dfrac{f(x+h)-f(x)}{h}=\dfrac{h(2x+h+1)}{h}=2x+h+1$

Step 4 $f'(x)=\lim\limits_{h\to 0}\dfrac{f(x+h)-f(x)}{h}=\lim\limits_{h\to 0}(2x+h+1)=2x+1.$

The instantaneous rate of change of y at $x=2$ is $f'(2)=5$ or 5 units per unit change in x.

c. The results in (a) suggest that the average rates of change of f at $x=2$ approach 5 as the interval $[2, 2+h]$ gets smaller and smaller ($h=1, 0.5,$ and 0.1). This number is the instantaneous rate of change of f at $x=2$ as computed in (b).

28. a. $f(x) = x^2 - 4x$

$$\frac{f(4) - f(3)}{4 - 3} = \frac{(16 - 16) - (9 - 12)}{1} = 3$$

$$\frac{f(3.5) - f(3)}{3.5 - 3} = \frac{(12.25 - 14) - (9 - 12)}{0.5} = 2.5$$

$$\frac{f(3.1) - f(3)}{3.1 - 3} = \frac{(9.61 - 12.4) - (9 - 12)}{0.1} = 2.1$$

b. We first compute $f'(x)$ using the four-step process:

Step 1 $f(x + h) = (x + h)^2 - 4(x + h) = x^2 + 2xh + h^2 - 4x - 4h$

Step 2 $f(x + h) - f(x) = (x^2 + 2xh + h^2 - 4x - 4h) - (x^2 - 4x)]$

$$= 2xh + h^2 - 4h = h(2x + h - 4)$$

Step 3 $\dfrac{f(x + h) - f(x)}{h} = \dfrac{h(2x + h - 4)}{h} = 2x + h - 4$

Step 4 $f'(x) = \lim\limits_{h \to 0} \dfrac{f(x + h) - f(x)}{h} = \lim\limits_{h \to 0} (2x + h - 4) = 2x - 4.$

The instantaneous rate of change of y at $x = 3$ is $f'(3) = 6 - 4 = 2$, or 2 units/unit change in x.

c. The results of (a) suggest that the average rates of change of f over smaller and smaller intervals (containing $x = 2$) approach the instantaneous rate of change of 2 units per unit change in x obtained in (b).

29 a. $f(t) = 2t^2 + 48t$. The average velocity of the car over $[20,21]$ is

$$\frac{f(21) - f(20)}{21 - 20} = \frac{[2(21)^2 + 48(21)] - [2(20)^2 + 48(20)]}{1} = 130 \text{ ft / sec}$$

Its average velocity over $[20,20.1]$ is

$$\frac{f(20.1) - f(20)}{20.1 - 20} = \frac{[2(20.1)^2 + 48(20.1)] - [2(20)^2 + 48(20)]}{0.1} = 128.2 \text{ ft / sec}$$

Its average velocity over $[20,20.01]$

$$\frac{f(20.01) - f(20)}{20.01 - 20} = \frac{[2(20.01)^2 + 48(20.01)] - [2(20)^2 + 48(20)]}{0.01} = 128.02 \text{ ft / sec}$$

b. We first compute $f'(t)$ using the four-step process.

Step 1 $f(t + h) = 2(t + h)^2 + 48(t + h) = 2t^2 + 4th + 2h^2 + 48t + 48h$

Step 2 $f(t+h) - f(t) = (2t^2 + 4th + 2h^2 + 48t + 48h) - (2t^2 + 48t)]$

$$= 4th + 2h^2 + 48h = h(4t + 2h + 48).$$

Step 3 $\dfrac{f(t+h) - f(t)}{h} = \dfrac{h(4t + 2h + 48)}{h} = 4t + 2h + 48$

Step 4 $f'(t) = \lim\limits_{t \to 0} \dfrac{f(t+h) - f(t)}{h} = \lim\limits_{t \to 0} 4t + 2h + 48 = 4t + 48$

The instantaneous velocity of the car at $t = 20$ is $f'(20) = 4(20) + 48$, or 128 ft/sec.

c. Our results shows that the average velocities do approach the instantaneous velocity as the intervals over which they are computed decreases.

30. a. The average velocity of the ball over the time interval [2,3] is

$$\frac{s(3) - s(2)}{3 - 2} = \frac{[128(3) - 16(3)^2] - [128(2) - 16(2)^2]}{1} = 48$$

or 48 ft/sec. Over the time interval [2,2.5]:

$$\frac{s(2.5) - s(2)}{2.5 - 2} = \frac{[128(2.5) - 16(2.5)^2] - [128(2) - 16(2)^2]}{0.5} = 56,$$

or 56 ft/sec. Over the time interval [2,2.1]:

$$\frac{s(2.1) - s(2)}{2.1 - 2} = \frac{[128(2.1) - 16(2.1)^2] - [128(2) - 16(2)^2]}{0.1} = 62.4$$

or 62.4 ft/sec.

b. Using the four–step process, we find that the instantaneous velocity of the ball at any time t is given by $v(t) = 128 - 32t$. In particular, the velocity of the ball at $t = 2$ is $v(2) = 128 - 32(2) = 64$, or 64 ft/sec.

c. At $t = 5$, $v(5) = 128 - 32(5) = -32$. So the velocity of the ball at $t = 5$ is -32 ft/sec and it is falling.

d. The ball hits the ground when $s(t) = 0$, that is, when $128t - 16^2 = 0$, $t(128 - 16t) = 0$, or $t = 0$ and $t = 8$. Thus, it will hit the ground when $t = 8$.

31. a. We solve the equation $16t^2 = 400$ obtaining $t = 5$ which is the time it takes the screw driver to reach the ground.

b. The average velocity over the time [0,5] is

$$\frac{f(5) - f(0)}{5 - 0} = \frac{16(25) - 0}{5} = 80, \text{ or 80 ft/sec.} \quad [\text{Let } s = f(t) = 16t^2]$$

c. The velocity of the screwdriver at time t is

$$v(t) = \lim\limits_{h \to 0} \frac{f(t+h) - f(t)}{h} = \lim\limits_{h \to 0} \frac{16(t+h)^2 - 16t^2}{h}$$

$$= \lim_{h \to 0} \frac{16t^2 + 32th + 16h^2 - 16t^2}{h} = \lim_{h \to 0} \frac{(32t + 16h)h}{h} = 32t \, .$$

In particular, the velocity of the screwdriver when it hits the ground (at $t = 5$) is
$$v(5) = 32(5) = 160, \text{ or } 160 \text{ ft/sec.}$$

32. a. Its height after 40 seconds is
$$f(40) = \tfrac{1}{2}(40)^2 + \tfrac{1}{2}(40) = 820 \qquad \text{[Writing } f(t) = \tfrac{1}{2}t^2 + \tfrac{1}{2}t \text{]}$$

b. Its average velocity over the interval $[0,40]$ is
$$\frac{f(40) - f(0)}{40 - 0} = \frac{820 - 0}{40} = 20.5, \text{ or } 20.5 \text{ ft/sec.}$$

c. Its velocity at time t is
$$v(t) = \lim_{h \to 0} \frac{f(t+h) - f(t)}{h} = \lim_{h \to 0} \frac{\tfrac{1}{2}(t+h)^2 + \tfrac{1}{2}(t+h) - (\tfrac{1}{2}t^2 + \tfrac{1}{2}t)}{h}$$

$$= \lim_{h \to 0} \frac{\tfrac{1}{2}t^2 + th + \tfrac{1}{2}h^2 + \tfrac{1}{2}t + \tfrac{1}{2}h - \tfrac{1}{2}t^2 - \tfrac{1}{2}t}{h}$$

$$= \lim_{h \to 0} \frac{th + \tfrac{1}{2}h^2 + \tfrac{1}{2}h}{h} = \lim_{h \to 0}(t + \tfrac{1}{2}h + \tfrac{1}{2}) = t + \tfrac{1}{2}$$

In particular, the velocity at the end of 40 seconds is

$$v(40) = 40 + \tfrac{1}{2}, \text{ or } 40\tfrac{1}{2} \text{ ft/sec.}$$

33. a. $V = \dfrac{1}{p}$. The average rate of change of V is
$$\frac{f(3) - f(2)}{3 - 2} = \frac{\tfrac{1}{3} - \tfrac{1}{2}}{1} = -\frac{1}{6}, \qquad \text{[Write } V = f(p) = \frac{1}{p} \text{]}$$

or a decrease of $\tfrac{1}{6}$ liter/atmosphere.

b.
$$V'(t) = \lim_{h \to 0} \frac{f(p+h) - f(p)}{h} = \lim_{h \to 0} \frac{\dfrac{1}{p+h} - \dfrac{1}{p}}{h \cdot}$$

$$= \lim_{h \to 0} \frac{p - (p+h)}{hp(p+h)} = \lim_{h \to 0} -\frac{1}{p(p+h)} = -\frac{1}{p^2}$$

In particular, the rate of change of V when $p = 2$ is

$$V'(2) = -\frac{1}{2^2}, \text{ or a decrease of } \frac{1}{4} \text{ liter/atmosphere}$$

34 $C(x) = -10x^2 + 300x + 130$

a. Using the four-step process, we find

$$C'(x) = \lim_{h \to 0} \frac{C(x+h) - C(x)}{h} = \lim_{h \to 0} \frac{h(-20x - 10h + 300)}{h} = -20x - 10h + 300$$

b. The rate of change is $C'(10) = -20(10) + 300 = 100$, or \$100/surfboard.

35 a. Using the four-step process, we find that

$$P'(x) = \lim_{h \to 0} \frac{P(x+h) - P(x)}{h}$$

$$= \lim_{h \to 0} \frac{-\frac{1}{3}(x^2 + 2xh + h^2) + 7x + 7h + 30 - (-\frac{1}{3}x^2 + 7x + 30)}{h}$$

$$P'(x) = \lim_{h \to 0} \frac{P(x+h) - P(x)}{h}$$

$$= \lim_{h \to 0} \frac{-\frac{2}{3}xh - \frac{1}{3}h + 7h}{h} = \lim_{h \to 0}(-\frac{2}{3}x - \frac{1}{3}h + 7) = -\frac{2}{3}x + 7$$

b. $P'(10) = -\frac{2}{3}(10) + 7 \approx 0.333$, or \$333 per quarter.

$P'(30) = -\frac{2}{3}(30) + 7 \approx -13$, or a decrease of \$13,000 per quarter.

36. a. $f(x) = -0.1x^2 - x + 40$

$$\frac{f(5.05) - f(5)}{5.05 - 5} = \frac{[-0.1(5.05)^2 - 5.05 + 40] - [-0.1(5)^2 - 5 + 40]}{0.05} = -2.005,$$

or approximately –\$2.01/1000 tents.

$$\frac{f(5.01) - f(5)}{5.01 - 5} = \frac{[-0.1(5.01)^2 - 5.01 + 40] - [-0.1(5)^2 - 5 + 40]}{0.01} = -2.001,$$

or approximately –\$2.00/1000 tents.

b. We compute $f'(x)$ using the four-step process obtaining

$$f'(x) = \lim_{h \to 0} \frac{f(x+h) - f(x)}{h}$$

$$= \frac{h(-0.2x - 0.h - 1)}{h} = \lim_{h \to 0}(-0.2x - 0.1h - 1) = -0.2x - 1.$$

The rate of change of the unit price if $x = 5000$ is $f'(5) = -0.2(5) - 1 = -2$, or a decrease of \$2/per 1000 tents.

37 $N(t) = t^2 + 2t + 50$. We first compute $N'(t)$ using the four–step process.

Step 1 $N(t + h) = (t + h)^2 + 2(t + h) + 50$
$$= t^2 + 2th + h^2 + 2t + 2h + 50$$

Step 2 $N(t + h) - N(t)$
$$= (t^2 + 2th + h^2 + 2t + 2h + 50) - (t^2 + 2t + 50)$$
$$= 2th + h^2 + 2h = h(2t + h + 2).$$

Step 3 $\dfrac{N(t+h) - N(t)}{h} = 2t + h + 2.$

Step 4 $N'(t) = \lim_{h \to 0}(2t + h + 2) = 2t + 2.$

The rate of change of the country's GNP two years from now will be $N'(2) = 6$, or \$6 billion/yr. The rate of change four years from now will be $N'(4) = 10$, or \$10 billion/yr.

38. $f(t) = 3t^2 + 2t + 1$ Using the four–step process, we obtain
$$f'(t) = \lim_{t \to 0}\frac{f(t+h) - f(t)}{h} = \lim_{t \to 0}\frac{h(6t + 3h + 2)}{h} = \lim_{t \to 0} 6t + 3h + 2 = 6t + 2.$$
Next, $f'(10) = 6(10) + 2 = 62$, and we conclude that the rate of bacteria growth at $t = 10$ is 62 bacteria per minute.

39. $\dfrac{f(a+h) - f(a)}{h}$ gives the average rate of change of the seal population over the time interval $[a, a + h]$.

$\lim_{h \to 0}\dfrac{f(a+h) - f(a)}{h}$ gives the instantaneous rate of change of the seal population at $x = a$.

40. $\dfrac{f(a+h) - f(a)}{h}$ gives the average rate of change of the prime interest rate over the time interval $[a, a + h]$. $\lim_{h \to 0}\dfrac{f(a+h) - f(a)}{h}$ gives the instantaneous rate of change of the prime interest rate at $x = a$.

41. $\dfrac{f(a+h)-f(a)}{h}$ gives the average rate of change of the country's industrial production over the time interval $[a, a+h]$.

$\displaystyle\lim_{h\to 0}\dfrac{f(a+h)-f(a)}{h}$ gives the instantaneous rate of change of the country's industrial production at $x = a$.

42. $\dfrac{f(a+h)-f(a)}{h}$ gives the average rate of change of the cost incurred in producing the commodity over the production level $[a, a+h]$. $\displaystyle\lim_{h\to 0}\dfrac{f(a+h)-f(a)}{h}$ gives the instantaneous rate of change of the cost of producing the commodity at $x = a$.

43 $\dfrac{f(a+h)-f(a)}{h}$ gives the average rate of change of the atmospheric pressure over the altitudes $[a, a+h]$.

$\displaystyle\lim_{h\to 0}\dfrac{f(a+h)-f(a)}{h}$ gives the instantaneous rate of change of the atmospheric pressure at $x = a$.

44. $\dfrac{f(a+h)-f(a)}{h}$ gives the average rate of change of the fuel economy of a car over the speeds $[a, a+h]$. $\displaystyle\lim_{h\to 0}\dfrac{f(a+h)-f(a)}{h}$ gives the instantaneous rate of change of the fuel economy of a car over the speeds $[a, a+h]$.

45. a. f has a limit at $x = a$.
b. f is not continuous at $x = a$ because $f(a)$ is not defined.
c. f is not differentiable at $x = a$ because it is not continuous there.

46. a. f has a limit at $x = a$.　　　b. f is continuous at $x = a$.
c. f is differentiable at $x = a$.

47. a. f has a limit at $x = a$.　　　b. f is continuous at $x = a$.
c. f is not differentiable at $x = a$ because f has a kink at the point $x = a$.

48. a. f does not have a limit at $x = a$ because the left-hand and right-hand limits are not equal.
b. f is not continuous at $x = a$ because the limit does not exist there.
c. f is not differentiable at $x = a$ because it is not continuous there.

49 a. f does not have a limit at $x = a$ because it is unbounded in the neighborhood of a.
b. f is not continuous at $x = a$.
c. f is not differentiable at $x = a$ because it is not continuous there.

50. a. f does not have a limit at $x = a$ because the left-hand and right-hand limits are unequal.
b. f is not continuous at $x = a$ because the limit does not exist there.
c. f is not differentiable at $x = a$ because it is not continuous there.

51 Our computations yield the following results:
32.1, 30.939, 30.814, 30.8014, 30.8001, 30.8000.
The motorcycle's instantaneous velocity at $t = 2$ is approximately 30.8 ft/sec.

52. Our computations yield the following results:
5.06060, 5.06006, 5.060006, 5.0600006, 5.06000006;
The rate of change of the total cost function when the level of production is 100 cases a day is approximately $5.06.

53. False. Let $f(x) = |x|$. Then f is continuous at $x = 0$, but is not differentiable there.

54. True. If g is differentiable at $x = a$, then it is continuous there. Therefore, the product fg is continuous. Therefore,
$$\lim_{x \to a} f(x)g(x) = \left[\lim_{x \to a} f(x) \right]\left[\lim_{x \to a} g(x) \right] = f(a)g(a).$$

55. Observe that the graph of f has a kink at $x = -1$. We have

$$\frac{f(-1+h) - f(-1)}{h} = 1 \text{ if } h > 0, \text{ and } -1 \text{ if } h < 0,$$

so that $\lim_{h \to 0} \dfrac{f(-1+h) - f(-1)}{h}$ does not exist.

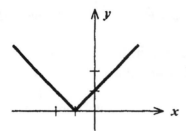

56. f does not have a derivative at $x = 1$ because it is not continuous there.

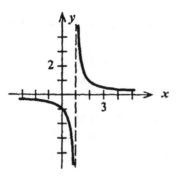

57 For continuity, we require that $f(1) = 1 = \lim_{x \to 1^+}(ax + b) = a + b$, or $a + b = 1$.

In order that the derivative exist at $x = 1$, we require that $\lim_{x \to 1^-} 2x = \lim_{x \to 1^+} a$, or $2 = a$.

Therefore, $b = -1$ and so $f(x) = \begin{cases} x^2 & \text{if } x \le 1 \\ 2x - 1 & \text{if } x > 1 \end{cases}$. The graph of f follows.

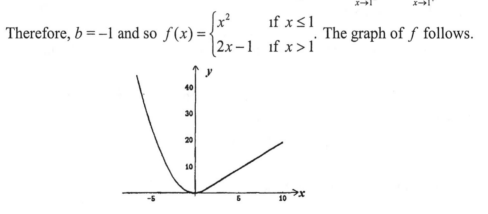

58. f is continuous at $x = 0$, but $f'(0)$ does not exist because the graph of f has a vertical tangent line at $x = 0$. The graph of f follows.

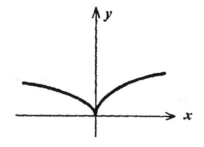

59 We have $f(x) = x$ if $x > 0$ and $f(x) = -x$ if $x < 0$. Therefore, when $x > 0$

$$f'(x) = \lim_{h \to 0} \frac{f(x+h) - f(x)}{h} = \lim_{h \to 0} \frac{x+h-x}{h} = \lim_{h \to 0} \frac{h}{h} = 1,$$

and when $x < 0$

$$f'(x) = \lim_{h \to 0} \frac{f(x+h) - f(x)}{h} = \lim_{h \to 0} \frac{-x-h-(-x)}{h} = \lim_{h \to 0} \frac{-h}{h} = -1.$$

Since the right–hand limit does not equal the left–hand limit, we conclude that $\lim_{h \to 0} f(x)$ does not exist.

60. From $f(x) - f(a) = \left[\dfrac{f(x) - f(a)}{x - a} \right](x - a)$, we see that

$$\lim_{x \to a}[f(x) - f(a)] = \lim_{x \to a}\left[\frac{f(x) - f(a)}{x - a} \right] \lim_{x \to a}(x - a) = f'(a) \cdot 0 = 0$$

and so $\lim_{x \to a} f(x) = f(a)$. This shows that f is continuous at $x = a$.

USING TECHNOLOGY EXERCISES 2.6, page 154

1   a. $y = 4x - 3$
    b.

2. a. $y = -7x - 8$
    b.

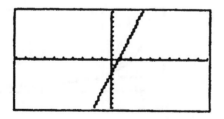

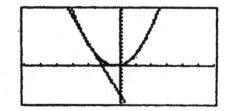

3   a. $y = 9x - 11$
     b.

4.   a. $y = 2$
     b.

5   a. $y = \frac{1}{4}x + 1$
     b.

6.   a. $y = -\frac{1}{16}x + \frac{3}{4}$
     b.

7   a. 4   b. $y = 4x - 1$
     c.

8.   a. 20   b. $y = 20x - 35$
     c.

9.   a. $\frac{3}{4}$ b. $y = \frac{3}{-4}x - 1$
     c.

10.   a. $-\frac{1}{4}$ b. $y = -\frac{1}{4}x + \frac{3}{4}$
     c.

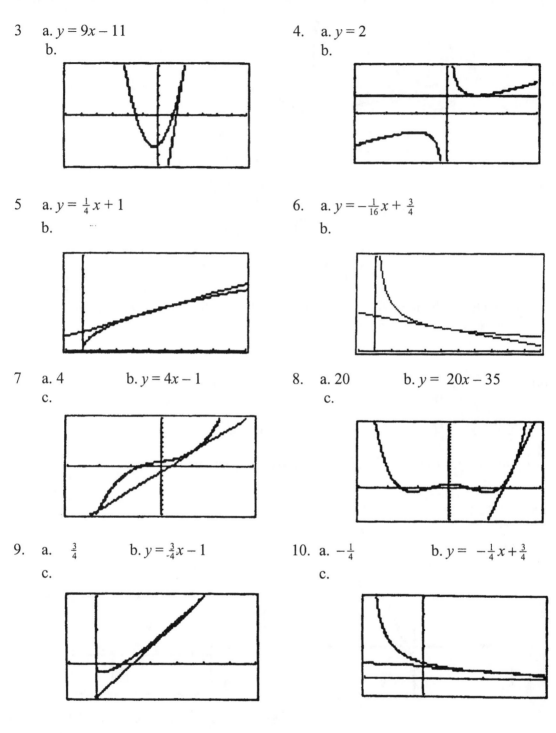

11. a. 4.02 b. $y = 4.02x - 3.57$

    c.

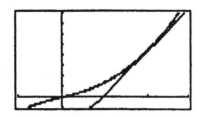

12. a. 0.35 b. $y = 0.35x + 1.06$

    c.

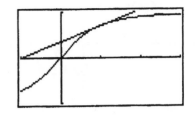

13. a.

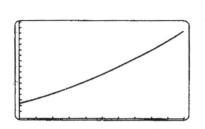

    b. 41.22 cents/mile

    c. 1.22 cents/mile/yr

14. a.

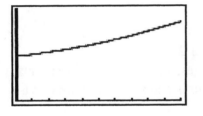

    b. $797.3896 million

    c. $53.1912 million/yr

CHAPTER 2 CONCEPT REVIEW, page 155

1 Domain; range; B 2. Domain; $f(x)$; vertical; point

3 $f(x) \pm g(x)$; $f(x)g(x)$; $\dfrac{f(x)}{g(x)}$; $A \cap B$; $A \cap B$; zero

4. $g[f(x)]$; f; $f(x)$; g

5 a. $P(x) = a_0 x^n + a_1 x^{n-1} + \cdots + a_{n-1}x + a_n$ $(a_0 \neq 0, n,$ a positive integer)

   b. Linear; quadratic; cubic

c. Quotient; polynomials   d. x^r, r, a real number

6. L, $f(x)$; L; a

7. a. L' b. $L \pm M$ c. LM d. $\dfrac{L}{M}$, $M \neq 0$

8. a. L; x b. M; negative; absolute   9 a. Right   b. Left   c. L, L

10. a. Continuous   b. Discontinuous   c. Every

11. a. a; a: $g(a)$ b. Everywhere   c. $Q(x)$

12. a. $[a,b]$, $f(c) = M$ b. $f(x) = 0$; (a,b)

13 a. $f'(a)$ b. $y - f(a) = m(x - a)$

14. a. $\dfrac{f(a+h) - f(a)}{h}$ b. $\displaystyle\lim_{h \to 0} \dfrac{f(a+h) - f(a)}{h}$

CHAPTER 2 REVIEW, page 156

1.   a. $9 - x \geq 0$ gives $x \leq 9$ and the domain is $(-\infty, 9]$.
     b. $2x^2 - x - 3 = (2x - 3)(x + 1)$, and $x = 3/2$ or $x = -1$.
     Since the denominator of the given expression is zero at these points, we see that
     the domain of f cannot include these points and so the domain of f is
     $(-\infty, -1) \cup (-1, \tfrac{3}{2}) \cup (\tfrac{3}{2}, \infty)$.

2.   a. $f(-2) = 3(-2)^2 + 5(-2) - 2 = 0$.
     b. $f(a + 2) = 3(a + 2)^2 + 5(a + 2) - 2 = 3a^2 + 12a + 12 + 5a + 10 - 2$
              $= 3a^2 + 17a + 20$.
     c. $f(2a) = 3(2a)^2 + 5(2a) - 2 = 12a^2 + 10a - 2$.
     d. $f(a + h) = 3(a + h)^2 + 5(a + h) - 2 = 3a^2 + 6ah + 3h^2 + 5a + 5h - 2$.

3   a.

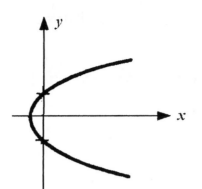

b. For each value of $x > 0$, there are two values of y. We conclude that y is not a function of x. Equivalently, the function fails the vertical line test.

c. Yes. For each value of y, there is only 1 value of x.

4.

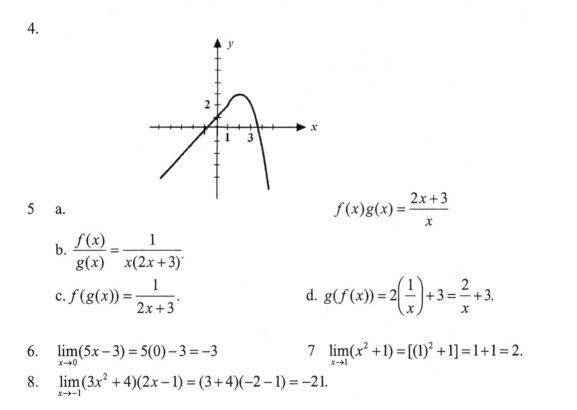

5   a. $\qquad\qquad\qquad\qquad\qquad f(x)g(x) = \dfrac{2x+3}{x}$

b. $\dfrac{f(x)}{g(x)} = \dfrac{1}{x(2x+3)}.$

c. $f(g(x)) = \dfrac{1}{2x+3}.$ d. $g(f(x)) = 2\left(\dfrac{1}{x}\right) + 3 = \dfrac{2}{x} + 3.$

6. $\lim_{x\to 0}(5x-3) = 5(0) - 3 = -3$ 7 $\lim_{x\to 1}(x^2+1) = [(1)^2 + 1] = 1 + 1 = 2.$

8. $\lim_{x\to -1}(3x^2+4)(2x-1) = (3+4)(-2-1) = -21.$

149   *2 Functions, Limits, and the Derivative*

9. $\lim\limits_{x\to 3}\dfrac{x-3}{x+4}=\dfrac{3-3}{3+4}=0.$

10. $\lim\limits_{x\to 2}\dfrac{x+3}{x^2-9}=\dfrac{2+3}{4-9}=-1.$

11. $\lim\limits_{x\to -2}\dfrac{x^2-2x-3}{x^2+5x+6}$ does not exist. (The denominator is 0 at $x=-2$.)

12. $\lim\limits_{x\to 3}\sqrt{2x^3-5}=\sqrt{2(27)-5}=7.$

13. $\lim\limits_{x\to 3}\dfrac{4x-3}{\sqrt{x+1}}=\dfrac{12-3}{\sqrt{4}}=\dfrac{9}{2}$

14. $\lim\limits_{x\to 1^+}\dfrac{x-1}{x(x-1)}=\lim\limits_{x\to 1^+}\dfrac{1}{x}=1.$

15. $\lim\limits_{x\to 1^-}\dfrac{\sqrt{x}-1}{x-1}=\lim\limits_{x\to 1^-}\dfrac{(\sqrt{x}-1)(\sqrt{x}+1)}{(x-1)(\sqrt{x}+1)}=\lim\limits_{x\to 1^-}\dfrac{x-1}{(x-1)(\sqrt{x}+1)}=\lim\limits_{x\to 1^-}\dfrac{1}{\sqrt{x}+1}=\dfrac{1}{2}$

16. $\lim\limits_{x\to\infty}\dfrac{x^2}{x^2-1}=\lim\limits_{x\to\infty}\dfrac{1}{1-\dfrac{1}{x^2}}=1.$

17. $\lim\limits_{x\to-\infty}\dfrac{x+1}{x}=\lim\limits_{x\to-\infty}\left(1+\dfrac{1}{x}\right)=1.$

18. $\lim\limits_{x\to\infty}\dfrac{3x^2+2x+4}{2x^2-3x+1}=\lim\limits_{x\to\infty}\dfrac{3+\dfrac{2}{x}+\dfrac{4}{x^2}}{2-\dfrac{3}{x}+\dfrac{1}{x^2}}=\dfrac{3}{2}$

19. $\lim\limits_{x\to-\infty}\dfrac{x^2}{x+1}=\lim\limits_{x\to-\infty}x\cdot\dfrac{1}{1+\dfrac{1}{x}}=-\infty$, so the limit does not exist.

20. $\lim\limits_{x\to 2^+}f(x)=\lim\limits_{x\to 2^+}(2x-3)$
$$=2(2)-3=4-3=1.$$

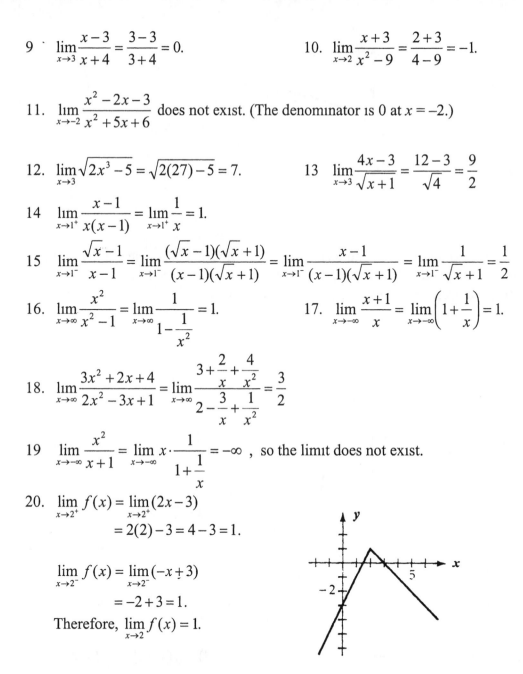

$\lim\limits_{x\to 2^-}f(x)=\lim\limits_{x\to 2^-}(-x+3)$
$$=-2+3=1.$$
Therefore, $\lim\limits_{x\to 2}f(x)=1.$

21. $\lim\limits_{x \to 2^+} f(x) = \lim\limits_{x \to 2^+} (x + 2) = 4;$

$\lim\limits_{x \to 2^-} f(x) = \lim\limits_{x \to 2^-} (4 - x) = 2.$

Therefore, $\lim\limits_{x \to 2} f(x)$ does not exist.

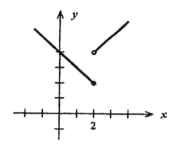

22. The function is discontinuous at $x = 2$.

23 Since the denominator
$$4x^2 - 2x - 2 = 2(2x^2 - x - 1) = 2(2x + 1)(x - 1) = 0$$
if $x = -1/2$ or 1, we see that f is discontinuous at these points.

24. Because $\lim\limits_{x \to -1} f(x) = \lim\limits_{x \to -1} \dfrac{1}{(x + 1)^2} = \infty$ (does not exist), we see that f is

discontinuous at $x = -1$.

25 The function is discontinuous at $x = 0$.

26. a. Let $f(x) = x^2 + 2$. Then the average rate of change of y over $[1,2]$ is
$$\frac{f(2) - f(1)}{2 - 1} = \frac{(4 + 2) - (1 + 2)}{1} = 3.$$
Over $[1, 1.5]$:
$$\frac{f(1.5) - f(1)}{1.5 - 1} = \frac{(2.25 + 2) - (1 + 2)}{0.5} = 2.5.$$
Over $[1, 1 1]$:
$$\frac{f(1.1) - f(1)}{1.1 - 1} = \frac{(1.21 + 2) - (1 + 2)}{0.1} = 2.1.$$
b. Computing $f'(x)$ using the four-step process, we obtain
$$f'(x) = \lim\limits_{h \to 0} \frac{f(x + h) - f(x)}{h} = \lim\limits_{h \to 0} \frac{h(2x + h)}{h} = \lim\limits_{h \to 0} (2x + h) = 2.$$
Therefore, the instantaneous rate of change of f at $x = 1$ is $f'(1) = 2$, or 2 units/unit change in x.

27 $f(x) = 3x + 5$. Using the four-step process, we find

Step 1 $f(x+h) = 3(x+h) + 5 = 3x + 3h + 5$

Step 2 $f(x+h) - f(x) = 3x + 3h + 5 - 3x - 5 = 3h$

Step 3 $\dfrac{f(x+h) - f(x)}{h} = \dfrac{3h}{h} = 3.$

Step 4 $f'(x) = \lim\limits_{h \to 0} \dfrac{f(x+h) - f(x)}{h} = \lim\limits_{h \to 0}(3) = 3.$

28. $f(x) = -\dfrac{1}{x}$. Now, using the four-step process, we obtain

Step 1 $f(x+h) = -\dfrac{1}{x+h}$

Step 2 $f(x+h) - f(x) = -\dfrac{1}{x+h} - \left(-\dfrac{1}{x}\right) = -\dfrac{1}{x+h} + \dfrac{1}{x} = \dfrac{h}{x(x+h)}$

Step 3 $\dfrac{f(x+h) - f(x)}{h} = -\dfrac{1}{x(x+h)}$

Step 4 $f'(x) = \lim\limits_{h \to 0} \dfrac{f(x+h) - f(x)}{h} = \lim\limits_{h \to 0}\dfrac{1}{x(x+h)} = \dfrac{1}{x^2}$

29 $f(x) = \frac{3}{2}x + 5$. We use the four-step process to obtain

Step 1 $f(x+h) = \frac{3}{2}(x+h) + 5 = \frac{3}{2}x + \frac{3}{2}h + 5.$

Step 2 $f(x+h) - f(x) = \frac{3}{2}x + \frac{3}{2}h + 5 - \frac{3}{2}x - 5 = \frac{3}{2}h.$

Step 3 $\dfrac{f(x+h) - f(x)}{h} = \dfrac{3}{2}.$

Step 4 $f'(x) = \lim\limits_{h \to 0} \dfrac{f(x+h) - f(x)}{h} = \lim\limits_{h \to 0}\dfrac{3}{2} = \dfrac{3}{2}$

Therefore, the slope of the tangent line to the graph of the function f at the point $(-2,2)$ is 3/2. To find the equation of the tangent line to the curve at the point $(-2,2)$, we use the point–slope form of the equation of a line obtaining
$$y - 2 = \tfrac{3}{2}[x - (-2)] \quad \text{or} \quad y = \tfrac{3}{2}x + 5.$$

30.. $f(x) = -x^2$. We use the four-step process to find $f'(x)$

Step 1 $f(x+h) = -(x+h)^2 = -x^2 - 2xh - h^2$

Step 2 $f(x+h) - f(x) = (-x^2 - 2xh - h^2) - (-x^2) = -2xh - h^2 = h(-2x - h).$

Step 3 $\dfrac{f(x+h) - f(x)}{h} = -2x - h$

Step 4 $f'(x) = \lim\limits_{h \to 0} \dfrac{f(x+h) - f(x)}{h} = \lim\limits_{h \to 0}(-2x - h) = -2x.$

The slope of the tangent line is $f'(2) = -2(2) = -4$. An equation of the tangent line is $y - (-4) = -4(x - 2)$, or $y = -4x + 4$.

31. a. f is continuous at $x = a$ because the three conditions for continuity are satisfied at $x = a$; that is,

    i. $f(x)$ is defined   *ii.* $\lim\limits_{x \to a} f(x)$ exists   *iii.* $\lim\limits_{x \to a} f(x) = f(a)$

b. f is not differentiable at $x = a$ because the graph of f has a kink at $x = a$.

32. $S(4) = 6000(4) + 30,000 = 54,000.$

33 a. The line passes through $(0, 2.4)$ and $(5, 7\ 4)$ and has slope $m = \dfrac{7\ 4 - 2.4}{5 - 0} = 1.$

Letting y denote the sales, we see that an equation of the line is
$$y - 2.4 = 1(t - 0), \text{ or } y = t + 2.4.$$
We can also write this in the form $S(t) = t + 2.4.$
b. The sales in 2003 were $S(3) = 3 + 2.4 = 5.4$, or $\$5.4$ million.

34. a. $C(x) = 6x + 30,000$ b. $R(x) = 10x$
c. $P(x) = R(x) - C(x) = 10x - (6x + 30,000) = 4x - 30,000.$
d. $P(6000) = 4(6000) - 30,000 = -6000$, or a loss of $\$6000$.
   $P(8000) = 4(8000) - 30,000 = 2000$, or a profit of $\$2000$.
   $P(12,000) = 4(12,000) - 30,000 = 18,000$, or a profit of $\$18,000$.

35 Substituting the first equation into the second yields
$$3x - 2(\tfrac{3}{4}x + 6) + 3 = 0 \quad \text{or} \quad \tfrac{3}{2}x - 12 + 3 = 0$$
or $x = 6$. Substituting this value of x into the first equation then gives $y = 21/2$, so the point of intersection is $(6, \tfrac{21}{2})$.

36. The profit function is given by
$$P(x) = R(x) - C(x) = 20x - (12x + 20000) = 8x - 20000$$

37. We solve the system
$$3x + p - 40 = 0$$
$$2x - p + 10 = 0.$$
Adding these two equations, we obtain $5x - 30 = 0$, or $x = 6$. So,
$$p = 2x + 10 = 12 + 10 = 22.$$
Therefore, the equilibrium quantity is 6000 and the equilibrium price is $22.

38. The child should receive $D(35) = \dfrac{500(35)}{150} = 117$, or 117 mg.

39. When 1000 units are produced,
$$R(1000) = -0.1(1000)^2 + 500(1000) = 400,000, \text{ or } \$400,000.$$

40. $R(30) = -\frac{1}{2}(30)^2 + 30(30) = 450$, or $45,000.

41. $N(0) = 200(4 + 0)^{1/2} = 400$, and so there are 400 members initially
$N(12) = 200(4 + 12)^{1/2} = 800$, and so there are 800 members a year later.

42. The population will increase by
$$P(9) - P(0) = [50,000 + 30(9)^{3/2} + 20(9)] - 50,000,$$
or 990 during the next 9 months. The population will increase by
$$P(16) - P(0) = [50,000 + 30(16)^{3/2} + 20(16)] - 50,000,$$
or 2240 during the next 16 months.

43. $T = f(n) = 4n\sqrt{n-4}$.
$f(4) = 0$, $f(5) = 20\sqrt{1} = 20$, $f(6) = 24\sqrt{2} \approx 33.9$, $f(7) = 28\sqrt{3} \approx 48.5$,
$f(8) = 32\sqrt{4} = 64$, $f(9) = 36\sqrt{5} \approx 80.5$, $f(10) = 40\sqrt{6} \approx 98$,
$f(11) = 44\sqrt{7} \approx 116$ and $f(12) = 48\sqrt{8} \approx 135.8$.

The graph of f follows:

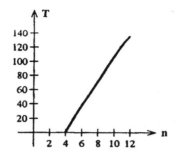

44. We need to find the point of intersection of the two straight lines representing the given linear functions. We solve the equation
$$2.3 + 0.4t = 1.2 + 0.6t$$
obtaining
$$1.1 = 0.2t,$$
or $t = 5.5$, and this tells us that the annual sales of the Cambridge Drug Store first surpasses that of the Crimson Drug store $5\frac{1}{2}$ years from now

45. We solve
$$-1 \ 1x^2 + 1.5x + 40 = 0.1x^2 + 0.5x + 15$$
$$1.2x^2 - x - 25 = 0$$
$$12x^2 - 10x - 250 = 0$$
$$6x^2 - 5x - 125 = 0; \quad (x - 5)(6x + 25) = 0.$$
Therefore, $x = 5$. Substituting this value of x into the second supply equation, we have $p = 0.1(5)^2 + 0.5(5) + 15 = 20$. So the equilibrium quantity is 5000 and the equilibrium price is $20.

46. a. $f(r) = \pi r^2$ b. $g(t) = 2t$
   c. $h(t) = (f \circ g)(t) = f(g(t)) = \pi[g(t)]^2 = 4\pi t^2$
   d. $h(30) = 4\pi(30^2) = 3600\pi$, or 3600π sq ft.

47.

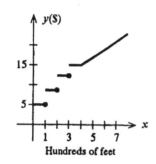

Hundreds of feet

48. $\lim_{x\to\infty}\overline{C}(x)=\lim_{x\to\infty}\left(20+\dfrac{400}{x}\right)=20.$ As the level of production increases without

bound, the average cost of producing the commodity steadily decreases and approaches \$20 per unit.

CHAPTER 2 BEFORE MOVING ON, page158

1. a. $f(-1)=-2(-1)+1=3$ b. $f(0)=2$ c. $f(\tfrac{3}{2})=(\tfrac{3}{2})^2+2=\tfrac{17}{4}.$

2. a. $(f+g)(x)=f(x)+g(x)=\dfrac{1}{x+1}+x^2+1$ b. $(fg)(x)=f(x)g(x)=\dfrac{x^2+1}{x+1}$

   c. $(f\pm g)(x)=f[g(x)]=\dfrac{1}{g(x)+1}=\dfrac{1}{x^2+2}$

   d. $(g\circ f)(x)=g[f(x)]^2+1=\dfrac{1}{(x+1)^2}+1$

3 $4x+\ell=108$ so $\ell=108-4x$

   Volume is $V=x^2\ell=x^2(108-4x)=108x^2-4x^3$

4. $\lim_{x\to-1}\dfrac{x^2+4x+3}{x^2+3x+2}=\lim_{x\to-1}\dfrac{(x+3)(x+1)}{(x+2)(x+1)}=2$

5 a. $\lim_{x\to1^-}f(x)=\lim_{x\to1^-}(x^2-1)=0$

   b. $\lim_{x\to1^+}f(x)=\lim_{x\to1^+}x^3=1.$

Since $\lim\limits_{x\to 1^-} f(x) \neq \lim\limits_{x\to 1^+} f(x)$, f is not continuous at 1.

6. The slope of the tangent line at any point is

$$\lim_{h\to 0}\frac{f(x+h)-f(x)}{h} = \lim_{h\to 0}\frac{(x+h)^2 - 3(x+h)+1-(x^2-3x+1)}{h}$$

$$= \lim_{h\to 0}\frac{x^2 + 2xh + h^2 - 3x - 3h - x^2 + 3x - 1}{h}$$

$$= \lim_{h\to 0}\frac{h(2x+h-3)}{h} = \lim_{h\to 0}(2x+h-3) = 2x-3$$

Therefore, the slope at 1 is $2(1) - 3 = -1$. An equation of the tangent line is

$$y - (-1) = -1(x - 1)$$

$$y + 1 = -x + 1 \quad , \text{ or } \quad y = -x$$

EXPLORE & DISCUSS

Page 72

1 $(g \circ f)(x) = g(f(x)) = [f(x)-1]^2 = [(\sqrt{x}+1)-1]^2 = (\sqrt{x})^2 = x.$

$(f \circ g)(x) = f(g(x)) = \sqrt{g(x)}+1 = \sqrt{(x-1)^2}+1 = (x-1)+1 = x.$

2. The graphs follow.

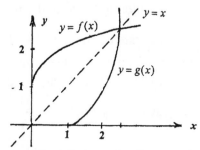

From the figure, we see that the graph of one is the mirror reflection of the other if we place a mirror along the line $y = x$.

Page 102

1. As x approaches 0 (from either direction), $h(x)$ oscillates more and more rapidly between -1 and 1 and therefore cannot approach a specific number. But this says $\lim_{x \to 0} h(x)$ does not exist.

2. The function f fails to have a limit at $x = 0$ because $f(x)$ approaches 1 from the right but -1 from the left. The function g fails to have a limit at $x = 0$ because $g(x)$ is unbounded on either side of $x = 0$. The function h here does not approach any number from either the right or the left and has no limit at 0 as explained earlier.

Page 110

1. $\lim_{x \to \infty} f(x)$ does not exist because no matter how large x is, $f(x)$ takes on values between -1 and 1. In other words, $f(x)$ does not approach a definite number as x approaches infinity. Similarly, $\lim_{x \to -\infty} f(x)$ fails to exist.

2. The function of Example 10 fails to have a limit at infinity (minus infinity) because $f(x)$ increases (decreases) without bound or x approaches infinity (minus infinity). On the other hand, the function whose graph is depicted here, though bounded (its values lie between -1 and 1), does not approach any specific number as x increases (decreases) without bound and this is the reason it fails to have a limit at infinity or minus infinity

Page 139

1 The average rate of change of a function f is measured over an interval. Thus, the average rate of change of f over the interval $[a, b]$ is the number $\dfrac{f(b) - f(a)}{b - a}$.

On the other hand, the instantaneous rate of change of a function measures the rate of change of the function at a point. As we have seen, this quantity can be found by taking the limit of an appropriate difference quotient. Specifically, the instantaneous rate of change of f at $x = a$ is $\lim_{h \to 0} \dfrac{f(a + h) - f(a)}{h}$

Page 141

1. Yes. Refer to the following figure. Here the line tangent to the graph of f at P also intersects the graph at the point Q lying on the graph of f.

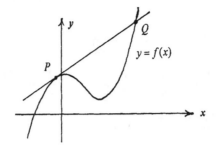

1 The quotient gives the slope of the secant line passing through $P(x-h, f(x-h))$ and $Q(x + h, f(x + h))$ [see figure].

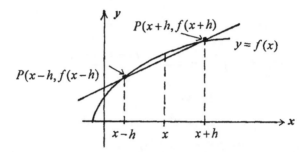

It also gives the average rate of change of f over the interval $[x - h, x + h]$.

2. The limit gives the slope of the tangent line to the graph of f at the point $(x, f(x))$ [see figure]. It also gives the (instantaneous) rate of change of f at the point $(x, f(x))$. As h gets smaller and smaller, the secant lines approach the tangent line T

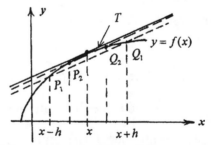

3. The observation in part (b) suggests that this definition makes sense. We can also justify this observation as follows: From the definition of $f'(x)$, we have

$$f'(x) = \lim_{h \to 0} \frac{f(x+h) - f(x)}{h}$$

Replacing h by $-h$ gives

$$f'(x) = \lim_{h \to 0} \frac{f(x-h)-f(x)}{-h} = \lim_{h \to 0} \frac{f(x)-f(x-h)}{h}$$

So

$$2f'(x) = \lim_{h \to 0}\left[\frac{f(x+h)-f(x)}{h} + \frac{f(x)-f(x-h)}{h}\right]$$

or

$$f'(x) = \lim_{h \to 0} \frac{f(x+h)-f(x-h)}{2h}$$

in agreement with the result of Example 3.

4   **Step 1**   Compute $f(x+h)$ and $f(x-h)$.

         Step 2   Form the difference $f(x+h)-f(x-h)$.

         Step 3   Form the quotient $\dfrac{f(x+h)-f(x-h)}{2h}$.

         Step 4   Compute $f'(x) = \lim\limits_{h \to 0} \dfrac{f(x+h)-f(x-h)}{2h}$

For the function $f(x) = x^2$, we have

         Step 1 $f(x+h) = (x+h)^2 = x^2 + 2xh + h^2$

                    $f(x-h) = (x-h)^2 = x^2 - 2xh + h^2$

         Step 2 $f(x+h)-f(x-h) = (x^2 + 2xh + h^2) - (x^2 - 2xh + h^2) = 4xh.$

         Step 3 $\dfrac{f(x+h)-f(x)}{2h} = \dfrac{4xh}{2h} = 2x.$

         Step 4 $f'(x) = \lim\limits_{h \to 0} \dfrac{f(x+h)-f(x)}{2h} = \lim\limits_{h \to 0} 2x = 2x$

in agreement with the result of Example 3

Page 146

1.   No. The slope of the tangent line to the graph of f at $(a, f(a))$ is defined by

$$f'(a) = \lim_{h \to 0} \frac{f(a+h)-f(a)}{h}$$ and since the limit must be unique (see the definition

of a limit), there is only one number $f'(a)$ giving the slope of the tangent line. Furthermore, since there can only be one straight line with a given slope, $f'(a)$, passing through a given point, $(a, f(a))$, our conclusion follows.

Page 55

1   2.

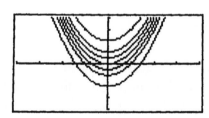   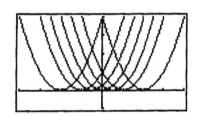

3

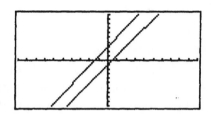

4. The graph of $f(x) + c$ is obtained by translating the graph of f along the y–axis by c units. The graph of $f(x + c)$ is obtained by translating the graph of f along the x–axis by c units. Finally, the graph of cf is obtained from that of f by expanding" $(c > 1)$ or "contracting" $(0 < c < 1)$ that of f. If $c < 0$, the graph of cf is obtained from that of f by reflecting it with respect to the x–axis as well as "expanding" it or "contracting" it.

Page 83

1   a.

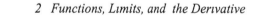

The lines seem to be parallel to each other and they don't appear to intersect.
b.

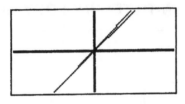

They appear to intersect. But finding the point of intersection using **TRACE** and **ZOOM** with any degree of accuracy seems to be an impossible task. Using the "intersection" function of the graphing utility yields the point of intersection $(-40,-81)$ immediately

c. Substituting the first equation into the second gives

$$2x - 1 = 2.1x + 3$$
$$- 4 = 0.1x,$$

or $x = -40$. The corresponding y-value is -81

d. The **Trace** and **Zoom** technique is not effective. The "intersection" function gives the desired result immediately The algebraic method also yields the answer with little effort and without the use of a graphing utility

2. a. Plotting the straight lines L_1 and L_2 and using **TRACE** and **ZOOM** repeatedly, you will see that the iterations approach the answer $(1,1)$. Using the "intersection"

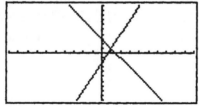

function of the graphing utility gives the result $x = 1$ and $y = 1$, immediately

b. Substituting the first equation into the second yields

$$3x - 2 = -2x + 3; \quad 5x = 5$$

and $x = 1$. Substituting this value of x into either equation gives $y = 1$.

c. The iterations obtained using **TRACE** and **ZOOM** converge to the solution $(1,1)$ with a little effort. The use of the "intersection" function is clearly superior to the first method. The algebraic method also yields the desired result accurately

Page 100

1. The graph of g follows.

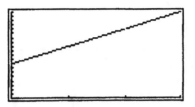

2. Using **ZOOM** and **TRACE** repeatedly, we find that $g(x)$ approaches 16 as x approaches 2.
3 If we try to use the "evaluation function" of the graphing utility to find $g(2)$ it will fail. It fails because $x = 2$ is not in the domain of g.
4. The results obtained here confirm those obtained in the preceding example.

Page 105

1. The graph of f follows.

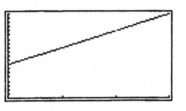

Using **TRACE**, we find $\lim\limits_{x \to 2} \dfrac{4(x^2 - 4)}{x - 2} = 16$.

2. The graph of g is shown below.

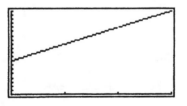

Using **TRACE**, we find $\lim\limits_{x \to 2} 4(x + 2) = 16$. When $x = 2$, $y = 16$. The function $f(x) = 4(x + 2)$ is defined at $x = 2$ and so $f(2) = 16$ is defined.
3 No.

4. As we saw in Example 5, the function f is not defined at $x = 2$ but g is defined there.

Page 106
1. The graph of g follows.

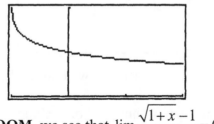

Using **TRACE** and **ZOOM**, we see that $\lim\limits_{x \to 0} \dfrac{\sqrt{1+x} - 1}{x} = 0.5$

2. The graph of f is the same as that of g except that the domain of f includes $x = 0$ (this will not be evident by just looking at the graphs!) Using the "evaluation" function to find the value of y, we obtain $y = 0.5$ when $x = 0$. This is to be expected since $x = 0$ lies in the domain of g

3. As mentioned in part (2), the graphs are indistinguishable even though $x = 0$ is in the domain of g but not in the domain of f.

4. The functions f and g are the same everywhere except at $x = 0$ and so
$$\lim_{x \to 0} \frac{\sqrt{1+x} - 1}{x} = \lim_{x \to 0} \frac{1}{\sqrt{1+x} + 1} = \frac{1}{2} \text{ as obtained in Example 6.}$$

Page 108
1. The graphs of the given functions follow

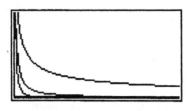

The results suggest that $\dfrac{1}{x^n}$ goes to zero (as x increases) with increasing rapidity as n gets larger. This is as predicted by Theorem 2.

2. The graphs of the given functions follow

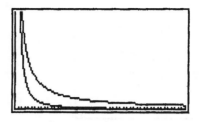

The results suggest that $\dfrac{1}{x^n}$ goes to zero (as x decreases) with increasing rapidity as n gets larger. This is as predicted by Theorem 2.

Page 141

1. The graph of g follows

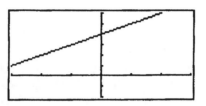

2. Using **ZOOM–IN** repeatedly, we find $\lim\limits_{x \to 0} g(x) = 4$.

3. That the limit found in (2) is $f'(2)$ is a consequence of the definition of a derivative.

Page 142

1. The graph of f and its tangent line at $(1,1)$ are shown in the figure that follows.

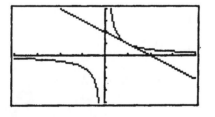

Page 146

1. The graph of f follows.

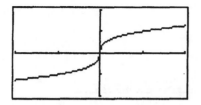

2. The graphing utility will indicate an error was made when you try to draw the tangent line to the graph of f at $(0,0)$. This happens because the slope of f is not defined when $x = 0$.

CHAPTER 3

3.1 CONCEPT QUESTIONS, page 167

1. a. The derivative of a constant is zero.
   b. The derivative of $f(x) = x^n$ is the power times x raised to the power $n - 1$.
   c. The derivative of a constant times a function is the constant times the derivative of the function.
   d. The derivative of the sum is the sum of the derivatives.
2. a. $h'(x) = 2f'(x)$ so $h'(2) = 2f'(2) = 2(3) = 6$
   b. $F'(x) = 3f'(x) - 4g'(x)$, so $F'(2) = 3f'(2) - 4g'(2) = 3(3) - 4(-2) = 17$

EXERCISES 3.1, page 167

1. $f'(x) = \dfrac{d}{dx}(-3) = 0.$

2. $f'(x) = \dfrac{d}{dx}(365) = 0.$

3. $f'(x) = \dfrac{d}{dx}(x^5) = 5x^4$

4. $f'(x) = \dfrac{d}{dx}(x^7) = 7x^6$

5. $f'(x) = \dfrac{d}{dx}(x^{2.1}) = 2.1x^{1.1}$

6. $f'(x) = \dfrac{d}{dx}(x^{0.8}) = 0.8x^{-0.2}$

7. $f'(x) = \dfrac{d}{dx}(3x^2) = 6x.$

8. $f'(x) = \dfrac{d}{dx}(-2x^3) = -6x^2.$

9. $f'(r) = \dfrac{d}{dr}(\pi r^2) = 2\pi r$

10. $f'(r) = \dfrac{d}{dr}\left(\dfrac{4}{3}\pi r^3\right) = 4\pi r^2.$

11. $f'(x) = \dfrac{d}{dx}(9x^{1/3}) = \dfrac{1}{3}(9)x^{(1/3-1)} = 3x^{-2/3}.$

12. $f'(x) = \dfrac{d}{dx}\left(\dfrac{5}{4}x^{4/5}\right) = \left(\dfrac{4}{5}\right)\left(\dfrac{5}{4}\right)x^{-1/5} = x^{-1/5}$

13. $f'(x) = \dfrac{d}{dx}(3\sqrt{x}) = \dfrac{d}{dx}(3x^{1/2}) = \dfrac{1}{2}(3)x^{-1/2} = \dfrac{3}{2}x^{-1/2} = \dfrac{3}{2\sqrt{x}}$

14. $f'(u) = \dfrac{d}{du}\left(\dfrac{2}{\sqrt{u}}\right)$, then $f'(u) = \dfrac{d}{du}(2u^{-1/2}) = -\dfrac{1}{2}(2)u^{-3/2} = -u^{-3/2}$

15: $f'(x) = \dfrac{d}{dx}\left(7x^{-12}\right) = (-12)(7)x^{(-12-1)} = -84x^{-13}$

16. $f'(x) = \dfrac{d}{dx}\left(0.3x^{-1.2}\right) = (0.3)(-1.2)x^{-2.2} = -0.36x^{-2.2}$

17 $f'(x) = \dfrac{d}{dx}\left(5x^2 - 3x + 7\right) = 10x - 3.$

18. $f'(x) = \dfrac{d}{dx}\left(x^3 - 3x^2 + 1\right) = 3x^2 - 6x.$

19. $f'(x) = \dfrac{d}{dx}\left(-x^3 + 2x^2 - 6\right) = -3x^2 + 4x.$

20. $f'(x) = \dfrac{d}{dx}\left(x^4 - 2x^2 + 5\right) = 4x^3 - 4x.$

21 $f'(x) = \dfrac{d}{dx}\left(0.03x^2 - 0.4x + 10\right) = 0.06x - 0.4.$

22. $f'(x) = \dfrac{d}{dx}\left(0.002x^3 - 0.05x^2 + 0.1x - 20\right) = 0.006x^2 - 0.1x + 0.1$

23 If $f(x) = \dfrac{x^3 - 4x^2 + 3}{x} = x^2 - 4x + \dfrac{3}{x}$,

then $f'(x) = \dfrac{d}{dx}\left(x^2 - 4x + 3x^{-1}\right) = 2x - 4 - \dfrac{3}{x^2}$

24 $f(x) = x^2 + 2x + 1 - x^{-1}$; $f'(x) = \dfrac{d}{dx}\left(x^2 + 2x + 1 - x^{-1}\right) = 2x + 2 + x^{-2}.$

25 $f'(x) = \dfrac{d}{dx}\left(4x^4 - 3x^{5/2} + 2\right) = 16x^3 - \frac{15}{2}x^{3/2}$

26. $f'(x) = \dfrac{d}{dx}\left(5x^{4/3} - \frac{2}{3}x^{3/2} + x^2 - 3x + 1\right) = \frac{20}{3}x^{1/3} - x^{1/2} + 2x - 3$

27 $f'(x) = \dfrac{d}{dx}\left(3x^{-1} + 4x^{-2}\right) = -3x^{-2} - 8x^{-3}$

28. $f'(x) = \dfrac{d}{dx}\left(-\frac{1}{3}(x^{-3} - x^6)\right) = -\frac{1}{3}(-3x^{-4} - 6x^5) = x^{-4} + 2x^5$

29: $f'(t) = \dfrac{d}{dt}\left(4t^{-4} - 3t^{-3} + 2t^{-1}\right) = -16t^{-5} + 9t^{-4} - 2t^{-2}$

30. $f'(x) = \dfrac{d}{dx}\left(5x^{-3} - 2x^{-2} - x^{-1} + 200\right) = -15x^{-4} + 4x^{-3} + x^{-2}$.

31. $f'(x) = \dfrac{d}{dx}\left(2x - 5x^{1/2}\right) = 2 - \dfrac{5}{2}x^{-1/2} = 2 - \dfrac{5}{2\sqrt{x}}$

32. $f'(t) = \dfrac{d}{dt}\left(2t^2 + t^{2/3}\right) = 4t + \dfrac{2}{3}t^{-1/3}$

33. $f'(x) = \dfrac{d}{dx}\left(2x^{-2} - 3x^{-1/3}\right) = -4x^{-3} + x^{-4/3} = -\dfrac{4}{x^3} + \dfrac{1}{x^{4/3}}$.

34. $f'(x) = \dfrac{d}{dx}\left(\dfrac{3}{x^3} + \dfrac{4}{\sqrt{x}} + 1\right) = \dfrac{d}{dx}(3x^{-3} + 4x^{-1/2} + 1) = -9x^{-4} - 2x^{-3/2}$

35. a. $f'(x) = \dfrac{d}{dx}\left(2x^3 - 4x\right) = 6x^2 - 4.$ $f'(-2) = 6(-2)^2 - 4 = 20.$

   b $f'(0) = 6(0) - 4 = -4.$ c. $f'(2) = 6(2)^2 - 4 = 20.$

36. $f'(x) = \dfrac{d}{dx}\left(4x^{5/4} + 2x^{3/2} + x\right) = 5x^{1/4} + 3x^{1/2} + 1.$

   a. $f'(0) = 1$ b $f'(16) = 5(16)^{1/4} + 3(16)^{1/2} + 1 = 10 + 12 + 1 = 23$

37 The given limit is $f'(1)$ where $f(x) = x^3$ Since $f'(x) = 3x^2$, we have
$$\lim_{h \to 0} \dfrac{(1+h)^3 - 1}{h} = f'(1) = 3.$$

38. Letting $h = x - 1$ or $x = h + 1$ and observing that $h \to 0$ as $x \to 1$, we find
$$\lim_{x \to 1} \dfrac{x^5 - 1}{x - 1} = \lim_{h \to 0} \dfrac{(h+1)^5 - 1}{h} = f'(1), \text{ where } f(x) = x^5. \text{ Since } f'(x) = 5x^4$$

we have $f'(1) = 5$, the value of the limit; that is, $\lim_{x \to 1} \dfrac{x^5 - 1}{x - 1} = 5.$

39 Let $f(x) = 3x^2 - x$. Then $\lim\limits_{h \to 0} \dfrac{3(2+h)^2 - (2+h) - 10}{h} = \lim\limits_{h \to 0} \dfrac{f(2+h) - f(2)}{h}$

because $f(2+h) - f(2) = 3(2+h)^2 - (2+h) - [3(4) - 2]$
$$= 3(2+h)^2 - (2+h) - 10.$$
But the last limit is $f'(2)$. Since $f'(x) = 6x - 1$, we have $f'(2) = 11$.

Therefore, $\lim\limits_{h \to 0} \dfrac{3(2+h)^2 - (2+h) - 10}{h} = 11$.

40. Write $\lim\limits_{t \to 0} \dfrac{1 - (1+t)^2}{t(1+t)^2} = \lim\limits_{t \to 0} \dfrac{1}{(1+t)^2} \cdot \lim\limits_{t \to 0} \dfrac{1 - (1+t)^2}{t}$

Let $f(t) = -t^2$. Then $\lim\limits_{t \to 0} \dfrac{1 - (1+t)^2}{t} = \lim\limits_{t \to 0} \dfrac{f(1+t) - f(1)}{t} = f'(1)$.

Since $f'(t) = -2t$, we find $f'(1) = -2$. Therefore,
$$\lim_{t \to 0} \dfrac{1 - (1+t)^2}{t(1+t)^2} = \lim_{t \to 0} \dfrac{1}{(1+t)^2} \cdot f'(1) = 1 \cdot (-2) = -2.$$

41 $f(x) = 2x^2 - 3x + 4$. The slope of the tangent line at any point $(x, f(x))$ on the graph of f is $f'(x) = 4x - 3$. In particular, the slope of the tangent line at the point $(2, 6)$ is $f'(2) = 4(2) - 3 = 5$ An equation of the required tangent line is
$$y - 6 = 5(x - 2) \qquad \text{or} \qquad y = 5x - 4.$$

42. $f(x) = -\frac{5}{3}x^2 + 2x + 2$. $f'(x) = -\frac{10}{3}x + 2$. The slope is $f'(-1) = \frac{10}{3} + 2 = \frac{16}{3}$.

An equation of the tangent line is $y + \frac{5}{3} = \frac{16}{3}(x + 1)$ or $y = \frac{16}{3}x + \frac{11}{3}$

43 $f(x) = x^4 - 3x^3 + 2x^2 - x + 1$. $f'(x) = 4x^3 - 9x^2 + 4x - 1$.
The slope is $f'(1) = 4 - 9 + 4 - 1 = -2$. An equation
of the tangent line is $y - 0 = -2(x - 1)$ or $y = -2x + 2$.

44. $f(x) = \sqrt{x} + 1/\sqrt{x}$. The slope of the tangent line at any point $(x, f(x))$ on the

graph of f is $f'(x) = \dfrac{1}{2}x^{-1/2} - \dfrac{1}{2}x^{-3/2} = \dfrac{1}{2\sqrt{x}} - \dfrac{1}{2\sqrt{x^3}}$ In particular, the slope of

the tangent line at the point $(4, \frac{5}{2})$ is $f'(4) = \frac{1}{4} - \frac{1}{16} = \frac{3}{16}$. The equation of the required tangent line is $y - \frac{5}{2} = \frac{3}{16}(x-4)$ or $y = \frac{3}{16}x + \frac{7}{4}$

45   a. $f'(x) = 3x^2$ At a point where the tangent line is horizontal,
$f'(x) = 0$, or $3x^2 = 0$ giving $x = 0$. Therefore, the point is (0,0).

b.

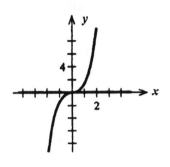

46. $f(x) = x^3 - 4x^2$. $f'(x) = 3x^2 - 8x = x(3x - 8) = 0$ implies $x = 0$ or $x = 8/3$.
Therefore, the points are (0,0) and $(\frac{8}{3}, -\frac{256}{27})$.

47   a. $f(x) = x^3 + 1$. The slope of the tangent line at any point $(x, f(x))$ on the graph
of f is $f'(x) = 3x^2$. At the point(s) where the slope is 12, we have
$3x^2 = 12$, or $x = \pm 2$. The required points are (-2,-7) and (2,9).
b. The tangent line at (-2,-7) has equation
$y - (-7) = 12[x - (-2)]$,   or $y = 12x + 17$,
and the tangent line at (2,9) has equation
$y - 9 = 12(x - 2)$,   or $y = 12x - 15$.
c.

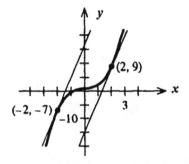

48. $f(x) = \frac{2}{3}x^3 + x^2 - 12x + 6$. $f'(x) = 2x^2 + 2x - 12$.
a. $f'(x) = -12$ gives $2x^2 + 2x - 12 = -12$, $2x^2 + 2x = 0$, $2x(x + 1) = 0$; that is,
$x = 0$ or $x = -1$.

171   3 Differentiation

b. $f'(x) = 0$ gives $2x^2 + 2x - 12 = 0$, $2(x^2 + x - 6) = 2(x + 3)(x - 2) = 0$, and so $x = -3$ or $x = 2$.

c. $f'(x) = 12$ gives $2x^2 + 2x - 12 = 12$, $2(x^2 + x - 12) = 2(x + 4)(x - 3) = 0$, and so $x = -4$ or $x = 3$

49 If $f(x) = \frac{1}{4}x^4 - \frac{1}{3}x^3 - x^2$, then $f'(x) = x^3 - x^2 - 2x$.

a. $f'(x) = x^3 - x^2 - 2x = -2x$

$$x^3 - x^2 = 0$$
$$x^2(x - 1) = 0 \quad \text{and} \quad x = 0 \text{ or } x = 1.$$
$$f(1) = \frac{1}{4}(1)^4 - \frac{1}{3}(1)^3 - (1)^2 = -\frac{13}{12}$$
$$f(0) = \frac{1}{4}(0)^4 - \frac{1}{3}(0)^3 - (0)^2 = 0.$$

We conclude that the corresponding points on the graph are $(1, -\frac{13}{12})$ and $(0,0)$.

b. $f'(x) = x^3 - x^2 - 2x = 0$

$$x(x^2 - x - 2) = 0$$
$$x(x - 2)(x + 1) = 0 \quad \text{and} \quad x = 0, 2, \text{ or } -1.$$
$$f(0) = 0$$
$$f(2) = \frac{1}{4}(2)^4 - \frac{1}{3}(2)^3 - (2)^2 = 4 - \frac{8}{3} - 4 = -\frac{8}{3}$$
$$f(-1) = \frac{1}{4}(-1)^4 - \frac{1}{3}(-1)^3 - (-1)^2 = \frac{1}{4} + \frac{1}{3} - 1 = -\frac{5}{12}.$$

We conclude that the corresponding points are $(0,0)$, $(2, -\frac{8}{3})$ and $(-1, -\frac{5}{12})$.

c. $f'(x) = x^3 - x^2 - 2x = 10x$

$$x^3 - x^2 - 12x = 0$$
$$x(x^2 - x - 12) = 0$$
$$x(x - 4)(x + 3) = 0$$

and $x = 0, 4,$ or -3.

$$f(0) = 0$$
$$f(4) = \frac{1}{4}(4)^4 - \frac{1}{3}(4)^3 - (4)^2 = 48 - \frac{64}{3} = \frac{80}{3}$$
$$f(-3) = \frac{1}{4}(-3)^4 - \frac{1}{3}(-3)^3 - (-3)^2 = \frac{81}{4} + 9 - 9 = \frac{81}{4}$$

We conclude that the corresponding points are $(0,0)$, $(4, \frac{80}{3})$ and $(-3, \frac{81}{4})$.

50. $y = x^3 - 3x + 1$. $\dfrac{dy}{dx} = 3x^2 - 3$. The slope of the tangent line to the given graph is

$$\left.\frac{dy}{dx}\right|_{x=2} = 3(4) - 3 = 9.$$

The slope of the normal line through the point (2,3) is $-\frac{1}{9}$. Therefore, a required equation of the normal line is $y - 3 = -\frac{1}{9}(x - 2)$ or $y = -\frac{1}{9}x + \frac{29}{9}$

51 $V(r) = \frac{4}{3}\pi r^3$. $V'(r) = 4\pi r^2$

a. $V'\left(\frac{2}{3}\right) = 4\pi\left(\frac{4}{9}\right) = \frac{16}{9}\pi$ cm³/cm. b. $V'\left(\frac{5}{4}\right) = 4\pi\left(\frac{25}{16}\right) = \frac{25}{4}\pi$ cm³/cm.

52. $v(r) = k(R^2 - r^2) = 1000(0.04 - r^2)$; $v(0.1) = 1000(0.04 - 0.1^2) = 1000(0.03) = 30$, and this says that the velocity of blood 0.1 cm from the central axis is 30 cm/sec. Next, $v'(r) = -2000r$ and so $v'(0.1) = -200$. This says that at a point that is 0.1 cm from the central axis, the velocity of blood is decreasing at the rate of 200 cm/sec per cm along a line transverse to the central axis.

53 a. $N(1) = 16.3(1^{0.8766}) = 16.3(1) = 16.3$, or 16.3 million cameras.

b. $N'(t) = (16.3)90.8766)t^{-0.1234}$; $N'(1) \approx 14.29$, or approximately 14.3 million cameras/yr.

c. $N(5) = 16.3(5^{0.8766}) \approx 66.82$, or approximately 66.8 million cameras.

d. $N'(5) = (16.3)(0.8766)(5^{-0.1234}) \approx 11\,71$, or approximately 11.7 million cameras/year.

54. a. $P(6) = 53(6^{0.12}) \equiv 65.7$, or 65 7%.

b. $P'(t) = 53(0.12t^{-0.88})$; $P'(6) = 53(0.12)(6^{-0.88}) \approx 1.3$, or 1.3%/yr.

55 a.

1970 ($t = 1$)	1980($t = 2$)	1990 ($t = 3$)	2000($t = 4$)
49.6%	41 1%	36.9%	34.1%

b. $P'(t) = (49.6)(-0.27t^{-1.27}) = -\dfrac{13.392}{t^{1.27}}$; In 1980, $P'(2) \approx -5.5$, or decreasing at 5.5%/decade. In 1990, $P'(3) \approx -3.3$, or decreasing at 3.3%/decade.

56. $\dfrac{dA}{dx} = 26.5\dfrac{d}{dx}(x^{-0.45}) = 26.5(-0.45)x^{-1.45} = -\dfrac{11.925}{x^{1.45}}$

Therefore, $\left.\dfrac{dA}{dx}\right|_{x=0.25} = -\dfrac{11.925}{(0.25)^{1.45}} \approx -89.01$ and $\left.\dfrac{dA}{dx}\right|_{x=2} = -\dfrac{11.925}{(2)^{1.45}} \approx -4.36$

Our computations reveal that if you make 0.25 stops per mile, your average speed will decrease at the rate of approximately 89.01 mph per stop per mile. If you make 2 stops per mile, your average speed will decrease at the rate of approximately 4.36 mph per stop per mile.

57   a. $P(9) = 24.4(9)^{0.34} = 51.5$, or 51.5%.

b. $P(t) = 24.4t^{0.34}$; $P'(t) = \dfrac{d}{dx}(24.4t^{0.34}) = (0.34)(24.4)t^{-0.66} = 8.296t^{-0.66}$

$P'(9) = 8.296(9)^{-0.66} = 1.946$, or approximately 1.95%/year.

58.   a. $f(x) = -0.1x^2 - 0.4x + 35$. $f'(x) = -0.2x - 0.4$
b. $f'(10) = -0.2(10) - 0.4 = -2.4$; that is, it is decreasing at the rate of $2.40 per 1000 lamps. The unit price at this level of demand is
$f(10) = -0.1(10^2) - 0.4(10) + 35$, or $21

59   a. $f(t) = 120t - 15t^2$. $v = f'(t) = 120 - 30t$ b. $v(0) = 120$ ft/sec
c. Setting $v = 0$ gives $120 - 30t = 0$, or $t = 4$. Therefore, the stopping distance is
$f(4) = 120(4) - 15(16)$ or 240 ft.

60.   a. $S(0) = 3.1$, or $3.1 billion. $S(5) = 0.14(5)^2 + 0.68(5) + 3.1 = 10$, or $10 million.
b. $S'(t) = 0.28t + 0.68$; $S'(0) = 0.28(0) + 0.68 = 0.68$, or $0.68 billion.
$S'(5) = 0.28(5) + 0.68 = 2.08$, or $2.08 billion/yr.

61. a. At the beginning of 1980, $P(0) = 5\%$. At the beginning of 1990,
$P(10) = -0.0105(10^2) + 0.735(10) + 5 \approx 11.3\%$. At the beginning of 2000,
$P(20) = -0.0105(20)^2 + 0.735(20) + 5 \approx 15.5\%$.
b. $P'(t) = -0.021t + 0.735$; At the beginning of 1985,
$P'(5) = -0.02(5) + 0.735 \approx 0.63\% /$ yr. At the beginning of 1990,
$P'(10) = -0.021(10) + 0.735 = 0.525\% /$ yr.

62. a. $P'(t) = 0.54t + 1.4$. In 2010, $P'(1) = 0.54(1) + 1.4 = 1.94$ or 1.94%/decade. In
2000, $P'(2) = 0.54(2) = 1.4 = 2.48\% /$ decade.
b. In 2010, $P(1) = 0.27(1^2) + 1.4(1) + 2.2 = 3.87\%$. In 2020,
$P(2) = 0.27(2^2) + 1.4(2) + 2.2 = 6.08\%$

63.. a $f(t) = 5.303t^2 - 53.977t + 253.8$. The rate of change of the groundfish
population at any time t is given by $f'(t) = 10.606t - 53.977$ The rate of change
at the beginning of 1994 is given by $f'(5) = 10.606(5) - 53.977 = -0.947$
and so the population is decreasing at the rate of 0.9 thousand metric tons/yr. At
the beginning of 1996, the rate of change is $f'(7) = 10.606(7) - 53.977 = 20.265$
and so the population is increasing at the rate of 20.3 thousand metric tons/yr.
b. Yes.

64.   a. $N(t) = -t^3 + 6t^2 + 15t$ The rate is given by $N'(t) = -3t^2 + 12t + 15$
b. The rate at which the average worker will be assembling walkie- talkies at
10 A.M. is $N'(2) = -3(2)^2 + 12(2) + 15 = 27$, or 27 walkie-talkies/hour. At
11 A.M., we have $N'(3) = -3(3)^2 + 12(3) + 15 = 24$, or 24 walkie-talkies/hour.
c. The number will be $N(3) - N(2) = (-27 + 54 + 45) - (-8 + 24 + 30)$
$$= 26, \text{ or 26 walkie-talkies.}$$

65   $I'(t) = -0.6t^2 + 6t$.
a. In 1999, it was changing at a rate of $I'(5) = -0.6(25) + 6(5)$, or 15 points/yr. In
2001, it was $I'(7) = -0.6(49) + 6(7)$, or 12.6 pts/yr. In 2004, it was
$I'(10) = -0.6(100) + 6(10)$, or 0 pts/yr.
b. The average rate of increase of the CPI over the period from 1999 to 2004 was
$$\frac{I(10) - I(5)}{5} = \frac{[-0.2(1000) + 3(100) + 100] - [-0.2(125) + 3(25) + 100]}{5}$$
$$= \frac{200 - 150}{5} = 10, \text{ or 10 pts/yr.}$$

66.   If $S(x) = -0.002x^3 + 0.6x^2 + x + 500$, then $S'(x) = -0.006x^2 + 1.2x + 1$
a. When $x = 100$, $S'(100) = -0.006(100)^2 + 1.2(100) + 1 = 61$,
or \$61,000 per thousand dollars.
b. When $x = 150$, $S'(150) = -0.006(150)^2 + 1.2(150) + 1 = 46$,
or \$46,000 per thousand dollars.We conclude that the company's total sales are
increasing at a faster rate when the amount of money spent on advertising is
(a) \$100,000.

67.   a. $f'(x) = \dfrac{d}{dx}\left[0.0001x^{5/4} + 10\right] = \dfrac{5}{4}(0.0001x^{1/4}) = 0.000125x^{1/4}$
b. $f'(10,000) = 0.000125(10,000)^{1/4} = 0.00125$, or \$0.00125/radio.

68. $P(t) = 50,000 + 30t^{3/2} + 20t$ The rate at which the population will be increasing at any time t is $P'(t) = 45t^{1/2} + 20$. Nine months from now the population will be increasing at the rate of $P'(9) = 45(3) + 20$, or 155 people/month. Sixteen months from now the population will be increasing at the rate of
$$P'(16) = 45(4) + 20, \text{ or } 200 \text{ people/month.}$$

69 a. $f(t) = 20t - 40\sqrt{t} + 50$ $f'(t) = 20 - 40\left(\dfrac{1}{2}\right)t^{-1/2} = 20\left(1 - \dfrac{1}{\sqrt{t}}\right)$.

   b. $f(0) = 20(0) - 40\sqrt{0} + 50 = 50$; $f(1) = 20(1) - 40\sqrt{1} + 50 = 30$
   $f(2) = 20(2) - 40\sqrt{2} + 50 \approx 33.43$.
   The average velocity at 6, 7, and 8 A.M. is 50 mph, 30 mph, and 33.43 mph, respectively

   c. $f'(\frac{1}{2}) = 20 - 20(\frac{1}{2})^{-1/2} \approx -8.28$. $f'(1) = 20 - 20(1)^{-1/2} \approx 0$.
   $f'(2) = 20 - 20(2)^{-1/2} \approx 5.86$.
   At 6:30 A.M. the average velocity is decreasing at the rate of 8.28 mph/hr; at 7 A.M., it is unchanged, and at 8 A.M., it is increasing at the rate of 5.86 mph.

70. $P(t) = -\frac{1}{3}t^3 + 64t + 3000$ $P'(t) = -t^2 + 64$. The rates of change at the end of years one, two, three and four, are
$$P'(1) = -1 + 64 = 63, \text{ or } 63,000 \text{ people/yr.}$$
$$P'(2) = -4 + 64 = 60, \text{ or } 60,000 \text{ people/yr.}$$
$$P'(3) = -9 + 64 = 55, \text{ or } 55,000 \text{ people/yr.}$$
$$P'(4) = -16 + 64 = 48, \text{ or } 48,000 \text{ people/yr.}$$
Evidently, the plan is working.

71. $N(t) = 2t^3 + 3t^2 - 4t + 1000$. $N'(t) = 6t^2 + 6t - 4$.
$N'(2) = 6(4) + 6(2) - 4 = 32$, or 32 turtles/yr.
$N'(8) = 6(64) + 6(8) - 4 = 428$, or 428 turtles/yr.
The population ten years after implementation of the conservation measures will be $N(10) = 2(10^3) + 3(10^2) - 4(10) + 1000$, or 3260 turtles.

72. a. $f(t) = -2t^3 + 114t^2 + 480t + 1$. $v = f'(t) = -6t^2 + 228t + 480$.
   b. $f'(0) = 480$, or 480 ft/sec; $f'(20) = -6(400) + 228(20) + 480 = 2640$ ft/sec
   $f'(40) = -6(1600) + 228(40) + 480 = 0$, or 0 ft/sec
   $f'(60) = -6(3600) + 228(60) + 480 = -7440$, or -7440 ft/sec.
   The rocket starts out at an initial velocity of 480 ft/sec. It climbs upward until a

maximum altitude is attained 40 seconds into flight. It then descends until it hits the ground.

c. At the highest point $v = 0$. But this occurs when $t = 40$ (see part(b)). The maximum altitude is $f(40) = -2(40)^3 + 114(40)^2 + 480(40) + 1$, or 73,601 feet.

73. a. At the beginning of 1991, $P(0) = 12\%$. At the beginning of 2004,

$P(13) = 0.0004(13^3) + 0.0036(13^2) + 0.8(13) + 12 \approx 23.9\%$.

b. $P'(t) = 0.0012t^2 + 0.0072t + 0.8$. At the beginning of 1991, $P'(0) = 0.8\% / \text{yr}$.

At the beginning of 2004, $P'(13) = 0.0012(13^2) + 0.0072(3) + 0.8 \approx 1.1\% / \text{yr}$.

74. a. $S(t) = 0.02836t^3 - 0.05167t^2 + 9.60881t + 41.9$

$S'(t) = 0.02836(3t^2) - 0.05167(2t) + 9.60881$

$\quad = 0.08508t^2 - 0.10334t + 9.60881$.

b. At the beginning of 1980, it was increasing at the rate of

$S'(15) = 0.08508(15^2) - 0.10334(15) + 9.60881$, or \$27.20171 billion/yr.

At the beginning of 2000, it was increasing at the rate of

$S'(35) = 0.08508(35^2) - 0.10334(35) + 9.60881$, or \$110.21491 billion/yr.

c. $S(15) = 0.02836(15)^3 - 0.05167(15)^2 + 9.60881(15) + 41.9$

$\quad = 270.1214$, or \$270.1214 billion.

$S(35) = 0.02836(35)^3 - 0.05167(35)^2 + 9.60881(35) + 41.9$

$\quad = 1530.8476$, or \$1530.8476 billion.

75 True. $\dfrac{d}{dx}[2f(x) - 5g(x)] = \dfrac{d}{dx}[2f(x)] - \dfrac{d}{dx}[5g(x)] = 2f'(x) - 5g'(x)$.

76. False. f is *not* a power function.

77. $\dfrac{d}{dx}(x^3) = \lim_{h \to 0} \dfrac{(x+h)^3 - x^3}{h} = \lim_{h \to 0} \dfrac{x^3 + 3x^2h + 3xh^2 + h^3 - x^3}{h}$

$\quad = \lim_{h \to 0} \dfrac{h(3x^2 + 3xh + h^2)}{h} = \lim_{h \to 0}(3x^2 + 3xh + h^2) = 3x^2$

USING TECHNOL0GY EXERCISES 3.1, page 172

1. 1   2. 3.072   3. 0.4226   4. 0.0732   5.   0.1613   6. 3.9730

7. a.

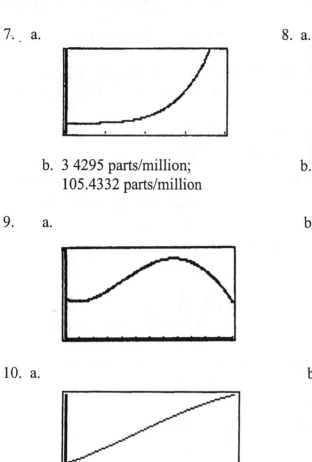

   b. 3 4295 parts/million;
      105.4332 parts/million

8. a.

   b. 3.0355 million/year

9. a.

    b. decreasing at the rate of 9 days/yr
       increasing at the rate of 13 days/yr

10. a.

    b. 42,272 cases/year

11. a.

    b. Increasing at the rate of 1 1557%/yr
       decreasing at the rate of 0.2116%/yr

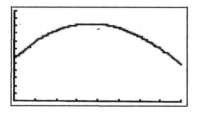

12.   a.

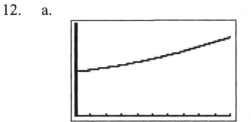

b. −43,371 metric tons; 20,265 metric tons

3.2 CONCEPT QUESTIONS, page 180

1   a. The derivative of the product of two functions is equal to the first function times the derivative of the second function plus the second function times the derivative of the first function.

b.   The derivative of the quotient of two functions is equal to the quotient whose numerator is given by the denominator times the derivative of the numerator minus the numerator times the derivative of the denominator and the denominator is the square of the denominator of the quotient.

2.   a. $h'(x) = f(x)g'(x) + f'(x)g(x)$. So

$$h'(1) = f(1)g'(1) + f'(1)g(1) = (3)(4) + (-1)(2) = 10$$

b. $F'(x) = \dfrac{g(x)f'(x) - f(x)g'(x)}{[g(x)]^2}$. So

$$F'(1) = \frac{g(1)f'(1) - f(1)g'(1)}{[g(1)]^2} = \frac{2(-1) - 3(4)}{2^2} = -\frac{7}{2}$$

EXERCISES 3.2, page 180

1. $f(x) = 2x(x^2 + 1)$.

$$f'(x) = 2x\frac{d}{dx}\left(x^2 + 1\right) + (x^2 + 1)\frac{d}{dx}(2x)$$
$$= 2x(2x) + (x^2 + 1)(2) = 6x^2 + 2.$$

2. $f(x) = 3x^2(x - 1)$

$$f'(x) = 3x^2\frac{d}{dx}(x - 1) + (x - 1)\frac{d}{dx}(3x^2) = 3x^2 + (x - 1)(6x) = 9x^2 - 6x.$$

3. $f(t) = (t - 1)(2t + 1)$

$$f'(t) = (t-1)\frac{d}{dt}(2t+1) + (2t+1)\frac{d}{dt}(t-1)$$
$$= (t-1)(2) + (2t+1)(1) = 4t - 1$$

4. $f(x) = (2x+3)(3x-4)$
$$f'(x) = (2x+3)\frac{d}{dx}(3x-4) + (3x-4)\frac{d}{dx}(2x+3)$$
$$= (2x+3)(3) + (3x-4)(2) = 12x + 1.$$

5. $f(x) = (3x+1)(x^2-2)$
$$f'(x) = (3x+1)\frac{d}{dx}(x^2-2) + (x^2-2)\frac{d}{dx}(3x+1)$$
$$= (3x+1)(2x) + (x^2-2)(3) = 9x^2 + 2x - 6.$$

6. $f(x) = (x+1)(2x^2-3x+1)$
$$f'(x) = (x+1)\frac{d}{dx}(2x^2-3x+1) + (2x^2-3x+1)\frac{d}{dx}(x+1)$$
$$= (x+1)(4x-3) + (2x^2-3x+1)(1) = 4x^2 - 3x + 4x - 3 + 2x^2 - 3x + 1$$
$$= 6x^2 - 2x - 2 = 2(3x^2 - x - 1).$$

7 $f(x) = (x^3-1)(x+1).$
$$f'(x) = (x^3-1)\frac{d}{dx}(x+1) + (x+1)\frac{d}{dx}(x^3-1)$$
$$= (x^3-1)(1) + (x+1)(3x^2) = 4x^3 + 3x^2 - 1.$$

8. $f(x) = (x^3-12x)(3x^2+2x)$
$$f'(x) = (x^3-12x)\frac{d}{dx}(3x^2+2x) + (3x^2+2x)\frac{d}{dx}(x^3-12x)$$
$$= (x^3-12x)(6x+2) + (3x^2+2x)(3x^2-12)$$
$$= 6x^4 + 2x^3 - 72x^2 - 24x + 9x^4 + 6x^3 - 36x^2 - 24x$$
$$= 15x^4 + 8x^3 - 108x^2 - 48x.$$

9 $f(w) = (w^3 - w^2 + w - 1)(w^2 + 2).$

$$f'(w) = (w^3 - w^2 + w - 1)\frac{d}{dw}(w^2 + 2) + (w^2 + 2)\frac{d}{dw}(w^3 - w^2 + w - 1)$$

$$= (w^3 - w^2 + w - 1)(2w) + (w^2 + 2)(3w^2 - 2w + 1)$$

$$= 2w^4 - 2w^3 + 2w^2 - 2w + 3w^4 - 2w^3 + w^2 + 6w^2 - 4w + 2$$

$$= 5w^4 - 4w^3 + 9w^2 - 6w + 2.$$

10. $f(x) = \frac{1}{5}x^5 + (x^2 + 1)(x^2 - x - 1) + 28$

$f'(x) = x^4 + (x^2 + 1)(2x - 1) + 2x(x^2 - x - 1)$

$\quad = x^4 + 2x^3 - x^2 + 2x - 1 + 2x^3 - 2x^2 - 2x = x^4 + 4x^3 - 3x^2 - 1.$

11. $f(x) = (5x^2 + 1)(2\sqrt{x} - 1)$

$f'(x) = (5x^2 + 1)\frac{d}{dx}(2x^{1/2} - 1) + (2x^{1/2} - 1)\frac{d}{dx}(5x^2 + 1)$

$\quad = (5x^2 + 1)(x^{-1/2}) + (2x^{1/2} - 1)(10x)$

$\quad = 5x^{3/2} + x^{-1/2} + 20x^{3/2} - 10x = \dfrac{25x^2 - 10x\sqrt{x} + 1}{\sqrt{x}}$

12. $f(t) = (1 + \sqrt{t})(2t^2 - 3)$

$f'(t) = (1 + t^{1/2})(4t) + (2t^2 - 3)(\frac{1}{2}t^{-1/2})$

$\quad = 4t + 4t^{3/2} + t^{3/2} - \frac{3}{2}t^{-1/2} = 5t^{3/2} + 4t - \frac{3}{2}t^{-1/2}$

13. $f(x) = (x^2 - 5x + 2)(x - \dfrac{2}{x})$

$f'(x) = (x^2 - 5x + 2)\dfrac{d}{dx}(x - \dfrac{2}{x}) + (x - \dfrac{2}{x})\dfrac{d}{dx}(x^2 - 5x + 2)$

$\quad = \dfrac{(x^2 - 5x + 2)(x^2 + 2)}{x^2} + \dfrac{(x^2 - 2)(2x - 5)}{x}$

$\quad = \dfrac{(x^2 - 5x + 2)(x^2 + 2) + x(x^2 - 2)(2x - 5)}{x^2}$

$\quad = \dfrac{x^4 + 2x^2 - 5x^3 - 10x + 2x^2 + 4 + 2x^4 - 5x^3 - 4x^2 + 10x}{x^2}$

$\quad = \dfrac{3x^4 - 10x^3 + 4}{x^2}.$

14. $f(x) = (x^3 + 2x + 1)(2 + \frac{1}{x^2}) = 2x^3 + 4x + 2 + x + \frac{2}{x} + \frac{1}{x^2}$

$f'(x) = \frac{d}{dx}\left(2x^3 + 5x + 2 + \frac{2}{x} + \frac{1}{x^2}\right) = 6x^2 + 5 - \frac{2}{x^2} - \frac{2}{x^3}$

$= \frac{6x^5 + 5x^3 - 2x - 2}{x^3}$

15. $f(x) = \frac{1}{x-2}$ $\quad f'(x) = \frac{(x-2)\frac{d}{dx}(1) - (1)\frac{d}{dx}(x-2)}{(x-2)^2} = \frac{0 - 1(1)}{(x-2)^2} = -\frac{1}{(x-2)^2}.$

16. $g(x) = \frac{3}{2x+4}$

$g'(x) = \frac{(2x+4)\frac{d}{dx}(3) - (3)\frac{d}{dx}(2x+4)}{(2x+4)^2} = \frac{0 - 3(2)}{(2x+4)^2} = -\frac{6}{(2x+4)^2} = -\frac{3}{2(x+2)^2}$

17. $f(x) = \frac{x-1}{2x+1}$

$f'(x) = \frac{(2x+1)\frac{d}{dx}(x-1) - (x-1)\frac{d}{dx}(2x+1)}{(2x+1)^2}$

$= \frac{2x+1 - (x-1)(2)}{(2x+1)^2} = \frac{3}{(2x+1)^2}$

18. $f(t) = \frac{1-2t}{1+3t}.$ $\quad f'(t) = \frac{(1+3t)(-2) - (1-2t)(3)}{(1+3t)^2} = \frac{-5}{(1+3t)^2}$

19. $f(x) = \frac{1}{x^2+1}$

$f'(x) = \frac{(x^2+1)\frac{d}{dx}(1) - (1)\frac{d}{dx}(x^2+1)}{(x^2+1)^2}$

$= \frac{(x^2+1)(0) - 1(2x)}{(x^2+1)^2} = -\frac{2x}{(x^2+1)^2}$

20. $f(u) = \dfrac{u}{u^2 + 1}$

$$f'(u) = \frac{(u^2 + 1)\dfrac{d}{du}(u) - u\dfrac{d}{du}(u^2 + 1)}{(u^2 + 1)^2} = \frac{(u^2 + 1)(1) - u(2u)}{(u^2 + 1)^2} = \frac{1 - u^2}{(u^2 + 1)^2}$$

21 $f(s) = \dfrac{s^2 - 4}{s + 1}.$

$$f'(s) = \frac{(s+1)\dfrac{d}{ds}(s^2 - 4) - (s^2 - 4)\dfrac{d}{ds}(s+1)}{(s+1)^2}$$

$$= \frac{(s+1)(2s) - (s^2 - 4)(1)}{(s+1)^2} = \frac{s^2 + 2s + 4}{(s+1)^2}.$$

22. $f(x) = \dfrac{x^3 - 2}{x^2 + 1}.$

$$f'(x) = \frac{(x^2 + 1)\dfrac{d}{dx}(x^3 - 2) - (x^3 - 2)\dfrac{d}{dx}(x^2 + 1)}{(x^2 + 1)^2}$$

$$= \frac{(x^2 + 1)(3x^2) - (x^3 - 2)(2x)}{(x^2 + 1)^2} = \frac{x(x^3 + 3x + 4)}{(x^2 + 1)^2}$$

23 $f(x) = \dfrac{\sqrt{x}}{x^2 + 1}$

$$f'(x) = \frac{(x^2 + 1)\dfrac{d}{dx}(x^{1/2}) - (x^{1/2})\dfrac{d}{dx}(x^2 + 1)}{(x^2 + 1)^2} = \frac{(x^2 + 1)(\frac{1}{2}x^{-1/2}) - (x^{1/2})(2x)}{(x^2 + 1)^2}$$

$$= \frac{(\frac{1}{2}x^{-1/2})[(x^2 + 1) - 4x^2]}{(x^2 + 1)^2} = \frac{1 - 3x^2}{2\sqrt{x}(x^2 + 1)^2}.$$

24. $f(x) = \dfrac{x^2 + 1}{\sqrt{x}}.$

$$f'(x) = \frac{x^{1/2}(2x) - (x^2 + 1)(\frac{1}{2}x^{-1/2})}{x} = \frac{\frac{1}{2}x^{-1/2}[4x^2 - (x^2 + 1)]}{x} = \frac{3x^2 - 1}{2x^{3/2}}.$$

3 Differentiation

25     $f(x) = \dfrac{x^2 + 2}{x^2 + x + 1}.$

$$f'(x) = \frac{(x^2 + x + 1)\dfrac{d}{dx}(x^2 + 2) - (x^2 + 2)\dfrac{d}{dx}(x^2 + x + 1)}{(x^2 + x + 1)^2}$$

$$= \frac{(x^2 + x + 1)(2x) - (x^2 + 2)(2x + 1)}{(x^2 + x + 1)^2}$$

$$= \frac{2x^3 + 2x^2 + 2x - 2x^3 - x^2 - 4x - 2}{(x^2 + x + 1)^2} = \frac{x^2 - 2x - 2}{(x^2 + x + 1)^2}$$

26. $f(x) = \dfrac{x + 1}{2x^2 + 2x + 3}$

$$f'(x) = \frac{(2x^2 + 2x + 3)(1) - (x + 1)(4x + 2)}{(2x^2 + 2x + 3)^2}$$

$$= \frac{2x^2 + 2x + 3 - 4x^2 - 2x - 4x - 2}{(2x^2 + 2x + 3)^2} = \frac{-2x^2 - 4x + 1}{(2x^2 + 2x + 3)^2}$$

27     $f(x) = \dfrac{(x + 1)(x^2 + 1)}{x - 2} = \dfrac{(x^3 + x^2 + x + 1)}{x - 2}.$

$$f'(x) = \frac{(x - 2)\dfrac{d}{dx}(x^3 + x^2 + x + 1) - (x^3 + x^2 + x + 1)\dfrac{d}{dx}(x - 2)}{(x - 2)^2}$$

$$= \frac{(x - 2)(3x^2 + 2x + 1) - (x^3 + x^2 + x + 1)}{(x - 2)^2}$$

$$= \frac{3x^3 + 2x^2 + x - 6x^2 - 4x - 2 - x^3 - x^2 - x - 1}{(x - 2)^2} = \frac{2x^3 - 5x^2 - 4x - 3}{(x - 2)^2}$$

28. $f(x) = (3x^2 - 1)(x^2 - \dfrac{1}{x}).$

$$f'(x) = 6x(x^2 - \frac{1}{x}) + (3x^2 - 1)(2x + \frac{1}{x^2})$$

$$= 6x^3 - 6 + 6x^3 + 3 - 2x - \frac{1}{x^2} = 12x^3 - 2x - 3 - \frac{1}{x^2}$$

29 $f(x) = \dfrac{x}{x^2 - 4} - \dfrac{x-1}{x^2 + 4} = \dfrac{x(x^2+4) - (x-1)(x^2-4)}{(x^2-4)(x^2+4)} = \dfrac{x^2 + 8x - 4}{(x^2-4)(x^2+4)}$

$$f'(x) = \frac{(x^2-4)(x^2+4)\dfrac{d}{dx}(x^2+8x-4) - (x^2+8x-4)\dfrac{d}{dx}(x^4-16)}{(x^2-4)^2(x^2+4)^2}$$

$$= \frac{(x^2-4)(x^2+4)(2x+8) - (x^2+8x-4)(4x^3)}{(x^2-4)^2(x^2+4)^2}$$

$$= \frac{2x^5 + 8x^4 - 32x - 128 - 4x^5 - 32x^4 + 16x^3}{(x^2-4)^2(x^2+4)^2}$$

$$= \frac{-2x^5 - 24x^4 + 16x^3 - 32x - 128}{(x^2-4)^2(x^2+4)^2}$$

30. $f(x) = \dfrac{x + \sqrt{3x}}{3x - 1}.$

$$f'(x) = \frac{(3x-1)(1 + \frac{1}{2}\sqrt{3}x^{-1/2}) - (x + \sqrt{3}x^{1/2})(3)}{(3x-1)^2}$$

$$= \frac{3x + \frac{3}{2}\sqrt{3}x^{1/2} - 1 - \frac{1}{2}\sqrt{3}x^{-1/2} - 3x - 3\sqrt{3}x^{1/2}}{(3x-1)^2} = -\frac{3\sqrt{3}x + 2\sqrt{x} + \sqrt{3}}{2\sqrt{x}(3x-1)^2}$$

31. $h'(x) = f(x)g'(x) + f'(x)g(x),$ by the Product Rule. Therefore,
$h'(1) = f(1)g'(1) + f'(1)g(1) = (2)(3) + (-1)(-2) = 8.$

32. $h'(x) = (x^2+1)g'(x) + \dfrac{d}{dx}(x^2+1) \cdot g(x) = (x^2+1)g'(x) + 2x\,g(x).$

Therefore $h\,'(1) = 2g\,'(1) + 2g\,(1) = (2)(3) + 2(-2) = 2.$

33 Using the Quotient Rule followed by the Product Rule, we have

$$h'(x) = \frac{[x+g(x)]\frac{d}{dx}[xf(x)] - xf(x)\frac{d}{dx}[x+g(x)]}{[x+g(x)]^2}$$

$$= \frac{[x+g(x)][xf'(x)+f(x)] - xf(x)[1+g'(x)]}{[x+g(x)]^2}$$

Therefore, $h'(1) = \dfrac{[1+g(1)][f'(1)+f(1)] - f(1)[1+g'(1)]}{[1+g(1)]^2}$

$$= \frac{(1-2)(-1+2) - 2(1+3)}{(1-2)^2} = \frac{-1-8}{1} = -9$$

34. Using the Quotient Rule followed by the Product Rule and the Sum Rule, we have

$$h'(x) = \frac{[f(x)-g(x)]\frac{d}{dx}[f(x)g(x)] - f(x)g(x)\frac{d}{dx}[f(x)-g(x)]}{[f(x)-g(x)]^2}$$

$$= \frac{[f(x)-g(x)][f(x)g'(x)+f'(x)g(x)] - f(x)g(x)[f'(x)-g'(x)]}{[f(x)-g(x)]^2}$$

Therefore,

$$h'(1) = \frac{[f(1)-g(1)][f(1)g'(1)+f'(1)g(1)] - f(1)g(1)[f'(1)-g'(1)]}{[f(1)-g(1)]^2}$$

$$= \frac{[2-(-2)][(2)(3)+(-1)(-2)] - (2)(-2)[(-1)-3]}{[2-(-2)]^2}$$

$$= \frac{(4)(8)-(-4)(-4)}{(-2)^2} = \frac{16}{4} = 4$$

35. $f(x) = (2x-1)(x^2+3)$

$$f'(x) = (2x-1)\frac{d}{dx}(x^2+3) + (x^2+3)\frac{d}{dx}(2x-1)$$

$$= (2x-1)(2x) + (x^2+3)(2) = 6x^2 - 2x + 6 = 2(3x^2 - x + 3).$$

At $x = 1, f'(1) = 2[3(1)^2 - (1) + 3] = 2(5) = 10.$

36. $f(x) = \dfrac{2x+1}{2x-1}.$

$$f'(x) = \frac{(2x-1)\dfrac{d}{dx}(2x+1) - (2x+1)\dfrac{d}{dx}(2x-1)}{(2x-1)^2}$$

$$= \frac{(2x-1)(2) - (2x+1)(2)}{(2x-1)^2} = \frac{4x-2-4x-2}{(2x-1)^2} = -\frac{4}{(2x-1)^2}$$

At $x = 2$, $f'(2) = \dfrac{-4}{[2(2)-1]^2} = -\dfrac{4}{9}$

37 $f(x) = \dfrac{x}{x^4 - 2x^2 - 1}$.

$$f'(x) = \frac{(x^4 - 2x^2 - 1)\dfrac{d}{dx}(x) - x\dfrac{d}{dx}(x^4 - 2x^2 - 1)}{(x^4 - 2x^2 - 1)^2}$$

$$= \frac{(x^4 - 2x^2 - 1)(1) - x(4x^3 - 4x)}{(x^4 - 2x^2 - 1)^2} = \frac{-3x^4 + 2x^2 - 1}{(x^4 - 2x^2 - 1)^2}$$

Therefore, $f'(-1) = \dfrac{-3+2-1}{(1-2-1)^2} = -\dfrac{2}{4} = -\dfrac{1}{2}$

38. $f(x) = (x^{1/2} + 2x)(x^{3/2} - x) = x^2 - x^{3/2} + 2x^{5/2} - 2x^2 = 2x^{5/2} - x^2 - x^{3/2}$

$f'(x) = 5x^{3/2} - 2x - \dfrac{3}{2}x^{1/2}$.

At $x = 4$, $f'(4) = 5(4)^{3/2} - 2(4) - \dfrac{3}{2}(4)^{1/2} = 5(8) - 2(4) - \dfrac{3}{2}(4)^{1/2} = 29$

39 $f(x) = (x^3 + 1)(x^2 - 2)$.

$$f'(x) = (x^3 + 1)\dfrac{d}{dx}(x^2 - 2) + (x^2 - 2)\dfrac{d}{dx}(x^3 + 1)$$

$$= (x^3 + 1)(2x) + (x^2 - 2)(3x^2).$$

The slope of the tangent line at $(2, 18)$ is $f'(2) = (8 + 1)(4) + (4 - 2)(12) = 60$.
An equation of the tangent line is $y - 18 = 60(x - 2)$, or $y = 60x - 102$.

40. $f(x) = \dfrac{x^2}{x+1}$ $f'(x) = \dfrac{(x+1)(2x) - x^2(1)}{(x+1)^2} = \dfrac{x^2 + 2x}{(x+1)^2}$.

The slope of the tangent line is $f'(2) = \frac{8}{9}$. An equation of the line is

$$y - \tfrac{4}{3} = \tfrac{8}{9}(x-2), \quad \text{or} \quad y = \tfrac{8}{9}x - \tfrac{4}{9}$$

41   $f(x) = \dfrac{x+1}{x^2+1}$

$$f'(x) = \dfrac{(x^2+1)\dfrac{d}{dx}(x+1) - (x+1)\dfrac{d}{dx}(x^2+1)}{(x^2+1)^2}$$

$$= \dfrac{(x^2+1)(1) - (x+1)(2x)}{(x^2+1)^2} = \dfrac{-x^2 - 2x + 1}{(x^2+1)^2}$$

At $x = 1$, $f'(1) = \dfrac{-1-2+1}{4} = -\dfrac{1}{2}$ Therefore, the slope of the tangent line at $x = 1$ is -1/2. Then an equation of the tangent line is
$$y - 1 = -\tfrac{1}{2}(x-1) \quad \text{or} \quad y = -\tfrac{1}{2}x + \tfrac{3}{2}$$

42. $f(x) = \dfrac{1+2x^{1/2}}{1+x^{3/2}}$. $f'(x) = \dfrac{(1+x^{3/2})(x^{-1/2}) - (1+2x^{1/2})(\tfrac{3}{2}x^{1/2})}{(1+x^{3/2})^2}$

The slope of the tangent line is $f'(4) = \dfrac{(1+8)(\tfrac{1}{2}) - (1+4)(3)}{9^2} = -\dfrac{7}{54}$

An equation of the line is $y - \tfrac{5}{9} = -\tfrac{7}{54}(x-4)$ or $y = -\tfrac{7}{54}x + \tfrac{29}{27}$

43   $f(x) = (x^3+1)(3x^2 - 4x + 2)$

$$f'(x) = (x^3+1)\dfrac{d}{dx}(3x^2 - 4x + 2) + (3x^2 - 4x + 2)\dfrac{d}{dx}(x^3+1)$$

$$= (x^3+1)(6x-4) + (3x^2 - 4x + 2)(3x^2)$$

$$= 6x^4 + 6x - 4x^3 - 4 + 9x^4 - 12x^3 + 6x^2$$

$$= 15x^4 - 16x^3 + 6x^2 + 6x - 4.$$

At $x = 1$, $f'(1) = 15(1)^4 - 16(1)^3 + 6(1) + 6(1) - 4 = 7$ The slope of the tangent line at the point $x = 1$ is 7. The equation of the tangent line is
$$y - 2 = 7(x-1), \quad \text{or} \quad y = 7x - 5.$$

44. $f(x) = \dfrac{3x}{x^2-2}$

The slope of the tangent line at any point $(x, f(x))$ lying on the graph of f is

$$f'(x) = \frac{(x^2-2)\frac{d}{dx}(3x) - (3x)\frac{d}{dx}(x^2-2)}{(x^2-2)^2}$$

$$= \frac{(x^2-2)(3) - 3x(2x)}{(x^2-2)^2} = \frac{-3x^2-6}{(x^2-2)^2} = \frac{-3(x^2+2)}{(x^2-2)^2}$$

In particular, the slope of the tangent line at $(2,3)$ is $f'(2) = \frac{-3(4+2)}{4} = -\frac{9}{2}$.

Therefore, an equation of the tangent line is
$$y - 3 = -\frac{9}{2}(x-2) \quad \text{or} \quad y = -\frac{9}{2}x + 12.$$

45    $f(x) = (x^2+1)(2-x)$

$$f'(x) = (x^2+1)\frac{d}{dx}(2-x) + (2-x)\frac{d}{dx}(x^2+1)$$

$$= (x^2+1)(-1) + (2-x)(2x) = -3x^2 + 4x - 1.$$

At a point where the tangent line is horizontal, we have
$$f'(x) = -3x^2 + 4x - 1 = 0$$
or $3x^2 - 4x + 1 = (3x-1)(x-1) = 0$, giving $x = 1/3$ or $x = 1$.

Since $f(\frac{1}{3}) = (\frac{1}{9}+1)(2-\frac{1}{3}) = \frac{50}{27}$, and $f(1) = 2(2-1) = 2$, we see that the required points are $(\frac{1}{3}, \frac{50}{27})$ and $(1, 2)$.

46. $f(x) = \dfrac{x}{x^2+1}$ $f'(x) = \dfrac{(x^2+1)(1) - x(2x)}{(x^2+1)^2} = \dfrac{1-x^2}{(x^2+1)^2}$

At a point where the tangent line is horizontal, we have $f'(x) = 0$ or $1 - x^2 = 0$ giving $x = \pm 1$. Therefore, the required points are $(-1, -\frac{1}{2})$ and $(1, \frac{1}{2})$.

47. $f(x) = (x^2+6)(x-5)$

$$f'(x) = (x^2+6)\frac{d}{dx}(x-5) + (x-5)\frac{d}{dx}(x^2+6)$$

$$= (x^2+6)(1) + (x-5)(2x) = x^2 + 6 + 2x^2 - 10x = 3x^2 - 10x + 6.$$

At a point where the slope of the tangent line is -2, we have
$$f'(x) = 3x^2 - 10x + 6 = -2.$$
This gives $3x^2 - 10x + 8 = (3x-4)(x-2) = 0$. So $x = \frac{4}{3}$ or $x = 2$.

Since $f(\frac{4}{3}) = (\frac{16}{9}+6)(\frac{4}{3}-5) = -\frac{770}{27}$ and $f(2) = (4+6)(2-5) = -30$, the required points are $(\frac{4}{3}, -\frac{770}{27})$ and $(2,-30)$.

48. $f(x) = \dfrac{x+1}{x-1}$

The slope of the tangent line at any point $(x, f(x))$ on the graph of f is

$$f'(x) = \frac{(x-1)\dfrac{d}{dx}(x+1)-(x+1)\dfrac{d}{dx}(x-1)}{(x-1)^2}$$

$$= \frac{(x-1)(1)-(x+1)(1)}{(x-1)^2} = -\frac{2}{(x-1)^2}.$$

At the point(s) where the slope is equal to -1/2, we have $-\dfrac{2}{(x-1)^2} = -\dfrac{1}{2}$

So $(x-1)^2 = 4$ and $x = 1 \pm 2 = -1$ or 3. Therefore, the required points are (-1,0) and (3,2).

49 $y = \dfrac{1}{1+x^2}$ $y' = \dfrac{(1+x^2)\dfrac{d}{dx}(1)-(1)\dfrac{d}{dx}(1+x^2)}{(1+x^2)^2} = \dfrac{-2x}{(1+x^2)^2}$

So, the slope of the tangent line at $(1,\frac{1}{2})$ is

$$y'\big|_{x=1} = \frac{-2x}{(1+x^2)^2}\bigg|_{x=1} = \frac{-2}{4} = -\frac{1}{2}$$

and the equation of the tangent line is $y - \frac{1}{2} = -\frac{1}{2}(x-1)$, or $y = -\frac{1}{2}x+1$.
Next, the slope of the required normal line is 2 and its equation is
$$y - \frac{1}{2} = 2(x-1), \quad \text{or} \quad y = 2x - \frac{3}{2}.$$

50. $C(t) = \dfrac{0.2t}{t^2+1}$

a.
$$C'(t) = \frac{(t^2+1)\dfrac{d}{dt}(0.2t)-(0.2t)\dfrac{d}{dt}(t^2+1)}{(t^2+1)^2}$$

$$= \frac{(t^2+1)(0.2)-(0.2t)(2t)}{(t^2+1)^2} = \frac{-0.2t^2+0.2}{(t^2+1)^2} = \frac{0.2(1-t^2)}{(t^2+1)^2}.$$

The rate of change of the concentration of the drug one-half hour after injection is $C'(\frac{1}{2}) = \dfrac{0.2(1-\frac{1}{4})}{(\frac{1}{4}+1)^2} = \dfrac{0.2(0.75)}{(1.25)^2} = 0.096$, or 0.096 percent/hr. The rate of change of the concentration of the drug one hour after injection is

$$C'(1) = \frac{0.2(1-1)}{(1+1)^2} = 0, \text{ or } 0 \text{ percent/hr.}$$

The rate of change of the concentration of the drug 2 hours after injection is

$$C'(2) = \frac{0.2(1-2^2)}{(2^2+1)^2} = \frac{0.2(-3)}{25} = -0.024, \text{ or } -0.024 \text{ percent/hr.}$$

51. $C(x) = \dfrac{0.5x}{100-x}$ $C'(x) = \dfrac{(100-x)(0.5)-0.5x(-1)}{(100-x)^2} = \dfrac{50}{(100-x)^2}.$

$C'(80) = \dfrac{50}{20^2} = 0.125 \ ;$ $C'(90) = \dfrac{50}{10^2} = 0.5,$

$C'(95) = \dfrac{50}{5^2} = 2;$ $C'(99) = \dfrac{50}{1} = 50.$

The rates of change of the cost in removing 80%, 90%, and 99% of the toxic waste are 0.125, 0.5, 2, and 50 million dollars per 1% more of the waste to be removed, respectively. It is too costly to remove *all* of the pollutant.

52. $D(t) = \dfrac{500t}{t+12}.$ So $D'(t) = \dfrac{(t+12)500-500t}{(t+12)^2} = \dfrac{6000}{(t+12)^2}.$

The rates of change for a six-year-old child and a ten-year-old child are

$$D'(6) = \frac{6000}{18^2} = 18.5 \text{ mg/yr} \quad \text{and} \quad D'(10) = \frac{6000}{22^2} = 12.4 \text{ mg/yr.}$$

53 $N(t) = \dfrac{10,000}{1+t^2} + 2000$

$N'(t) = \dfrac{d}{dt}[10,000(1+t^2)^{-1} + 2000] = -\dfrac{10,000}{(1+t^2)^2}(2t) = -\dfrac{20,000t}{(1+t^2)^2}.$

The rate of change after 1 minute and after 2 minutes is

$$N'(1) = -\frac{20,000}{(1+1^2)^2} = -5000; \ N'(2) = -\frac{20,000(2)}{(1+2^2)^2} = -1600.$$

The population of bacteria after one minute is $N(1) = \dfrac{10,000}{1+1} + 2000 = 7000$

The population after two minutes is $N(2) = \dfrac{10,000}{1+4} + 2000 = 4000.$

54. $d(x) = \dfrac{50}{0.01x^2 + 1}$, $d'(x) = \dfrac{(0.01x^2 + 1)(0) - 50(0.02x)}{(0.01x^2 + 1)^2} = -\dfrac{x}{(0.01x^2 + 1)^2}$

a. $d'(5) = -\dfrac{5}{(0.25 + 1)^2} = -3.2$, $d'(10) = -\dfrac{10}{(2)^2} = -2.5$, $d'(15) = -\dfrac{15}{(3.25)^2} = -1.4$,

So the rate of change of the quantity demanded when the quantity demanded is 5,000, 10,000, and 15,000, is decreasing at the rate of 3200, 2500, and 1400 per 1000 watches, respectively.

55 a. $N(t) = \dfrac{60t + 180}{t + 6}$.

$$N'(t) = \dfrac{(t+6)\dfrac{d}{dt}(60t + 180) - (60t + 180)\dfrac{d}{dt}(t+6)}{(t+6)^2}$$

$$= \dfrac{(t+6)(60) - (60t + 180)(1)}{(t+6)^2} = \dfrac{180}{(t+6)^2}$$

b. $N'(1) = \dfrac{180}{(1+6)^2} = 3.7$, $N'(3) = \dfrac{180}{(3+6)^2} = 2.2$, $N'(4) = \dfrac{180}{(4+6)^2} = 1.8$,

$N'(7) = \dfrac{180}{(7+6)^2} = 1.1$

We conclude that the rate at which the average student is increasing his or her speed one week, three weeks, four weeks, and seven weeks into the course is 3.7, 2.2, 1.8, and 1.1 words per minute, respectively

c. Yes

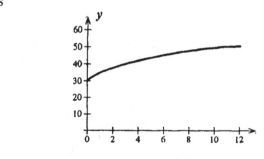

d. $N(12) = \dfrac{60(12) + 180}{12 + 6} = 50$, or 50 words/minute.

56. $T(x) = \dfrac{120x^2}{x^2 + 4}$.

$$T'(x) = \dfrac{(x^2 + 4)\dfrac{d}{dx}(120x^2) - (120x^2)\dfrac{d}{dx}(x^2 + 4)}{(x^2 + 4)^2}$$

$$= \dfrac{(x^2 + 4)(240x) - (120x^2)(2x)}{(x^2 + 4)^2} = \dfrac{960x}{(x^2 + 4)^2}$$

$T'(1) = \dfrac{960}{(1 + 4)^2} = \dfrac{960}{25} = 38.4$, or \$38.4 million per year. $T'(3) = \dfrac{960(3)}{(9 + 4)^2} = 17.04$,

or \$17.04 million per year.

$T'(5) = \dfrac{960(5)}{(25 + 4)^2} = 5.71$, or \$5.71 million per year.

57. $f(t) = \dfrac{0.055t + 0.26}{t + 2}$; $f'(t) = \dfrac{(t + 2)(0.055) - (0.055t + 0.26)(1)}{(t + 2)^2} = -\dfrac{0.15}{(t + 2)^2}$

At the beginning, the formaldehyde level is changing at the rate of

$$f'(0) = -\dfrac{0.15}{4} = -0.0375;$$

that is, it is dropping at the rate of 0.0375 parts per million per year. Next,

$$f'(3) = -\dfrac{0.15}{5^2} = -0.006,$$

and so the level is dropping at the rate of 0.006 parts per million per year at the beginning of the fourth year ($t = 3$).

58. a. $P(t) = \dfrac{25t^2 + 125t + 200}{t^2 + 5t + 40}$. The rate at which Glen Cove's population is

changing with respect to time is given by

$$P'(t) = \dfrac{(t^2 + 5t + 40)\dfrac{d}{dt}(25t^2 + 125t + 200) - (25t^2 + 125t + 200)\dfrac{d}{dt}(t^2 + 5t + 40)}{(t^2 + 5t + 40)^2}$$

$$= \dfrac{(t^2 + 5t + 40)(50t + 125) - (25t^2 + 125t + 200)(2t + 5)}{(t^2 + 5t + 40)^2}$$

$$= \dfrac{25(2t + 5)(t^2 + 5t + 40 - t^2 - 5t - 8)}{(t^2 + 5t + 40)^2} = \dfrac{(25)(32)(2t + 5)}{(t^2 + 5t + 40)^2} = \dfrac{800(2t + 5)}{(t^2 + 5t + 40)^2}.$$

b. After ten years the population will be

$$P(10) = \frac{25(10)^2 + 125(10) + 200}{(10)^2 + 5(10) + 40} = \frac{3950}{190} = 20.790, \quad \text{or } 20,790.$$

After ten years the population will be increasing at the rate of

$$P'(10) = \frac{800[2(10) + 5]}{[(10)^2 + 5(10) + 40]^2} = \frac{20,000}{190^2} = 0.554, \quad \text{or } 554 \text{ people per year.}$$

59. False. Take $f(x) = x$ and $g(x) = x$. Then $f(x)g(x) = x^2$ So

$$\frac{d}{dx}[f(x)g(x)] = \frac{d}{dx}(x^2) = 2x \neq f'(x)g'(x) = 1$$

60. True. Using the Product Rule,

$$\frac{d}{dx}[x f(x)] = f(x)\frac{d}{dx}(x) + x\frac{d}{dx}[f(x)] = f(x)(1) + xf'(x)$$

61. False. Let $f(x) = x^3$. Then

$$\frac{d}{dx}\left[\frac{f(x)}{x^2}\right] = \frac{d}{dx}\left(\frac{x^3}{x^2}\right) = \frac{d}{dx}(x) = 1 \neq \frac{f'(x)}{2x} = \frac{3x^2}{2x} = \frac{3}{2}x.$$

62. True. Using the Quotient Rule followed by the Product Rule

$$\frac{d}{dx}\left[\frac{f(x)g(x)}{h(x)}\right] = \frac{h(x)\frac{d}{dx}[f(x)g(x)] - f(x)g(x)\frac{d}{dx}[h(x)]}{[h(x)]^2}$$

$$= \frac{h(x)[f'(x)g(x) + f(x)g'(x)] - f(x)g(x)h'(x)}{[h(x)]^2}.$$

63. Let $f(x) = u(x)v(x)$ and $g(x) = w(x)$. Then $h(x) = f(x)g(x)$. Therefore,
$$h'(x) = f'(x)g(x) + f(x)g'(x).$$
But $\quad f'(x) = u(x)v'(x) + u'(x)v(x)$.
Therefore, $h'(x) = [u(x)v'(x) + u'(x)v(x)]g(x) + u(x)v(x)w'(x)$
$$= u(x)v(x)w'(x) + u(x)v'(x)w(x) + u'(x)v(x)w(x).$$

64. Let $k(x) = f(x)/g(x)$. Then

a.
$$\frac{k(x+h)-k(x)}{h}=\frac{\dfrac{f(x+h)}{g(x+h)}-\dfrac{f(x)}{g(x)}}{h}=\frac{f(x+h)g(x)-f(x)g(x+h)}{hg(x+h)g(x)}$$

b. By adding $[-f(x)g(x)+f(x)g(x)]$, which is zero, to the numerator, and simplifying, we have

$$\frac{k(x+h)-k(x)}{h}=\frac{1}{g(x+h)g(x)}\left\{\left[\frac{f(x+h)-f(x)}{h}\right]g(x)-\left[\frac{g(x+h)-g(x)}{h}\right]f(x)\right\}$$

c. Taking the limit and using the definition of the derivative, we find

$$k'(x)=\lim_{h\to 0}\frac{k(x+h)-k(x)}{h}=\frac{1}{[g(x)]^2}\left[f'(x)g(x)-g'(x)f(x)\right]$$

$$=\frac{f'(x)g(x)-g'(x)f(x)}{[g(x)]^2}$$

USING TECHNOLOGY EXERCISES 3.2, page 184

1. 0.8750   2. 16.7987   3 0.0774   4. -0.1314   5. -0.5000   6. 2.875
7 87,322 per year   8. a. 20,790   b. 554/year

3.3 CONCEPT QUESTIONS, page 192

1. The derivative of $h(x)=g[f(x)]$ is equal to the derivative of g evaluated at $f(x)$ times the derivative of f.

2. $h'(x)=\dfrac{d}{dx}[(f(x))]^n=n[f(x)]^{n-1}f'(x)$

EXERCISES 3.3, page 192

1. $f(x)=(2x-1)^4.$ $f'(x)=4(2x-1)^3\dfrac{d}{dx}(2x-1)=4(2x-1)^3(2)=8(2x-1)^3$

2. $f(x)=(1-x)^3;$ $f'(x)=3(1-x)^2(-1)=-3(1-x)^2$

3. $f(x)=(x^2+2)^5.$ $f'(x)=5(x^2+2)^4(2x)=10x(x^2+2)^4$

4. $f(t) = 2(t^3 - 1)^5$; $f'(t) = (2)(5)(t^3 - 1)^4 (3t^2) = 30t^2 (t^3 - 1)^4$.

5. $f(x) = (2x - x^2)^3$.

   $f'(x) = 3(2x - x^2)^2 \dfrac{d}{dx}(2x - x^2) = 3(2x - x^2)^2 (2 - 2x) = 6x^2 (1 - x)(2 - x)^2$

6. $f(x) = 3(x^3 - x)^4$. $f'(x) = (3)(4)(x^3 - x)^3 (3x^2 - 1) = 12(3x^2 - 1)(x^3 - x)^3$.

7. $f(x) = (2x + 1)^{-2}$

   $f'(x) = -2(2x + 1)^{-3} \dfrac{d}{dx}(2x + 1) = -2(2x + 1)^{-3}(2) = -4(2x + 1)^{-3}$

8. $f(t) = \frac{1}{2}(2t^2 + t)^{-3}$. $f'(t) = \frac{1}{2}(-3)(2t^2 + t)^{-4}(4t + 1) = -\dfrac{3(1 + 4t)}{2(2t^2 + t)^4}$

9. $f(x) = (x^2 - 4)^{3/2}$.

   $f'(x) = \frac{3}{2}(x^2 - 4)^{1/2} \dfrac{d}{dx}(x^2 - 4) = \frac{3}{2}(x^2 - 4)^{1/2}(2x) = 3x(x^2 - 4)^{1/2}$

10. $f(t) = (3t^2 - 2t + 1)^{3/2}$. $f'(t) = \frac{3}{2}(3t^2 - 2t + 1)^{1/2}(6t - 2) = 3(3t - 1)(3t^2 - 2t + 1)^{1/2}$

11. $f(x) = \sqrt{3x - 2} = (3x - 2)^{1/2}$

    $f'(x) = \dfrac{1}{2}(3x - 2)^{-1/2}(3) = \dfrac{3}{2}(3x - 2)^{-1/2} = \dfrac{3}{2\sqrt{3x - 2}}$.

12. $f(t) = \sqrt{3t^2 - t} = (3t^2 - t)^{1/2}$. $f'(t) = \frac{1}{2}(3t^2 - t)^{-1/2}(6t - 1) = \dfrac{6t - 1}{2\sqrt{3t^2 - t}}$

13. $f(x) = \sqrt[3]{1 - x^2}$.

    $f'(x) = \dfrac{d}{dx}(1 - x^2)^{1/3} = \dfrac{1}{3}(1 - x^2)^{-2/3} \dfrac{d}{dx}(1 - x^2)$

    $= \dfrac{1}{3}(1 - x^2)^{-2/3}(-2x) = -\dfrac{2}{3}x(1 - x^2)^{-2/3} = \dfrac{-2x}{3(1 - x^2)^{2/3}}$

14. $f(x) = \sqrt{2x^2 - 2x + 3}$.

$$f'(x) = \tfrac{1}{2}(2x^2 - 2x + 3)^{-1/2}(4x - 2) = (2x - 1)(2x^2 - 2x + 3)^{-1/2}$$

15. $f(x) = \dfrac{1}{(2x + 3)^3} = (2x + 3)^{-3}$

$$f'(x) = -3(2x + 3)^{-4}(2) = -6(2x + 3)^{-4} = -\dfrac{6}{(2x + 3)^4}.$$

16. $f(x) = \dfrac{2}{(x^2 - 1)^4}.$

$$f'(x) = 2\dfrac{d}{dx}(x^2 - 1)^{-4} = 2(-4)(x^2 - 1)^{-5}(2x) = -16x(x^2 - 1)^{-5}$$

17. $f(t) = \dfrac{1}{\sqrt{2t - 3}}.$

$$f'(t) = \dfrac{d}{dt}(2t - 3)^{-1/2} = -\dfrac{1}{2}(2t - 3)^{-3/2}(2) = -(2t - 3)^{-3/2} = -\dfrac{1}{(2t - 3)^{3/2}}$$

18. $f(x) = \dfrac{1}{\sqrt{2x^2 - 1}} = (2x^2 - 1)^{-1/2} \quad f'(x) = -\dfrac{1}{2}(2x^2 - 1)^{-3/2}(4x) = -\dfrac{2x}{\sqrt{2x^2 - 1)^3}}.$

19 $y = \dfrac{1}{(4x^4 + x)^{3/2}}.$

$$\dfrac{dy}{dx} = \dfrac{d}{dx}(4x^4 + x)^{-3/2} = -\dfrac{3}{2}(4x^4 + x)^{-5/2}(16x^3 + 1) = -\dfrac{3}{2}(16x^3 + 1)(4x^4 + x)^{-5/2}$$

20. $f(t) = \dfrac{4}{\sqrt[3]{2t^2 + t}}.$

$$f'(t) = 4\dfrac{d}{dt}(2t^2 + t)^{-1/3} = -\dfrac{4}{3}(2t^2 + t)^{-4/3}(4t + 1) = -\dfrac{4}{3}(4t + 1)(2t^2 + t)^{-4/3}$$

21. $f(x) = (3x^2 + 2x + 1)^{-2}.$

$$f'(x) = -2(3x^2 + 2x + 1)^{-3}\dfrac{d}{dx}(3x^2 + 2x + 1)$$

$$= -2(3x^2 + 2x + 1)^{-3}(6x + 2) = -4(3x + 1)(3x^2 + 2x + 1)^{-3}$$

22. $f(t) = (5t^3 + 2t^2 - t + 4)^{-3}$ $f'(t) = -3(5t^3 + 2t^2 - t + 4)^{-4}(15t^2 + 4t - 1)$.

23 $f(x) = (x^2 + 1)^3 - (x^3 + 1)^2$

$$f'(x) = 3(x^2 + 1)^2 \frac{d}{dx}(x^2 + 1) - 2(x^3 + 1)\frac{d}{dx}(x^3 + 1)$$
$$= 3(x^2 + 1)^2(2x) - 2(x^3 + 1)(3x^2)$$
$$= 6x[(x^2 + 1)^2 - x(x^3 + 1)] = 6x(2x^2 - x + 1).$$

24. $f(t) = (2t - 1)^4 + (2t + 1)^4$

$$f'(t) = 4(2t - 1)^3(2) + 4(2t + 1)^3(2) = 8[(2t - 1)^3 + (2t + 1)^3].$$

25 $f(t) = (t^{-1} - t^{-2})^3$. $f'(t) = 3(t^{-1} - t^{-2})^2 \dfrac{d}{dt}(t^{-1} - t^{-2}) = 3(t^{-1} - t^{-2})^2(-t^{-2} + 2t^{-3})$.

26. $f(v) = (v^{-3} + 4v^{-2})^3$. $f'(v) = 3(v^{-3} + 4v^{-2})^2(-3v^{-4} - 8v^{-3})$.

27 $f(x) = \sqrt{x + 1} + \sqrt{x - 1} = (x + 1)^{1/2} + (x - 1)^{1/2}$

$$f'(x) = \tfrac{1}{2}(x + 1)^{-1/2}(1) + \tfrac{1}{2}(x - 1)^{-1/2}(1) = \tfrac{1}{2}[(x + 1)^{-1/2} + (x - 1)^{-1/2}].$$

28. $f(u) = (2u + 1)^{3/2} + (u^2 - 1)^{-3/2}$.

$$f'(u) = \tfrac{3}{2}(2u + 1)^{1/2}(2) - \tfrac{3}{2}(u^2 - 1)^{-5/2}(2u) = 3(2u + 1)^{1/2} - 3u(u^2 - 1)^{-5/2}$$

29 $f(x) = 2x^2(3 - 4x)^4$.

$$f'(x) = 2x^2(4)(3 - 4x)^3(-4) + (3 - 4x)^4(4x) = 4x(3 - 4x)^3(-8x + 3 - 4x)$$
$$= 4x(3 - 4x)^3(-12x + 3) = (-12x)(4x - 1)(3 - 4x)^3.$$

30. $h(t) = t^2(3t + 4)^3$

$$h'(t) = 2t(3t + 4)^3 + t^2(3)(3t + 4)^2(3) = t(3t + 4)^2[2(3t + 4) + 9t]$$
$$= t(15t + 8)(3t + 4)^2.$$

31. $f(x) = (x - 1)^2(2x + 1)^4$

$$f'(x) = (x-1)^2 \frac{d}{dx}(2x+1)^4 + (2x+1)^4 \frac{d}{dx}(x-1)^2 \quad \text{[Product Rule]}$$

$$= (x-1)^2(4)(2x+1)^3 \frac{d}{dx}(2x+1) + (2x+1)^4(2)(x-1)\frac{d}{dx}(x-1)$$

$$= 8(x-1)^2(2x+1)^3 + 2(x-1)(2x+1)^4$$

$$= 2(x-1)(2x+1)^3(4x-4+2x+1) = 6(x-1)(2x-1)(2x+1)^3$$

32. $g(u) = (1+u^2)^5(1-2u^2)^8.$

$$g'(u) = (1+u^2)^5(8)(1-2u^2)^7(-4u) + (1-2u^2)^8(5)(1+u^2)^4(2u)$$

$$= -2u(1+u^2)^4(1-2u^2)^7[16(1+u^2) - 5(1-2u^2)]$$

$$= -2u(26u^2+11)(1+u^2)^4(1-2u^2)^7.$$

33. $f(x) = \left(\dfrac{x+3}{x-2}\right)^3$

$$f'(x) = 3\left(\frac{x+3}{x-2}\right)^2 \frac{d}{dx}\left(\frac{x-3}{x-2}\right) = 3\left(\frac{x+3}{x-2}\right)^2\left[\frac{(x-2)(1)-(x+3)(1)}{(x-2)^2}\right]$$

$$= 3\left(\frac{x+3}{x-2}\right)^2\left[-\frac{5}{(x-2)^2}\right] = -\frac{15(x+3)^2}{(x-2)^4}$$

34. $f(x) = \left(\dfrac{x+1}{x-1}\right)^5.$ $f'(x) = 5\left(\dfrac{x+1}{x-1}\right)^4\left[\dfrac{(x-1)(1)-(x+1)(1)}{(x-1)^2}\right] = -\dfrac{10(x+1)^4}{(x-1)^6}$

35. $s(t) = \left(\dfrac{t}{2t+1}\right)^{3/2}.$

$$s'(t) = \frac{3}{2}\left(\frac{t}{2t+1}\right)^{1/2} \frac{d}{dt}\left(\frac{t}{2t+1}\right) = \frac{3}{2}\left(\frac{t}{2t+1}\right)^{1/2}\left[\frac{(2t+1)(1)-t(2)}{(2t+1)^2}\right]$$

$$= \frac{3}{2}\left(\frac{t}{2t+1}\right)^{1/2}\left[\frac{1}{(2t+1)^2}\right] = \frac{3t^{1/2}}{2(2t+1)^{5/2}}$$

36. $g(s) = \left(s^2 + \dfrac{1}{s}\right)^{3/2} = (s^2 + s^{-1})^{3/2}$

$$g'(s) = \frac{3}{2}(s^2 + s^{-1})^{1/2}(2s - s^{-2}) = \frac{3}{2}(s^2 + \frac{1}{s})^{1/2}(2s - \frac{1}{s^2}) = \frac{3}{2}(\frac{s^3+1}{s})^{1/2}(\frac{2s^3-1}{s^2}).$$

37 $g(u) = \left(\dfrac{u+1}{3u+2}\right)^{1/2}.$

$$g'(u) = \frac{1}{2}\left(\frac{u+1}{3u+2}\right)^{-1/2} \frac{d}{du}\left(\frac{u+1}{3u+2}\right)$$

$$= \frac{1}{2}\left(\frac{u+1}{3u+2}\right)^{-1/2}\left[\frac{(3u+2)(1)-(u+1)(3)}{(3u+2)^2}\right] = -\frac{1}{2\sqrt{u+1}(3u+2)^{3/2}}$$

38. $g(x) = \left(\dfrac{2x+1}{2x-1}\right)^{1/2}.$

$$g'(x) = \frac{1}{2}\left(\frac{2x+1}{2x-1}\right)^{-1/2}\left[\frac{(2x-1)(2)-(2x+1)(2)}{(2x-1)^2}\right]$$

$$= \frac{1}{2}\left(\frac{2x+1}{2x-1}\right)^{-1/2}\left(-\frac{4}{(2x-1)^2}\right) = -\frac{2}{(2x+1)^{1/2}(2x-1)^{3/2}}$$

39 $f(x) = \dfrac{x^2}{(x^2-1)^4}.$

$$f'(x) = \frac{(x^2-1)^4 \dfrac{d}{dx}(x^2) - (x^2)\dfrac{d}{dx}(x^2-1)^4}{\left[(x^2-1)^4\right]^2}$$

$$= \frac{(x^2-1)^4(2x) - x^2(4)(x^2-1)^3(2x)}{(x^2-1)^8}$$

$$= \frac{(x^2-1)^3(2x)(x^2-1-4x^2)}{(x^2-1)^8} = \frac{(-2x)(3x^2+1)}{(x^2-1)^5}$$

40. $g(u) = \dfrac{2u^2}{(u^2+u)^3}$

$$g'(u) = \frac{(u^2+u)^3(4u) - (2u^2)3(u^2+u)^2(2u+1)}{(u^2+u)^6}$$

$$= \frac{2u(u^2+u)^2[2(u^2+u) - 3u(2u+1)]}{(u^2+u)^6} = \frac{-2u(4u^2+u)}{(u^2+u)^4} = \frac{-2u^2(4u+1)}{(u^2+u)^4}.$$

41 $h(x) = \dfrac{(3x^2+1)^3}{(x^2-1)^4}$.

$h'(x) = \dfrac{(x^2-1)^4(3)(3x^2+1)^2(6x) - (3x^2+1)^3(4)(x^2-1)^3(2x)}{(x^2-1)^8}$

$\quad\quad = \dfrac{2x(x^2-1)^3(3x^2+1)^2[9(x^2-1)-4(3x^2+1)]}{(x^2-1)^8}$

$\quad\quad = -\dfrac{2x(3x^2+13)(3x^2+1)^2}{(x^2-1)^5}$

42. $g(t) = \dfrac{(2t-1)^2}{(3t+2)^4}$.

$g'(t) = \dfrac{(3t+2)^4(2)(2t-1)(2) - (2t-1)^2(4)(3t+2)^3(3)}{(3t+2)^8}$

$\quad\quad = \dfrac{2(3t+2)^3(2t-1)[2(3t+2)-6(2t-1)]}{(3t+2)^8} = \dfrac{4(2t-1)(5-3t)}{(3t+2)^5}$

43 $f(x) = \dfrac{\sqrt{2x+1}}{x^2-1}$.

$f'(x) = \dfrac{(x^2-1)(\frac{1}{2})(2x+1)^{-1/2}(2) - (2x+1)^{1/2}(2x)}{(x^2-1)^2}$

$\quad\quad = \dfrac{(2x+1)^{-1/2}[(x^2-1)-(2x+1)(2x)]}{(x^2-1)^2} = -\dfrac{3x^2+2x+1}{\sqrt{2x+1}(x^2-1)^2}$

44. $f(t) = \dfrac{4t^2}{\sqrt{2t^2+2t-1}} = \dfrac{4t^2}{(2t^2+2t-1)^{1/2}}$

$f'(t) = \dfrac{(2t^2+2t-1)^{1/2}\dfrac{d}{dt}(4t^2) - 4t^2\dfrac{d}{dt}(2t^2+2t-1)^{1/2}}{[(2t^2+2t-1)^{1/2}]^2}$

$\quad\quad = \dfrac{(2t^2+2t-1)^{1/2}(8t) - 4t^2(\frac{1}{2})(2t^2+2t-1)^{-1/2}(4t+2)}{2t^2+2t-1}$

$$= \frac{4t(2t^2 + 2t - 1)^{-1/2}[2(2t^2 + 2t - 1) - t(2t + 1)]}{2t^2 + 2t - 1} = \frac{4t(2t^2 + 3t - 2)}{\left(\sqrt{2t^2 + 2t - 1}\right)^3}$$

45 $g(t) = \dfrac{(t+1)^{1/2}}{(t^2+1)^{1/2}}.$

$$g'(t) = \frac{(t^2+1)^{1/2} \dfrac{d}{dt}(t+1)^{1/2} - (t+1)^{1/2} \dfrac{d}{dt}(t^2+1)^{1/2}}{t^2+1}$$

$$= \frac{(t^2+1)^{1/2}(\frac{1}{2})(t+1)^{-1/2}(1) - (t+1)^{1/2}(\frac{1}{2})(t^2+1)^{-1/2}(2t)}{t^2+1}$$

$$= \frac{\frac{1}{2}(t+1)^{-1/2}(t^2+1)^{-1/2}[(t^2+1) - 2t(t+1)]}{t^2+1} = -\frac{t^2+2t-1}{2\sqrt{t+1}(t^2+1)^{3/2}}$$

46. $f(x) = \dfrac{(x^2+1)^{1/2}}{(x^2-1)^{1/2}}.$

$$f'(x) = \frac{(x^2-1)^{1/2}(\frac{1}{2})(x^2+1)^{-1/2}(2x) - (x^2+1)^{1/2}(\frac{1}{2})(x^2-1)^{-1/2}(2x)}{x^2-1}$$

$$= \frac{x(x^2-1)^{-1/2}(x^2+1)^{-1/2}[(x^2-1) - (x^2+1)]}{x^2-1} = -\frac{2x}{\sqrt{x^2+1}(x^2-1)^{3/2}}$$

47. $f(x) = (3x+1)^4(x^2-x+1)^3$

$$f'(x) = (3x+1)^4 \cdot \frac{d}{dx}(x^2-x+1)^3 + (x^2-x+1)^3 \frac{d}{dx}(3x+1)^4$$

$$= (3x+1)^4 \; 3(x^2-x+1)^2(2x-1) + (x^2-x+1)^3 \cdot 4(3x+1)^3 \cdot 3$$

$$= 3(3x+1)^3(x^2-x+1)^2[(3x+1)(2x-1) + 4(x^2-x+1)]$$

$$= 3(3x+1)^3(x^2-x+1)^2(6x^2-3x+2x-1+4x^2-4x+4)$$

$$= 3(3x+1)^3(x^2-x+1)^2(10x^2-5x+3)$$

48. $g(t) = (2t+3)^2(3t^2-1)^{-3}$

$$g'(t) = (2t+3)^2 \frac{d}{dt}(3t^2-1)^{-3} + (3t^2-1)^{-3} \frac{d}{dt}(2t+3)^2$$

$$= (2t+3)^2(-3)(3t^2-1)^{-4}(6t) + (3t^2-1)^{-3}(2)(2t+3)(2)$$

$$= 2(2t+3)(3t^2-1)^{-4}[-9t(2t+3)+2(3t^2-1)]$$
$$= 2(2t+3)(3t^2-1)^{-4}(-18t^2-27t+6t^2-2)$$
$$= -2(12t^2+27t+2)(2t+3)(3t^2-1)^{-4}$$

49 $y = g(u) = u^{4/3}$ and $\dfrac{dy}{du} = \dfrac{4}{3}u^{1/3}$, $u = f(x) = 3x^2 - 1$, and $\dfrac{du}{dx} = 6x$.

So $\dfrac{dy}{dx} = \dfrac{dy}{du} \cdot \dfrac{du}{dx} = \tfrac{4}{3}u^{1/3}(6x) = \tfrac{4}{3}(3x^2-1)^{1/3}6x = 8x(3x^2-1)^{1/3}$

50. $\dfrac{dy}{du} = \tfrac{1}{2}u^{-1/2}$, $\dfrac{du}{dx} = 7-4x$. Therefore, $\dfrac{dy}{dx} = \dfrac{dy}{du} \cdot \dfrac{du}{dx} = \dfrac{7-4x}{2\sqrt{u}} = \dfrac{7-4x}{2\sqrt{7x-2x^2}}$

51. $\dfrac{dy}{du} = -\dfrac{2}{3}u^{-5/3} = -\dfrac{2}{3u^{5/3}}$, $\dfrac{du}{dx} = 6x^2 - 1$.

$\dfrac{dy}{dx} = \dfrac{dy}{du} \cdot \dfrac{du}{dx} = -\dfrac{2(6x^2-1)}{3u^{5/3}} = -\dfrac{2(6x^2-1)}{3(2x^3-x+1)^{5/3}}$.

52. $\dfrac{dy}{du} = 4u$, $\dfrac{du}{dx} = 2x$. $\dfrac{dy}{dx} = \dfrac{dy}{du} \cdot \dfrac{du}{dx} = 4u(2x) = 8xu = 8x(x^2+1)$.

53 $\dfrac{dy}{du} = \tfrac{1}{2}u^{-1/2} - \tfrac{1}{2}u^{-3/2}$, $\dfrac{du}{dx} = 3x^2 - 1$.

$\dfrac{dy}{dx} = \dfrac{dy}{du} \cdot \dfrac{du}{dx} = \left[\dfrac{1}{2\sqrt{x^3-x}} - \dfrac{1}{2(x^3-x)^{3/2}} \right](3x^2-1)$

$= \dfrac{(3x^2-1)(x^3-x-1)}{2(x^3-x)^{3/2}}$

54. $\dfrac{dy}{du} = -\dfrac{1}{u^2}$, $\dfrac{du}{dx} = \dfrac{1}{2}x^{-1/2}$; $\dfrac{dy}{dx} = \dfrac{dy}{du} \cdot \dfrac{du}{dx} = -\dfrac{1}{u^2} \cdot \left(\dfrac{1}{2}x^{-1/2}\right) = -\dfrac{1}{2\sqrt{x}(\sqrt{x}+1)^2}$

55. $F(x) = g(f(x))$; $F'(x) = g'(f(x))f'(x)$ and $F'(2) = g'(3)(-3) = (4)(-3) = -12$

56. $h = f(g(x))$; $h'(0) = f'(g(0))g'(0) = f'(5)\ 3 = -2 \cdot 3 = -6$.

57. Let $g(x) = x^2 + 1$, then $F(x) = f(g(x))$. Next, $F'(x) = f'(g(x))g'(x)$
and $F'(1) = f'(2)(2x) = (3)(2) = 6$.

58. No. Let $F(x) = f(f(x))$. Then $F'(x) = f'(f(x))f'(x)$. Then let $f(x) = x^2$.
$f(f(x)) = f(x^2) = x^4$; $F'(x) = 4x^3$, $f'(x) = 2x$; and $[f'(x)]^2 = 4x^2$

59. No. Suppose $h = g(f(x))$. Let $f(x) = x$ and $g(x) = x^2$. Then
$h = g(f(x)) = g(x) = x^2$ and $h'(x) = 2x \neq g'(f'(x)) = g'(1) = 2(1) = 2$.

60. $h = f(g(x))$; $h' = f'(g(x))g'(x)$ and $f' \circ g = f'(g(x))$; $(f' \circ g)g' = f'(g(x)g'(x))$

61. $f(x) = (1-x)(x^2-1)^2$
$f'(x) = (1-x)2(x^2-1)(2x) + (-1)(x^2-1)^2$
$= (x^2-1)(4x-4x^2-x^2+1) = (x^2-1)(-5x^2+4x+1)$.
Therefore, the slope of the tangent line at $(2,-9)$ is
$f'(2) = [(2)^2-1][-5(2)^2+4(2)+1] = -33$.
Then the required equation is $y+9 = -33(x-2)$, or $y = -33x + 57$.

62. $f(x) = \left(\dfrac{x+1}{x-1}\right)^2$

$f'(x) = 2\left(\dfrac{x+1}{x-1}\right)\left[\dfrac{(x-1)(1)-(x+1)(1)}{(x-1)^2}\right] = 2\left(\dfrac{x+1}{x-1}\right)\left[-\dfrac{2}{(x-1)^2}\right]$.

The slope of the tangent line is $f'(3) = 2(\frac{4}{2})(-\frac{2}{4}) = -2$.
An equation of the tangent line is $y - 4 = -2(x-3)$, or $y = -2x + 10$.

63. $f(x) = x\sqrt{2x^2+7}$. $f'(x) = \sqrt{2x^2+7} + x(\frac{1}{2})(2x^2+7)^{-1/2}(4x)$.
The slope of the tangent line is $f'(3) = \sqrt{25} + (\frac{3}{2})(25)^{-1/2}(12) = \frac{43}{5}$.
An equation of the tangent line is $y - 15 = \frac{43}{5}(x-3)$ or $y = \frac{43}{5}x - \frac{54}{5}$.

64. $f(x) = \dfrac{8}{\sqrt{x^2+6x}} = 8(x^2+6x)^{-1/2}$
$f'(x) = -\frac{1}{2}(8)(x^2+6x)^{-3/2}(2x+6) = -4(2x+6)(x^2+6x)^{-3/2}$

Therefore, the slope of the tangent line at (2,2) is
$$f'(2) = -4(10)(4+12)^{-3/2} = -4(10)(16)^{-3/2} = -40(\tfrac{1}{64}) = -\tfrac{5}{8}.$$
An equation of the tangent line is $y - 2 = -\tfrac{5}{8}x + \tfrac{13}{4}$, or $y = -\tfrac{5}{8}x + \tfrac{21}{4}$.

65. $N(t) = (60+2t)^{2/3}$. $N'(t) = \tfrac{2}{3}(60+2t)^{-1/3}\dfrac{d}{dt}(60+2t) = \tfrac{4}{3}(60+2t)^{-1/3}$

The rate of increase at the end of the second week is
$$N'(2) = \tfrac{4}{3}(64)^{-1/3} = \tfrac{1}{3}, \text{ or } \tfrac{1}{3}\text{ million/week}$$
At the end of the 12th week, $N'(12) = \tfrac{4}{3}(84)^{-1/3} \approx 0.3$ million/wk. The number of viewers in the 2nd and 24th week are $N(2) = (60+4)^{2/3} = 16$ million and $N(24) = (60+48)^{2/3} = 22.7$ million, respectively.

66. $N'(t) = 0.0018425(2.5)(t+5)^{1.5} = 0.00460625(t+5)^{1.5}$. In 2005,
$N'(5) = 0.00460625(10^{1.5}) \approx 0.145662$, or 145,662/yr. In 2010,
$N'(10) = 0.00460625(15^{1.5}) \approx 0.267599$, or 267,599/yr.

67. $P(t) = 33.55(t+5)^{0.205}$. $P'(t) = 33.55(0.205)(t+5)^{-0.795}(1) = 6.87775(t+5)^{-0.795}$
The rate of change at the beginning of 2000 is
$$P'(20) = 6.87775(25)^{-0.795} \approx 0.5322 \text{ or } 0.53\%/\text{yr}.$$
The percent of these mothers was $P(20) = 33.55(25)^{0.205} \approx 64.90$, or 64.9%.

68. $A'(t) = 699\dfrac{d}{dt}(t+1)^{-0.94} = -657.06(t+1)^{-1.94}$

At the beginning of 2002, $A'(0) = -657.06$ so, it is falling at the rate of \$657.06/yr. At the beginning of 2006, $A'(4) = 28.95$. So it will be falling at the rate of \$28.95/yr.

69. a. $f(t) = 23.7(0.2t+1)^{1.32}$. The rate of change at any time t is given by
$$f'(t) = (23.7)(1.32)(0.2t+1)^{0.32}(0.2) = 6.2568(0.2t+1)^{0.32}$$
At the beginning of 2000, the rate of change is
$$f'(9) = 6.2568[0.2(9)+1]^{0.32} \approx 8.6985, \text{ or approximately } \$8.7 \text{ billion/yr}.$$
b. The assets were $f(9) = 92.256$, or \$92.3 billion.

70. $f(t) = 10.72(0.9t+10)^{0.3}$. The rate of change at any time t is given by

$f'(t) = 10.72(0.3)(0.9t + 10)^{-0.7}(0.9) = 2.8944(0.9t + 10)^{-0.7}$ At the beginning of 2000, we find $f'(0) = 2.8944(10)^{-0.7} \approx 0.5775$, or 0.6%/yr. At the beginning of 2010, we have $f'(10) = 2.8944(9 + 10)^{-0.7} \approx 0.3685$, or 0.4% / yr.

The percent of the population of Americans age 55 or over in 2010 is

$$f(10) = 10.72(9 + 10)^{0.3} \approx 25.93, \text{ or } 25.9\%.$$

71. $C(t) = 0.01(0.2t^2 + 4t + 64)^{2/3}$.

   a. $C'(t) = 0.01(\frac{2}{3})(0.2t^2 + 4t + 64)^{-1/3} \dfrac{d}{dt}(0.2t^2 + 4t + 64)$

            $= (0.01)(0.667)(0.4t + 4)(0.2t^2 + 4t + 4)^{-1/3}$

            $= 0.027(0.1t + 1)(0.2t^2 + 4t + 64)^{-1/3}$

   b. $C'(5) = 0.007[0.4(5) + 4][0.2(25) + 4(5) + 64]^{-1/3} \approx 0.009$,

   or 0.009 parts per million per year.

72. $N(t) = -\dfrac{20{,}000}{\sqrt{1 + 0.2t}} + 21{,}000.$ $N'(t) = -20{,}000(-\frac{1}{2})(1 + 0.2t)^{-3/2}(0.2) = \dfrac{2000}{(1 + 0.2t)^{3/2}}$

   $N'(0) = 2000$, or 2000 students/yr. $N'(5) = \dfrac{2000}{[1 + 0.2(5)]^{3/2}} \approx 707$, or 707 students/yr.

73. a. $A(t) = 0.03t^3(t - 7)^4 + 60.2$

      $A'(t) = 0.03[3t^2(t - 7)^4 + t^3(4)(t - 7)^3] = 0.03t^2(t - 7)^3[3(t - 7) + 4t]$

      $= 0.21t^2(t - 3)(t - 7)^3$.

   b. $A'(1) = 0.21(-2)(-6)^3 = 90.72$; $A'(3) = 0$. $A'(4) = 0.21(16)(1)(-3)^3 = -90.72$.

   The amount of pollutant is increasing at the rate of 90.72 units/hr at 8 A.M. Its rate of change is 0 units/hr at 10 A.M.; its rate of change is –90.72 units/hr at 11 A.M.

74. $N(x) = (10{,}000 - 40x - 0.02x^2)^{1/2}$

   $N'(x) = \frac{1}{2}(10{,}000 - 40x - 0.02x^2)^{-1/2}(-40 - 0.04x)$.

   Then, $N'(10) = \frac{1}{2}(10{,}000 - 400 - 2)^{-1/2}(-40 - 0.4) = \frac{1}{2}(9598)^{-1/2}(-40.4) = -0.2062$,

   or a 20.6 percent drop in consumption/percentage increase in tax.

   Similarly, $N'(100) \approx -0.2889$, or a drop of 28.9%, and $N'(150) \approx -0.3860$, or a drop of 38.6%.

75. $P(t) = \dfrac{300\sqrt{\frac{1}{2}t^2 + 2t + 25}}{t + 25} = \dfrac{300(\frac{1}{2}t^2 + 2t + 25)^{1/2}}{t + 25}$.

$$P'(t) = 300\left[\frac{(t+25)\frac{1}{2}(\frac{1}{2}t^2+2t+25)^{-1/2}(t+2)-(\frac{1}{2}t^2+2t+25)^{1/2}(1)}{(t+25)^2}\right]$$

$$= 300\left[\frac{(\frac{1}{2}t^2+2t+25)^{-1/2}[(t+25)(t+2)-2(\frac{1}{2}t^2+2t+25)]}{(t+25)^2}\right]$$

$$= \frac{3450t}{(t+25)^2\sqrt{\frac{1}{2}t^2+2t+25}}$$

Ten seconds into the run, the athlete's pulse rate is increasing at

$$P'(10) = \frac{3450(10)}{(35)^2\sqrt{50+20+25}} \approx 2.9, \text{ or approximately 2.9 beats per minute per}$$

minute. Sixty seconds into the run, it is increasing at

$$P'(60) = \frac{3450(60)}{(85)^2\sqrt{1800+120+25}} \approx 0.65, \text{ or approximately 0.7 beats per minute per}$$

minute. Two minutes into the run, it is increasing at

$$P'(120) = \frac{3450(120)}{(145)^2\sqrt{7200+240+25}} \approx 0.23, \text{ or approximately 0.2 beats per minute}$$

per minute. The pulse rate two minutes into the run is given by

$$P(120) = \frac{300\sqrt{7200+240+25}}{120+25} \approx 178.8, \text{ or approximately 179 beats per minute.}$$

76. a. $\quad \dfrac{dT}{dn} = A(n-b)^{1/2} + An(\frac{1}{2})(n-b)^{-1/2} = \frac{1}{2}A(n-b)^{-1/2}[2(n-b)+n]$

$$= \frac{(3n-2b)A}{2\sqrt{n-b}},$$

and this gives the rate of change of the learning time with respect to the length of the list.

b. $\quad \dfrac{dT}{dn} = \dfrac{(3n-8)4}{2\sqrt{n-4}}$. if $A = 4$ and $b = 4$. $\quad f'(13) = \dfrac{(39-8)4}{2\sqrt{9}} \approx 20.7, \text{ or}$

approximately 21 units of time per unit increase in the word list.

$$f'(29) = \frac{(87-8)4}{2\sqrt{25}} \approx 31.6, \text{ or approximately 32 units of time per units}$$

increase in the word list.

77 The area is given by $A = \pi r^2$. The rate at which the area is increasing is given by

dA/dt, that is, $\dfrac{dA}{dt} = \dfrac{d}{dt}(\pi r^2) = \dfrac{d}{dt}(\pi r^2)\dfrac{dr}{dt} = 2\pi r\dfrac{dr}{dt}$

3 Differentiation

If $r = 40$ and $dr/dt = 2$, then $\dfrac{dA}{dt} = 2\pi(40)(2) = 160\pi$, that is, it is increasing at the rate of 160π, or approximately 503, sq ft/sec.

78. $g(t) = 0.5t^2(t^2 + 10)^{-1}$

$g'(t) = 0.5(2t)(t^2 + 10)^{-1} + 0.5t^2(-1)(t^2 + 10)^{-2}(2t)$

$\quad = t(t^2 + 10)^{-2}[(t^2 + 10) - t^2] = \dfrac{10t}{(t^2 + 10)^2}.$

$g'(5) = \dfrac{50}{(35)^2} \approx 0.04$ cm/yr.

79 $f(t) = 6.25t^2 + 19\,75t + 74.75 \quad g(x) = -0.00075x^2 + 67.5.$

$\dfrac{dS}{dt} = g'(x)f'(t) = (-0.0015x)(12.5t + 19\,75).$

When $t = 4$, we have $x = f(4) = 6.25(16) + 19.75(4) + 74.75 = 253\,75$

and $\dfrac{dS}{dt}\bigg|_{t=4} = (-0.0015)(253.75)[12.5(4) + 19\,75] \approx -26.55;$

that is, the average speed will be dropping at the rate of approximately 27 mph per decade. The average speed of traffic flow at that time will be

$\quad S = g(f(4)) = -0.00075(253.75^2) + 67.5 = 19.2,$ or approximately 19 mph.

80. $r(t) = \frac{10}{81}t^3 - \frac{10}{3}t^2 + \frac{200}{9}t + 60$ and $R(r) = -\frac{3}{5000}r^3 + \frac{9}{50}r^2$

a. The rate of change of Wonderland's occupancy rate with respect to time is given by $r'(t) = \frac{30}{81}t^2 - \frac{20}{3}t + \frac{200}{9}$

b. The rate of change of Wonderlands' monthly revenue with respect to the occupancy rate is given by $R'(r) = -\dfrac{9}{5000}r^2 + \dfrac{9}{25}r$

c. When $t = 0$, $r(0) = \frac{10}{81}(0)^3 - \frac{10}{3}(0)^2 + \frac{200}{9}(0) + 60 = 60;$

$r'(0) = \frac{30}{81}(0)^2 - \frac{20}{3}(0) + \frac{200}{9} = \frac{200}{9}; R'(60) = -\frac{9}{5000}(60)^2 + \frac{9}{25}(60) = 15.12;$

$R'(r(0))r'(0) = (15.12)(\frac{200}{9}) = 336.$

And the rate of change of Wonderland's monthly revenue with respect to time at the beginning of January is approximately \$336,000/month. Next, when $t = 6$

$\quad r(6) = \frac{10}{81}(6)^3 - \frac{10}{3}(6)^2 + \frac{200}{9}(6) + 60 = 100;$

$r'(6) = \frac{30}{81}(6)^2 - \frac{20}{3}(6) + \frac{200}{9} = -4.44; R'(100) = -\frac{9}{5000}(100)^2 + \frac{9}{25}(100) = 18.$

$R'(r(6))r'(6) = (18)(-4.44) \approx -80$

and the rate of change of Wonderlands' monthly revenue with respect to time at the beginning of June is approximately –\$80,000/month; that is, the revenue is decreasing at the rate of \$80,000/month.

81. $N(x) = 1.42x$ and $x(t) = \dfrac{7t^2 + 140t + 700}{3t^2 + 80t + 550}$ The number of construction jobs as a function of time is $n(t) = N[x(t)]$. Using the Chain Rule,

$$n'(t) = \frac{dN}{dx} \cdot \frac{dx}{dt} = 1.42 \frac{dx}{dt}$$

$$= (1.42) \left[\frac{(3t^2 + 80t + 550)(14t + 140) - (7t^2 + 140t + 700)(6t + 80)}{(3t^2 + 80t + 550)^2} \right]$$

$$= \frac{1.42(140t^2 + 3500t + 21000)}{(3t^2 + 80t + 550)^2}.$$

$$n'(1) = \frac{1.42(140 + 3500 + 21000)}{(3 + 80 + 550)^2} \approx 0.0873216, \text{ or approximately 87,322 jobs/year.}$$

82. $x = f(p) = \frac{100}{9}\sqrt{810,000 - p^2}$ and $p(t) = \dfrac{400}{1 + \frac{1}{8}\sqrt{t}} + 200.$

We want $\dfrac{dx}{dt} = \dfrac{dx}{dp} \cdot \dfrac{dp}{dt}.$ But

$$\frac{dx}{dp} = \frac{100}{9}\left(\frac{1}{2}\right)(810,000 - p^2)^{-1/2}(-2p) = -\frac{100p}{9\sqrt{810,000 - p^2}}$$

and $\dfrac{dp}{dt} = 400\dfrac{d}{dt}(1 + \frac{1}{8}t^{1/2})^{-1} + \dfrac{d}{dt}(200) = -400(1 + \frac{1}{8}t^{1/2})^{-2}(\frac{1}{8})(\frac{1}{2}t^{-1/2})$

$$= -\frac{25}{\sqrt{t}(1 + \frac{1}{8}\sqrt{t})^2}$$

So $\dfrac{dx}{dt} = \dfrac{2500p}{9\sqrt{t}\sqrt{810,000 - p^2}(1 + \frac{1}{8}\sqrt{t})^2}$

and when $t = 16$, $p = \dfrac{400}{1 + \frac{1}{8}\sqrt{16}} + 200 = \dfrac{1400}{3}$ Therefore,

$$\frac{dx}{dt} = \frac{2500(\frac{1400}{3})}{9\sqrt{16}\sqrt{810,000 - (\frac{1400}{3})^2}\,(1 + \frac{1}{8}\sqrt{16})^2} \approx 18.7$$

So the quantity demanded will be changing at the rate of approximately 19 computers/month.

83. $x = f(p) = 10\sqrt{\dfrac{50-p}{p}}$,

$$\frac{dx}{dp} = \frac{d}{dp}\left[10\left(\frac{50-p}{p}\right)^{1/2}\right] = (10)(\tfrac{1}{2})\left(\frac{50-p}{p}\right)^{-1/2}\frac{d}{dp}\left(\frac{50-p}{p}\right)$$

$$= 5\left(\frac{50-p}{p}\right)^{-1/2}\cdot\frac{d}{dp}\left(\frac{50}{p}-1\right)$$

$$= 5\left(\frac{50-p}{p}\right)^{-1/2}\left(-\frac{50}{p^2}\right) = -\frac{250}{p^2\left(\frac{50-p}{p}\right)^{1/2}}$$

$$\left.\frac{dx}{dp}\right|_{p=25} = -\frac{250}{p^2\left(\frac{50-p}{p}\right)^{1/2}} = -\frac{250}{(625)\left(\frac{25}{25}\right)^{1/2}} = -0.4$$

So the quantity demanded is falling at the rate of 0.4(1000) or 400 wristwatches per dollar increase in price.

84. $p = f(t) = 50\left(\dfrac{t^2 + 2t + 4}{t^2 + 4t + 8}\right)$; $R(p) = 1000\left(\dfrac{p+4}{p+2}\right)$. We want $\dfrac{dR}{dt} = \dfrac{dR}{dp}\cdot\dfrac{dp}{dt}$ Now

$$\frac{dR}{dp} = 1000\left[\frac{(p+2)(1)-(p+4)(1)}{(p+2)^2}\right] = -\frac{2000}{(p+2)^2}$$

$$\frac{dp}{dt} = 50\left[\frac{(t^2+4t+8)(2t+2)-(t^2+2t+4)(2t+4)}{(t^2+4t+8)^2}\right] = \frac{100t(t+4)}{(t^2+4t+8)^2}$$

When $t = 2$, $p = 50\left(\dfrac{2^2+2(2)+4}{2^2+4(2)+8}\right) = 30$, and

$$\frac{dR}{dt} = -\frac{2000}{(p+2)^2}\cdot\frac{100t(t+4)}{(t^2+4t+8)^2}\bigg|_{t=2} = -\frac{2000}{(32)^2}\cdot\frac{100(2)(6)}{(4+8+8)^2}$$

$$\approx -5.86, \text{ that is, the passage will decrease at the rate of}$$

approximately $5.86 per passenger per year.

85. True. This is just the statement of the Chain Rule.

86. True. $\dfrac{d}{dx}[f(cx)] = f'(cx)\dfrac{d}{dx}(cx) = f'(cx)\cdot c.$

87. True. $\dfrac{d}{dx}\sqrt{f(x)} = \dfrac{d}{dx}[f(x)]^{1/2} = \dfrac{1}{2}[f(x)]^{-1/2}f'(x) = \dfrac{f'(x)}{2\sqrt{f(x)}}.$

88. False. Let $f(x) = x$. Then $f\left(\dfrac{1}{x}\right) = \dfrac{1}{x}$ and so $f'(x) = -\dfrac{1}{x^2}$ But $f'(x) = 1$ and so and so $f'\left(\dfrac{1}{x}\right) = 1.$

89. Let $f(x) = x^{1/n}$ so that $[f(x)]^n = x.$
Differentiating both sides with respect to x, we get
$$n[f(x)]^{n-1}f'(x) = 1$$
$$f'(x) = \dfrac{1}{n[f(x)]^{n-1}} = \dfrac{1}{n[x^{1/n}]^{n-1}} = \dfrac{1}{nx^{1-(1/n)}} = \dfrac{1}{n}x^{(1/n)-1}.$$
as was to be shown.

90. Let $f(x) = x^r = x^{m/n} = (x^m)^{1/n}$ Then $[f(x)]^n = x^m.$
Therefore, $n[f(x)]^{n-1}f'(x) = \dfrac{m}{n}[f(x)]^{-n+1}x^{m-1} = \dfrac{m}{n}(x^{m/n})^{-n+1}x^{m-1}$
$$= \dfrac{m}{n}x^{[m(-n+1)/n]+m-1} = \dfrac{m}{n}x^{(m-n)/n} = \dfrac{m}{n}x^{(m/n)-1} = rx^{r-1}$$

USING TECHNOLOGY EXERCISES 3.3 page 197

1. 0.5774   2. 1.4364   3. 0.9390   4. 3.9051   5. –4.9498 6. 0.1056

7. a. 10,146,200/decade   b. 7,810,520/decade

8. a. 42.1766 million   b. 0.522296 million/year

3.4 CONCEPT QUESTIONS, page 208

1. a. The marginal cost function is the derivative of the cost function.
   b. The average cost function is equal to the total cost function divided by the total number of the commodity produced.
   c. The marginal average cost function is the derivative of the average cost function.
   d. The marginal revenue function is the derivative of the revenue function.
   e. The marginal profit function is the derivative of the profit function.

2. a. The elasticity of demand at a price P is $E(p) = -\dfrac{pf'(p)}{f(p)}$, where f is the demand function $x = f(p)$
   b. The elasticity of demand is elastic if $E(p) > 1$, unitary if $E9p) = 1$, and inelastic if $E(p) < 1$. If $E(p) > 1$, then an increase in the unit price will cause the revenue to decrease, whereas a decrease in the unit price will cause the revenue to increase. If $E(p) = 1$, then an increase in the unit price will cause the revenue to stay the same. If $E(p) < 1$, then an increase in the unit price will cause the revenue to increase, and a decrease in the unit price will cause the revenue to decrease.

EXERCISES 3.4, page 208

1. a. $C(x)$ is always increasing because as x, the number of units produced, increases, the greater the amount of money that must be spent on production.
   b. This occurs at $x = 4$, or a production level of 4000. You can see this by looking at the slopes of the tangent lines for x less than, equal to, and a little larger then $x = 4$.

2. a. If very few units of the commodity are produced then the cost/unit of production will be very large. Next, if x is very large the typical total cost is very large due to overtime, excessive cost of raw material, breakdowns of machines, etc., so that $A(x)$ is very large as well; in fact, for a typical total cost function, $C(x)$ ultimately $A(x)$ grows faster than x, that is, $\lim\limits_{x \to \infty} \dfrac{C(x)}{x} = \infty$.
   b. The average cost per unit is smallest, ($\$y_0$) when the level of production is x_0 units.

3. a. The actual cost incurred in the production of the 1001st record is given by
   $$C(1001) - C(1000) = [2000 + 2(1001) - 0.0001(1001)^2]$$

$$-[2000 + 2(1000) - 0.0001(1000)^2]$$
$$= 3901.7999 - 3900 = 1.7999,$$

or \$1.80. The actual cost incurred in the production of the 2001st record is given
by $C(2001) - C(2000) = [2000 + 2(2001) - 0.0001(2001)^2]$
$$-[2000 + 2(2000) - 0.0001(2000)^2]$$
$$= 5601.5999 - 5600 = 1.5999, \text{ or } \$1.60.$$

b. The marginal cost is $C'(x) = 2 - 0.0002x$. In particular
$$C'(1000) = 2 - 0.0002(1000) = 1.80$$
and $\qquad C'(2000) = 2 - 0.0002(2000) = 1.60.$

4. a. $C(101) - C(100) = [0.0002(101)^3 - 0.06(101)^2 + 120(101) + 5000]$
$$- [0.0002(100)^3 - 0.06(100)^2 + 120(100) + 5000]$$
$$\approx 114, \text{ or approximately } \$114$$

Similarly, we find $C(201) - C(200) \approx \$120.16; \quad C(301) - C(300) \approx \$138.12.$
b. We compute $C'(x) = 0.0006x^2 - 0.12x + 120$. So the required quantities are
$$C'(100) = 0.0006(100)^2 - 0.12(100) + 120 = 114, \text{ or } \$114,$$
$$C'(200) = 0.0006(200)^2 - 0.12(200) + 120 = 120, \text{ or } \$120,$$
and $C'(300) = 0.0006(300)^2 - 0.12(300) + 120 = 138, \text{ or } \$138.$

5   a. $\overline{C}(x) = \dfrac{C(x)}{x} = \dfrac{100x + 200,000}{x} = 100 + \dfrac{200,000}{x}$

b. $\overline{C}'(x) = \dfrac{d}{dx}(100) + \dfrac{d}{dx}(200,000x^{-1}) = -200,000x^{-2} = -\dfrac{200,000}{x^2}.$

c. $\displaystyle\lim_{x\to\infty} \overline{C}(x) = \lim_{x\to\infty}\left[100 + \dfrac{200,000}{x}\right] = 100$

and this says that the average cost approaches \$100 per unit if the production level
is very high.

6. a. $\overline{C}(x) = \dfrac{C(x)}{x} = \dfrac{5000}{x} + 2.$ $\qquad$ b. $\overline{C}'(x) = -\dfrac{5000}{x^2}$

c. Since the marginal average cost function is negative for $x > 0$, the rate of change
of the average cost function is negative for all $x > 0$.

7. $\overline{C}(x) = \dfrac{C(x)}{x} = \dfrac{2000 + 2x - 0.0001x^2}{x} = \dfrac{2000}{x} + 2 - 0.0001x.$

$\overline{C}'(x) = -\dfrac{2000}{x^2} + 0 - 0.0001 = -\dfrac{2000}{x^2} - 0.0001.$

8. $\overline{C}(x) = \dfrac{C(x)}{x} = \dfrac{0.0002x^3 - 0.06x^2 + 120x + 5000}{x} = 0.0002x^2 - 0.06x + 120 + \dfrac{5000}{x}$

$\overline{C}'(x) = 0.0004x - 0.06 - \dfrac{5000}{x^2}$

9   a. $R'(x) = \dfrac{d}{dx}(8000x - 100x^2) = 8000 - 200x.$

      b. $R'(39) = 8000 - 200(39) = 200.$ $R'(40) = 8000 - 200(40) = 0$
         $R'(41) = 8000 - 200(41) = -200$

      c. This suggests the total revenue is maximized if the price charged/ passenger is
$40.

10. a. $R(x) = px = x(-0.04x + 800) = -0.04x^2 + 800x$
     b. $R'(x) = -0.08x + 800$ c. $R'(5000) = -0.08(5000) + 800 = 400.$
     This says that when the level of production is 5000 units the production of the next
     speaker system will bring an additional revenue of $400.

11. a. $P(x) = R(x) - C(x) = (-0.04x^2 + 800x) - (200x + 300{,}000)$
           $= -0.04x^2 + 600x - 300{,}000.$
     b. $P'(x) = -0.08x + 600$
     c. $P'(5000) = -0.08(5000) + 600 = 200$ $P'(8000) = -0.08(8000) + 600 = -40.$
     d.

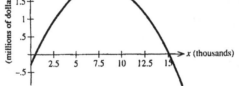

The profit realized by the company increases as production increases, peaking at a
level of production of 7500 units. Beyond this level of production, the profit begins
to fall.

12. a. $P(x) = -10x^2 + 1760x - 50{,}000.$ To find the actual profit realized from renting
     the 51st unit, assuming that 50 units have already been rented, we compute
     $P(51) - P(50) = [-10(51)^2 + 1760(51) - 50{,}000] - [-10(50)^2 + 1760(50) - 50{,}000]$
            $= -26{,}010 + 89{,}760 - 50{,}000 + 25{,}000 - 88{,}000 + 50{,}000 = 750,$
     or $750.
     b. The marginal profit is given by $P'(x) = -20x + 1760.$ When $x = 50,$

$$P'(50) = -20(50) + 1760 = 760, \text{ or } \$760.$$

13 a. The revenue function is $R(x) = px = (600 - 0.05x)x = 600x - 0.05x^2$
and the profit function is
$$P(x) = R(x) - C(x)$$
$$= (600x - 0.05x^2) - (0.000002x^3 - 0.03x^2 + 400x + 80,000)$$
$$= -0.000002x^3 - 0.02x^2 + 200x - 80,000.$$

b. $C'(x) = \dfrac{d}{dx}(0.000002x^3 - 0.03x^2 + 400x + 80,000) = 0.000006x^2 - 0.06x + 400.$

$R'(x) = \dfrac{d}{dx}(600x - 0.05x^2) = 600 - 0.1x.$

$P'(x) = \dfrac{d}{dx}(-0.000002x^3 - 0.02x^2 + 200x - 80,000)$

$\qquad = -0.000006x^2 - 0.04x + 200.$

c. $C'(2000) = 0.000006(2000)^2 - 0.06(2000) + 400 = 304$, and this says that at a
level of production of 2000 units, the cost for producing the 2001st unit is \$304.
$R'(2000) = 600 - 0.1(2000) = 400$ and this says that the revenue realized in selling
the 2001st unit is \$400. $P'(2000) = R'(2000) - C'(2000) = 400 - 304 = 96$, and this
says that the revenue realized in selling the 2001st unit is \$96.

d.

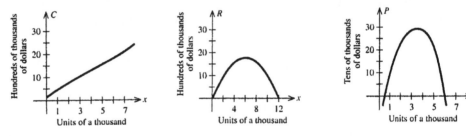

14. a. $R(x) = xp(x) = -0.006x^2 + 180x$
$\qquad P(x) = R(x) - C(x)$
$$= -0.006x^2 + 180x - (0.000002x^3 - 0.02x^2 + 120x + 60,000)$$
$$= -0.000002x^3 + 0.014x^2 + 60x - 60,000.$$

b. $C'(x) = 0.000006x^2 - 0.04x + 120;\ R'(x) = -0.012x + 180$
$\qquad P'(x) = -0.000006x^2 + 0.028x + 60.$

c. $C'(2000) = 0.000006(2000)^2 - 0.04(2000) + 120 = 64;$
$\qquad R'(2000) = -0.012(2000) + 180 = 156$
$\qquad P'(2000) = -0.000006(2000)^2 + 0.028(2000) + 60 = 92.$

3 Differentiation

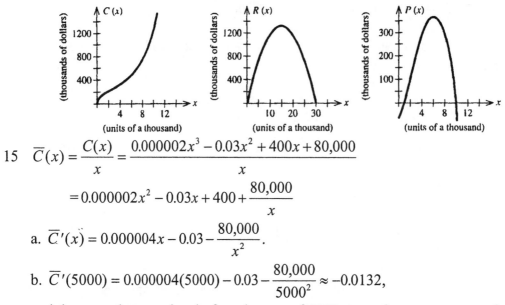

15 $\overline{C}(x) = \dfrac{C(x)}{x} = \dfrac{0.000002x^3 - 0.03x^2 + 400x + 80{,}000}{x}$

$$= 0.000002x^2 - 0.03x + 400 + \dfrac{80{,}000}{x}$$

a. $\overline{C}'(x) = 0.000004x - 0.03 - \dfrac{80{,}000}{x^2}.$

b. $\overline{C}'(5000) = 0.000004(5000) - 0.03 - \dfrac{80{,}000}{5000^2} \approx -0.0132,$

and this says that, at a level of production of 5000 units, the average cost of production is dropping at the rate of approximately a penny per unit.

$$\overline{C}'(10{,}000) = 0.000004(10000) - 0.03 - \dfrac{80{,}000}{10{,}000^2} \approx 0.0092,$$

and this says that, at a level of production of 10,000 units, the average cost of production is increasing at the rate of approximately a penny per unit.

c.

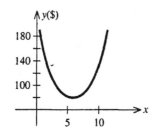

16. $C(x) = 0.000002x^3 - 0.02x^2 + 120x + 60{,}000$

$\overline{C}(x) = 0.000002x^2 - 0.02x + 120 + \dfrac{60{,}000}{x}$

a. The marginal average cost function is given by

$$\overline{C}'(x) = 0.000004x - 0.02 - \frac{60{,}000}{x^2}$$

b. $\overline{C}'(5000) = 0.000004(5000) - 0.02 - \dfrac{60{,}000}{(5000)^2} = 0.02 - 0.02 - 0.0024 = -0.0024$

$\overline{C}'(10000) = 0.000004(10000) - 0.02 - \dfrac{60{,}000}{(10000)^2} = 0.04 - 0.02 - 0.0006 = 0.0194.$

We conclude that the average cost is decreasing when 5000 TV sets are produced and increasing when 10,000 units are produced.

17 a. $R(x) = px = \dfrac{50x}{0.01x^2 + 1}$ b. $R'(x) = \dfrac{(0.01x^2 + 1)50 - 50x(0.02x)}{(0.01x^2 + 1)^2} = \dfrac{50 - 0.5x^2}{(0.01x^2 + 1)^2}$

c. $R'(2) = \dfrac{50 - 0.5(4)}{[0.01(4) + 1]^2} \approx 44.379$

This result says that at a level of sale of 2000 units, the revenue increases at the rate of approximately $44,379 per sales of 1000 units.

18. $\dfrac{dC}{dx} = \dfrac{d}{dx}(0.712x + 95.05) = 0.712.$

19 $C(x) = 0.873x^{1.1} + 20.34, \quad C'(x) = 0.873(1.1)x^{0.1}$
$C'(10) = 0.873(1.1)(10)^{0.1} = 1.21$, or \$1.21 billion per billion dollars.

20. $\dfrac{dS}{dx} = \dfrac{d}{dx}[x - C(x)] = 1 - \dfrac{dC}{dx}$

21 The consumption function is given by $C(x) = 0.712x + 95.05$. The marginal propensity to consume is given by $\dfrac{dC}{dx} = 0.712$. The marginal propensity to save is given by $\dfrac{dS}{dx} = 1 - \dfrac{dC}{dx} = 1 - 0.712 = 0.288$, or \$0.288 billion per billion dollars.

22. Here $C(x) = 0.873x^{1.1} + 20.34$. So $C'(x) = 0.9603x^{0.1}$ and
$\dfrac{dS}{dx} = 1 - \dfrac{dC}{dx} = 1 - 0.9603x^{0.1}$ When $x = 10$, we have
$\dfrac{dS}{dx} = 1 - 0.9603(10)^{0.1} = -0.209$, or $-\$0.209$ billion per billion dollars.

23. Here $x = f(p) = -\frac{5}{4}p + 20$ and so $f'(p) = -\frac{5}{4}$ Therefore,

$$E(p) = -\frac{pf'(p)}{f(p)} = -\frac{p(-\frac{5}{4})}{-\frac{5}{4}p + 20} = \frac{5p}{80 - 5p}.$$

$$E(10) = \frac{5(10)}{80 - 5(10)} = \frac{50}{30} = \frac{5}{3} > 1, \text{ and so the demand is elastic.}$$

24. $f(p) = -\frac{3}{2}p + 9$; $f'(p) = -\frac{3}{2}$. Then the elasticity of demand is given by

$$E(p) = -\frac{pf'(p)}{f(p)} = -\frac{p(-\frac{3}{2})}{-\frac{3}{2}p + 9}.$$

Therefore, when $p = 2$,

$$E(2) = -\frac{2(-\frac{3}{2})}{-\frac{3}{2}(2) + 9} = \frac{3}{6} = \frac{1}{2} < 1,$$

and we conclude that the demand is inelastic at this price.

25. $f(p) = -\frac{1}{3}p + 20$; $f'(p) = -\frac{1}{3}$.

Then the elasticity of demand is given by

$$E(p) = -\frac{p(-\frac{1}{3})}{-\frac{1}{3}p + 20},$$

and $\quad E(30) = -\frac{30(-\frac{1}{3})}{-\frac{1}{3}(30) + 20} = 1,$

and we conclude that the demand is unitary at this price.

26. Solving the demand equation for x, we have

$$0.4x = -p + 20 \quad \text{or} \quad x = f(p) = -\frac{5}{2}p + 50.$$

Then $f'(p) = -\frac{5}{2}$, and so

$$E(p) = -\frac{pf'(p)}{f(p)} = -\frac{p(-\frac{5}{2})}{-\frac{5}{2}p + 50} = \frac{5p}{100 - 5p}$$

$$E(10) = \frac{50}{50} = 1, \text{ and so the demand is unitary.}$$

27. $x^2 = 169 - p$ and $f(p) = (169 - p)^{1/2}$

Next, $\quad f'(p) = \frac{1}{2}(169 - p)^{-1/2}(-1) = -\frac{1}{2}(169 - p)^{-1/2}$

Then the elasticity of demand is given by

$$E(p) = -\frac{pf'(p)}{f(p)} = -\frac{p\left(-\frac{1}{2}\right)(169-p)^{-1/2}}{(169-p)^{1/2}} = \frac{\frac{1}{2}p}{169-p}.$$

Therefore, when $p = 29$,

$$E(p) = \frac{\frac{1}{2}(29)}{169-29} = \frac{14.5}{140} = 0.104.$$

Since $E(p) < 1$, we conclude that demand is inelastic at this price.

28. Solving the demand equation for x, we find
$$x^2 = 144 - p, \text{ or } x = \sqrt{144 - p} \qquad [x \text{ must be nonnegative}]$$
With $x = f(p) = (144 - p)^{1/2}$, we have
$$f'(p) = \frac{1}{2}(144-p)^{-1/2}(-1) = -\frac{1}{2\sqrt{144-p}}$$

Therefore, $E(p) = -\dfrac{pf'(p)}{f(p)} = -\dfrac{p\left(-\dfrac{1}{2\sqrt{144-p}}\right)}{\sqrt{144-p}} = \dfrac{p}{2(144-p)}$

$E(96) = \dfrac{96}{2(48)} = 1$, and so the demand equation is unitary.

29. $f(p) = \frac{1}{5}(225 - p^2); \quad f'(p) = \frac{1}{5}(-2p) = -\frac{2}{5}p$

Then the elasticity of demand is given by
$$E(p) = -\frac{pf'(p)}{f(p)} = -\frac{p\left(-\frac{2}{5}p\right)}{\frac{1}{5}(225-p^2)} = \frac{2p^2}{225-p^2}.$$

a. When $p = 8$, $E(8) = \dfrac{2(64)}{225-64} = 0.8 < 1$ and the demand is inelastic. When $p = 10$,

$$E(10) = \frac{2(100)}{225-100} = 1.6 > 1$$

and the demand is elastic.

b. The demand is unitary when $E = 1$. Solving $\dfrac{2p^2}{225-p^2} = 1$ we find $2p^2 = 225 - p^2$,

$3p^2 = 225$, and $p = 8.66$. So the demand is unitary when $p = 8.66$.

c. Since demand is elastic when $p = 10$, lowering the unit price will cause the revenue to increase.

d. Since the demand is inelastic at $p = 8$, a slight increase in the unit price will cause the revenue to increase.

30. $f(p) = (144 - p)^{1/2}$; $f'(p) = \frac{1}{2}(144 - p)^{-1/2}(-1)$.

Then the elasticity of demand is given by

$$E(p) = -\frac{pf'(p)}{f(p)} = -\frac{p(-\frac{1}{2})(144 - p)^{-1/2}}{(144 - p)^{1/2}} = \frac{p}{2(144 - p)}$$

a. $E(63) = \frac{63}{2(144 - 63)} \approx 0.39.$ $E(96) = \frac{96}{2(144 - 96)} = 1.$

$$E(108) = \frac{108}{2(144 - 108)} = 1.5.$$

b. When the price is set at $63, an increase of $1 in the price per tire will result in a decrease of approximately 0.39 percent in the quantity demanded. When the unit price is set at $96, an increase of $1 in the unit price will cause a decrease of 1 percent in the quantity demanded.

c. The demand is inelastic when $p = 63$, unitary when $p = 96$, and elastic when $p = 108$.

31. $f(p) = \frac{2}{3}(36 - p^2)^{1/2}$

$f'(p) = \frac{2}{3}(\frac{1}{2})(36 - p^2)^{-1/2}(-2p) = -\frac{2}{3}p(36 - p^2)^{-1/2}$

Then the elasticity of demand is given by

$$E(p) = -\frac{pf'(p)}{f(p)} = -\frac{-\frac{2}{3}p(36 - p^2)^{-1/2}\,p}{\frac{2}{3}(36 - p^2)^{1/2}} = \frac{p^2}{36 - p^2}$$

When $p = 2$, $E(2) = \frac{4}{36 - 4} = \frac{1}{8} < 1$, and we conclude that the demand is inelastic.

b. Since the demand is inelastic, the revenue will increase when the rental price is increased.

32. Here $x = f(p) = \sqrt{400 - 5p} = (400 - 5p)^{1/2}$ Therefore,

$$f'(p) = \frac{1}{2}(400 - 5p)^{-1/2}(-5) = -\frac{5}{2\sqrt{400 - 5p}}.$$

Therefore, $E(p) = -\frac{pf'(p)}{f(p)} = -\frac{p\left(-\dfrac{5}{2\sqrt{400 - 5p}}\right)}{\sqrt{400 - 5p}} = \frac{5p}{400 - 5p}$

a. $E(40) = \dfrac{5(40)}{2[400 - 5(40)]} = 0.5,$

and so the demand is inelastic when $p = 40$. $E(60) = \dfrac{5(60)}{2[400 - 5(60)]} = 1.5$

and so the demand is elastic when $p = 60$.

b. The demand is unitary if $\dfrac{5p}{2(400 - 5p)} = 1$, or $5p = 800 - 10p$,

that is, when $p = 53\frac{1}{3}$. (This also follows from part (a)).

c. Since the demand is elastic at $p = 60$, lowering the unit price a little will cause the revenue to increase.

d. Since the demand is inelastic at $p = 40$, a slight increase of the unit price will cause the revenue to increase.

33 We first solve the demand equation for x in terms of p. Thus,
$$p = \sqrt{9 - 0.02x}$$
$$p^2 = 9 - 0.02x$$
or $x = -50p^2 + 450$. With $f(p) = -50p^2 + 450$, we find
$$E(p) = -\frac{pf'(p)}{f(p)} = -\frac{p(-100p)}{-50p^2 + 450} = \frac{2p^2}{9 - p^2}.$$
Setting $E(p) = 1$ gives $2p^2 = 9 - p^2$, so $p = \sqrt{3}$ So the demand is inelastic in $[0, \sqrt{3}]$, unitary when $p = \sqrt{3}$, and elastic in $(\sqrt{3}, 3)$.

34. $f(p) = 10\left(\dfrac{50 - p}{p}\right)^{1/2} = 10\left(\dfrac{50}{p} - 1\right)^{1/2}$

$f'(p) = 10(\tfrac{1}{2})\left(\dfrac{50}{p} - 1\right)^{-1/2}\left(-\dfrac{50}{p^2}\right) = -\dfrac{250}{p^2}\left(\dfrac{50}{p} - 1\right)^{-1/2}$

Then the elasticity of demand is given by

$E(p) = -\dfrac{pf'(p)}{f(p)} = -\dfrac{p\left(-\dfrac{250}{p^2}\right)\left(\dfrac{50}{p} - 1\right)^{-1/2}}{10\left(\dfrac{50}{p} - 1\right)^{1/2}} = -\dfrac{\dfrac{250}{p}}{10\left(\dfrac{50}{p} - 1\right)} = \dfrac{25}{p\left(\dfrac{50 - p}{p}\right)} = \dfrac{25}{50 - p}$

Setting $E = 1$, gives $1 = \dfrac{25}{50-p}$ and so $25 = 50 - p$, and $p = 25$

Thus, if $p > 25$, then $E > 1$, and the demand is elastic; if $p = 25$, then $E = 1$ and the demand is unitary; and if $p < 25$, then $E < 1$ and the demand is inelastic.

35 True. $\overline{C}'(x) = \dfrac{d}{dx}\left[\dfrac{C(x)}{x}\right] = \dfrac{xC'(x) - C(x)\dfrac{d}{dx}(x)}{x^2} = \dfrac{xC'(x) - C(x)}{x^2}$

36. False. In fact, it makes good sense to *increase* the level of production since, in this instance, the profit increases by $f'(a)$ units/unit increase in x.

3.5 CONCEPT QUESTIONS, page 216

1. a. The second derivative of f is the derivative of f'.
    b. To find the second derivative of f we differentiate f'
2. $f'(t)$ measures its velocity at time t and $f''(t)$ measures its acceleration at time t.
3. The relative rate of change is $I'(c)/I(c)$

EXERCISES 3.5, page 216

1. $f(x) = 4x^2 - 2x + 1$; $f'(x) = 8x - 2$; $f''(x) = 8.$

2. $f(x) = -0.2x^2 + 0.3x + 4$; $f'(x) = -0.4x + 0.3$ and $f''(x) = -0.4.$

3   $f(x) = 2x^3 - 3x^2 + 1$; $f'(x) = 6x^2 - 6x$; $f''(x) = 12x - 6 = 6(2x - 1).$

4   $g(x) = -3x^3 + 24x^2 + 6x - 64$; $g'(x) = -9x^2 + 48x + 6$; $g''(x) = -18x + 48.$

5. $h(t) = t^4 - 2t^3 + 6t^2 - 3t + 10$; $h'(t) = 4t^3 - 6t^2 + 12t - 3$
    $h''(t) = 12t^2 - 12t + 12 = 12(t^2 - t + 1).$

6. $f(x) = x^5 - x^4 + x^3 - x^2 + x - 1$; $f'(x) = 5x^4 - 4x^3 + 3x^2 - 2x + 1$;
    $f''(x) = 20x^3 - 12x^2 + 6x - 2.$

7   $f(x) = (x^2 + 2)^5$; $f'(x) = 5(x^2 + 2)^4(2x) = 10x(x^2 + 2)^4$ and

$$f''(x) = 10(x^2 + 2)^4 + 10x(x^2 + 2)^3(2x)$$
$$= 10(x^2 + 2)^3[(x^2 + 2) + 8x^2] = 10(9x^2 + 2)(x^2 + 2)^3$$

8. $g(t) = t^2(3t + 1)^4$;

$$g'(t) = 2t(3t + 1)^4 + t^2(4)(3t + 1)^3(3) = 2t(3t + 1)^3[(3t + 1) + 6t]$$
$$= (3t + 1)^3(18t^2 + 2t);$$
$$g''(t) = 2t(9t + 1)^3(3t + 1)^2(3) + (3t + 1)^3(36t + 2)$$
$$= 2(3t + 1)^2[9t(9t + 1) + (3t + 1)(18t + 1)]$$
$$= 2(3t + 1)^2(81t^2 + 9t + 54t^2 + 3t + 18t + 1) = 2(135t^2 + 30t + 1)(3t + 1)^2$$

9 $g(t) = (2t^2 - 1)^2(3t^2)$;

$$g'(t) = 2(2t^2 - 1)(4t)(3t^2) - (2t^2 - 1)^2(6t)$$
$$= 6t(2t^2 - 1)[4t^2 + (2t^2 - 1)] = 6t(2t^2 - 1)(6t^2 - 1)$$
$$= 6t(12t^4 - 8t^2 + 1) = 72t^5 - 48t^3 + 6t.$$
$$g''(t) = 360t^4 - 144t^2 + 6 = 6(60t^4 - 24t^2 + 1)$$

10. $h(x) = (x^2 + 1)^2(x - 1)$.

$$h'(x) = 2(x^2 + 1)(2x)(x - 1) + (x^2 + 1)^2(1)$$
$$= (x^2 + 1)[4x(x - 1) + (x^2 + 1)] = (x^2 + 1)(5x^2 - 4x + 1);$$
$$h''(x) = 2x(5x^2 - 4x + 1) + (x^2 + 1)(10x - 4)$$
$$= 10x^3 - 8x^2 + 2x + 10x^3 - 4x^2 + 10x - 4$$
$$= 20x^3 - 12x^2 + 12x - 4 = 4(5x^3 - 3x^2 + 3x - 1).$$

11. $f(x) = (2x^2 + 2)^{7/2}$; $f'(x) = \frac{7}{2}(2x^2 + 2)^{5/2}(4x) = 14x(2x^2 + 2)^{5/2}$,

$$f''(x) = 14(2x^2 + 2)^{5/2} + 14x(\frac{5}{2})(2x^2 + 2)^{3/2}(4x)$$
$$= 14(2x^2 + 2)^{3/2}[(2x^2 + 2) + 10x^2] = 28(6x^2 + 1)(2x^2 + 2)^{3/2}$$

12. $h(w) = (w^2 + 2w + 4)^{5/2}$;

$$h'(w) = \frac{5}{2}(w^2 + 2w + 4)^{3/2}(2w + 2) = 5(w + 1)(w^2 + 2w + 4)^{3/2};$$

3 Differentiation

$$h''(w) = 5(w^2 + 2w + 4)^{3/2} + 5(w+1)(\tfrac{3}{2})(w^2 + 2w + 4)^{1/2}(2w+2)$$
$$= 5(w^2 + 2w + 4)^{1/2}[(w^2 + 2w + 4) + 3(w+1)^2]$$
$$= 5(4w^2 + 8w + 7)(w^2 + 2w + 4)^{1/2}.$$

13. $f(x) = x(x^2 + 1)^2,$
$$f'(x) = (x^2 + 1)^2 + x(2)(x^2 + 1)(2x)$$
$$= (x^2 + 1)[(x^2 + 1) + 4x^2] = (x^2 + 1)(5x^2 + 1);$$
$$f''(x) = 2x(5x^2 + 1) + (x^2 + 1)(10x) = 2x(5x^2 + 1 + 5x^2 + 5) = 4x(5x^2 + 3).$$

14. $g(u) = \ddot{u}(2u - 1)^3;$
$$g'(u) = (2u - 1)^3 + u(3)(2u - 1)^2(2) = (2u - 1)^2[(2u - 1) + 6u] = (8u - 1)(2u - 1)^2;$$
$$g''(u) = 8(2u - 1)^2 + (8u - 1)(2)(2u - 1)(2)$$
$$= 4(2u - 1)[2(2u - 1) + (8u - 1)] = 12(2u - 1)(4u - 1).$$

15. $f(x) = \dfrac{x}{2x + 1},$ $f'(x) = \dfrac{(2x + 1)(1) - x(2)}{(2x + 1)^2} = \dfrac{1}{(2x + 1)^2};$
$$f''(x) = \frac{d}{dx}(2x + 1)^{-2} = -2(2x + 1)^{-3}(2) = -\frac{4}{(2x + 1)^3}$$

16. $g(t) = \dfrac{t^2}{t - 1};$ $g'(t) = \dfrac{(t - 1)(2t) - t^2(1)}{(t - 1)^2} = \dfrac{t^2 - 2t}{(t - 1)^2} = \dfrac{t(t - 2)}{(t - 1)^2},$
$$g''(t) = \frac{(t - 1)^2(2t - 2) - t(t - 2)2(t - 1)}{(t - 1)^4} = \frac{2(t - 1)[(t - 1)^2 - t(t - 2)]}{(t - 1)^4} = \frac{2}{(t - 1)^3}$$

17 $f(s) = \dfrac{s - 1}{s + 1};$ $f'(s) = \dfrac{(s + 1)(1) - (s - 1)(1)}{(s + 1)^2} = \dfrac{2}{(s + 1)^2}$
$$f''(s) = 2\frac{d}{ds}(s + 1)^{-2} = -4(s + 1)^{-3} = -\frac{4}{(s + 1)^3}$$

18. $f(u) = \dfrac{u}{u^2 + 1},$ $f'(u) = \dfrac{(u^2 + 1)(1) - (u)(2u)}{(u^2 + 1)^2} = \dfrac{-u^2 + 1}{(u^2 + 1)^2};$

$$f'(u) = \frac{(u^2+1)(1)-(u)(2u)}{(u^2+1)^2} = \frac{-u^2+1}{(u^2+1)^2};$$

$$f''(u) = \frac{(u^2+1)^2(-2u)-(-u^2+1)(2)(u^2+1)(2u)}{(u^2+1)^4}$$

$$= \frac{2u(u^2+1)(-u^2-1+2u^2-2)}{(u^2+1)^4} = \frac{2u(u^2-3)}{(u^2+1)^3};$$

19 $f(u) = \sqrt{4-3u} = (4-3u)^{1/2}.$ $f'(u) = \frac{1}{2}(4-3u)^{-1/2}(-3) = -\dfrac{3}{2\sqrt{4-3u}}$

$$f''(u) = -\frac{3}{2}\cdot\frac{d}{du}(4-3u)^{-1/2} = -\frac{3}{2}\left(-\frac{1}{2}\right)(4-3u)^{-3/2}(-3) = -\frac{9}{4(4-3u)^{3/2}}$$

20. $f(x) = \sqrt{2x-1} = (2x-1)^{1/2}$

$$f'(x) = \frac{1}{2}(2x-1)^{-1/2}(2) = (2x-1)^{-1/2} = \frac{1}{\sqrt{2x-1}}$$

$$f''(x) = -\frac{1}{2}(2x-1)^{-3/2}(2) = -(2x-1)^{-3/2} = -\frac{1}{\sqrt{(2x-1)^3}}.$$

21. $f(x) = 3x^4 - 4x^3,$ $f'(x) = 12x^3 - 12x^2,$ $f''(x) = 36x^2 - 24x;$ $f'''(x) = 72x - 24.$

22. $f(x) = 3x^5 - 6x^4 + 2x^2 - 8x + 12;$ $f'(x) = 15x^4 - 24x^3 + 4x - 8;$
$f''(x) = 60x^3 - 72x^2 + 4;$ $f'''(x) = 180x^2 - 144x.$

23 $f(x) = \dfrac{1}{x};$ $f'(x) = \dfrac{d}{dx}(x^{-1}) = -x^{-2};$ $f''(x) = 2x^{-3};$ $f'''(x) = -6x^{-4} = -\dfrac{6}{x^4}.$

24. $f(x) = \dfrac{2}{x^2};$ $f'(x) = 2\dfrac{d}{dx}(x^{-2}) = -4x^{-3};$ $f''(x) = 12x^{-4},$ $f'''(x) = -48x^{-5} = -\dfrac{48}{x^5}$

25. $g(s) = (3s-2)^{1/2};$ $g'(s) = \dfrac{1}{2}(3s-2)^{-1/2}(3) = \dfrac{3}{2(3s-2)^{1/2}};$

$$g''(s) = \frac{3}{2}\left(-\frac{1}{2}\right)(3s-2)^{-3/2}(3) = -\frac{9}{4}(3s-2)^{-3/2} = -\frac{9}{4(3s-2)^{3/2}};$$

$$g'''(s) = \frac{27}{8}(3s-2)^{-5/2}(3) = \frac{81}{8}(3s-2)^{-5/2} = \frac{81}{8(3s-2)^{5/2}}.$$

26. $g(t) = \sqrt{2t+3}$; $g'(t) = \frac{1}{2}(2t+3)^{-1/2}(2) = (2t+3)^{-1/2}$;

$g''(t) = -\frac{1}{2}(2t+3)^{-3/2}(2) = -(2t+3)^{-3/2}$; $g'''(t) = \frac{3}{2}(2t+3)^{-5/2}(2) = \frac{3}{(2t+3)^{5/2}}$

27. $f(x) = (2x-3)^4$, $f'(x) = 4(2x-3)^3(2) = 8(2x-3)^3$

$f''(x) = 24(2x-3)^2(2) = 48(2x-3)^2$; $f'''(x) = 96(2x-3)(2) = 192(2x-3)$.

28. $g(t) = (\frac{1}{2}t^2 - 1)^5$; $g'(t) = 5(\frac{1}{2}t^2 - 1)^4(t) = 5t(\frac{1}{2}t^2 - 1)^4$

$g''(t) = 5(\frac{1}{2}t^2 - 1)^4 + 5t(4)(\frac{1}{2}t^2 - 1)^3(t) = 5(\frac{1}{2}t^2 - 1)^3[(\frac{1}{2}t^2 - 1) + 4t^2]$

$\quad = \frac{5}{2}(9t^2 - 2)(\frac{1}{2}t^2 - 1)^3$.

$g'''(t) = \frac{5}{2}[18t(\frac{1}{2}t^2 - 1)^3 + (9t^2 - 2)3(\frac{1}{2}t^2 - 1)^2(t)]$

$\quad = \frac{15}{2}t(\frac{1}{2}t^2 - 1)^2[6(\frac{1}{2}t^2 - 1) + (9t^2 - 2)] = 30t(3t^2 - 2)(\frac{1}{2}t^2 - 1)^2$.

29. Its velocity at any time t is $v(t) = \dfrac{d}{dt}(16t^2) = 32t$ The hammer strikes the ground

when $16t^2 = 256$ or $t = 4$ (we reject the negative   root). Therefore, its velocity at the instant it strikes the ground is $v(4) = 32(4) = 128$ ft/sec. Its acceleration at time

t is $a(t) = \dfrac{d}{dt}(32t) = 32$. In particular, its acceleration at $t = 4$ is 32 ft/sec^2.

30. $s(t) = 20t + 8t^2 - t^3$; $s'(t) = 20 + 16t - 3t^2$, $s''(t) = 16 - 6t$.

$s''(\frac{8}{3}) = 16 - 6(\frac{8}{3}) = 16 - \frac{48}{3} = 0$.

We conclude that the acceleration of the car at $t = 8/3$ seconds is zero and that the car will start to decelerate at that point in time.

31. $N(t) = -0.1t^3 + 1.5t^2 + 100$.

a. $N'(t) = -0.3t^2 + 3t = 0.3t(10 - t)$. Since $N'(t) > 0$ for $t = 0, 1, 2, ..., 7$, it is evident that $N(t)$ (and therefore the crime rate) was increasing from 1988 through 1995.

b. $N''(t) = -0.6t + 3 = 0.6(5 - t)$. Now $N''(4) = 0.6 > 0$, $N''(5) = 0$, $N''(6) = -0.6 < 0$ and $N''(7) = -1.2 < 0$. This shows that the rate of the rate of change was decreasing beyond $t = 5$ (1990). This shows that the program was working.

32. $G(t) = -0.2t^3 + 2.4t^2 + 60$.
   a. $G'(t) = -0.6t^2 + 4.8t = 0.6t(8 - t)$
   $G'(0) = 0$, $G'(1) = 4.2$, $G'(2) = 7.2$, $G'(3) = 9$, $G'(4) = 9.6$, $G'(5) = 9$, $G'(6) = 7.2$, $G'(7) = 4.2$, $G'(8) = 0$.
   b. $G''(t) = -1.2t + 4.8 = 1.2(4 - t)$
   $G''(0) = 4.8$, $G''(1) = 3.6$, $G''(2) = 2.4$, $G''(3) = 1.2$, $G''(4) = 0$,
   $G''(5) = -1.2$, $G''(6) = -2.4$, $G''(7) = -3.6$, $G''(8) = -4.8$.
   c. Our computations show that the GDP is increasing at an increasing rate in the first five years. Even though the GDP continues to rise from that point on, the negativity of $G''(t)$ shows that the rate of increase is slowing down.

33. $N(t) = 0.00037t^3 - 0.0242t^2 + 0.52t + 5.3 \qquad (0 \le t \le 10)$
   $N'(t) = 0.00111t^2 - 0.0484t + 0.52$
   $N''(t) = 0.00222t - 0.0484$
   So $\quad N(8) = 0.00037(8)^3 - 0.0242(8)^2 + 5.3 = 8.1$
   $\qquad N'(8) = 0.00111(8)^2 - 0.0484(8) + 0.52 \approx 0.204$.
   $\qquad N''(8) = 0.00222(8) - 0.0484 = -0.031$.
   We conclude that at the beginning of 1998, there were 8.1 million persons receiving disability benefits, the number is increasing at the rate of 0.2 million/yr, and the rate of the rate of change of the number of persons is decreasing at the rate of 0.03 million persons/yr^2.

34 $P'(t) = 0.00012t^2 + 0.0072t + 0.8$; $\quad P'(t) \le 0.8$ for $(0 \le t \le 13)$
   $P''(t) = 0.00024t + 0.0072 \quad$ For $0 \le t \le 13$, $P''(t) > 0 \quad$ This means that the percent of the U.S. population was increasing at an increasing rate from 1991 through 2004.

35. a. $h(t) = \frac{1}{16}t^4 - t^3 + 4t^2 \quad h'(t) = \frac{1}{4}t^3 - 3t^2 + 8t$
   b. $h'(0) = 0$ or zero feet per second.
   $\qquad h'(4) = \frac{1}{4}(64) - 3(16) + 8(4) = 0$, or zero feet per second.
   $\qquad h'(8) = \frac{1}{4}(8)^3 - 3(64) + 8(8) = 0$, or zero feet per second.
   c. $h''(t) = \frac{3}{4}t^2 - 6t + 8$
   d. $h''(0) = 8 \ \text{ft/sec}^2$; $\quad h''(4) = \frac{3}{4}(16) - 6(4) + 8 = -4 \ \text{ft/sec}^2$

$h''(8) = \frac{3}{4}(64) - 6(8) + 8 = 8$ ft/sec^2

e. $h(0) = 0$ feet; $h(4) = \frac{1}{16}(4)^4 - (4)^3 + 4(4)^2 = 16$ feet.

$h(8) = \frac{1}{16}(8)^4 - (8)^3 + 4(8)^2 = 0$ feet.

36. $A(t) = 100 - 17.63t + 1.915t^2 - 0.1316t^3 + 0.00468t^4 - 0.00006t^5$
$A'(t) = -17.63 + 3.83t - 0.3948t^2 + 0.01872t^3 - 0.0003t^4$
$A''(t) = 3.83 - 0.7896t + 0.05616t^2 - 0.0012t^3$.
So, $A'(10) = -3.09$ and $A''(10) = 0.35$
Our computations show that 10 minutes after the start of the test, the smoke remaining is decreasing at a rate of 3 percent per minute but the rate at which the rate of smoke is decreasing is increasing at the rate of 0.35 percent per minute per minute.

37 $f(t) = 10.72(0.9t + 10)^{0.3}$.
$f'(t) = 10.72(0.3)(0.9t + 10)^{-0.7}(0.9) = 2.8944(0.9t + 10)^{-0.7}$
$f''(t) = 2.8944(-0.7)(0.9t + 10)^{-1.7}(0.9) = -1.823472(0.9t + 10)^{-1.7}$
So $f''(10) = -1.823472(19)^{-1.7} \approx -0.01222$. And this says that the rate of the rate of change of the population is decreasing at the rate of 0.01%/ yr^2

38. $P(t) = 33.55(t + 5)^{0.205}$; $P'(t) = 33.55(0.205)(t + 5)^{-0.795} = 6.87775(t + 5)^{-0.795}$
$P''(t) = 6.87775(-0.795)(t + 5)^{-1.795} = -5.46781125(t + 5)^{-1.795}$
So $P''(20) = 6.87775(-0.795)(t + 5)^{-1.795} = -5.46781125(t + 5)^{-1.795}$
And this says that the rate of the rate of change of such mothers is decreasing at the rate of 0.02%/ yr^2

39 False. If f has derivatives of order two at $x = a$, then $f''(a) = [f'(a)]^2$.

40. True. If $h = fg$ where f and g have derivatives of order 2. Then
$h''(x) = f''(x)g(x) + 2f'(x)g'(x) + f(x)g''(x)$.

41 True. If $f(x)$ is a polynomial function of degree n, then $f^{(n+1)}(x) = 0$.

42. True. Suppose $P(t)$ represents the population of bacteria at time t and suppose $P'(t) > 0$ and $P''(t) < 0$, then the population is increasing at time t but at a

decreasing rate.

43. True. Using the chain rule, $h'(x) = f'(2x) \cdot \dfrac{d}{dx}(2x) = f'(x) \cdot 2 = 2f'(2x)$

   Using the chain rule again, $h''(x) = 2f''(2x) \cdot 2 = 4f''(2x)$.

44. $f'(x) = \frac{7}{3}x^{5/3}$, $f''(x) = \frac{35}{9}x^{2/3}$, and so f' and f'' exist everywhere.

   But $f'''(x) = \frac{70}{27}x^{-1/3} = \dfrac{70}{27x^{1/3}}$ is not defined at $x = 0$.

45 Consider the function $f(x) = x^{(2n+1)/2} = x^{n+(1/2)}$

   Then $f'(x) = (n+\frac{1}{2})x^{n-(1/2)}$

   $f''(x) = (n+\frac{1}{2})(n-\frac{1}{2})x^{n-(3/2)}$

   ....

   $f^{(n)}(x) = (n+\frac{1}{2})(n-\frac{1}{2}) \cdots \frac{3}{2}x^{1/2}$

   $f^{(n+1)}(x) = (n+\frac{1}{2})(n-\frac{1}{2}) \cdots \frac{1}{2}x^{-1/2}$.

   The first n derivatives exist at $x = 0$, but the $(n + 1)$st derivative fails to be defined there.

46. Let $P(x) = a_0x^n + a_1x^{n-1} + a_2x^{n-2} + \cdots + a_n$. Then
   $P'(x) = na_0x^{n-1} + (n-1)a_1x^{n-2} + \cdots a_{n-1}$.
   Eventually, $P^{(n)}(x) = a_0$, $P^{(n+1)}(x) = P^{(n+2)}(x) = P^{(n+3)}(x) = \cdots = 0$.
   So P has derivatives of all orders.

USING TECHNOLOGY EXERCISES 3.5, page 220

1. –18   2. 425.25   3. 15.2762   4. 128.7540

5. –0.6255   6. –13.9463   7 0.1973   8. –0.0163

9   $f''(6) = -68.46214$ and it tells us that at the beginning of 1988, the rate of the rate of the rate at which banks were failing was 68 banks per year per year per year.

10. $S''(7) = -0.6444$ and this says that at the beginning of 1997, the rate of change in the sales of the multimedia market were dropping at the rate of 0.644 billion

dollars per year per year per year.

3.6 CONCEPT QUESTIONS, page 229

1. a. We differentiate both sides of $F(x, y) = 0$ with respect to x. Then solve for dy/dx.

   b. The chain rule is used to differentiate any expression involving the dependent variable y.

2. $xg(y) + yf(x) = 0$. Differentiating both sides with respect to x gives
$$xg'(y) + g(y) + y'f(x) + yf'(x) = 0$$
$$[xg'(y) + f(x)]y' = -[g(y) + yf'(x)]$$
$$y' = -\frac{g(y) + yf'(x)}{f(x) + xg'(y)}$$

3. Suppose x and y are two variables that are related by an equation. Furthermore, suppose x and y are both functions of a third variable t. (Normally, t represents time). Then a related rates problem involves finding dx/dt or dy/dt.

4. See page 227 in the text.

EXERCISES 3.6, page 229

1. a. Solving for y in terms of x, we have $y = -\frac{1}{2}x + \frac{5}{2}$. Therefore, $y' = -\frac{1}{2}$.

   b. Next, differentiating $x + 2y = 5$ implicitly, we have $1 + 2y' = 0$, or $y' = -\frac{1}{2}$.

2. a. Solving for y in terms of x, we have $y = -\frac{3}{4}x + \frac{3}{2}$. Therefore, $y' = -\frac{3}{4}$

   b. Next, differentiating $3x + 4y = 6$ implicitly, we obtain $3 + 4y' = 0$, or $y' = -\frac{3}{4}$.

3. a. $xy = 1$, $y = \dfrac{1}{x}$, and $\dfrac{dy}{dx} = -\dfrac{1}{x^2}$.

   b. $\quad x\dfrac{dy}{dx} + y = 0$
$$x\frac{dy}{dx} = -y$$
$$\frac{dy}{dx} = -\frac{y}{x} = \frac{-\frac{1}{x}}{x} = -\frac{1}{x^2}.$$

4. a. Solving for y, we have $y(x - 1) = 1$ or $y = (x - 1)^{-1}$ Therefore,
$$y' = -(x-1)^{-2} = -\frac{1}{(x-1)^2}.$$
   b. Next, differentiating $xy - y - 1 = 0$ implicitly, we obtain
$$y + xy' - y' = 0, \text{ or } y'(x - 1) = -y \quad \text{or} \quad y' = -\frac{y}{x-1} = -\frac{1}{(x-1)^2}$$

5. $x^3 - x^2 - xy = 4.$
   a. $-xy = 4 - x^3 + x^2$
$$y = -\frac{4}{x} + x^2 - x \text{ and } y' = \frac{4}{x^2} + 2x - 1.$$
   b. $x^3 - x^2 - xy = 4$
$$-x\frac{dy}{dx} = -3x^2 + 2x + y$$
$$\frac{dy}{dx} = 3x - 2 - \frac{y}{x}$$
$$= 3x - 2 - \frac{1}{x}(-\frac{4}{x} + x^2 - x) = 3x - 2 + \frac{4}{x^2} - x + 1$$
$$= \frac{4}{x^2} + 2x - 1.$$

6. $x^2y - x^2 + y - 1 = 0.$
   a. $(x^2 + 1)y = 1 + x^2$, or $y = \frac{1+x^2}{1+x^2} = 1$. Therefore, $\frac{dy}{dx} = 0$.
   b. Differentiating implicitly,
$$x^2y' + 2xy - 2x + y' = 0; \quad (x^2 + 1)y' = 2x(1 - y); \quad y' = \frac{2x(1-y)}{x^2+1}$$
   But from part (1), we know that $y = 1$, so $y' = \frac{2x(1-1)}{x^2+1} = 0$.

7 a. $\frac{x}{y} - x^2 = 1$ is equivalent to $\frac{x}{y} = x^2 + 1$, or $y = \frac{x}{x^2+1}$. Therefore,

$$y' = \frac{(x^2+1) - x(2x)}{(x^2+1)^2} = \frac{1-x^2}{(x^2+1)^2}.$$

b. Next, differentiating the equation $x - x^2y = y$ implicitly, we obtain

$$1 - 2xy - x^2y' = y', \ y'(1+x^2) = 1 - 2xy, \ \text{or} \ y' = \frac{1-2xy}{(1+x^2)}$$

(This may also be written in the form $-2y^2 + \frac{y}{x}$.) To show that this is equivalent to

the results obtained earlier, use the value of y obtained before, to get

$$y' = \frac{1 - 2x\left(\frac{x}{x^2+1}\right)}{1+x^2} = \frac{x^2 + 1 - 2x^2}{(1+x^2)^2} = \frac{1-x^2}{(1+x^2)^2}$$

8. a. $\frac{y}{x} - 2x^3 = 4$ is equivalent to $y = 2x^4 + 4x$. Therefore, $y' = 8x^3 + 4$.

b. Next, differentiating the equation $y - 2x^4 = 4x$ implicitly, we obtain
$$y' - 8x^3 = 4 \quad \text{and so} \ y' = 8x^3 + 4$$
as obtained earlier.

9 $x^2 + y^2 = 16$. Differentiating both sides of the equation implicitly, we obtain
$$2x + 2yy' = 0 \ \text{and so} \ y' = -\frac{x}{y}.$$

10. $2x^2 + y^2 = 16, \ 4x + 2y\frac{dy}{dx} = 0 \ \text{and} \ \frac{dy}{dx} = -\frac{2x}{y}.$

11. $x^2 - 2y^2 = 16$. Differentiating implicitly with respect to x, we have
$$2x - 4y\frac{dy}{dx} = 0 \ \text{and} \ \frac{dy}{dx} = \frac{x}{2y}.$$

12. $x^3 + y^3 + y - 4 = 0$. Differentiating both sides of the equation implicitly, we obtain
$$3x^2 + 3y^2y' + y' = 0 \ \text{or} \ y'(3y^2 + 1) = -3x^2. \ \text{Therefore,} \ y' = -\frac{3x^2}{3y^2+1}$$

13. $x^2 - 2xy = 6$. Differentiating both sides of the equation implicitly, we obtain

$2x - 2y - 2xy' = 0$ and so $y' = \dfrac{x-y}{x} = 1 - \dfrac{y}{x}$.

14 $x^2 + 5xy + y^2 = 10$. Differentiating both sides of the equation implicitly, we obtain

$2x + 5y + 5xy' + 2yy' = 0$, $2x + 5y + y'(5x + 2y) = 0$ and so $\;\; y' = -\dfrac{2x+5y}{5x+2y}$.

15. $x^2y^2 - xy = 8$. Differentiating both sides of the equation implicitly, we obtain

$$2xy^2 + 2x^2yy' - y - xy' = 0,\; 2xy^2 - y + y'(2x^2y - x) = 0$$

and so $\qquad\qquad y' = \dfrac{y(1-2xy)}{x(2xy-1)} = -\dfrac{y}{x}.$

16. $x^2y^3 - 2xy^2 = 5$. Differentiating both sides of the equation implicitly, we obtain

$$2xy^3 + 3x^2y^2y' - 2y^2 - 4xyy' = 0,\;\; 2y^2(xy-1) + xy(3xy-4)y' = 0,$$

So $\qquad\qquad y' = \dfrac{2y(1-xy)}{x(3xy-4)}$

17 $x^{1/2} + y^{1/2} = 1$. Differentiating implicitly with respect to x, we have

$$\tfrac{1}{2}x^{-1/2} + \tfrac{1}{2}y^{-1/2}\dfrac{dy}{dx} = 0. \;\; \text{Therefore,} \;\; \dfrac{dy}{dx} = -\dfrac{x^{-1/2}}{y^{-1/2}} = -\dfrac{\sqrt{y}}{\sqrt{x}}$$

18. $x^{1/3} + y^{1/3} = 1$. Differentiating both sides of the equation implicitly, we obtain

$$\tfrac{1}{3}x^{-2/3} + \tfrac{1}{3}y^{-2/3}y' = 0 \;\; \text{and so} \;\; y' = -\dfrac{x^{-2/3}}{y^{-2/3}} = -\dfrac{y^{2/3}}{x^{2/3}} = -\left(\dfrac{y}{x}\right)^{2/3}.$$

19. $\sqrt{x+y} = x$. Differentiating both sides of the equation implicitly, we obtain

$$\tfrac{1}{2}(x+y)^{-1/2}(1+y') = 1,\;\; 1 + y' = 2(x+y)^{1/2},$$

or $\qquad\qquad y' = 2\sqrt{x+y} - 1.$

20. $(2x+3y)^{1/3} = x^2$. Differentiating both sides of the equation implicitly, we obtain

$$\tfrac{1}{3}(2x+3y)^{-2/3}(2+3y') = 2x,\;\; 2 + 3y' = 6x(2x+3y)^{2/3}$$

or $\qquad\qquad y' = \tfrac{2}{3}[3x(2x+3y)^{2/3} - 1].$

21. $\dfrac{1}{x^2}+\dfrac{1}{y^2}=1.$ Differentiating both sides of the equation implicitly, we obtain

$$-\dfrac{2}{x^3}-\dfrac{2}{y^3}y'=0, \text{ or } y'=-\dfrac{y^3}{x^3}.$$

22. $\dfrac{1}{x^3}+\dfrac{1}{y^3}=5.$ Differentiating both sides of the equation implicitly, we obtain

$$-\dfrac{3}{x^4}-\dfrac{3}{y^4}y'=0, \text{ or } y'=-\dfrac{y^4}{x^4}.$$

23. $\sqrt{xy}=x+y$ Differentiating both sides of the equation implicitly, we obtain

$$\tfrac{1}{2}(xy)^{-1/2}(xy'+y)=1+y'$$
$$xy'+y=2\sqrt{xy}(1+y')$$
$$y'(x-2\sqrt{xy})=2\sqrt{xy}-y$$

or
$$y'=-\dfrac{(2\sqrt{xy}-y)}{(2\sqrt{xy}-x)}=\dfrac{2\sqrt{xy}-y}{x-2\sqrt{xy}}$$

24. $\sqrt{xy}=2x+y^2.$ Differentiating both sides of the equation implicitly, we obtain

$$\tfrac{1}{2}(xy)^{-1/2}(xy'+y)=2+2yy'$$
$$xy'+y=4\sqrt{xy}+4\sqrt{xy}\,yy' \;\Rightarrow\; y'(x-4y\sqrt{xy})=4\sqrt{xy}-y$$

and
$$y'=\dfrac{4\sqrt{xy}-y}{x-4y\sqrt{xy}}.$$

25. $\dfrac{x+y}{x-y}=3x,$ or $x+y=3x^2-3xy.$ Differentiating both sides of the equation implicitly, we obtain $\quad 1+y'=6x-3xy'-3y$ or $y'=\dfrac{6x-3y-1}{3x+1}$

26. $\dfrac{x-y}{2x+3y}=2x,$ or $x-y=4x^2+6xy.$ Differentiating both sides of the equation implicitly, we have $1-y'=8x+6y+6xy'$ or $y'=-\dfrac{8x+6y-1}{6x+1}.$

27. $xy^{3/2} = x^2 + y^2$. Differentiating implicitly with respect to x, we obtain

$$y^{3/2} + x\left(\tfrac{3}{2}\right)y^{1/2}\frac{dy}{dx} = 2x + 2y\frac{dy}{dx}$$

$$2y^{3/2} + 3xy^{1/2}\frac{dy}{dx} = 4x + 4y\frac{dy}{dx} \qquad \text{(Multiplying by 2.)}$$

$$(3xy^{1/2} - 4y)\frac{dy}{dx} = 4x - 2y^{3/2}$$

$$\frac{dy}{dx} = \frac{2(2x - y^{3/2})}{3xy^{1/2} - 4y}.$$

28. $x^2 y^{1/2} = x + 2y^3$. Differentiating implicitly with respect to x, we have

$$2xy^{1/2} + \tfrac{1}{2}x^2 y^{-1/2}y' = 1 + 6y^2 y' \Rightarrow 4xy + x^2 y' = 2y^{1/2} + 12y^{5/2}y'$$

or

$$y' = \frac{2\sqrt{y} - 4xy}{x^2 - 12y^{5/2}}.$$

29. $(x + y)^3 + x^3 + y^3 = 0$. Differentiating implicitly with respect to x, we obtain

$$3(x + y)^2\left(1 + \frac{dy}{dx}\right) + 3x^2 + 3y^2\frac{dy}{dx} = 0$$

$$(x + y)^2 + (x + y)^2\frac{dy}{dx} + x^2 + y^2\frac{dy}{dx} = 0$$

$$[(x + y)^2 + y^2]\frac{dy}{dx} = -[(x + y)^2 + x^2]$$

$$\frac{dy}{dx} = -\frac{2x^2 + 2xy + y^2}{x^2 + 2xy + 2y^2}.$$

30. $(x + y^2)^{10} = x^2 + 25$. Differentiating both sides of the equation with respect to x, we obtain $10(x + y^2)^9(1 + 2yy') = 2x$, or $y' = \dfrac{x - 5(x + y^2)^9}{10y(x + y^2)^9}.$

31 $4x^2 + 9y^2 = 36$. Differentiating the equation implicitly, we obtain
$$8x + 18yy' = 0.$$
At the point $(0,2)$, we have $0 + 36y' = 0$ and the slope of the tangent line is 0. Therefore, an equation of the tangent line is $y = 2$.

32. $y^2 - x^2 = 16$. Differentiating both sides of the equation implicitly, we obtain $2yy' - 2x = 0$. At the point $(2, 2\sqrt{5})$, we have $4\sqrt{5}y' - 4 = 0$, or $m = \frac{1}{\sqrt{5}} = \frac{\sqrt{5}}{5}$
Using the point–slope form of an equation of a line, we have $y = \frac{\sqrt{5}}{5}x + \frac{8\sqrt{5}}{5}$

33. $x^2y^3 - y^2 + xy - 1 = 0$. Differentiating implicitly with respect to x, we have
$$2xy^3 + 3x^2y^2\frac{dy}{dx} - 2y\frac{dy}{dx} + y + x\frac{dy}{dx} = 0.$$
At $(1,1)$, $2 + 3\frac{dy}{dx} - 2\frac{dy}{dx} + 1 + \frac{dy}{dx} = 0$, and
$$2\frac{dy}{dx} = -3 \quad \text{and} \quad \frac{dy}{dx} = -\frac{3}{2}$$
Using the point-slope form of an equation of a line, we have
$y - 1 = -\frac{3}{2}(x - 1)$, and the equation of the tangent line to the graph of the function
f at $(1,1)$ is $y = -\frac{3}{2}x + \frac{5}{2}$.

34. $(x - y - 1)^3 = x$. Differentiating both sides of the given equation implicitly, we obtain $3(x - y - 1)^2(1 - y') = 1$. At the point $(1,-1)$, $3(1 + 1 - 1)^2(1 - y') = 1$ or $y' = \frac{2}{3}$
Using the point–slope form of an equation of a line, we have
$$y + 1 = \frac{2}{3}(x - 1) \quad \text{or} \quad y = \frac{2}{3}x - \frac{5}{3}.$$

35. $xy = 1$. Differentiating implicitly, we have $xy' + y = 0$, or $y' = -\frac{y}{x}$.

Differentiating implicitly once again, we have $xy'' + y' + y' = 0$

Therefore, $y'' = -\frac{2y'}{x} = \frac{2\left(\frac{y}{x}\right)}{x} = \frac{2y}{x^2}$.

36. $x^3 + y^3 = 28$. Differentiating implicitly, we have
$$3x^2 + 3y^2y' = 0, \quad \text{or} \quad y' = -\frac{x^2}{y^2}.$$

Differentiating again, we have $6x + 3y^2y'' + 6y(y')^2 = 0$.

So $y'' = -\frac{2y(y')^2 + 2x}{y^2}$. But $\frac{dy}{dx} = -\frac{x^2}{y^2}$, and, therefore,

$$y'' = -\frac{2y\left(\dfrac{x^4}{y^4}\right) + 2x}{y^2} = -\frac{2\left(\dfrac{x^4}{y^3} + x\right)}{y^2} = -\frac{2x(x^3 + y^3)}{y^5}$$

37. $y^2 - xy = 8$. Differentiating implicitly we have $2yy' - y - xy' = 0$

and $y' = \dfrac{y}{2y - x}$. Differentiating implicitly again, we have

$$2(y')^2 + 2yy'' - y' - y' - xy'' = 0, \quad \text{or} \quad y'' = \frac{2y' - 2(y')^2}{2y - x}.$$

Then $\quad y'' = \dfrac{2\left(\dfrac{y}{2y - x}\right)\left(1 - \dfrac{y}{2y - x}\right)}{2y - x} = \dfrac{2y(2y - x - y)}{(2y - x)^3} = \dfrac{2y(y - x)}{(2y - x)^3}$

38. Differentiating implicitly, we have $\frac{1}{3}x^{-2/3} + \frac{1}{3}y^{-2/3}y' = 0$ and $y' = -\dfrac{y^{2/3}}{x^{2/3}}$.

Differentiating implicitly once again, we have

$$y'' = -\frac{x^{2/3}\left(\frac{2}{3}\right)y^{-1/3}y' - y^{2/3}\left(\frac{2}{3}\right)x^{-1/3}}{x^{4/3}} = \frac{-\dfrac{2}{3}x^{2/3}y^{-1/3}\left(-\dfrac{y^{2/3}}{x^{2/3}}\right) + \dfrac{2}{3}y^{2/3}x^{-1/3}}{x^{4/3}}$$

$$= \frac{2}{3}\left(\frac{y^{1/3} + y^{2/3}x^{-1/3}}{x^{4/3}}\right) = \frac{2y^{1/3}(x^{1/3} + y^{1/3})}{3x^{4/3}x^{1/3}} = \frac{2y^{1/3}}{3x^{5/3}}.$$

39 a. Differentiating the given equation with respect to t, we obtain

$$\frac{dV}{dt} = \pi r^2 \frac{dh}{dt} + 2\pi rh \frac{dr}{dt} = \pi r\left(r\frac{dh}{dt} + 2h\frac{dr}{dt}\right).$$

b. Substituting $r = 2$, $h = 6$, $\dfrac{dr}{dt} = 0.1$ and $\dfrac{dh}{dt} = 0.3$ into the expression for $\dfrac{dV}{dt}$

we obtain $\dfrac{dV}{dt} = \pi(2)[2(0.3) + 2(6)(0.1)] = 3.6\pi$, and so the volume is increasing at

the rate of 3.6π cu in/sec.

40. Let $(x, 0)$ and $(0, y)$ denote the position of the two cars. Then $D^2 = x^2 + y^2$.

Differentiating with respect to t, we obtain

or $\quad D\dfrac{dD}{dt} = x\dfrac{dx}{dt} + y\dfrac{dy}{dt}$

$\quad 2D\dfrac{dD}{dt} = 2x\dfrac{dx}{dt} + 2y\dfrac{dy}{dt}$

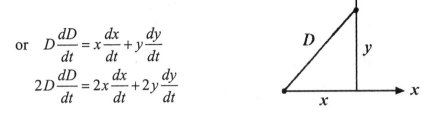

When $t = 4$, $x = -20$, and $y = 28$, $\dfrac{dx}{dt} = -9$, and $\dfrac{dy}{dt} = 11$.

Therefore, $\left(\sqrt{(-20)^2 + (28)^2}\right)\dfrac{dD}{dt} = (-20)(-9) + (28)(11) = 488$

and $\qquad\qquad \dfrac{dD}{dt} = \dfrac{488}{\sqrt{1184}} = 14.18$ ft/sec.

That is, the distance is changing at the rate of 14 18 ft/sec.

41. We are given $\dfrac{dp}{dt} = 2$ and are required to find $\dfrac{dx}{dt}$ when $x = 9$ and $p = 63$.

Differentiating the equation $p + x^2 = 144$ with respect to t, we obtain

$$\dfrac{dp}{dt} + 2x\dfrac{dx}{dt} = 0.$$

When $x = 9$, $p = 63$, and $\dfrac{dp}{dt} = 2$,

$$2 + 2(9)\dfrac{dx}{dt} = 0$$

and $\qquad\qquad \dfrac{dx}{dt} = -\dfrac{1}{9} \approx -0.111,$

or the quantity demanded is decreasing at the rate of 111 tires per week.

42. $p = \frac{1}{2}x^2 + 48$. Differentiating implicitly, we have

$$\dfrac{dp}{dt} - x\dfrac{dx}{dt} = 0, \text{ and } \quad -x\dfrac{dx}{dt} = -\dfrac{dp}{dt}, \quad \text{or} \quad \dfrac{dx}{dt} = \dfrac{\dfrac{dp}{dt}}{x}.$$

When $x = 6$, $p = 66$, and $\dfrac{dp}{dt} = -3$, we have $\dfrac{dx}{dt} = -\dfrac{3}{6} = -\dfrac{1}{2}$, or $\left(-\tfrac{1}{2}\right)(1000) = -500$ tires/week.

43. $100x^2 + 9p^2 = 3600$. Differentiating the given equation implicitly with respect to t,
we have $200x\dfrac{dx}{dt} + 18p\dfrac{dp}{dt} = 0$. Next, when $p = 14$, the given equation yields
$$100x^2 + 9(14)^2 = 3600$$
$$100x^2 = 1836,$$
or $x = 4.2849$. When $p = 14$, $\dfrac{dp}{dt} = -0.15$, and $x = 4.2849$, we have
$$200(4.2849)\dfrac{dx}{dt} + 18(14)(-0.15) = 0$$
$$\dfrac{dx}{dt} = 0.0441.$$
So the quantity demanded is increasing at the rate of 44 ten–packs per week.

44. $625p^2 - x^2 = 100$. Differentiating the given equation implicitly with respect to t,
we have $1250p\dfrac{dp}{dt} - 2x\dfrac{dx}{dt} = 0$. To find p when $x = 25$, we solve the equation
$$625p^2 - 625 = 100 \text{ giving } \quad p = \sqrt{\dfrac{725}{625}} \approx 1.0770.$$
Therefore, $\quad 1250(1.077)(-0.02) - 2(25)\dfrac{dx}{dt} = 0 \quad$ and $\dfrac{dx}{dt} = -0.5385.$
We conclude that the supply is falling at the rate of 539 dozen eggs per week.

45. From the results of Problem 44, we have
$$1250p\dfrac{dp}{dt} - 2x\dfrac{dx}{dt} = 0.$$
When $p = 1.0770$, $x = 25$, and $\dfrac{dx}{dt} = -1$, we find that
$$1250(1.077)\dfrac{dp}{dt} - 2(25)(-1) = 0,$$
and $\qquad \dfrac{dp}{dt} = -\dfrac{50}{1250(1.077)} = -0.037.$
We conclude that the price is decreasing at the rate of 3.7 cents per carton.

46. $p = -0.01x^2 - 0.1x + 6$. Differentiating the given equation with respect to t, we obtain

$$1 = -0.02x\frac{dx}{dp} - 0.1\frac{dx}{dp}$$

$$= -(0.02x + 0.1)\frac{dx}{dp}.$$

When $x = 10$, we have

$$1 = -[0.02(10) + 0.1]\frac{dx}{dp} \text{ ,or} \qquad \frac{dx}{dp} = -\frac{1}{0.3} = -\frac{10}{3}.$$

Also, for this value of x, $p = -0.01(100) - 0.1(10) + 6 = 4$.

Therefore, for these values of x and p,

$$E(p) = -\frac{pf'(p)}{f(p)} = -\frac{4\left(-\dfrac{10}{3}\right)}{10} = \frac{4}{3} > 1 \qquad \left[f'(p) = \frac{dx}{dp}\right]$$

and the demand is elastic.

47. $p = -0.01x^2 - 0.2x + 8$. Differentiating the given equation implicitly with respect to p, we have

$$1 = -0.02x\frac{dx}{dp} - 0.2\frac{dx}{dp} = [0.02x + 0.2]\frac{dx}{dp}$$

or $\qquad \dfrac{dx}{dp} = -\dfrac{1}{0.02x + 0.2}.$

When $x = 15$, $p = -0.01(15)^2 - 0.2(15) + 8 = 2.75$

and $\qquad \dfrac{dx}{dp} = -\dfrac{1}{0.02(15) + 0.2} = -2.$

Therefore, $\quad E(p) = -\dfrac{pf'(p)}{f(p)} = -\dfrac{(2.75)(-2)}{15} = 0.37 < 1$,

and the demand is inelastic.

48. $V = x^3$. $\dfrac{dV}{dt} = 3x^2 \dfrac{dx}{dt} \Rightarrow \dfrac{dV}{dt} = 3(25)(0.1) = 7.5$ cu in/sec.

49. $A = \pi r^2$ Differentiating with respect to t, we obtain

$$\frac{dA}{dt} = 2\pi r \frac{dr}{dt}$$

When the radius of the circle is 40 ft and increasing at the rate of 2 ft/sec,

$$\frac{dA}{dt} = 2\pi(40)(2) = 160\pi, \text{ or } 160\pi \text{ ft}^2 / \text{sec}$$

50. Let D denote the distance between the two ships, x the distance that Ship A traveled north, and y the distance that Ship B traveled east. Then $D^2 = x^2 + y^2$. Differentiating implicitly, we have

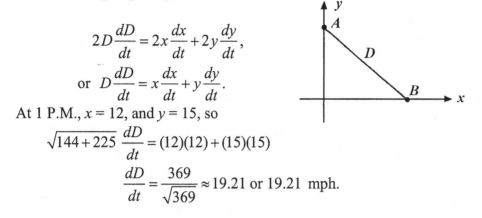

$$2D\frac{dD}{dt} = 2x\frac{dx}{dt} + 2y\frac{dy}{dt},$$

or $D\frac{dD}{dt} = x\frac{dx}{dt} + y\frac{dy}{dt}.$

At 1 P.M., $x = 12$, and $y = 15$, so

$$\sqrt{144 + 225}\,\frac{dD}{dt} = (12)(12) + (15)(15)$$

$$\frac{dD}{dt} = \frac{369}{\sqrt{369}} \approx 19.21 \text{ or } 19.21 \text{ mph.}$$

51. Let D denote the distance between the two cars, x the distance traveled by the car heading east, and y the distance traveled by the car heading north as shown in the diagram at the right. Then $D^2 = x^2 + y^2$. Differentiating with respect to t, we have

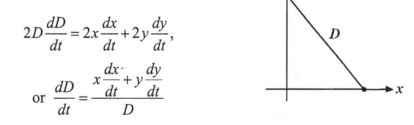

$$2D\frac{dD}{dt} = 2x\frac{dx}{dt} + 2y\frac{dy}{dt},$$

or $\dfrac{dD}{dt} = \dfrac{x\dfrac{dx}{dt} + y\dfrac{dy}{dt}}{D}$

When $t = 5$, $x = 30, y = 40, \dfrac{dx}{dt} = 2(5) + 1 = 11$, and $\dfrac{dy}{dt} = 2(5) + 3 = 13$

Therefore, $\dfrac{dD}{dt} = \dfrac{(30)(11) + (40)(13)}{\sqrt{900 + 1600}} = 17$, or 17 ft/sec.

52. $D^2 = x^2 + (50)^2 = x^2 + 2500$. Differentiating implicitly with respect to t, we have

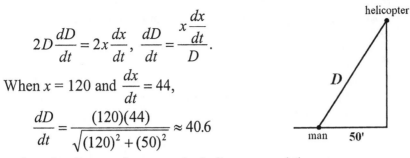

$$2D\frac{dD}{dt} = 2x\frac{dx}{dt}, \quad \frac{dD}{dt} = \frac{x\dfrac{dx}{dt}}{D}.$$

When $x = 120$ and $\dfrac{dx}{dt} = 44$,

$$\frac{dD}{dt} = \frac{(120)(44)}{\sqrt{(120)^2 + (50)^2}} \approx 40.6$$

and so the distance between the helicopter and the man is increasing at the rate of 40.6 ft/sec.

53. Referring to the diagram at the right, we see that
$$D^2 = 120^2 + x^2.$$
Differentiating this last equation with respect to t, we have

$$2D\frac{dD}{dt} = 2x\frac{dx}{dt} \quad \text{and} \quad \frac{dD}{dt} = \frac{x\dfrac{dx}{dt}}{D}.$$

When $x = 50$, $D = \sqrt{120^2 + 50^2} = 130$ and
$$\frac{dD}{dt} = \frac{(20)(50)}{130} \approx 7.69, \quad \text{or } 7.69 \text{ ft/sec.}$$

54. Refer to the diagram at the right. By the Pythagorean Theorem,
$$s^2 = x^2 + 4^2 = x^2 + 16.$$
We want to find $\dfrac{dx}{dt}$ when $x = 25$,

given that $\dfrac{ds}{dt} = -3$. Differentiating

both sides of the equation with respect to t yields

$$2s\frac{ds}{dt} = 2x\frac{dx}{dt} \quad \text{or} \quad \frac{dx}{dt} = \frac{s\dfrac{ds}{dt}}{x}.$$

Now, when $x = 25$, $s^2 = 25^2 + 16 = 241$ and $s = \sqrt{241}$. Therefore, when $x = 25$, we have $\dfrac{dx}{dt} = \dfrac{\sqrt{241}(-3)}{25} \approx -1.86$; that is, the boat is approaching the dock at the rate of approximately 1.86 ft/sec.

55. Let V and S denote its volume and surface area. Then we are given that

$\dfrac{dV}{dt} = -kS$, where k is the constant of proportionality. But from $V = \left(\dfrac{4}{3}\right)\pi r^3$,

we find, upon differentiating both sides with respect to t, that

$$\frac{dV}{dt} = \left(\frac{4}{3}\right)\pi(3\pi r^2)\frac{dr}{dt} = 4\pi^2 r^2 \frac{dr}{dt}$$

and using the fact stated earlier,

$$\frac{dV}{dt} = 4\pi^2 r^2 \frac{dr}{dt} = -kS = -k(4\pi r^2).$$

Therefore, $\dfrac{dr}{dt} = -\dfrac{k(4\pi r^2)}{4\pi^2 r^2} = -\dfrac{k}{\pi}$ and this proves that the radius is decreasing at the constant rate of (k/π) units/unit time.

56. Let V denote the volume of the soap bubble, and r its radius. Then, we are given

$\dfrac{dV}{dt} = 8$. From the formula, $V = \dfrac{4}{3}\pi r^3$, we find, upon differentiating with respect

to t, $\quad \dfrac{dV}{dt} = \left(\dfrac{4}{3}\right)\left(3\pi r^2 \dfrac{dr}{dt}\right) = 4\pi r^2 \dfrac{dr}{dt}$.

So, $\quad \dfrac{dr}{dt} = \dfrac{\dfrac{dV}{dt}}{4\pi r^2}$. At the instant of time that $r = 10$, we have

$\dfrac{dr}{dt} = \dfrac{8}{4\pi(10^2)} \approx 0.0064$. So, the radius is increasing at the rate of approximately

0.0064 cm/sec. From $s = 4\pi r^2$, we find $\dfrac{ds}{dt} = 4\pi(2r)\dfrac{dr}{dt} = 8\pi r \dfrac{dr}{dt}$. Therefore,

when $r = 10$, we have $\dfrac{ds}{dt} \approx 8\pi(10)(0.0064) = 1.6$. So, the surface area is increasing

at the rate of approximately 1.6 $cm^2 / \sec$.

57. Refer to the figure at the right.

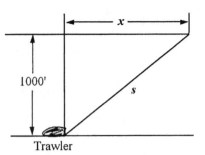

We are given that $\dfrac{dx}{dt} = 264$. Using the

Pythagorean Theorem,
$$s^2 = x^2 + 1000^2 = x^2 + 1000000.$$

We want to find $\dfrac{ds}{dt}$ when $s = 1500$.

Differentiating both sides of the equation with respect to t, we have

$$2s\frac{ds}{dt} = 2x\frac{dx}{dt} \quad \text{and so} \quad \frac{ds}{dt} = \frac{x\dfrac{dx}{dt}}{s}$$

Now, when $s = 1500$, we have
$$1500^2 = x^2 + 10000 \quad \text{or} \quad x = \sqrt{1250000}.$$

Therefore, $\qquad \dfrac{ds}{dt} = \dfrac{\sqrt{1250000} \cdot (264)}{1500} \approx 196.8$,

that is, the aircraft is receding from the trawler at the speed of approximately 196.8 ft/sec.

58. The volume V of the water in the pot is $V = \pi r^2 h = \pi(16)h = 16\pi h$. Differentiating

with respect to t, we obtain $\dfrac{dV}{dt} = 16\pi\dfrac{dh}{dt}$ Therefore, with $\dfrac{dh}{dt} = 0.4$, we find

$\dfrac{dV}{dt} = 16\pi(0.4) \approx 20.1$; that is, water is being poured into the pot at the rate of

approximately 20.1 cm^2/sec.

59. Refer to the diagram at the right.

$$\frac{y}{6} = \frac{y+x}{18}, \quad 18y = 6(y+x)$$
$$3y = y + x, \quad 2y = x, \quad y = \tfrac{1}{2}x.$$

Then $D = y + x = \tfrac{3}{2}x$. Differentiating

implicitly, we have $\qquad \dfrac{dD}{dt} = \dfrac{3}{2} \bullet \dfrac{dx}{dt}$

and when $\dfrac{dx}{dt} = 6$, $\dfrac{dD}{dt} = \dfrac{3}{2}(6) = 9$, or 9 ft / sec.

60. Differentiating $x^2 + y^2 = 400$ with respect to t gives $2x\dfrac{dx}{dt} + 2y\dfrac{dy}{dt} = 0$

When $x = 12$, we have $144 + y^2 = 400$, or $y = \sqrt{256} = 16$. Therefore, with

$x = 12$, $\dfrac{dx}{dt} = 5$, and $y = 16$, we find $2(12)(5) + 2(16)\dfrac{dy}{dt} = 0$, or $\dfrac{dy}{dt} = -3.75$,

that is, the top of the ladder is sliding down the wall at 3.75 ft/sec.

61 Differentiating $x^2 + y^2 = 13^2 = 169$ with respect to t gives

$$2x\dfrac{dx}{dt} + 2y\dfrac{dy}{dt} = 0.$$

When $x = 12$, we have

$$144 + y^2 = 169 \quad \text{or} \quad y = 5.$$

Therefore, with $x = 12$, $y = 5$, and $\dfrac{dx}{dt} = 8$, we

find $\quad 2(12)(8) + 2(5)\dfrac{dy}{dt} = 0$, or

$\dfrac{dy}{dt} = -19.2$, that is, the top of the ladder is sliding down the wall at 19.2 ft/sec.

62. Differentiating the equation $2h^{1/2} + \dfrac{1}{25}t - 2\sqrt{20} = 0$ with respect to t gives

$2\left(\dfrac{1}{2}h^{-1/2}\right)\dfrac{dh}{dt} + \dfrac{1}{25} = 0$, or $\dfrac{dh}{dt} = -\dfrac{\sqrt{h}}{25}$. Therefore, with $h = 8$, we have

$\dfrac{dh}{dt} = \dfrac{\sqrt{8}}{25} \approx -0.113$. That is, the height of the water is decreasing at the rate of

approximately 0.11 ft/sec.

63. True. Differentiating both sides of the equation with respect to x, we have

$$\frac{d}{dx}[f(x)g(y)] = \frac{d}{dx}(0)$$

$$f(x)g'(y)\frac{dy}{dx} + f'(x)g(y) = 0$$

$$\frac{dy}{dx} = -\frac{f'(x)g(y)}{f(x)g'(y)}$$

provided $f(x) \neq 0$ and $g'(y) \neq 0$.

64. True. Differentiating both sides of the equation with respect to x,

$$\frac{d}{dx}[f(x) + g(y)] = \frac{d}{dx}(0); \quad f'(x) + g'(y)\frac{dy}{dx} = 0, \text{ or } \frac{dy}{dx} = -\frac{f'(x)}{g'(y)}.$$

3.7 CONCEPT QUESTIONS, page 237

1. The differential of x is dx. The differential of y is $dy = f'(x)\,dx$
2. $\Delta y = f(x + \Delta x) - f(x) \approx dy$

EXERCISES 3.7, page 238

1. $f(x) = 2x^2$ and $dy = 4x\,dx$.

2. $f(x) = 3x^2 + 1$ and $dy = 6x\,dx$.

3. $f(x) = x^3 - x$ and $dy = (3x^2 - 1)\,dx$.

4. $f(x) = 2x^3 + x$ and $dy = (6x^2 + 1)\,dx$.

5. $f(x) = \sqrt{x+1} = (x+1)^{1/2}$ and $dy = \frac{1}{2}(x+1)^{-1/2}\,dx = \frac{dx}{2\sqrt{x+1}}$.

6. $f(x) = 3x^{-1/2}$ and $dy = -\frac{3}{2x^{3/2}}\,dx$.

7. $f(x) = 2x^{3/2} + x^{1/2}$ and $dy = (3x^{1/2} + \frac{1}{2}x^{-1/2})\,dx = \frac{1}{2}x^{-1/2}(6x + 1)\,dx = \frac{6x+1}{2\sqrt{x}}\,dx$.

8. $f(x) = 3x^{5/6} + 7x^{2/3}$ and $dy = (\frac{5}{2}x^{-1/6} + \frac{14}{3}x^{-1/3})\,dx$

9. $f(x) = x + \frac{2}{x}$ and $dy = \left(1 - \frac{2}{x^2}\right)\,dx = \frac{x^2 - 2}{x^2}\,dx$.

10. $f(x) = \dfrac{3}{x-1}$ and $dy = -\dfrac{3}{(x-1)^2} dx.$

11. $f(x) = \dfrac{x-1}{x^2+1}$ and $dy = \dfrac{x^2+1-(x-1)2x}{(x^2+1)^2} dx = \dfrac{-x^2+2x+1}{(x^2+1)^2} dx.$

12. $f(x) = \dfrac{2x^2+1}{x+1}$ and $dy = \dfrac{(x+1)(4x)-(2x^2+1)}{(x+1)^2} dx = \dfrac{2x^2+4x-1}{(x+1)^2} dx.$

13. $f(x) = \sqrt{3x^2-x} = (3x^2-x)^{1/2}$ and

$$dy = \frac{1}{2}(3x^2-x)^{-1/2}(6x-1)dx = \frac{6x-1}{2\sqrt{3x^2-x}} dx.$$

14. $f(x) = (2x^2+3)^{1/3}$ and $dy = \dfrac{1}{3}(2x^2+3)^{-2/3}(4x)dx = \dfrac{4x}{3(2x^2+3)^{2/3}} dx.$

15. $f(x) = x^2-1.$
    a. $dy = 2x\, dx.$ b. $dy \approx 2(1)(0.02) = 0.04.$
    c. $\Delta y = [(1.02)^2 - 1] - [1 - 1] = 0.0404.$

16. $f(x) = 3x^2 - 2x + 6;$
    a. $dy = (6x-2)\, dx$ b. $dy \approx 10(-0.03) = -0.3.$
    c. $\Delta y = [3(1.97)^2 - 2(1.97) + 6] - [3(2)^2 - 2(2) + 6] = -0.2973.$

17. $f(x) = \dfrac{1}{x}.$
    a. $dy = -\dfrac{dx}{x^2}$ b. $dy \approx -0.05$ c. $\Delta y = \dfrac{1}{-0.95} - \dfrac{1}{-1} = -0.05263.$

18. $f(x) = \sqrt{2x+1} = (2x+1)^{1/2}.$
    a. $dy = \dfrac{1}{2}(2x+1)^{-1/2}(2) = \dfrac{dx}{\sqrt{2x+1}}.$ b. $dy \approx \dfrac{0.1}{\sqrt{9}} = 0.03333$
    c. $\Delta y = [2(4.1) + 1]^{1/2} - [2(4) + 1]^{1/2} = 0.03315.$

19. $y = \sqrt{x}$ and $dy = \dfrac{dx}{2\sqrt{x}}$ Therefore, $\sqrt{10} \approx 3 + \dfrac{1}{2\sqrt{9}} = 3\ 167$.

20. $y = \sqrt{x}$ and $dy = \dfrac{dx}{2\sqrt{x}}$ Therefore, $\sqrt{17} \approx 4 + \dfrac{1}{2 \cdot 4} = 4.125$

21. $y = \sqrt{x}$ and $dy = \dfrac{dx}{2\sqrt{x}}$. Therefore, $\sqrt{49.5} \approx 7 + \dfrac{0.5}{2 \cdot 7} = 7.0357$.

22. $y = \sqrt{x}$ and $dy = \dfrac{dx}{2\sqrt{x}}$. Therefore, $\sqrt{99.7} \approx 10 - \dfrac{0.3}{2 \cdot 10} = 9.85$

23. $y = x^{1/3}$ and $dy = \frac{1}{3}x^{-2/3}\ dx$. Therefore, $\sqrt[3]{7.8} \approx 2 - \dfrac{0.2}{3 \cdot 4} = 1.983$.

24. $y = x^{1/4}$ and $dy = \frac{1}{4}x^{-3/4}\ dx$. Therefore, $\sqrt[4]{81.6} \approx 3 + \dfrac{0.6}{4\ 27} = 3.0056$.

25. $y = \sqrt{x}$ and $dy = \dfrac{dx}{2\sqrt{x}}$. Therefore, $\sqrt{0.089} \approx \frac{1}{10}\sqrt{8.9} = \frac{1}{10}\left[3 - \dfrac{0.1}{2\ 3}\right] \approx 0.298$.

26. $y = \sqrt[3]{x}$ and $dy = \dfrac{dx}{3x^{2/3}}$. Therefore,

$$\sqrt[3]{0.00096} = \dfrac{1}{100}\sqrt[3]{960} \approx \dfrac{1}{100}\left[10 - \dfrac{40}{3(100)}\right] \approx 0.0987.$$

27. $y = f(x) = \sqrt{x} + \dfrac{1}{\sqrt{x}} = x^{1/2} + x^{-1/2}$. Therefore,

$$\dfrac{dy}{dx} = \dfrac{1}{2}x^{-1/2} - \dfrac{1}{2}x^{-3/2}$$

$$dy = \left(\dfrac{1}{2x^{1/2}} - \dfrac{1}{2x^{3/2}}\right)dx.$$

Letting $x = 4$ and $dx = 0.02$, we find

$$\sqrt{4.02} + \frac{1}{\sqrt{4.02}} - f(4) = f(4.02) - f(4) = \Delta y \approx dy$$

$$\sqrt{4.02} + \frac{1}{\sqrt{4.02}} \approx f(4) + dy\Big|_{\substack{x=4 \\ dx=0.02}}$$

$$\approx 2 + \frac{1}{2} + \left(\frac{1}{2 \cdot 2} - \frac{1}{2 \cdot 2\sqrt{2}} \right)(0.02) \approx 2.50146.$$

28. Let $y = f(x) = \dfrac{2x}{x^2 + 1}$.

Then $\dfrac{dy}{dx} = \dfrac{(x^2 + 1)(2) - 2x(2x)}{(x^2 + 1)^2} = \dfrac{2(1 - x^2)}{(x^2 + 1)^2}$

and $dy = \dfrac{2(1 - x^2)}{(x^2 + 1)^2} dx$. Letting $x = 5$ and $dx = -0.02$, we find

$$f(5) - f(4.98) = \frac{2(5)}{5^2 + 1} - \frac{2(4.98)}{(4.98)^2 + 1} = \Delta y \approx dy.$$

$$\frac{2(4.98)}{(4.98)^2 + 1} \approx \frac{10}{26} - \frac{2(1 - 5^2)}{(5^2 + 1)^2}(-0.02) \approx 0.3832.$$

29. The volume of the cube is given by $V = x^3$. Then $dV = 3x^2\,dx$ and when $x = 12$ and $dx = 0.02$, $dV = 3(144)(\pm 0.02) = \pm 8.64$, and the possible error that might occur in calculating the volume is ± 8.64 cm^3.

30. The volume of a cube of side x cm is $V = x^3$. The amount of paint required is $\Delta V \approx dV = 3x^2 \Delta x$. With $x = 30$ and $\Delta x = 2(0.05)$ (twice the thickness of the paint), we find $\Delta V \approx 3(30^2)(0.01) = 270$, or 270 cu cm.

31. The volume of the hemisphere is given by $V = \frac{2}{3}\pi r^3$ The amount of rust-proofer needed is

$$\Delta V = \frac{2}{3}\pi(r + \Delta r)^3 - \frac{2}{3}\pi r^3$$

$$\approx dV = \left(\frac{2}{3} \right)(3\pi r^2)\,dr.$$

So, with $r = 60$, and $dr = \dfrac{1}{12}(0.01)$, we have

$$\Delta V \approx 2\pi(60^2)\left(\frac{1}{12}\right)(0.01) \approx 18.85$$

So we need approximately 18.85 ft^3 of rust-proofer.

32. The volume of the tumor is given by $V = \frac{4}{3}\pi r^3$. Then $dV = 4\pi r^2\, dr$. When $r = 1.1$ and $dr = 0.005$, $dV = 4\pi(1.1)^2(\pm 0.005) = \pm 0.076 \text{ cm}^3$.

33. $dR = \dfrac{d}{dr}(k\ell r^{-4})dr = -4k\ell r^{-5}\,dr$ With $\dfrac{dr}{r} = 0.1$, we find

$$\frac{dR}{R} = -\frac{4k\ell r^{-5}}{k\ell r^{-4}}\,dr = -4\frac{dr}{r} = -4(0.1) = -0.4.$$

In other words, the resistance will drop by 40%.

34. $f(x) = 640x^{1/5}$ and $df = 128x^{-4/5}\,dx$. When $x = 243$ and $dx = 5$, we have $df = 128\left(\frac{5}{81}\right) \approx 7.9$, or approximately 7.9 billion dollars.

35. $f(n) = 4n\sqrt{n-4} = 4n(n-4)^{1/2}$.

Then $df = 4[(n-4)^{1/2} + \frac{1}{2}n(n-4)^{-1/2}]dn$

When $n = 85$ and $dn = 5$, $df = 4[9 + \frac{85}{2.9}]5 \approx 274$ seconds.

36. $P(x) = -\frac{1}{8}x^2 + 7x + 30$ and $dP = (-\frac{1}{4}x + 7)dx$. To estimate the increase in profits when the amount spent on advertising each quarter is increased from \$24,000 to \$26,000, we compute

$$dP = (-\tfrac{24}{4} + 7)(2) = 2, \qquad (dx = 2,\ x = 24)$$

or \$2000 dollars.

37 $N(r) = \dfrac{7}{1 + 0.02r^2}$ and $dN = -\dfrac{0.28r}{(1 + 0.02r^2)^2}\,dr$ To estimate the decrease in the number of housing starts when the mortgage rate is increased from 12 to 12.5 percent, we compute

$$dN = -\frac{(0.28)(12)(0.5)}{(3.88)^2} \approx -0.111595 \quad (r = 12, \, dr = 0.5)$$

or 111,595 fewer housing starts.

38. $s(x) = 0.3\sqrt{x} + 10$ and $s' = \frac{0.15}{\sqrt{x}}dx$. To estimate the change in price when the quantity supplied is increased from 10,000 units to 10,500 units, we compute
$$ds = \frac{(0.15)500}{100} = 0.75, \text{ or } 75 \text{ cents.}$$

39 $p = \frac{30}{0.02x^2 + 1}$ and $dp = -\frac{(1.2x)}{(0.02x^2 + 1)^2}dx$. To estimate the change in the price p when the quantity demanded changed from 5000 to 5500 units ($x = 5$ to $x = 5.5$) per week, we compute $dp = \frac{(-1.2)(5)(0.5)}{[0.02(25)+1]^2} \approx -1.33$, or a decrease of \$1.33.

40. $S = kW^{2/3}$ and $dS = \frac{0.2}{3W^{1/3}}dW$. To determine the percentage error in the calculation of the surface area of a horse that weighs 300 kg when the maximum error in measurement is 0.6 kg and $k = 0.1$, we compute
$$\frac{dS}{S} = \frac{0.2}{3W^{1/3}}dW \cdot \frac{1}{0.1W^{2/3}} = \frac{2}{3W}dW = \frac{2(0.6)}{3(300)} = 0.00133, \text{ or } 0.133 \text{ percent.}$$

41 $P(x) = -0.000032x^3 + 6x - 100$ and $dP = (-0.000096x^2 + 6)\,dx$. To determine the error in the estimate of Trappee's profits corresponding to a maximum error in the forecast of 15 percent $[dx = \pm0.15(200)]$, we compute
$$dP = [(-0.000096)(200)^2 + 6]\,(\pm30) = (2.16)(30) = \pm64.80$$
or $\pm$ \$64,800.

42. $p = \frac{55}{2x^2 + 1}$ and $dp = -\frac{220x}{(2x^2 + 1)^2}dx$. To find the error corresponding to a possible error of 15 percent in a forecast of 1.8 billion bushels, we compute
$$dp = -\frac{(220)(1.8)(\pm 0.27)}{[2(1.8)^2 + 1]^2} \approx 1.91, \text{ or approximately } \pm 1.91 \text{ percent.}$$

43. $N(\dot{x}) = \dfrac{500(400+20x)^{1/2}}{(5+0.2x)^2}$ and

$$N'(x) = \dfrac{(5+0.2x)^2 250(400+20x)^{-1/2}(20) - 500(400+20x)^{1/2}(2)(5+0.2x)(0.2)}{(5+0.2x)^4}\, dx.$$

To estimate the change in the number of crimes if the level of reinvestment changes from 20 cents per dollars deposited to 22 cents per dollar deposited, we compute

$$dN = \dfrac{(5+4)^2(250)(800)^{-1/2}(20) - 500(400+400)^{1/2}(2)(9)(0.2)}{(5+4)^4}(2)$$

$$= \dfrac{(14318.91 - 50911.69)}{9^4}(2) \approx -11$$

or a decrease of approximately 11 crimes per year.

44. a. $P = \dfrac{10{,}000r}{1 - \left(1 + \dfrac{r}{12}\right)^{-360}}$ and

$$dP = \dfrac{\left[1 - \left(1 + \frac{r}{12}\right)^{-360}\right]10{,}000 - 10{,}000r(360)\left(1 + \frac{r}{12}\right)^{-361}\left(\frac{1}{12}\right)}{\left[1 - \left(1 + \frac{r}{12}\right)^{-360}\right]^2}\, dr$$

$$= \dfrac{10{,}000\left\{1 - \left(1 + \frac{r}{12}\right)^{-360} - 30r\left(1 + \frac{r}{12}\right)^{-361}\right\}}{\left[1 - \left(1 + \frac{r}{12}\right)^{-360}\right]^2}\, dr$$

b. When $x = 0.09$, $dP = \dfrac{10{,}000(0.932113992 - 0.181927761)}{(0.932113992)^2}\, dr \approx 8634.378\, dr$.

When the interest rate increases from 9% per year to 9.2% per year,
$dP = 8634.378(0.002) \approx 17.27$, or approximately \$17.27.
When the interest rate increases from 9% per year to 9.3% per year,
$dP = 8634.378(0.003) \approx 25.90$, or approximately \$25.90.
When the interest rate increases from 9% per year to 9.4% per year,
$dP = 8634.378(0.004) \approx 34.54$, or approximately \$34.54.
When the interest rate increases from 9% per year to 9.5% per year,
$dP = 8634.378(0.005) \approx 43.17$, or approximately \$43.17.

45 $A = 10,000\left(1+\dfrac{r}{12}\right)^{120}$

   a. $dA = 10,000(120)\left(1+\dfrac{r}{12}\right)^{119}\left(\dfrac{1}{12}\right)dr = 100,000\left(1+\dfrac{r}{12}\right)^{119}dr.$

   b. At 8.1%, it will be worth $100,000\left(1+\dfrac{0.08}{12}\right)^{119}(0.001)$, or \$220.49 more.

      At 8.2%, it will be worth $100,000\left(1+\dfrac{0.08}{12}\right)^{119}(0.002)$, or \$440.99 more.

      At 8.3%, it will be worth $100,000\left(1+\dfrac{0.08}{12}\right)^{119}(0.003)$, or \$661.48 more.

46. $S = \dfrac{24000\left[\left(1+\frac{r}{12}\right)^{300}-1\right]}{r}$

   a. $dS = 24000\left[\dfrac{(r)300\left(1+\frac{r}{12}\right)^{299}\left(\frac{1}{12}\right)-\left(1+\frac{r}{12}\right)^{300}+1}{r^2}\right]dr$

   b. With $r = 0.09$, we find $dS = 37342023.87\,dr$
      Therefore, if John's account earned 9.1%, 9.2%, and 9.3%, it would be worth
      $\qquad dS = 37342023.87(0.001)$ or \$37,342.02
      $\qquad dS = 37342023.87(0.002)$ or \$74,684.05
      and $dS = 37342023.87(0.003)$ or \$112,026.0 more, respectively.

47 True. $dy = f'(x)\,dx = \dfrac{d}{dx}(ax+b)\,dx = a\,dx$. On the other hand,
      $\Delta y = f(x+\Delta x) - f(x) = [a(x+\Delta x)+b] - (ax+b) = a\Delta x = a\,dx.$

48. True. The percentage change in A is approximately

      $\dfrac{100[f(x+\Delta x) - f(x)]}{f(x)} \approx \dfrac{100 f'(x)\,dx}{f(x)}.$

USING TECHNOLOGY EXERCISES 3.7, page 242

1. $dy = f'(3)\,dx = 757.87(0.01) \approx 7.5787.$

2. $dy = f'(2)\,dx = -0.125639152666(-0.04) \approx -0.005025566107.$

3. $dy = f'(1)\,dx = 1.04067285926(0.03) \approx 0.031220185778.$

4. $dy = f'(2)(-0.02) = 9.66379267622(-0.02) = -0.193275853524.$

5. $dy = f'(4)(0.1) = -0.198761598(0.1) = -0.0198761598.$

6. $dy = f'(3)(-0.05) = 12.3113248654(-0.05) = -0.61556624327.$

7. If the interest rate changes from 10% to 10.3% per year, the monthly payment will increase by
    $$dP = f'(0.1)(0.003) \approx 26.60279,$$
    or approximately \$26.60 per month. If the interest rate changes from 10% to 10.4% per year, it will be \$35 47 per month. If the interest rate changes from 10% to 10.5% per year, it will be \$44.34 per month.

8. $A = \pi r^2.$ Then $dA = 2\pi r\,dr.$ The area of the ring is approximately
    $$dA = 2\pi(53{,}200)(15) \text{ or } 5{,}013{,}981 \text{ sq km.}$$

9   $dx = f'(40)(2) \approx -0.625.$ That is, the quantity demanded will decrease by 625 watches per week.

10. $T'(22{,}000) = 0.0000570472;\ \ \Delta T \approx T'(22{,}000)\Delta d \approx -0.02536.$ The period decreases by $(-0.025236)(24) \approx -0.6845664$, or approximately 0.69 hours.

CHAPTER 3, CONCEPT REVIEW QUESTIONS, page 243

1. a. 0   b. nx^{n-1} c. $cf'(x)$ d. $f'(x) \pm g'(x)$

2. a. $f(x)g'(x) + g(x)f'(x)$ b. $\dfrac{g(x)f'(x) - f(x)g'(x)}{[g(x)]^2}$

3. a. $g'[f(x)]f'(x)$ b. $n[f(x)]^{n-1}f'(x)$

4. Marginal cost; marginal revenue; marginal profit; marginal average cost

5 a. $-\dfrac{pf'(p)}{f(p)}$ b. Elastic; unitary; inelastic

6. Both sides; dy/dx 7. y; dy/dt; a 8. $-x/y$; $-y/x$

9. a. $x_2 - x_1$ b. $f(x + \Delta x) - f(x)$ 10. Δx; Δx; x; $f'(x)\,dx$

CHAPTER 3 REVIEW, page 243

1. $f'(x) = \dfrac{d}{dx}(3x^5 - 2x^4 + 3x^2 - 2x + 1) = 15x^4 - 8x^3 + 6x - 2.$

2. $f'(x) = \dfrac{d}{dx}(4x^6 + 2x^4 + 3x^2 - 2) = 24x^5 + 8x^3 + 6x.$

3. $g'(x) = \dfrac{d}{dx}(-2x^{-3} + 3x^{-1} + 2) = 6x^{-4} - 3x^{-2}$

4. $f'(t) = \dfrac{d}{dt}(2t^2 - 3t^3 - t^{-1/2}) = 4t - 9t^2 + \tfrac{1}{2}t^{-3/2}.$

5. $g'(t) = \dfrac{d}{dt}(2t^{-1/2} + 4t^{-3/2} + 2) = -t^{-3/2} - 6t^{-5/2}.$

6. $h'(x) = \dfrac{d}{dx}\left(x^2 + \dfrac{2}{x}\right) = 2x - \dfrac{2}{x^2}.$

7   $f'(t) = \dfrac{d}{dt}(t + 2t^{-1} + 3t^{-2}) = 1 - 2t^{-2} - 6t^{-3} = 1 - \dfrac{2}{t^2} - \dfrac{6}{t^3}$

8. $g'(s) = \dfrac{d}{ds}(2s^2 - 4s^{-1} + 2s^{-1/2}) = 4s + 4s^{-2} - s^{-3/2} = 4s + \dfrac{4}{s^2} - \dfrac{1}{s^{3/2}}.$

9   $h'(x) = \dfrac{d}{dx}(x^2 - 2x^{-3/2}) = 2x + 3x^{-5/2} = 2x + \dfrac{3}{x^{5/2}}.$

10. $f(x) = \dfrac{x+1}{2x-1}.$ $f'(x) = \dfrac{(2x-1)(1) - (x+1)(2)}{(2x-1)^2} = -\dfrac{3}{(2x-1)^2}$

11. $g(t) = \dfrac{t^2}{2t^2 + 1}.$

$$g'(t) = \frac{(2t^2+1)\frac{d}{dt}(t^2) - t^2\frac{d}{dt}(2t^2+1)}{(2t^2+1)^2}$$

$$= \frac{(2t^2+1)(2t) - t^2(4t)}{(2t^2+1)^2} = \frac{2t}{(2t^2+1)^2}.$$

12. $h(t) = \dfrac{t^{1/2}}{t^{1/2}+1}.$ $h'(t) = \dfrac{(t^{1/2}+1)\frac{1}{2}t^{-1/2} - t^{1/2}(\frac{1}{2}t^{-1/2})}{(t^{1/2}+1)^2} = \dfrac{1}{2\sqrt{t}(\sqrt{t}+1)^2}$

13. $f(x) = \dfrac{\sqrt{x}-1}{\sqrt{x}+1} = \dfrac{x^{1/2}-1}{x^{1/2}+1}.$

$$f'(x) = \frac{(x^{1/2}+1)(\frac{1}{2}x^{-1/2}) - (x^{1/2}-1)(\frac{1}{2}x^{-1/2})}{(x^{1/2}+1)^2}$$

$$= \frac{\frac{1}{2} + \frac{1}{2}x^{-1/2} - \frac{1}{2} + \frac{1}{2}x^{-1/2}}{(x^{1/2}+1)^2} = \frac{x^{-1/2}}{(x^{1/2}+1)^2} = \frac{1}{\sqrt{x}(\sqrt{x}+1)^2}.$$

14. $f(t) = \dfrac{t}{2t^2+1}$ $f'(t) = \dfrac{(2t^2+1)(1) - t(4t)}{(2t^2+1)^2} = \dfrac{1-2t^2}{(2t^2+1)^2}$

15. $f(x) = \dfrac{x^2(x^2+1)}{x^2-1}$

$$f'(x) = \frac{(x^2-1)\frac{d}{dx}(x^4+x^2) - (x^4+x^2)\frac{d}{dx}(x^2-1)}{(x^2-1)^2}$$

$$= \frac{(x^2-1)(4x^3+2x) - (x^4+x^2)(2x)}{(x^2-1)^2}$$

$$= \frac{4x^5+2x^3-4x^3-2x-2x^5-2x^3}{(x^2-1)^2}$$

$$= \frac{2x^5-4x^3-2x}{(x^2-1)^2} = \frac{2x(x^4-2x^2-1)}{(x^2-1)^2}.$$

16. $f'(x) = 3(2x^2 + x)^2 \dfrac{d}{dx}(2x^2 + x) = 3(4x + 1)(2x^2 + x)^2$

17. $f(x) = (3x^3 - 2)^8$; $f'(x) = 8(3x^3 - 2)^7(9x^2) = 72x^2(3x^3 - 2)^7$.

18. $h'(x) = 5(x^{1/2} + 2)^4 \dfrac{d}{dx}x^{1/2} = 5(x^{1/2} + 2)^4 \cdot \dfrac{1}{2}x^{-1/2} = \dfrac{5(\sqrt{x} + 2)^4}{2\sqrt{x}}$

19. $f'(t) = \dfrac{d}{dt}(2t^2 + 1)^{1/2} = \dfrac{1}{2}(2t^2 + 1)^{-1/2}\dfrac{d}{dt}(2t^2 + 1)$

$= \dfrac{1}{2}(2t^2 + 1)^{-1/2}(4t) = \dfrac{2t}{\sqrt{2t^2 + 1}}$.

20. $g(t) = \sqrt[3]{1 - 2t^3} = (1 - 2t^3)^{1/3}$

$g'(t) = \frac{1}{3}(1 - 2t^3)^{-2/3}(-6t^2) = -2t^2(1 - 2t^3)^{-2/3}$

21. $s(t) = (3t^2 - 2t + 5)^{-2}$

$s'(t) = -2(3t^2 - 2t + 5)^{-3}(6t - 2) = -4(3t^2 - 2t + 5)^{-3}(3t - 1)$

$= -\dfrac{4(3t - 1)}{(3t^2 - 2t + 5)^3}$.

22. $f(x) = (2x^3 - 3x^2 + 1)^{-3/2}$.

$f'(x) = -\frac{3}{2}(2x^3 - 3x^2 + 1)^{-5/2}(6x^2 - 6x) = -9x(x - 1)(2x^3 - 3x^2 + 1)^{-5/2}$

23. $h(x) = \left(x + \dfrac{1}{x}\right)^2 = (x + x^{-1})^2$

$h'(x) = 2(x + x^{-1})(1 - x^{-2}) = 2\left(x + \dfrac{1}{x}\right)\left(1 - \dfrac{1}{x^2}\right)$

$= 2\left(\dfrac{x^2 + 1}{x}\right)\left(\dfrac{x^2 - 1}{x^2}\right) = \dfrac{2(x^2 + 1)(x^2 - 1)}{x^3}$.

3 Differentiation

24. $h(x) = \dfrac{1+x}{(2x^2+1)^2}$.

$$h'(x) = \frac{(2x^2+1)^2(1) - (1+x)2(2x^2+1)(4x)}{(2x^2+1)^4}$$

$$= \frac{(2x^2+1)[(2x^2+1) - 8x - 8x^2]}{(2x^2+1)^4} = -\frac{6x^2+8x-1}{(2x^2+1)^3}$$

25. $h'(t) = (t^2+t)^4 \dfrac{d}{dt}(2t^2) + 2t^2 \dfrac{d}{dt}(t^2+t)^4$

$$= (t^2+t)^4(4t) + 2t^2 \cdot 4(t^2+t)^3(2t+1)$$

$$= 4t(t^2+t)^3[(t^2+t) + 4t^2 + 2t] = 4t^2(5t+3)(t^2+t)^3.$$

26. $f(x) = (2x+1)^3(x^2+x)^2$

$$f'(x) = (2x+1)^3 \cdot 2(x^2+x)(2x+1) + (x^2+x)^2 3(2x+1)^2(2)$$

$$= 2(2x+1)^2(x^2+x)[(2x+1)^2 + 3(x^2+x)]$$

$$= 2(2x+1)^2(x^2+x)(7x^2+7x+1).$$

27. $g(x) = x^{1/2}(x^2-1)^3$.

$$g'(x) = \frac{d}{dx}[x^{1/2}(x^2-1)^3] = x^{1/2} \cdot 3(x^2-1)^2(2x) + (x^2-1)^3 \cdot \tfrac{1}{2}x^{-1/2}$$

$$= \tfrac{1}{2}x^{-1/2}(x^2-1)^2[12x^2 + (x^2-1)]$$

$$= \frac{(13x^2-1)(x^2-1)^2}{2\sqrt{x}}.$$

28. $f(x) = \dfrac{x}{(x^3+2)^{1/2}}$.

$$f'(x) = \frac{(x^3+2)^{1/2}(1) - x \cdot \tfrac{1}{2}(x^3+2)^{-1/2} \cdot 3x^2}{x^3+2}$$

$$= \frac{\tfrac{1}{2}(x^3+2)^{-1/2}[2(x^3+2) - 3x^3]}{x^3+2} = \frac{4-x^3}{2(x^3+2)^{3/2}}.$$

29. $h(x) = \dfrac{(3x+2)^{1/2}}{4x-3}$.

$$h'(x) = \frac{(4x-3)\frac{1}{2}(3x+2)^{-1/2}(3) - (3x+2)^{1/2}(4)}{(4x-3)^2}$$

$$= \frac{\frac{1}{2}(3x+2)^{-1/2}[3(4x-3) - 8(3x+2)]}{(4x-3)^2} = -\frac{12x+25}{2\sqrt{3x+2}(4x-3)^2}.$$

30. $f(t) = \dfrac{(2t+1)^{1/2}}{(t+1)^3}$.

$$f'(t) = \frac{(t+1)^3 \frac{1}{2}(2t+1)^{-1/2}(2) - (2t+1)^{1/2} \; 3(t+1)^2(1)}{(t+1)^6}$$

$$= \frac{(2t+1)^{-1/2}(t+1)^2[(t+1) - 3(2t+1)]}{(t+1)^6} = -\frac{5t+2}{\sqrt{2t+1}(t+1)^4}$$

31. $f(x) = 2x^4 - 3x^3 + 2x^2 + x + 4$.

$$f'(x) = \frac{d}{dx}(2x^4 - 3x^3 + 2x^2 + x + 4) = 8x^3 - 9x^2 + 4x + 1.$$

$$f''(x) = \frac{d}{dx}(8x^3 - 9x^2 + 4x + 1) = 24x^2 - 18x + 4 = 2(12x^2 - 9x + 2).$$

32. $g(x) = x^{1/2} + x^{-1/2}$. $g'(x) = \frac{1}{2}x^{-1/2} - \frac{1}{2}x^{-3/2}$

$$g''(x) = -\frac{1}{4}x^{-3/2} + \frac{3}{4}x^{-5/2} = -\frac{1}{4x^{3/2}} + \frac{3}{4x^{5/2}}.$$

33 $h(t) = \dfrac{t}{t^2+4}$. $h'(t) = \dfrac{(t^2+4)(1) - t(2t)}{(t^2+4)^2} = \dfrac{4-t^2}{(t^2+4)^2}$.

$$h''(t) = \frac{(t^2+4)^2(-2t) - (4-t^2)2(t^2+4)(2t)}{(t^2+4)^4}$$

$$= \frac{-2t(t^2+4)[(t^2+4) + 2(4-t^2)]}{(t^2+4)^4} = \frac{2t(t^2-12)}{(t^2+4)^3}$$

3 Differentiation

34. $f(x) = (x^3 + x + 1)^2$.

$f'(x) = 2(x^3 + x + 1)(3x^2 + 1) = 2(3x^5 + 3x^3 + 3x^2 + x^3 + x + 1)$

$\qquad = 2(3x^5 + 4x^3 + 3x^2 + x + 1)$.

$f''(x) = 2(15x^4 + 12x^2 + 6x + 1)$.

35. $f'(x) = \dfrac{d}{dx}(2x^2 + 1)^{1/2} = \dfrac{1}{2}(2x^2 + 1)^{-1/2}(4x) = 2x(2x^2 + 1)^{-1/2}$

$f''(x) = 2(2x^2 + 1)^{-1/2} + 2x \cdot (-\tfrac{1}{2})(2x^2 + 1)^{-3/2}(4x)$

$\qquad = 2(2x^2 + 1)^{-3/2}[(2x^2 + 1) - 2x^2] = \dfrac{2}{(2x^2 + 1)^{3/2}}$

36. $f(t) = t(t^2 + 1)^3$

$f'(t) = (t^2 + 1)^3 + t \cdot 3(t^2 + 1)^2(2t) = (t^2 + 1)^2[(t^2 + 1) + 6t^2]$

$\qquad = (t^2 + 1)^2(7t^2 + 1)$.

$f''(t) = (t^2 + 1)(14t) + (7t^2 + 1)(2)(t^2 + 1)(2t)$

$\qquad = 2t(t^2 + 1)[7(t^2 + 1) + 2(7t^2 + 1)] = 6t(t^2 + 1)(7t^2 + 3)$.

37. $6x^2 - 3y^2 = 9$ so $12x - 6y\dfrac{dy}{dx} = 0$ and $-6y\dfrac{dy}{dx} = -12x$.

Therefore, $\dfrac{dy}{dx} = \dfrac{-12x}{-6y} = \dfrac{2x}{y}$

38. $2x^3 - 3xy = 4$. $\quad 6x^2 - 3y - 3x\dfrac{dy}{dx} = 0$, so $\dfrac{dy}{dx} = \dfrac{2x^2 - y}{x}$.

39. $y^3 + 3x^2 = 3y$, so $3y^2 y' + 6x = 3y'$, $3y^2 y' - 3y' = -6x$,

and $y'(3y^2 - 3) = -6x$. Therefore, $y' = -\dfrac{6x}{3(y^2 - 1)} = -\dfrac{2x}{y^2 - 1}$.

40. $x^2 + 2x^2 y^2 + y^2 = 10$.

$2x + 4xy^2 + 2x^2(2yy') + 2yy' = 0$,

$\qquad\qquad 2yy'(2x^2 + 1) = -2x(1 + 2y^2)$

$$y' = -\frac{x(1+2y^2)}{y(2x^2+1)}.$$

41. $x^2 - 4xy - y^2 = 12$ so $2x - 4xy' - 4y - 2yy' = 0$ and $y'(-4x-2y) = -2x+4y$

So $y' = \dfrac{-2(x-2y)}{-2(2x+y)} = \dfrac{x-2y}{2x+y}.$

42. $3x^2y - 4xy + x - 2y = 6.$

$$6xy + 3x^2y' - 4y - 4xy' + 1 - 2y' = 0$$
$$y'(3x^2 - 4x - 2) = 4y - 6xy - 1$$
$$y' = \frac{4y - 6xy - 1}{3x^2 - 4x - 2}$$

43 $df = f'(x)dx = (2x - 2x^{-3})dx = \left(2x - \dfrac{2}{x^3}\right)dx = \dfrac{2(x^4 - 1)}{x^3}dx$

44. $df = f'(x)dx = \dfrac{d}{dx}(x^3+1)^{-1/2}\,dx = -\tfrac{1}{2}(x^3+1)^{-3/2}(3x^2)dx = -\dfrac{3x^2}{2(x^3+1)^{3/2}}dx$

45. a. $df = f'(x)dx = \dfrac{d}{dx}(2x^2+4)^{1/2}\,dx = \dfrac{1}{2}(2x^2+4)^{-1/2}(4x) = \dfrac{2x}{\sqrt{2x^2+4}}dx$

  b. $\Delta f \approx df\big|_{\substack{x=4 \\ dx=0.1}} = \dfrac{2(4)(0.1)}{\sqrt{2(16)+4}} = \dfrac{0.8}{6} = \dfrac{8}{60} = \dfrac{2}{15}.$

  c. $\Delta f = f(4.1) - f(4) = \sqrt{2(4.1)^2 + 4} - \sqrt{2(16) + 4} = 0.1335$

  From (b), $\Delta f \approx \dfrac{2}{15} \approx 0.1333.$

46. Take $y = f(x) = x^{1/3}$, $x = 27$. Then $\Delta x = dx = 26.8 - 27 = -0.2$

$\Delta y \approx dy = f'(x)\Delta x = \dfrac{1}{3}x^{-2/3}\bigg|_{x=27} \cdot (-0.2) = \dfrac{1}{3(9)}(-0.2) = -\dfrac{2}{270} = -\dfrac{1}{135}$

3 Differentiation

Therefore, $\sqrt[3]{26.8} - \sqrt[3]{27} = \Delta y = -\dfrac{1}{135}$; $\sqrt[3]{26.8} = \sqrt[3]{27} - \dfrac{1}{135} = 3 - \dfrac{1}{135} \approx 2.9926.$

47. $f(x) = 2x^3 - 3x^2 - 16x + 3$ and $f'(x) = 6x^2 - 6x - 16.$

a. To find the point(s) on the graph of f where the slope of the tangent line is equal to –4, we solve
$$6x^2 - 6x - 16 = -4, \ 6x^2 - 6x - 12 = 0, \ 6(x^2 - x - 2) = 0$$
$$6(x - 2)(x + 1) = 0$$
and $x = 2$ or $x = -1$. Then $f(2) = 2(2)^3 - 3(2)^2 - 16(2) + 3 = -25$ and
$f(-1) = 2(-1)^3 - 3(-1)^2 - 16(-1) + 3 = 14$ and the points are $(2,-25)$ and $(-1,14)$.
b. Using the point-slope form of the equation of a line, we find
that $\quad y - (-25) = -4(x - 2), \ y + 25 = -4x + 8,$ or $y = -4x - 17$
and $\quad y - 14 = -4(x + 1),$ or $y = -4x + 10$
are the equations of the tangent lines at $(2,-25)$ and $(-1,14)$.

48. $f(x) = \frac{1}{3}x^3 + \frac{1}{2}x^2 - 4x + 1.$ $f'(x) = x^2 + x - 4.$

a. Set $x^2 + x - 4 = -2, \ x^2 + x - 2 = (x + 2)(x - 1) = 0,$ so $x = -2$
or 1. Therefore, the points are $(-2, \frac{25}{3})$ and $(1, -\frac{13}{6})$.

b. $y - \frac{25}{3} = -2(x + 2),$ or $y = -2x + \frac{13}{3}$, and $y + \frac{13}{6} = -2(x - 1),$ or $y = -2x - \frac{1}{6}$

49. $y = (4 - x^2)^{1/2}.$ $y' = \frac{1}{2}(4 - x^2)^{-1/2}(-2x) = -\dfrac{x}{\sqrt{4 - x^2}}$

The slope of the tangent line is obtained by letting $x = 1$, giving
$$m = -\dfrac{1}{\sqrt{3}} = -\dfrac{\sqrt{3}}{3}$$
Therefore, an equation of the tangent line is
$$y - \sqrt{3} = -\dfrac{\sqrt{3}}{3}(x - 1), \quad \text{or} \quad y = -\dfrac{\sqrt{3}}{3}x + \dfrac{4\sqrt{3}}{3}.$$

50. $y = x(x + 1)^5$
$$y' = (x + 1)^5 + x \cdot 5(x + 1)^4(1) = (x + 1)^4[(x + 1) + 5x] = (6x + 1)(x + 1)^4$$
The slope of the tangent line is obtained by letting $x = 1$. Then
$$m = (6 + 1)(2)^4 = 112.$$
An equation of the tangent line is $y - 32 = 112(x - 1),$ or $y = 112x - 80.$

51. $f(x) = (2x-1)^{-1};\ f'(x) = -2(2x-1)^{-2},\ f''(x) = 8(2x-1)^{-3} = \dfrac{8}{(2x-1)^3}$.

$f'''(x) = -48(2x-1)^4 = -\dfrac{48}{(2x-1)^4}$.

Since $(2x-1)^4 = 0$ when $x = 1/2$, we see that the domain of f''' is $(-\infty, \frac{1}{2}) \cup (\frac{1}{2}, \infty)$.

52. $x = f(p) = -\dfrac{5}{2}p + 30;\ f'(p) = -\dfrac{5}{2};\ E(p) = -\dfrac{pf'(p)}{f(p)} = -\dfrac{p\left(-\frac{5}{2}\right)}{-\frac{5}{2}p + 30} = \dfrac{p}{12 - p}$

   a. $E(3) = \frac{3}{9} = \frac{1}{3}$ and demand is inelastic. b. $E(6) = \frac{6}{12-6} = 1$ and demand is unitary

   c. $E(9) = \frac{9}{12-9} = 3$ and demand is elastic.

53 $x = \dfrac{25}{\sqrt{p}} - 1;\quad f'(p) = -\dfrac{25}{2p^{3/2}};\quad E(p) = -\dfrac{p\left(-\frac{25}{2p^{3/2}}\right)}{\frac{25}{p^{1/2}} - 1} = \dfrac{\frac{25}{2p^{1/2}}}{\frac{25 - p^{1/2}}{p^{1/2}}} = \dfrac{25}{2(25 - p^{1/2})}$

   Since $E(p) = 1$,

$$2(25 - p^{1/2}) = 25,$$
$$25 - p^{1/2} = \tfrac{25}{2},\quad p^{1/2} = \tfrac{25}{2}, \text{ and } p = \tfrac{625}{4}$$

   $E(p) > 1$ and demand is elastic if $p > 156.25$; $E(p) = 1$ and demand is unitary if $p = 156.25$; and $E(p) < 1$ and demand is inelastic, if $p < 156.25$.

54. $x = 100 - 0.01p^2;\ f'(p) = -0.02p;\ E(p) = -\dfrac{p(-0.02p)}{100 - 0.01p^2} = \dfrac{p^2}{5000 - \frac{1}{2}p^2}$

   a. $E(40) = \dfrac{1600}{5000 - \frac{1}{2}(1600)} = \dfrac{1600}{4200} = \dfrac{8}{21} < 1$ and so demand is inelastic.

   b. Since demand is inelastic, raising the unit price slightly will cause the revenue to increase.

55. $p = 9\sqrt[3]{1000 - x}\ ;\ \sqrt[3]{1000 - x} = \dfrac{p}{9};\ 1000 - x = \dfrac{p^3}{729};\ x = 1000 - \dfrac{p^3}{729}$

   Therefore, $x = f(p) = \dfrac{729,000 - p^3}{729}$ and $f'(x) = -\dfrac{3p^2}{729} = -\dfrac{p^2}{243}$.

Then $E(p) = -\dfrac{p(-\frac{p^2}{243})}{\frac{729,000-p^3}{729}} = \dfrac{3p^3}{729,000-p^3}.$

So $E(60) = \dfrac{3(60)^3}{729,000-60^3} = \dfrac{648,000}{513,000} = \dfrac{648}{513} > 1,$ and so demand is elastic.

Therefore, raising the price slightly will cause the revenue to decrease.

56. a. $P(0) = 15$, or 15%;

$P(22) = 0.01484(22)^2 + 0.446(22) + 15 = 31.99,$ or 31.99%.

b. $P'(t) = 2(0.01484)t + 0.446 = 0.02968t + 0.446$

$P'(2) = 0.02968(2) + 0.446 = 0.50536,$ or 0.51%/yr;

$P'(20) = 0.02968(20) + 0.446 = 1.0396,$ or 1.04%/yr.

57 $N(x) = 1000(1 + 2x)^{1/2}.$ $N'(x) = 1000(\tfrac{1}{2})(1+2x)^{-1/2}(2) = \dfrac{1000}{\sqrt{1+2x}}.$

The rate of increase at the end of the twelfth week is $N'(12) = \dfrac{1000}{\sqrt{25}} = 200,$

or 200 subscribers/week.

58. $f(t) = 31.88(1+t)^{-0.45}$ $f'(t) = 31.88(-0.45)(1+t)^{-1.45} = -14.346(1+t)^{-1.45}$

It is changing at the rate of $f'(2) = -2.917;$ that is, decreasing at the rate of 2.9 cents/minute/yr. The average price/minute at the beginning of 2000 was

$f(2) = 31.88(1+2)^{-0.45},$ or 19.45 cents/minute.

59 He can expect to live $f(100) = 46.9[1+1.09(100)]^{0.1} \approx 75.0433$, or approximately 75.04 years. $f'(t) = 46.9(0.1)(1+1.09t)^{-0.9}(1.09) = 5\;1121(1+1.09t)^{-0.9}$

So the required rate of change is $f'(100) = 5\;1121(1+1.09)^{-0.9} = 0.074,$ or approximately 0.07 yr/yr.

60. $C(x) = 2500 + 2.2x.$

a. The marginal cost is $C'(x) = 2.2.$ The marginal cost when $x = 1000$ is $C'(1000) = 2.2.$ The marginal cost when $x = 2000$ is $C'(2000) = 2.2.$

b. $\overline{C}(x) = \dfrac{C(x)}{x} = \dfrac{2500+2.2x}{x} = 2.2 + \dfrac{2500}{x}.$

$$\overline{C}'(x) = -\frac{2500}{x^2}$$

c. $\displaystyle\lim_{x\to\infty} \overline{C}(x) = \lim_{x\to\infty}\left(2.2 + \frac{2500}{x}\right) = 2.2.$

61. a. $R(x) = px = (-0.02x + 600)x = -0.02x^2 + 600x$
b. $R'(x) = -0.04x + 600$
c. $R'(10,000) = -0.04(10,000) + 600 = 200$ and this says that the sale of the 10,001st phone will bring a revenue of $200.

62. a. $R(x) = px = (2000 - 0.04x)x = 2000x - 0.04x^2.$
$P(x) = R(x) - C(x)$
$\quad = (2000x - 0.04x^2) - (0.000002x^3 - 0.02x^2 + 1000x + 120,000)$
$\quad = -0.000002x^3 - 0.02x^2 + 1000x - 120,000.$
$$\overline{C}(x) = \frac{C(x)}{x} = \frac{0.000002x^3 - 0.02x^2 + 1000x + 120,000}{x}$$
$$= 0.000002x^2 - 0.02x + 1000 + \frac{120,000}{x}$$

b. $C'(x) = \dfrac{d}{dx}(0.000002x^3 - 0.02x^2 + 1000x + 120,000)$
$\quad = 0.000006x^2 - 0.04x + 1000.$
$R'(x) = \dfrac{d}{dx}(2000x - 0.04x^2) = 2000 - 0.08x.$
$P'(x) = \dfrac{d}{dx}(-0.000002x^3 - 0.02x^2 + 1000x - 120,000)$
$\quad = -0.000006x^2 - 0.04x + 1000$
$\overline{C}'(x) = \dfrac{d}{dx}(0.000002x^2 - 0.02x + 1000 + 120,000x^{-1})$
$\quad = 0.000004x - 0.02 - 120,000x^{-2}.$

c. $C'(3000) = 0.000006(3000)^2 - 0.04(3000) + 1000 = 934$
$R'(3000) = 2000 - 0.08(3000) = 1760.$
$P'(3000) = -0.000006(3000)^2 - 0.04(3000) + 1000 = 826.$
d. $\overline{C}'(5000) = 0.000004(5000) - 0.02 - 120,000(5000)^{-2} = -0.0048$
$\overline{C}'(8000) = 0.000004(8000) - 0.02 - 120,000(8000)^{-2} = 0.0101.$
At a level of production of 5000 machines, the average cost of each additional unit is decreasing at a rate of 0.48 cents. At a level of production of 8000

machines, the average cost of each additional unit is increasing at a rate of 1 cent per unit.

CHAPTER 3, BEFORE MOVING ON, page 245

1. $f'(x) = 2(3x^2) - 3(\frac{1}{3}x^{-2/3}) + 5(-\frac{2}{3}x^{-5/3}) = 6x^2 - x^{-2/3} - \frac{10}{3}x^{-5/3}$

2. $g'(x) = \dfrac{d}{dx}[x(2x^2-1)^{1/2}] = (2x^2-1)^{1/2} + x(\frac{1}{2})(2x^2-1)^{-1/2}\dfrac{d}{dx}(2x^2-1)$

    $= (2x^2-1)^{1/2} + \frac{1}{2}x(2x^2-1)^{-1/2}(4x) = (2x^2-1)^{-1/2}[(2x^2-1)+2x^2]$

    $= \dfrac{4x^2-1}{\sqrt{2x^2-1}}$

3. $\dfrac{dy}{dx} = \dfrac{(x^2+x+1)(2)-(2x+1)(2x+1)}{(x^2+x+1)^2} = \dfrac{2x^2+2x+2-(4x^2+4x+1)}{(x^2+x+1)^2}$

    $= -\dfrac{2x^2+2x-1}{(x^2+x+1)^2}.$

4. $f'(x) = \dfrac{d}{dx}(x+1)^{-1/2} = -\dfrac{1}{2}(x+1)^{-3/2} = -\dfrac{1}{2(x+1)^{3/2}}$

    $f''(x) = -\dfrac{1}{2}\left(-\dfrac{3}{2}\right)(x+1)^{-5/2} = \dfrac{3}{4}(x+1)^{-5/2} = \dfrac{3}{4(x+1)^{5/2}}$

    $f'''(x) = \dfrac{3}{4}\left(-\dfrac{5}{2}\right)(x+1)^{-7/2} = -\dfrac{15}{8}(x+1)^{-7/2} = -\dfrac{15}{8(x+1)^{7/2}}$

5. Differentiating both sides of the equation with respect to x gives

    $y^2 + x(2yy') - 2xy - x^2y' + 3x^2 = 0$

    $(2xy - x^2)y' + (y^2 - 2xy + 3x^2) = 0$

    $$y' = \dfrac{-y^2 + 2xy - 3x^2}{2xy - x^2} = \dfrac{-y^2 + 2xy - 3x^2}{x(2y-x)}$$

6. a. $dy = \dfrac{d}{dx}[x(x^2+5)^{1/2}]dx = [(x^2+5)^{1/2}(2x)]dx$

    $= (x^2+5)^{-1/2}[(x^2+5)+x^2]dx = \dfrac{2x^2+5}{\sqrt{x^2+5}}dx$

    Here $dx = \Delta x = 2.01 - 2 = 0.01$. Therefore,

$$\Delta y \approx dy\Big|_{\substack{x=2 \\ dx=0.01}} = \frac{2(4)+5}{\sqrt{4+5}}(0.01) = \frac{0.13}{3} \approx 0.043$$

EXPLORE & DISCUSS

Page 178

1. $R'(x) = p(x) + xp'(x)$. It says that the rate of change of the revenue (marginal revenue) is equal to the sum of the unit price of the product plus the product of the number of units sold and the rate of change of the unit price.

2. If $p(x)$ is a constant, say p, then $R'(x) = p$. In other words, the marginal revenue is equal to the unit price. This is expected because if the unit price is constant, then the revenue realized in selling one more unit (the marginal revenue) should just be p

Page 190

1. The required expression is $\dfrac{dP}{dx} = g'(x)$. 2. The required expression is $\dfrac{dx}{dt} = f'(t)$.

3 $P = g(x) = g[f(x)]$. Using the Chain Rule, we have $\dfrac{dP}{dt} = g'[f(x)]f'(x)$.

Page 191

1. $\dfrac{dP}{dt}$ measures the rate of change of the population P with respect to the temperature of the medium.

2. $\dfrac{dT}{dt}$ measures the rate of change of the temperature of the medium with respect to time.

3. $\dfrac{dP}{dt} = \dfrac{dP}{dT} \cdot \dfrac{dT}{dt} = f'(T)g'(t)$ measures the rate of change of the population with respect to time.

4 $(f \circ g)(t) = f[g(t)] = P$ gives the population of bacteria at any time t.

5. $f'[g(t)]g'(t) = \dfrac{dP}{dt}$ (by the Chain Rule) and gives the rate of change of the population with respect to time (see part (c)).

3 Differentiation

Page 222

1. Thinking of x as a function of y and differentiating the given equation with respect to the *independent variable y*, we obtain $\dfrac{d}{dy}(y^3 - y + 2x^3 - x) = \dfrac{d}{dy}(8)$.

$$\frac{d}{dy}(y^3) - \frac{d}{dy}(y) + \frac{d}{dy}(2x^3) + \frac{d}{dy}(-x) = 0; \quad 3y^2 - 1 + 2\left(3x^2 \frac{dx}{dy}\right) - \frac{dx}{dy} = 0$$

$$(6x^2 - 1)\frac{dx}{dy} = 1 - 3y^2 \quad \text{and} \quad \frac{dx}{dy} = \frac{1 - 3y^2}{6x^2 - 1}.$$

Page 224

1. The graph of y is shown at the right.

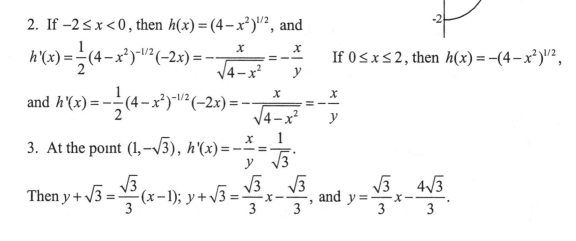

2. If $-2 \le x < 0$, then $h(x) = (4 - x^2)^{1/2}$, and

$$h'(x) = \frac{1}{2}(4 - x^2)^{-1/2}(-2x) = -\frac{x}{\sqrt{4 - x^2}} = -\frac{x}{y} \qquad \text{If } 0 \le x \le 2, \text{ then } h(x) = -(4 - x^2)^{1/2},$$

and $h'(x) = -\dfrac{1}{2}(4 - x^2)^{-1/2}(-2x) = -\dfrac{x}{\sqrt{4 - x^2}} = -\dfrac{x}{y}$

3. At the point $(1, -\sqrt{3})$, $h'(x) = -\dfrac{x}{y} = \dfrac{1}{\sqrt{3}}$.

Then $y + \sqrt{3} = \dfrac{\sqrt{3}}{3}(x - 1)$; $y + \sqrt{3} = \dfrac{\sqrt{3}}{3}x - \dfrac{\sqrt{3}}{3}$, and $y = \dfrac{\sqrt{3}}{3}x - \dfrac{4\sqrt{3}}{3}$.

EXPLORING WITH TECHNOLOGY QUESTIONS

Page 166

1.
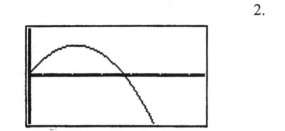

2.
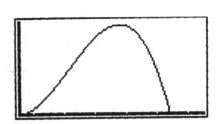

3   We see that $f(t) = 0$ when $t = 98$. We conclude that the rocket returns to Earth 98 seconds later.

Page 177

1.
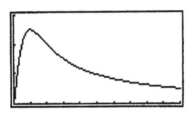

2. The highest point on the graph of S is $(1, 2.5)$, and this tells us that the sales of the laser disc reach a maximum of $2.5 million one year after its release.

Page 189

1
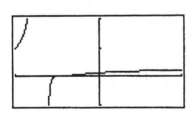

2.
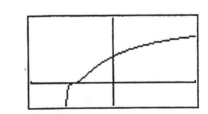

3 The slope of the tangent line is 0.1875, as expected.

1.   2.

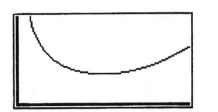 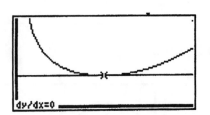

The slope is zero. Yes, the point of tangency is the lowest point on the graph of $\overline{C}$

3 Yes. At the lowest point on the graph of $\overline{C}$, the derivative of $\overline{C}$ must be zero.

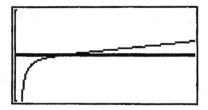

CHAPTER 4

4.1 CONCEPT QUESTIONS, page 258

1. a. f is increasing on I if whenever x_1 and x_2 are in I with $x_1 < x_2$, then
   $f(x_1) < f(x_2)$

   b. f is decreasing on I if whenever x_1 and x_2 are in I with $x_1 < x_2$, then
   $f(x_1) > f(x_2)$.

2. Find all numbers such that $f'(x)$ does not exist or $f'(x)$ is not defined. Using test points if necessary, draw the sign diagram for f'. On a subinterval where $f'(x) < 0$. f is decreasing on that subinterval; on a subinterval where $f'(x) > 0$, f is increasing on that subinterval.

3 a. f has a relative maximum at $x = a$ if there is an open interval I containing a such that $f(x) \le f(a)$ for all x in I.

   b. f has a relative minimum at $x = a$ if there is an open interval I containing a such that $f(x) \le f(a)$ for all x in I.

4. a. A critical number of f is a number c in the domain of f such that $f'(c) = 0$ or $f'(c) = 0$ or f' does not exist at c.

   b. f has a relative extremum at c, then c must be a critical number of f

5. See text page 255.

EXERCISES 4.1, page 258

1. f is decreasing on $(-\infty, 0)$ and increasing on $(0, \infty)$.

2. f is decreasing on $(-\infty, -1)$, constant on $(-1, 1)$, and increasing on $(1, \infty)$.

3 f is increasing on $(-\infty, -1) \cup (1, \infty)$, and decreasing on $(-1, 1)$.

4. f is increasing on $(-\infty, -1) \cup (1, \infty)$ and decreasing on $(-1, 0) \cup (0, 1)$.

5 f is increasing on $(0, 2)$ and decreasing on $(-\infty, 0) \cup (2, \infty)$.

6. f is increasing on $(-1, 0) \cup (1, \infty)$ and decreasing on $(-\infty, -1) \cup (0, 1)$.

7. f is decreasing on $(-\infty,-1) \cup (1,\infty)$ and increasing on $(-1,1)$.

8. f is increasing on $(-\infty,-1) \cup (-1,0) \cup (0,\infty)$.

9. Increasing on $(20.2, 20.6) \cup (21.7, 21.8)$, constant on $(19.6, 20.2) \cup (20.6, 21.1)$, and decreasing on $(21.1, 21.7) \cup (21.8, 22.7)$,

10. a. f is decreasing on $(0, 4)$.   b. f is constant on $(4, 12)$.
    c. f is increasing on $(12, 24)$.

11. $f(x) = 3x + 5; f'(x) = 3 > 0$ for all x and so f is increasing on $(-\infty,\infty)$.

12. $f(x) = 4 - 5x.$ $f'(x) = -5$ and, therefore, f is decreasing everywhere, that is, f is decreasing on $(-\infty,\infty)$.

13. $f(x) = x^2 - 3x.$ $f'(x) = 2x - 3$ is continuous everywhere and is equal to zero when $x = 3/2$. From the following sign diagram

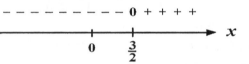

we see that f is decreasing on $(-\infty, \frac{3}{2})$ and increasing on $(\frac{3}{2}, \infty)$.

14. $f(x) = 2x^2 + x + 1; f'(x) = 4x + 1 = 0$, if $x = -1/4$. From the sign diagram of f'

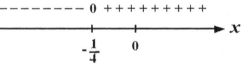

we see that f is decreasing on $(-\infty,-\frac{1}{4})$ and increasing on $(-\frac{1}{4}, \infty)$.

15. $g(x) = x - x^3.$ $g'(x) = 1 - 3x^2$ is continuous everywhere and is equal to zero when $1 - 3x^2 = 0$, or $x = \pm\frac{\sqrt{3}}{3}$ From the following sign diagram

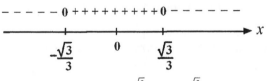

we see that f is decreasing on $(-\infty, -\frac{\sqrt{3}}{3}) \cup (\frac{\sqrt{3}}{3}, \infty)$ and increasing on

$\left(-\frac{\sqrt{3}}{3}, \frac{\sqrt{3}}{3}\right)$.

16. $f(x) = x^3 - 3x^2$. $f'(x) = 3x^2 - 6x = 3x(x-2) = 0$ if $x = 0$ or 2. From the sign

$$+++++++0--0++++++$$

$$\xrightarrow{} x$$

$$0 \qquad 2$$

diagram of f', we see that f is increasing on $(-\infty,0) \cup (2,\infty)$ and decreasing on $(0,2)$.

17. $g(x) = x^3 + 3x^2 + 1$; $g'(x) = 3x^2 + 6x = 3x(x+2)$.
    From the following sign diagram

$$++++++++0--0++++++$$

$$\xrightarrow{} x$$

$$-2 \qquad 0$$

we see that g is increasing on $(-\infty,-2) \cup (0,\infty)$ and decreasing on $(-2,0)$.

18. $f(x) = x^3 - 3x + 4$. $f'(x) = 3x^2 - 3$ is continuous everywhere and is equal to zero when $x = \pm 1$. From the sign diagram

$$+++++ 0--------0++++++$$

$$\xrightarrow{} x$$

$$-1 \qquad 0 \qquad 1$$

we see that f is increasing on $(-\infty,-1) \cup (1,\infty)$ and decreasing on $(-1,1)$.

19. $f(x) = \frac{1}{3}x^3 - 3x^2 + 9x + 20$; $f'(x) = x^2 - 6x + 9 = (x-3)^2 > 0$ for all x except $x = 3$, at which point $f'(3) = 0$. Therefore, f is increasing on $(-\infty,3) \cup (3,\infty)$.

20. $f(x) = \frac{2}{3}x^3 - 2x^2 - 6x - 2$; $f'(x) = 2x^2 - 4x - 6 = 2(x^2 - 2x - 3) = 2(x-3)(x+1) = 0$ if $x = -1$ or 3. From the sign diagram of f',

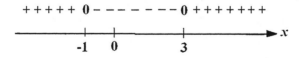

$$+++++ 0--------0+++++++$$

$$\xrightarrow{} x$$

$$-1 \quad 0 \qquad 3$$

we see that f is increasing on $(-\infty,-1) \cup (3,\infty)$ and decreasing on $(-1,3)$.

21. $h(x) = x^4 - 4x^3 + 10$; $h'(x) = 4x^3 - 12x^2 = 4x^2(x - 3)$ if $x = 0$ or 3. From the sign diagram of h',

```
- - - - - - - 0 - - - - - 0 + + + + + +
————————————+——————————————+————————————▸ x
            0              3
```

we see that h is increasing on $(3,\infty)$ and decreasing on $(-\infty,0) \cup (0,3)$.

22. $g(x) = x^4 - 2x^2 + 4$. $g'(x) = 4x^3 - 4x = 4x(x^2 - 1)$ is continuous everywhere and is equal to zero when $x = 0$, 1, and -1. From the sign diagram

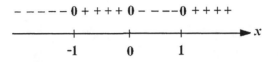

we see that g is decreasing on $(-\infty,-1) \cup (0,1)$ and increasing on $(-1,0) \cup (1,\infty)$.

23. $f(x) = \dfrac{1}{x-2} = (x-2)^{-1}$. $f'(x) = -1(x-2)^{-2}(1) = -\dfrac{1}{(x-2)^2}$ is discontinuous at $x = 2$ and is continuous everywhere else. From the sign diagram

```
                              f' not defined here
                                    ↓
    - - - - - - - - - - - - - - - - ' - - - - - -
    ————————————————+———————————————+———————————▸ x
                    0               2
```

we see that f is decreasing on $(-\infty,2) \cup (2,\infty)$.

24. $h(x) = \dfrac{1}{2x+3}$, $h'(x) = \dfrac{-2}{(2x+3)^2}$ and we see that h' is not defined at $x = -3/2$.

But $h'(x) < 0$ for all x except $x = -3/2$. Therefore, h is decreasing on $(-\infty,-\frac{3}{2}) \cup (-\frac{3}{2},\infty)$.

25 $h(t) = \dfrac{t}{t-1}$ $h'(t) = \dfrac{(t-1)(1) - t(1)}{(t-1)^2} = -\dfrac{1}{(t-1)^2}$.

From the following sign diagram,

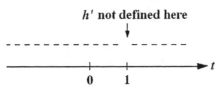

we see that $h'(t) < 0$ whenever it is defined. We conclude that h is decreasing on $(-\infty,1) \cup (1,\infty)$.

26. $g(t) = \dfrac{2t}{t^2+1}$; $g'(t) = \dfrac{(t^2+1)(2)-(2t)(2t)}{(t^2+1)^2} = \dfrac{2t^2+2-4t^2}{(t^2+1)^2} = -\dfrac{2(t^2-1)}{(t^2+1)^2}$

Next, $g'(t) = 0$ if $t = \pm 1$. From the sign diagram of g',

$$- \; - \; - \; -0+++\; + \; + \; +0- \; - \; -$$

we see that g is increasing on $(-1,1)$ and decreasing on $(-\infty,-1) \cup (1,\infty)$.

27. $f(x) = x^{3/5}$. $f'(x) = \dfrac{3}{5}x^{-2/5} = \dfrac{3}{5x^{2/5}}$. Observe that $f'(x)$ is not defined at $x = 0$, but is positive everywhere else and therefore increasing on $(-\infty,0) \cup (0,\infty)$.

28. $f(x) = x^{2/3} + 5$, $f'(x) = \dfrac{2}{3}x^{-1/3} = \dfrac{2}{3x^{1/3}}$ and so f' is not defined at $x = 0$. Now $f'(x) < 0$ if $x < 0$ and $f'(x) > 0$ if $x > 0$, and so f is decreasing on $(-\infty,0)$ and increasing on $(0,\infty)$.

29. $f(x) = \sqrt{x+1}$. $f'(x) = \dfrac{d}{dx}(x+1)^{1/2} = \dfrac{1}{2}(x+1)^{-1/2} = \dfrac{1}{2\sqrt{x+1}}$ and we see that $f'(x) > 0$ if $x > -1$. Therefore, f is increasing on $(-1, \infty)$.

30. $f(x) = (x-5)^{2/3}$; $f'(x) = \dfrac{2}{3}(x-5)^{-1/3} = \dfrac{2}{3(x-5)^{1/3}}$, and we have the following sign diagram.

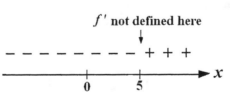

So, f is decreasing on $(-\infty,5)$ and is increasing on $(5,\infty)$.

31. $f(x) = \sqrt{16-x^2} = (16-x^2)^{1/2}$. $f'(x) = \dfrac{1}{2}(16-x^2)^{-1/2}(-2x) = -\dfrac{x}{\sqrt{16-x^2}}$

Since the domain of f is [-4,4], we consider the sign diagram for f' on this interval. Thus,

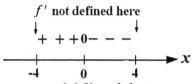

and we see that f is increasing on (-4,0) and decreasing on (0,4).

32. $g(x) = x(x+1)^{1/2}$.
$g'(x) = (x+1)^{1/2} + x(\tfrac{1}{2})(x+1)^{-1/2} = (x+1)^{-1/2}(x+1+\tfrac{1}{2}x)$

$$= (x+1)^{-1/2}(\tfrac{3}{2}x+1) = \dfrac{3x+2}{2\sqrt{x+1}}.$$

Then g' is continuous on $(-1,\infty)$ and has a zero at $x = -2/3$. From the sign diagram

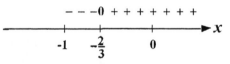

we see that g is decreasing on $(-1,-\tfrac{2}{3})$ and increasing on $(-\tfrac{2}{3},\infty)$.

33. $f'(x) = \dfrac{d}{dx}(x-x^{-1}) = 1+\dfrac{1}{x^2} = \dfrac{x^2+1}{x^2}$ and so $f'(x) > 0$ for all $x \neq 0$.

Therefore, f is increasing on $(-\infty,0) \cup (0,\infty)$.

34. $h(x) = \dfrac{x^2}{x-1}$. $h'(x) = \dfrac{(x-1)(2x)-x^2}{(x-1)^2} = \dfrac{x^2-2x}{(x-1)^2} = \dfrac{x(x-2)}{(x-1)^2}$

Then, h' is continuous everywhere except at $x = 1$ and has zeros at $x = 0$ and $x = 2$. From the sign diagram

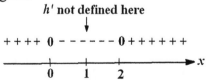

we see that h is increasing on $(-\infty,0) \cup (2,\infty)$ and decreasing on $(0,1) \cup (1,2)$.

35. f has a relative maximum of $f(0) = 1$ and relative minima of $f(-1) = 0$ and $f(1) = 0$.

36. f has a relative maximum of $f(0) = 1$ and relative minima of $f(-1) = 0$ and $f(1) = 0$.

37 f has a relative maximum of $f(-1) = 2$ and a relative minimum of $f(1) = -2$.

38. f has a relative maximum at $x = 0$ with value of 0; it has a relative minimum at $(4,-32)$. --

39. f has a relative maximum of $f(1) = 3$ and a relative minimum of $f(2) = 2$.

40. f has a relative minimum at $(-1,0)$.   41. f has a relative minimum at $(0,2)$.

42. f has a relative maximum at $(-3, -\frac{9}{2})$ and a relative minimum at $(3, \frac{9}{2})$.

43 a   44. c   45. d   46. b

47. $f(x) = x^2 - 4x.$ $f'(x) = 2x - 4 = 2(x - 2)$ has a critical point at $x = 2$. From the following sign diagram

we see that $f(2) = -4$ is a relative minimum by the First Derivative Test.

48. $g(x) = x^2 + 3x + 8;$ $g'(x) = 2x + 3$ has a critical point at $x = -3/2$. From the following sign diagram

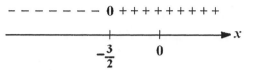

we see that $g(-\frac{3}{2}) = \frac{23}{4}$ is a relative minimum by the First Derivative Test.

49. $h(t) = -t^2 + 6t + 6$; $h'(t) = -2t + 6 = -2(t - 3) = 0$ if $t = 3$, a critical point. The sign

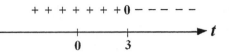

diagram and the First Derivative Test imply that h has a relative maximum at 3 with value $f(3) = -9 + 18 + 6 = 15$.

50. $f(x) = \frac{1}{2}x^2 - 2x + 4$. $f'(x) = x - 2$ giving the critical point $x = 2$. The sign diagram for f' is

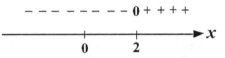

and we see that $f(2) = 2$ is a relative minimum.

51. $f(x) = x^{5/3}$ $f'(x) = \frac{5}{3}x^{2/3}$ giving $x = 0$ as the critical point of f.
From the sign diagram

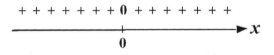

we see that f' does not change sign as we move across $x = 0$, and conclude that f has no relative extremum.

52. $f(x) = x^{2/3} + 2$. $f'(x) = \frac{2}{3}x^{-1/3} = \frac{2}{3x^{1/3}}$ and is discontinuous at $x = 0$, a critical point. From the sign diagram

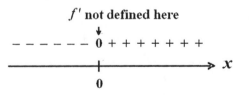

and the First Derivative Test we see that f has a relative minimum at $(0,2)$.

53. $g(x) = x^3 - 3x^2 + 4$. $g'(x) = 3x^2 - 6x = 3x(x - 2) = 0$ if $x = 0$ or 2. From the sign diagram, we see that the critical point $x = 0$ gives a relative maximum, whereas,

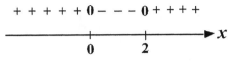

$x = 2$ gives a relative minimum. The values are $g(0) = 4$ and $g(2) = 8 - 12 + 4 = 0$.

54. $f(x) = x^3 - 3x + 6$. Setting $f'(x) = 3x^2 - 3 = 3(x^2 - 1) = 3(x + 1)(x - 1) = 0$ gives $x = -1$ and $x = 1$ as critical points. The sign diagram of f'

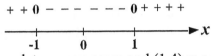

shows that $(-1,8)$ is a relative maximum and $(1,4)$ is a relative minimum.

55. $f(x) = \frac{1}{2}x^4 - x^2$ $f'(x) = 2x^3 - 2x = 2x(x^2 - 1) = 2x(x + 1)(x - 1)$ is continuous everywhere and has zeros as $x = -1$, $x = 0$, and $x = 1$, the critical points of f. Using the First Derivative Test and the following sign diagram of f'

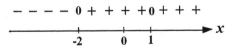

we see that $f(-1) = -1/2$ and $f(1) = -1/2$ are relative minima of f and $f(0) = 0$ is a relative maximum of f.

56. $h(x) = \frac{1}{2}x^4 - 3x^2 + 4x - 8$;
$h'(x) = 2x^3 - 6x + 4 = 2(x^3 - 3x + 2) = 2(x - 1)(x^2 + x - 2)$
$= 2(x - 1)(x - 1)(x + 2) = 2(x - 1)^2(x + 2)$.
We see that $h'(x) = 0$ at $x = -2$ and $x = 1$; both are critical points of h. From the sign diagram of h'

we see that h has a relative minimum at $(-2,-20)$.

57. $F(x) = \frac{1}{3}x^3 - x^2 - 3x + 4$. Setting $F'(x) = x^2 - 2x - 3 = (x-3)(x+1) = 0$ gives $x = -1$ and $x = 3$ as critical points. From the sign diagram

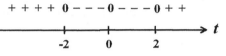

we see that $x = -1$ gives a relative maximum and $x = 3$ gives a relative minimum. The values are
$$F(-1) = -\frac{1}{3} - 1 + 3 + 4 = \frac{17}{3} \quad \text{and} \quad F(3) = 9 - 9 - 9 + 4 = -5,$$
respectively

58. $F(t) = 3t^5 - 20t^3 + 20$. Setting
$F'(t) = 15t^4 - 60t^2 = 15t^2(t^2 - 4) = 15t^2(t+2)(t-2) = 0$
gives $t = -2, 0,$ and 2 as critical points. From the sign diagram

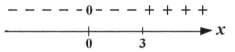

we see that $t = -2$ gives a relative maximum and $t = 2$ gives a relative minimum. The values are $F(-2) = 3(-32) - 20(-8) + 20 = 84$ and $F(2) = 3(32) - 20(8) + 20 = -44$, respectively.

59. $g(x) = x^4 - 4x^3 + 8$. Setting $g'(x) = 4x^3 - 12x^2 = 4x^2(x - 3) = 0$ gives $x = 0$ and $x = 3$ as critical points. From the sign diagram

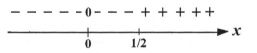

we see that $x = 3$ gives a relative minimum. Its value is $g(3) = 3^4 - 4(3)^3 + 8 = -19$.

60. $f(x) = 3x^4 - 2x^3 + 4$; $f'(x) = 12x^3 - 6x^2 = 6x^2(2x - 1) = 0$ if $x = 0$ or $1/2$. The sign diagram of f' is shown below.

and shows that f has a relative minimum at $(\frac{1}{2}, \frac{63}{16})$.

61. $g'(x) = \dfrac{d}{dx}\left(1 + \dfrac{1}{x}\right) = -\dfrac{1}{x^2}$ Observe that g' is never zero for all values of x.

Furthermore, g' is undefined at $x = 0$, but $x = 0$ is not in the domain of g.
Therefore g has no critical points and so g has no relative extrema.

62. $h(x) = \dfrac{x}{x+1}$. $h'(x) = \dfrac{(x+1)(1) - x(1)}{(x+1)^2} = \dfrac{1}{(x+1)^2}$, Since $x = -1$ is not in the domain

of h, we see that $x = -1$ is not a critical point of h and conclude that h has no
relative extrema.

63. $f(x) = x + \dfrac{9}{x} + 2$. Setting $f'(x) = 1 - \dfrac{9}{x^2} = \dfrac{x^2 - 9}{x^2} = \dfrac{(x+3)(x-3)}{x^2} = 0$

gives $x = -3$ and $x = 3$ as critical points. From the sign diagram

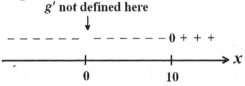

we see that $(-3, -4)$ is a relative maximum and $(3, 8)$ is a relative minimum.

64. $g(x) = 2x^2 + \dfrac{4000}{x} + 10$. $g'(x) = 4x - \dfrac{4000}{x^2} = \dfrac{4(x^3 - 1000)}{x^2}$. The only critical

point of g is $x = 10$; $x = 0$ is not a critical point of g since $g(x)$ is not defined there.
The sign diagram of g' is

g' not defined here

we $-$ $-$ $-$ $-$ $-$ $-$ $-$ $-$ $-$ $-$ $-$ $-$ $-0+++$

0 10

Using the First Derivative Test, we conclude that the point $(10, 610)$ is a relative
minimum of g

65. $f(x) = \dfrac{x}{1+x^2}$. $f'(x) = \dfrac{(1+x^2)(1) - x(2x)}{(1+x^2)^2} = \dfrac{1 - x^2}{(1+x^2)^2} = \dfrac{(1-x)(1+x)}{(1+x^2)^2} = 0$ if $x = \pm 1$,

and these are critical points of f. From the sign diagram of f'

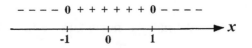

we see that f has a relative minimum at $(-1, -\frac{1}{2})$ and a relative maximum at $(1, \frac{1}{2})$.

66. $g(x) = \dfrac{x}{x^2 - 1}$. Observe that $g'(x) = \dfrac{(x^2 - 1) - x(2x)}{(x^2 - 1)^2} = -\dfrac{1 + x^2}{(x^2 - 1)^2}$ is never zero.

Furthermore, $x \pm 1$ are not critical points since they are not in the domain of g. So g has no relative extrema.

67. $f(x) = (x - 1)^{2/3}$. $f'(x) = \dfrac{2}{3}(x - 1)^{-1/3} = \dfrac{2}{3(x - 1)^{1/3}}$.

$f'(x)$ is discontinuous at $x = 1$. The sign diagram for f' is

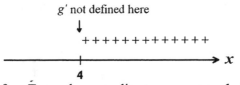

We conclude that $f(1) = 0$ is a relative minimum.

68. $g(x) = x\sqrt{x - 4} = x(x - 4)^{1/2}$.

$g'(x) = (x - 4)^{1/2} + x(\frac{1}{2})(x - 4)^{-1/2} = \frac{1}{2}(x - 4)^{-1/2}[2(x - 4) + x] = \dfrac{3x - 8}{2\sqrt{x - 4}}$

is continuous everywhere except at $x = 4$ and has a zero at $x = 8/3$. Only the point $x = 4$ lies in the domain of g which is the interval $[4, \infty)$. Thus, $x = 4$ is the only

g' not defined here
$\downarrow$
$+ + + + + + + + + + + + + +$

$\xrightarrow{\qquad\qquad\qquad\qquad\qquad} x$
$\qquad\quad 4$

critical point of g. From the sign diagram, we conclude that $g(4) = 0$ is a relative minimum of g.

69. $h(t) = -16t^2 + 64t + 80$. $h'(t) = -32t + 64 = -32(t - 2)$ and has sign diagram

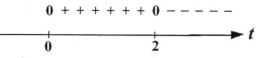

This tells us that the stone is rising on the time interval (0,2) and falling when $t > 2$. It hits the ground when $h(t) = -16t^2 + 64t + 80 = 0$
or $t^2 - 4t - 5 = (t - 5)(t + 1) = 0$ or $t = 5$ (we reject the root $t = -1$.)

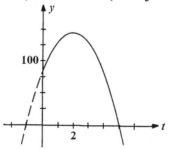

70. $P(x) = -0.001x^2 + 8x - 5000$. $P'(x) = -0.002x + 8 = 0$ if $x = 4000$. Observe that $P'(x) > 0$ if $x < 4000$ and $P'(x) < 0$ if $x > 4000$. So P is increasing on $(0,4000)$ and decreasing on $(4000, \infty)$.

71. $P'(x) = \dfrac{d}{dx}(0.0726x^2 + 0.7902x + 4.9623) = 0.1452x + 0.7902$.

Since $P'(x) > 0$ on $(0, 25)$, we see that P is increasing on the interval in question. Our result tells us that the percent of the population afflicted with Alzheimer's disease increases with age for those that are 65 and over.

72. a. $f'(t) = \dfrac{d}{dt}(0.469t^2 + 0.758t + 0.44) = 0.938t + 0.758$

Since $f'(t) > 0$ for t in $(0, 6)$, we conclude that f is increasing on that interval.
b. The result of part (a) tells us that sales in managed services will grow from 1999 through 2005.

73 $h(t) = -\frac{1}{3}t^3 + 16t^2 + 33t + 10$; $h'(t) = -t^2 + 32t + 33 = -(t + 1)(t - 33)$.
The sign diagram for h' is

The rocket is rising on the time interval $(0,33)$ and descending on $(33,T)$ for some positive number T. The parachute is deployed 33 seconds after liftoff.

74. $I(t) = \frac{1}{3}t^3 - \frac{5}{2}t^2 + 80;$ $I'(t) = t^2 - 5t = t(t-5) = 0$ if $t = 0$ or 5 From the sign

$$0 \; - \; - \; - \; 0 + \; + \; +$$

diagram, we see that I is decreasing on $(0,5)$ and increasing on $(5,10)$. After declining from 1984 through 1989, the index begins to increase after 1989.

75. $f(t) = 20t - 40\sqrt{t} + 50 = 20t - 40t^{1/2} + 50.$

$$f'(t) = 20 - 40(\frac{1}{2}t^{-1/2}) = 20(1 - \frac{1}{\sqrt{t}}) = \frac{20(\sqrt{t} - 1)}{\sqrt{t}}.$$

Then f' is continuous on $(0,4)$ and is equal to zero at $t = 1$. From the sign diagram

$$0 \; - \; - \; 0 + \; + \; + \; + \; + \; + \; + \; + \; +$$

$$\xrightarrow{\qquad \qquad \qquad \qquad \qquad} t$$
$$\qquad 0 \quad 1 \qquad \qquad 4$$

we see that f is decreasing on $(0,1)$ and increasing on $(1,4)$. We conclude that the average speed decreases from 6 A.M. to 7 A.M. and then picks up from 7 A.M. to 10 A. M.

76. $\overline{C}(x) = -0.0001x + 2 + \dfrac{2000}{x}.$ $\overline{C}'(x) = -0.0001 - \dfrac{2000}{x^2} < 0$ for all values of x and so $\overline{C}$ is always decreasing.

77. a. $f'(t) = \dfrac{d}{dt}(-0.05t^3 + 0.56t^2 + 5.47t + 7.5) = -0.15t^2 + 1.12t + 5.47$

Setting $f'(t) = 0$ gives $-0.15t^2 + 1.12t + 5.47 = 0.$ Using the quadratic formula, we find

$$t = \frac{-1.12 \pm \sqrt{(1.12)^2 - 4(-0.15)(5.47)}}{-0.3}$$

that is, $t = -3.37$, or 10.83. Since f' is continuous, the only critical points of f are $t = -3.4$ and $t = 10.8$, both of which lie outside the interval of interest.

Nevertheless this result can be used to tell us that f' does not change sign in the interval (-3.4, 10.8). Using $t = 0$ as the test point, we see that $f'(0) = 5.47 > 0$ and so we see that f is increasing on (-3.4, 10.8), and , in particular, in the interval (0, 6). Thus, we conclude that f is increasing on (0, 6).

b. The result of part (a) tells us that sales in the Web-hosting industry will be increasing throughout the years from 1999 through 2005.

78. a. $R'(t) = \dfrac{d}{dt}(0.03056t^3 - 0.45357t^2 + 4.81111t + 31.7)$

$= 0.09168t^2 - 0.90714t + 4.8111$

Observe that R' is continuous everywhere. Setting $R'(t) = 0$ gives

$$t = \frac{0.90714 \pm \sqrt{0.90714^2 - 4(0.09168)(4.81111)}}{2(0.09168)}$$

But the expression inside the radical is $-1.76 < 0$, and so there is no solution. We see that R has no critical points. Since $R'(0) = 4.81111 > 0$, we see that R is always increasing. In particular, R is increasing on (0, 6).

b. The result of part (a) shows that the revenue is always increasing over the period in question.

79 a. $P'(t) = 0.00279t^2 - 0.036t - 0.51$. Setting $P'(t) = 0$ and solving the resulting equation, we have

$$t = \frac{0.036 \pm \sqrt{(-0.036)^2 - 4(0.00279)(-0.51)}}{2(0.00279)}$$

≈ -8.53 or 21.43

The sign diagram for P' follows. [Take t = -10, 0, 25 as test points.]

From the sign diagram, we see that P is decreasing on [0, 21.43] and increasing on [21.43, 30].

b. The percent of men 65 years and older in the workforce was decreasing from 1970 through about the middle of 1991, then starting increasing from then through the year 2000.

80. a. $N'(t) = -0.0999t^2 + 0.94t - 3.8.$ Setting $N'(t) = 0$ and solving the resulting equation gives

$$t = \frac{-0.94 \pm \sqrt{(0.94)^2 - 4(-0.0999)(-3.8)}}{2(-0.0999)}$$

But this discriminant is negative (it's equal to –0.63488). Therefore there are no solutions to the equation. Since $N'(0) = -3.8 < 0$, we see that N is decreasing on [0, 6]; that is, the number of medical school applicants had been declining over the period in question.

b. The largest number of medical school applicants occur at $t = 0$ (1997-1998) an is given by $N(0) = 47$ or 47,000.

81. $S'(t) = \dfrac{d}{dt}(0.46t^3 - 2.22t^2 + 6.21t + 17.25) = 0.96t^2 - 4\,44t + 6.21.$

Observe that S' is continuous everywhere. Setting $S'(t) = 0$ and solving, we find

$$t = \frac{4.44\sqrt{4.44^2 - 4(0.96)(6.21)}}{2(0.96)}$$

Now, the discriminant is –4.1328 < 0 which shows that the equation has no real roots. Since $S'(0) = 6.21 > 0$, we conclude that $S'(t) > 0$ for all t, in particular, for t in the interval (0,4). This shows that S is increasing on (0,4).

82. $A(t) = -96.6t^4 + 403.6t^3 + 660.9t^2 + 250$
$A'(t) = -386.4t^3 + 1210.8t^2 + 1321.8t = t(386.4t^2 + 1210.8t + 1321.8).$
Solving $A'(t) = 0$, we find $t = 0$ and

$$t = \frac{-1210.8 \pm \sqrt{(1210.8)^2 - 4(-386.4)(1321.8)}}{-2(386.4)} = \frac{-1210.8 \pm 1873.2}{-2(386.4)} \approx 4.$$

Since t lies in the interval [0,5], we see that the continuous function A' has zeros at $t = 0$ and $t = 4$. From the sign diagram

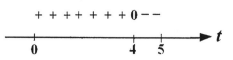

we see that f is increasing on (0,4) and decreasing on (4,5). We conclude that the cash in the Central Provident Trust Funds will be increasing from 1995 to 2035 and decreasing from 2035 to 2045.

83 $S'(t) = -6.945t^2 + 68.65t + 1.32$. Setting $S'(t) = 0$ and solving the resulting equation, we obtain

$$t = \frac{-68.65 \pm \sqrt{(68.65)^2 - 4(-6.945)(1.32)}}{2(-6.945)} \approx -0.02 \text{ or } 9.90.$$

The sign diagram for S' follows.

From the sign diagram, we see that S' is increasing on the interval $[0, 5]$. We conclude that U.S. telephone company spending was projected to be increasing from 2001 through 2006

84. $A(t) = 0.03t^3(t - 7)^4 + 60.2$.
$A'(t) = 0.09t^2(t - 7)^4 + 0.03t^3(4)(t - 7)^3$
$= 0.03t^2(t - 7)^3[3(t - 7) + 4t] = 0.21t^2(t - 3)(t - 7)^3$.
From the sign diagram of A' on $(0,7)$

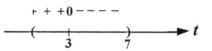

we see that A is increasing on $(0,3)$ and decreasing on $(3,7)$. This says that the pollution is increasing from 7 A.M. to 10 A.M. and decreasing from 10 A.M. to 2 P.M.

85. $C(t) = \frac{t^2}{2t^3 + 1}$; $C'(t) = \frac{(2t^3 + 1)(2t) - t^2(6t^2)}{(2t^3 + 1)^2} = \frac{2t - 2t^4}{(2t^3 + 1)^2} = \frac{2t(1 - t^3)}{(2t^3 + 1)^2}$.
From the sign diagram of C' on $(0,\infty)$,

We see that the drug concentration is increasing on $(0,1)$ and decreasing on $(1,4)$.

86. $f(x) = 15(0.08333x^2 + 1.91667x + 1)^{-1}$. So by the Chain Rule,

$$f'(x) = -15(0.08333x^2 + 1.91667x + 1)^{-2} \frac{d}{dx}(0.08333x^2 + 1.91667x + 1)$$

$$= \frac{-15(0.16666x + 1.91667)}{(0.08333x^2 + 1.91667x + 1)^2} < 0$$

for all x in (0, 11). Therefore f is decreasing on (0, 11). Our result shows that as the age of the driver increases from 16 years old to 27 years old, the predicted crash fatalities drop.

87. $A(t) = \dfrac{136}{1 + 0.25(t - 4.5)^2} + 28.$

$$A'(t) = 136\frac{d}{dt}[1 + 0.25(t - 4.5)^2]^{-1} = -136[1 + 0.25(t - 4.5)^2]^{-2}2(0.25)(t - 4.5)$$

$$= -\frac{68(t - 4.5)}{[1 + 0.25(t - 4.5)^2]^2}.$$

Observe that $A'(t) > 0$ if $t < 4.5$ and $A'(t) < 0$ if $t > 4.5$, so the pollution is increasing from 7 A.M. to 11:30 A.M. and decreasing from 11:30 A.M. to 6 P.M.

88. $G(t) = N(t) - C(t) = (3.5t^2 + 26.7t + 436.2) - (24.3t + 365)$
    $\quad = 3.5t^2 + 2.4t + 71.2.$
$G'(t) = 7t + 2.4 > 0$ on (0,10). This says that the gap is always increasing on the time interval (0,10).

89. a. $G(t) = (D - S)(t) = D(t) - S(t)$

$\quad\quad = (0.0007t^2 + 0.0265t + 2) - (-0.0014t^2 + 0.0326t + 1.9)$

$\quad\quad = 0.0021t^2 - 0.0061t + 0.1$

b. $G'(t) = 0.0042t - 0.0061 = 0$ implies $t \approx 1.45$ The sign diagram of G' follows:

We see that G is decreasing on (0, 1.5) and increasing on (1.5, 15). This shows that the gap between the demand and supply of nurses eas increasing from 2000 through the middle of 2001 but starts widening from the middle of 2001 through 2015.

c. The relative minimum of G occurs at $t = 1.5$ and is $f(1.45) \approx 0.0956$. This says that at its best there is a shortage of approximately 96,000.

90. False. The function $f(x) = \begin{cases} -x+1 & x < 0 \\ -\dfrac{1}{2}x+1 & x \geq 0 \end{cases}$

is decreasing on $(-1,1)$, but $f'(0)$ does not exist.

91. True. Let $a < x_1 < x_2 < b$. Then $f(x_2) > f(x_1)$ and $g(x_2) > g(x_1)$. Therefore,
$$(f+g)(x_2) = f(x_2) + g(x_2) > f(x_1) + g(x_1) = (f+g)(x_1)$$
and so $f + g$ is increasing on (a, b).

92. False. Let $f(x) = -x$ and $g(x) = -2x$. then both f and g are decreasing on $(-\infty, \infty)$, but $f(x) - g(x) = x - (-2x) = x$ is increasing on $(-\infty, \infty)$

93. True. Let $a < x_1 < x_2 < b$, then $f(x_1) < f(x_2)$ and $g(x_1) < g(x_2)$ We find
$$\begin{aligned} (fg)(x_2) - (fg)(x_1) &= f(x_2)g(x_2) - f(x_1)g(x_1) \\ &= f(x_2)g(x_2) - f(x_2)g(x_1) + f(x_2)g(x_1) - f(x_1)g(x_1) \\ &= f(x_2)[g(x_2) - g(x_1)] + g(x_1)[f(x_2) - f(x_1)] \\ &> 0 \end{aligned}$$
So $(fg)(x_2) > (fg)(x_1)$ and fg is increasing on (a, b).

94. False. Let $f(x) = x^3$. then $f'(0) = 3x^2\big|_{x=0} = 0$. But f does not have a relative extremum at $x = 0$.

95. False. Let $f(x) = |x|$. Then f has a relative minimum at $x = 0$, but $f'(0)$ does not exist.

96. We compute $f'(x) = m$. If $m > 0$, then $f'(x) > 0$ for all x and f is increasing; if $m < 0$, then $f'(x) < 0$ for all x and f is decreasing; if $m = 0$, then $f'(x) = 0$ for all x and f is a constant function.

97. $f'(x) = 3x^2 + 1$ is continuous on $(-\infty, \infty)$ and is always greater than or equal to 1. So f has no critical points in $(-\infty, \infty)$. Therefore f has no relative extrema on $(-\infty, \infty)$.

98. a. $f'(x) = \begin{cases} -3 & \text{if } x < 0 \\ 2 & \text{if } x > 0 \end{cases}$

$f'(-1) = -3$ and $f'(1) = 2$, so $f'(x)$ changes sign as we move across $x = 0$.

b. No. f does not have a relative minimum at $x = 0$ because $f(0) = 4$ but $f(x) < 4$ if x is a little less than 4. This does not contradict the First Derivative Test because f' is not continuous at $x = 0$.

99 a. $f'(x) = -2x$ if $x \neq 0$. $f'(-1) = 2$ and $f'(1) = -2$ so $f'(x)$ changes sign from positive to negative as we move across $x = 0$.

b. f does not have a relative maximum at $x = 0$ because $f(0) = 2$ but a neighborhood of $x = 0$, for example $(-\frac{1}{2}, \frac{1}{2})$, contains points with values larger than 2. This does not contradict the First Derivative Test because f is not continuous at $x = 0$.

100. a. $f'(x) = \begin{cases} -\dfrac{2}{x^3} & x > 0 \\ 2x & x < 0 \end{cases}$

The sign diagram of f' that follows

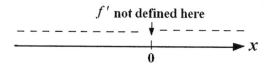

shows that f' does not change sign as we move across $x = 0$.

b. From the graph of f we see that f has a relative minimum at $x = 0$. This does not contradict the first derivative text since f is not a continuous function.

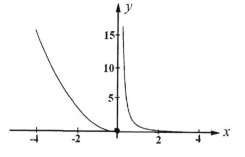

101. $f(x) = ax^2 + bx + c$. Setting $f'(x) = 2ax + b = 2a\left(x + \frac{b}{2a}\right) = 0$ gives $x = -\frac{b}{2a}$ as the

only critical point of f. If $a < 0$, we have the sign diagram

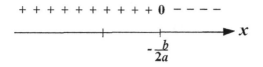

from which we see that $x = -b/2a$ gives a relative maximum. Similarly, you can show that if $a > 0$, then $x = -b/2a$ gives a relative minimum.

102. $f(x) = ax^3 + bx^2 + cx + d$; $f'(x) = 3ax^2 + 2bx + c$. The roots of $f'(x) = 0$ are
$$x = \frac{-2b \pm \sqrt{4b^2 - 12ac}}{6a}$$
There is no relative extremum if and only if the roots are not real or are repeated. This occurs if and only if $4b^2 - 12ac = 4(b^2 - 3ac) \leq 0$ or $b^2 - 3ac \leq 0$.

103 a. $f'(x) = 3x^2 + 1$ and so $f'(x) > 1$ on the interval $(0,1)$. Therefore, f is increasing on $(0,1)$.
b. $f(0) = -1$ and $f(1) = 1 + 1 - 1 = 1$. So the Intermediate Value Theorem guarantees that there is at least one root of $f(x) = 0$ in $(0,1)$. Since f is increasing on $(0,1)$, the graph of f can cross the x-axis at only one point in $(0,1)$. So $f(x) = 0$ has exactly one root.

104. $f'(x) = \dfrac{(cx+d)a - (ax+b)c}{(cx+d)^2} = \dfrac{acx + ad - acx - bc}{(cx+d)^2} = \dfrac{ad - bc}{(cx+d)^2}$.
So, if $ad - bc \neq 0$, then $f'(x) \neq 0$ for all x and f has no critical points. Therefore, f has no relative extremum in this case. If $ad - bc = 0$, then $f'(x) = 0$ for all x and so f is a constant function.

USING TECHNOLOGY EXERCISES 4.1, page 226

1. a. f is decreasing on $(-\infty, -0.2934)$ and increasing on $(-0.2934, \infty)$.
   b. Relative minimum: $f(-0.2934) = -2.5435$

2. a. f is decreasing on $(-\infty, -0.4067) \cup (0.4563, 3.7421)$ and increasing on $(-0.4067, 0.4563) \cup (3.7421, \infty)$.
   b. Relative maximum: $(0.4563, -2.5050)$
   relative minima: $(-0.4067, -5.3721)$; $(3.7421, -109 1789)$

3 a. f is increasing on $(-\infty,-1.6144) \cup (0.2390,\infty)$ and decreasing on $(-1.6144, 0.2390)$

   b. Relative maximum: $f(-1.6144) = 26.7991$; relative minimum: $f(0.2390) = 1.6733$

4. a. f is increasing on $(-\infty,\infty)$.   b. None

5. a. f is decreasing on $(-\infty,-1) \cup (0.33,\infty)$ and increasing on $(-1,0.33)$

    b. Relative maximum: $f(0.33) = 1.11$; relative minimum: $f(-1) = -0.63$.

6. a. f is increasing on $(-\infty,-0.87) \cup (0.89,\infty)$ and decreasing on $(-0.87,0) \cup (0, 0.89)$

    b. Relative maximum: $(-0.87, -2.23)$; relative minimum: $(0.89, 0.51)$

7. a. f is decreasing on $(-1,-0.71)$ and increasing on $(-0.71,1)$.

    b. f has a relative minimum at $(-0.71,-1.41)$.

8. a. f is decreasing on $(0,2) \cup (2, 2.47)$ and increasing on $(2.47,\infty)$

    b. Relative minimum: $(2.47,87.01)$

9. a.

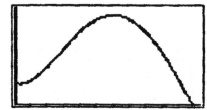

   b. f is decreasing on $(0,0.2398) \cup (6.8758,12)$ and increasing on $(0.2398,6.8758)$
   c. $(6.8758, 200.14)$; The rate at which the number of banks were failing reached a peak of 200/yr during the latter part of 1988 $(t = 6.8758)$.

10. a.

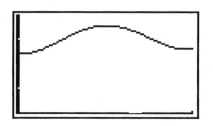

b. *V* is increasing on (0, 11). It tells us that the volume of cargo moved is always on the rise.

c. $V'(t) = 0.0283995t^2 - 0.10555t + 0.39895 > 0$ for all $t \in [0,11]$ because $V'(0) = 0.39895 > 0$ and the discriminant

$$b^2 - 4ac = (-0.10555)^2 - 4(0.0283995) = -0.0348 < 0$$

11. a.

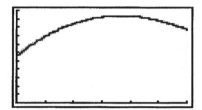

b. increasing on (0,3.6676) and decreasing on (3.6676, 6).

12. a.

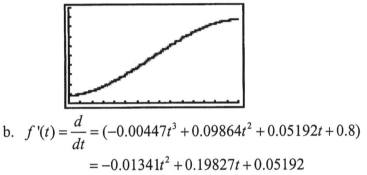

b. $f'(t) = \dfrac{d}{dt} = (-0.00447t^3 + 0.09864t^2 + 0.05192t + 0.8)$

$$= -0.013411t^2 + 0.19827t + 0.05192$$

The graph of f' in the viewing window $[0, 15] \times \{0, 2\}$ shown below shows that $f'(t) > 0$ on (0, 15). This shows that *f* is increasing on (0, 15).

13. *f* is decreasing on the interval (0,1) and increasing on (1,4). The relative minimum occurs at the point (1,32). These results indicate that the speed of traffic flow drops between 6 A.M. and 7 A.M. reaching a low of 32 mph. Thereafter, it increases till 10 A.M.

14. The PSI is increasing on the interval (0, 4.5) and decreasing on (4.5, 11). It is highest when $t = 4.5$ (11:30 A.M.) and has value 164.

4.2 CONCEPT QUESTIONS, page 276

1. a. f is concave upward on (a,b) if f' is increasing on (a,b)
   f is concave downward on (a,b) if f' is decreasing on (a,b).
   b. To determine where f is concave upward and concave downward, see page 269.
2. An inflection point of the graph of f is a point on the graph of f where its concavity changes from upward to downward or vice versa. See text page 270 for the procedure for finding inflection points.
3. The second derivatve test is stated in the text on page 274. In general, if f'' is easy to compute, then use the second derivative test. However, keep in mind that (1) in order to use this test f'' must exist, (2) the test is inconclusive if $f''(c) = 0$, and (3) the test is inconvenient to use if f'' is difficult to compute.

EXERCISES 4.2, page 276

1. f is concave downward on $(-\infty,0)$ and concave upward on $(0,\infty)$. f has an inflection point at $(0,0)$.

2. f is concave downward on $(0, \frac{3}{2})$ and concave upward on $(\frac{3}{2}, \infty)$. f has an inflection point at $(\frac{3}{2}, 2)$.

3. f is concave downward on $(-\infty,0) \cup (0,\infty)$.

4. f is concave upward on $(-\infty,-4) \cup (4,\infty)$; concave downward on $(-4,4)$.

5. f is concave upward on $(-\infty,0) \cup (1,\infty)$ and concave downward on $(0,1)$. $(0,0)$ and $(1,-1)$ are inflection points of f.

6. f is concave upward on $(0,1) \cup (5,\infty)$ and concave downward on $(1,5)$.

7. f is concave downward on $(-\infty,-2) \cup (-2,2) \cup (2,\infty)$.

8. f is concave downward on $(-\infty,0)$ and concave upward on $(0,\infty)$. $(0,1)$ is an inflection point.

9. a   10. b   11. b   12. c

13. a. $D_1'(t) > 0$, $D_2'(t) > 0$, $D_1''(t) > 0$, and $D_2''(t) < 0$ on $(0,12)$.

b. With or without the proposed promotional campaign, the deposits will increase, but with the promotion, the deposits will increase at an increasing rate whereas without the promotion, the deposits will increase at a decreasing rate.

14. If you look at the tangent lines to the graph of P, you will see that the tangent line at P has the greatest slope. This means that the rate at which the average worker is assembling transistor radios is the greatest-- that is, she is most efficient-- at $t = 2$, or at 10 A.M.

15. The significance of the inflection point Q is that the restoration process is working at its peak at the time t_0 corresponding to its t-coordinate.

16. The rumor spreads with increasing speed initially. The rate at which the rumor is spread reaches a maximum at the time corresponding to the t-coordinate of the point P on the curve. Thereafter, the speed at which the rumor is spread decreases.

17. $f(x) = 4x^2 - 12x + 7$. $f'(x) = 8x - 12$ and $f''(x) = 8$. So, $f''(x) > 0$ everywhere and therefore f is concave upward everywhere.

18. $g(x) = x^4 + \frac{1}{2}x^2 + 6x + 10$; $g'(x) = 4x^3 + x + 6$ and $g''(x) = 12x^2 + 1$. We see that $g''(x) \geq 1$ for all values of x and so g is concave upward everywhere.

19. $f(x) = \dfrac{1}{x^4} = x^{-4}$; $f'(x) = -\dfrac{4}{x^5}$ and $f''(x) = \dfrac{20}{x^6} > 0$ for all values of x in
$(-\infty,0) \cup (0,\infty)$ and so f is concave upward everywhere.

20. $g(x) = -\sqrt{4-x^2}$. $g'(x) = \dfrac{d}{dx}\left[-(4-x^2)^{1/2}\right] = -\frac{1}{2}(4-x^2)^{-1/2}(-2x) = x(4-x^2)^{-1/2}$.
$g''(x) = (4-x^2)^{-1/2} + x(-\frac{1}{2})(4-x^2)^{-3/2}(-2x)$
$\qquad = (4-x^2)^{-3/2}[(4-x^2)+x^2] = \dfrac{4}{(4-x^2)^{3/2}} > 0,$

whenever it is defined and so g is concave upward wherever it is defined.

21. $f(x) = 2x^2 - 3x + 4$; $f'(x) = 4x - 3$ and $f''(x) = 4 > 0$ for all values of x. So f is concave upward on $(-\infty,\infty)$.

22. $g(x) = -x^2 + 3x + 4$; $g'(x) = -2x + 3$ and $g''(x) = -2 < 0$ for all values of x. So g is concave downward on $(-\infty,\infty)$.

23 $f(x) = x^3 - 1$. $f'(x) = 3x^2$ and $f''(x) = 6x$. The sign diagram of f'' follows.

$$- - - - - - - - - - 0 + + + + + + + + +$$

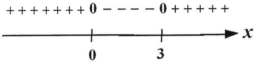

We see that f is concave downward on $(-\infty,0)$ and concave upward on $(0,\infty)$.

24. $g(x) = x^3 - x$. $g'(x) = 3x^2 - 1$ and $g''(x) = 6x$. Since $g''(x) < 0$ if $x < 0$ and $g''(x) > 0$ if $x > 0$, we see that g is concave downward on $(-\infty,0)$ and concave upward on $(0,\infty)$.

25 $f(x) = x^4 - 6x^3 + 2x + 8$; $f'(x) = 4x^3 - 18x^2 + 2$ and $f''(x) = 12x^2 - 36x = 12x(x - 3)$. The sign diagram of f''

$$+ + + + + + + 0 - - - - 0 + + + + +$$

shows that f is concave upward on $(-\infty,0) \cup (3,\infty)$ and concave downward on $(0,3)$.

26. $f(x) = 3x^4 - 6x^3 + x - 8$. $f'(x) = 12x^3 - 18x^2 + 1$ and $f''(x) = 36x^2 - 36x = 36x(x - 1)$.   From the sign diagram of f''

$$+ + + + + + + 0 - - 0 + + + + ++ + + +$$

we conclude that f is concave upward on $(-\infty,0) \cup (1,\infty)$ and concave downward on $(0,1)$.

27 $f(x) = x^{4/7}$. $f'(x) = \dfrac{4}{7}x^{-3/7}$ and $f''(x) = -\dfrac{12}{49}x^{-10/7} = -\dfrac{12}{49x^{10/7}}$.

Observe that $f''(x) < 0$ for all x different from zero. So f is concave downward on $(-\infty,0) \cup (0,\infty)$.

28. $f(x) = x^{1/3}$, $f'(x) = \dfrac{1}{3}x^{-2/3}$ and $f''(x) = -\dfrac{2}{9}x^{-5/3} = -\dfrac{2}{9x^{5/3}}$.

From the sign diagram of f'',

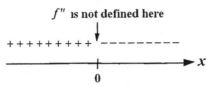

f'' is not defined here

we see that f is concave upward on $(-\infty,0)$ and concave downward on $(0,\infty)$.

29. $f(x) = (4-x)^{1/2}$ $f'(x) = \frac{1}{2}(4-x)^{-1/2}(-1) = -\frac{1}{2}(4-x)^{-1/2}$;

$f''(x) = \frac{1}{4}(4-x)^{-3/2}(-1) = -\frac{1}{4(4-x)^{3/2}} < 0.$

whenever it is defined. So f is concave downward on $(-\infty,4)$.

30. $g(x) = \sqrt{x-2} = (x-2)^{1/2}$. $g'(x) = \frac{1}{2}(x-2)^{-1/2}$

and $g''(x) = -\frac{1}{4}(x-2)^{-3/2} = -\frac{1}{4(x-2)^{3/2}}$, which is negative for $x > 2$. Next, the

domain of g is $[2,\infty)$, and we conclude that g is concave downward on $(2,\infty)$.

31. $f'(x) = \frac{d}{dx}(x-2)^{-1} = -(x-2)^{-2}$ and $f''(x) = 2(x-2)^{-3} = \frac{2}{(x-2)^3}$.

The sign diagram of f'' shows that f is concave downward on $(-\infty,2)$ and concave upward on $(2,\infty)$.

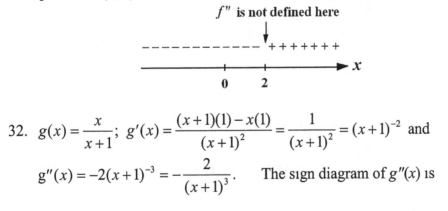

f'' is not defined here

32. $g(x) = \frac{x}{x+1}$; $g'(x) = \frac{(x+1)(1) - x(1)}{(x+1)^2} = \frac{1}{(x+1)^2} = (x+1)^{-2}$ and

$g''(x) = -2(x+1)^{-3} = -\frac{2}{(x+1)^3}$.   The sign diagram of $g''(x)$ is

297   *4 Applications of the Derivative*

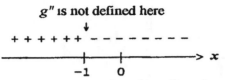

and we see that g is concave upward on $(-\infty,-1)$ and concave downward on $(-1,\infty)$.

33. $f'(x) = \dfrac{d}{dx}(2+x^2)^{-1} = -(2+x^2)^{-2}(2x) = -2x(2+x^2)^{-2}$ and

$f''(x) = -2(2+x^2)^{-2} - 2x(-2)(2+x^2)^{-3}(2x)$

$\qquad = 2(2+x^2)^{-3}[-(2+x^2)+4x^2] = \dfrac{2(3x^2-2)}{(2+x^2)^3} = 0$ if $x = \pm\sqrt{2/3}$

From the sign diagram of f''

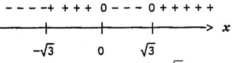

we see that f is concave upward on $(-\infty,-\sqrt{2/3}) \cup (\sqrt{2/3}, \infty)$ and concave
downward on $(-\sqrt{2/3}, \sqrt{2/3})$.

34. $g(x) = \dfrac{x}{1+x^2}$; $g'(x) = \dfrac{(1+x^2)(1) - x(2x)}{(1+x^2)^2} = \dfrac{1-x^2}{(1+x^2)^2}$

$g''(x) = \dfrac{(1+x^2)^2(-2x) - (1-x^2)2(1+x^2)(2x)}{(1+x^2)^4}$

$\qquad = \dfrac{-2x(1+x^2)(1+x^2+2-2x^2)}{(1+x^2)^4} = -\dfrac{2x(3-x^2)}{(1+x^2)^3}.$

The sign diagram for g'' follows:

We see that g is concave downward on $(-\infty,-\sqrt{3}) \cup (0, \sqrt{3})$ and concave upward

on $(-\sqrt{3},0) \cup (\sqrt{3},\infty)$.

35. $h(t) = \dfrac{t^2}{t-1}$; $h'(t) = \dfrac{(t-1)(2t) - t^2(1)}{(t-1)^2} = \dfrac{t^2 - 2t}{(t-1)^2}$;

$h''(t) = \dfrac{(t-1)^2(2t-2) - (t^2 - 2t)2(t-1)}{(t-1)^4}$

$= \dfrac{(t-1)(2t^2 - 4t + 2 - 2t^2 + 4t)}{(t-1)^4} = \dfrac{2}{(t-1)^3}$

The sign diagram of h'' is

h'' is not defined here

$\downarrow$

$-\ -\ -\ -\ -\ -$ $+\ +\ +\ +\ +\ +\ +$

$\xrightarrow{\hspace{4cm}} t$

$\quad$ 0 $\quad$ 1

and tells us that h is concave downward on $(-\infty, 1)$ and concave upward on $(1, \infty)$.

36. $f(x) = \dfrac{x+1}{x-1}$; $f'(x) = \dfrac{(x-1)(1) - (x+1)(1)}{(x-1)^2} = -\dfrac{2}{(x-1)^2} = -2(x-1)^{-2}$ and

$f''(x) = (-2)(-2)(x-1)^{-3} = \dfrac{4}{(x-1)^3}$.

The sign diagram of f'' is

f'' is not defined here

$\downarrow$

$-\ -\ -\ -\ -\ -\ -\ -$ $+\ +\ +\ +\ +\ +\ +$

$\xrightarrow{\hspace{4cm}} x$

$\quad$ 0 $\quad$ 1

and we conclude that f is concave downward on $(-\infty, 1)$ and concave upward on $(1, \infty)$.

37. $g(x) = x + \dfrac{1}{x^2}$; $g'(x) = 1 - 2x^{-3}$ and $g''(x) = 6x^{-4} = \dfrac{6}{x^4} > 0$ whenever $x \neq 0$.

Therefore, g is concave upward on $(-\infty, 0) \cup (0, \infty)$.

38. $h(r) = -(r-2)^{-2}$; $h'(r) = 2(r-2)^{-3}$; $h''(r) = -6(r-2)^{-4} < 0$ for all $r \neq 2$.

So h is concave downward on $(-\infty, 2) \cup (2, \infty)$.

39. $g(t) = (2t-4)^{1/3}$. $g'(t) = \ = \dfrac{1}{3}(2t-4)^{-2/3}(2) = \dfrac{2}{3}(2t-4)^{-2/3}$.

4 Applications of the Derivative

$$g''(t) = -\frac{4}{9}(2t-4)^{-5/3} = -\frac{4}{9(2t-4)^{5/3}}.$$ The sign diagram of g''

g'' is not defined here

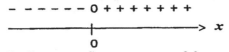

tells us that g is concave upward on $(-\infty,2)$ and concave downward on $(2,\infty)$.

40. $f(x) = (x-2)^{2/3}$.

$$f'(x) = \frac{2}{3}(x-2)^{-1/3} \text{ and } f''(x) = -\frac{2}{9}(x-2)^{-4/3} = -\frac{2}{9(x-2)^{4/3}} < 0$$

for all $x \neq 2$. Therefore, f is concave downward on $(-\infty,2) \cup (2,\infty)$.

41. $f(x) = x^3 - 2. \ f'(x) = 3x^2$ and $f''(x) = 6x. \ f''(x)$ is continuous everywhere and has a zero at $x = 0$. From the sign diagram of f''

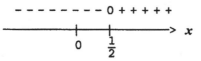

we conclude that $(0,-2)$ is an inflection point of f.

42. $g(x) = x^3 - 6x. \ g'(x) = 3x^2 - 6$ and $g''(x) = 6x$. Observe that $g''(x) = 0$ if $x = 0$. Since $g''(x) < 0$ if $x < 0$ and $g''(x) > 0$ if $x > 0$, we see that $(0,0)$ is an inflection point of g.

43. $f(x) = 6x^3 - 18x^2 + 12x - 15; f'(x) = 18x^2 - 36x + 12$ and $f''(x) = 36x - 36 = 36(x-1) = 0$ if $x = 1$. The sign diagram of f''

tells us that f has an inflection point at $(1,-15)$.

44. $g(x) = 2x^3 - 3x^2 + 18x - 8, \ g'(x) = 6x^2 - 6x + 18$ and $g''(x) = 12x - 6 = 6(2x - 1)$. From the sign diagram of g''

we conclude that $(\frac{1}{2},\frac{1}{2})$ is an inflection point of g.

45. $f(x) = 3x^4 - 4x^3 + 1.\, f'(x) = 12x^3 - 12x^2$ and $f''(x) = 36x^2 - 24x = 12x(3x-2) = 0$ if $x = 0$ or 2/3. These are candidates for inflection points. The sign diagram of f''

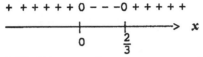

shows that $(0,1)$ and $(\frac{2}{3},\frac{11}{27})$ are inflection points of f

46. $f(x) = x^4 - 2x^3 + 6.\, f'(x) = 4x^3 - 6x^2$ and $f''(x) = 12x^2 - 12x = 12x(x-1).\, f''(x)$ is continuous everywhere and has zeros at $x = 0$ and $x = 1$. From the sign diagram of f''

```
+ + + + + 0 - - 0 + + + + +
————————————+———+————————> x
            0   1
```

we conclude that $(0,6)$ and $(1,5)$ are inflection points of f.

47. $g(t) = t^{1/3}$, $g'(t) = \frac{1}{3}t^{-2/3}$ and $g''(t) = -\frac{2}{9}t^{-5/3} = -\dfrac{2}{9t^{5/3}}$ Observe that $t = 0$ is in the

domain of g. Next, since $g''(t) > 0$ if $t < 0$ and $g''(t) < 0$, if $t > 0$, we see that $(0,0)$ is an inflection point of g.

48. $f(x) = x^{1/5}.\, f'(x) = \frac{1}{5}x^{-4/5}$ and $f''(x) = -\frac{4}{25}x^{-9/5} = -\dfrac{4}{25x^{9/5}}$. Observe that

$f''(x) > 0$ if $x < 0$ and $f''(x) < 0$ if $x > 0$. Therefore, $(0,0)$ is an inflection point.

49. $f(x) = (x-1)^3 + 2.\, f'(x) = 3(x-1)^2$ and $f''(x) = 6(x-1)$. Observe that $f''(x) < 0$ if $x < 1$ and $f''(x) > 0$ if $x > 1$ and so $(1,2)$ is an inflection point of f.

50. $f(x) = (x-2)^{4/3}.\, f'(x) = \frac{4}{3}(x-2)^{1/3}.\, f''(x) = \frac{4}{9}(x-2)^{-2/3} = \dfrac{4}{9(x-2)^{2/3}}$.

$x = 2$ is a candidate for an inflection point of f, but $f''(x) > 0$ for all values of $x = 2$ and so f has no inflection point.

51. $f(x) = \dfrac{2}{1+x^2} = 2(1+x^2)^{-1}.\, f'(x) = -2(1+x^2)^{-2}(2x) = -4x(1+x^2)^{-2}$

$$f''(x) = -4(1+x^2)^{-2} - 4x(-2)(1+x^2)^{-3}(2x)$$

$$= 4(1+x^2)^{-3}[-(1+x^2)+4x^2] = \frac{4(3x^2-1)}{(1+x^2)^3},$$

is continuous everywhere and has zeros at $x = \pm\frac{\sqrt{3}}{3}$. From the sign diagram of f'' we conclude that $\left(-\frac{\sqrt{3}}{3},\frac{3}{2}\right)$ and $\left(\frac{\sqrt{3}}{3},\frac{3}{2}\right)$ are inflection points of f.

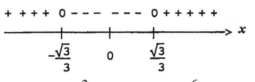

52. $f(x) = 2 + \dfrac{3}{x}$. $f'(x) = -\dfrac{3}{x^2}$ and $f''(x) = \dfrac{6}{x^3}$ Now f'' changes sign as we move across $x = 0$ but $x = 0$ is not in the domain of f so f has no inflection points.

53. $f(x) = -x^2 + 2x + 4$ and $f'(x) = -2x + 2$. The critical point of f is $x = 1$. Since $f''(x) = -2$ and $f''(1) = -2 < 0$, we conclude that $f(1) = 5$ is a relative maximum of f.

54. $g(x) = 2x^2 + 3x + 7$; $g'(x) = 4x + 3 = 0$ if $x = -3/4$ and this is a critical point of g. Next, $g''(x) = 4$ and so $g''(-\frac{3}{4}) = 4 > 0$. So $\left(-\frac{3}{4}, \frac{47}{8}\right)$ is a relative minimum.

55 $f(x) = 2x^3 + 1$; $f'(x) = 6x^2 = 0$ if $x = 0$ and this is a critical point of f. Next, $f''(x) = 12x$ and so $f''(0) = 0$. Thus, the Second Derivative Test fails. But the First Derivative Test shows that $(0,0)$ is not a relative extremum.

56. $g(x) = x^3 - 6x$. $g'(x) = 3x^2 - 6 = 3(x^2 - 2) = 0$ implies $x = \pm\sqrt{2}$, are the critical points of g. Next, $g''(x) = 6x$. Since $g''(-\sqrt{2}) = -6\sqrt{2} < 0$ and $g''(\sqrt{2}) = 6\sqrt{2} > 0$, we conclude, by the Second Derivative Test, that $(-\sqrt{2}, 4\sqrt{2})$ is a relative maximum and $(\sqrt{2}, -4\sqrt{2})$ is a relative minimum of g.

57. $f(x) = \frac{1}{3}x^3 - 2x^2 - 5x - 10$. $f'(x) = x^2 - 4x - 5 = (x - 5)(x + 1)$ and this gives $x = -1$ and $x = 5$ as critical points of f. Next, $f''(x) = 2x - 4$. Since $f''(-1) = -6 < 0$, we see that $(-1, -\frac{22}{3})$ is a relative maximum. Next, $f''(5) = 6 > 0$ and this shows that $(5, -\frac{130}{3})$ is a relative minimum.

58. $f(x) = 2x^3 + 3x^2 - 12x - 4$; $f'(x) = 6x^2 + 6x - 12 = 6(x^2 + x - 2) = 6(x + 2)(x - 1)$.

The critical points of f are $x = -2$ and $x = 1$. $f''(x) = 12x + 6 = 6(2x + 1)$. Then $f''(-2) = 6(-4 + 1) = -18 < 0$ and $f''(1) = 6(2 + 1) = 18 > 0$. Using the Second Derivative Test, we conclude that $f(-2) = 16$ is a relative maximum and $f(1) = -11$ is a relative minimum.

59 $g(t) = t + \dfrac{9}{t}$. $g'(t) = 1 - \dfrac{9}{t^2} = \dfrac{t^2 - 9}{t^2} = \dfrac{(t+3)(t-3)}{t^2}$ and this shows that $t = \pm 3$ are

critical points of g. Now, $g''(t) = 18t^{-3} = \dfrac{18}{t^3}$. Since $g''(-3) = -\dfrac{18}{27} < 0$ the Second

Derivative Test implies that g has a relative maximum at $(-3,-6)$. Also,

$g''(3) = \dfrac{18}{27} > 0$ and so g has a relative minimum at $(3,6)$.

60. $f(t) = 2t + 3t^{-1}$. $f'(t) = 2 - 3t^{-2}$. Setting $f'(t) = 0$ gives $3t^{-2} = 2$ or $t^2 = 3/2$, so that

$t = \pm\sqrt{3/2}$ are critical points of f. Next, we compute $f''(t) = 6/t^3$ Since

$f''(-\sqrt{3/2}) < 0$ and $f''(\sqrt{3/2}) > 0$, we see that $f(-\sqrt{3/2}) = -2\sqrt{3/2} - 3\sqrt{2/3}$ is

a relative maximum and $f(\sqrt{3/2}) = 2\sqrt{3/2} + 3\sqrt{2/3}$ is a relative minimum of f.

61. $f(x) = \dfrac{x}{1-x}$. $f'(x) = \dfrac{(1-x)(1) - x(-1)}{(1-x)^2} = \dfrac{1}{(1-x)^2}$ is never zero.

So there are no critical points and f has no relative extrema.

62. $f(x) = \dfrac{2x}{x^2 + 1}$. $f'(x) = \dfrac{(x^2 + 1)(2) - 2x(2x)}{(x^2 + 1)^2} = \dfrac{2(1 - x^2)}{(x^2 + 1)^2} = 0$ if $x = \pm 1$.

So $x = \pm 1$ are critical points of f.

Next, $f''(x) = \dfrac{(x^2 + 1)^2(-4x) - 2(1 - x^2)2(x^2 + 1)(2x)}{(x^2 + 1)^4}$

$= \dfrac{2x(x^2 + 1)(-2x^2 - 2 - 4 + 4x^2)}{(x^2 + 1)^4} = \dfrac{4x(x^2 - 3)}{(x^2 + 1)^3}$.

Since $f''(-1) = \dfrac{-2(-4)}{2^3} = 1 > 0$, we see that $(-1,-1)$ is a relative minimum and

$f''(-1) = \dfrac{-2(-4)}{2^3} = 1 < 0$, we see that $(1,1)$ is a relative maximum.

63. $f(t) = t^2 - \dfrac{16}{t}$. $f'(t) = 2t + \dfrac{16}{t^2} = \dfrac{2t^3 + 16}{t^2} = \dfrac{2(t^3 + 8)}{t^2}$. Setting

$f'(t) = 0$ gives $t = -2$ as a critical point. Next, we compute

$f''(t) = \dfrac{d}{dt}(2t + 16t^{-2}) = 2 - 32t^{-3} = 2 - \dfrac{32}{t^3}$. Since $f''(-2) = 2 - \dfrac{32}{(-8)} = 6 > 0$, we

see that $(-2, 12)$ is a relative minimum.

64. $g(x) = x^2 + \dfrac{2}{x}$. $g'(x) = 2x - \dfrac{2}{x^2}$. Setting $g'(x) = 0$ gives $x^3 = 1$ or $x = 1$. Thus, $x = 1$

is the only critical point of g. Next, $g''(x) = 2 + \dfrac{4}{x^3}$. Since $g''(1) = 6 > 0$, we

conclude that $g(1) = 3$ is a relative minimum of g.

65. $g(s) = \dfrac{s}{1 + s^2}$; $g'(s) = \dfrac{(1 + s^2)(1) - s(2s)}{(1 + s^2)^2} = \dfrac{1 - s^2}{(1 + s^2)^2} = 0$ gives $s = -1$ and $s = 1$

as critical points of g. Next, we compute

$$g''(s) = \dfrac{(1 + s^2)^2(-2s) - (1 - s^2)2(1 + s^2)(2s)}{(1 + s^2)^4}$$

$$= \dfrac{2s(1 + s^2)(-1 - s^2 - 2 + 2s^2)}{(1 + s^2)^4} = \dfrac{2s(s^2 - 3)}{(1 + s^2)^3}$$

Now, $g''(-1) = \tfrac{1}{2} > 0$ and so $g(-1) = -\tfrac{1}{2}$ is a relative minimum of g. Next,

$g''(1) = -\tfrac{1}{2} < 0$ and so $g(1) = \tfrac{1}{2}$ is a relative maximum of g.

66. $g'(x) = \dfrac{d}{dx}(1 + x^2)^{-1} = -(1 + x^2)^{-2}(2x) = -\dfrac{2x}{(1 + x^2)^2}$. Setting $g'(x) = 0$ gives $x = 0$

as the only critical point. Next, we find

$$g'(x) = \dfrac{(1 + x^2)^2(-2) + 2x(2)(1 + x^2)(2x)}{(1 + x^2)^4} = \dfrac{-2(1 + x^2)(1 + x^2 - 4x^2)}{(1 + x^2)^4} = -\dfrac{2(1 - 3x^2)}{(1 + x^2)^3}.$$

Since $g''(0) = -2 < 0$, we see that $(0,1)$ is a relative maximum.

67. $f(x) = \dfrac{x^4}{x - 1}$.

$$f'(x) = \frac{(x-1)(4x^3) - x^4(1)}{(x-1)^2} = \frac{4x^4 - 4x^3 - x^4}{(x-1)^2} = \frac{3x^4 - 4x^3}{(x-1)^2} = \frac{x^3(3x-4)}{(x-1)^2}$$

and so $x = 0$ and $x = 4/3$ are critical points of f. Next,

$$f''(x) = \frac{(x-1)^2(12x^3 - 12x^2) - (3x^4 - 4x^3)(2)(x-1)}{(x-1)^4}$$

$$= \frac{(x-1)(12x^4 - 12x^3 - 12x^3 + 12x^2 - 6x^4 + 8x^3)}{(x-1)^4}$$

$$= \frac{6x^4 - 16x^3 + 12x^2}{(x-1)^3} = \frac{2x^2(3x^2 - 8x + 6)}{(x-1)^3}.$$

Since $f''(\frac{4}{3}) > 0$, we see that $f(\frac{4}{3}) = \frac{256}{27}$ is a relative minimum. Since $f''(0) = 0$, the Second Derivative Test fails. Using the sign diagram for f',

f' is not defined here

$$+++++0----\downarrow-\ 0++++++$$

and the First Derivative Test, we see that $f(0) = 0$ is a relative maximum.

68. $f(x) = \dfrac{x^2}{x^2+1}$. $f'(x) = \dfrac{(1+x^2)(2x) - x^2(2x)}{(1+x^2)^2} = \dfrac{2x}{(1+x^2)^2}$.

Setting $f'(x) = 0$ gives $x = 0$ as the only critical point of f.

$$f''(x) = \frac{(1+x^2)^2(2) - 2x(2)(1+x^2)(2x)}{(1+x^2)^4} = \frac{2(1+x^2)[(1+x^2) - 4x^2]}{(1+x^2)^4} = \frac{2(1-3x^2)}{(1+x^2)^3}.$$

Since $f''(0) = 2 > 0$, we see that $(0,0)$ is a relative minimum.

69.

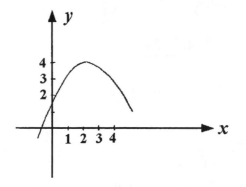

70.

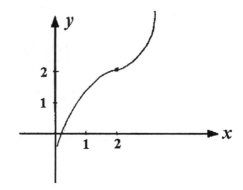

71.

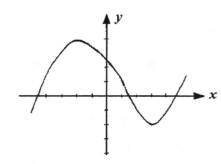

72.

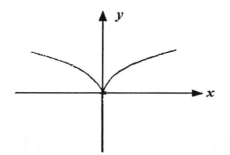

73.

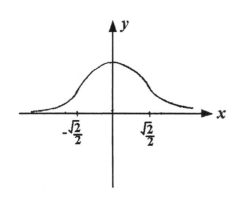

74.

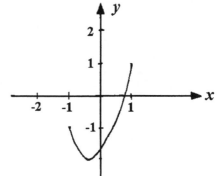

75 a. $N'(t)$ is positive because N is increasing on $(0,12)$.
   b. $N''(t) < 0$ on $(0,6)$ and $N''(t) > 0$ on $(6,12)$.
   c. The rate of growth of the number of help-wanted advertisements was decreasing over the first six months of the year and increasing over the last six months.

76. a. Both $N_1(t)$ and $N_2(t)$ are increasing on $(0,12)$.
   b. $N_1''(t) < 0$ and $N_2''(t) > 0$ on $(0,12)$.
   c. Although the projected number of crimes will increase in either case, a cut in the budget will see an accelerated increase in the number of crimes committed. With the budget intact, the rate of increase of crimes committed will continue to drop.

77. $f(t)$ increases at an increasing rate until the water level reaches the middle of the vase at which time (and this corresponds to the inflection point of f), $f(t)$ is increasing at the fastest rate. Though $f(t)$ still increases until the vase is filled, it does so at a decreasing rate.

78. The behavior of $f(t)$ is just the opposite of that given in the solution to exercise 76. $f(t)$ increases at a decreasing rate until the water level reaches the middle of the vase (and this corresponds to the inflection point of f). After that $f(t)$ increases until the vase is filled and does so at an increasing rate (see the following figure).

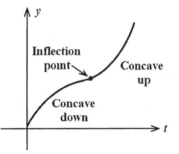

79. a. $S'(t) = 0.39t + 0.32 > 0$ on $[0, 7]$. So sales were increasing through the years in question.
   b. $S''(t) = 0.39 > 0$ on $[0,7]$. So sales continued to accelerate through the years.

80. a. $S'(t) = 0.328t + 0.85$ and $S''(t) = 0.328$

b. These results follow from the fact that both $S'(t)$ and $S''(t)$ are positive over the interval (0,4).

81. We wish to find the inflection point of the function $N(t) = -t^3 + 6t^2 + 15t$. Now, $N'(t) = -3t^2 + 12t + 15$ and $N''(t) = -6t + 12 = -6(t - 2)$ giving $t = 2$ as the only candidate for an inflection point of N. From the sign diagram

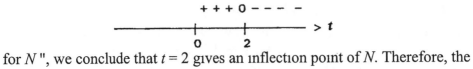

for N'', we conclude that $t = 2$ gives an inflection point of N. Therefore, the average worker is performing at peak efficiency at 10 A.M.

82. $s = f(t) = -t^3 + 54t^2 + 480t + 6$. The velocity of the rocket is
$$v = f'(t) = -3t^2 + 108t + 480$$
and its acceleration is $a = f''(t) = -6t + 108 = -6(t - 18)$. From the sign diagram

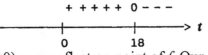

we see that (18, 20,310) is an inflection point of f. Our computations reveal that the maximum velocity of the rocket is attained when $t = 18$. The maximum velocity is
$$f'(18) = -3(18)^2 + 108(18) + 480 = 1452, \text{ or } 1452 \text{ ft/sec}$$

83. $S'(t) = -5.64t^2 + 60.66t - 76.14$; $S''(t) = -11.28t + 60.66 = 0$ if $t \approx 5.38$
The sign diagram of S'' follows:

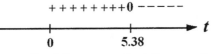

From the sign diagram for S'', we see that the graph of S is concave upward on (0,5). This says that the rate of business spending on technology is increasing from 2000 through 2005.

84. a. $f'(t) = \dfrac{d}{dt}(0.0117t^3 + 0.0037t^2 + 0.7563t + 4.1)$
$$= 0.0351t^2 + 0.0074t + 0.7563 \geq 0.7563$$
for all t in the interval [0, 9]. This shows that f is increasing on (0, 9). It tells us that the projected amount of AMT will keep on increasing over the years in question.

b. $f''(t) = \dfrac{d}{dt}(0.0351t^2 + 0.0074t + 0.7563) = 0.0702t + 0.0074 \geq 0.0074.$

This shows that f' is increasing on (0, 9). Out result tells us that not only is the amount of AMT paid increasing over the period in question, but it is actually accelerating!

85. a. $R'(x) = -0.009x^2 + 2.7x + 2;\ R''(x) = -0.018x + 2.7.$ Setting $R''(x) = 0$ gives $x = 150.$ Since $R''(x) > 0$ if $x < 150$ and $R''(x) < 0$ if $x > 150$, we see that the graph of R is concave upward on (0, 150) and concave downward on (150,400). So $x = 150$ gives rise to an inflection point of R. $R(150) = 28,850.$ So the inflection point is (150, 28,850).

b. $R''(140) = 0.18;\ R''(160) = -0.18$ This shows that at $x = 140$, a slight increase in x (spending) would result in the revenue increasing. At $x = 160$, the opposite conclusion holds. So it would be more beneficial to increase the expenditure when it is \$140,000 than when it's at \$160,000.

86. $P(t) = t^3 - 9t^2 + 40t + 50.\ P'(t) = 3t^2 - 18t + 40$ and $P''(t) = 6t - 18 = 6(t - 3).$
The sign diagram of P''

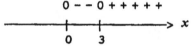

shows that (3,116) is an inflection point. This analysis reveals that after declining the first 3 years, the growth rate of the company's profit is once again on the rise.

87. a. $A'(t) = 0.92(0.61)(t+1)^{-0.39} = \dfrac{0.5612}{(t+1)^{0.39}} > 0$ on (0,4), so A is increasing on (0,4).

his tells us that the spending is increasing over the years in question.

b. $A''(t) = (0.5612)(-0.39)(t+1)^{-1.39} = -\dfrac{0.218868}{(t+1)^{1.39}} < 0$ on (0,4). And so A'' is

concave downward on (0,4). This tells us that the spending is increasing but at a decreasing rate.

88. a. $S'(t) = 6.8(0.49)(t+1.03)^{-0.51} = \dfrac{3.332}{(t+1.03)^{0.51}} > 0$ on (0,4). So S is decreasing on

(0,4). This tells us that the sales are increasing from 2003 through 2007.

b. $S''(t) = 3.332(-0.51)(t+1.03)^{-1.51} = -\dfrac{1.69932}{(t+1.03)^{1.51}} < 0$ on (0,4). This tells us that

the graph of S is concave downward on (0,4), and that the sales are increasing but at a decreasing rate.

89. $S'(t) = -5.418t^2 + 20.476t + 93.35; \ S''(t) = -10.836t + 20.476 = 0$ if $t \approx 1.9$. The

sign diagram for S'' follows.

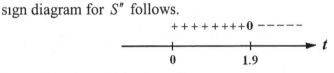

$$++++++++0\ -----$$

t

0   1.9

Since $S(1.9) = 784.9$, the inflection point is approximately (1.9, 784.9). The rate of annual spending slows down near the end of 2000.

90. a. $N'(t) = 2.25t^2 - 3t + 8.25$

$N''(t) = 4.5t - 3 = 0$ implies $t \approx 0.67$. The sign diagram of N'' follows:

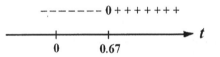

$$--------0+++++++$$

t

0   0.67

The graph of N is concave downward on (0, 0.67) and concave upward on (0.67,4).

b. From the sign diagram, we see that an inflection point occurs when $t = 0.67$. Since $N(0.67) \approx 138.1$, the inflection point occurs when $t = 0.67$. Since $N(0.67) \approx 138.1$, the inflection point is approximately (0.67,138.1). The rate of increase of shipments is slowest at $t = 0.67$; that is a little after the middle of 2001.

91. a. $R'(t) = 74.925t^2 - 99.62t + 41.25$

$R''(t) = 149.85t - 99.62$

b. In solving the equation $R'(t) = 0$, we see that the discriminant is

$$(-99.62)^2 - 4(74.925)(41.25) = -2438.4806 < 0$$

and so R' has no zeros. Since $R'(0) = 41.25 > 0$, we see that $R'(t) > 0$ in (0,4). This shows that the revenue is always increasing from 1999 through 2003.

c. $R''(t) = 0$ implies $t = 0.66$. The sign diagram of R'' follows.

```
------- 0 + + + + + + +
```

                    ───────────────────────► t
                    0   0.66

92. a. $P'(t) = \dfrac{d}{dt}(44560t^3 - 89394t^2 + 234633t + 273288)$

   $= 133680t^2 - 178788 + 234633$

   Observe that P' is continuous everywhere and $P'(t) = 0$ has no real solution since the discriminant

   $$b^2 - 4ac = (-178788)^2 - 4(133680)(234633)$$
   $$= -93497808816 < 0$$

   Since $P'(0) = 234633 > 0$, we may conclude that $P'(t) > 0$ for all t in $(0, 4)$. So the population is always increasing.

   b. $P''(t) = 267360t - 178788 = 0$ implies $t = 0.67$. The sign diagram of P'' shows that $t = 0.67$ is an inflection point of the graph of P. This shows that the population was increasing at the slowest pace sometime toward the middle of August of 1976.

93. $A(t) = 1.0974t^3 - 0.0915t^4$. $A'(t) = 3.2922t^2 - 0.366t^3$ and $A''(t) = 6.5844t - 1.098t^2$.
   Setting $A'(t) = 0$, we obtain $t^2(3.2922 - 0.366t) = 0$, and this gives $t = 0$ or
   $t \approx 8.995 \approx 9$ Using the Second Derivative Test, we find
   $A''(9) = 6.5844(9) - 1.098(81) = -29.6784 < 0$, and this tells us that $t \approx 9$ gives rise to a relative maximum of A. Our analysis tells us that on that May day, the level of ozone peaked at approximately 4 P.M. in the afternoon.

94. a. $R'(t) = -6t^3 + 42t^2 - 50.8t + 64$; $R''(t) = -18t^2 + 84t - 50.8$. Solving the equation
   $R''(t) = 0$, we obtain

   $$t = \frac{-84 \pm \sqrt{84^2 - 4(-18)(-50.8)}}{-36} \approx 0.714 \text{ or } 3.95.$$

   The sign diagram of R'' follows.

```
----- 0 + + + + + + + + + 0 --
```

                    ───────────────────────► t
               0   0.714   4

   We see that the inflection points are $(0.714, 327.5)$ and $(3.95, 644.5)$. The cash reserve is growing at the greatest rate at $t = 3.95$, that is, at approximately the beginning of 2002.

95 a. $N'(t) = \dfrac{d}{dt}(-0.9307t^3 + 74.04t^2 + 46.8667t + 3967)$

$= -2.7921t^2 + 148.08t + 46.8667$

N' is continuous everywhere and has no zeros at

$$t = \dfrac{-146.08 \pm \sqrt{(148.08)^2 - 4(-0.9307)(46.86667)}}{2(-2.7921)}$$

that is, at $t = -0.1053$ or 53.1406. Both these points lie outside the interval of interest. Picking $t = 0$ for a test point, we see that $N'(0) = 46.86667 > 0$ and conclude that N is increasing on $(0, 16)$. This shows that the number of participants is increasing over the years in question.

b. $N''(t) = \dfrac{d}{dt}(-2.7921t^2 + 148.08t + 46.86667) = -5.5842t + 148.08 = 0$

if $t = 26.518$. So $N''(t)$ does not change sign in the interval $(0, 16)$. Since $N''(0) = 148.08 > 0$, we see that $N'(t)$ is increasing on $(0, 16)$ and the desired conclusion follows.

96. a. $R'(t) = 0.02924t^3 - 0.522t^2 + 3.056t + 0.48$; $R''(t) = 0.08772t^2 - 1.044t + 3.056$

Solving the equation $R''(t) = 0$, we obtain

$$t = \dfrac{1.044 \pm \sqrt{(-1.044)^2 - 4(0.08772)(3.056)}}{2(0.08772)} \approx 5.19 \text{ or } 6.71.$$

The sign diagram of R'' follows.

From the sign diagram, we see that the inflection points are approximately $(5.19, 43.95)$ and $(6.71, 53.56)$. We see that the dependency ratio will be increasing at the greatest pace around $t = 5.2$, that is, at around 205.2.

b. The dependency ratio will be $R(5.2) \approx 43.95$, or approximately 44.

97. True. If f' is increasing on (a,b), then $-f'$ is decreasing on (a,b), and so if the graph of f is concave upward on (a,b), the graph of $-f$ must be concave downward on (a,b).

98. False. Let $f(x) = x + \dfrac{1}{x}$ (see Example 2). Then f is concave downward on $(-\infty, 0)$ and concave upward on , but f does not have an inflection point at 0.

99 True. The given conditions imply that $f''(0) < 0$ and the Second Derivative Test gives the desired conclusion.

100. True. Suppose the degree of P is n $n \geq 3$. Thus $P''(x) = 0$ can have at most $(n - 2)$ zeros.

101. $f(x) = ax^2 + bx + c$. $f'(x) = 2ax + b$ and $f''(x) = 2a$. So $f''(x) > 0$ if $a > 0$, and the parabola opens upward. If $a < 0$, then $f''(x) < 0$ and the parabola opens downward.

102. a. $f'(x) = 3x^2$, $g'(x) = 4x^3$, and $h'(x) = -4x^3$. Setting $f'(x) = 0$, $g'(x) = 0$, and $h'(x) = 0$, respectively, gives $x = 0$ as a critical point of each function.
b. $f''(x) = 6x$, $g''(x) = 12x^2$, and $h''(x) = -12x^2$, so that $f''(0) = 0$, $g''(0) = 0$, and $h''(0) = 0$. Thus, the second derivative test yields no conclusion in these cases.
c. Since $f'(x) > 0$ for both $x > 0$ and $x < 0$, $f'(x)$ does not change sign as we move across the critical point $x = 0$ by the First Derivative Test. Next, $g'(x)$ changes sign from negative to positive as we move. Finally, we see that $h'(x) < 0$ for $x > 0$, so h has a relative maximum at $x = 0$.

USING TECHNOLOGY EXERCISES 4.2, page 283

1. a. f is concave upward on $(-\infty, 0) \cup (1.1667, \infty)$ and concave downward on $(0, 1.1667)$.
    b. $(1.1667, 1.1153)$; $(0,2)$

2. a. f is concave downward on $(-\infty, -0.1740) \cup (0.9121, \infty)$ and concave upward on $(-0.1740, 0.9121)$.
    b. $(-0.1740, 1.4173)$; $(0.9121, 2.8507)$

3. a. f is concave downward on $(-\infty, 0)$ and concave upward on $(0, \infty)$.
    b. $(0,2)$

4. a. f is concave upward on $(-\infty, -0.7702) \cup (0.2743, 0.4958)$ and concave downward on $(-0.7702, 0.2743) \cup (0.4958, \infty)$.
    b. $(-0.7702, -9.4325)$; $(0.2743, -2.9506)$; $(0.4958, -2.1312)$

5. a. *f* is concave downward on (-∞,0) and concave upward on (0, ∞).
    b. (0,0)

6. a. *f* is concave downward on (-∞,0.3335) ∪ (0.7885, 1), and concave upward on
       (0.3335, 0.7885) ∪ (1, ∞).
    b. (0.3335, -0.9930), (0.7885, -0.0824), (1, 0)

7. a. *f* is concave downward on (-∞,-2.4495) ∪ (0, 2.4495); *f* is concave upward on
       (-2.4495, 0) ∪ (2.4495, ∞).   b. (-2.4495, -0.3402); (2.4495, 0.3402)

8. a. *f* is concave upward on (0, 2.5); *f* is concave downward on (2.5, 2.2136)
    b. (2.5, 2.2136)

9. a.

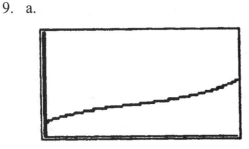

    b. (5.5318, 35.9483)
    c. *t* = 5.5318

10. a.

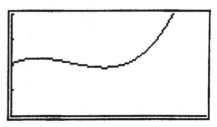

    b. (2.4286, 2.0891);
    manufacturing capacity was
    increasing at the fastest rate in 1990
    (*t* = 2.4286).

11. a.

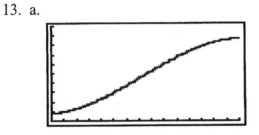

12. a.

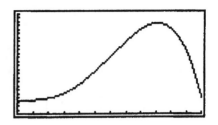

b. (3.9024, 77.0919);
sales of houses were increasing
at the fastest rate in late 1988.

b.   The inflection point occurs
at (6.1542,14.7446). It reveals that the
the sales of the Multimedia market
are projected to have the highest
increase in the level of sales in
approximately the middle of 1996 with
sales of $14.75 billion.

13. a.

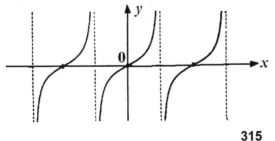

b. April 1993 ($t = 7.36$)

4.3 CONCEPT QUESTIONS, page 293

1. a. See the definition on page 287 of the text.
   b. See the definition on page 287 of the text.
2. a. There is no restriction to the number of vertical asymptotes. the graph of a
   function can have:

b. The graph of a function can have at most two horizontal asymptotes.

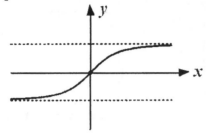

3. See the procedure given on page 287 of the text.
4. See the procedure given on page 290 of the text.

EXERCISES 4.3, page 293

1. $y = 0$ is a horizontal asymptote.

2. $y = 0$ is a horizontal asymptote and $x = -1$ is a vertical asymptote.

3. $y = 0$ is a horizontal asymptote and $x = 0$ is a vertical asymptote.

4. $y = 0$ is a horizontal asymptote.

5. $y = 0$ is a horizontal asymptote and $x = -1$ and $x = 1$ are vertical asymptotes.

6. $y = 0$ is a horizontal asymptote.

7. $y = 3$ is a horizontal asymptote and $x = 0$ is a vertical asymptote.

8. $y = 0$ is a horizontal asymptote, and $x = -2$ is a vertical asymptote.

9. $y = 1$ and $y = -1$ are horizontal asymptotes.

10. $y = 1$ is a horizontal asymptote and $x = \pm 1$ are vertical asymptotes.

11. $\lim\limits_{x \to \infty} \dfrac{1}{x} = 0$ and so $y = 0$ is a horizontal asymptote. Next, since the numerator of the rational expression is not equal to zero and the denominator is zero at $x = 0$, we see that $x = 0$ is a vertical asymptote.

12. $\lim\limits_{x \to \infty} \dfrac{1}{x+2} = 0$ and so $y = 0$ is a horizontal asymptote, Next, observe that the numerator of the rational function is not equal to zero but the denominator is equal to zero at $x = -2$ and so $x = -2$ is a vertical asymptote.

13. $f(x) = -\dfrac{2}{x^2}$ $\lim\limits_{x \to \infty} -\dfrac{2}{x^2} = 0$, so $y = 0$ is a horizontal asymptote. Next, the denominator of $f(x)$ is equal to zero at $x = 0$. Since the numerator of $f(x)$ is not equal to zero at $x = 0$, we see that $x = 0$ is a vertical asymptote.

14. $\lim\limits_{x \to \infty} \dfrac{1}{1+2x^2} = 0$ and so $y = 0$ is a horizontal asymptote, Next, observe that the denominator $1 + 2x^2 \neq 0$ and so there are no vertical asymptotes.

15. $\lim\limits_{x \to \infty} \dfrac{x-1}{x+1} = \lim\limits_{x \to \infty} \dfrac{1-\frac{1}{x}}{1+\frac{1}{x}} = 1$, and so $y = 1$ is a horizontal asymptote. Next, the denominator is equal to zero at $x = -1$ and the numerator is not equal to zero at this point, so $x = -1$ is a vertical asymptote.

16. $\lim\limits_{t \to \infty} \dfrac{t+1}{2t-1} = \lim\limits_{t \to \infty} \dfrac{1+\frac{1}{t}}{2-\frac{1}{t}} = \dfrac{1}{2}$, and so $y = 1/2$ is a horizontal asymptote. Next, observe that the denominator of the rational expression is zero at $t = 1/2$, but the numerator is not equal to zero at this point, and so $t = 1/2$ is a vertical asymptote.

17. $h(x) = x^3 - 3x^2 + x + 1$. $h(x)$ is a polynomial function and, therefore, it does not have any horizontal or vertical asymptotes.

18. The function g is a polynomial, and so the graph of g has no horizontal or vertical asymptotes.

19. $\lim\limits_{t \to \infty} \dfrac{t^2}{t^2-9} = \lim\limits_{t \to \infty} \dfrac{1}{1-\frac{9}{t^2}} = 1$, and so $y = 1$ is a horizontal asymptote. Next, observe that the denominator of the rational expression $t^2 - 9 = (t+3)(t-3) = 0$ if $t = -3$ and $t = 3$. But the numerator is not equal to zero at these points. Therefore, $t = -3$ and $t = 3$ are vertical asymptotes.

20. $\displaystyle\lim_{x\to\infty}\frac{x^3}{x^2-4}=\lim_{x\to\infty}\frac{x}{1-\frac{4}{x^2}}=\infty$, and, similarly, $\displaystyle\lim_{x\to\infty}\frac{x^3}{x^2-4}=-\infty$. Therefore, there

are no horizontal asymptotes. Next, note that the denominator of $g(x)$ equals zero at $x\pm 2$. Since the numerator of $g(x)$ is not equal to zero at $x\pm 2$, we see that $x=-2$ and $x=2$ are vertical asymptotes.

21. $\displaystyle\lim_{x\to\infty}\frac{3x}{x^2-x-6}=\lim_{x\to\infty}\frac{\frac{3}{x}}{1-\frac{1}{x}-\frac{6}{x^2}}=0$ and so $y=0$ is a horizontal asymptote. Next,

observe that the denominator $x^2-x-6=(x-3)(x+2)=0$ if $x=-2$ or $x=3$. But the numerator $3x$ is not equal to zero at these points. Therefore, $x=-2$ and $x=3$ are vertical asymptotes.

22. $\displaystyle\lim_{x\to\infty}\frac{2x}{x^2+x-2}=\lim_{x\to\infty}\frac{\frac{2}{x}}{1+\frac{1}{x}-\frac{2}{x^2}}=0$, and so $y=0$ is a horizontal asymptote. Next,

observe that the denominator $x^2+x-2=(x+2)(x-1)=0$, if $x=-2$ or $x=1$. The numerator is not equal to zero at these points, and so $x=-2$ and $x=1$ are vertical asymptotes.

23. $\displaystyle\lim_{t\to\infty}\left[2+\frac{5}{(t-2)^2}\right]=2$, and so $y=2$ is a horizontal asymptote. Next observe that

$\displaystyle\lim_{t\to 2^+}g(t)=\lim_{t\to 2^-}\left[2+\frac{5}{(t-2)^2}\right]=\infty$, and so $t=2$ is a vertical asymptote.

24. $\displaystyle\lim_{x\to\infty}\left[1+\frac{2}{x-3}\right]=1$ and $\displaystyle\lim_{x\to-\infty}\left[1+\frac{2}{x-3}\right]=1$, so $y=1$ is a horizontal asymptote.

Next, we write $\quad f(x)=1+\dfrac{2}{x-3}=\dfrac{x-3+2}{x-3}=\dfrac{x-1}{x-3},\qquad$ and observe that the

denominator of $f(x)$ is equal to zero at $x=3$. However, since the numerator of $f(x)$ is not equal to zero at $x=3$, we see that $x=3$ is a vertical asymptote.

25. $\displaystyle\lim_{x\to\infty}\frac{x^2-2}{x^2-4}=\lim_{x\to\infty}\frac{1-\frac{2}{x^2}}{1-\frac{4}{x^2}}=1$ and so $y=1$ is a horizontal asymptote. Next, observe

that the denominator $x^2-4=(x+2)(x-2)=0$ if $x=-2$ or 2. Since the numerator x^2-2 is not equal to zero at these points, the lines $x=-2$ and $x=2$ are vertical asymptotes.

26. $\lim_{x\to\infty} \dfrac{2-x^2}{x^2+x} = \lim_{x\to\infty} \dfrac{\frac{2}{x^2}-1}{1+\frac{1}{x}} = -1$, and so $y = 1$ is a horizontal asymptote. Next observe

that the denominator $x^2 + x = x(x+1) = 0$ if $x = 0$ or $x = -1$. Since the numerator $2 - x^2$ is not equal to zero at these values of x, we see that $x = 0$ and $x = -1$ are vertical asymptotes.

27. $g(x) = \dfrac{x^3 - x}{x(x+1)}$; Rewrite $g(x)$ as $g(x) = \dfrac{x^2 - 1}{x+1}$ $(x \neq 0)$ and note that

$\lim_{x\to-\infty} g(x) = \lim_{x\to-\infty} \dfrac{x - \frac{1}{x}}{1 + \frac{1}{x}} = -\infty$ and $\lim_{x\to\infty} g(x) = \infty$. Therefore, there are no horizontal

asymptotes. Next, note that the denominator of $g(x)$ is equal to zero at $x = 0$ and $x = -1$. However, since the numerator of $g(x)$ is also equal to zero when $x = 0$, we see that $x = 0$ is not a vertical asymptote. Also, the numerator of $g(x)$ is equal to zero when $x = -1$, so $x = -1$ is not a vertical asymptote.

28. $\lim_{x\to\infty} \dfrac{x^4 - x^2}{x(x-1)(x+2)} = \lim_{x\to\infty} x \cdot \dfrac{1 - \frac{1}{x^2}}{\left(1 - \frac{1}{x}\right)\left(1 + \frac{2}{x}\right)} = \infty$, so there are no horizontal

asymptotes. Next, observe that the denominator is zero at $x = 0$, $x = 1$, or $x = -2$. Of these values, only $x = -2$ is a vertical asymptote because the numerator is not also equal to zero at this value.

29. f is the derivative function of the function g. Observe that at a relative maximum (relative minimum) of g, $f(x) = 0$.

30. f is the derivative function of the function g. Observe that at a relative maximum (relative minimum) of g, $f(x) = 0$.

31.

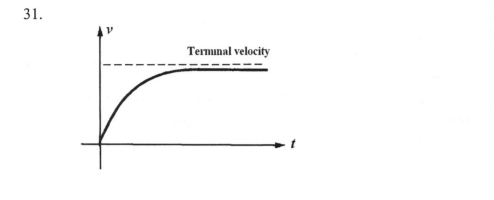

32.

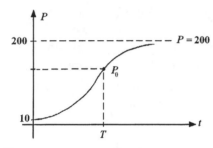

33.

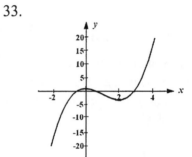

a. f is increasing on $(0,\infty)$.

b. Yes, $P = 200$

c. Concave up on $(0,T)$ and concave down on (T,∞).

d. Yes; at P_0. $P(t)$ is increasing fastest at $t = T$

34.

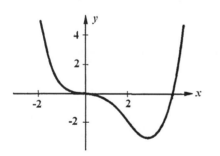

35

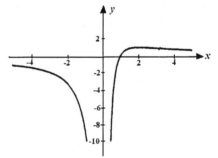

36.

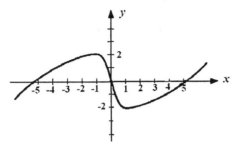

37. $g(x) = 4 - 3x - 2x^3$.

We first gather the following information on the graph of f.

1. The domain of f is $(-\infty, \infty)$.

2. Setting $x = 0$ gives $y = 4$ as the y-intercept. Setting $y = g(x) = 0$ gives a cubic equation which is not easily solved and we will not attempt to find the x-intercepts.

3. $\lim_{x \to -\infty} g(x) = \infty$ and $\lim_{x \to \infty} g(x) = -\infty$. 4. There are no asymptotes of g.

5 $g'(x) = -3 - 6x^2 = -3(2x^2 + 1) < 0$ for all values of x and so g is decreasing on $(-\infty, \infty)$.

6. The results of 5 show that g has no critical points and hence has no relative extrema.

7 $g''(x) = -12x$. Since $g''(x) > 0$ for $x < 0$ and $g''(x) < 0$ for $x > 0$, we see that g is concave upward on $(-\infty, 0)$ and concave downward on $(0, \infty)$.

8. From the results of (7), we see that $(0,4)$ is an inflection point of g

The graph of g follows.

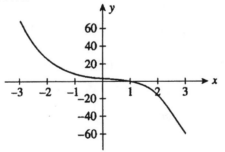

38. $f(x) = x^2 - 2x + 3$

We first gather the following information on the graph of f.

1. The domain of f is $(-\infty, \infty)$.

2. Setting $x = 0$ gives the y-intercept as 3. There are no x-intercepts since $x^2 - 2x + 3 = 0$ has no real solution.

4 Applications of the Derivative

3. $\lim\limits_{x\to\infty} x^2 - 2x + 3 = \lim\limits_{x\to-\infty} x^2 - 2x + 3 = \infty.$

4. There are no asymptotes since $f(x)$ is a polynomial.

5. $f'(x) = 2x - 2 = 2(x - 1) = 0$ if $x = 1$. The sign diagram follows.

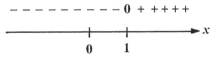

It tells us that f is decreasing on $(-\infty, 1)$ and increasing on $(1, \infty)$.

6. The point $(1,2)$ is a relative minimum.

7. $f''(x) = 2 > 0$ for all x and so the graph of f is concave upward on $(-\infty, \infty)$.

8. Since $f''(x) \neq 0$ for all values of x, there are no inflection points.
The graph of f follows.

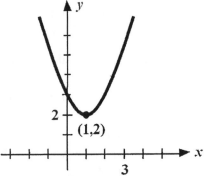

39. $h(x) = x^3 - 3x + 1$

We first gather the following information on the graph of h.

1. The domain of h is $(-\infty, \infty)$.

2. Setting $x = 0$ gives 1 as the y-intercept. We will not find the x-intercept.

3. $\lim\limits_{x\to-\infty} (x^3 - 3x + 1) = -\infty$ and $\lim\limits_{x\to\infty} (x^3 - 3x + 1) = \infty$

4. There are no asymptotes since $h(x)$ is a polynomial.

5. $h'(x) = 3x^2 - 3 = 3(x + 1)(x - 1)$, and we see that $x = -1$ and $x = 1$ are critical points. From the sign diagram

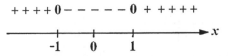

we see that h is increasing on $(-\infty, -1) \cup (1, \infty)$ and decreasing on $(-1, 1)$.

6. The results of (5) shows that $(-1, 3)$ is a relative maximum and $(1, -1)$ is a

relative minimum.

7. $h''(x) = 6x$ and $h''(x) < 0$ if $x < 0$ and $h''(x) > 0$ if $x > 0$. So the graph of h is concave downward on $(-\infty, 0)$ and concave upward on $(0, \infty)$.

8. The results of (7) show that $(0,1)$ is an inflection point of h.
The graph of h follows.

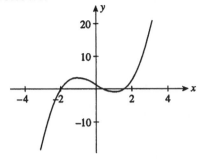

40. $f(x) = 2x^3 + 1$

We first gather the following information on the graph of f.

1. The domain of f is $(-\infty, \infty)$.

2. Setting $x = 0$ gives 1 as the y-intercept. Next, observe that

$$2x^3 = -1. \quad x^3 = -\frac{1}{2}, \quad \text{so } x = -\frac{1}{\sqrt[3]{2}} \approx -0.8$$

is the x-intercept.

3. $\lim\limits_{x \to \infty}(2x^3 + 1) = \infty$ and $\lim\limits_{x \to -\infty}(2x^3 + 1) = -\infty$.

4. Since $f(x)$ is a polynomial, there are no asymptotes.

5. $f'(x) = 6x^2 = 0$ if $x = 0$, a critical point of f. Since $f'(x) > 0$ for all $x \neq 0$, we see that f is increasing on $(-\infty, 0) \cup (0, \infty)$.

6. Using the results of (5), we see that f has no relative extrema.

7. $f''(x) = 12x = 0$ if $x = 0$. Since $f''(x) < 0$ if $x < 0$ and $f''(x) > 0$ if $x > 0$, we see that f is concave downward if $x < 0$ and concave upward if $x > 0$.

8. The results of (7) show that $(0,1)$ is an inflection point.
The graph of f follows.

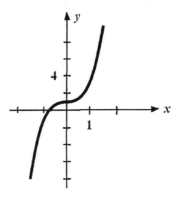

41. $f(x) = -2x^3 + 3x^2 + 12x + 2$

We first gather the following information on the graph of f

1. The domain of f is $(-\infty, \infty)$.

2. Setting $x = 0$ gives 2 as the y-intercept.

3. $\lim_{x \to -\infty} (-2x^3 + 3x^2 + 12x + 2) = \infty$ and $\lim_{x \to \infty} (-2x^3 + 3x^2 + 12x + 2) = -\infty$

4. There are no asymptotes because $f(x)$ is a polynomial function.

5. $f'(x) = -6x^2 + 6x + 12 = -6(x^2 - x - 2) = -6(x - 2)(x + 1) = 0$ if $x = -1$ or $x = 2$, the critical points of f. From the sign diagram

$$- - - - - - 0 + + + + + + + + 0 - - -$$

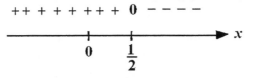

we see that f is decreasing on $(-\infty, -1) \cup (2, \infty)$ and increasing on $(-1, 2)$.

6. The results of (5) show that $(-1, -5)$ is a relative minimum and $(2, 22)$ is a relative maximum.

7. $f''(x) = -12x + 6 = 0$ if $x = 1/2$. The sign diagram of f''

$$+ + + + + + + + 0 - - - -$$

shows that the graph of f is concave upward on $(-\infty, 1/2)$ and concave downward on $(1/2, \infty)$.

8. The results of (7) show that $(\frac{1}{2}, \frac{17}{2})$ is an inflection point.

The graph of f follows.

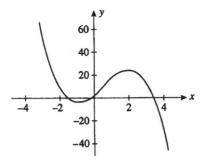

42. $f(t) = 2t^3 - 15t^2 + 36t - 20.$

We first gather the following information on the graph of f

1. The domain of f is $(-\infty, \infty)$.

2. Setting $t = 0$ gives -20 as the y-intercept. Setting $y = f(t) = 0$ leads to a cubic equation which is not easily solved and we will not attempt to find the t-intercepts.

3. $\lim\limits_{t \to -\infty} f(t) = -\infty$ and $\lim\limits_{t \to \infty} f(t) = \infty$.

4. There are no asymptotes of f.

5 $f'(t) = 6t^2 - 30t + 36 = 6(t^2 - 5t + 6) = 6(t - 3)(t - 2)$. The sign diagram for f' is

$$+ + + + + + + + + + +\ 0\ - - -0 + + +$$

We see that f is increasing on $(-\infty, 2) \cup (3, \infty)$ and decreasing on $(2, 3)$.

6. The results of (5) show that $(2,8)$ is a relative maximum and $(3,7)$ is a relative minimum.

7. $f''(t) = 12t - 30 = 6(2t - 5)$. Setting $f''(t) = 0$ gives $t = 5/2$ as a candidate for an inflection point of f. Since $f''(t) < 0$ for $t < 5/2$ and $f''(t) > 0$ for $t > 5/2$, we see that f is concave downward on $(-\infty, \frac{5}{2})$ and concave upward on $(\frac{5}{2}, \infty)$.

8. From the results of (7), we see that $(\frac{5}{2}, \frac{15}{2})$ is an inflection point of f.

The graph of f follows.

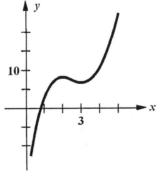

43 $h(x) = \frac{3}{2}x^4 - 2x^3 - 6x^2 + 8$

We first gather the following information on the graph of h.

1. The domain of h is $(-\infty, \infty)$.

2. Setting $x = 0$ gives 8 as the y-intercept.

3. $\lim\limits_{x \to -\infty} h(x) = \lim\limits_{x \to \infty} h(x) = \infty$

4. There are no asymptotes.

5. $h'(x) = 6x^3 - 6x^2 - 12x = 6x(x^2 - x - 2) = 6x(x-2)(x+1) = 0$ if $x = -1, 0,$ or 2, and these are the critical points of h. The sign diagram of h' is

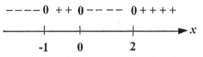

and this tells us that h is increasing on $(-1, 0) \cup (2, \infty)$ and decreasing on $(-\infty, -1) \cup (0, 2)$.

6. The results of (5) show that $(-1, \frac{11}{2})$ and $(2, -8)$ are relative minima of h and $(0, 8)$ is a relative maximum of h.

7. $h''(x) = 18x^2 - 12x - 12 = 6(3x^2 - 2x - 2)$. The zeros of h'' are

$$x = \frac{2 \pm \sqrt{4 + 24}}{6} \approx -0.5 \text{ or } 1.2.$$

The sign diagram of h'' is

and tells us that the graph of h is concave upward on $(-\infty, -0.5) \cup (1.2, \infty)$ and is concave downward on $(0.5, 1.2)$.

8. The results of (7) also show that $(-0.5, 6.8)$ and $(1.2, -1)$ are inflection points. The graph of h follows.

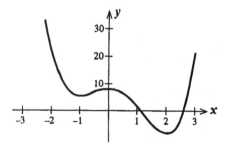

44. $f(t) = 3t^4 + 4t^3 = t^3(3t + 4)$.

We first gather the following information on f.

1. The domain of f is $(-\infty, \infty)$.

2. Setting $t = 0$ gives 0 as the y-intercept. Next, setting $y = f(t) = 0$ gives
$$3t^4 + 4t^3 = t^3(3t + 4) = 0$$
and $t = -4/3$ and $t = 0$ as the t-intercepts.

3. $\lim\limits_{t \to \infty} f(t) = \infty$ and $\lim\limits_{t \to -\infty} f(t) = \infty$.

4. There are no asymptotes.

5. $f'(t) = 12t^3 + 12t^2 = 12t^2(t + 1)$. From the sign diagram for f',

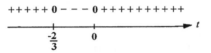

we see that f is increasing on $(-1, 0) \cup (0, \infty)$ and decreasing on $(-\infty, -1)$.

6. From the results of (5), we see that has a relative minimum at $(-1, -1)$.

7. $f''(t) = 36t^2 + 24t = 12t(3t + 2)$. Setting $f''(t) = 0$ gives $t = -2/3$ and $t = 0$ as candidates for inflection points of f. The sign diagram for f'' is

++++++ 0 − − − 0 ++++++++++++
-2/3   0

8. We see that f is concave upward on $(-\infty, -\frac{2}{3}) \cup (0, \infty)$ and concave downward on $(-\frac{2}{3}, 0)$. The results of (7) imply that $(-\frac{2}{3}, -\frac{16}{27})$ and $(0, 0)$ are inflection points of f.

The graph of f follows.

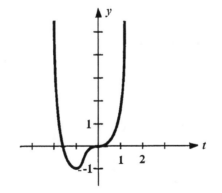

4 Applications of the Derivative

45. $f(t) = \sqrt{t^2 - 4}$.

We first gather the following information on f.

1. The domain of f is found by solving $t^2 - 4 \geq 0$ giving it as $(-\infty, -2] \cup [2, \infty)$.

2. Since $t \neq 0$, there is no y-intercept. Next, setting $y = f(t) = 0$ gives the t-intercepts as -2 and 2.

3. $\lim\limits_{t \to -\infty} f(t) = \lim\limits_{t \to \infty} f(t) = \infty$ 4. There are no asymptotes.

5. $f'(t) = \frac{1}{2}(t^2 - 4)^{-1/2}(2t) = t(t^2 - 4)^{-1/2} = \dfrac{t}{\sqrt{t^2 - 4}}$

Setting $f'(t) = 0$ gives $t = 0$. But $t = 0$ is not in the domain of f and so there are no critical points. The sign diagram for f' is

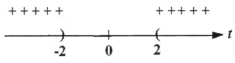

We see that f is increasing on $(2, \infty)$ and decreasing on $(-\infty, -2)$.

6. From the results of (5) we see that there are no relative extrema.

7. $f''(t) = (t^2 - 4)^{-1/2} + t(-\frac{1}{2})(t^2 - 4)^{-3/2}(2t) = (t^2 - 4)^{-3/2}(t^2 - 4 - t^2)$

$= -\dfrac{4}{(t^2 - 4)^{3/2}}.$

8. Since $f''(t) < 0$ for all t in the domain of f, we see that f is concave downward everywhere. From the results of (7), we see that there are no inflection points. The graph of f follows.

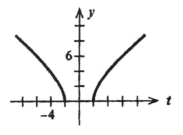

46. $f(x) = \sqrt{x^2 + 5}$.

We first gather the following information on the graph of f.

1. The domain of f is $(-\infty, \infty)$.

2. Setting $x = 0$ gives $\sqrt{5} \approx 2.2$ as the y-intercept.

3. $\lim\limits_{x \to -\infty} \sqrt{x^2 + 5} = \lim\limits_{x \to \infty} \sqrt{x^2 + 5} = \infty$.

4. The results of (3) show that there are no horizontal asymptotes. There are also no vertical asymptotes.

5. $f'(x) = \frac{1}{2}(x^2+5)^{-1/2}(2x) = \frac{x}{\sqrt{x^2+5}}$ and this shows that $x = 0$ is a critical point of f. Since $f'(x) < 0$ if $x < 0$ and $f'(x) > 0$ is $x > 0$, we see that f is decreasing on $(-\infty, 0)$ and increasing on $(0, \infty)$.

6. The results of (5) show that $(0, \sqrt{5})$ is a relative minimum of f.

7. $f''(x) = \frac{d}{dx} x(x^2+5)^{-1/2} = (x^2+5)^{-1/2} + x(-\frac{1}{2})(x^2+5)^{-3/2}(2x)$

$$= (x^2+5)^{-3/2}[(x^2+5) - x^2] = \frac{5}{(x^2+5)^{3/2}} > 0$$

for all values of x. So the graph of f is concave upward on $(-\infty, \infty)$.

8. The results of (7) also show that there are no inflection points. The graph of f follows.

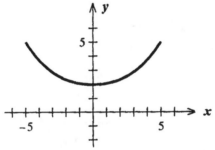

47 $g(x) = \frac{1}{2}x - \sqrt{x}$.

We first gather the following information on g.

1. The domain of g is $[0, \infty)$.

2. The y-intercept is 0. To find the x-intercept, set $y = 0$, giving

$$\frac{1}{2}x - \sqrt{x} = 0$$

$$x = 2\sqrt{x}$$

$$x^2 = 4x$$

$$x(x-4) = 0, \text{ and } x = 0 \text{ or } x = 4$$

3. $\lim_{x \to \infty} (\frac{1}{2}x - \sqrt{x}) = \lim_{x \to \infty} \frac{1}{2}x(1 - \frac{2}{\sqrt{x}}) = \infty.$

4. There are no asymptotes.

5. $g'(x) = \frac{1}{2} - \frac{1}{2}x^{-1/2} = \frac{1}{2}x^{-1/2}(x^{1/2} - 1) = \frac{\sqrt{x}-1}{2\sqrt{x}}$

which is zero when $x = 1$. From the sign diagram for g'

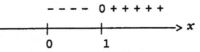

we see that g is decreasing on $(0,1)$ and increasing on $(1,\infty)$.

6. From the sign diagram of g', we see that $g(1) = -1/2$ is a relative minimum.

7   $g''(x) = (-\frac{1}{2})(-\frac{1}{2})x^{-3/2} = \dfrac{1}{4x^{3/2}} > 0$ for $x > 0$, and so g is concave upward on

$(0,\infty)$.

8. There are no inflection points.

The graph of g follows.

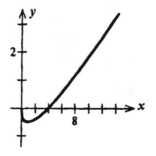

48. $f(x) = \sqrt[3]{x^2}$.

We first gather the following information on the graph of f.

1. The domain of f is $(-\infty, \infty)$ since $x^2 \geq 0$ for all x.

2. Setting $x = 0$ gives the y-intercept as 0. Similarly, setting $y = 0$ gives 0 as the x-intercept.

3. $\lim\limits_{x \to -\infty} \sqrt[3]{x^2} = \lim\limits_{x \to \infty} \sqrt[3]{x^2} = \infty$.   4. There are no asymptotes.

5. $f'(x) = \dfrac{d}{dx} x^{2/3} = \dfrac{2}{3} x^{-1/3} = \dfrac{2}{3\sqrt[3]{x}}$. The sign diagram of f' follows.

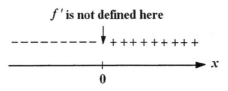

and shows that f is decreasing on $(-\infty,0)$ and increasing on $(0,\infty)$.

6. Since f has no critical points, f has no relative extrema.

7. $f''(x) = \dfrac{d}{dx}(\dfrac{2}{3}x^{-1/3}) = -\dfrac{2}{9}x^{-4/3} = -\dfrac{2}{9x^{4/3}} > 0$ for all $x \neq 0$ and so f

is concave downward on $(-\infty,0) \cup (0,\infty)$.

8. Since $f''(x) \neq 0$, there are no inflection points.
The graph of f follows.

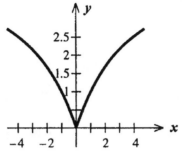

49. $g(x) = \dfrac{2}{x-1}.$ We first gather the following information on g.

1. The domain of g is $(-\infty,1) \cup (1,\infty)$.

2. Setting $x = 0$ gives -2 as the y-intercept. There are no x-intercepts since

$\dfrac{2}{x-1} \neq 0$ for all values of x.

3 $\lim\limits_{x \to -\infty} \dfrac{2}{x-1} = 0$ and $\lim\limits_{x \to \infty} \dfrac{2}{x-1} = 0$

4. The results of (3) show that $y = 0$ is a horizontal asymptote. Furthermore, the denominator of $g(x)$ is equal to zero at $x = 1$ but the numerator is not equal to zero there. Therefore, $x = 1$ is a vertical asymptote.

5. $g'(x) = -2(x-1)^{-2} = -\dfrac{2}{(x-1)^2} < 0$ for all $x \neq 1$ and so g is decreasing on

$(-\infty,1)$ and $(1,\infty)$.

6. Since g has no critical points, there are no relative extrema.

7. $g''(x) = \dfrac{4}{(x-1)^3}$ and so $g''(x) < 0$ if $x < 1$ and $g''(x) > 0$ if $x > 1$. Therefore, the

graph of g is concave downward on $(-\infty,1)$ and concave upward on $(1,\infty)$.

8. Since $g''(x) \neq 0$, there are no inflection points.
The graph of g follows.

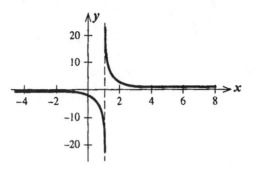

50. $f(x) = \dfrac{1}{x+1}$. We first gather the following information on f

1. Since the denominator is zero when $x = -1$, we see that the domain of f is $(-\infty,-1) \cup (-1,\infty)$.

2. Setting $x = 0$ gives the y-intercept as 1. Since $y \neq 0$, there is no x-intercept.

3. $\displaystyle\lim_{x\to-\infty} f(x) = \lim_{x\to\infty} f(x) = 0$.

4. From the results of (3), we see that $y = 0$ is a horizontal asymptote of f. Next, setting the denominator of f equal to zero gives $x = -1$. Furthermore, $\displaystyle\lim_{x\to-1^-} f(x) = -\infty$ and $\displaystyle\lim_{x\to-1^+} f(x) = \infty$, and so $x = -1$ is a vertical asymptote of f.

5. $f'(x) = -\dfrac{1}{(x+1)^2}$. Note that $f'(x)$ is not defined at $x = -1$. Since $f'(x) < 0$ whenever x is defined, we see that f is decreasing everywhere.

6. The results of (5) show that there are no critical points ($x = -1$ does not belong to the domain of f.) Thus, there are no relative extrema.

7. $f''(x) = \dfrac{2}{(x+1)^3}$. We see that $f''(x) < 0$ for $x < -1$ and $f''(x) > 0$ for $x > -1$.

Therefore, f is concave downward on $(-\infty,-1)$ and concave upward on $(-1,\infty)$.

8. Since there are no critical points, f has no inflection points.
The graph of f follows.

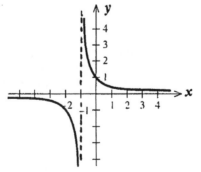

51. $h(x) = \dfrac{x+2}{x-2}$.

We first gather the following information on the graph of h.

1. The domain of h is $(-\infty, 2) \cup (2, \infty)$.

2. Setting $x = 0$ gives $y = -1$ as the y-intercept. Next, setting $y = 0$ gives $x = -2$ as the x-intercept.

3. $\displaystyle \lim_{x \to \infty} h(x) = \lim_{x \to -\infty} \dfrac{1 + \dfrac{2}{x}}{1 - \dfrac{2}{x}} = \lim_{x \to -\infty} h(x) = 1$.

4. Setting $x - 2 = 0$ gives $x = 2$. Furthermore,

$$\lim_{x \to 2^+} \frac{x+2}{x-2} = \infty \quad \text{and} \quad \lim_{x \to 2^+} \frac{x+2}{x-2} = -\infty$$

So $x = 2$ is a vertical asymptote of h. Also, from the results of (3), we see that $y = 1$ is a horizontal asymptote of h.

5. $h'(x) = \dfrac{(x-2)(1) - (x+2)(1)}{(x-2)^2} = -\dfrac{4}{(x-2)^2}$.

We see that there are no critical points of h. (Note $x = 2$ does not belong to the domain of h.) The sign diagram of h' follows.

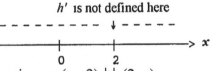

h' is not defined here

We see that h is decreasing on $(-\infty, 2) \cup (2, \infty)$.

6. From the results of (5), we see that there is no relative extremum.

7. $h''(x) = \dfrac{8}{(x-2)^3}$. Note that $x = 2$ is not a candidate for an inflection point because $h(2)$ is not defined. Since $h''(x) < 0$ for $x < 2$ and $h''(x) > 0$ for $x > 2$, we see that h is concave downward on $(-\infty, 2)$ and concave upward on $(2, \infty)$.

8. From the results of (7), we see that there are no inflection points.
The graph of h follows.

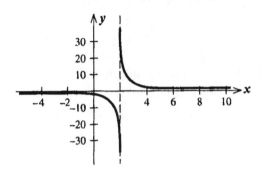

52. $g(x) = \dfrac{x}{x-1}$.

We first gather the following information on g.

1. The domain of g is $(-\infty, 1) \cup (1, \infty)$.

2. Setting $x = 0$ gives 0 as the y-intercept. Similarly, setting $y = 0$ gives 0 as the x-intercept.

3. $\displaystyle\lim_{x \to -\infty} \frac{x}{x-1} = 1$ and $\displaystyle\lim_{x \to \infty} \frac{x}{x-1} = 1$.

4. The results of (3) show that $y = 1$ is a horizontal asymptote. Next, since the denominator is zero at $x = 1$, but the numerator is not equal to zero at this value of x, we see that $x = 1$ is a vertical asymptote of the graph of g.

5. $g'(x) = \dfrac{(x-1)(1) - x(1)}{(x-1)^2} = -\dfrac{1}{(x-1)^2} < 0$ if $x \neq 1$ and so f is decreasing on $(-\infty, 1) \cup (1, \infty)$.

6. Since $g'(x) \neq 0$ for all x, there are no critical points and so g has no relative

extrema.

7. $g''(x) = \dfrac{2}{(x-1)^3}$ and so $g''(x) < 0$ if $x < 1$ and $g''(x) > 0$ if $x > 1$. Therefore, the graph of g is concave downward on $(-\infty, 1)$ and concave upward on $(1, \infty)$.

8. Since $g''(x) \neq 0$ for all x, we see that there are no inflection points.
The graph of g follows.

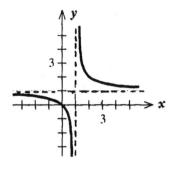

53. $f(t) = \dfrac{t^2}{1+t^2}$

We first gather the following information on the graph of f

1 The domain of f is $(-\infty, \infty)$.

2. Setting $t = 0$ gives the y-intercept as 0. Similarly, setting $y = 0$ gives the t-intercept   as 0.

3. $\displaystyle\lim_{t\to-\infty}\frac{t^2}{1+t^2} = \lim_{t\to\infty}\frac{t^2}{1+t^2} = 1.$

4. The results of (3) show that $y = 1$ is a horizontal asymptote. There are no vertical asymptotes since the denominator is not equal to zero.

5 $f'(t) = \dfrac{(1+t^2)(2t) - t^2(2t)}{(1+t^2)^2} = \dfrac{2t}{(1+t^2)^2} = 0$, if $t = 0$, the only critical point of f.

Since $f'(t) < 0$ if $t < 0$ and $f'(t) > 0$ if $t > 0$, we see that f is decreasing on $(-\infty,0)$ and increasing on $(0,\infty)$.

6. The results of (5) show that $(0,0)$ is a relative minimum.

7. $f''(t) = \dfrac{(1+t^2)^2(2) - 2t(2)(1+t^2)(2t)}{(1+t^2)^4} = \dfrac{2(1+t^2)[(1+t^2) - 4t^2]}{(1+t^2)^4}$

$= \dfrac{2(1-3t^2)}{(1+t^2)^3} = 0$ if $t = \pm\dfrac{\sqrt{3}}{3}.$

The sign diagram of f'' is

$$- \ - \ - \ - \ \ 0 + + + \ + + + + \ 0 - - - -$$

$$\xrightarrow{\hspace{6cm}} x$$

$$-\frac{\sqrt{3}}{3} \qquad 0 \qquad \frac{\sqrt{3}}{3}$$

and shows that f is concave downward on $(-\infty,-\frac{\sqrt{3}}{3}) \cup (\frac{\sqrt{3}}{3},\infty)$ and concave

upward on $(-\frac{\sqrt{3}}{3},\frac{\sqrt{3}}{3})$.

8. The results of (7) show that $(-\frac{\sqrt{3}}{3}, \frac{1}{4})$ and $(\frac{\sqrt{3}}{3}, \frac{1}{4})$ are inflection points. The graph of f follows.

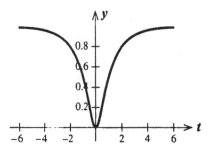

54. $g(x) = \dfrac{x}{x^2 - 4} = \dfrac{x}{(x+2)(x-2)}$.

We first gather the following information on the graph of g.

1. The denominator of $g(x)$ is zero when $x = \pm 2$, and so the domain of g is $(-\infty, -2) \cup (-2, 2) \cup (2, \infty)$.

2. Setting $x = 0$ gives 0 as the y-intercept. Next, setting $y = 0$ gives 0 as the x-intercept.

3. $\displaystyle\lim_{x \to -\infty} \frac{x}{x^2 - 4} = \lim_{x \to \infty} \frac{\frac{1}{x}}{1 - \frac{4}{x^2}} = 0$. Similarly, $\displaystyle\lim_{x \to \infty} g(x) = 0$.

4. From the results of (3), we see that $y = 0$ is a horizontal asymptote of g. Next, observe that the denominator of $g(x)$ is zero when $x = \pm 2$. Now,

$$\lim_{x \to -2^-} \frac{x}{(x+2)(x-2)} = -\infty; \quad \lim_{x \to -2^+} \frac{x}{(x+2)(x-2)} = \infty;$$

$$\lim_{x \to 2^-} \frac{x}{(x+2)(x-2)} = -\infty; \quad \lim_{x \to 2^+} \frac{x}{(x+2)(x-2)} = \infty.$$

Therefore, $x = -2$ and $x = 2$ are vertical asymptotes.

5. $g'(x) = \dfrac{(x^2 - 4)(1) - x(2x)}{(x^2 - 4)^2} = -\dfrac{x^2 + 4}{(x^2 - 4)^2}$. Since $g'(x) < 0$ whenever it is defined, we see that g is decreasing everywhere.

6. From the results of (5), we see that there are no relative extrema.

7 $g''(x) = \dfrac{(x^2 - 4)^2(-2x) + (x^2 + 4)2(x^2 - 4)(2x)}{(x^2 - 4)^4}$

$= \dfrac{2x(x^2 - 4)(-x^2 + 4 + 2x^2 + 8)}{(x^2 - 4)^4} = \dfrac{2x(x^2 + 12)}{(x^2 - 4)^3}$.

Setting $g''(x) = 0$ gives $x = 0$ as the only candidate for a point of inflection. The sign diagram for g'' is

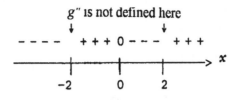

We see that g is concave upward on $(-2,0) \cup (2,\infty)$ and is concave downward on $(-\infty,-2) \cup (0,2)$.

8. From the results of (7), we see that $(0,0)$ is an inflection point of g.
The graph of g follows.

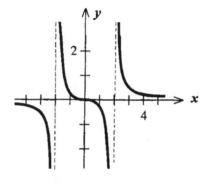

55. $g(t) = -\dfrac{t^2 - 2}{t - 1}$.

First we obtain the following information on g.
1. The domain of g is $(-\infty, 1) \cup (1, \infty)$.
2. Setting $t = 0$ gives -2 as the y-intercept.
3. $\displaystyle\lim_{t \to -\infty} -\frac{t^2 - 2}{t - 1} = \infty$ and $\displaystyle\lim_{t \to \infty} -\frac{t^2 - 2}{t - 1} = -\infty$.

4. There are no horizontal asymptotes. The denominator is equal to zero at $t = 1$ at which point the numerator is not equal to zero. Therefore $t = 1$ is a vertical asymptote.

$5 \quad g'(t) = -\dfrac{(t-1)(2t)-(t^2-2)(1)}{(t-1)^2} = -\dfrac{t^2-2t+2}{(t-1)^2} \neq 0$

for all values of t. The sign diagram of g'

f

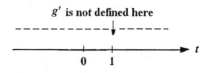

g′ is not defined here

shows that g is decreasing on $(-\infty, 1) \cup (1, \infty)$.

6. Since there are no critical points, g has no relative extrema.

7. $g''(t) = -\dfrac{(t-1)^2(2t-2)-(t^2-2t+2)(2)(t-1)}{(t-1)^4}$

$= \dfrac{-2(t-1)(t^2-2t+1-t^2+2t-2)}{(t-1)^4} = \dfrac{2}{(t-1)^3}$

The sign diagram of g''

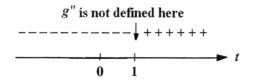

g″ is not defined here

shows that the graph of g is concave upward on $(1, \infty)$ and concave downward on $(-\infty, 1)$.

8. There are no inflection points since $g''(x) \neq 0$ for all x.
The graph of g follows.

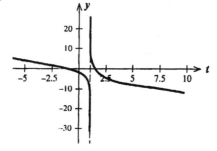

56. $f(x) = \dfrac{x^2-9}{x^2-4}$.

1. The domain is $(-\infty, -2) \cup (-2, 2) \cup (2, \infty)$.

2. The y-intercept is 9/4 and the x-intercepts are -3 and 3

3. $\lim\limits_{x\to\infty}\dfrac{x^2-9}{x^2-4}=\lim\limits_{x\to\infty}\dfrac{1-\frac{9}{x^2}}{1-\frac{4}{x^2}}=1.$

Similarly, $\lim\limits_{x\to-\infty}\dfrac{x^2-9}{x^2-4}=1.$

4. From the results of (3), we see that $y=1$ is a horizontal asymptote. Next, $x^2-4=0$ implies $x=\pm2$. Since the numerator (x^2-9) is not zero at $x=\pm2$, we see that $x=-2$ and $x=2$ are vertical asymptotes.

5. $f'(x)=\dfrac{(x^2-4)(2x)-(x^2-9)(2x)}{(x^2-4)^2}=\dfrac{10x}{(x^2-4)^2}$ is zero at $x=0$ and

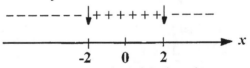

discontinuous at $x=\pm2$. From the sign diagram for f', we see that f is increasing on $(0,2)\cup(2,\infty)$ and decreasing on $(-\infty,-2)\cup(-2,0)$.

6. The point $(0,\frac{9}{4})$ is a relative minimum.

7   $f''(x)=\dfrac{(x^2-4)^2(10)-(10x)(2)(x^2-4)(2x)}{(x^2-4)^4}$

$=\dfrac{10(x^2-4)(x^2-4-4x^2)}{(x^2-4)^4}=\dfrac{-10(3x^2+4)}{(x^2-4)^3}$

which is not defined at $x=\pm2$. From the sign diagram for f''

f'' is not defined here

$-\,-\,-\,-\,-\,-\,-\,\big\downarrow+\,+\,+\,+\,+\,+\,+\big\downarrow-\,-\,-\,-$

$\xrightarrow{}x$

-202

we see that f is concave upward on $(-2,2)$ and concave downward on $(-\infty,-2)\cup(2,\infty)$.

8. There are no inflection points. Note that both $x=-2$ and $x=2$ are not in the domain of f.

The graph of f follows.

4 Applications of the Derivative

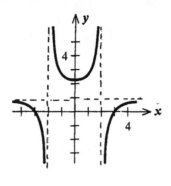

57. $g(t) = \dfrac{t^2}{t^2 - 1}$.

We first gather some information on the graph of g.

1. Since $t^2 - 1 = 0$ if $t = \pm 1$, we see that the domain of g is $(-\infty, -1) \cup (-1,1) \cup (1, \infty)$.

2. Setting $t = 0$ gives 0 as the y-intercept. Setting $y = 0$ gives 0 as the t-intercept.

3. $\displaystyle\lim_{t \to -\infty} g(t) = \lim_{t \to \infty} g(t) = 1$.

4. The results of (3) show that $y = 1$ is a horizontal asymptote. Since the denominator (but not the numerator) is zero at $t = \pm 1$, we see that $t = \pm 1$ are vertical asymptotes.

5. $g'(t) = \dfrac{(t^2 - 1)(2t) - (t^2)(2t)}{(t^2 - 1)^2} = -\dfrac{2t}{(t^2 - 1)^2} = 0$, if $t = 0$.

The sign diagram of g' is

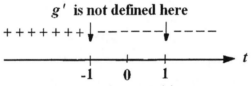

We see that g is increasing on $(-\infty,-1) \cup (-1, 0)$ and decreasing on $(0, 1) \cup (1, \infty)$.

6. From the results of (5), we see that g has a relative maximum at $t = 0$

7. $g''(t) = \dfrac{(t^2 - 1)^2(-2) - (-2t)(2)(t^2 - 1)(2t)}{(t^2 - 1)^4}$

$= \dfrac{2(t^2 - 1)^2[-(t^2 - 1) + 4t^2]}{(t^2 - 1)^3}$

$= \dfrac{2(-t^2 + 1 + 4t^2)}{(t^2 - 1)^3} = \dfrac{2(3t^2 + 1)}{(t^2 - 1)^3}$

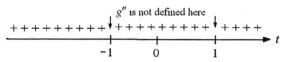

g″ is not defined here

From the sign diagram we see that the graph of g is concave up on $(-\infty, -1) \cup (-1,1) \cup (1,\infty)$.

8. From (7), we see that the graph of g has no inflection points. The graph of g follows.

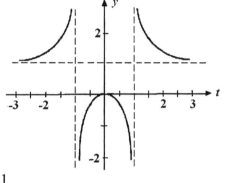

58. $h(x) = \dfrac{1}{x^2 - x - 2}$

We first gather the following information on h.

1. Since $x^2 - x - 2 = (x - 2)(x + 1) = 0$ if $x = -1$ or $x = 2$, we see that the domain of h is $(-\infty,-1) \cup (-1,2) \cup (2,\infty)$.

2. Setting $x = 0$ gives $-1/2$ as the y-intercept.

3. $\displaystyle\lim_{x \to -\infty} h(x) = \lim_{x \to \infty} h(x) = 0$.

4. The results of (3) show that $y = 0$ is a horizontal asymptote. Furthermore, the denominator is equal to zero at $x = -1$ or 2, where the numerator is not equal to zero. Therefore, $x = -1$ and $x = 2$ are vertical asymptotes.

5. $h'(x) = \dfrac{d}{dx}(x^2 - x - 2)^{-1} = -(x^2 - x - 2)^{-2}(2x - 1) = \dfrac{1 - 2x}{(x^2 - x - 2)^2}$.

Setting $h'(x) = 0$ gives $x = 1/2$ as a critical point. The sign diagram of h' is

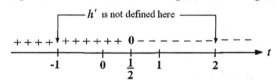

h′ is not defined here

It tells us that h is increasing on $(-\infty,-1) \cup (-1, \frac{1}{2})$ and decreasing on $(\frac{1}{2}, 2) \cup (2,\infty)$.

6. The results of (5) show that $(\frac{1}{2}, -\frac{4}{9})$ is a relative maximum.

7. $h''(x) = \dfrac{(x^2 - x - 2)^2(-2) - (1 - 2x)2(x^2 - x - 2)(2x - 1)}{(x^2 - x - 2)^4}$

$= \dfrac{2(x^2 - x - 2)[-(x^2 - x - 2) + (2x - 1)^2]}{(x^2 - x - 2)^4} = \dfrac{6(x^2 - x + 1)}{(x^2 - x - 2)^3}$

$h''(x)$ has no zeros and is discontinuous at $x = -1$ and $x = 2$. The sign diagram of h'' is

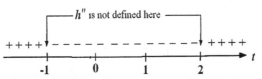

and tells us that the graph of h is concave upward on $(-\infty, -1) \cup (2, \infty)$ and concave downward on $(-1, 2)$.

8. Since $h''(x) \neq 0$, there are no inflection points. The graph of h follows.

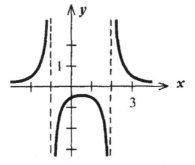

59. $h(x) = (x - 1)^{2/3} + 1$.

We begin by obtaining the following information on h.

1. The domain of h is $(-\infty, \infty)$.

2. Setting $x = 0$ gives 2 as the y-intercept; since $h(x) \neq 0$ there is no x-intercept.

3. $\lim\limits_{x \to \infty} [(x - 1)^{2/3} + 1] = \infty$. Similarly, $\lim\limits_{x \to -\infty} [(x - 1)^{2/3} + 1] = \infty$.

4. There are no asymptotes.

5. $h'(x) = \frac{2}{3}(x - 1)^{-1/3}$ and is positive if $x > 1$ and negative if $x < 1$. So h is increasing on $(1, \infty)$, and decreasing on $(-\infty, 1)$.

6. From (5), we see that h has a relative minimum at $(1, 1)$.

7. $h''(x) = \frac{2}{3}(-\frac{1}{3})(x - 1)^{-4/3} = -\frac{2}{9}(x - 1)^{-4/3} = -\dfrac{2}{(x - 1)^{4/3}}$. Since $h''(x) < 0$ on

$(-\infty,1) \cup (1,\infty)$, we see that h is concave downward on $(-\infty,1) \cup (1,\infty)$. Note that $h''(x)$ is not defined at $x = 1$.

8. From the results of (7), we see h has no inflection points.
The graph of h follows.

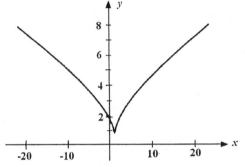

60. $g(x) = (x+2)^{3/2} + 1.$

We first gather the following information on g.

1. The domain of g is $[-2,\infty)$.

2. Setting $x = 0$ gives $2^{3/2} + 1 \approx 3.8$ as the y-intercept.

3. $\lim\limits_{x \to \infty} g(x) = \lim\limits_{x \to \infty}(x+2)^{3/2} + 1 = \infty$.

4. There are no asymptotes.

5   $g'(x) = \frac{3}{2}(x+2)^{1/2} \geq 0$ if $x \geq -2$, and so g is increasing on $(-2,\infty)$.

6. There are no relative extrema since $g'(x) \neq 0$ on $(-2,\infty)$.

7. $g''(x) = \frac{3}{4}(x+2)^{-1/2} = \dfrac{3}{4\sqrt{x+2}} > 0$ if $x > 0$ and so the graph of g is concave

upward on $(2,\infty)$.

8. There are no inflection points since $g''(x) \neq 0$.
The graph of g is shown below.

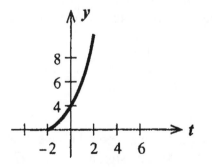

4 Applications of the Derivative

61. a. The denominator of $C(x)$ is equal to zero if $x = 100$. Also,
$$\lim_{x \to 100^-} \frac{0.5x}{100-x} = \infty \quad \text{and} \quad \lim_{x \to 100^+} \frac{0.5x}{100-x} = -\infty$$
Therefore, $x = 100$ is a vertical asymptote of C.
b. No, because the denominator will be equal to zero in that case.

62. a. $\lim\limits_{x \to \infty} \overline{C}(x) = \lim\limits_{x \to \infty}(2.2 + \dfrac{2500}{x}) = 2.2$, and so $y = 2.2$ is a horizontal asymptote.

b. The limiting value is 2.2, or \$2.20 per disc.

63 a. Since $\lim\limits_{t \to \infty} C(t) = \lim\limits_{t \to \infty} \dfrac{0.2t}{t^2+1} = \lim\limits_{t \to \infty} \left[\dfrac{0.2}{t + \frac{1}{t^2}} \right] = 0$, $y = 0$ is a horizontal asymptote.

b. Our results reveal that as time passes, the concentration of the drug decreases and approaches zero.

64. a. $\lim\limits_{x \to \infty} \dfrac{ax}{x+b} = \lim\limits_{x \to \infty} \dfrac{a}{1 + \frac{b}{x}} = a.$

b. The initial speed of the reaction approaches a moles/liter/sec as the amount of substrate becomes arbitrarily large.

65. $G(t) = -0.2t^3 + 2.4t^2 + 60$.
We first gather the following information on the graph of G.
1. The domain of G is $(0, \infty)$.
2. Setting $t = 0$ gives 60 as the y-intercept.
Note that Step 3 is not necessary in this case because of the restricted domain.
4. There are no asymptotes since G is a polynomial function.
5. $G'(t) = -0.6t^2 + 4.8t = -0.6t(t - 8) = 0$, if $t = 0$ or $t = 8$. But these points do not lie in the interval $(0,8)$, so they are not critical points. The sign diagram of G'

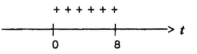

shows that G is increasing on $(0,8)$.
6. The results of (5) tell us that there are no relative extrema.
7. $G''(t) = -1.2t + 4.8 = -1.2(t - 4)$. The sign diagram of G'' is

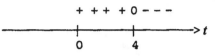

and shows that G is concave upward on $(0,4)$ and concave downward on $(4,8)$.
6. The results of (7) shows that $(4,85.6)$ is an inflection point.
The graph of G follows.

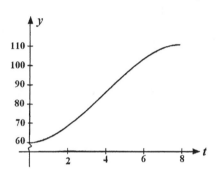

66. $N(t) = -\frac{1}{2}t^3 + 3t^2 + 10t.$

We first gather the following information on N.
1. The domain of N is $(0,4)$ because of the restriction put on it.
2. The y-intercept is 0.
3   Step 3 does not apply because the domain of $N(t)$ is $(0,4)$.
4. There are no asymptotes.
5   $N'(t) = -\frac{3}{2}t^2 + 6t + 10 = -\frac{1}{2}(3t^2 - 12t - 20)$ is never zero. Therefore, N is increasing on $(0,4)$.
6. There are no relative extrema in $(0,4)$.
7. $N''(t) = -3t + 6 = -3(t-2)$ and is zero when $t = 2$.
From the sign diagram of N''

```
        + + + 0  - - - - -
    ─────────┼────┼────────→ t
             0    2
```

we see that N is concave upward on $(0,2)$ and concave downward on $(2,\infty)$.
8. The point $(2, 28)$ is an inflection point.
The graph of $N(t)$ follows.

4 Applications of the Derivative

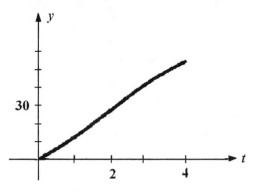

67. $C(t) = \dfrac{0.2t}{t^2 + 1}$.

We first gather the following information on the function C.

1. The domain of C is $[0, \infty)$.

2. If $t = 0$, then $y = 0$. Also, if $y = 0$, then $t = 0$.

3. $\lim\limits_{t \to \infty} \dfrac{0.2t}{t^2 + 1} = 0$.

4. The results of (3) imply that $y = 0$ is a horizontal asymptote.

5. $C'(t) = \dfrac{(t^2 + 1)(0.2) - 0.2t(2t)}{(t^2 + 1)^2} = \dfrac{0.2(t^2 + 1 - 2t^2)}{(t^2 + 1)^2} = \dfrac{0.2(1 - t^2)}{(t^2 + 1)^2}$

and this is equal to zero at $t = \pm 1$, so $t = 1$ is a critical point of C. The sign diagram of C' is

$$\begin{array}{c} + + + 0 - - - - \\ \hline \quad\quad\; 0 \quad 1 \quad\quad\quad \longrightarrow t \end{array}$$

and tells us that C is decreasing on $(1, \infty)$ and increasing on $(0, 1)$.

6. The results of (5) tell us that $(1, 0.1)$ is a relative maximum.

7. $C''(t) = 0.2 \left[\dfrac{(t^2 + 1)^2(-2t) - (1 - t^2)2(t^2 + 1)(2t)}{(t^2 + 1)^4} \right]$

$= \dfrac{0.2(t^2 + 1)(2t)(-t^2 - 1 - 2 + 2t^2)}{(t^2 + 1)^4} = \dfrac{0.4t(t^2 - 3)}{(t^2 + 1)^3}$.

The sign diagram of C'' is

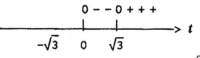

and so the graph of C is concave downward on $(0, \sqrt{3}\,)$ and concave upward on $(\sqrt{3}\,, \infty)$.

8. The results of (7) show that $(\sqrt{3}, 0.05\sqrt{3})$ is an inflection point. The graph of C follows.

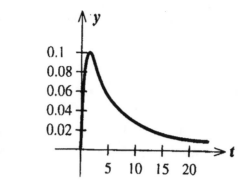

68. $f(t) = 100\left(\dfrac{t^2 - 4t + 4}{t^2 + 4}\right).$

We first gather the following information on the function f.
1. The domain of f is restricted to $[0,\infty)$.
2. Setting $t = 0$ gives $y = 100$. Next, setting $y = 0$ gives $t = 2$.
3. $\displaystyle\lim_{t\to\infty} 100\left[\dfrac{t^2 - 4t + 4}{t^2 + 4}\right] = 100 \lim_{t\to\infty}\left[\dfrac{1 - \frac{4}{t} + \frac{4}{t^2}}{1 + \frac{4}{t^2}}\right] = 100$

4. From the results of (3), we see that $y = 100$ is a horizontal asymptote. There are no vertical asymptotes.
5. $f'(t) = 100\left[\dfrac{(t^2 + 4)(2t - 4) - (t^2 - 4t + 4)(2t)}{(t^2 + 4)^2}\right]$

$= \dfrac{400(t^2 - 4)}{(t^2 + 4)^2} = \dfrac{400(t - 2)(t + 2)}{(t^2 + 4)^2}.$

Setting $f'(t) = 0$ gives $t = 2$ as a critical point of f. ($t = -2$ is not in the domain of f.) Since $f'(t) < 0$ when $t < 2$ and $f'(t) > 0$ when $t > 2$, we see that f is decreasing on $(0,2)$ and increasing on $(2,\infty)$.
6. The results of (5) imply that $f(2) = 0$ is a relative minimum.
7.
$$f''(t) = 400\left[\dfrac{(t^2 + 4)^2(2t) - (t^2 - 4)2(t^2 + 4)(2t)}{(t^2 + 4)^4}\right]$$

$$= 400\left[\frac{(2t)(t^2+4)(t^2+4-2t^2+8)}{(t^2+4)^4}\right] = -\frac{800t(t^2-12)}{(t^2+4)^3}.$$

Setting $f''(t) = 0$ gives $t = 2\sqrt{3}$ as a candidate for a point of inflection. The sign diagram for f'' is

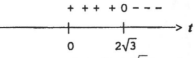

We see that f is concave upward on $(0, 2\sqrt{3})$ and concave downward on $(2\sqrt{3}, \infty)$.

8. From the results of (7), we see that $(2\sqrt{3}, 50(2 - \sqrt{3}))$ is an inflection point of f The graph of f follows.

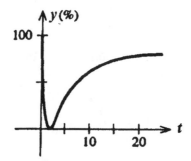

69. $T(x) = \dfrac{120x^2}{x^2+4}$.

We first gather the following information on the function T.

1. The domain of T is $[0, \infty)$.
2. Setting $x = 0$ gives 0 as the y-intercept.
3. $\displaystyle\lim_{x\to\infty} \frac{120x^2}{x^2+4} = 120$.
4. The results of (3) show that $y = 120$ is a horizontal asymptote.
5. $T'(x) = 120\left[\dfrac{(x^2+4)2x - x^2(2x)}{(x^2+4)^2}\right] = \dfrac{960x}{(x^2+4)^2}$. Since $T'(x) > 0$

if $x > 0$, we see that T is increasing on $(0, \infty)$.
6. There are no relative extrema in $(0, \infty)$.
7. $T''(x) = 960\left[\dfrac{(x^2+4)^2 - x(2)(x^2+4)(2x)}{(x^2+4)^4}\right]$

$$= \frac{960(x^2+4)[(x^2+4)-4x^2]}{(x^2+4)^4} = \frac{960(4-3x^2)}{(x^2+4)^3}$$

The sign diagram for T'' is

```
              + + + 0 - - -
    ─────────(───┼──────────────→ x
              0   2√3
                  ──
                   3
```

We see that T is concave downward on $(\frac{2\sqrt{3}}{3},\infty)$ and concave upward on $(0, \frac{2\sqrt{3}}{3})$.

8. We see from the results of (7) that $(\frac{2\sqrt{3}}{3}, 30)$ is an inflection point.

The graph of T follows.

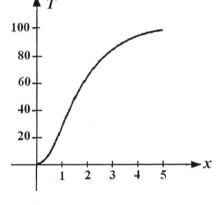

70. $C(x) = \frac{0.5x}{100-x}$

We first gather the following information on the graph of C.

1. The domain of C is $[0,100)$.
2. Setting $x = 0$ gives the y-intercept as 0.

Because of the restricted domain, we omit steps 3 and 4

5. $C'(x) = 0.5\left[\frac{(100-x)(1)-x(-1)}{(100-x)^2}\right] = \frac{50}{(100-x)^2} > 0$ for all $x \neq 100$. Therefore C

is increasing on $(0,100)$.

6. There are no relative extrema.

7. $C''(x) = -\frac{100}{(100-x)^3}$. So $C''(x) > 0$ if $x < 100$ and the graph of C is concave

upward on $(0,100)$.

8. There are no inflection points.

4 Applications of the Derivative

The graph of C follows.

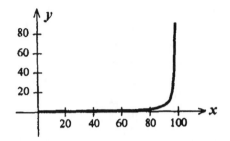

USING TECHNOLOGY EXERCISES 4.3, page 299

1.

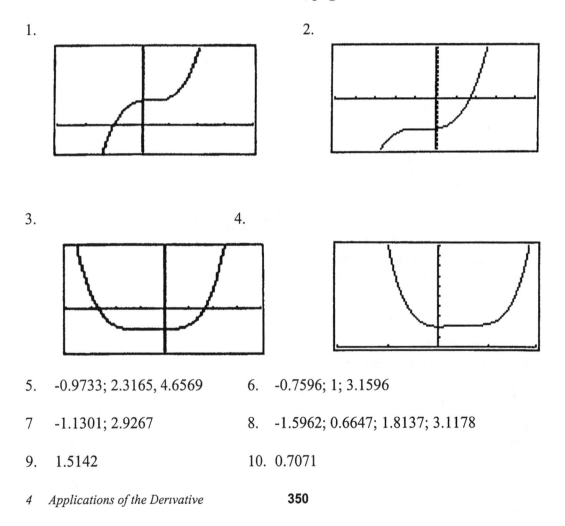

2.

3.

4.

5.   -0.9733; 2.3165, 4.6569

6.   -0.7596; 1; 3.1596

7   -1.1301; 2.9267

8.   -1.5962; 0.6647; 1.8137; 3.1178

9.   1.5142

10. 0.7071

4.4 . CONCEPT QUESTIONS, page 307

1. a. A function f has an absolute maximum at a if $f(x) \le f(a)$ for all x in the domain of f.

   b. A function f has an absolute minimum at a if $f(x) \ge f(a)$ for all x in the domain of f.

2. See the procedure given on page 302 of the text.

EXERCISES 4.4, page 308

1. f has no absolute extrema.

2. f has an absolute minimum at $(-2,-\frac{1}{2})$ and an absolute maximum at $(2, \frac{1}{2})$.

3. f has an absolute minimum at $(0,0)$.

4. f has an absolute minimum at $(0,0)$. f has no absolute maximum.

5. f has an absolute minimum at $(0,-2)$ and an absolute maximum at $(1,3)$.

6. f has no absolute extrema.

7. f has an absolute minimum at $(\frac{3}{2},-\frac{27}{16})$ and an absolute maximum at $(-1,3)$.

8. f has an absolute minimum at $(0,-3)$ and an absolute maximum at $(3,1)$.

9. The graph of $f(x) = 2x^2 + 3x - 4$ is a parabola that opens upward. Therefore, the vertex of the parabola is the absolute minimum of f. To find the vertex, we solve the equation $f'(x) = 4x + 3 = 0$ giving $x = -3/4$. We conclude that the absolute minimum value is $f(-\frac{3}{4}) = -\frac{41}{8}$.

10. The graph of $g(x) = -x^2 + 4x + 3$ is a parabola that opens downward. Therefore, the vertex of the parabola is the absolute maximum of f. To find the vertex, we solve the equation $g'(x) = -2x + 4 = 0$ giving $x = 2$. We conclude that the absolute maximum value is $f(2) = 7$.

11. Since $\lim_{x \to -\infty} x^{1/3} = -\infty$ and $\lim_{x \to \infty} x^{1/3} = \infty$, we see that h is unbounded. Therefore it has

4 *Applications of the Derivative*

no absolute extrema.

12. From the graph of f (see Figure 19, page 255, in the text), we see that $(0,0)$ affords absolute minimum of f. There is no absolute maximum since $\lim\limits_{x \to \infty} x^{2/3} = \infty$.

13. $f(x) = \dfrac{1}{1+x^2}$

Using the techniques of graphing, we sketch the graph of f (see Figure 40, page 272, in the text). The absolute maximum of f is $f(0) = 1$. Alternatively, observe that $1 + x^2 \geq 1$ for all real values of x. Therefore, $f(x) \leq 1$ for all x, and we see that the absolute maximum is attained when $x = 0$.

14. $f(x) = \dfrac{x}{1+x^2}$. Since f is defined for all x in $(-\infty, \infty)$, we use the graphical method.

Using the techniques of graphing, we sketch the graph of f as follows.

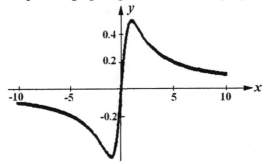

From the graph we see that f has an absolute maximum at $(1, \frac{1}{2})$ and an absolute minimum at $(-1, -\frac{1}{2})$.

15. $f(x) = x^2 - 2x - 3$ and $f'(x) = 2x - 2 = 0$, so $x = 1$ is a critical point. From the table,

x	-2	1	3
$f(x)$	5	-4	0

we conclude that the absolute maximum value is $f(-2) = 5$ and the absolute minimum value is $f(1) = -4$.

16. $g(x) = x^2 - 2x - 3$; $g'(x) = 2x - 2 = 0$ so $x = 1$ is a critical point.

x	0	1	4
$f(x)$	-3	-4	5

So g has an absolute minimum at $(1,-4)$ and an absolute maximum at $(4, 5)$.

17. $f(x) = -x^2 + 4x + 6$; The function f is continuous and defined on the closed interval $[0,5]$. $f'(x) = -2x + 4$ and $x = 2$ is a critical point. From the table

x	0	2	5
$f(x)$	6	10	1

we conclude that $f(2) = 10$ is the absolute maximum value and $f(5) = 1$ is the absolute minimum value.

18. $f(x) = -x^2 + 4x + 6$; The function f is continuous and defined on the closed interval $[3,6]$. $f'(x) = -2x + 4$ and $x = 2$ is a critical point. But this point lies outside the given interval. From the table

x	3	6
$f(x)$	9	-6

we conclude that $f(3) = 9$ is the absolute maximum value and $f(6) = -6$ is the absolute minimum value.

19 The function $f(x) = x^3 + 3x^2 - 1$ is continuous and defined on the closed interval $[-3,2]$ and differentiable in $(-3,2)$. The critical points of f are found by solving
$$f'(x) = 3x^2 + 6x = 3x(x + 2)$$
giving $x = -2$ and $x = 0$. Next, we compute the values of f given in the following table.

x	-3	-2	0	2
$f(x)$	-1	3	-1	19

From the table, we see that the absolute maximum value of f is $f(2) = 19$ and the absolute minimum value is $f(-3) = -1$ and $f(0) = -1$.

20. The function $g(x) = x^3 + 3x^2 - 1$ is continuous and defined on the closed interval

4 Applications of the Derivative

[-3,1] and differentiable in (-3,1). The critical points of g are found by solving
$$g'(x) = 3x^2 + 6x = 3x(x + 2) = 0$$
giving $x = -2$ and $x = 0$. We next compute the values given in the following table.

x	-3	-2	0	1
$g(x)$	-1	3	-1	3

From the table we see that the absolute maximum value of g is given by $g(1) = 3$ and $g(-2) = 3$ and the absolute minimum value of g is given by $g(-3) = -1$ and $g(0) = -1$.

21. The function $g(x) = 3x^4 + 4x^3$ is continuous and differentiable on the closed interval $[-2,1]$ and differentiable in $(-2,1)$. The critical points of g are found by solving
$$g'(x) = 12x^3 + 12x^2 = 12x^2(x + 1)$$
giving $x = 0$ and $x = -1$. We next compute the values of g shown in the following table.

x	-2	-1	0	1
$g(x)$	16	-1	0	7

From the table we see that $g(-2) = 16$ is the absolute maximum value of g and $g(-1) = -1$ is the absolute minimum value of g.

22. $f(x) = \frac{1}{2}x^4 - \frac{2}{3}x^3 - 2x^2 + 3$ is continuous on the closed interval $[-2,3]$ and differentiable in the open interval $(-2,3)$. The critical points of f are found by solving
$$f'(x) = 2x^3 - 2x^2 - 4x = 2x(x^2 - x - 2) = 2x(x - 2)(x + 1) = 0$$
giving $x = -1, 0,$ and 2 as critical points. We compute

x	-2	-1	0	2	3
$f(x)$	25/3	13/6	3	-7/3	15/2

From the table we see that the absolute maximum value of f is $f(-2) = 25/3$, and the absolute minimum value of f is $f(2) = -7/3$.

23. $f(x) = \dfrac{x+1}{x-1}$ on [2,4]. Next, we compute,

$$f'(x) = \frac{(x-1)(1)-(x+1)(1)}{(x-1)^2} = -\frac{2}{(x-1)^2}.$$

Since there are no critical points, ($x = 1$ is not in the domain of f), we need only test the endpoints. From the table

x	2	4
$g(x)$	3	5/3

we conclude that $f(4) = 5/3$ is the absolute minimum value and $f(2) = 3$ is the absolute maximum value.

24. $g(t) = \dfrac{t}{t-1}$; $g'(t) = \dfrac{(t-1)-t}{(t-1)^2} = -\dfrac{1}{(t-1)^2}$. Since there are no critical points,

($t = 1$ is not in the domain of g), we need only test the endpoints. From the table

t	2	4
$g(t)$	2	4/3

we conclude that $g(2) = 2$ is the absolute maximum value and $g(4) = 4/3$ is the absolute minimum value.

25. $f(x) = 4x + \dfrac{1}{x}$ is continuous on [1,3] and differentiable in (1,3). To find the critical points of f, we solve $f'(x) = 4 - \dfrac{1}{x^2} = 0$, obtaining $x = \pm\frac{1}{2}$. Since these critical points lie outside the interval [1,3], they are not candidates for the absolute extrema of f. Evaluating f at the endpoints of the interval [1,3], we find that the absolute maximum value of f is $f(3) = \frac{37}{3}$, and the absolute minimum value of f is $f(1) = 5$.

26. $f(x) = 9x - \dfrac{1}{x}$ is continuous on [1,3] and differentiable in (1,3). To find the critical points of f, we solve $f'(x) = 9 + \dfrac{1}{x^2} = 0$, obtaining $x^2 = -1/9$ which has no

solution. Evaluating f at the endpoints of the interval $[1,3]$, we find that the absolute minimum value is $f(1) = 8$ and the absolute maximum value is $f(3) = \frac{80}{3}$.

27. $f(x) = \frac{1}{2}x^2 - 2\sqrt{x} = \frac{1}{2}x^2 - 2x^{1/2}$. To find the critical points of f, we solve
$$f'(x) = x - x^{-1/2} = 0, \quad \text{or} \qquad x^{3/2} - 1 = 0,$$
obtaining $x = 1$. From the table

x	0	1	3
$f(x)$	0	$-\frac{3}{2}$	$\frac{9}{2} - 2\sqrt{3} \approx 1.04$

we conclude that $f(3) \approx 1.04$ is the absolute maximum value and $f(1) = -3/2$ is the absolute minimum value.

28. The function $g(x) = \frac{1}{8}x^2 - 4\sqrt{x} = \frac{1}{8}x^2 - 4x^{1/2}$ is continuous on the closed interval $[0,9]$ and differentiable in $(0,9)$. To find the critical points of g, we first compute
$$g'(x) = \frac{1}{4}x - 2x^{-1/2} = \frac{1}{4}x^{-1/2}(x^{3/2} - 8).$$
Setting $g'(x) = 0$, we have $x^{3/2} = 8$, or $x = 4$. Next, we compute the values of g shown in the following table.

x	0	4	9
$f(x)$	0	-6	-15/8

We conclude that $g(4) = -6$ is the absolute minimum value and $g(0) = 0$ is the absolute maximum value of g.

29. The graph of $f(x) = 1/x$ over the interval $(0,\infty)$ follows.

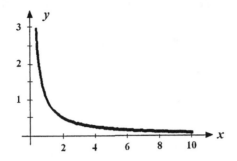

From the graph of f, we conclude that f has no absolute extrema.

30. The graph of $g(x) = \dfrac{1}{x+1}$ on $(0,\infty)$ follows.

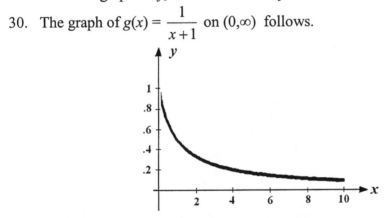

From the graph of g, we conclude that g has no absolute extrema.

31. $f(x) = 3x^{2/3} - 2x$. The function f is continuous on $[0,3]$ and differentiable on $(0,3)$. To find the critical points of f, we solve
$$f'(x) = 2x^{-1/3} - 2 = 0$$
obtaining $x = 1$ as the critical point. From the table,

x	0	1	3
$f(x)$	0	1	$3^{5/3} - 6 \approx 0.24$

we conclude that the absolute maximum value is $f(1) = 1$ and the absolute minimum value is $f(0) = 0$.

4 Applications of the Derivative

32. $g(x) = x^2 + 2x^{2/3}$. $g'(x) = 2x + \frac{4}{3}x^{-1/3} = \frac{2}{3}x^{-1/3}(3x^{4/3} + 2)$ is never zero, but $g'(x)$ is not defined at $x = 0$, which is a critical point of g. From the following table,

x	-2	0	2
$f(x)$	$4 + 2^{5/3}$	0	$4 + 2^{5/3}$

we conclude that $g(-2) = 4 + 2^{5/3}$ and $g(2) = 4 + 2^{5/3}$ give the absolute maximum value and $g(0) = 0$ gives the absolute minimum value.

33. $f(x) = x^{2/3}(x^2 - 4)$.
$$f'(x) = x^{2/3}(2x) + \frac{2}{3}x^{-1/3}(x^2 - 4) = \frac{2}{3}x^{-1/3}[3x^2 + (x^2 - 4)]$$
$$= \frac{8(x^2 - 1)}{3x^{1/3}} = 0.$$

Observe that f' is not defined at $x = 0$. Furthermore, $f'(x) = 0$ at $x \pm 1$. So the critical points of f are -1, 0, 1. From the following table,

x	-1	0	1	2
$f(x)$	-3	0	-3	0

we see that f has an absolute minimum at $(-1,-3)$ and $(1,-3)$ and absolute maxima at $(0,0)$ and $(2,0)$.

34. The function is the same as that of Exercise 33. Using the results from Exercise 33, we have the following table.

x	-1	0	1	3
$f(x)$	-3	0	-3	$5 \cdot 3^{2/3}$

We see that f has an absolute minimum at $(-1,-3)$ and $(1,-3)$ and an absolute maximum at $(3, 5 \cdot 3^{2/3})$.

35   $f(x) = \dfrac{x}{x^2+2}$ To find the critical points of f, we solve

$$f'(x) = \frac{(x^2+2) - x(2x)}{(x^2+2)^2} = \frac{2-x^2}{(x^2+2)^2} = 0$$

obtaining $x = \pm\sqrt{2}$. Since $x = -\sqrt{2}$ lies outside $[-1,2]$, $x = \sqrt{2}$ is the only critical point in the given interval. From the table

x	-1	$\sqrt{2}$	2
$f(x)$	$-\frac{1}{3}$	$\sqrt{2}/4 \approx 0.35$	$\frac{1}{3}$

we conclude that $f(\sqrt{2})) = \sqrt{2}/4 \approx 0.35$ is the absolute maximum value and $f(-1) = -1/3$ is the absolute minimum value.

36. $f'(x) = \frac{d}{dx}(x^2+2x+5)^{-1} = -(x^2+2x+5)^{-2}(2x+2) = \dfrac{-2(x+1)}{(x^2+2x+5)^2}$.

Setting $f'(x) = 0$ gives $x = -1$ as a critical point.

x	-2	-1	1
$f(x)$	1/5	1/4	1/8

From the table, we see that f has an absolute minimum at $(1, \frac{1}{8})$ and an absolute maximum at $(-1, \frac{1}{4})$.

37. The function $f(x) = \dfrac{x}{\sqrt{x^2+1}} = \dfrac{x}{(x^2+1)^{1/2}}$ is continuous and defined on the closed interval $[-1,1]$ and differentiable on $(-1,1)$. To find the critical points of f, we first compute

$$f'(x) = \frac{(x^2+1)^{1/2}(1) - x(\frac{1}{2})(x^2+1)^{-1/2}(2x)}{[(x^2+1)^{1/2}]^2}$$

$$= \frac{(x^2+1)^{-1/2}[x^2+1-x^2]}{x^2+1} = \frac{1}{(x^2+1)^{3/2}}$$

which is never equal to zero. Next, we compute the values of f shown in the following table.

4 Applications of the Derivative

x	-1	1
$f(x)$	$-\sqrt{2}/2$	$\sqrt{2}/2$

We conclude that $f(-1) = -\sqrt{2}/2$ is the absolute minimum value and $f(1) = \sqrt{2}/2$ is the absolute maximum value.

38. $g(x) = x(4 - x^2)^{1/2}$ on $[0,2]$.
$$g'(x) = (4-x^2)^{1/2} + x(\tfrac{1}{2})(4-x^2)^{-1/2}(-2x)$$
$$= (4-x^2)^{-1/2}(4-x^2-x^2) = -\frac{2(x^2-2)}{\sqrt{4-x^2}}.$$

The critical point of g in $(0,2)$ is $\sqrt{2}$. Next, we compute the values of g shown in the following table.

x	0	$\sqrt{2}$	2
$f(x)$	0	2	0

We conclude that $(g(\sqrt{2})) = 2$ is the absolute maximum value and $g(0) = 0$ and $g(2) = 0$ gives the absolute minimum value.

39. $h(t) = -16t^2 + 64t + 80$. To find the maximum value of h, we solve
$$h'(t) = -32t + 64 = -32(t - 2) = 0$$
giving $t = 2$ as the critical point of h. Furthermore, this value of t gives rise to the absolute maximum value of h since the graph of h is a parabola that opens downward. The maximum height is given by
$$h(2) = -16(4) + 64(2) + 80 = 144, \text{ or } 144 \text{ feet.}$$

40. $P(x) = -10x^2 + 1760x - 50,000$; $P'(x) = -20x + 1760 = 0$ if $x = 88$ and this is a critical point of P. Now $P(88) = -10(88)^2 + 1760(88) - 50,000 = 27,440$. The graph of P is a parabola that opens downward. So, the point $(88, 27,440)$ is an absolute maximum of P So if 88 units are rented out, the maximum monthly profit realizable is \$27,440.

41. $P'(t) = 0.027t - 1.126 = 0$ implies $t \approx 41.7$, a critical number for P. $P''(t) = 0.027$

and $P''(41.7) = 0.027 > 0$. Therefore, $t = 41.7$ gives a minimum of P. This is around September of 1991. The percent is approximately $P(41.7) \approx 17.7$.

42. $h(t) = -\frac{1}{3}t^3 + 4t^2 + 20t + 2$; $h'(t) = -t^2 + 8t + 20 = -(t^2 - 8t - 20) = -(t - 10)(t + 2) = 0$ if $t = -2$ or $t = 10$. Rejecting the negative root, we take $t = 10$. Next, we compute $h''(t) = -2t + 8$. Since $h''(10) = -20 + 8 = -12 < 0$, using the Second Derivative Test we see that the point $t = 10$ gives a relative maximum. From physical considerations, or from a sketch of the graph of h, we conclude that the rocket attains its maximum altitude at $t = 10$ with a maximum height of
$$h(10) = -\frac{1}{3}(10)^3 + 4(10)^2 + 20(10) + 2, \text{ or } 268.7 \text{ ft.}$$

43. $N(t) = 0.81t - 1.14\sqrt{t} + 1.53$. $N'(t) = 0.81 - 1.14(\frac{1}{2}t^{-1/2}) = 0.81 - \dfrac{0.57}{t^{1/2}}$ Setting $N'(t) = 0$ gives $t^{1/2} = \dfrac{0.57}{0.81}$, or $t = 0.4952$ as a critical point of N. Evaluating $N(t)$ at the endpoints $t = 0$ and $t = 6$ as well as at the critical point, we have

t	0	0.4952	6
$N(t)$	1.53	1.13	3.60

From the table, we see that the absolute maximum of N occurs at $t = 6$ and the absolute minimum occurs at $t \approx 0.5$. Our results tell us that the number of nonfarm full-time self-employed women over the time interval from 1963 to 1993 was the highest in 1993 and stood at approximately 3.6 million.

44. Observe that f is continuous on $[0, 4]$. Next, we compute
$$f'(t) = \frac{d}{dt}(20t - 40t^{1/2} + 50)$$
$$= 20 - 20t^{-1/2} = 20t^{-1/2}(t^{1/2} - 1) = \frac{\sqrt{t} - 1}{20\sqrt{t}}$$
Observe that $t = 1$ is the only critical point of f in $(0, 4)$. Since
$$f(0) = 50, \quad f(1) = 30, \quad f(4) = 50$$
we conclude that f attains its minimum value of 30 at $t = 1$. This tells us that the traffic is moving at the slowest rate at 9 A.M. and the average speed of a vehicle at that time is 30 mph.

45. $P(x) = -0.000002x^3 + 6x - 400$. $P'(x) = -0.000006x^2 + 6 = 0$ if $x = \pm 1000$. We reject the negative root. Next, we compute $P''(x) = -0.000012x$. Since $P''(1000) = -0.012 < 0$, the Second Derivative Test shows that $x = 1000$ affords a relative maximum of f. From physical considerations, or from a sketch of the graph of f, we see that the maximum profit is realized if 1000 cases are produced per day. The profit is $P(1000) = -0.000002(1000)^3 + 6(1000) - 400$, or $3600/day.

46. The revenue is $R(x) = px = -0.00042x^2 + 6x$. Therefore, the profit is
$$P(x) = R(x) - C(x) = -0.00042x^2 + 6x - (600 + 2x - 0.00002x^2)$$
$$= -0.0004x^2 + 4x - 600.$$
$$P'(x) = -0.0008x + 4 = 0$$
if $x = 5000$, a critical point of P. From the following table

x	0	5000	12000
$P(x)$	-600	9400	-10200

we see that Phonola should produce 5000 discs/month.

47. The revenue is $R(x) = px = -0.0004x^2 + 10x$, and the profit is
$$P(x) = R(x) - C(x) = -0.0004x^2 + 10x - (400 + 4x + 0.0001x^2)$$
$$= -0.0005x^2 + 6x - 400.$$
$$P'(x) = -0.001x + 6 = 0$$
if $x = 6000$, a critical point. Since $P''(x) = -0.001 < 0$ for all x, we see that the graph of P is a parabola that opens downward. Therefore, a level of production of 6000 rackets/day will yield a maximum profit.

48. $R(x) = px = -0.05x^2 + 600x$
$P(x) = R(x) - C(x) = -0.05x^2 + 600x - (0.000002x^3 - 0.03x^2 + 400x + 80000)$
$$= -0.000002x^3 - 0.02x^2 + 200x - 80000.$$
We want to maximize P on $[0, 12,000]$. $P'(x) = -0.000006x^2 - 0.04x + 200$.
Setting $P'(x) = 0$ gives $3x^2 + 20,000x - 100,000,000 = 0$

or $x = \dfrac{-20,000 \pm \sqrt{20,000^2 + 1,200,000,000}}{6} = -10,000$, or 3,333.3

So $x = 3,333.3$ is a critical point in the interval $[0, 12,000]$.

x	0	3,333	12,000
$f(x)$	-80,000	290,370	-4,016,000

From the table, we see that a level of production of 3,333 units will yield a maximum profit.

49 The total cost function is given by
$$C(x) = V(x) + 20,000$$
$$= 0.000001x^3 - 0.01x^2 + 50x + 20,000$$

The profit function is
$$P(x) = R(x) - C(x)$$
$$= -0.02x^2 + 150x - 0.000001x^3 + 0.01x^2 - 50x + 20,000$$
$$= -0.000001x^3 - 0.01x^2 + 100x - 20,000$$

We want to maximize P on $[0, 7000]$.
$$P'(x) = -0.000003x^2 - 0.02x + 100$$

Setting $P'(x) = 0$ gives $3x^2 + 20,000x - 100,000,000 = 0$

or $x = \dfrac{-20,000 \pm \sqrt{20,000^2 + 1,200,000,000}}{6} = -10,000$ or $3,333.3$

So $x = 3,333.30$ is a critical point in the interval $[0, 7000]$.

x	0	3,333	7,000
$P(x)$	-20,000	165,185	-519,700

From the table, we see that a level of production of 3,333 pagers per week will yield a maximum profit of $165,185 per week.

50. The cost function is $C(x) = 0.2(0.01x^2 + 120)$ and the average cost function is
$$\overline{C}(x) = \frac{C(x)}{x} = 0.2(0.01x + \tfrac{120}{x}) = 0.002x + \tfrac{24}{x}.$$

To find the minimum average cost, we first compute $\overline{C}'(x) = 0.002 - \dfrac{24}{x^2}$.

Setting $\overline{C}'(x) = 0$ gives $0.002 - \dfrac{24}{x^2} = 0$, $x^2 = \dfrac{24}{0.002} = 12,000$, $x \approx \pm 110$.

We reject the negative root, leaving $x = 110$ as the only critical point of $\overline{C}(x)$. Since $\overline{C}''(x) = 48x^{-3} > 0$ for all $x > 0$, we see that $\overline{C}(x)$ is concave upward on $(0, \infty)$. We conclude that $\overline{C}(110) \approx 0.44$ is the absolute minimum value of $\overline{C}(x)$ and that the average cost is minimized when $x = 110$ units.

51. a. $\overline{C}(x) = \dfrac{C(x)}{x} = 0.0025x + 80 + \dfrac{10{,}000}{x}$.

b. $\overline{C}'(x) = 0.0025 - \dfrac{10{,}000}{x^2} = 0$ if $0.0025x^2 = 10{,}000$, or $x = 2000$.

Since $\overline{C}''(x) = \dfrac{20{,}000}{x^3}$, we see that $\overline{C}''(x) > 0$ for $x > 0$ and so $\overline{C}$ is concave upward on $(0, \infty)$. Therefore, $x = 2000$ yields a minimum.

c. We solve $\overline{C}(x) = C'(x)$. $0.0025x + 80 + \dfrac{10{,}000}{x} = 0.005x + 80$,

$0.0025x^2 = 10{,}000$, or $x = 2000$.

d. It appears that we can solve the problem in two ways.
NOTE This can be proved.

52. a. $C(x) = 0.000002x^3 + 5x + 400$; $\overline{C}(x) = \dfrac{C(x)}{x} = 0.000002x^2 + 5 + \dfrac{400}{x}$

b. $\overline{C}'(x) = 0.000004x - \dfrac{400}{x^2} = \dfrac{0.00004x^3 - 400}{x^2} = \dfrac{0.000004(x^3 - 100{,}000{,}000)}{x^2}$.

Setting $\overline{C}'(x) = 0$ gives $x = 464$, the only critical point of $\overline{C}$. Next,

$$\overline{C}''(x) = 0.000004 + \dfrac{800}{x^3}.$$

So $\overline{C}''(464) > 0$ and by the Second Derivative Test, the point $x = 464$ gives rise to a relative minimum. Since $\overline{C}''(x) > 0$ for all $x > 0$, $\overline{C}$ is concave upward on $(0, \infty)$ and $x = 464$ gives rise to an absolute minimum of $\overline{C}$. Thus, the smallest average product cost occurs when the level of production is 464 cases per day.

c. We want to solve the equation $\overline{C}(x) = C'(x)$, that is,

$$0.000002x^2 + 5 + \dfrac{400}{x} = 0.000006x^2 + 5,$$

$0.000004x^3 = 400$, $x^3 = 100{,}000{,}000$ and $x = 464$.

d. The results are the same as expected.

53. The demand equation is $p = \sqrt{800-x} = (800-x)^{1/2}$ The revenue function is
$R(x) = xp = x(800-x)^{1/2}$. To find the maximum of R, we compute

$$R'(x) = \tfrac{1}{2}(800-x)^{-1/2}(-1)(x) + (800-x)^{1/2}$$
$$= \tfrac{1}{2}(800-x)^{-1/2}[-x + 2(800-x)]$$
$$= \tfrac{1}{2}(800-x)^{-1/2}(1600-3x).$$

Next, $R'(x) = 0$ implies $x = 800$ or $x = 1600/3$ are critical points of R. Next, we compute the values of R given in the following table.

x	0	800	1600/3
$R(x)$	0	0	8709

We conclude that $R(\frac{1600}{3}) = 8709$ is the absolute maximum value. Therefore, the revenue is maximized by producing $1600/3 \approx 533$ dresses.

54. The revenue function is $R(x) = xp = \dfrac{50x}{0.01x^2 + 1}$ To find the maximum value of R,

we compute $R'(x) = \dfrac{(0.01x^2 + 1)50 - 50x(0.02x)}{(0.01x^2 + 1)^2} = -\dfrac{0.5(x^2 - 100)}{(0.01x^2 + 1)^2}$. Now, $R'(x) = 0$

implies $x = -10$ or $x = 10$. The first root is rejected since x must be greater than or equal to zero. Thus, $x = 10$ is the only critical point. Next, we compute

x	0	10	20
$R(x)$	0	250	200

and conclude that $R(10) = 250$ is the absolute maximum value of R. Thus, the revenue is maximized by selling 10,000 watches.

55. $f(t) = 100\left[\dfrac{t^2 - 4t + 4}{t^2 + 4}\right]$.

 a. $f'(t) = 100\left[\dfrac{(t^2 + 4)(2t - 4) - (t^2 - 4t + 4)(2t)}{(t^2 + 4)^2}\right] = \dfrac{400(t^2 - 4)}{(t^2 + 4)^2}$

$$= \frac{400(t-2)(t+2)}{(t^2+4)^2}.$$

From the sign diagram for f'

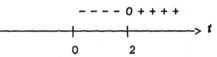

we see that $t = 2$ gives a relative minimum, and we conclude that the oxygen content is the lowest 2 days after the organic waste has been dumped into the pond.

b.

$$f''(t) = 400\left[\frac{(t^2+4)^2(2t)-(t^2-4)2(t^2+4)(2t)}{(t+4)^4}\right] = 400\left[\frac{(2t)(t^2+4)(t^2+4-2t^2+8)}{(t^2+4)^4}\right]$$

$$= -\frac{800t(t^2-12)}{(t^2+4)^3}$$

and $f''(t) = 0$ when $t = 0$ and $t = \pm 2\sqrt{3}$. We reject $t = 0$ and $t = -2\sqrt{3}$ From the sign diagram for f'',

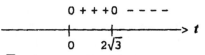

we see that $f'(2\sqrt{3})$ gives an inflection point of f and we conclude that this is an absolute maximum. Therefore, the rate of oxygen regeneration is greatest 3.5 days after the organic waste has been dumped into the pond.

56. $A'(t) = 136\dfrac{d}{dt}[1+0.25(t-4.5)^2]^{-1} = (136)(-1)[1+0.25(t-4.5)^2]^{-2}(0.25)2(t-4.5)$

$$= -\frac{68(t-4.5)}{[1+0.25(t-4.5)^2]^2}.$$

Setting $A'(t) = 0$ gives $t = 4.5$ as a critical point of A.

x	0	4.5	11
$R(x)$	50.4	164	39.8

We see that the maximum of A occurs when $t = 4.5$, that is, at 11:30 A.M.

57 We compute $\bar{R}'(x) = \dfrac{xR'(x) - R(x)}{x^2}$. Setting $\bar{R}'(x) = 0$ gives $xR'(x) - R(x) = 0$

or $R'(x) = \dfrac{R(x)}{x} = \bar{R}(x)$, so a critical point of $\bar{R}$ occurs when $\bar{R}(x) = R'(x)$.

Next, we compute

$$\bar{R}''(x) = \dfrac{x^2[R'(x) + xR''(x) - R'(x)] - [xR'(x) - R(x)](2x)}{x^4} = \dfrac{R''(x)}{x} < 0.$$

So, by the Second Derivative Test, the critical point does give a maximum revenue.

58. $v'(r) = -2kr = 0$ if $r = 0$. So there are no critical points in $(0,R)$.

r	0	R
$v(r)$	kR^2	0

From the table we see that v has an absolute maximum at $r = 0$. So the velocity is greatest along the central axis.

59. The growth rate is $G'(t) = -0.6t^2 + 4.8t$. To find the maximum growth rate, we compute $G''(t) = -1.2t + 4.8$. Setting $G''(t) = 0$ gives $t = 4$ as a critical point.

t	0	4	8
$G'(t)$	0	9.6	0

From the table, we see that G is maximal at $t = 4$; that is, the growth rate is greatest in 2001.

60. $N(t) = -0.1t^3 + 1.5t^2 + 100$ and $N'(t) = -0.3t^2 + 3t$. We want to maximize the function $N'(t)$. Now, $N''(t) = -0.6t + 3$. Setting $N''(t) = 0$ gives $t = 5$ as the critical point of $N'(t)$. $N'''(5) = -0.6 < 0$ and $t = 5$ does give rise to a maximum for $N'(t)$, that is the growth rate was maximal in 1992, as we wished to show.

61. $P'(t) = 0.13089t^2 - 0.534t - 1.59 = 0$ gives

$$t = \frac{0.534 \pm \sqrt{(0.534)^2 - 4(0.13089)(-1.59)}}{2(0.13089)} \approx -2 \text{ or } 6.08$$

We reject the negative root. Since
$$P''(t) = 0.26178t - 0.534 \quad \text{and} \quad P''(6.08) \approx 1.06 > 0$$
we conclude that $t = 6.08$ gives a minimum of P, and this number corresponds to approximately early 1970.

62. $P'(t) = -0.549t^2 + 9.3t - 17.3 = 0$ gives
$$t = \frac{-9.3 \pm \sqrt{9.3^2 - 4(-0.549)(-17.3)}}{2(-0.549)} \approx 2.13, \text{ or } 14.81.$$
The root 14.8 lies outside the interval [0, 12] and is rejected. Since
$$P''(t) = -0.732t + 9.3 \quad \text{and} \quad P''(2.13) \approx 7.74 > 0$$
we see that $t = 2.13$ gives rise to a relative minimum of P_1. So the price is lowest at $t = 2$ or around the beginning of 1992. The lowest average annual price is given by
$$P(2.13) \approx 182.5$$
or approximately \$182,500.

63. $R'(t) = -2.133t^2 + 7.52t + 0.2 = 0$ implies
$$t = \frac{-7.52 \pm \sqrt{7.52^2 - 4(-2.133)(0.2)}}{2(-2.133)} \approx -0.026, \text{ or } 3.55.$$
The root -0.026 lies outside the interval [0, 5], and is rejected.
$$R''(t) = -4.266t + 7.52 \text{ and } R''(3.55) \approx -7.62 > 0$$
and so $t = 3.55$ gives a relative maximum. This is around the middle of 2000. The highest office space rent was given by $R(3.55) \approx 52.79$, or approximately \$52.79/sq ft.

64. a. $P'(t) = 0.00222t^2 - 0.1408t + 0.89 = 0$ implies
$$t = \frac{0.1408 \pm \sqrt{(0.1408)^2 - 4(0.00222)(0.89)}}{2(0.00222)} \approx 7.12, \text{ or } 56.3$$
The root 56.3 is rejected because it lies outside the interval [0, 10].
$P''(t) = 0.00444t - 0.1408$ and $P''(7.12) = -0.109 < 0$ and so $t \approx 7.12$ gives a relative maximum. This occurs around 2071.
b. The population will peak at $P(7.12) \approx 9.07499$ billion.

65. a. On [0,3]: $f(t) = 0.6t^2 + 2.4t + 7.6$; $f'(t) = 1.2t + 2.4 = 0$ implies $t = -2$ which lies outside the interval $[0, 3]$.

t	0	3
$f(t)$	7.6	20.2

On [3, 5]: $f(t) = 3t^2 + 18.8t - 63.2$, $f'(t) = 6t + 18.8 = 0$ implies $t = -3.13$ which lies outside the interval $[3, 5]$.

t	3	5
$f(t)$	20.2	105.8

On [5, 8]: $f(t) = -3.3167t^3 + 80.1t^2 - 642.583t + 1730.8025$
$$f'(t) = -9.9501t^2 + 160.2t - 642.583$$
Solving the equation $f'(t) = 0$, we find

$$t = \frac{-160.2 \pm \sqrt{160.2^2 - 4(-9.9501)(642.583)}}{2(-9.9501)} \approx 7.58, \text{ or } 8.52.$$

Only the critical number $t = 7.58$ lies inside the interval $[5, 8]$.

t	5	7.58	8
$f(t)$	105.8	17.8	18.4

From the tables, we see that the investment peaked when $t = 5$, that is, in 2000. The amount was $105.8 billion.
b. The investment ($7.6 billion) was lowest when $t = 0$.

66. We want to minimize the function $E(v) = \dfrac{aLv^3}{v - u}$. Since $v > u$, the function has no points of discontinuity. To find the critical points of $E(v)$, we solve the equation

$$E'(v) = \frac{(v-u)3aLv^2 - aLv^3}{(v-u)^2} = \frac{aLv^2(2v - 3u)}{(v-u)^2} = \frac{aLv^2(2v - 3u)}{(v-u)^2} = 0$$

obtaining $v = (3/2)u$ or $v = 0$. Now $v \neq 0$ since $u < v$ so $v = (3/2)u$ is the only critical point of interest. Since $E'(v) < 0$ if $v < (3/2)u$ and $E'(v) > 0$ if $v > (3/2)u$, we see that $v = (3/2)u$ gives a relative minimum. The nature of the problem suggests that $v = (3/2)u$ gives the absolute minimum of E (or we can verify that by sketching the graph of E). Therefore, the fish must swim at $(3/2)u$ ft/sec in order to minimize the total energy expended.

67 $R = D^2 \left(\dfrac{k}{2} - \dfrac{D}{3} \right) = \dfrac{kD^2}{2} - \dfrac{D^3}{3}$. $\dfrac{dR}{dD} = \dfrac{2kD}{2} - \dfrac{3D^2}{3} = kD - D^2 = D(k - D)$

Setting $\dfrac{dR}{dD} = 0$, we have $D = 0$ or $k = D$. We only consider $k = D$

(since $D > 0$). If $k > 0$, $\dfrac{dR}{dD} > 0$ and if $k < 0$, $\dfrac{dR}{dD} < 0$. Therefore $k = D$ provides a

relative maximum. The nature of the problem suggests that $k = D$ gives the absolute maximum of R. We can also verify this by graphing R.

68. $\dfrac{dR}{dD} = kD - D^2;$ $\dfrac{d^2R}{dD^2} = k - 2D;$ Setting this last equation equal to zero,

we have $k = 2D$ or $D = \dfrac{k}{2}$ Since $\dfrac{d^2R}{dD^2} > 0$ for $k < 2D$ and $\dfrac{d^2R}{dD^2} < 0$ for $k > 2D$,

we see that $k = 2D$ provides the relative (absolute) maximum.

69. False. Let $f(x) = \begin{cases} |x| & \text{if } x \neq 0 \\ 1 & \text{if } x = 0 \end{cases}$ on $[-1, 1]$.

70. False. Let $f(x) = x^2$ on $(-1, 1)$.

71. False. Let $f(x) = \begin{cases} -x & \text{if } -1 \leq x < 0 \\ \dfrac{1}{2} & \text{if } 0 \leq x < 1 \end{cases}$. Then f is discontinuous at $x = 0$. But f

has an absolute maximum value of 1 attained at $x = -1$.

72. True. $f''(x) < 0$ on (a, b) says the graph of f is concave downward on (a, b). Therefore, the relative maximum value at $x = c$ must, in fact, be the absolute maximum value.

73. Since $f(x) = c$ for all x, the function f satisfies $f(x) \leq c$ for all x and so f has an absolute maximum at all points of x. Similarly, f has an absolute minimum at all

points of x.

74. Suppose f is a nonconstant polynomial function. Then
$$f(x) = a_0x^n + a_1x^{n-1} + \cdots + a_n, \text{ where } a_0 \neq 0 \text{ and } n \geq 1.$$
First, let us suppose that $a_0 > 0$. There are two cases to consider:
(1) If n is odd, then $\lim\limits_{x \to -\infty} f(x) = -\infty$ and $\lim\limits_{x \to \infty} f(x) = \infty$ and so f has no absolute

maximum or absolute minimum.
(2) If n is even, then $\lim\limits_{x \to -\infty} f(x) = \lim\limits_{x \to \infty} f(x) = \infty$ so f cannot have an absolute

minimum. A similar argument is used in the case where $a_0 < 0$.

75 a. f is not continuous at $x = 0$ because $\lim\limits_{x \to 0} f(x)$ does not exist.

b. $\lim\limits_{x \to 0} f(x) = \lim\limits_{x \to 0^-} \dfrac{1}{x} = -\infty$ and $\lim\limits_{x \to 0^+} f(x) = \lim\limits_{x \to 0^+} \dfrac{1}{x} = \infty$

c.

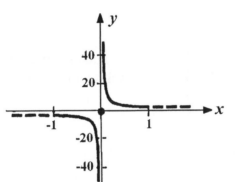

76. $f(x)$ can be made as close to -1 as we please by taking x sufficiently close to -1. But, the value -1 is never attained since x must be greater than -1. Similarly, 1 is never attained. Therefore, f has neither an absolute minimum value or an absolute maximum value.

USING TECHNOLOGY EXERCISES 4.4, page 314

1. Absolute maximum value: 145.8985; absolute minimum value: -4.3834

2. Absolute maximum value: 26.3997; absolute minimum value: -4.4372

4 Applications of the Derivative

3. Absolute maximum value: 16; absolute minimum value: -0.1257

4. Absolute maximum value: 11.2016; absolute minimum value: 9

5. Absolute maximum value: 2.8889; absolute minimum value: 0

6. No maximum value; Absolute minimum value: 18.8535

7. a.

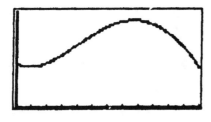

b. 200.1410 banks/yr

8. a.

b. Absolute maximum value: 108.8756;
   absolute minimum value: 49 7773

9. a.

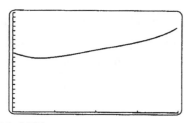

b.   21.51%

10. a.

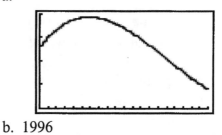

b. 1996

11. b. 1145

12.a.

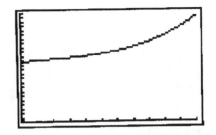

b. Lowest in 1996; highest in early 2000

c. Lowest: $\approx \$37,000$; highest: $\approx \$54,000$

13. a.

14. a.

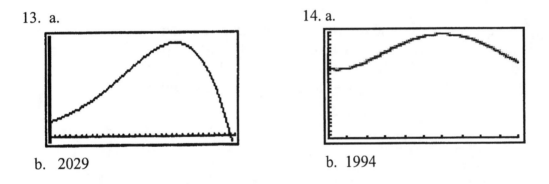

b. 2029

b. 1994

4.5 CONCEPT QUESTIONS, page 322

1   We could solve the problem by sketching the graph of f and checking to see if there is (are) an absolute extrema.

2. $S = 2\pi r^2 + 2\pi rh$. From $\pi r^2 h = 54$, we see that $r = \left(\dfrac{54}{\pi h}\right)^{1/2}$. Therefore,

$$S = 2\pi\left(\frac{54}{\pi h}\right) + 2\pi h\sqrt{\frac{54}{\pi}} \cdot \frac{1}{h^{1/2}} = \frac{108}{h} + 2\sqrt{54\pi}\,h^{1/2}$$

$$S' = -\frac{108}{h^2} + 2\sqrt{54\pi}\left(\frac{1}{2}h^{-1/2}\right) = -\frac{108}{h^2} + \frac{\sqrt{54\pi}}{h^{1/2}} = 0 \text{ implies}$$

$$\frac{108}{h^2} = \frac{\sqrt{54\pi}}{h^{1/2}}, \quad h^{3/2} = \frac{108}{\sqrt{54\pi}}$$

and so

$$h = \left[\frac{108}{(54\pi)^{1/2}}\right]^{2/3} = \frac{108^{2/3}}{(54\pi)^{1/3}} = \left(\frac{108}{54\pi}\right)^{1/3} = \frac{6}{\sqrt[3]{\pi}}$$

as obtained in Example 4. Writing S in terms of r seems to be a better choice.

EXERCISES 4.5, page 322

1. Refer to the following figure.

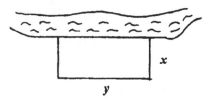

We have $2x + y = 3000$ and we want to maximize the function
$$A = f(x) = xy = x(3000 - 2x) = 3000x - 2x^2$$
on the interval $[0,1500]$. The critical point of A is obtained by solving
$f'(x) = 3000 - 4x = 0$, giving $x = 750$. From the table of values

x	0	750	1500
$f(x)$	0	1,125,000	0

we conclude that $x = 750$ yields the absolute maximum value of A. Thus, the required dimensions are 750×1500 yards. The maximum area is 1,125,000 sq yd.

2. Refer to the following figure.

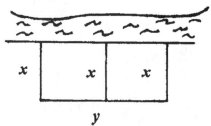

Let x denote the length of one of the sides. Then $y = 3000 - 3x = 3(1000 - x)$. The

area is $A(x) = xy = 3x(1000 - x) = -3x^2 + 3000x$ for $0 \le x \le 1000$. Next,
$A'(x) = -6x + 3000 = -6(x - 500)$. Setting $A'(x) = 0$ gives $x = 500$ as the critical
point. From the table of values

x	0	500	1000
$A(x)$	0	750,000	0

we see that $f(500) = 750,000$ is the absolute maximum value. Next,
$y = 3(1000 - 500) = 1500$. Therefore, the required dimensions are 500 yd × 1500
yd. The area is 750,000 sq yd.

3 Let x denote the length of the side made of wood and y the length of the side made
of steel. The cost of construction will be $C = 6(2x) + 3y$. But $xy = 800$. So

$y = 800/x$ and therefore $C = f(x) = 12x + 3\left(\dfrac{800}{x}\right) = 12x + \dfrac{2400}{x}$. To minimize C,

we compute

$$f'(x) = 12 - \frac{2400}{x^2} = \frac{12x^2 - 2400}{x^2} = \frac{12(x^2 - 200)}{x^2}.$$

Setting $f'(x) = 0$ gives $x = \pm\sqrt{200}$ as critical points of f. The sign diagram of f'

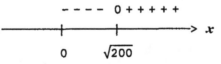

shows that $x = \pm\sqrt{200}$ gives a relative minimum of f. $f''(x) = \dfrac{4800}{x^3} > 0$

if $x > 0$ and so f is concave upward for $x > 0$. Therefore $x = \sqrt{200} = 10\sqrt{2}$ actually
yields the absolute minimum. So the dimensions of the enclosure should be

$$10\sqrt{2} \text{ ft} \times \frac{800}{10\sqrt{2}} \text{ ft, or } 14.1 \text{ ft} \times 56.6 \text{ ft.}$$

4. Refer to the following figures.

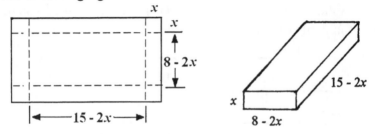

The volume of the box is given by
$$V = f(x) = (8 - 2x)(15 - 2x)x = 4x^3 - 46x^2 + 120x.$$
Since the sides of the box must be nonnegative, we must have
$$8 - 2x \geq 0 \text{ or } x \leq 4$$
and $\qquad 15 - 2x \geq 0 \text{ or } x \leq \frac{15}{2}$

The problem is equivalent to the following: Find the absolute maximum of f on $[0,4]$. Now, $f'(x) = 12x^2 - 92x + 120 = 4(3x^2 - 23x + 30) = 4(3x - 5)(x - 6)$ so that $f'(x) = 0$ implies $x = 5/3$ or $x = 6$. Since $x = 6$ is outside the interval $[0,4]$, only $x = 5/3$ qualifies as the critical point of f. From the table of values

x	0	5/3	4
$f(x)$	0	2450/27	0

we see that $x = 5/3$ gives rise to an absolute maximum of f. Thus, the dimensions which yield the maximum volume are $\frac{14}{3}'' \times \frac{35}{3}'' \times \frac{5}{3}''$. The maximum volume is $\frac{2450}{27}$, or approximately 90.7 cubic inches.

5. Let the dimensions of each square that is cut out be $x'' \times x''$. Refer to the following diagram.

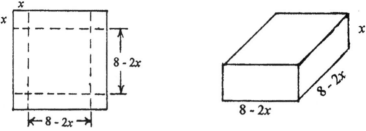

Then the dimensions of the box will be $(8 - 2x)''$ by $(8 - 2x)''$ by x''. Its volume will be $V = f(x) = x(8 - 2x)^2$. We want to maximize f on $[0,4]$.

$$f'(x) = (8 - 2x)^2 + x(2)(8 - 2x)(-2) \qquad \text{[Using the Product Rule.]}$$
$$= (8 - 2x)[(8 - 2x) - 4x] = (8 - 2x)(8 - 6x) = 0$$

if $x = 4$ or $4/3$. The latter is a critical point in $(0,4)$.

x	0	4/3	4
$f(x)$	0	1024/27	0

We see that $x = 4/3$ yields an absolute maximum for f. So the dimensions of the box should be $\frac{16}{3}'' \times \frac{16}{3}'' \times \frac{4}{3}''$.

6. Let the dimensions of the box be $x'' \times x'' \times y''$ Since its volume is 108 cubic inches, we have $x^2 y = 108$. We want to minimize $S = x^2 + 4xy$. But $y = 108/x^2$ and so we want to minimize $S = x^2 + 4x\left(\dfrac{108}{x^2}\right) = x^2 + \dfrac{432}{x}$ $(x > 0)$. Now

$$S' = 2x - \frac{432}{x^2} = \frac{2(x^3 - 216)}{x^2}.$$

Setting $S' = 0$ gives $x = 6$ as a critical point of S. The sign diagram

$$---- 0 + + + + +$$

shows that $x = 6$ gives a relative minimum of S. Next,

$$S'' = 2 + \frac{864}{x^3} > 0 \text{ if } x > 0$$

and this says that S is concave upward on $(0,\infty)$. Therefore, $x = 6$ gives an absolute minimum. So the dimensions of the box should be $6'' \times 6'' \times 3''$

7. Let x denote the length of the sides of the box and y denote its height. Referring to the following figure, we see that the volume of the box is given by $x^2 y = 128$. The

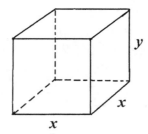

amount of material used is given by

$$S = f(x) = 2x^2 + 4xy$$

$$= 2x^2 + 4x\left(\frac{128}{x^2}\right)$$

$$= 2x^2 + \frac{512}{x} \text{ square inches.}$$

We want to minimize f subject to the condition that $x > 0$. Now

$$f'(x) = 4x - \frac{512}{x^2} = \frac{4x^3 - 512}{x^2} = \frac{4(x^3 - 128)}{x^2}.$$

Setting $f'(x) = 0$ yields $x = 5.04$, a critical point of f. Next,

$$f''(x) = 4 + \frac{1024}{x^3} > 0$$

for all $x > 0$. Thus, the graph of f is concave upward and so $x = 5.04$ yields an absolute minimum of f. Thus, the required dimensions are 5.04" $\times$ 5.04" $\times$ 5.04"

8. From the given figure, we see that $x^2y = 20$ and $y = 20/x^2$, and

$$C = 30x^2 + 10(4xy) + 20x^2 = 50x^2 + 40x\left(\frac{20}{x^2}\right) = 50x^2 + \frac{800}{x}.$$

To find the critical points of C, we solve $C' = 100x - \frac{800}{x^2} = 0$, obtaining,

$100x^3 = 800$, $x^3 = 8$, or $x = 2$. Next, $C'' = \frac{1600}{x^3} > 0$ for all $x > 0$, we see that $x = 2$

gives the absolute minimum value of C. Since $y = 20/4 = 5$, we see that the dimensions are 2 ft $\times$ 2 ft $\times$ 5 ft.

9. The length plus the girth of the box is $4x + h = 108$ and $h = 108 - 4x$. Then
$$V = x^2h = x^2(108 - 4x) = 108x^2 - 4x^3$$
and $V' = 216x - 12x^2$. We want to maximize V on the interval $[0,27]$. Setting

$V'(x) = 0$ and solving for x, we obtain $x = 18$ and $x = 0$. Evaluating $V(x)$ at $x = 0$, $x = 18$, and $x = 27$, we obtain

$$V(0) = 0, \ V(18) = 11,664, \ \text{and} \ V(27) = 0$$

Thus, the dimensions of the box are $18'' \times 18'' \times 36''$ and its maximum volume is approximately 11,664 cu in.

10. $xy = 50$ and so $y = 50/x$. The area of the printed area is

$$A = (x-1)(y-2) = (x-1)(\tfrac{50}{x} - 2) = (x-1)(\tfrac{50-2x}{x}) = -2x + 52 - \tfrac{50}{x}$$

$$A' = -2 + \tfrac{50}{x^2} = \tfrac{-2(x^2-25)}{x^2} = 0 \ \text{if} \ x = \pm 5. \ \text{From the sign diagram}$$

$$+ + + + + 0 - - - - -$$

for A', we see that $x = 5$ yields a maximum. Since

$$A'' = -\frac{100}{x^3} < 0 \ \text{if} \ x > 0$$

we see that the graph of A is concave downward on $(0,\infty)$ and so $x = 5$ yields an absolute maximum. The dimensions of the paper should, therefore, be $5'' \times 10''$.

11. We take $2\pi r + \ell = 108$. We want to maximize

$$V = \pi r^2 \ell = \pi r^2 (-2\pi r + 108) = -2\pi^2 r^3 + 108\pi r^2$$

subject to the condition that $0 \le r \le \tfrac{54}{\pi}$. Now

$$V'(r) = -6\pi^2 r^2 + 216\pi r = -6\pi r(\pi r - 36).$$

Since $V' = 0$, we find $r = 0$ or $r = 36/\pi$, the critical points of V. From the table

r	0	36/π	54/π
V	0	46,656/π	0

we conclude that the maximum volume occurs when $r = 36/\pi \approx 11.5$ inches and $\ell = 108 - 2\pi\left(\tfrac{36}{\pi}\right) = 36$ inches and its volume is $46,656/\pi$ cu in .

12. Let r and h denote the radius and height of the container. Since its capacity is to be 36 cu in, we have $\pi r^2 h = 36$ or $h = 36/\pi r^2$. We want to minimize $S = 2\pi r^2 + 2\pi rh$ or

$$S = f(r) = 2\pi r^2 + 2\pi r\left(\frac{36}{\pi r^2}\right) = 2\pi r^2 + \tfrac{72}{r},$$

4 Applications of the Derivative

over the interval $(0, \infty)$. Now

$$f'(r) = 4\pi r - \frac{72}{\pi r^2} = 0 \text{ gives } 4\pi r^3 = 72, \text{ or } r = \left(\frac{18}{\pi}\right)^{1/3},$$

as the only critical point of f. Next, observe that $f''(r) = 4\pi + \frac{144}{\pi r} > 0$ for r in

$(0,\infty)$. So f is concave upward on $(0,\infty)$ and $r = \left(\frac{18}{\pi}\right)^{1/3}$ gives rise to the absolute

minimum of f. We find $h = \dfrac{36}{\pi\left(\frac{18}{\pi}\right)^{2/3}} = \dfrac{2\cdot 18}{\pi^{1/3}18^{2/3}} = 2\left(\dfrac{18}{\pi}\right)^{1/3}$ or twice the radius.

13. Let y denote the height and x the width of the cabinet. Then $y = (3/2)x$. Since the volume is to be 2.4 cu ft, we have $xyd = 2.4$, where d is the depth of the cabinet.

We have $\quad x\left(\dfrac{3}{2}x\right)d = 2.4 \text{ or } d = \dfrac{2.4(2)}{3x^2} = \dfrac{1.6}{x^2}$.

The cost for constructing the cabinet is

$$C = 40(2xd + 2yd) + 20(2xy) = 80\left[\frac{1.6}{x} + \left(\frac{3}{2}x\right)\left(\frac{1.6}{x^2}\right)\right] + 40x\left(\frac{3}{2}x\right)$$

$$= \frac{320}{x} + 60x^2.$$

$$C'(x) = -\frac{320}{x^2} + 120x = \frac{120x^3 - 320}{x^2} = 0 \text{ if } x = \sqrt[3]{\frac{8}{3}} = \frac{2}{\sqrt[3]{3}} = \frac{2}{3}\sqrt[3]{9}$$

Therefore, $x = \frac{2}{3}\sqrt[3]{9}$ is a critical point of C. The sign diagram

$$\begin{array}{c} \text{- - - -- 0 + + + + + + + + + +} \\ \hline \qquad\qquad +\qquad\quad +\qquad\qquad\longrightarrow x \\ \qquad\qquad 0\qquad\quad \frac{2}{3}\sqrt[3]{9} \end{array}$$

shows that $x = \frac{2}{3}\sqrt[3]{9}$ gives a relative minimum. Next, $C''(x) = \dfrac{640}{x^3} + 120 > 0$

for all $x > 0$ tells us that the graph of C is concave upward. So $x = \frac{2}{3}\sqrt[3]{9}$ yields an

absolute minimum. The required dimensions are $\frac{2}{3}\sqrt[3]{9}\,' \times \sqrt[3]{9}\,' \times \frac{2}{5}\sqrt[3]{9}\,'$.

14. Since the perimeter of the window is 28 ft, we have

$$2x + 2y + \pi x = 28 \text{ or } y = \tfrac{1}{2}(28 - \pi x - 2x)$$

We want to maximize

$$A = 2xy + \tfrac{1}{2}\pi x^2 = \tfrac{1}{2}\pi x^2 + x(28 - \pi x - 2x) = \tfrac{1}{2}\pi x^2 + 28x - \pi x^2 - 2x^2$$
$$= 28x - \tfrac{\pi}{2}x^2 - 2x^2.$$

Now $A' = 28 - \pi x - 4x = 0$ gives $x = \frac{28}{4+\pi}$ as a critical point of A. Since

$A'' = -\pi - 4 < 0$, the point yields a maximum of A. Finally,

$$y = \frac{1}{2}\left[28 - \frac{28\pi}{4+\pi} - \frac{56}{4+\pi}\right] = \frac{1}{2}\left[\frac{112 + 28\pi - 28\pi - 56}{4+\pi}\right] = \frac{28}{4+\pi}$$

15   We want to maximize the function
$$R(x) = (200 + x)(300 - x) = -x^2 + 100x + 60000.$$
Then $R'(x) = -2x + 100 = 0$
gives $x = 50$ and this is a critical point of R. Since $R''(x) = -2 < 0$, we see that $x = 50$ gives an absolute maximum of R. Therefore, the number of passengers should be 250. The fare will then be \$250/passenger and the revenue will be \$62,500.

16. Let x denote the number of trees beyond 22 per acre. Then the yield is
$$Y = (36 - 2x)(22 + x) = -2x^2 - 8x + 792.$$
Next, $Y' = -4x - 8 = 0$ gives $x = -2$ as the critical point of Y. Now $Y'' = -4 < 0$ and so $x = -2$ gives the absolute maximum of Y. So we should plant 20 trees/acre.

17   Let x denote the number of people beyond 20 who sign up for the cruise. Then the revenue is $R(x) = (20 + x)(600 - 4x) = -4x^2 + 520x + 12,000$ We want to maximize R on the closed bounded interval $[0, 70]$.
$$R'(x) = -8x + 520 = 0 \text{ implies } x = 65,$$
a critical point of R. Evaluating R at this critical point and the endpoints, we have

x	0	65	70
$R(x)$	12,000	28,900	28,800

From this table, we see that R is maximized if $x = 65$. Therefore, 85 passengers will result in a maximum revenue of \$28,900. The fare would be \$340/passenger.

18. Let x denote the number of bottles beyond 10,000. Then the profit is
$$P(x) = (10,000 + x)(5 - 0.0002x) = -0.0002x^2 + 3x + 50,000$$
We want to maximize P on $[0, \infty)$.
$$P'(x) = -0.0004x + 3 = 0$$

implies $x = 7500$. Since $P''(x) = -0.0004 < 0$, the graph of P is concave downward, and we see that $x = 7500$ gives the absolute maximum of P. So Phillip should produce 17,000 bottles of wine giving a profit of

$$P(7500) = -0.0002(7500)^2 + 3(7500) + 50,000 \quad \text{or } \$61,250.$$

The price will be $5 - 0.0002(7500)$ or \$3.50/bottle.

19. We want to maximize $S = kh^2w$. But $h^2 + w^2 = 24^2$ or $h^2 = 576 - w^2$ So
$S = f(w) = kw(576 - w^2) = k(576w - w^3)$. Now, setting
$$f'(w) = k(576 - 3w^2) = 0$$
gives $w = \pm\sqrt{192} \approx \pm 13.86$. Only the positive root is a critical point of interest. Next, we find $f''(w) = -6kw$, and in particular,
$$f''(\sqrt{192}) = -6\sqrt{192}\, k < 0,$$
so that $w = \pm\sqrt{192} \approx \pm 13.86$ gives a relative maximum of f. Since $f''(w) < 0$ for $w > 0$, we see that the graph of f is concave downward on $(0,\infty)$ and so, $w = \sqrt{192}$ gives an absolute maximum of f. We find $h^2 = 576 - 192 = 384$ or $h \approx 19.60$. So the width and height of the log should be approximately 13.86 inches and 19.60 inches, respectively.

20. We want to minimize $S = 3\pi r^2 + 2\pi rh$. But $\pi r^2 h + \frac{2}{3}\pi r^3 = 504\pi$, or
$$h = \frac{1}{r^2}(504 - \frac{2}{3}r^3)$$
Therefore, $\quad S = f(r) = 3\pi r^2 + 2\pi r \cdot \frac{1}{r^2}(504 - \frac{2}{3}r^3)$

$$= 3\pi r^2 + \frac{1008\pi}{r} - \frac{4\pi r^2}{3} = \frac{5\pi r^2}{3} + \frac{1008\pi}{r}.$$

Now, $\quad f'(r) = \frac{10\pi r}{3} - \frac{1008\pi}{r^2} = \frac{10\pi r^3 - 3024\pi}{3r^2}.$

So $f'(r) = 0$ if $r^3 = \frac{3024\pi}{10\pi}$ or $r = \left(\frac{1512}{5}\right)^{1/3} \approx 6.7$ is a critical point of f. Since

$f''(r) = \frac{10\pi}{3} + \frac{2016\pi}{r^3} > 0$ for all r in $(0,\infty)$, we see that $r \approx 6.7$ does yield an

absolute minimum of h. Therefore, the radius should be approximately 6.7 ft and the height should be approximately 6.7 ft.

21 We want to minimize $C(x) = 1.50(10,000 - x) + 2.50\sqrt{3000^2 + x^2}$ subject to $0 \leq x \leq 10,000$. Now

$$C'(x) = -1.50 + 2.5(\tfrac{1}{2})(9,000,000 + x^2)^{-1/2}(2x) = -1.50 + \frac{2.50x}{\sqrt{9,000,000 + x^2}}$$

$$C'(x) = 0 \Rightarrow 2.5x = 1.50\sqrt{9,000,000 + x^2}$$

$$6.25x^2 = 2.25(9,000,000 + x^2) \quad \text{or} \quad 4x^2 = 20250000, \ x = 2250.$$

x	0	2250	10000
$f(x)$	22500	21000	26101

From the table, we see that $x = 2250$ gives the absolute minimum.

22. We need to minimize $\hat{V} = \dfrac{16r^2}{(r + \tfrac{1}{2})^2} - r^2$.   Now,

$$\hat{V}' = \frac{(r + \tfrac{1}{2})^2(32r) - 16r^2 \cdot 2(r + \tfrac{1}{2})}{(r + \tfrac{1}{2})^4} - 2r = \frac{32r(r + \tfrac{1}{2})(r + \tfrac{1}{2} - r) - 2r(r + \tfrac{1}{2})^4}{(r + \tfrac{1}{2})^3}$$

$$= \frac{16r(r + \tfrac{1}{2}) - 2r(r + \tfrac{1}{2})^4}{(r + \tfrac{1}{2})^3} = \frac{2r\left[8 - (r + \tfrac{1}{2})^3\right]}{(r + \tfrac{1}{2})^3} = 0$$

implies $8 - (r + \tfrac{1}{2})^3 = 0$, $(r + \tfrac{1}{2})^3 = 8$, $r + \tfrac{1}{2} = 2$, or $r = \tfrac{3}{2}$

Next, $\hat{V}(\tfrac{3}{2}) = \dfrac{16(\tfrac{3}{2})^2}{2^2} - (\tfrac{3}{2})^2 = (\tfrac{3}{2})^2 (4 - 1) = 3(\tfrac{9}{4}) = \tfrac{27}{4}$

$$h = \frac{16}{(r + \tfrac{1}{2})^2} - 1 = \frac{16}{4} - 1 = 3$$

So the dimensions are $r = \tfrac{3}{2}$, and $h = 3$. From the table

r	0	$\tfrac{3}{2}$	$\tfrac{7}{2}$
$\hat{V}$	0	$\tfrac{27}{4}$	0

We see that V is maximized if $r = \tfrac{3}{2}$. So the radius is 1.5 ft, and the height is 3'.

23. The time taken for the flight is

$$T = f(x) = \frac{12 - x}{6} + \frac{\sqrt{x^2 + 9}}{4}.$$

$$f'(x) = -\frac{1}{6} + \frac{1}{4}\left(\frac{1}{2}\right)(x^2 + 9)^{-1/2}(2x) = -\frac{1}{6} + \frac{x}{4\sqrt{x^2 + 9}}$$

$$= \frac{3x - 2\sqrt{x^2 + 9}}{12\sqrt{x^2 + 9}} .$$

Setting $f'(x) = 0$ gives $3x = 2\sqrt{x^2 + 9}$, $9x^2 = 4(x^2 + 9)$ or $5x^2 = 36$. Therefore, $x = \pm 6/\sqrt{5} = \pm 6\sqrt{5}/5$. Only the critical point $x = 6\sqrt{5}/5$ is of interest. The nature of the problem suggests $x \approx 2.68$ gives an absolute minimum for T.

24. The fuel cost is $x/400$ dollars per mile, and the labor cost is $8/x$ dollars per mile. Therefore, the total cost is $C(x) = \dfrac{8}{x} + \dfrac{x}{400}$; $C'(x) = -\dfrac{8}{x^2} + \dfrac{1}{400}$.

Setting $C'(x) = 0$ gives $-\dfrac{8}{x^2} = -\dfrac{1}{400}$; $x^2 = 3200$, and $x = 56.57$

Next, $C''(x) = \dfrac{16}{x^3} > 0$ for all $x > 0$ so C is concave upward. Therefore, $x = 56.57$

gives the absolute minimum. So the most economical speed is 56.57 mph.

25. The area enclosed by the rectangular region of the racetrack is $A = (\ell)(2r) = 2r\ell$. The length of the racetrack is $2\pi r + 2\ell$, and is equal to 1760. That is,
$$2(\pi r + \ell) = 1760; \ \pi r + \ell = 880, \ \text{or} \ \ell = 880 - \pi r$$

Therefore, we want to maximize $A = f(r) = 2r(880 - \pi r) = 1760r - 2\pi r^2$.

The restricition on r is $0 \le r \le \frac{880}{\pi}$. To maximize A, we compute

$f'(r) = 1760 - 4\pi r$. Setting $f'(r) = 0$ gives $r = \dfrac{1760}{4\pi} = \dfrac{440}{\pi} \approx 140$. Since

$f(0) = f\left(\frac{880}{\pi}\right) = 0$, we see that the maximum rectangular area is enclosed if we

take $r = \frac{440}{\pi}$ and $\ell = 880 - \pi\left(\frac{440}{\pi}\right) = 440$. So $r = 140$ and $\ell = 440$. The total area

enclosed is $2r\ell + \pi r^2 = 2\left(\frac{440}{\pi}\right)(440) + \pi\left(\frac{440}{\pi}\right)^2 = \frac{2(440)^2}{\pi} + \frac{440^2}{\pi} = \frac{580,800}{\pi} \approx 184,874$ sq ft.

26. Let x denote the number of motorcycle tires in each order. We want to minimize
$$C(x) = 400\left(\frac{40,000}{x}\right) + x = \frac{16,000,000}{x} + x.$$

We compute $C'(x) = -\dfrac{16,000,000}{x^2} + 1 = \dfrac{x^2 - 16,000,000}{x^2}$.

Setting $C'(x) = 0$ gives $x = 4000$, a critical point of C. Since

$$C''(x) = \frac{32,000,000}{x^3} > 0 \text{ for all } x > 0,$$

we see that the graph of C is concave upward and so $x = 4000$ gives an absolute minimum of C. So there should be 10 orders per year, each order of 4000 tires.

27. Let x denote the number of bottles in each order. We want to minimize

$$C(x) = 200\left(\frac{2,000,000}{x}\right) + \frac{x}{2}(0.40) = \frac{400,000,000}{x} + 0.2x.$$

We compute $C'(x) = -\frac{400,000,000}{x^2} + 0.2$. Setting $C'(x) = 0$ gives

$$x^2 = \frac{400,000,000}{0.2} = 2,000,000,000, \text{ or } x = 44,721, \text{ a critical point of } C.$$

$$C'(x) = \frac{800,000,000}{x^3} > 0 \text{ for all } x > 0, \text{ and we see that the graph of } C \text{ is concave}$$

upward and so $x = 44,721$ gives an absolute minimum of C. Therefore, there should be $2,000,000/x \approx 45$ orders per year (since we can not have fractions of an order.) Then each order should be for $2,000,000/45 \approx 44,445$ bottles.

28. We want to minimize the function $C(x) = \frac{500,000,000}{x} + 0.2x + 500,000$ on the

interval $(0, 1,000,000)$. Differentiating $C(x)$, we have $C'(x) = -\frac{500,000,000}{x^2} + 0.2$.

Setting $C'(x) = 0$ and solving the resulting equation, we find $0.2x^2 = 500,000,000$

and $x = \sqrt{2,500,000,000}$ or $x = 50,000$. Next, we find

$$C''(x) = \frac{1,000,000,000}{x^3} > 0 \text{ for all } x \text{ and so the graph of } C \text{ is concave upward on}$$

$(0, \infty)$. Thus, $x = 50,000$ gives rise to the absolute minimum of C. So, the company should produce 50,000 containers of cookies per production run.

29. a. Since the sales are assumed to be at a steady rate and D units are expected to be sold per year, the number of orders/yr is D/x. Since is costs $\$K$ per order, the ordering cost is KD/x. The purchasing cost is PD (cost per item times number purchased). Finally, the holding cost is $(x/2)h$ (the average number on hand times holding cost per item). Therefore

$$C(x) = \frac{KD}{x} + pD + \frac{hx}{2}$$

4 Applications of the Derivative

b. $C'(x) = -\dfrac{KD}{x^2} + \dfrac{h}{2} = 0$

implies $\dfrac{KD}{x^2} = \dfrac{h}{2}$

$$x^2 = \dfrac{2KD}{h}$$

$$x = \pm\sqrt{\dfrac{2KD}{h}}$$

We reject the negative root. So $x = \sqrt{\dfrac{2KD}{h}}$ is the only critical number. Next,

$$C''(x) = \dfrac{2KD}{x^3} > 0 \text{ for } x > 0$$

So $C''\left(\sqrt{\dfrac{2KD}{h}}\right) > 0$ and the second derivative test shows that $x = \sqrt{\dfrac{2KD}{h}}$ does

give a relative minimum and because C is concave upward, the absolute minimum.

30 a. We use the result of Exercise 29 with $D = 960$, $K = 10$, $p = 80$, and $h = 12$, obtaining

$$x = \sqrt{\dfrac{2KD}{h}} = \sqrt{\dfrac{2(10)(960)}{12}} = 40$$

and the EOQ..

  b. The number of orders to be placed each year is $\dfrac{960}{40} = 24$.

  c. The interval between orders is $\dfrac{12}{24} = \dfrac{1}{2}$ or one-half month.

CHAPTER 4 CONCEPT REVIEW, page 327

1. a. $f(x_1) < f(x_2)$ b. $f(x_1) > f(x_2)$
2. a. Increasing   b. $f'(x) < 0$ c. Constant
3 a. $f(x) \le f(c)$ b. $f(x) \ge f(c)$
4. a. Domain; $= 0$; exist b. Critical number
   c. Relative extremum
5. a. $f'(x)$ b. > 0 c. Concavity   d. Relative maximum; relative extremum

6. $\pm\infty$; $\pm\infty$ 7. 0; 0   8. b; b

9. a. $f(x) \le f(c)$; absolute maximum value   b. $f(x) \ge f(c)$; open interval

10. Continuous; absolute; absolute

CHAPTER 4 REVIEW, page 328

1. a. $f(x) = \frac{1}{3}x^3 - x^2 + x - 6$. $f'(x) = x^2 - 2x + 1 = (x - 1)^2$. $f'(x) = 0$ gives $x = 1$, the critical point of f. Now, $f'(x) > 0$ for all $x \ne 1$. Thus, f is increasing on $(-\infty, 1) \cup (1, \infty)$.

    b. Since $f'(x)$ does not change sign as we move across the critical point $x = 1$, the First Derivative Test implies that $x = 1$ does not give rise to a relative extremum of f.

    c. $f''(x) = 2(x - 1)$. Setting $f''(x) = 0$ gives $x = 1$ as a candidate for an inflection point of f. Since $f''(x) < 0$ for $x < 1$, and $f''(x) > 0$ for $x > 1$, we see that f is concave downward on $(-\infty, 1)$ and concave upward on $(1, \infty)$.

    d. The results of (c) imply that $(1, -\frac{17}{3})$ is an inflection point.

2. a. $f(x) = (x - 2)^3$; $f'(x) = 3(x - 2)^2 > 0$ for all $x \ne 2$. Therefore, f is increasing on $(-\infty, 2) \cup (2, \infty)$.

    b. There are no relative extrema.

    c. $f''(x) = 6(x - 2)$. Since $f''(x) < 0$ if $x < 2$ and $f''(x) > 0$ if $x > 2$, we see that f is concave downward on $(-\infty, 2)$ and concave upward on $(2, \infty)$,

    d. The results of (c) show that $(2, 0)$ is an inflection point.

3. a. $f(x) = x^4 - 2x^2$. $f'(x) = 4x^3 - 4x = 4x(x^2 - 1) = 4x(x + 1)(x - 1)$. The sign diagram of f' shows that f is decreasing on $(-\infty, -1) \cup (0, 1)$ and increasing on $(-1, 0) \cup (1, \infty)$.

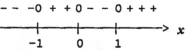

    b. The results of (a) and the First Derivative Test show that $(-1, -1)$ and $(1, -1)$ are relative minima and $(0, 0)$ is a relative maximum.

    c. $f''(x) = 12x^2 - 4 = 4(3x^2 - 1) = 0$ if $x = \pm\sqrt{3}/3$. The sign diagram

$+ + + + \ 0 - - - - - - - \ 0 \ + + + +$

```
        +----+----+----+---->  x
     -√3/3    0    √3/3
```

shows that f is concave upward on $(-\infty, -\sqrt{3}/3) \cup (\sqrt{3}/3, \infty)$ and concave downward on $(-\sqrt{3}/3, \sqrt{3}/3)$.

d. The results of (c) show that $(-\sqrt{3}/3, -5/9)$ and $(\sqrt{3}/3, -5/9)$ are inflection points.

4. $f(x) = x + \frac{4}{x}$. $f'(x) = 1 - \frac{4}{x^2} = \frac{x^2-4}{x^2} = \frac{(x-2)(x+2)}{x^2}$. Setting $f'(x) = 0$ gives $x = -2$ and $x = 2$ as critical points of f. $f'(x)$ is undefined at $x = 0$ as well. The sign diagram for f' is

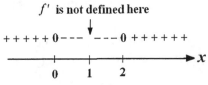

a. f is increasing on $(-\infty, -2) \cup (2, \infty)$ and decreasing on $(-2, 0) \cup (0, 2)$.

b. $f(-2) = -4$ is a relative maximum and $f(2) = 4$ is a relative minimum.

c. Next, we compute $f''(x) = \frac{8}{x^3}$. Since $f''(x) < 0$ for $x < 0$ and $f''(x) > 0$ for $x > 0$, we see that f is concave downward on $(-\infty, 0)$ and concave upward on $(0, \infty)$.

d. There are no inflection points. Note that $x = 0$ is not in the domain of f and is therefore not a candidate for an inflection point.

5. a. $f(x) = \frac{x^2}{x-1}$. $f'(x) = \frac{(x-1)(2x) - x^2(1)}{(x-1)^2} = \frac{x^2-2x}{(x-1)^2} = \frac{x(x-2)}{(x-1)^2}$.

The sign diagram of f'

f' is not defined here

$$+++++\,0---\,\downarrow\,---\,0\,++++++$$

$$0 \qquad 1 \qquad 2 \qquad \longrightarrow x$$

shows that f is increasing on $(-\infty, 0) \cup (2, \infty)$ and decreasing on $(0, 1) \cup (1, 2)$.

b. The results of (a) show that $(0, 0)$ is a relative maximum and $(2, 4)$ is a relative minimum.

c. $f''(x) = \frac{(x-1)^2(2x-2) - x(x-2)2(x-1)}{(x-1)^4} = \frac{2(x-1)[(x-1)^2 - x(x-2)]}{(x-1)^4}$

$$= \frac{2}{(x-1)^3}.$$

Since $f''(x) < 0$ if $x < 1$ and $f''(x) > 0$ if $x > 1$, we see that f is concave downward on $(-\infty, 1)$ and concave upward on $(1, \infty)$.

d. Since $x = 1$ is not in the domain of f, there are no inflection points.

6. a. $f(x) = \sqrt{x-1}$ $f'(x) = \frac{1}{2}(x-1)^{-1/2} = \dfrac{1}{2\sqrt{x-1}}$

Since $f'(x) > 0$ if $x > 1$, we see that f is increasing on $(1,\infty)$.

b. Since there are no critical points in $(1,\infty)$, f has no relative extrema.

c. $f''(x) = -\dfrac{1}{4}(x-1)^{-3/2} = -\dfrac{1}{4(x-1)^{3/2}} < 0$ if $x > 1$, and so f is concave downward on $(1,\infty)$.

d. There are no inflection points since $f''(x) \neq 0$ for all x in $(1,\infty)$.

7. $f(x) = (1 - x)^{1/3}$ $f'(x) = -\dfrac{1}{3}(1-x)^{-2/3} = -\dfrac{1}{3(1-x)^{2/3}}$

The sign diagram for f' is

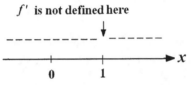

a. f is decreasing on $(-\infty,1) \cup (1,\infty)$.

b. There are no relative extrema.

c. Next, we compute $f''(x) = -\dfrac{2}{9}(1-x)^{-5/3} = -\dfrac{2}{9(1-x)^{5/3}}$.

The sign diagram for f'' is

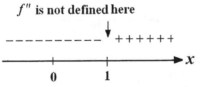

We find f is concave downward on $(-\infty,1)$ and concave upward on $(1,\infty)$.

d. $x = 1$ is a candidate for an inflection point of f. Referring to the sign diagram for f'', we see that $(1,0)$ is an inflection point.

8. $f(x) = x\sqrt{x-1} = x(x-1)^{1/2}$

a. $f'(x) = x(\frac{1}{2})(x-1)^{-1/2} + (x-1)^{1/2} = \frac{1}{2}(x-1)^{-1/2}[x+2(x-1)] = \dfrac{3x-2}{2(x-1)^{1/2}}$

4 Applications of the Derivative

Setting $f'(x) = 0$ gives $x = 2/3$. But, this point lies outside the domain of f which is $[1,\infty)$. Thus, there are no critical points of f. Now, $f'(x) > 0$ for all $x \in (1,\infty)$ so f is increasing there.

b. Since there are no critical points, f has no relative minimum.

c. $\quad f''(x) = \dfrac{1}{2}\left[\dfrac{(x-1)^{1/2}(3)-(3x-2)\frac{1}{2}(x-1)^{-1/2}}{(x-1)}\right]$

$\qquad = \dfrac{1}{2}\left[\dfrac{\frac{1}{2}(x-1)^{-1/2}[6(x-1)-(3x-2)]}{(x-1)}\right] = \dfrac{3x-4}{4(x-1)^{3/2}}.$

Next, $f''(x) = 0$ implies that $x = 4/3$. $f''(x) < 0$ if $x < 4/3$, and $f''(x) > 0$ if $x > 4/3$, so f is concave downward on $(1,\frac{4}{3})$ and concave upward on $(\frac{4}{3},\infty)$.

d. From the results of (c), we conclude that $(\frac{4}{3},\frac{4\sqrt{3}}{9})$ is an inflection point of f

9. a. $f(x) = \dfrac{2x}{x+1}$. $\ f'(x) = \dfrac{(x+1)(2)-2x(1)}{(x+1)^2} = \dfrac{2}{(x+1)^2} > 0$ if $x \neq -1$.

Therefore f is increasing on $(-\infty,-1) \cup (-1,\infty)$.

b. Since there are no critical points, f has no relative extrema.

c. $f''(x) = -4(x+1)^{-3} = -\dfrac{4}{(x+1)^3}$. Since $f''(x) > 0$ if $x < -1$ and $f''(x) < 0$ if $x > -1$,

we see that f is concave upward on $(-\infty,-1)$ and concave downward on $(-1,\infty)$.

d. There are no inflection points since $f''(x) \neq 0$ for all x in the domain of f.

10. $f(x) = -\dfrac{1}{1+x^2}$; $\ f'(x) = \dfrac{2x}{(1+x^2)^2}.$

Setting $f'(x) = 0$ gives $x = 0$ as the only critical point of f. For $x < 0$, $f'(x) < 0$ and for $x > 0$, $f'(x) > 0$. Therefore,

a. f is decreasing on $(-\infty,0)$ and increasing on $(0,\infty)$.

b. f has a relative minimum at $f(0) = -1$.

c. Next, we compute

$$f''(x) = \dfrac{(1+x^2)^2(2)-2x(2)(1+x^2)(2x)}{(1+x^2)^4} = \dfrac{2(1+x^2)(1+x^2-4x^2)}{(1+x^2)^4} = -\dfrac{2(3x^2-1)}{(1+x^2)^3}$$

and we see that $x = \pm 1/\sqrt{3}$ are candidates for inflection points of f The sign diagram for f'' is

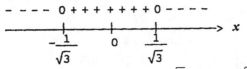

Therefore f is concave downward on $(-\infty, -1/\sqrt{3}) \cup (1/\sqrt{3}, \infty)$ and concave upward on $(-1/\sqrt{3}, 1/\sqrt{3})$.

   d. $(-1/\sqrt{3}, -3/4)$ and $(1/\sqrt{3}, -3/4)$ are inflection points of f

11. $f(x) = x^2 - 5x + 5$

   1. The domain of f is $(-\infty, \infty)$.

   2. Setting $x = 0$ gives 5 as the y-intercept.

   3 $\lim\limits_{x \to -\infty} (x^2 - 5x + 5) = \lim\limits_{x \to \infty} (x^2 - 5x + 5) = \infty$.

   4. There are no asymptotes because f is a quadratic function.

   5. $f'(x) = 2x - 5 = 0$ if $x = 5/2$. The sign diagram

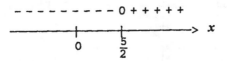

   shows that f is increasing on $(\frac{5}{2}, \infty)$ and decreasing on $(-\infty, \frac{5}{2})$.

   6. The First Derivative Test implies that $(\frac{5}{2}, -\frac{5}{4})$ is a relative minimum.

   7. $f''(x) = 2 > 0$ and so f is concave upward on $(-\infty, \infty)$.

   8. There are no inflection points.

The graph of f follows.

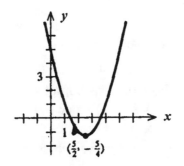

12. $f(x) = -2x^2 - x + 1$

   1. The domain of f is $(-\infty, \infty)$.

   2. Setting $x = 0$ gives 1 as the y-intercept.

         4 Applications of the Derivative

3. $\lim\limits_{x \to -\infty} (-2x^2 - x + 1) = \lim\limits_{x \to \infty} (-2x^2 - x + 1) = -\infty$.

4. There are no asymptotes because f is a polynomial function.

5. $f'(x) = -4x - 1 = 0$ if $x = -1/4$. The sign diagram of f'

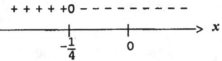

shows that f is increasing on $(-\infty, -\frac{1}{4})$ and decreasing on $(-\frac{1}{4}, \infty)$.

6. The results of (5) show that $(-\frac{1}{4}, \frac{9}{8})$ is a relative maximum.

7. $f''(x) = -4 < 0$ for all x in $(-\infty, \infty)$ and so f is concave downward on $(-\infty, \infty)$.

8. There are no inflection points.

The graph of f follows.

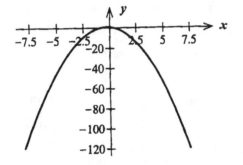

13. $g(x) = 2x^3 - 6x^2 + 6x + 1$.

1. The domain of g is $(-\infty, \infty)$.

2. Setting $x = 0$ gives 1 as the y-intercept.

3. $\lim\limits_{x \to -\infty} g(x) = -\infty$, $\lim\limits_{x \to \infty} g(x) = \infty$.

4. There are no vertical or horizontal asymptotes.

5. $g'(x) = 6x^2 - 12x + 6 = 6(x^2 - 2x + 1) = 6(x - 1)^2$. Since $g'(x) > 0$ for all $x \neq 1$, we see that g is increasing on $(-\infty, 1) \cup (1, \infty)$.

6. $g'(x)$ does not change sign as we move across the critical point $x = 1$, so there is no extremum.

7. $g''(x) = 12x - 12 = 12(x - 1)$. Since $g''(x) < 0$ if $x < 1$ and $g''(x) > 0$ if $x > 1$, we see that g is concave upward on $(1, \infty)$ and concave downward on $(-\infty, 1)$.

8. The point $x = 1$ gives rise to the inflection point $(1, 3)$.

9. The graph of g follows.

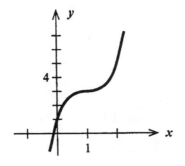

14. $g(x) = \frac{1}{3}x^3 - x^2 + x - 3$

   1. The domain of g is $(-\infty, \infty)$.
   2. Setting $x = 0$ gives -3 as the y-intercept.
   3. $\lim\limits_{x \to -\infty} (\frac{1}{3}x^3 - x^2 + x - 3) = -\infty$ and $\lim\limits_{x \to \infty} (\frac{1}{3}x^3 - x^2 + x - 3) = \infty$
   4. There are no asymptotes because $g(x)$ is a polynomial.
   5. $g'(x) = x^2 - 2x + 1 = (x - 1)^2 = 0$ if $x = 1$, a critical point of g. Observe that $g'(x) > 0$ if $x \neq 1$, and so g is increasing on $(-\infty,1) \cup (1,\infty)$.
   6. The results of (5) show that there are no relative extrema.
   7. $g''(x) = 2x - 2 = 2(x - 1) = 0$ if $x = 1$. Observe that $g''(x) < 0$ if $x < 1$ and $g''(x) > 0$ if $x > 1$ and so g is concave downward on $(-\infty,1)$ and is concave upward on $(1,\infty)$.
   8. The results of (7) show that $(1,-\frac{8}{3})$ is an inflection point.

   The graph of g follows.

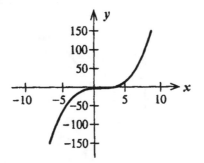

15 $h(x) = x\sqrt{x - 2}$.

   1. The domain of h is $[2,\infty)$.
   2. There are no y-intercepts. Next, setting $y = 0$ gives 2 as the x-intercept.
   3. $\lim\limits_{x \to \infty} x\sqrt{x - 2} = \infty$.

4   Applications of the Derivative

4. There are no asymptotes.

5. $h'(x) = (x-2)^{1/2} + x(\frac{1}{2})(x-2)^{-1/2} = \frac{1}{2}(x-2)^{-1/2}[2(x-2)+x]$

$$= \frac{3x-4}{2\sqrt{x-2}} > 0 \quad \text{on } [2,\infty)$$

and so h is increasing on $[2,\infty)$.

6. Since h has no critical points in $(2,\infty)$, there are no relative extrema.

7. $h''(x) = \frac{1}{2}\left[\dfrac{(x-2)^{1/2}(3)-(3x-4)\frac{1}{2}(x-2)^{-1/2}}{x-2}\right]$

$$= \frac{(x-2)^{-1/2}[6(x-2)-(3x-4)]}{4(x-2)} = \frac{3x-8}{4(x-2)^{3/2}}$$

The sign diagram for h''

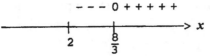

shows that h is concave downward on $(2,\frac{8}{3})$ and concave upward on $(\frac{8}{3},\infty)$

8. The results of (7) tell us that $(\frac{8}{3}, \frac{8\sqrt{6}}{9})$ is an inflection point.

The graph of h follows.

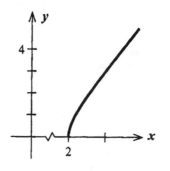

16. $h(x) = \dfrac{2x}{1+x^2}$.

1. The domain of h is $(-\infty, \infty)$.

2. Setting $x = 0$ gives 0 as the y-intercept.

3. $\displaystyle\lim_{x\to-\infty}\frac{2x}{1+x^2} = \lim_{x\to\infty}\frac{2x}{1+x^2} = 0$.

4. The results of (3) tell us that $y = 0$ is a horizontal asymptote.

5. $h'(x) = \dfrac{(1+x^2)(2) - 2x(2x)}{(1+x^2)^2} = \dfrac{2(1-x^2)}{(1+x^2)^2} = \dfrac{2(1-x)(1+x)}{(1+x^2)^2}.$

The sign diagram of h'

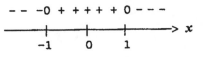

tells us that h is decreasing on $(-\infty,-1) \cup (1,\infty)$ and increasing on $(-1,1)$.

6. The results of (6) show that $(-1,-1)$ is a relative minimum and $(1,1)$ is a relative maximum.

7. $h''(x) = 2\left[\dfrac{(1+x^2)^2(-2x) - (1-x^2)2(1+x^2)(2x)}{(1+x^2)^4}\right]$

$= \dfrac{4x(1+x^2)[-(1+x^2) - 2(1-x^2)]}{(1+x^2)^4} = \dfrac{4x(x^2 - 3)}{(1+x^2)^3}.$

The sign diagram of h''

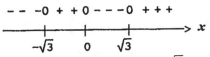

shows that h is concave downward on $(-\infty,-\sqrt{3}) \cup (0,\sqrt{3})$ and concave upward on $(-\sqrt{3},0) \cup (\sqrt{3},\infty)$.

8. The results of (6) also tell us that $(-\sqrt{3},-\frac{\sqrt{3}}{2})$ and $(\sqrt{3},\frac{\sqrt{3}}{2})$ are inflection points. The graph of h follows.

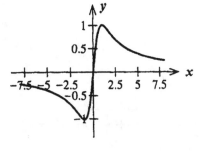

17. $f(x) = \dfrac{x-2}{x+2}$

   1. The domain of f is $(-\infty,-2) \cup (-2,\infty)$.
   2. Setting $x = 0$ gives -1 as the y-intercept. Setting $y = 0$ gives 2 as the x-intercept.

4 Applications of the Derivative

3. $\lim\limits_{x \to -\infty} \dfrac{x-2}{x+2} = \lim\limits_{x \to \infty} \dfrac{x-2}{x+2} = 1.$

4 The results of (3) tell us that $y = 1$ is a horizontal asymptote. Next, observe that the denominator of $f(x)$ is equal to zero at $x = -2$, but its numerator is not equal to zero there. Therefore, $x = -2$ is a vertical asymptote.

5. $\qquad f'(x) = \dfrac{(x+2)(1)-(x-2)(1)}{(x+2)^2} = \dfrac{4}{(x+2)^2}$

The sign diagram of f'

f' is not defined here

$$\downarrow$$
$$+++++\ \blacktriangledown\ ++++++++++++$$

$$\overset{\mid}{\underset{-2}{}} \qquad \overset{\mid}{\underset{0}{}} \longrightarrow x$$

tells us that f is increasing on $(-\infty,-2) \cup (-2,\infty)$.

6. The results of (5) tells us that there are no relative extrema.

7. $f''(x) = -\dfrac{8}{(x+2)^3}$. The sign diagram of f'' follows

f'' is not defined here

$$\downarrow$$
$$+++++\ \blacktriangledown\ -\ -\ -\ -\ -\ -\ -\ -\ -\ -\ -$$

$$\overset{\mid}{\underset{-2}{}} \qquad \overset{\mid}{\underset{0}{}} \longrightarrow x$$

and it shows that f is concave upward on $(-\infty,-2)$ and concave downward on $(-2,\infty)$.

8. There are no inflection points.
The graph of f follows.

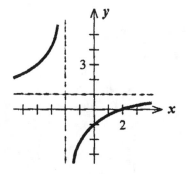

18. $f(x) = x - \dfrac{1}{x}$.

1. The domain of f is $(-\infty, 0) \cup (0, \infty)$.

2. There are no y-intercepts. Next, setting $y = 0$ gives $\dfrac{x^2 - 1}{x} = \dfrac{(x+1)(x-1)}{x} = 0$

and so the x-intercepts are -1 and 1.

3. $\lim\limits_{x \to -\infty} \left(x - \dfrac{1}{x} \right) = -\infty$ and $\lim\limits_{x \to \infty} \left(x - \dfrac{1}{x} \right) = \infty$.

4. There are no horizontal asymptotes. But from $f(x) = \dfrac{x^2 - 1}{x}$

we see that the denominator of $f(x)$ is equal to zero at $x = 0$. Since the numerator is not equal to zero there, we conclude that $x = 0$ is a vertical asymptote.

5 $f'(x) = 1 + \dfrac{1}{x^2} = \dfrac{x^2 + 1}{x^2} > 0$ for all $x \neq 0$. Therefore, f is increasing on

$(-\infty, 0) \cup (0, \infty)$.

6. The results of (5) show that f has no relative extrema.

7. $f''(x) = -\dfrac{2}{x^3}$. Observe that $f''(x) > 0$ if $x < 0$ and $f''(x) < 0$ if $x > 0$. Therefore, f

is concave upward on $(-\infty, 0)$ and concave downward on $(0, \infty)$.

8. There are no inflection points.

The graph of f follows.

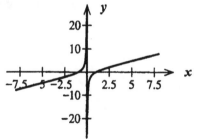

19. $\lim\limits_{x \to -\infty} \dfrac{1}{2x + 3} = \lim\limits_{x \to \infty} \dfrac{1}{2x + 3} = 0$ and so $y = 0$ is a horizontal asymptote. Since the

denominator is equal to zero at $x = -3/2$, but the numerator is not equal to zero there, we see that $x = -3/2$ is a vertical asymptote.

20. $\lim\limits_{x\to-\infty}\dfrac{2x}{x+1}=\lim\limits_{x\to\infty}\dfrac{2x}{x+1}=2$ and so $y=2$ is a horizontal asymptote. Since the denominator is equal to zero at $x=-1$, but the numerator is not equal to zero there, we see that $x=-1$ is a vertical asymptote.

21. $\lim\limits_{x\to-\infty}\dfrac{5x}{x^2-2x-8}=\lim\limits_{x\to\infty}\dfrac{5x}{x^2-2x-8}=0$ and so $y=0$ is a horizontal asymptote. Next, note that the denominator is zero if $x^2-2x-8=(x-4)(x+2)=0$, or $x=-2$ or $x=4$. Since the numerator is not equal to zero at these points, we see that $x=-2$ and $x=4$ are vertical asymptotes.

22. $\lim\limits_{x\to-\infty}\dfrac{x^2+x}{x^2-x}=\lim\limits_{x\to\infty}\dfrac{x^2+x}{x^2-x}=1$, we see that $y=1$ is a horizontal asymptote. Next observe that the denominator is equal to zero at $x=0$ or $x=1$. Since the numerator is not equal to zero at $x=1$, we see that $x=1$ is a vertical asymptote.

23. $f(x)=2x^2+3x-2$; $f'(x)=4x+3$. Setting $f'(x)=0$ gives $x=-3/4$ as a critical point of f. Next, $f''(x)=4>0$ for all x, so f is concave upward on $(-\infty,\infty)$. Therefore, $f(-\tfrac{3}{4})=-\tfrac{25}{8}$ is an absolute minimum of f. There is no absolute maximum.

24. $g(x)=x^{2/3}$. $g'(x)=\tfrac{2}{3}x^{-1/3}=\dfrac{2}{3x^{1/3}}$ and so $x=0$ is a critical point. Since $g'(x)<0$ if $x<0$ and $g'(x)>0$ if $x>0$, we see that $(0,0)$ is a relative minimum. The graph of g shows that $(0,0)$ is an absolute minimum.

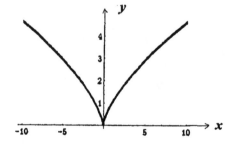

25 $g(t)=\sqrt{25-t^2}=(25-t^2)^{1/2}$. Differentiating $g(t)$, we have

$$g'(t)=\tfrac{1}{2}(25-t^2)^{-1/2}(-2t)=-\dfrac{t}{\sqrt{25-t^2}}$$

Setting $g'(t) = 0$ gives $t = 0$ as a critical point of g. The domain of g is given by solving the inequality $25 - t^2 \geq 0$ or $(5 - t)(5 + t) \geq 0$ which implies that $t \in [-5,5]$. From the table

t	-5	0	5
$g(t)$	0	5	0

we conclude that $g(0) = 5$ is the absolute maximum of g and $g(-5) = 0$ and $g(5) = 0$ is the absolute minimum value of g.

26. $f(x) = \frac{1}{3}x^3 - x^2 + x + 1$; $f'(x) = x^2 - 2x + 1 = (x - 1)^2$. Therefore, $x = 1$ is a critical point of f.

x	0	1	2
$f(x)$	1	4/3	5/3

From the table, we see that $f(0) = 1$ is the absolute minimum value and $f(2) = 5/3$ is the absolute maximum value of f.

27. $h(t) = t^3 - 6t^2$. $h'(t) = 3t^2 - 12t = 3t(t - 4) = 0$ if $t = 0$ or $t = 4$, critical points of h. But only $t = 4$ lies in $(2,5)$.

t	2	4	5
$h(t)$	-16	-32	-25

From the table, we see that there is an absolute minimum at $(4,-32)$ and an absolute maximum at $(2,-16)$.

28. $g(x) = \dfrac{x}{x^2 + 1}$. $g'(x) = \dfrac{(x^2 + 1)(1) - x(2x)}{(x^2 + 1)^2} = \dfrac{1 - x^2}{(x^2 + 1)^2} = 0$, if $x = \pm 1$. But only the critical point $x = 1$ lies in $(0,5)$.

4 *Applications of the Derivative*

x	0	1	5
$g(x)$	0	1/2	5/26

From the table, we see that $(0,0)$ is an absolute minimum and $(1,\frac{1}{2})$ is an absolute maximum.

29. $f(x) = x - \dfrac{1}{x}$ on $[1,3]$. $f'(x) = 1 + \dfrac{1}{x^2}$. Since $f'(x)$ is never zero, f has no critical point.

x	1	3
$f(x)$	0	$\frac{8}{3}$

We see that $f(1) = 0$ is the absolute minimum value and $f(3) = 8/3$ is the absolute maximum value.

30. $h(t) = 8t - \dfrac{1}{t^2}$ on $[1,3]$. $h'(t) = 8 + \dfrac{2}{t^3} = \dfrac{8t^3 + 2}{t^3} = 0$ if $t = -\dfrac{1}{4^{1/3}}$. But this critical point does not lie in $(1,3)$. Furthermore, $t = 0$ is not a critical point of h nor does it lie in $(1,3)$.

t	1	3
$h(t)$	7	$\frac{215}{9}$

From the table, we se that $(1,7)$ gives an absolute minimum of h and $(3, \frac{215}{9})$ gives an absolute maximum of h.

31. $f(s) = s\sqrt{1-s^2}$ on $[-1,1]$. The function f is continuous on $[-1,1]$ and differentiable on $(-1,1)$. Next,

$$f'(s) = (1-s^2)^{1/2} + s(\tfrac{1}{2})(1-s^2)^{-1/2}(-2s) = \frac{1-2s^2}{\sqrt{1-s^2}}.$$

Setting $f'(s) = 0$, we have $s = \pm\sqrt{2}/2$, giving the critical points of f From the table

x	-1	$-\sqrt{2}/2$	$\sqrt{2}/2$	1
$f(x)$	0	-1/2	1/2	0

we see that $f(-\sqrt{2}/2) = -1/2$ is the absolute minimum value and
$f(\sqrt{2}/2) = 1/2$ is the absolute maximum value of f.

32. $f(x) = \dfrac{x^2}{x-1}$. Observe that $\lim\limits_{x \to 1^-} \dfrac{x^2}{x-1} = -\infty$ and $\lim\limits_{x \to 1^+} \dfrac{x^2}{x-1} = \infty$. Therefore, there are
no absolute extrema.

33. We want to maximize $P(x) = -x^2 + 8x + 20$. Now, $P'(x) = -2x + 8 = 0$ if $x = 4$, a
critical point of P. Since $P''(x) = -2 < 0$, the graph of P is concave downward.
Therefore, the critical point $x = 4$ yields an absolute maximum. So, to maximize
profit, the company should spend $4000 on advertising per month.

34. a. $f'(t) = \dfrac{d}{dt}(0.157t^2 + 1.175t + 2.03) = 0.314t + 1 \ 75 > 0$ on (0, 6) and so f is

increasing on (0, 6).

b. $f'(t) = \dfrac{d}{dt}(0.314t + 1.175) = 0.314 > 0$ and so f is concave upward on (0, 6).

c. Online travel spending is increasing at an increasing rate over the years in
question.

35. a. $N'(t) = 16.25t + 24.625$; Since $N'(t) > 0$ for $0 < t < 3$, we see that sales of
camera phones is always increasing between 2002 and 2005
b. $N''(t) = 16.25$; Since $N''(t) > 0$ for $0 < t < 3$, we see that the rate of sales is
increasing between 2002 and 2005.

36. $S(x) = -0.002x^3 + 0.6x^2 + x + 500$; $S'(x) = -0.006x^2 + 1.2x + 1$;
$S''(x) = -0.012x + 1.2$. $x = 100$ is a candidate for an inflection point of S.
The sign diagram for S'' is

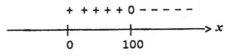

We see that (100,4600) is an inflection point of S.

37 $C(x) = 0.0001x^3 - 0.08x^2 + 40x + 5000;\ C'(x) = 0.0003x^2 - 0.16x + 40;$
$C''(x) = 0.0006x - 0.16.$ Thus, $x = 266.67$ is a candidate for an inflection point of C.
The sign diagram for C'' is

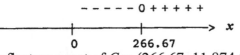

$$- - - - - 0 + + + + +$$

We see that the inflection point of C is (266.67, 11,874.08).

38. a. $I(t) = \dfrac{50t^2 + 600}{t^2 + 10}.$

$I'(t) = \dfrac{(t^2 + 10)(100t) - (50t^2 + 600)(2t)}{(t^2 + 10)^2} = -\dfrac{200t}{(t^2 + 10)^2} < 0$ on (0,10) and so I is

decreasing on (0,10).

b. $I''(t) = -200\left[\dfrac{(t^2 + 10)^2(1) - t(2)(t^2 + 10)(2t)}{(t^2 + 10)^4}\right]$

$= \dfrac{-200(t^2 + 10)[(t^2 + 10) - 4t^2]}{(t^2 + 10)^4} = -\dfrac{200(10 - 3t^2)}{(t^2 + 10)^3}.$

The sign diagram of I'' (for $t > 0$)

$$- - - - \ 0 + + + + + + +$$

shows that I is concave downward on $(0, \sqrt{10/3})$ and concave upward on
$(\sqrt{10/3}, \infty)$.

c.

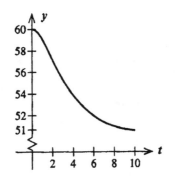

d. The rate of decline in the environmental quality of the wildlife was increasing the first 1.8 years. After that time the rate of decline decreased.

39. The revenue is $R(x) = px = x(-0.0005x^2 + 60) = -0.0005x^3 + 60x$. Therefore, the total profit is $P(x) = R(x) - C(x) = -0.0005x^3 + 0.001x^2 + 42x - 4000$.
$P'(x) = -0.0015x^2 + 0.002x + 42$. Setting $P'(x) = 0$, we have
$3x^2 - 4x - 84,000 = 0$. Solving for x, we find
$$x = \frac{4 \pm \sqrt{16 - 4(3)(84,000)}}{2(3)} = \frac{4 \pm 1004}{6} = 168, \text{ or } -167.$$
We reject the negative root. Next, $P''(x) = -0.003x + 0.002$ and $P''(168) = -0.003(168) + 0.002 = -0.502 < 0$. By the Second Derivative Test, $x = 168$ gives a relative maximum. Therefore, the required level of production is 168 DVDs.

40. $P(x) = -0.04x^2 + 240x - 10,000$. We compute $P'(x) = -0.08x + 240$. Setting $P'(x) = 0$ gives $x = 3000$. The graph of P is a parabola that opens downward and so $x = 3000$ gives rise to the absolute maximum of P. Thus, to maximize profits, the company should produce 3000 cameras per month.

41. a. $C(x) = 0.001x^2 + 100x + 4000$.
$$\overline{C}(x) = \frac{C(x)}{x} = \frac{0.001x^2 + 100x + 4000}{x} = 0.001x + 100 + \frac{4000}{x}$$

b. $\overline{C}'(x) = 0.001 - \dfrac{4000}{x^2} = \dfrac{0.001x^2 - 4000}{x^2} = \dfrac{0.001(x^2 - 4,000,000)}{x^2}$

Setting $\overline{C}'(x) = 0$ gives $x = \pm 2000$. We reject the negative root.

```
- - - - - - 0 + + + + + +
```

```
              +           +           → x
              0         2000
```

The sign diagram of $\overline{C}'$ shows that $x = 2000$ gives rise to a relative minimum of $\overline{C}$
Since $\overline{C}''(x) = \dfrac{8000}{x^3} > 0$ if $x > 0$, we see that $\overline{C}$ is concave upward on $(0,\infty)$. So $x = 2000$ yields an absolute minimum. So the required production level is 2000 units.

42. $N(t) = -2t^3 + 12t^2 + 2t$. We wish to find the inflection point of the function N.
Now, $N'(t) = -6t^2 + 24t + 2$ and $N''(t) = -12t + 24 = -12(t-2)$.
Setting $N''(t) = 0$ gives $t = 2$. Furthermore, $N''(t) > 0$ when $t < 2$ and
$N''(t) < 0$ when $t > 2$. Therefore, $t = 2$ is an inflection point of N. Thus, the
average worker is performing at peak efficiency at 10 A.M.

43. a. $P'(t) = -0.0006t^2 + 0.036t - 0.36$; Setting $P'(t) = 0$ gives
$$-0.0006t^2 + 0.036t - 0.36 = 0$$
$$t^2 - 60t + 600 = 0$$

So
$$t = \frac{60 \pm \sqrt{60^2 - 4(1)(600)}}{2} \approx 12.7 \text{ or } 47.3$$

We reject the root 47.3 because it lies outside [0, 30]. The sign diagram for P'
follows.

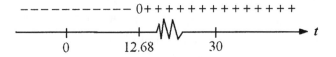

So P is decreasing on (0, 12.7) and increasing on (12.7, 30).
b. The absolute minimum of P occurs at $t = 12.7$ and $P(12.7) \approx 7.9$

44. $R'(x) = k\dfrac{d}{dx}x(M-x) = k\left[(M-x) + x(-1)\right] = k(M-2x)$

Setting $R'(x) = 0$ gives $M - 2x = 0$, or $x = \frac{M}{2}$, a critical point of R. Since
$R''(x) = -2k < 0$, we see that $x = M/2$ affords a maximum; that is R is greatest
when half the population is infected.

45. The volume is $V = f(x) = x(10 - 2x)^2$ cubic units for $0 \le x \le 5$.

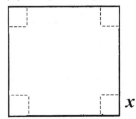

To maximize V, we compute
$$f'(x) = 12x^2 - 80x + 100 = 4(3x^2 - 20x + 25) = 4(3x - 5)(x - 5)$$
Setting $f'(x) = 0$ gives $x = 5/3$, or 5 as critical points of f. From the table

x	0	5/3	5
$f(x)$	0	2000/27 ≈ 74.07	0

We see that the box has a maximum volume of 74.07 cu in.

46. Suppose the radius is r and the height is h. Then the capacity is $\pi r^2 h$ and we want

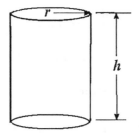

it to be 32π cu ft; that is, $\pi r^2 h = 32\pi$. Let the cost for the side by c/sq ft. Then
the cost of construction is $C = 2\pi rhc + 2(\pi r^2)(2c) = 2\pi crh + 4\pi cr^2$. But
$h = \dfrac{32\pi}{\pi r^2} = \dfrac{32}{r^2}$. Therefore,

$$C = f(r) = -\frac{64\pi c}{r^2} + 8\pi cr = \frac{-64\pi c + 8\pi cr^3}{r^2} = \frac{8\pi c(-8 + r^3)}{r^2}$$

Setting $f'(r) = 0$ gives $r^3 = 8$ or $r = 2$. Next, $f''(r) = \dfrac{128\pi c}{r^3} + 8\pi c$ and so
$f''(2) > 0$. Therefore, $r = 2$ minimizes f. The required dimensions are $r = 2$ and
$h = \dfrac{32}{4} = 8$. That is, its radius is 2 ft and its height is 8 ft.

47. Refer to the following picture.

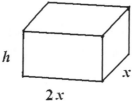

$$C(x) = 30(2)(2x)(x) + 20(2)(2xh + xh) = 120x^2 + 120xh. \quad \text{But } x(2x)h = 4, \text{ or } h = \frac{2}{x^2}.$$

Therefore, $C(x) = 120x^2 + 120x\left(\frac{2}{x^2}\right) = 120x^2 + \frac{240}{x}$

$$C'(x) = 240x - \frac{240}{x^2}.$$

Setting $C'(x) = 0$ gives $240x - \frac{240}{x^2} = 0$, or $x^3 = 1$. Therefore, $x = 1$.

$C''(x) = 240 + \frac{480}{x^3}.$ In particular, $C''(1) > 0$. Therefore, the cost is minimized by

taking $x = 1$. The required dimensions are 1 ft $\times$ 2 ft $\times$ 2 ft.

48. Let x denote the number of cases in each order. Then the average number of cases
of beer in storage during the year is $x/2$. The storage cost is $2(x/2)$, or x dollars.
Next, we see that the number of orders required is $800,000/x$, and so the ordering
cost is

$$\frac{500(800,000)}{x} = \frac{400,000,000}{x}$$

dollars. Thus, the total cost incurred by the company per year is given by

$$C(x) = x + \frac{400,000,000}{x}$$

We want to minimize C in the interval $(0, \infty)$. Now

$$C'(x) = 1 - \frac{400,000,000}{x^2}.$$

Setting $C'(x) = 0$ gives $x^2 = 400,000,000$, or $x = 20,000$ (we reject $x = -20,000$).

Next, $C''(x) = \frac{800,000,000}{x^3} > 0$ for all x, so C is concave upward. Thus,

$x = 20,000$ gives rise to the absolute minimum of C. Thus, the company should
order 20,000 cases of beer per order.

49. $f(x) = ax^2 + bx + c$; $f'(x) = 2ax + b = 2a\left(x + \frac{b}{2a}\right)$. Then f' is continuous everywhere and has a zero at $x = -\frac{b}{2a}$. The sign diagram of f' is

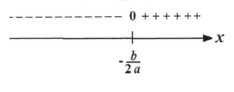

when $a > 0$, or

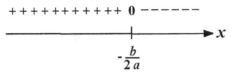

when $a < 0$. Therefore, if $a > 0$, f is decreasing on $(-\infty, -\frac{b}{2a})$ and increasing on $(-\frac{b}{2a}, \infty)$, and if $a < 0$, f is increasing on $(-\infty, -\frac{b}{2a})$ and decreasing on $(-\frac{b}{2a}, \infty)$.

50. a. $f'(x) = 3x^2$ if $x \neq 0$. We see that $f'(x) > 0$ for $x < 0$ as well as for $x > 0$. In other words $f'(x)$ does not change sign.
b. $f(0) = 2$ and is larger than $f(x)$ for x near $x = 0$. Therefore, f has a relative maximum at $x = 0$. This does not contradict the First Derivative Test because f is not continuous at $x = 0$.

CHAPTER 4, BEFORE MOVING ON, page 330

1. $f'(x) = \dfrac{(1-x)(2x) - x^2(-1)}{(1-x)^2} = \dfrac{2x - 2x^2 + x^2}{(1-x)^2} = \dfrac{x(2-x)}{(1-x)^2}$; f' is not defined at $= 1$ and has zeros at $x = 0$ and $x = 2$. The sign diagram of f follows:

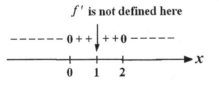

We see that f is decreasing on $(-\infty, 0) \cup (2, \infty)$ and increasing on $(0,1) \cup (1,2)$.

2. $f'(x) = 4x - 4x^{-2/3} = 4x^{-2/3}(x^{5/3} - 1) = \dfrac{4(x^{5/3} - 1)}{x^{2/3}}$; f' is discontinuous at $x = 0$ and has a zero where $x^{5/3} = 1$ or $x = 1$. Therefore, f has critical numbers at 0 and 1. The sign diagram for f' follows:

4 Applications of the Derivative

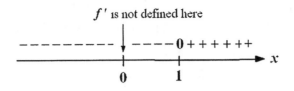

f' is not defined here

We see that $x = 1$ gives a relative minimum. Since $f(1) = 2 - 12 = -10$, the relative minimum is $(1,-10)$. There are no relative maxima.

3. $f'(x) = x^2 - \frac{1}{2}x - \frac{1}{2}$; $f''(x) = 2x - \frac{1}{2}$; $f''(x) = 0$ gives $x = \frac{1}{4}$. The sign diagram of f'' follows:

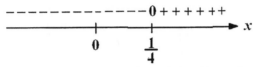

We see that f is concave downward on $(-\infty, \frac{1}{4})$ and concave upward on $(\frac{1}{4}, \infty)$. Since

$$f(\tfrac{1}{4}) = \tfrac{1}{3}(\tfrac{1}{4})^3 - \tfrac{1}{4}(\tfrac{1}{4})^2 - \tfrac{1}{2}(\tfrac{1}{4}) + 1 = \frac{83}{96}$$

the inflection point is $(\frac{1}{4}, \frac{83}{96})$

4. $f(x) = 2x^3 - 9x^2 + 12x - 1$
   1. Domain of f is $(-\infty, \infty)$.
   2. Setting $y = f(x) = 0$ gives -1 as the y-intercept of f.
   3. $\lim\limits_{x \to -\infty} f(x) = -\infty$ and $\lim\limits_{x \to \infty} f(x) = \infty$.
   4. There are no asymptotes.
   5. $f'(x) = 6x^2 - 18x + 12 = 6(x^2 - 3x + 2) = 6(x - 2)(x - 1)$. The sign diagram of f'

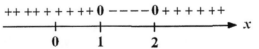

   shows that f is increasing on $(-\infty, 1) \cup (2, \infty)$ and decreasing on $(1, 2)$.
   6. We see that $(1, 4)$ is a relative maximum and $(2, 3)$ is a relative minimum.
   7. $f''(x) = 12x - 18 = 6(2x - 3)$. The sign diagram of f'' is

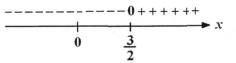

and shows that f is concave downward on $(-\infty, \frac{3}{2})$ and concave upward on $(\frac{3}{2}, \infty)$.

8. $f(\frac{3}{2}) = 2(\frac{3}{2})^3 - 9(\frac{3}{2})^2 + 12(\frac{3}{2}) - 1 = \frac{7}{2}$; So $(\frac{3}{2}, \frac{7}{2})$ is an inflection point of f

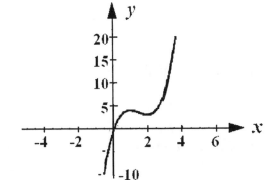

5. f is continuous on a closed interval [-2, 3]. $f'(x) = 6x^2 + 6x = 6x(x+1)$. The critical numbers of f are -1 and 0.

x	-2	-1	0	3
y	-5	0	-1	80

The absolute maximum value of f is 80; the absolute minimum value is -5.

6. The amount of material used (the surface area) is

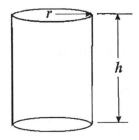

$A = \pi r^2 + 2\pi rh$. But $V = \pi r^2 h = 1$ and so $h = \dfrac{1}{\pi r^2}$. Therefore,

4 Applications of the Derivative

$$A = \pi r^2 + 2\pi r h\left(\frac{1}{\pi r^2}\right) = \pi r^2 + \frac{2}{r}; \quad A' = 2\pi r - \frac{2}{r^2} = 0 \text{ implies}$$

$$2\pi r = \frac{2}{r^2}, \ r^3 = \frac{2}{r^2}, \ r^3 = \frac{1}{\pi}, \text{ or } r = \frac{1}{\sqrt[3]{\pi}}; \quad \text{Since } A'' = 2\pi + \frac{4}{r^3} > 0 \text{ for } r > 0, \text{ we see}$$

that $r = \dfrac{1}{\sqrt[3]{\pi}}$ does give an absolute maximum. Also

$$h = \frac{1}{\pi r^2} = \frac{1}{\pi} \pi^{2/3} = \frac{1}{\pi^{1/3}} = \frac{1}{\sqrt[3]{\pi}}$$

Therefore both the radius and height should be $\dfrac{1}{\sqrt[3]{\pi}}$ ft.

EXPLORE & DISCUSS

Page 250
1. This is false. Consider $f(x) = x^3$ which is continuous at c. Now, f is increasing at $x = 0$ because if we pick any interval containing c, then f is increasing on that interval. This fact can be established rigorously, but we will accept a "geometric proof." (Just make a sketch of the graph of f.) But $f'(x) = 3x^2$, so that $f'(c) = f'(0) = 0$.

Page 252
1. $P'(x) = R'(x) - C'(x)$
2. a. P is increasing at $x = a$ if $P'(a) = R'(a) - C'(a) > 0$, or $R'(a) > C'(a)$.
   b. P is decreasing at $x = a$ if $R'(a) < C'(a)$. c. P is constant at $x = a$ if $R'(a) = C'(a)$.
3. a. The profit is increasing when the level of production is a if the revenue is increasing faster than the cost at a.
   b. The profit is decreasing when the level of production is a if the revenue is decreasing faster than the cost at a.
   c. The profit is flat if the revenue is increasing at the same pace as the cost.

Page 256

1. $\overline{C}'(x) = \dfrac{xC'(x) - C(x)}{x^2} = \dfrac{C'(x) - \dfrac{C(x)}{x}}{x} = \dfrac{C'(x) - \overline{C}(x)}{x}.$

2. Since $x > 0$, we see that $C'(x) < \overline{C}(x)$ implies $\overline{C}'(x) < 0$, and so $\overline{C}'(x) < 0$, and so $\overline{C}$ is decreasing for values of x satisfying the condition $C'(x) < \overline{C}(x)$. Similarly, we see that $\overline{C}$ is increasing for values of x for which $C'(x) > \overline{C}(x)$. Finally, $\overline{C}$ is constant for values of x satisfying $C'(x) = \overline{C}(x)$.

3. The results of (b) tell us that the marginal average cost is (a) decreasing for values of x for which the marginal cost is less than the average cost, (b) increasing for values of x for which the marginal cost is greater than the average cost, and (c) constant for values of x for which the marginal cost is equal to the average cost.

Page 272

1. No, consider $f(x) = x^3$. Then f has an inflection point at $(0,0)$. But f has no extremum at $x = 0$.

2. True. Consider $f(x) = ax^3 + bx^2 + cx + d$ $(a \neq 0)$. Without loss of generality, assume $a > 0$. Thus $f'(x) = 3ax^2 + 2bx + c$; $f''(x) = 6ax + 2b = 6a\left(x + \dfrac{b}{3a}\right)$

   Observe that $f''(0) = 0$ implies $x = -\dfrac{b}{3a}$. The sign diagram for f'' is either

   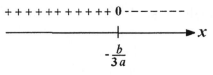

   if $b > 0$, or

   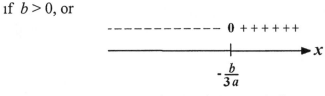

   if $b < 0$. Therefore, $\left(-\frac{b}{3a}, f\left(-\frac{b}{3a}\right)\right)$ is an inflection point of f, and the only one.

Page 275

1. First of all, $f'(c) = 0$ tells us that $x = c$ is a critical number of f. Since $f''(x) > 0$ for

all x in (a, b), we see that $f''(c) > 0$, and so by the Second Derivative Test, the point $(c, f(c))$ is a relative minimum of f. If Property 1 is replaced by the property that $f''(x) < 0$ for all x in (a,b), then the Second Derivative Test implies that $(c, f(c))$ is a relative maximum of f.

Page 291

1. a. On $(0,1)$: $f'(t) > 0$ and $f''(t) > 0$; On $(1,2)$: $f'(t) > 0$ and $f''(t) < 0$
    On $(2,3)$: $f'(t) < 0$ and $f''(t) < 0$.
    b.

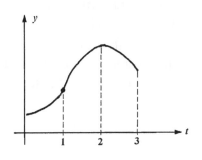

Page 304

1. At the level of production x_0, $P'(x_0) = 0$. This means $P'(x_0) = R'(x_0) - C'(x_0) = 0$ or $R'(x_0) = C'(x_0)$. Furthermore, since x_0 gives a relative maximum, $P''(x_0) < 0$ and this translates into the condition $P''(x_0) = R''(x_0) - C''(x_0) < 0$ or $R''(x_0) < C''(x_0)$.

2. The first condition $R''(x_0) > C''(x_0) R'(x_0) = C'(x_0)$ says that at the maximal level of production, the marginal revenue equals the marginal cost. This makes sense because at that level of production, we can expect that the rate of change of revenue should not exceed or be smaller than the rate of growth of the total cost. The second condition says that at the maximal level of production, the rate of change of the marginal revenue, should be smaller than that of the marginal cost function. This makes sense because, assuming the contrary, $R'(x_0) > C''(x_0)$, we see that the level of production can be increased to increase the profit since the rate of the rate of change of revenue is greater than the corresponding quantity associated with the cost.

Page 305

1. The average cost is $\overline{C}(x) = \dfrac{C(x)}{x}$. Then $\overline{C}'(x) = \dfrac{xC'(x) - C(x)}{x^2}$. Setting $\overline{C}'(x) = 0$ gives $x = \dfrac{C(x)}{C'(x)}$ as the sole critical number of $\overline{C}$. Next,

$$\overline{C}''(x) = \frac{x^2[C'(x) + xC''(x) - C'(x)] - [xC'(x) - C(x)]2x}{x^4}$$

$$= \frac{C''(x)}{x} - \frac{2}{x^3}[xC'(x) - C(x)].$$

2. At the critical number, $xC'(x) - C(x) = 0$, and so $\overline{C}''(x) = \frac{C''(x)}{x} > 0$ since C is concave upward. Therefore $x = C(x)/C'(x)$ does give the minimum value. Rewriting, we have $C'(x) = \frac{C(x)}{x} = \overline{C}(x)$ and the proof is complete.

EXPLORING WITH TECHNOLOGY QUESTIONS

Page 250
1.

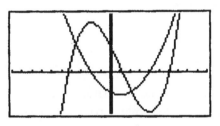

2. Yes. Because f is increasing over an interval where $f'(x) > 0$ and decreasing over an interval where $f'(x) < 0$.
Page 252

1.

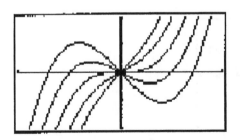

2. f is increasing on $(-\infty, \infty)$ if and only if $a = 0$.

3. If $a = 0$, then $f(x) = x^3$ Since $f'(x) = 3x^2 > 0$ for all x in $(-\infty, 0)$ and $(0, \infty)$, we see that f is increasing on $(-\infty, \infty)$. Next, if $a \neq 0$, without loss of generality, suppose

$a > 0$. Then $f'(x) = 3x^2 - a$ giving $x = -\sqrt{\frac{a}{3}}$ and $x = \sqrt{\frac{a}{3}}$ as critical numberss. The sign diagram of f' follows.

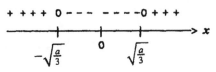

This shows that f has relative extrema at two points. The proof is similar if $a < 0$. Thus f is increasing only if $a = 0$.

Page 257
1 The graphs of f and f' are shown in the following figure.

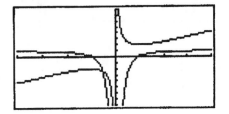

2. From the graph of f', we see that $x = \pm 1$ are critical numbers of f. The sign of $f'(x)$ changes from positive to negative as we move across $x = -1$ showing that the point $(-1,-2)$ is a relative maximum. The sign of $f'(x)$ changes from negative to positive as we move across $x = 1$ and so $(1,2)$ is a relative minimum. These conclusions are the same as those arrived at in Example 8, as expected.

Page 269
1.   2. Yes.

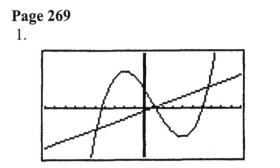

1.   2.

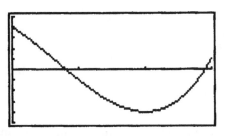   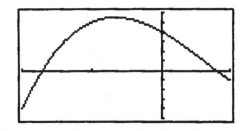

$f'(x) = 3x^2 - 4x - 4 = (3x + 2)(x - 2) = 0$ gives $x = -\frac{2}{3}$, or 2. The number $-\frac{2}{3}$ lies in [-2,1] and is a critical number of f. From the table

x	-2	$-\frac{3}{2}$	1
$f(x)$	-4	$\frac{17}{8}$	-1

we see that the absolute minimum occurs at (-2,-4) and the absolute maximum occurs at $(-\frac{3}{2}, \frac{17}{8})$.

Page 306
1.

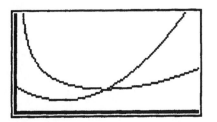

2. The point of intersection of the graphs of $\overline{C}$ and C' is (500,35). This is as predicted by the Explore & Discuss question on page 305.

1.

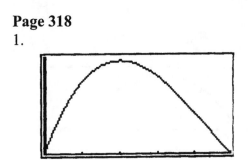

2.   The value of $f(x)$ is zero at $x = 0$, increases to a maximum value somewhere in the interval $[0,5]$, then decreases until it again takes on the value zero at $x = 5$ If $x = 0$, the volume of the box, $f(0)$, is zero because there is really no box for $x = 0$. If $x = 5$, we have cut clear across the cardboard and once again there is no box so the volume is zero. For $0 < x < 5$, a square is removed from each corner and the volume of the resulting box increases, then decreases, as the length of the square increases. So there is a definite size for the squares to be removed so that the volume of the resulting box is the largest possible.

CHAPTER 5

5.1 CONCEPT QUESTIONS, page 335

1. $f(x) = b^x$; $a < b$, $b \neq 1$. Its domain is $(-\infty, \infty)$.
2. a. Domain is $(-\infty, \infty)$; Range is $(0, \infty)$. b. Its y-intercept is 1.
   b. It is continuous on $(-\infty, \infty)$.
   c. It is increasing on $(-\infty, \infty)$ if $b > 1$ and decreasing on $(-\infty, \infty)$ if $b < 1$.

EXERCISES 5.1, page 335

1. a. $4^{-3} \times 4^5 = 4^{-3+5} = 4^2 = 16$

   b. $3^{-3} \times 3^6 = 3^{6-3} = 3^3 = 27$.

2. a. $(2^{-1})^3 = 2^{-3} = \dfrac{1}{2^3} = \dfrac{1}{8}$.

   b. $(3^{-2})^3 = 3^{-6} = \dfrac{1}{3^6} = \dfrac{1}{729}$

3. a. $9(9)^{-1/2} = \dfrac{9}{9^{1/2}} = \dfrac{9}{3} = 3$.

   b. $5(5)^{-1/2} = 5^{1/2} = \sqrt{5}$

4. a. $[(-\frac{1}{2})^3]^{-2} = (-\frac{1}{2})^{-6} = \dfrac{(-1)^{-6}}{2^{-6}} = 2^6 = 64$.

   b. $[(-\frac{1}{3})^2]^{-3} = (-\frac{1}{3})^{-6} = \dfrac{(-1)^{-6}}{3^{-6}} = 3^6 = 729$.

5. a. $\dfrac{(-3)^4(-3)^5}{(-3)^8} = (-3)^{4+5-8} = (-3)^1 = -3$.   b. $\dfrac{(2^{-4})(2^6)}{2^{-1}} = 2^{-4+6+1} = 2^3 = 8$.

6. a. $3^{1/4} \times 9^{-5/8} = 3^{1/4}(3^2)^{-5/8} = 3^{1/4} \times 3^{-5/4} = 3^{(1/4)-(5/4)} = 3^{-1} = \frac{1}{3}$.

   b. $2^{3/4} \times 4^{-3/2} = 2^{3/4}(2^2)^{-3/2} = 2^{3/4} \times 2^{-3} = 2^{(3/4)-3} = 2^{-9/4} = \dfrac{1}{2^{9/4}}$.

7. a. $\dfrac{5^{3.3} \cdot 5^{-1.6}}{5^{-0.3}} = \dfrac{5^{3.3-1.6}}{5^{-0.3}} = 5^{1.7+(0.3)} = 5^2 = 25$

   b. $\dfrac{4^{2.7} \cdot 4^{-1.3}}{4^{-0.4}} = 4^{2.7-1.3+0.4} = 4^{1.8} \approx 12.1257$.

8. a. $\left(\dfrac{1}{16}\right)^{-1/4}\left(\dfrac{27}{64}\right)^{-1/3} = (16)^{1/4}\left(\dfrac{64}{27}\right)^{1/3} = 2\left(\dfrac{4}{3}\right) = \dfrac{8}{3}$.

b. $\left(\dfrac{8}{27}\right)^{-1/3}\left(\dfrac{81}{256}\right)^{-1/4} = \left(\dfrac{27}{8}\right)^{1/3}\left(\dfrac{256}{81}\right)^{1/4} = \dfrac{3}{2}\cdot\dfrac{4}{3} = 2.$

9. a. $(64x^9)^{1/3} = 64^{1/3}(x^{9/3}) = 4x^3.$

    b. $(25x^3y^4)^{1/2} = 25^{1/2}(x^{3/2})(y^{4/2}) = 5x^{3/2}y^2 = 5xy^2\sqrt{x}$

10. a. $(2x^3)(-4x^{-2}) = -8x^{3-2} = -8x$ b. $(4x^{-2})(-3x^5) = -12x^{-2+5} = -12x^3$

11. a. $\dfrac{6a^{-5}}{3a^{-3}} = 2a^{-5+3} = 2a^{-2} = \dfrac{2}{a^2}.$ b. $\dfrac{4b^{-4}}{12b^{-6}} = \dfrac{1}{3}b^{-4+6} = \dfrac{1}{3}b^2.$

12. a. $y^{-3/2}y^{5/3} = y^{(-3/2)+(5/3)} = y^{1/6}$ b. $x^{-3/5}x^{8/3} = x^{(-3/5)+(8/3)} = x^{31/15}.$

13. a. $(2x^3y^2)^3 = 2^3 \times x^{3(3)} \times y^{2(3)} = 8x^9y^6.$

    b. $(4x^2y^2z^3)^2 = 4^2 \times x^{2(2)} \times y^{2(2)} \times z^{3(2)} = 16x^4y^4z^6.$

14. a. $(x^{r/s})^{s/r} = x^{(r/s)(s/r)} = x$ b. $(x^{-b/a})^{-a/b} = x^{(-b/a)(-a/b)} = x.$

15. a. $\dfrac{5^0}{(2^{-3}x^{-3}y^2)^2} = \dfrac{1}{2^{-3(2)}x^{-3(2)}y^{2(2)}} = \dfrac{2^6x^6}{y^4} = \dfrac{64x^6}{y^4}.$

    b. $\dfrac{(x+y)(x-y)}{(x-y)^0} = (x+y)(x-y).$

16. a. $\dfrac{(a^m \cdot a^{-n})^{-2}}{(a^{m+n})^2} = \dfrac{a^{-2m} \cdot a^{2n}}{a^{2(m+n)}} = a^{-2m+2n-2(m+n)} = \dfrac{1}{a^{4m}}.$

    b. $\left(\dfrac{x^{2n-2}y^{2n}}{x^{5n+1}y^{-n}}\right)^{1/3} = \left(\dfrac{y^{3n}}{x^{3n+3}}\right)^{1/3} = \dfrac{y^n}{x^{n+1}}.$

17 $6^{2x} = 6^4$ if and only if $2x = 4$ or $x = 2.$ 18. $5^{-x} = 5^3$ if and only if $-x = 3$ or $x = -3.$

19. $3^{3x-4} = 3^5$ if and only if $3x - 4 = 5$, $3x = 9$, or $x = 3.$

20. $10^{2x-1} = 10^{x+3}$ if and only if $2x - 1 = x + 3$, or $x = 4.$

21. $(2.1)^{x+2} = (2.1)^5$ if and only if $x + 2 = 5$, or $x = 3.$

22. $(-1.3)^{x-2} = (-1.3)^{2x+1}$ if and only if $x - 2 = 2x + 1$, or $x = -3$.

23. $8^x = (\frac{1}{32})^{x-2}$, $(2^3)^x = (32)^{2-x} = (2^5)^{2-x}$, so $2^{3x} = 2^{5(2-x)}$, $3x = 10 - 5x$, $8x = 10$, or $x = 5/4$.

24. $3^{x-x^2} = \frac{1}{9^x} = (3^2)^{-x} = 3^{-2x}$ This is true if and only if $x - x^2 = -2x$, $x^2 - 3x = x(x - 3) = 0$, so $x = 0$ or 3.

25. Let $y = 3^x$, then the given equation is equivalent to
$$y^2 - 12y + 27 = 0$$
$$(y - 9)(y - 3) = 0$$
giving $y = 3$ or 9. So $3^x = 3$ or $3^x = 9$, and therefore, $x = 1$ or $x = 2$.

26. $2^{2x} - 4 \cdot 2^x + 4 = 0$, $(2^x)^2 - 4(2^x) + 4 = 0$. Let $y = 2^x$, then we have
$y^2 - 4y + 4 = (y - 2)^2 = 0$, or $y = 2$. So we have $2^x = 2$ or $x = 1$.

27 $y = 2^x, y = 3^x$, and $y = 4^x$

28. $y = (\frac{1}{2})^x$, $y = (\frac{1}{3})^x$, and $y = (\frac{1}{4})^x$.

29. $y = 2^{-x}, y = 3^{-x}$, and $y = 4^{-x}$

30. $y = 4^{0.5x}$ and $y = 4^{-0.5x}$

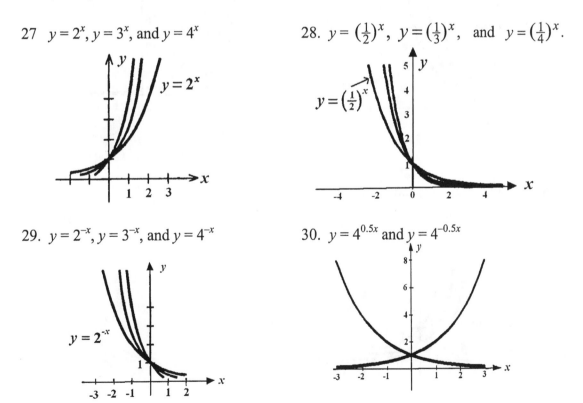

31. $y = 4^{0.5x}$, $y = 4x$, and $y = 4^{2x}$

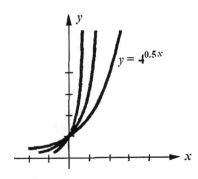

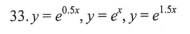

32. $y = e^x$, $y = 2e^x$, and $y = 3e^x$

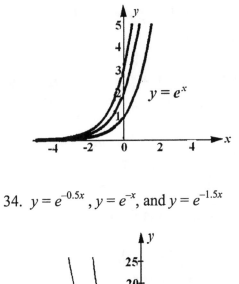

33. $y = e^{0.5x}$, $y = e^x$, $y = e^{1.5x}$

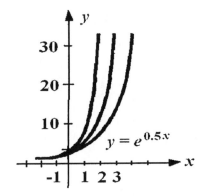

34. $y = e^{-0.5x}$, $y = e^{-x}$, and $y = e^{-1.5x}$

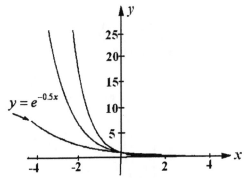

35. $y = 0.5e^{-x}$, $y = e^{-x}$, and $y = 2e^{-x}$

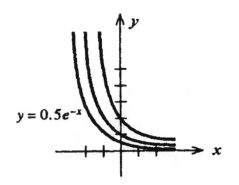

36. $y = 1 - e^{-x}$ and $y = 1 - e^{-0.5x}$

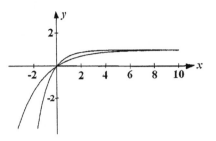

37 a. $R(t) = 26.3e^{-0.016t}$; In 1982, the rate was $R(0) = 26.3\%$. In 1986, the rate was $R(4) = 24.7\%$. In 1994, the rate was $R(12) = 21.7\%$. In 2000, the rate was $R(18) = 19.7\%$.

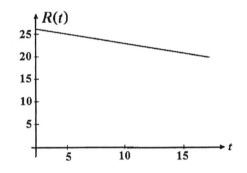

38. a. $N(t) = 0.6e^{0.17t}$; The number installed in 2000 was $N(0) = 0.6$, or 0.6 million. The number projected to be installed in 2005 is $N(5) = 0.6e^{0.17(5)} = 1.40379$, or 1.4 million.

b.

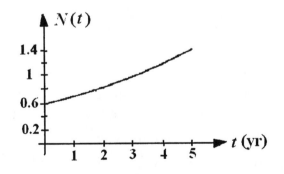

39. a.

Year	0	1	2	3	4	5
Number (billions)	0.45	0.80	1.41	2.49	4.39	7 76

b.

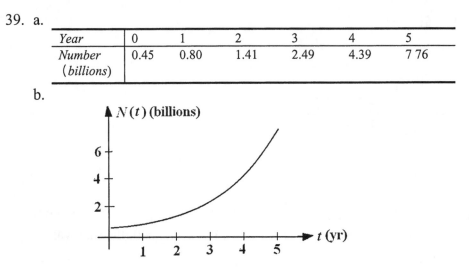

40. a. $P(t) = 86.9e^{-0.05t}$; The percent in 1970 was $P(0) = 86.9$. The percent in 1980 was $P(1) = 82.7$. The percent in 1990 was $P(2) = 78.6$. The percent in 2000 was $P(3) = 74.8$.

b.

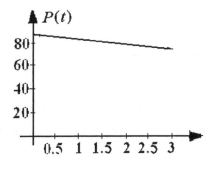

41. $N(t) = \dfrac{35.5}{1+6.89e^{-0.8674t}}$; $\quad N(6) = \dfrac{35.5}{1+6.89e^{-0.8674(6)}} \approx 34.2056$, or 34.21 million.

42. a. The initial concentration is given by $C(0) = 0.3(0) - 18(1 - e^{-(0)/60})$, or 0 g/cm^3

   b. The concentration after 10 seconds is given by
   $$C(10) = 0.3(10) - 18(1 - e^{-(10)/60}) = 0.23667, \text{ or } 0.2367 \text{ g/cm}^3.$$

   c. The concentration after 30 seconds is given by
   $$C(30) = 18e^{-(30)/60} - 12e^{-(30-20)/60} = 0.75977, \text{ or } 0.7598 \text{ g/cm}^3.$$

   d. The concentration of the drug in the long run is given by

$$\lim_{t \to \infty} C(t) = \lim_{t \to \infty}[18e^{-t/60} - 12e^{-\frac{t-20}{60}}] = 0$$

43. a. The concentration initially is given by

$$N(0) = 0.08 + 0.12(1 - e^{-0.02(0)}) = 0.08 \text{ , or } 0.08 \text{ g/cm}^3.$$

b. The concentration after 20 seconds is given by

$$N(20) = 0.08 + 0.12(1 - e^{-0.02(20)}) = 0.11956, \text{ or } 0.1196 \text{ g/cm}^3.$$

c. The concentration in the long run is given by

$$\lim_{t \to \infty} x(t) = \lim_{t \to \infty}[0.08 + 0.12(1 - e^{-0.02t})] = 0.2, \text{ or } 0.2 \text{ g/cm}^3.$$

d.

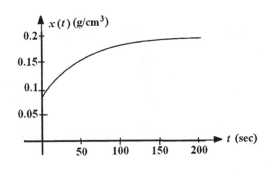

44. a. The amount of drug in Jane's body immediately after the second dosage is

$$A(1) = 100(1 + e^{1.4})e^{-1.4(1)} = 100(e^{-1.4} + 1), \text{ or } 124.66 \text{ mg.}$$

b. The amount of drug in Jane's body after 2 days is

$$A(2) = 100(1 + e^{1.4})e^{-1.4(2)} = 30.741, \text{ or } 30.74 \text{ mg.}$$

c. The amount of drug in Jane's body in the long run is given by

$$\lim_{t \to \infty} A(t) = \lim_{t \to \infty}[100(1 + e^{1.4})e^{-1.4t}] = 0, \text{ or } 0 \text{ mg.}$$

d.

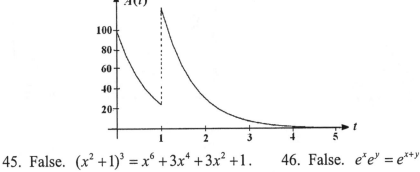

45. False. $(x^2 + 1)^3 = x^6 + 3x^4 + 3x^2 + 1$.   46. False. $e^x e^y = e^{x+y}$

47. True. $f(x) = e^x$ is an increasing function and so if $x < y$, then $f(x) < f(y)$, or $e^x < e^y$.

48. True. If $0 < b < 1$, then $f(x) = b^x$ is a decreasing function of x and so if $x < y$, then $f(x) > f(y)$ or $b^x > b^y$.

USING TECHNOLOGY EXERCISES 5.1, page 338

1.

2.

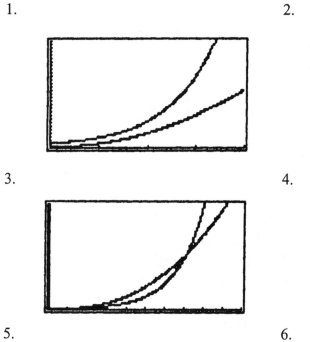

3.

4.

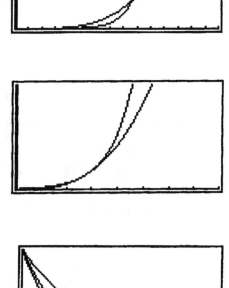

5.

6.

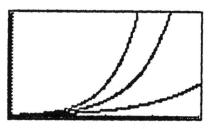

7.

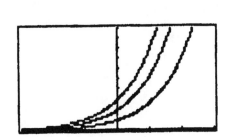

8.

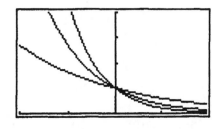

9.

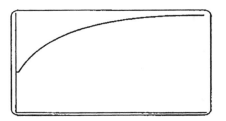

10.

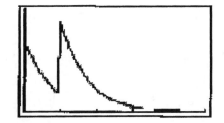

11. a.

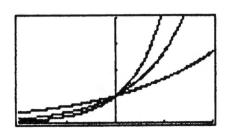

12. a.

b. 0.08 g/cm^3 c. 0.12 g/cm^3
d. 0.2 g/cm^3

13. a.

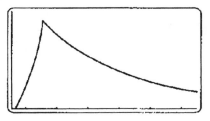

b. 20 sec.   c. 35 1 sec

5.2 CONCEPT QUESTIONS, page 345

1. a. $y = \log_b x$ if and only if $x = b^y$; $b > 0$, $b \neq 1$; Its domain is $(0, \infty)$.
2. a. Domain is $(0, \infty)$, Range is $(-\infty, \infty)$.
   b. Its x-intercept is 1.
   c. It is continuous on $(0, \infty)$.
   d. It is increasing on $(0, \infty)$ if $b > 1$ and decreasing on $(0, \infty)$ if $b < 1$.
3. a. $e^{\ln x} = x$ b. $\ln e^x = x$

EXERCISES 5.2 , page 345

1. $\log_2 64 = 6$ 2. $\log_3 243 = 5$ 3. $\log_3 \dfrac{1}{9} = -2$ 4. $\log_5 \dfrac{1}{125} = -3$

5. $\log_{1/3} \dfrac{1}{3} = 1$ 6. $\log_{1/2} 16 = -4$ 7. $\log_{32} 8 = \dfrac{3}{5}$ 8. $\log_{81} 27 = \dfrac{3}{4}$

9. $\log_{10} 0.001 = -3$ 10. $\log_{16} 0.5 = -\dfrac{1}{4}$.

11. $\log 12 = \log 4 \times 3 = \log 4 + \log 3 = 0.6021 + 0.4771 = 1.0792$.

12. $\log \frac{3}{4} = \log 3 - \log 4 = 0.4771 - 0.6021 = -0.125$.

13. $\log 16 = \log 4^2 = 2 \log 4 = 2(0.6021) = 1.2042$.

14. $\log \sqrt{3} = \log 3^{1/2} = \frac{1}{2} \log 3 = \frac{1}{2}(0.4771) = 0.2386$.

15. $\log 48 = \log 3 \times 4^2 = \log 3 + 2 \log 4 = 0.4771 + 2(0.6021) = 1.6813$

16. $\log \frac{1}{300} = \log 1 - \log 300 = - \log 300 = - \log (3 \times 100)$
    $= -(\log 3 + \log 100) = - (\log 3 + 2 \log 10) = - (\log 3 + 2) = -2.4771$.

17. $2 \ln a + 3 \ln b = \ln a^2 b^3$.   18. $\dfrac{1}{2} \ln x + 2 \ln y - 3 \ln z = \ln \dfrac{x^{1/2} y^2}{3z} = \ln \dfrac{\sqrt{x} y^2}{3z}$

19. $\ln 3 + \dfrac{1}{2} \ln x + \ln y - \dfrac{1}{3} \ln z = \ln \dfrac{3\sqrt{x} y}{\sqrt[3]{z}}$

20. $\ln 2 + \dfrac{1}{2}\ln(x+1) - 2\ln(1+\sqrt{x}) = \ln\dfrac{2(x+1)^{1/2}}{(1+\sqrt{x})^2}$

21. $\log x(x+1)^4 = \log x + \log (x+1)^4 = \log x + 4\log (x+1)$.

22. $\log x(x^2+1)^{-1/2} = \log x - \frac{1}{2}\log (x^2+1)$.

23. $\log \dfrac{\sqrt{x+1}}{x^2+1} = \log (x+1)^{1/2} - \log(x^2+1) = \frac{1}{2}\log (x+1) - \log (x^2+1)$

24. $\ln \dfrac{e^x}{1+e^x} = x - \ln (1+e^x)$.

25. $\ln xe^{-x^2} = \ln x - x^2$.

26. $\ln x(x+1)(x+2) = \ln x + \ln (x+1) + \ln (x+2)$.

27. $\ln \left(\dfrac{x^{1/2}}{x^2\sqrt{1+x^2}}\right) = \ln x^{1/2} - \ln x^2 - \ln (1+x^2)^{1/2}$

$\qquad\qquad = \frac{1}{2}\ln x - 2\ln x - \frac{1}{2}\ln (1+x^2) = -\frac{3}{2}\ln x - \frac{1}{2}\ln (1+x^2)$.

28. $\ln \dfrac{x^2}{\sqrt{x}(1+x)^2} = 2\ln x - \frac{1}{2}\ln x - 2\ln (1+x) = \frac{3}{2}\ln x - 2\ln (1+x)$.

29. $y = \log_3 x$ 30. $y = \log_{1/3} x$

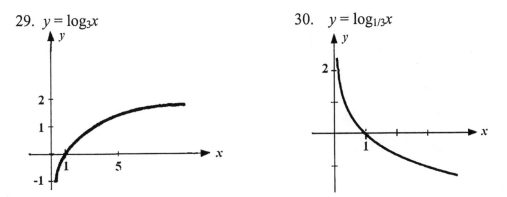

31. $y = \ln 2x$

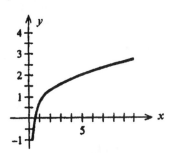

32. $y = \ln \frac{1}{2}x$

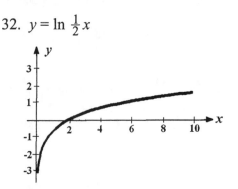

33. $y = 2^x$ and $y = \log_2 x$

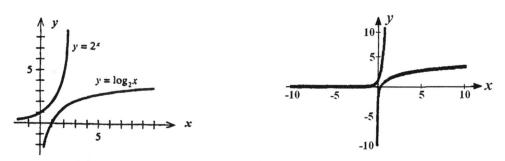

34. $y = e^{3x}$ and $y = \ln 3x$

35. $e^{0.4t} = 8$, $0.4t \ln e = \ln 8$, and $0.4t = \ln 8$ ($\ln e = 1$.) So, $t = \dfrac{\ln 8}{0.4} = 5.1986$.

36. $\frac{1}{3}e^{-3t} = 0.9$, $e^{-3t} = 2.7$. Taking the logarithm, we have

$$-3t \ln e = \ln 2.7, \quad t = -\frac{\ln 2.7}{3} \approx -0.3311.$$

37 $5e^{-2t} = 6$, $e^{-2t} = \frac{6}{5} = 1.2$. Taking the logarithm, we have

$$-2t \ln e = \ln 1.2, \quad \text{or } t = -\frac{\ln 1.2}{2} \approx -0.0912.$$

38. $4e^{t-1} = 4$, $e^{t-1} = 1$, $\ln e^{t-1} = \ln 1$, $(t-1)\ln e = 0$, $t = 1$.

39 $2e^{-0.2t} - 4 = 6$, $2e^{-0.2t} = 10$. Taking the logarithm on both sides of this last equation, we have $\ln e^{-0.2t} = \ln 5$; $-0.2t \ln e = \ln 5$; $-0.2t = \ln 5$;

and $\quad t = -\dfrac{\ln 5}{0.2} \approx -8.0472$.

40. $12 - e^{0.4t} = 3$, $e^{0.4t} = 9$, $\ln e^{0.4t} = \ln 9$, $0.4t \ln e = \ln 9$, $0.4t = \ln 9$,

so $t = \dfrac{\ln 9}{0.4} \approx 5.4931$.

41. $\dfrac{50}{1+4e^{0.2t}} = 20$, $1+4e^{0.2t} = \dfrac{50}{20} = 2.5$, $4e^{0.2t} = 1.5$,

$e^{0.2t} = \dfrac{1.5}{4} = 0.375$, $\ln e^{0.2t} = \ln 0.375$, $0.2t = \ln 0.375$. So $t = \dfrac{\ln 0.375}{0.2} \approx -4.9041$.

42. $\dfrac{200}{1+3e^{-0.3t}} = 100$, $1+3e^{-0.3t} = \dfrac{200}{100} = 2$, $3e^{-0.3t} = 1$; $e^{-0.3t} = \dfrac{1}{3}$,

$\ln e^{-0.3t} = \ln \dfrac{1}{3} = \ln 1 - \ln 3 = -\ln 3$. So $-0.3t \ln e = -\ln 3$, or $0.3t = \ln 3$.

So $t = \dfrac{\ln 3}{0.3} \approx 3.6620$.

43. Taking the logarithm on both sides, we obtain

$\ln A = \ln Be^{-t/2}$, $\ln A = \ln B + \ln e^{-t/2}$, $\ln A - \ln B = -t/2 \ln e$,

$\ln \dfrac{A}{B} = -\dfrac{t}{2}$ or $t = -2 \ln \dfrac{A}{B} = 2 \ln \dfrac{B}{A}$

44. $\dfrac{A}{1+Be^{t/2}} = C$, $A = C + BCe^{t/2}$, $A - C = BCe^{t/2}$;

$\dfrac{A-C}{BC} = e^{t/2}$, $\dfrac{t}{2} = \ln \dfrac{A-C}{BC}$, $t = 2 \ln\left(\dfrac{A-C}{BC}\right)$.

45. $p(x) = 19.4 \ln x + 18$. For a child weighing 92 lb, we find
    $p(92) = 19.4 \ln 92 + 18 = 105.72$ millimeters of mercury.

46. a. $5 = \log \dfrac{I}{I_0}$, $\dfrac{I}{I_0} = 10^5$, or $I = 10^5 I_0 = 100{,}000\, I_0$.

    b. $8 = \log \dfrac{I}{I_0}$, from which we find, $I = 10^8 I_0$ and so it is 1000 times greater.

c. $8.2 = \log \dfrac{I}{I_0}$ gives $I = 10^{8.2} I_0$. So it is $\dfrac{10^{8.2}}{10^5} = 10^{3.2}$, or 1585 times greater than one with magnitude 5.

47. a. $30 = 10 \log \dfrac{I}{I_0}$; $3 = \log \dfrac{I}{I_0}$; $\dfrac{I}{I_0} = 10^3 = 1000$. So $I = 1000\, I_0$.

b. When $D = 80$, $I = 10^8 I_0$ and when $D = 30$, $I = 10^3 I_0$. Therefore, an 80–decibel sound is $10^8/10^3$ or $10^5 = 100{,}000$ times louder than a 30–decibel sound.

c. It is $10^{15}/10^8 = 10^7$, or 10,000,000, times louder.

48. We solve the equation $29.92e^{-0.2x} = 20$, $e^{-0.2x} = \dfrac{20}{29.92} = 0.6684$; $-0.2x = \ln 0.6684$,

and $x = -\dfrac{\ln 0.6684}{0.2} \approx 2.01$. So, the balloonist's altitude is 2.01 miles.

49. We solve the following equation for t. Thus,

$$\dfrac{160}{1+240e^{-0.2t}} = 80; \quad 1 + 240e^{-0.2t} = \dfrac{160}{80},$$

$$240e^{-0.2t} = 2 - 1 = 1; \quad e^{-0.2t} = \dfrac{1}{240}; \quad -0.2t = \ln \dfrac{1}{240}$$

$$t = -\dfrac{1}{0.2}\ln\dfrac{1}{240} \approx 27.40, \text{ or approximately 27.4 years old.}$$

50. a. The temperature when it was first poured is given by
$$T(0) = 70 + 100e^0 = 170, \text{ or } 170\ {}^\circ F.$$

b. We solve the equation

$$70 + 100e^{-0.0446t} = 120; \quad 100e^{-0.0446t} = 50; \quad e^{-0.0446t} = \dfrac{50}{100} = \dfrac{1}{2}$$

$$\ln e^{-0.0446t} = \ln \dfrac{1}{2} = \ln 1 - \ln 2 = -\ln 2; \quad -0.0446t = -\ln 2$$

$$t = \dfrac{\ln 2}{0.0446} \approx 15.54.$$

So, it will take approximately 15.54 minutes.

51. We solve the following equation for t:
$$200(1 - 0.956e^{-0.18t}) = 140$$

$$1 - 0.956e^{-0.18t} = \frac{140}{200} = 0.7$$

$$-0.956e^{-0.18t} = 0.7 - 1 = -0.3$$

$$e^{-0.18t} = \frac{0.3}{0.956}$$

$$-0.18t = \ln\left(\frac{0.3}{0.956}\right)$$

$$t = -\frac{\ln\left(\frac{0.3}{0.956}\right)}{0.18} \approx 6.43875.$$

So, its approximate age is 6.44 years.

52. a. We solve the equation $0.08(1 - e^{-0.02t}) = 0.02$, obtaining

$$1 - e^{-0.02t} = \frac{0.02}{0.08} = \frac{1}{4}; \; -e^{-0.02t} = \frac{1}{4} - 1 = -\frac{3}{4}; \; e^{-0.02t} = \frac{3}{4}$$

$$\ln e^{-0.02t} = \ln\frac{3}{4}; \; -0.02t = \ln\frac{3}{4}; \; t \approx 14.38, \text{ or } 14.38 \text{ seconds.}$$

b. $1 - e^{-0.02t} = \frac{0.04}{0.08}; \; -e^{-0.02t} = \frac{1}{2} - 1 = -\frac{1}{2}; \; t \approx 34.66, \text{ or } 34.66 \text{ seconds.}$

53. a. We solve the equation $0.08 + 0.12e^{-0.02t} = 0.18$.

$$0.12e^{-0.02t} = 0.1; \; e^{-0.02t} = \frac{0.1}{0.12} = \frac{1}{1.2}$$

$$\ln e^{-0.02t} = \ln\frac{1}{1.2} = \ln 1 - \ln 1.2 = -\ln 1.2$$

$$-0.02t = -\ln 1.2$$

$$t = \frac{\ln 1.2}{0.02} \approx 9.116, \text{ or } 9.12 \text{ sec.}$$

b. We solve the equation $0.08 + 0.12e^{-0.02t} = 0.16$.

$$0.12e^{-0.02t} = 0.08; \; e^{-0.02t} = \frac{0.08}{0.12} = \frac{2}{3}; \; -0.02t = \ln\frac{2}{3}$$

$$t = -\frac{\ln\left(\frac{2}{3}\right)}{0.02} \approx 20.2733, \text{ or } 20.27 \text{ sec.}$$

54. With $T_0 = 70$, $T_1 = 98.6$, and $T = 80$, we have

$$80 = 70 + (98.6 - 70)(0.97)^t$$

$$28.6(0.97)^t = 10; \quad (0.97)^t = 0.34965.$$

Taking logarithms, we have $\ln (0.97)^t = \ln 0.34965$, or $t = \dfrac{\ln 0.34965}{\ln 0.97} \approx 34.50$.

So he was killed 34½ hours earlier at 1:30 P.M.

55. False. Take $x = e$. Then $(\ln e)^3 = 1^3 = 1 \neq 3 \ln e = 3$.

56. False. Take $a = 2e$ and $b = e$. Then
$$\ln a - \ln b = \ln 2e - \ln e = \ln 2 + \ln e - \ln e = \ln 2.$$
But $\ln(a - b) = \ln(2e - e) = \ln e = 1$.

57. True. $g(x) = \ln x$ is continuous and greater than zero on $(1, \infty)$. Therefore,
$$f(x) = \frac{1}{\ln x} \text{ is continuous on } (1, \infty).$$

58. True. If $x > 0$, then $|x| = x$ and $f(x) = \ln|x| = \ln x$ is continuous on $(0, \infty)$. If $x < 0$, then $|x| = -x$ and so $f(x) = \ln|x| = \ln(-x)$ is continuous on $(-\infty, 0)$.

59. a. Taking the logarithm on both sides gives $\ln 2^x = \ln e^{kx}$, $x \ln 2 = kx(\ln e) = kx$. So, $x(\ln 2 - k) = 0$ for all x and this implies that $k = \ln 2$.
b. Tracing the same steps as done in (a), we find that $k = \ln b$.

60. a. Let $p = \log_b m$ and $q = \log_b n$ so that $m = b^p$ and $n = b^q$. Then $mn = b^p b^q = b^{p+q}$ and by definition, $p + q = \log_b mn$; that is, $\log_b mn = \log_b m + \log_b n$.

b. $\dfrac{m}{n} = \dfrac{b^p}{b^q} = b^{p-q}$. So, by definition, $p - q = \log_b \dfrac{m}{n}$; that is
$$\log_b \frac{m}{n} = \log_b m - \log_b n.$$

61. Let $\log_b m = p$, then $m = b^p$. Therefore, $m^n = (b^p)^n = b^{np}$. Therefore,
$$\log_b m^n = \log_b b^{np} = np \log_b b = np \qquad (\text{Since } \log_b b = 1.)$$
$$= n \log_b m,$$
as was to be shown.

62. a. By definition $\log_b 1 = 0$ means $1 = b^0 = 1$.
b. By definition $\log_b b = 1$ means $b = b^1 = b$.

5.3 CONCEPT QUESTIONS, page 357

1. a. In simple interest, the interest is based on the original principal. In compound interest, interest earned is periodically added to the principal and thereafter earns interest at the same rate.

   b. Simple interest formula: $A = P(1+rt)$;

   Compound interest formula: $A = \left(1+\dfrac{r}{m}\right)^{mt}$

2. a. The effective rate of interest is the simple interest that would produce the same amount in 1 year as the nominal rate compounded m times a year.

   b. $r_{eff} = \left(1+\dfrac{r}{m}\right)^{m} - 1$

3. $P = A\left(1+\dfrac{r}{m}\right)^{-mt}$

4. $A = Pe^{rt}$

EXERCISES 5.3, page 357

1. $A = 2500\left(1+\dfrac{0.07}{2}\right)^{20} = 4974.47,$ or $4974.47.

2. $A = 12{,}000\left(1+\dfrac{0.08}{4}\right)^{40} = 26{,}496.48,$ or $26,496.48.

3. $A = 150{,}000\left(1+\dfrac{0.1}{12}\right)^{48} = 223{,}403.11,$ or $223,403.11

4. $A = 150{,}000\left(1+\dfrac{0.09}{365}\right)^{1095} = 196{,}488.13$ or $196,488.13.

5. a. Using the formula $r_{eff} = \left(1+\dfrac{r}{m}\right)^{m} - 1$ with $r = 0.10$ and $m = 2$, we have

   $r_{eff} = \left(1+\dfrac{0.10}{2}\right)^{2} - 1 = 0.1025,$ or 10.25 percent/yr

b.   Using the formula $r_{eff} = \left(1+\dfrac{r}{m}\right)^m - 1$ with $r = 0.09$ and $m = 4$, we have

$$r_{eff} = \left(1+\dfrac{0.09}{4}\right)^4 - 1 = 0.09308, \text{ or } 9.308 \text{ percent/yr.}$$

6. a.   Using the formula $r_{eff} = \left(1+\dfrac{r}{m}\right)^m - 1$ with $r = 0.08$ and $m = 12$, we have

$$r_{eff} = \left(1+\dfrac{0.08}{12}\right)^{12} - 1 = 0.08300, \quad \text{or } 8.3 \text{ percent/yr.}$$

b.   The effective rate is given by $R = \left(1+\dfrac{0.08}{365}\right)^{365} - 1 = 0.08328,$

or 8.328 percent/yr.

7. a.   The present value is given by $P = 40{,}000\left(1+\dfrac{0.08}{2}\right)^{-8} = 29{,}227.61,$

or \$29,227.61.

b.   The present value is given by $P = 40{,}000\left(1+\dfrac{0.08}{4}\right)^{-16} = 29{,}137.83,$ or

\$29,137.83.

8. a.   The present value is given by

$$P = 40{,}000\left(1+\dfrac{0.07}{12}\right)^{-48} = 30{,}255.95, \quad \text{or } \$30{,}255.95.$$

b.   The present value is given by

$$P = 40{,}000\left(1+\dfrac{0.09}{365}\right)^{-(365)(4)} = 27{,}908.29, \quad \text{or } \$27{,}908.29$$

9. $A = 5000e^{0.08(4)} \approx 6885.64, \quad \text{or } \$6{,}885.64.$

10. $A = 25000(1+0.07)^6 \approx 37{,}518.26,$ or approximately \$37,518.26.
The interest earned is \$12,518.26.

11. We use formula (6) with $A = 7500$, $P = 5000$, $m = 12$, and $t = 3$. Thus
$$7500 = 5000\left(1+\tfrac{r}{12}\right)^{36};$$

$$\left(1+\tfrac{r}{12}\right)^{36} = \tfrac{7500}{5000} = \tfrac{3}{2}, \quad \ln\left(1+\tfrac{r}{12}\right)^{36} = \ln 1.5;$$

$$36\left(1+\tfrac{r}{12}\right) = \ln 1.5$$

$$\left(1+\tfrac{r}{12}\right) = \tfrac{\ln 1.5}{36} = 0.0112629$$

$$1+\tfrac{r}{12} = e^{0.0112629} = 1.011327; \tfrac{r}{12} = 0.011327;$$

$$r = 0.13592$$

So the interest rate is 13.59% per year.

12. We use formula (6) with $A = 7500$, $P = 5000$, $m = 4$, and $t = 3$. Thus

$$7500 = 5000\left(1+\tfrac{r}{4}\right)^{12}$$

$$\left(1+\tfrac{r}{4}\right)^{12} = \tfrac{7500}{5000} = \tfrac{3}{2}, \quad \ln\left(1+\tfrac{r}{4}\right)^{12} = \ln 1.5;$$

$$12\left(1+\tfrac{r}{4}\right) = \ln 1.5; \quad \left(1+\tfrac{r}{4}\right) = \tfrac{\ln 1.5}{12} = 0.0337888$$

$$1+\tfrac{r}{4} = e^{0.0337888} = 1.034366; \tfrac{r}{4} = 0.034366$$

$$r = 0.034366$$

So the required interest rate is 13.75% per year.

13 We use formula (6) with $A = 8000$, $P = 5000$, $m = 2$, and $t = 4$. Thus

$$8000 = 5000\left(1+\tfrac{r}{2}\right)^{8}$$

$$\left(1+\tfrac{r}{2}\right)^{8} = \tfrac{8000}{5000} = 1.6, \quad \ln\left(1+\tfrac{r}{2}\right)^{8} = \ln 1.6;$$

$$8\ln\left(1+\tfrac{r}{2}\right) = \ln 1.6$$

$$\ln\left(1+\tfrac{r}{2}\right) = \tfrac{\ln 1.6}{8} = 0.05875$$

$$1+\tfrac{r}{2} = e^{0.05875} = 1.06051; \tfrac{r}{2} = 0.06051$$

$$r = 0.1210$$

So the required interest rate is 12.1% per year.

14. We use formula (6) with $A = 5500$, $P = 5000$, $m = 12$, and $t = \tfrac{1}{2}$. Thus

$$5500 = 5000\left(1+\tfrac{r}{12}\right)^{6}; \quad \left(1+\tfrac{r}{12}\right)^{6} = \tfrac{5500}{5000} = 1.1$$

Proceeding as in the previous problem, we find $r = 0.1921$. So the required interest rate is 19.21% per year.

15. We use formula (6) with $A = 4000$, $P = 2000$, $m = 1$, and $t = 5$. Thus

$$4000 = 2000\left(1+r\right)^{5}; \quad \left(1+r\right)^{5} = 2 ; 5\ln(1+r) = \ln 2; \quad \ln(1+r) = \tfrac{\ln 2}{5} = 0.138629$$

$1 + r = e^{0.138629} = 1.148698; \ r = 0.1487$

So the required interst rate is 14.87% per year.

16. We use formula (6) with $A = 6000$, $P = 2000$, $m = 12$, and $t = 5$. Thus

$$6000 = 2000\left(1 + \frac{r}{12}\right)^{60}$$

Proceeding as in the previous problem, we find $r = 22.17$. So the required interest rate is 22.17% per year.

17. We use formula (6) with $A = 6500$, $P = 5000$, $m = 12$, and $r = 0.12$. Thus

$$6500 = 5000\left(1 + \frac{0.12}{12}\right)^{12t} ; \quad (1.01)^{12t} = \frac{6500}{5000} = 1.3; \quad 12t \ln(1.01) = \ln 1.3$$

$$t = \frac{\ln 1.3}{12 \ln 1.01} \approx 2.197$$

So, it will take approximately 2.2 years.

18. We use formula (6) with $A = 15000$, $P = 12000$, $m = 12$, and $r = 0.08$. Thus,

$$15000 = 12000\left(1 + \frac{0.08}{12}\right)^{12t}$$

Proceeding as in the previous exercise, we find $r = 2.799$. So it will take approximately 2.8 years.

19. We use formula (6) with $A = 4000$, $P = 2000$, $m = 12$, and $r = 0.09$. Thus,

$$4000 = 2000\left(1 + \frac{0.09}{12}\right)^{12t}$$

$$\left(1 + \frac{0.09}{12}\right)^{12t} = 2$$

$$12t \ln\left(1 + \frac{0.09}{12}\right) = \ln 2 \quad \text{and} \quad t = \frac{\ln 2}{12 \ln\left(1 + \frac{0.09}{12}\right)} \approx 7.73.$$

So it will take approximately 7.7 years.

20. We use formula (6) with $A = 15000$, $P = 5000$, $m = 365$, and $r = 0.08$. Thus

$$15000 = 5000\left(1 + \frac{0.08}{365}\right)^{365t}$$

to obtain $\quad t = \dfrac{\ln\left(\frac{15000}{5000}\right)}{365 \ln\left(1 + \frac{0.08}{365}\right)} \approx 13.73.$ So, it will take approximately 13.7 years.

21. We use formula (10) with $A = 6000$, $P = 5000$, and $t = 3$. Thus,

$$6000 = 5000e^{3r}$$

$$e^{3r} = \frac{6000}{5000} = 1.2; \qquad 3r = \ln 1.2$$

$$r = \frac{\ln 1.2}{3} \approx 0.6077$$

So the interest rate is 6.08% per year.

22. We use formula (10) with $A = 8000$, $P = 4000$, and $t = 5$. Thus
$$8000 = 4000e^{5r}$$

obtaining $\qquad r = \dfrac{\ln\left(\frac{8000}{4000}\right)}{5} \approx 0.13863$. So the interest rate is 13.86% per year.

23. We use formula (10) formula (6) with $A = 7000$, $P = 6000$, and $r = 0.075$ Thus
$$7000 = 6000e^{0.075t}; \quad e^{0.075t} = \tfrac{7000}{6000} = \tfrac{7}{6}$$

$$0.075t \ln e = \ln \tfrac{7}{6} \quad \text{and} \quad t = \frac{\ln \tfrac{7}{6}}{0.075} \approx 2.055.$$

So, it will take 2.06 years.

24. We use formula (10) with $A = 16{,}000$, $P = 8000$, and $r = 0.08$. Thus
$$16{,}000 = 8000e^{0.08t}$$

obtaining $t = \dfrac{\ln 2}{0.08} \approx 8.664$. So, it will take 8.7 years.

25. The Estradas can expect to pay $180{,}000(1 + 0.09)^4$, or approximately $254,084.69.

26. The utility company will have to increase its generating capacity by a factor of $(1.08)^{10}$, or 2.16 times.

27. The investment will be worth
$$A = 1.5\left(1 + \frac{0.065}{2}\right)^{20} = 2.84376 \text{ , or approximately } \$2.844 \text{million.}$$

28. Bernie originally invested $P = 22{,}289.22\left(1 + \dfrac{0.08}{4}\right)^{-20} = 15{,}000$, or $15,000.

29. The present value of the $8000 loan due in 3 years is given by

$$P = 8000\left(1 + \frac{0.10}{2}\right)^{-6} = 5969.72, \text{ or } \$5969\ 72.$$

The present value of the \$15,000 loan due in 6 years is given by

$$P = 15,000\left(1 + \frac{0.10}{2}\right)^{-12} = 8352.56, \text{ or } \$8352.56.$$

Therefore, the amount the proprietors of the inn will be required to pay at the end

of 5 years is given by $A = 14,322.28\left(1 + \frac{0.10}{2}\right)^{10} = 23,329.48,$ or \$23,329.48.

30. a. The accumulated amount before taxes is $A = 25,000\left(1 + \frac{0.12}{1}\right)^{10} \approx 77,646.21.$

After taxes, it is worth \$55,905.27.
b. The accumulated amount (tax-free) is $A = 25,000(1 + 0.864)^{10} \approx 57,258.19,$
or \$57,258.19. After taxes, it is worth $0.72(57,258.19) = 41,225.90,$ or \$41,225.90.

31. He can expect the minimum revenue for 2007 to be
$240,000(1.2)(1.3)(1.25)^3 \approx 731,250$ or \$731,250.

32. The projected online sales for 2008 are
$23.5(1.332)(1.278)(1.305)(1.199)(1.243)(1.14)(1.176)(1.105) \approx 115.25$
or approximately \$115.3 billion.

33. We want the value of a 2004 dollar in the year 2000. Denoting this value by x, we
have
$(1.034)(1.028)(1.016)(1.023)x = 1$
or $x \approx 0.9051.$ Thus, the purchasing power is approximately 91 cents.

34. We solve the equation $216,000 = 160,000(1 + R)^6,\ (1 + R)^6 = 1.35,$
$1 + R = (1.35)^{1/6} \approx 1.051289$ and $r = 0.051289,$ or 5.13%.

35. The effective annual rate of return on his investment is found by solving the
equation $(1 + r)^2 = \dfrac{32100}{25250}$

$$1 + r = \left(\frac{32100}{25250}\right)^{1/2}$$

$1 + r \approx 1.1275$ and $r = 0.1275,$ or 12.75 percent.

36. Suppose $1 is invested in each investment.

Investment A: Accumulated amount is $\left(1+\frac{0.1}{2}\right)^8 \approx 1.47746$.

Investment B: Accumulated amount is $e^{0.0975(4)} \approx 1.47698$.

So Investment A has a higher rate of return.

37. $P = Ae^{-rt} = 59673e^{-(0.08)5} \approx 40,000.008$, or approximately $40,000.

38. We solve the equation $3.6 = 1.4e^{6r}$, $e^{6r} = \dfrac{3.6}{1.4}$, or $6r \ln e \approx \ln \dfrac{3.6}{1.4}$,

$6r = 0.944462$, $r = 0.1574$, or approximately 15 7%.

39. a. If they invest the money at 10.5 percent compounded quarterly, they should set aside $P = 70,000\left(1+\frac{0.105}{4}\right)^{-28} \approx 33,885\ 14$, or $33,885.14

b. If they invest the money at 10.5 percent compounded continuously, they should set aside $P = 70,000e^{-(0.105)(7)} = 33,565.38$, or $33,565.38.

40. He needs $35,000e^{0.06(10)} \approx 63,774.16$ or approximately $63,744 a year.

41. a. If inflation over the next 15 years is 6 percent, then Eleni's first year's pension will be worth $P = 40,000e^{-0.9} = 16,262.79$, or $16,262.79

b. If inflation over the next 15 years is 8 percent, then Eleni's first year's pension will be worth $P = 40,000e^{-1.2} = 12,047.77$, or $12,047.77.

c. If inflation over the next 15 years is 12 percent, then Eleni's first year's pension will be worth $P = 40,000e^{-1.8} = 6611.96$, or $6,611.96.

42. $P(t) = V(t)e^{-rt} = 80,000e^{\sqrt{t}/2}e^{-rt} = 80,000e^{(\sqrt{t}/2 - 0.09t)}$

$P(4) = 80,000e^{1-0.09(4)} \approx 151,718.47$, or approximately $151,718.

43. $r_{eff} = \lim\limits_{m\to\infty}\left(1+\dfrac{r}{m}\right)^m - 1 = e^r - 1$.

44. a. $r_{eff} = \left(1+\dfrac{0.1}{4}\right)^4 - 1 \approx 0.1038$, or 10.38%.

b. $r_{eff} = \left(1 + \dfrac{0.1}{12}\right)^{12} - 1 \approx 0.1047$, or 10.47%. c. $r_{eff} = e^{0.1} - 1 \approx 0.1052$, or 10.52%.

45. The effective rate of interest at Bank A is given by
$$R = \left(1 + \tfrac{0.07}{4}\right)^4 - 1 = 0.07186,$$
or 7 186 percent. The effective rate at Bank B is given by
$$R = e^r - 1 = e^{0.07125} - 1 = 0.07385$$
or 7.385 percent. We conclude that Bank B has the higher effective rate of interest.

46. $\left(1 + \tfrac{r}{12}\right)^{12} - 1 = r_{eff},\ \left(1 + \tfrac{r}{12}\right)^{12} = 1.10,\ 1 + \tfrac{r}{12} = 1.10^{1/12}$
$\tfrac{r}{12} = 1.10^{1/12} - 1$ and $r = 12(1.10^{1/2} - 1) = 0.09569$, or 9.59 percent.

47. The nominal rate of interest that, when compounded continuously, yields an effective rate of interest of 10 percent per year is found by solving the equation
$$R = e^r - 1,\ 0.10 = e^r - 1,\ 1.10 = e^r,\quad \ln 1.10 = r \ln e,\ r = \ln 1.10 \approx 0.09531,$$
or 9.531 percent.

48. $\displaystyle \lim_{i \to 0} R\left[\dfrac{(1+i)^n - 1}{i}\right] = R \lim_{i \to 0}\left[\dfrac{(1+i)^n - 1}{i}\right]$. Consider the function $f(x) = x^n$ Then by

definition of the derivative $f'(1) = \displaystyle\lim_{h \to 0}\dfrac{(1+h)^n - 1}{h}$. With the variable h taken to be

i, we see that $\displaystyle\lim_{i \to 0} R\left[\dfrac{(1+i)^n - 1}{i}\right] = Rf'(1) = Rnx^{n-1}\big|_{x=1} = nR$. Thus, if the interest

rate is 0, then after n payments of R dollars each, the future value of the annuity will be nR dollars as expected.

5.4 CONCEPT QUESTIONS, page 365

1. a. $f'(x) = e^x$ b. $g'(x) = e^{f(x)} \cdot f'(x)$
2. a. $f'(x) = ke^{kx}$
   b. If $k > 0$, then $f'(x) > 0$ and f is increasing on $(-\infty, \infty)$. If $k < 0$, then $f'(x) < 0$, and f is decreasing on $(-\infty, \infty)$.

EXERCISES 5.4 , page 365

1. $f(x) = e^{3x};\ f'(x) = 3e^{3x}$

2. $f(x) = 3e^x,\ f'(x) = 3e^x$

3. $g(t) = e^{-t};\ g'(t) = -e^{-t}$

4. $f(x) = e^{-2x};\ f'(x) = -2e^{-2x}$

5. $f(x) = e^x + x;\ f'(x) = e^x + 1$

6. $f(x) = 2e^x - x^2,\ f'(x) = 2e^x - 2x = 2(e^x - x).$

7. $f(x) = x^3 e^x,\ f'(x) = x^3 e^x + e^x(3x^2) = x^2 e^x(x + 3).$

8. $f(u) = u^2 e^{-u},\ f'(u) = 2ue^{-u} + u^2 e^{-u}(-1) = u(2 - u)e^{-u}.$

9. $f(x) = \dfrac{2e^x}{x},\quad f'(x) = \dfrac{x(2e^x) - 2e^x(1)}{x^2} = \dfrac{2e^x(x-1)}{x^2}$

10. $f(x) = \dfrac{x}{e^x}\ ;\ f'(x) = \dfrac{e^x(1) - xe^x}{e^{2x}} = \dfrac{1-x}{e^x}.$

11. $f(x) = 3(e^x + e^{-x});\ f'(x) = 3(e^x - e^{-x}).$

12. $f(x) = \dfrac{e^x + e^{-x}}{2}\ ;\ f'(x) = \dfrac{e^x - e^{-x}}{2}$

13. $f(w) = \dfrac{e^w + 1}{e^w} = 1 + \dfrac{1}{e^w} = 1 + e^{-w}.\ f'(w) = -e^{-w} = -\dfrac{1}{e^w}.$

14. $f(x) = \dfrac{e^x}{e^x + 1};\ f'(x) = \dfrac{(e^x + 1)e^x - e^x(e^x)}{(e^x + 1)^2} = \dfrac{e^x}{(e^x + 1)^2}.$

15. $f(x) = 2e^{3x-1},\ f'(x) = 2e^{3x-1}(3) = 6e^{3x-1}.$

16. $f(t) = 4e^{3t+2};\ f'(t) = 4e^{3t+2}(3) = 12e^{3t+2}$

17. $h(x) = e^{-x^2};\ h'(x) = e^{-x^2}(-2x) = -2xe^{-x^2}.$

18. $f(x) = e^{x^2-1};\ f'(x) = e^{x^2-1}(2x) = 2xe^{x^2-1}.$

19. $f(x) = 3e^{-1/x};\ f'(x) = 3e^{-1/x} \cdot \dfrac{d}{dx}\left(-\dfrac{1}{x}\right) = 3e^{-1/x}\left(\dfrac{1}{x^2}\right) = \dfrac{3e^{-1/x}}{x^2}.$

20. $f(x) = e^{1/(2x)}$; $f'(x) = e^{1/2x} \cdot \dfrac{d}{dx}\left(\dfrac{1}{2x}\right) = \dfrac{1}{2}e^{1/2x} \cdot -x^{-2} = -\dfrac{e^{1/2x}}{2x^2}$

21. $f(x) = (e^x + 1)^{25}$, $f'(x) = 25(e^x + 1)^{24}e^x = 25e^x(e^x + 1)^{24}$.

22. $f(x) = (4 - e^{-3x})^3$; $f'(x) = 3(4 - e^{-3x})^2(-e^{-3x})(-3) = 9e^{-3x}(4 - e^{-3x})^2$

23. $f(x) = e^{\sqrt{x}}$; $f'(x) = e^{\sqrt{x}}\dfrac{d}{dx}x^{1/2} = e^{\sqrt{x}}\dfrac{1}{2}x^{-1/2} = \dfrac{e^{\sqrt{x}}}{2\sqrt{x}}$.

24. $f(t) = -e^{-\sqrt{2t}}$; $f'(t) = -e^{-\sqrt{2t}}\dfrac{d}{dt}(-\sqrt{2t}) = e^{-\sqrt{2t}}\left(\dfrac{1}{2}\right)(2t)^{-1/2}(2) = \dfrac{e^{-\sqrt{2t}}}{\sqrt{2t}}$

25. $f(x) = (x - 1)e^{3x+2}$; $f'(x) = (x - 1)(3)e^{3x+2} + e^{3x+2} = e^{3x+2}(3x - 3 + 1) = e^{3x+2}(3x - 2)$.

26. $f(s) = (s^2 + 1)e^{-s^2}$; $f'(s) = 2se^{-s^2} + (s^2 + 1)e^{-s^2}(-2s) = -2s^3e^{-s^2}$.

27 $f(x) = \dfrac{e^x - 1}{e^x + 1}$; $f'(x) = \dfrac{(e^x + 1)(e^x) - (e^x - 1)(e^x)}{(e^x + 1)^2} = \dfrac{e^x(e^x + 1 - e^x + 1)}{(e^x + 1)^2} = \dfrac{2e^x}{(e^x + 1)^2}$.

28. $g(t) = \dfrac{e^{-t}}{1 + t^2}$;

$g'(t) = \dfrac{(1 + t^2)(-e^{-t}) - (e^{-t})(2t)}{(1 + t^2)^2} = \dfrac{e^{-t}(-1 - t^2 - 2t)}{(1 + t^2)^2} = \dfrac{-e^{-t}(t^2 + 2t + 1)}{(1 + t^2)^2} = \dfrac{-e^{-t}(t + 1)^2}{(1 + t^2)^2}$.

29. $f(x) = e^{-4x} + 2e^{3x}$; $f'(x) = -4e^{-4x} + 6e^{3x}$ and
    $f''(x) = 16e^{-4x} + 18e^{3x} = 2(8e^{-4x} + 9e^{3x})$.

30. $f(t) = 3e^{-2t} - 5e^{-t}$; $f'(t) = -6e^{-2t} + 5e^{-t}$ and $f''(t) = 12e^{-2t} - 5e^{-t}$.

31. $f(x) = 2xe^{3x}$; $f'(x) = 2e^{3x} + 2xe^{3x}(3) = 2(3x + 1)e^{3x}$.
    $f''(x) \quad = 6e^{3x} + 2(3x + 1)e^{3x}(3) = 6(3x + 2)e^{3x}$.

32. $f(t) = t^2e^{-2t}$; $f'(t) = 2te^{-2t} + t^2e^{-2t}(-2) = 2t(1 - t)e^{-2t}$.
    $f''(t) = (2 - 4t)e^{-2t} + 2t(1 - t)e^{-2t}(-2) = 2(2t^2 - 4t + 1)e^{-2t}$.

33. $y = f(x) = e^{2x-3}$. $f'(x) = 2e^{2x-3}$. To find the slope of the tangent line to the graph
    of f at $x = 3/2$, we compute $f'(\frac{3}{2}) = 2e^{3-3} = 2$. Next, using the point–slope form of

the equation of a line, we find that
$$y - 1 = 2(x - \tfrac{3}{2})$$
$$= 2x - 3, \quad \text{or} \quad y = 2x - 2.$$

34. $y = e^{-x^2}$. The slope of the tangent line at any point is $y' = e^{-x^2}(-2x) = -2xe^{-x^2}$. The slope of the tangent line when $x = 1$ is $m = -2e^{-1}$. Therefore, an equation of the tangent line is $y - \tfrac{1}{e} = -\tfrac{2}{e}(x-1)$, or $y = -\tfrac{2}{e} + \tfrac{3}{e}$.

35 $f(x) = e^{-x^2/2}$, $f'(x) = e^{-x^2/2}(-x) = -xe^{-x^2/2}$. Setting $f'(x) = 0$, gives $x = 0$ as the only critical point of f. From the sign diagram,

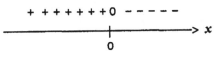

we conclude that f is increasing on $(-\infty,0)$ and decreasing on $(0,\infty)$.

36. $f(x) = x^2 e^{-x}$; $f'(x) = 2xe^{-x} + x^2 e^{-x}(-1) = x(2 - x)e^{-x}$. Observe that $f'(x) = 0$ if $x = 0$ or 2. The sign diagram of f'

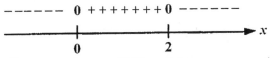

shows that f is increasing on $(0,2)$ and decreasing on $(-\infty,0) \cup (2,\infty)$.

37. $f(x) = \tfrac{1}{2}e^x - \tfrac{1}{2}e^{-x}$, $f'(x) = \tfrac{1}{2}(e^x + e^{-x})$, $f''(x) = \tfrac{1}{2}(e^x - e^{-x})$. Setting $f''(x) = 0$, gives $e^x = e^{-x}$ or $e^{2x} = 1$, and $x = 0$. From the sign diagram for f'',

+ + + + + + + + + + + 0 – – – – – – – –
———————————+————————→ x
                       0

we conclude that f is concave upward on $(0,\infty)$ and concave downward on $(-\infty,0)$.

38. $f(x) = xe^x$. $f'(x) = e^x + xe^x = (x + 1)e^x$. $f''(x) = (x + 1)e^x + e^x = (x + 2)e^x$. Setting $f''(x) = 0$ gives $x = -2$. The sign diagram of f''

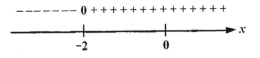

shows that f is concave downward on $(-\infty,-2)$ and concave upward on $(-2,\infty)$.

39. $f(x) = xe^{-2x}$. $f'(x) = e^{-2x} + xe^{-2x}(-2) = (1 - 2x)e^{-2x}$.
$f''(x) = -2e^{-2x} + (1 - 2x)e^{-2x}(-2) = 4(x - 1)e^{-2x}$.
Observe that $f''(x) = 0$ if $x = 1$. The sign diagram of f''

$$- - - - - - - - - - - - \ 0 + + + + + + + + + + + +$$
$$\xrightarrow{\hspace{2cm}\underset{1}{|}\hspace{4cm}} x$$

shows that $(1, e^{-2})$ is an inflection point.

40. $f(x) = 2e^{-x^2} = 2(e^{-x^2})$, $f'(x) = 2(-2x)e^{-x^2} = -4xe^{-x^2}$
$f''(x) = -4x(-2x)e^{-x^2} - 4e^{-x^2} = -4e^{-x^2}(-2x^2 + 1) = 4e^{-x^2}(2x^2 - 1)$.
Setting $f''(x) = 0$ gives $2x^2 = 1$, $x^2 = 1/2$, or $x = \pm \frac{\sqrt{2}}{2}$.
The sign diagram for f'' is

$$+ + + + + + 0 - - - - - - - - - - 0 + + + + + +$$
$$\xrightarrow{\hspace{1cm}\underset{-\frac{\sqrt{2}}{2}}{|}\hspace{1.5cm}\underset{0}{|}\hspace{1.5cm}\underset{\frac{\sqrt{2}}{2}}{|}\hspace{2cm}} x$$

We see that $(-\frac{\sqrt{2}}{2}, 2e^{-1/2})$ and $(\frac{\sqrt{2}}{2}, 2e^{-1/2})$ are inflection points.

41. $f(x) = e^{-x^2}$, $f'(x) = -2xe^{-x^2}$;
$f''(x) = -2e^{-x^2} - 2xe^{-x^2} \cdot (-2x) = -2e^{-x^2(1-2x^2)=0}$ implies $x = \pm\frac{\sqrt{2}}{2}$. The sign diagram of f'' follows:

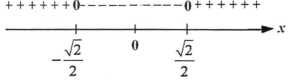

$$+ + + + + + 0 - - - - - - - - - - 0 + + + + + +$$
$$\xrightarrow{\hspace{1cm}\underset{-\frac{\sqrt{2}}{2}}{|}\hspace{1.5cm}\underset{0}{|}\hspace{1.5cm}\underset{\frac{\sqrt{2}}{2}}{|}\hspace{2cm}} x$$

We see that the graph of f has inflection points at $(-\frac{\sqrt{2}}{2}, e^{-1/2})$ and $(\frac{\sqrt{2}}{2}, e^{-1/2})$. The slope of the tangent line at $(-\frac{\sqrt{2}}{2}, e^{-1/2})$ is $f'(-\frac{\sqrt{2}}{2}) = \sqrt{2}e^{-1/2}$. The tangent line has equation

$$y - e^{-1/2} = \sqrt{2}e^{-1/2}(x + \frac{\sqrt{2}}{2}) \text{ or } y = \sqrt{\frac{2}{e}}x + \frac{2}{\sqrt{e}} \text{ or } e^{-1/2}(\sqrt{2}x + 2)$$

The slope of the tangent line at $(\frac{\sqrt{2}}{2}, e^{-1/2})$ is $f'(\frac{\sqrt{2}}{2}) = -\sqrt{2}e^{-1/2}$. The tangent line has equation

$$y - e^{-1/2} = -\sqrt{2}e^{-1/2}(x - \tfrac{\sqrt{2}}{2}) \quad \text{or} \quad y = e^{-1/2}(-\sqrt{2}x + 2)$$

42. $f(x) = xe^{-x}$, $f'(x) = e^{-x} + xe^{-x}(-1) = (1-x)e^{-x}$

$f''(x) = -e^{-x} + (1-x)e^{-x}(-1) = (x-2)e^{-x} = 0$ implies $x - 2 = 0$ or $x = 2$. The sign diagram of f'' follows:

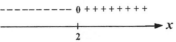

We see that the graph of f has an inflection point at $(2, 2e^{-2})$. The slope of the tangent line at that point is $f'(2) = -e^{-2}$. The tangent line has equation

$$y - 2e^{-2} = -e^{-2}(x-2) = -e^{-2}x + 4e^{-2}$$

or $\qquad y = -\dfrac{x}{e^{-2}} + \dfrac{4}{e^2}$

43. $f(x) = e^{-x^2}$. $f'(x) = -2xe^{-x^2} = 0$ if $x = 0$, the only critical point of f.

x	-1	0	1
$f(x)$	e^{-1}	1	e^{-1}

From the table, we see that f has an absolute minimum value of e^{-1} attained at $x = -1$ and $x = 1$. It has an absolute maximum at $(0,1)$.

44. $h(x) = e^{x^2-4}$, $h'(x) = 2xe^{x^2-4}$. Setting $h'(x) = 0$ gives $x = 0$ as the only critical point of h.

x	-2	0	2
$h(x)$	1	e^{-4}	1

We see that $h(0) = e^{-4}$ is the absolute minimum and $h(-2) = 1$ and $h(2) = 1$ are the absolute maximum values of h.

45. $g(x) = (2x - 1)e^{-x}$; $g'(x) = 2e^{-x} + (2x - 1)e^{-x}(-1) = (3 - 2x)e^{-x} = 0$, if $x = 3/2$. The graph of g shows that $(\tfrac{3}{2}, 2e^{-3/2})$ is an absolute maximum, and $(0,-1)$ is an absolute minimum.

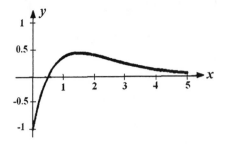

46. $f(x) = xe^{-x^2}$; $f'(x) = e^{-x^2} + xe^{-x^2}(-2x) = (1 - 2x^2)e^{-x^2} = 0$, if $x = \pm\frac{\sqrt{2}}{2}$.

x	0	$\frac{\sqrt{2}}{2}$	2
$f(x)$	0	$\frac{\sqrt{2}}{2}e^{-1/2}$	$2e^{-4}$

From the table, we see that f has an absolute minimum at $(0,0)$ and an absolute maximum at $(\frac{\sqrt{2}}{2}, \frac{\sqrt{2}}{2}e^{-1/2})$.

47. $f(t) = e^t - t$;
We first gather the following information on f.
1. The domain of f is $(-\infty,\infty)$.
2. Setting $t = 0$ gives 1 as the y–intercept.
3. $\lim_{t \to -\infty} (e^t - t) = \infty$ and $\lim_{t \to \infty} (e^t - t) = \infty$.
4. There are no asymptotes.
5. $f'(t) = e^t - 1$ if $t = 0$, a critical point of f. From the sign diagram for f'

$$- \; - \; - \; - \; - \; - \; - \; -0 + + + + ++ + + +$$
$$\xrightarrow{\qquad \underset{0}{+} \qquad\qquad} t$$

we see that f is decreasing on $(-\infty,0)$ and increasing on $(0,\infty)$.
6. From the results of (5), we see that $(0,1)$ is a relative minimum of f
7. $f''(t) = e^t > 0$ for all t in $(-\infty,\infty)$. So the graph of f is concave upward on $(-\infty,\infty)$.
8. There are no inflection points.
The graph of f follows.

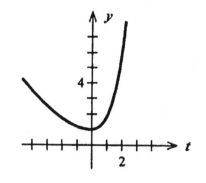

48. $h(x) = \dfrac{e^x + e^{-x}}{2}$.

We first gather the following information on h.
1. The domain of h is $(-\infty,\infty)$.
2. Setting $x = 0$ gives 1 as the y–intercept.
3. $\lim\limits_{x\to-\infty} h(x) = \lim\limits_{x\to\infty} h(x) = \infty$.
4. There are no asymptotes.
5 $h'(x) = \frac{1}{2}(e^x - e^{-x}) = 0$ if $e^x = e^{-x}$, $e^{2x} = 1$ or $x = 0$, a critical point of h. The sign diagram of h'

$$- \ - \ - \ - \ \ - \ - \ - \ -0 + + + \ ++ \ + + +$$

$$\xrightarrow{\hspace{2cm}\underset{0}{|}\hspace{2.5cm}} x$$

shows that h is decreasing on $(-\infty,0)$ and increasing on $(0,\infty)$.
6. The results of (5) show that $(0,1)$ is a relative minimum of h.
7. $h''(x) = \frac{1}{2}(e^x + e^{-x})$ is always positive. So the graph of h is always concave upward.
8. The results of (7) show that h has no inflection points.
The graph of h follows.

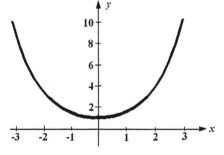

49. $f(x) = 2 - e^{-x}$

We first gather the following information on f.
1. The domain of f is $(-\infty,\infty)$.
2. Setting $x = 0$ gives 1 as the y-intercept.
3. $\lim\limits_{x \to -\infty} (2 - e^{-x}) = -\infty$ and $\lim\limits_{x \to \infty} (2 - e^{-x}) = 2$,
4. From the results of (3), we see that $y = 2$ is a horizontal asymptote of f.
5. $f'(x) = e^{-x}$. Observe that $f'(x) > 0$ for all x in $(-\infty,\infty)$ and so f is increasing on $(-\infty,\infty)$.
6. Since there are no critical points, f has no relative extrema.
7. $f''(x) = -e^{-x} < 0$ for all x in $(-\infty,\infty)$ and so the graph of f is concave downward on $(-\infty,\infty)$.
8. There are no inflection points
The graph of f follows.

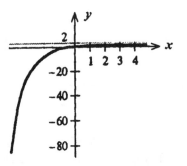

50. $f(x) = \dfrac{3}{1+e^{-x}}$.

We first gather the following information on f.
1. The domain of f is $(-\infty,\infty)$.
2. Letting $x = 0$ gives 3/2 as the y-intercept.
3. $\lim\limits_{x \to -\infty} \dfrac{3}{1+e^{-x}} = 3$ and $\lim\limits_{x \to \infty} \dfrac{3}{1+e^{-x}} = 0$.
4. From the results of (3), we see that $y = 0$ and $y = 3$ are horizontal asymptotes of f.
5. $f'(x) = 3\dfrac{d}{dx}(1+e^{-x})^{-1} = -3(1+e^{-x})^{-2}(e^{-x})(-1) = \dfrac{3e^{-x}}{(1+e^{-x})^2}$. Observe that $f'(x) > 0$ for all x in $(-\infty,\infty)$ and so f is increasing on $(-\infty,\infty)$.
6. f has no relative extrema since there are no critical points.

7. $f''(x) = \dfrac{(1+e^{-x})^2(-3e^{-x}) - 3e^{-x}(2)(1+e^{-x})(-e^{-x})}{(1+e^{-x})^4}$

$= \dfrac{3e^{-x}(1+e^{-x})[2e^{-x}-(1+e^{-x})]}{(1+e^{-x})^4} = \dfrac{3e^{-x}(e^{-x}-1)}{(1+e^{-x})^3}$.

Observe that $f''(x) = 0$ if $e^{-x} = 1$ or $x = 0$. The sign diagram of f''

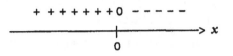

shows that f is concave upward on $(-\infty,0)$ and concave downward on $(0,\infty)$.
8. The results of (7) show that $(0,3/2)$ is an inflection point of f.
The graph of f follows.

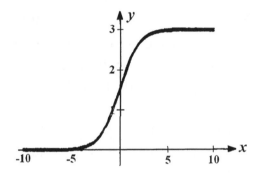

51. $P'(t) = 20.6(-0.009)e^{-0.009t} = -0.1854e^{-0.009t}$
$P'(10) = -0.1694$, $P'(20) = -0.1549$, and $P'(30) = -0.1415$,
and this tells us that the percentage of the total population relocating was
decreasing at the rate of 0.17% in 1970, 0.15% in 1980, and 0.14% in 1990.

52. a. The percent is $N(3) = 15.5719$, or 15.6.
    b. $f'(t) = 1.5(0.78)e^{0.78t} = 1.17e^{0.78t}$. So the required rate is $f'(3) = 12.146$, or
    12.1% per year.
    c. $f''(t) = 1.17(0.78)e^{0.78t} = 0.9126e^{0.78t}$. So the required rate is $f''(3) = 9.474$, or
    9.5%/yr/yr.

53. a. The population at the beginning of 2000 was $P(0) = 0.07$, or 70,000. The

population at the beginning of 2030 will be $P(3) = 0.3537$, or approximately 353,700.

b. $P'(t) = 0.0378e^{0.54t}$; The population was changing at the rate of $P'(0) = 0.0378$ or 37,800/decade at the beginning of 2000. At the beginning of 2030, it was changing at the rate of $P'(3) \approx 0.191$, or approximately 191,000/decade.

54. a. The projected annual average population growth rate in 2020 will be
$G(3) \approx 0.834$, or approximately 0.83%/decade.

b. $G'(t) = -0.33654e^{-0.213t}$; the projected annual average population growth rate will be changing at the rate of $G'(3) = -0.1776$, that is, it is decreasing at approximately 0.18%/decade/decade.

55. a. The total loans outstanding in 1998 were $L(0) = 4.6$, or \$4.6 trillion. The total loans outstanding in 2004 were $L(6) = 3.6$, or \$3.6 trillion.

b. $L'(t) = -0.184e^{-0.04t}$; The total loans outstanding were changing at the rate of $L'(0) = -0.184$, that is, they were declining at the rate of \$0.18 trillion/yr in 1998. In 2004, they were changing at $L'(16) \approx -0.145$ or declining at the rate of \$0.15 trillion/yr.

c. $L''(t) = 0.00736e^{-0.04t}$; Since $L''(t) > 0$ on the interval (0, 6), we see L is decreasing but at a slower rate and this proves the assertion.

56. $C(t) = 1486e^{-0.073t} + 500$.

    a. The average energy consumption of the York refrigerator/freezer at the beginning of 1972 is given by
$C(0) = 1486e^{-0.073(0)} + 500 = 1486 + 500 = 1986,$ or 1986 kwh/yr.

    b. To show that the average energy consumption of the York refrigerator is decreasing over the years in question, we compute
$C'(t) = 1486e^{-0.073t}(-0.073) = -108.48e^{-0.073t},$
and note that $C'(t) < 0$ for all t. Therefore, $C(t)$ is decreasing over the interval $(0 \le t \le 20)$.

    c. To see if the York refrigerator/freezer satisfied the 1990 requirement we compute
$C(18) = 1486e^{-0.073(18)} + 500 = 399.35 + 500 = 899.35,$
or 899.35 kwh/yr. Since this is less than the 950 kwh/yr, we conclude that York satisfied the requirement.

57. a. $S(t) = 20,000(1 + e^{-0.5t})$

$S'(t) = 20,000(-0.5e^{-0.5t}) = -10,000e^{-0.5t};$
$S'(1) = -10,000e^{-0.5} = -6065,$ or $-\$6065/\text{day}.$
$S'(2) = -10,000e^{-1} = -3679,$ or $-\$3679/\text{day}.$
$S'(3) = -10,000(e^{-1.5}) = -2231,$ or $-\$2231/\text{day}.$
$S'(4) = -10,000e^{-2} = -1353,$ or $-\$1353/\text{day}.$

b. $S(t) = 20,000(1 + e^{-0.5t}) = 27,400$

$$1 + e^{-0.5t} = \frac{27,400}{20,000}$$

$$e^{-0.5t} = \frac{274}{200} - 1$$

$$-0.5t = \ln\left(\frac{274}{200} - 1\right)$$

$$t = \frac{\ln\left(\dfrac{274}{200} - 1\right)}{-0.5} \approx 2, \text{ or 2 days}$$

58. a. $A(t) = 0.23te^{-0.4t};$ $A(\frac{1}{2}) = 0.23(\frac{1}{2})e^{-0.2} = 0.094;$ $A(8) = 0.23(8)e^{-3.2} = 0.075.$

   b. $A'(t) = 0.23[t(-0.4)e^{-0.4t} + e^{-0.4t}] = 0.23e^{-0.4t}(-0.4t + 1)$
   $A'(\frac{1}{2}) = 0.23e^{-0.2}(0.8) = 0.151;$ $A'(8) = 0.23e^{-3.2}(-2.2) = -0.021.$

59. $N(t) = 5.3e^{0.095t^2 - 0.85t}.$
   a. $N'(t) = 5.3e^{0.095t^2 - 0.85t}(0.19t - 0.85).$ Since $N'(t)$ is negative for $(0 \le t \le 4)$, we see that $N(t)$ is decreasing over that interval.
   b. To find the rate at which the number of polio cases was decreasing at the beginning of 1959, we compute
   $$N'(0) = 5.3e^{0.095(0^2) - 0.85(0)}(0.85) = 5.3(-0.85) = -4.505$$
   (t is measured in thousands), or 4,505 cases per year. To find the rate at which the number of polio cases was decreasing at the beginning of 1962, we compute
   $$N'(3) = 5.3e^{0.095(9) - 0.85(3)}(0.57 - 0.85)$$
   $$= (-0.28)(0.9731) \approx -0.273, \text{ or 273 cases per year.}$$

60. a. $R(x) = px = 100xe^{-0.0001x}.$

   b. $R'(x) = 100e^{-0.0001x} + 100xe^{-0.0001x} \cdot (-0.0001)$
   $$= 100(1 - 0.0001x)e^{-0.0001x}.$$

   c. $R'(10) = 100(1 - 0.001)e^{-0.001} \approx 99.800,$ or $\$99.80/\text{thousand pair.}$

61. From the results of Exercise 60, we see that $R'(x) = 100(1 - 0.0001x)e^{-0.0001x}$.
Setting $R'(x) = 0$ gives $x = 10,000$, a critical point of R. From the graph of R

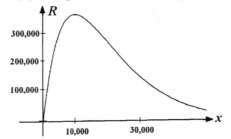

we see that the revenue is maximized when $x = 10,000$. So 10,000 pairs must be sold, yielding a maximum revenue of $R(10,000) = 367,879.44$, or $367,879.

62. The demand equation is
$$p(x) = 100e^{-0.0002x} + 150.$$
Next, $p'(x) = 100(-0.0002)e^{-0.0002x} = -0.02e^{-0.0002x}$.
a. To find the rate of change of the price per bottle when $x = 1000$, we compute
$$p'(1000) = -0.02e^{-0.0002(1000)} = -0.02e^{-0.2} \approx -0.0163, \text{ or } -1.63 \text{ cents per bottle.}$$
To find the rate of change of the price per bottle when $x = 2000$, we compute
$$p'(2000) = -0.02e^{-0.0002(2000)} = -0.02e^{-0.4} \approx -0.0134,$$
or -1.34 cents per bottle.
b. The price per bottle when $x = 1000$ is given by
$$p(1000) = 100e^{-0.0002(1000)} + 150 \approx 231.87,$$
or $231.87/bottle. The price per bottle when $x = 2000$ is given by
$$p(2000) = 100e^{-0.0002(2000)} + 150 \approx 217.03, \text{ or } \$217.03/bottle.$$

63 $p = 240\left(1 - \dfrac{3}{3 + e^{-0.0005x}}\right) = 240[1 - 3(3 + e^{-0.0005x})^{-1}]$.
$p' = 720(3 + e^{-0.0005x})^{-2}(-0.0005e^{-0.0005x})$

$p'(1000) = 720(3 + e^{-0.0005(1000)})^{-2}(-0.0005e^{-0.0005(1000)})$
$$= -\frac{0.36(0.606531)}{(3 + 0.606531)^2} \approx -0.0168, \quad \text{or } -1.68 \text{ cents per case.}$$

$$p(1000) = 240(1 - \frac{3}{3.606531}) \approx 40.36, \quad \text{or } \$40.36/\text{case.}$$

64. a. $N(0) = \dfrac{3000}{1 + 99} = 30.$

b. $N'(x) = 3000\dfrac{d}{dx}(1 + 99e^{-x})^{-1} = -3000(1 + 99e^{-x})^{-2}(-99e^{-x}) = \dfrac{297{,}000e^{-x}}{(1+99e^{-x})^2}$

Since $N'(x) > 0$ for all x in $(0,\infty)$, we see that N is increasing on $(0,\infty)$.

c. The graph of N follows.

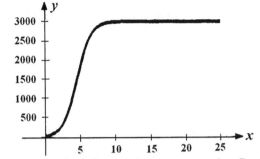

The total number of students who contracted influenza during that particular epidemic is approximately

$$\lim_{x\to\infty}\frac{3000}{1+99e^{-x}} = 3000.$$

65. a. $W = 2.4e^{1.84h}$; $W = 2.4e^{1.84(16)} \approx 45.58$, or approximately 45.6 kg.

b. $\Delta W \approx dW = (2.4)(1.84)e^{1.84h}dh$. With $h = 1.6$ and $dh = \Delta h = 1.65 - 1.6 = 0.05$, we find

$$\Delta W \approx (2.4)(1.84)e^{1.84(1.6)}\cdot(0.05) \approx 4.19\text{, or approximately 4.2 kg.}$$

66. We want to find the maximum of dT/dt:

$$T'(t) = -1000\frac{d}{dt}(t + 10)e^{-0.1t} = -1000[e^{-0.1t} + (t + 10)e^{-0.1t}(-0.1)] = 100te^{-0.1t}.$$

$$T''(t) = 100\frac{d}{dt}(te^{-0.1t}) = 100[e^{-0.1t} + te^{-0.1t}(-0.1)] = 100e^{-0.1t}(1 - 0.1t).$$

Observe that $T''(t) = 0$ if $t = 10$, a critical point of T' From the sign diagram of

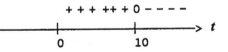

T'', we see that $t = 10$ gives a relative maximum of T'. This is, in fact, an absolute maximum. So the maximum production will be reached in the 10th year of operation.

67. $P(t) = 80{,}000\, e^{\sqrt{t}/2 - 0.09t} = 80{,}000\, e^{\frac{1}{2}t^{1/2} - 0.09t}$.

$$P'(t) = 80{,}000(\tfrac{1}{4}t^{-1/2} - 0.09)e^{\frac{1}{2}t^{1/2} - 0.09t}.$$

Setting $P'(t) = 0$, we have

$$\tfrac{1}{4}t^{-1/2} = 0.09, \ \ t^{-1/2} = 0.36, \ \ \frac{1}{\sqrt{t}} = 0.36, \ \ t = \left(\frac{1}{0.36}\right)^2 \approx 7.72.$$

Evaluating $P(t)$ at each of its endpoints and at the point $t = 7.72$, we find

t	$P(t)$
0	80,000
7.72	160,207.69
8	160,170.71

We conclude that P is optimized at $t = 7.72$. The optimal price is $160,207.69.

68. $A'(t) = 0.23(1 = 0.4t)e^{-0.4t}$. Setting $A'(t) = 0$ gives $t = \frac{1}{0.4} = \frac{5}{2}$. From the graph of A,

we see that the percent of alcohol is highest $2\tfrac{1}{2}$ hours after drinking. The level is given by $A = \left(\tfrac{5}{2}\right) = 0.2115$, or 0.2115%.

69. $f(t) = 1.5 + 1.8te^{-1.2t}$

$$f'(t) = 1.8\frac{d}{dt}(te^{-1.2t}) = 1.8[e^{-1.2t} + te^{-1.2t}(-1.2)] = 1.8e^{-1.2t}(1 - 1.2t).$$

$f'(0) = 1.8$, $f'(1) = -0.11$, $f'(2) = -0.23$, and $f'(3) = -0.13$,
and this tells us that the rate of change of the amount of oil used is 1.8 barrels per $1000 of output per decade in 1965; it is decreasing at the rate of 0.11 barrels per $1000 of output per decade in 1966, and so on.

70. a. The price at $t = 0$ is $18 - 3e^0 - 6e^0 = 9$, or $9/unit.

b. $\dfrac{dp}{dt} = 6e^{-2t} + 2e^{-t/3}$ $\qquad \dfrac{dp}{dt}\bigg|_{t=0} = 6e^{0} + 2e^{0} = 8$

and so the price is increasing at the rate of $8/week.

c. The equilibrium price is given by

$$\lim_{t\to\infty} p = \lim_{t\to\infty}(18 - 3e^{-2t} - 6e^{-t/3}) = 18, \quad \text{or } \$18/\text{unit.}$$

71. a. The price at $t = 0$ is $8 + 4$, or 12, dollars per unit.

b. $\dfrac{dp}{dt} = -8e^{-2t} + e^{-2t} - 2te^{-2t}.$

$\dfrac{dp}{dt}\bigg|_{t=0} = -8e^{-2t} + e^{-2t} - 2te^{-2t}\bigg|_{t=0} = -8 + 1 = -7.$

That is, the price is decreasing at the rate of $7/week.

c. The equilibrium price is $\lim_{t\to\infty}(8 + 4e^{-2t} + te^{-2t}) = 8 + 0 + 0$, or $8 per unit.

72. a.

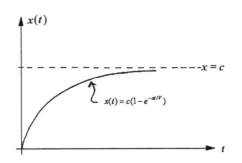

b. $x(t) = c(1 - e^{-at/V})$; $\quad x'(t) = \dfrac{d}{dt}[c - ce^{-at/V}] = \dfrac{ac}{V}e^{-at/V}.$

Since $a > 0$, $c > 0$, and $V > 0$, we see that $x'(t)$ is always positive and we conclude that $x(t)$ is always increasing.

73. We are given that

$$c(1 - e^{-at/V}) < m$$

$$1 - e^{-at/V} < \dfrac{m}{c}$$

$$-e^{-at/V} < \dfrac{m}{c} - 1 \quad \text{and} \quad e^{-at/V} > 1 - \dfrac{m}{c}.$$

Taking the log of both sides of the inequality, we have

$$-\frac{at}{V}\ln e > \ln\frac{c-m}{c}$$

$$-\frac{at}{V} > \ln\frac{c-m}{c}$$

$$-t > \frac{V}{a}\ln\frac{c-m}{c} \quad \text{or} \quad t < \frac{V}{a}\left(-\ln\frac{c-m}{c}\right) = \frac{V}{a}\ln\left(\frac{c}{c-m}\right).$$

Therefore the liquid must not be allowed to enter the organ for a time longer than

$$t = \frac{V}{a}\ln\left(\frac{c}{c-m}\right) \text{ minutes.}$$

74. a. $y' = c(-be^{-bt} + ae^{-at}) = ca(-\frac{b}{a}e^{-bt} + e^{-at}) = cae^{-at}(-\frac{b}{a}e^{(a-b)t} + 1).$

Setting $y' = 0$ gives $-\frac{b}{a}e^{(a-b)t} + 1 = 0$; $e^{(a-b)t} = \frac{a}{b}$; $\ln e^{(a-b)t} = \ln\left(\frac{a}{b}\right)$; $t = \frac{\ln\left(\frac{a}{b}\right)}{a-b}$

Since $y(0) = 0$ and $\lim\limits_{t\to\infty} y = 0$, $t = \frac{\ln\left(\frac{a}{b}\right)}{a-b}$ gives the time at which the

concentration is maximal.

b. $y'' = c(b^2 e^{-bt} - a^2 e^{-at}) = ca^2 e^{-at}\left(\frac{b^2}{a^2}e^{(a-b)t} - 1\right).$ Setting $y'' = 0$ gives

$e^{(a-b)t} = \frac{a^2}{b^2}$; $t = \frac{2\ln\left(\frac{a}{b}\right)}{(a-b)}$. From the sign diagram of y''

```
      ------ 0 ++++++++++++++++
     ┼────────────┼──────────▶ t
     0         2 ln(ᵃ⁄ᵦ)
              ─────────
              (a−b)
```

we see that the concentration of the drug is increasing most rapidly when

$$t = \frac{2\ln\left(\frac{a}{b}\right)}{(a-b)}$$

75. $C'(t) = \begin{cases} 0.3 + 18e^{-t/60}(-\frac{1}{60}) & 0 \le t \le 20 \\ -\frac{18}{60}e^{-t/60} + \frac{12}{60}e^{-(t-20)/60} & t > 20 \end{cases} = \begin{cases} 0.3(1-e^{-t/60}) & 0 \le t \le 20 \\ -0.3e^{-t/60} + 0.2e^{-(t-20)/60} & t > 20 \end{cases}$

a. $C'(10) = 0.3(1 - e^{-10/60}) \approx 0.05$ or 0.05 g/cm^3/sec.

b. $C'(30) = -0.3e^{-30/60} + 0.2e^{-10/60} \approx -0.01$, or decreasing at the rate of

0.01 g/ cm^3/sec.

c. On the interval $(0, 20)$, $C'(t) = 0$ implies $1 - e^{-t/60} = 0$, or $t = 0$.

Therefore, C attains its absolute maximum value at an endpoint. In this

case, at $t = 20$. On the interval $[20, \infty)$, $C'(t) = 0$ implies

$$-0.3e^{-t/60} = -0.2e^{-(t-20)/60}$$

$$\frac{e^{-\left(\frac{t-20}{60}\right)}}{e^{-t/60}} = \frac{3}{2}; \text{ or } e^{1/3} = \frac{3}{2},$$

which is not possible. Therefore $C'(t) \neq 0$ on $[20, \infty)$. Since $C(t) \rightarrow 0$ as $t \rightarrow \infty$, the absolute maximum of c occurs at $t = 20$. Thus, the concentration of the drug reaches a maximum at $t = 20$.

d. The maximum concentration is $C(20) = 0.90$ g/cm^3.

76. a. $A'(t) = \begin{cases} -140e^{-1.4t} & 0 < t < 1 \\ -140(1+e^{1.4})e^{-1.4t} & t > 1 \end{cases}$

So after 12 hr, the amount of drug is changing at the rate of

$$A'\left(\tfrac{1}{2}\right) = -140e^{-0.7} \approx -69.52$$

or decreasing at the rate of 70 mg/day. After 2 days, it is changing at the rate of

$$A'(2) = -140(1+e^{1.4})e^{-2.8} \approx -43.04,$$

or decreasing at the rate of 43 mg/day.

b. From the graph of A

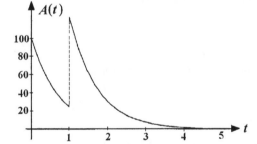

we see that the maximum occurs at $t = 1$, that, at the time when she takes the second dose. The maximum amount is

$$A(1) = 100(1+e^{1.4})e^{-1.4} \approx 124.66, \text{ or } 125 \text{ mg.}$$

77. False. $f(x) = 3^x = e^{x \ln 3}$ and so $f'(x) = e^{x \ln 3} \cdot \dfrac{d}{dx}(x \ln 3) = (\ln 3)e^{x \ln 3} = (\ln 3)3^x$.

78. False. $f(x) = e^{\pi}$ is a constant function and so $f'(x) = 0$.

79. False. $f'(x) = (\ln \pi)\pi^x$. See Exercise 74.

80. True. Differentiating both sides of the equation with respect to x, we have

$$\frac{d}{dx}(x^2 + e^y) = \frac{d}{dx}(10); \quad 2x + e^y \frac{dy}{dx} = 0 \quad \text{and} \quad \frac{dy}{dx} = -\frac{2x}{e^y}.$$

USING TECHNOLOGY EXERCISES 5.4, page 370

1. 5 4366   2. –0.5123   3. 12.3929   4. 0.0926   5 0.1861   6. –1.0311

7. a. The initial population of crocodiles is $P(0) = \frac{300}{6} = 50$.

b. $\displaystyle \lim_{t \to 0} P(t) = \lim_{t \to 0} \frac{300e^{-0.024t}}{5e^{-0.024t} + 1} = \frac{0}{0 + 1} = 0$.

c.
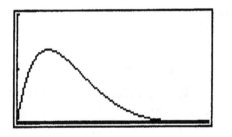

8. a.

b. 57,972/$1000; –$23,418/$1000

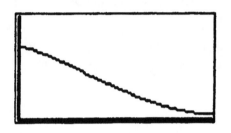

9. a.

b. 4.2720 billion/half century

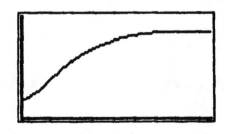

10. a.

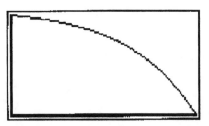

b. Initially, they owe $160,000, and their debt is decreasing at the rate of $87.07 per month. After 180 payments, they owe $126,982.78, and their debt is decreasing at the rate of $334.18 per month.

11. a. Using the function evaluation capabilities of a graphing utility, we find
$f(11) = 153.024$ and $g(11) = 235.180977624$
and this tells us that the number of violent-crime arrests will be 153,024 at the beginning of the year 2000, but if trends like inner-city drug use and wider availability of guns continue, then the number of arrests will be 235,181.
b. Using the differentiation capability of a graphing utility, we find
$f'(11) = -0.634$ and $g'(11) = 18.4005596893$
and this tells us that the number of violent-crime arrests will be decreasing at the rate of 634 per year at the beginning of the year 2000. But if the trends like inner-city drug use and wider availability of guns continues, then the number of arrests will be increasing at the rate of 18,401 per year at the beginning of the year 2000.

12. a. At the beginning of June, there are $F(1) = 196.20$ or approximately 196 aphids in a typical bean stem. At the beginning of July the number is $F(2) = 180.02$, or approximately 180 aphids per bean stem.
b. At the beginning of June, the population of aphids is changing at the rate of $F'(1) = 226.02$; that is, it is increasing at the rate of 226 aphids on a typical bean stem per month. At the beginning of July, the population is changing at the rate of $F'(2) = -238.3$; that is, it is decreasing at the rate of 238 aphids per month.

13. a. $P(10) = \dfrac{74}{1 + 2.6e^{-0.166(10) + 0.04536(10)^2 - 0.0066(10)^3}} \approx 69.63$ percent.

b. $P'(10) = 5.09361$, or 5.09361%/decade

5.5 CONCEPT QUESTIONS, page 376

1. a. $f'(x) = \dfrac{1}{x}$; $g'(x) = \dfrac{f'(x)}{f(x)}$

2. See the procedure given in the text on page 375

EXERCISES 5.5, page 379

1. $f(x) = 5 \ln x;\ f'(x) = 5\left(\dfrac{1}{x}\right) = \dfrac{5}{x}.$

2. $f(x) = \ln 5x;\ f'(x) = \dfrac{5}{5x} = \dfrac{1}{x}$

3. $f(x) = \ln (x + 1);\ f'(x) = \dfrac{1}{x+1}.$

4. $g(x) = \ln (2x + 1);\ g'(x) = \dfrac{2}{2x+1}.$

5. $f(x) = \ln x^8;\ f'(x) = \dfrac{8x^7}{x^8} = \dfrac{8}{x}.$

6. $h(t) = 2 \ln t^5;\ h(t) = 10 \ln t$ and so $h'(t) = \dfrac{10}{t}.$

7. $f(x) = \ln x^{1/2};\ f'(x) = \dfrac{\frac{1}{2}x^{-1/2}}{x^{1/2}} = \dfrac{1}{2x}.$

8. $f(x) = \ln (x^{1/2} + 1);\ f'(x) = \dfrac{\frac{1}{2}x^{-1/2}}{x^{1/2}+1} = \dfrac{1}{2\sqrt{x}(\sqrt{x}+1)}.$

9. $f(x) = \ln \left(\dfrac{1}{x^2}\right) = \ln x^{-2} = -2 \ln x;\ f'(x) = -\dfrac{2}{x}.$

10. $f(x) = \ln \dfrac{1}{2x^3} = \ln 1 - \ln (2x^3) = -\ln 2 - 3 \ln x.$ So $f'(x) = -\dfrac{3}{x}$

11. $f(x) = \ln (4x^2 - 6x + 3);\ f'(x) = \dfrac{8x-6}{4x^2-6x+3} = \dfrac{2(4x-3)}{4x^2-6x+3}.$

12. $f(x) = \ln (3x^2 - 2x + 1);\ f'(x) = \dfrac{6x-2}{3x^2-2x+1} = \dfrac{2(3x-1)}{3x^2-2x+1}.$

13. $f(x) = \ln \left(\dfrac{2x}{x+1}\right) = \ln 2x - \ln (x + 1).$

$f'(x) = \dfrac{2}{2x} - \dfrac{1}{x+1} = \dfrac{2(x+1)-2x}{2x(x+1)} = \dfrac{2x+2-2x}{2x(x+1)} = \dfrac{2}{2x(x+1)} = \dfrac{1}{x(x+1)}.$

14. $f(x) = \ln (x + 1) - \ln (x - 1).$

So $f'(x) = \dfrac{1}{x+1} - \dfrac{1}{x-1} = \dfrac{(x-1)-(x+1)}{x^2-1} = -\dfrac{2}{x^2-1}.$

15. $f(x) = x^2 \ln x$; $f'(x) = x^2\left(\frac{1}{x}\right) + (\ln x)(2x) = x + 2x \ln x = x(1 + 2 \ln x)$

16. $f(x) = 3x^2 \ln 2x$; $f'(x) = 6x \ln 2x + 3x^2 \cdot \frac{2}{2x} = 6x \ln 2x + 3x = 3x(2 \ln 2x + 1)$.

17. $f(x) = \dfrac{2 \ln x}{x}$. $\quad f'(x) = \dfrac{x\left(\frac{2}{x}\right) - 2 \ln x}{x^2} = \dfrac{2(1 - \ln x)}{x^2}$.

18. $f(x) = \dfrac{3 \ln x}{x^2}$. $\quad f'(x) = \dfrac{x^2\left(\frac{3}{x}\right) - (3 \ln x)(2x)}{x^4} = \dfrac{3x(1 - 2 \ln x)}{x^4}$.

19. $f(u) = \ln (u - 2)^3$; $f'(u) = \dfrac{3(u-2)^2}{(u-2)^3} = \dfrac{3}{u-2}$.

20. $f(x) = \ln (x^3 - 3)^4 = 4 \ln (x^3 - 3)$. $\quad f'(x) = \dfrac{4(3x^2)}{x^3 - 3} = \dfrac{12x^2}{x^3 - 3}$.

21. $f(x) = (\ln x)^{1/2}$ and $f'(x) = \dfrac{1}{2}(\ln x)^{-1/2}\left(\dfrac{1}{x}\right) = \dfrac{1}{2x\sqrt{\ln x}}$.

22. $f(x) = (\ln x + x)^{1/2}$; $f'(x) = \dfrac{1}{2}(\ln x + x)^{-1/2}\left(\dfrac{1}{x} + 1\right) = \dfrac{x+1}{2x\sqrt{\ln x + x}}$

23. $f(x) = (\ln x)^3$; $f'(x) = 3(\ln x)^2\left(\dfrac{1}{x}\right) = \dfrac{3(\ln x)^2}{x}$.

24. $f(x) = 2(\ln x)^{3/2}$; $f'(x) = 2\left(\dfrac{3}{2}\right)(\ln x)^{1/2}\left(\dfrac{1}{x}\right) = \dfrac{3(\ln x)^{1/2}}{x}$.

25. $f(x) = \ln (x^3 + 1)$; $f'(x) = \dfrac{3x^2}{x^3 + 1}$.

26. $f(x) = \ln (x^2 - 4)^{1/2} = \frac{1}{2} \ln (x^2 - 4)$. So $f'(x) = \dfrac{2x}{2(x^2 - 4)} = \dfrac{x}{x^2 - 4}$.

27. $f(x) = e^x \ln x$. $f'(x) = e^x \ln x + e^x\left(\dfrac{1}{x}\right) = \dfrac{e^x(x \ln x + 1)}{x}$.

28. $f(x) = e^x \ln \sqrt{x+3} = \frac{1}{2}e^x \ln(x+3)$.

$f'(x) = \dfrac{1}{2}\left[e^x \ln(x+3) + e^x \cdot \dfrac{1}{x+3}\right] = \dfrac{e^x[(x+3)\ln(x+3) + 1]}{2(x+3)}$

29. $f(t) = e^{2t} \ln (t + 1)$

$$f'(t) = e^{2t}\left(\frac{1}{t+1}\right) + \ln(t+1) \cdot (2e^{2t}) = \frac{[2(t+1)\ln(t+1)+1]e^{2t}}{t+1}.$$

30. $g(t) = t^2 \ln(e^{2t} + 1);$

$$g'(t) = 2t \ln (e^{2t} + 1) + t^2\left(\frac{2e^{2t}}{e^{2t}+1}\right) = \frac{2t[(e^{2t}+1)\ln(e^{2t}+1)+te^{2t}]}{e^{2t}+1}$$

31. $f(x)\ \dfrac{\ln x}{x}.$ $f'(x) = \dfrac{x(\frac{1}{x}) - \ln x}{x^2} = \dfrac{1 - \ln x}{x^2}$

32. $g(t) = \dfrac{t}{\ln t};$ $g'(t) = \dfrac{(\ln t)(1) - t(\frac{1}{t})}{(\ln t)^2} = \dfrac{\ln t - 1}{(\ln t)^2}.$

33. $f(x) = \ln 2 + \ln x;$ So $f'(x) = \dfrac{1}{x}$ and $f''(x) = -\dfrac{1}{x^2}.$

34. $f(x) = \ln (x + 5);$ $f'(x) = \dfrac{1}{x+5}$ and so

$$f''(x) = \frac{d}{dx}(x+5)^{-1} = -(x+5)^{-2} = -\frac{1}{(x+5)^2}.$$

35. $f(x) = \ln (x^2 + 2);$ $f'(x) = \dfrac{2x}{(x^2+2)}$ and

$$f''(x) = \frac{(x^2+2)(2) - 2x(2x)}{(x^2+2)^2} = \frac{2(2-x^2)}{(x^2+2)^2}.$$

36. $f(x) = (\ln x)^2;$ $f'(x) = 2(\ln x)\left(\dfrac{1}{x}\right) = \dfrac{2\ln x}{x}$ and

$$f''(x) = \frac{x(\frac{2}{x}) - 2\ln x}{x^2} = \frac{2(1 - \ln x)}{x^2}.$$

37. $y = (x + 1)^2(x + 2)^3$

$\ln y = \ln (x + 1)^2(x + 2)^3 = \ln (x + 1)^2 + \ln (x + 2)^3$

$\qquad = 2 \ln (x + 1) + 3 \ln (x + 2).$

$$\frac{y'}{y} = \frac{2}{x+1} + \frac{3}{x+2} = \frac{2(x+2)+3(x+1)}{(x+1)(x+2)} = \frac{5x+7}{(x+1)(x+2)}$$

$$y' = \frac{(5x+7)(x+1)^2(x+2)^3}{(x+1)(x+2)} = (5x+7)(x+1)(x+2)^2.$$

38. $y = (3x + 2)^4(5x - 1)^2$; $\ln y = 4 \ln (3x + 2) + 2 \ln (5x - 1)$

$$\frac{dy}{dx} \cdot \frac{1}{y} = \frac{4(3)}{3x+2} + \frac{2(5)}{5x-1} = \frac{12(5x-1)+10(3x+2)}{(3x+2)(5x-1)}$$

$$= \frac{60x-12+30x+20}{(3x+2)(5x-1)} = \frac{2(45x+4)}{(3x+2)(5x-1)}.$$

$$\frac{dy}{dx} = \frac{2(3x+2)^4(5x-1)^2(45x+4)}{(3x+2)(5x-1)} = 2(3x+2)^3(5x-1)(45x+4).$$

39. $y = (x - 1)^2(x + 1)^3(x + 3)^4$

$\ln y = 2 \ln (x - 1) + 3 \ln (x + 1) + 4 \ln (x + 3)$

$$\frac{y'}{y} = \frac{2}{x-1} + \frac{3}{x+1} + \frac{4}{x+3}$$

$$= \frac{2(x+1)(x+3)+3(x-1)(x+3)+4(x-1)(x+1)}{(x-1)(x+1)(x+3)}$$

$$= \frac{2x^2+8x+6+3x^2+6x-9+4x^2-4}{(x-1)(x+1)(x+3)} = \frac{9x^2+14x-7}{(x-1)(x+1)(x+3)}$$

Therefore,

$$y' = \frac{9x^2+14x-7}{(x-1)(x+1)(x+3)} \cdot y$$

$$= \frac{(9x^2+14x-7)(x-1)^2(x+1)^3(x+3)^4}{(x-1)(x+1)(x+3)}$$

$$= (9x^2+14x-7)(x-1)(x+1)^2(x+3)^3.$$

40. $y = (3x + 5)^{1/2}(2x - 3)^4$; $\ln y = \frac{1}{2} \ln (3x + 5) + 4 \ln (2x - 3)$

$$\frac{y'}{y} = \frac{1}{2}\left(\frac{1(3)}{3x+5}\right) + 4\left(\frac{2}{2x-3}\right) = \frac{3}{2(3x+5)} + \frac{8}{2x-3}$$

$$= \frac{3(2x-3)+16(3x+5)}{2(3x+5)(2x-3)} = \frac{54x+71}{2(3x+5)(2x-3)}.$$

Therefore,

$$y' = \left(\frac{54x+71}{2}\right)(3x+5)^{-1}(2x-3)^{-1}y$$

$$= \left(\frac{54x+71}{2}\right)(3x+5)^{-1}(2x-3)^{-1}(3x+5)^{1/2}(2x-3)^4$$

$$= \tfrac{1}{2}(2x-3)^3(54x+71)(3x+5)^{-1/2}.$$

41. $y = \dfrac{(2x^2-1)^5}{\sqrt{x+1}}$

$\ln y = \ln \dfrac{(2x^2-1)^5}{(x+1)^{1/2}} = 5\ln(2x^2-1) - \dfrac{1}{2}\ln(x+1)$

So $\dfrac{y'}{y} = \dfrac{20x}{2x^2-1} - \dfrac{1}{2(x+1)} = \dfrac{40x(x+1)-(2x^2-1)}{2(2x^2-1)(x+1)}$

$$= \dfrac{38x^2+40x+1}{2(2x^2-1)(x+1)}.$$

$$y' = \dfrac{38x^2+40x+1}{2(2x^2-1)(x+1)} \cdot \dfrac{(2x^2-1)^5}{\sqrt{x+1}} = \dfrac{(38x^2+40x+1)(2x^2-1)^4}{2(x+1)^{3/2}}.$$

42. $y = \dfrac{\sqrt{4+3x^2}}{\sqrt[3]{x^2+1}}$; $\ln y = \dfrac{1}{2}\ln(4+3x^2) - \dfrac{1}{3}(x^2+1)$.

$\dfrac{y'}{y} = \dfrac{6x}{2(4+3x^2)} - \dfrac{2x}{3(x^2+1)} = \dfrac{9x(x^2+1)-2x(4+3x^2)}{3(4+3x^2)(x^2+1)}$

$$y' = \dfrac{3x^3+x}{3(4+3x^2)(x^2+1)} \cdot \dfrac{\sqrt{4+3x^2}}{(x^2+1)^{1/3}} = \dfrac{x(3x^2+1)}{3(4x^2+1)^{1/2}(x^2+1)^{4/3}}.$$

43 $y = 3^x$; $\ln y = x\ln 3$; $\dfrac{1}{y}\cdot\dfrac{dy}{dx} = \ln 3$; $\dfrac{dy}{dx} = y\ln 3 = 3^x\ln 3$.

44. $y = x^{x+2}$ $\ln y = \ln x^{x+2} = (x+2)\ln x$.

So $\dfrac{y'}{y} = \ln x + (x+2)\left(\dfrac{1}{x}\right) = \dfrac{x\ln x + x + 2}{x}$ and $y' = \dfrac{(x\ln x + x + 2)x^{x+2}}{x}$.

45. $y = (x^2+1)^x$; $\ln y = \ln(x^2+1)^x = x\ln(x^2+1)$. So

$$\dfrac{y'}{y} = \ln(x^2+1) + x\left(\dfrac{2x}{x^2+1}\right) = \dfrac{(x^2+1)\ln(x^2+1)+2x^2}{x^2+1}.$$

$$y' = \frac{[(x^2+1)\ln(x^2+1)+2x^2](x^2+1)^x}{x^2+1}$$

46. $y = x^{\ln x}$; $\ln y = \ln x^{\ln x} = (\ln x)^2$. So $\dfrac{y'}{y} = 2(\ln x)\left(\dfrac{1}{x}\right) = \dfrac{2\ln x}{x}$

and $y' = \dfrac{2\ln x}{x} \cdot x^{\ln x} = 2(\ln x)x^{\ln x - 1}$.

47. $y = x \ln x$. The slope of the tangent line at any point is
$$y' = \ln x + x\left(\tfrac{1}{x}\right) = \ln x + 1.$$
In particular, the slope of the tangent line at $(1,0)$ where $x = 1$ is $m = \ln 1 + 1 = 1$. So, an equation of the tangent line is $y - 0 = 1(x - 1)$ or $y = x - 1$

48. $y = \ln x^2 = 2 \ln x$ and $y' = 2/x$, and this gives the slope of the tangent line at any point (x, y) on the graph of $y = \ln x^2$. In particular, the slope of the tangent line at $(2, \ln 4)$ is $m = 2/2 = 1$. Therefore, the required equation is
$$y - \ln 4 = 1(x - 2) \text{ or } y = x + \ln 4 - 2.$$

49. $f(x) = \ln x^2 = 2 \ln x$ and so $f'(x) = 2/x$. Since $f'(x) < 0$ if $x < 0$, and $f'(x) > 0$ if $x > 0$, we see that f is decreasing on $(-\infty, 0)$ and increasing on $(0, \infty)$.

50. $f(x) = \dfrac{\ln x}{x}$. $f'(x) = \dfrac{x\frac{1}{x} - \ln x}{x^2} = \dfrac{1 - \ln x}{x^2}$. Observe that $f'(x) = 0$ if $1 - \ln x = 0$ or $x = e$. The sign diagram of f' on $(0, \infty)$.

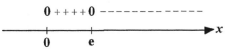

shows that f is increasing on $(0, e)$ and decreasing on (e, ∞).

51. $f(x) = x^2 + \ln x^2$; $f'(x) = 2x + \dfrac{2x}{x^2} = 2x + \dfrac{2}{x}$; $f''(x) = 2 - \dfrac{2}{x^2}$.

To find the intervals of concavity for f, we first set $f''(x) = 0$ giving
$$2 - \frac{2}{x^2} = 0, \quad 2 = \frac{2}{x^2}, \quad 2x^2 = 2$$
or
$$x^2 = 1 \text{ and } x = \pm 1.$$

Next, we construct the sign diagram for f''

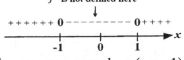

and conclude that f is concave upward on $(-\infty,-1) \cup (1,\infty)$ and concave downward on $(-1,0) \cup (0,1)$.

52. $f(x) = \dfrac{\ln x}{x}$. From Problem 50, we have $f'(x) = \dfrac{1 - \ln x}{x^2}$. Then

$$f''(x) = \dfrac{x^2\left(-\frac{1}{x}\right) - (1 - \ln x)(2x)}{x^4} = \dfrac{(2\ln x - 3)}{x^3}.$$

Observe that $f''x) = 0$ implies $2 \ln x - 3 = 0$, $\ln x = 3/2$, or $x = e^{3/2}$. From the sign diagram of f'' on $(0,\infty)$,

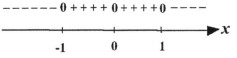

we see that the graph of f is concave downward on $(0,e^{3/2})$ and is concave upward on $(e^{3/2},\infty)$.

53. $f(x) = \ln(x^2 + 1)$. $f'(x) = \dfrac{2x}{x^2 + 1}$; $f''(x) = \dfrac{(x^2 + 1)(2) - (2x)(2x)}{(x^2 + 1)^2} = -\dfrac{2(x^2 - 1)}{(x^2 + 1)^2}$.

Setting $f''(x) = 0$ gives $x = \pm 1$ as candidates for inflection points of f.

$$ - - - - - - 0 + + + + 0 + + + + 0 - - - - $$
$$ \overset{\hspace{3.2cm}}{\underset{\hspace{1cm}-1 \hspace{1cm} 0 \hspace{1cm} 1}{\vert \hspace{1.5cm} \vert \hspace{1.5cm} \vert}} \rightarrow x $$

From the sign diagram for f'', we see that $(-1, \ln 2)$ and $(1, \ln 2)$ are inflection points of f

54. $f(x) = x^2 \ln x$; $f'(x) = 2x \ln x + x^2\left(\frac{1}{x}\right) = 2x \ln x + x$ and

$f''(x) = 2 \ln x + 2x\left(\frac{1}{x}\right) + 1 = 2 \ln x + 3$. Observe that $f''(x) = 0$ if

$2 \ln x + 3 = 0$, $\ln x = -3/2$, or $x = e^{-3/2}$. From the sign diagram of f''

we see that $(e^{-3/2}, -\frac{3}{2}e^{-3})$ is an inflection point of f.

55. $f(x) = x^2 + 2\ln x$, $f'(x) = 2x + \dfrac{2}{x}$, $f''(x) = 2 - \dfrac{2}{x^2} = 0$ implies

$2 - \dfrac{2}{x^2} = 0$, $x^2 = 1$, or $x = \pm 1$. We reject the negative root because the domain of f

is $(0, \infty)$. The sign diagram of f'' follows:

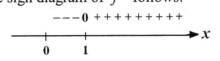

We see that $(1,1)$ is an inflection point of the graph of f. $f'(1) = 4$. So, an equation
of the required tangent line is
$$y - 1 = 4(x - 1) \quad \text{or} \quad y = 4x - 3$$

56. $f(x) = e^{x/2} \ln x$, $f'(x) = e^{x/2}\left(\dfrac{1}{x}\right) + \dfrac{1}{2}e^{x/2} \ln x = \left(\dfrac{1}{x} + \dfrac{\ln x}{2}\right)e^{x/2}$

$f''(x) = \left(-\dfrac{1}{x^2} + \dfrac{1}{2x}\right)e^{x/2} + \left(\dfrac{1}{x} + \dfrac{\ln x}{2}\right)e^{x/2}\left(\dfrac{1}{2}\right) = \left(-\dfrac{1}{x^2} + \dfrac{1}{x} + \dfrac{1}{4}\ln x\right)e^{x/2}$

$f''(1) = 0$. The sign diagram of f'' follows:

$$\text{---}0 ++++++++++$$

We see that $(1,0)$ is an inflection point.

$f(1) = 0$ and $f'(1) = e^{1/2}$. So an equation of the required tangent line is
$$y - 0 = \sqrt{e}(x - 1) \quad \text{or} \quad y = \sqrt{e}x - \sqrt{e}$$

57. $f(x) = x - \ln x$; $f'(x) = 1 - \dfrac{1}{x} = \dfrac{x-1}{x} = 0$ if $x = 1$, a critical point of f.

x	1/2	1	3
$f(x)$	$1/2 + \ln 2$	1	3 - ln 3

From the table, we see that f has an absolute minimum at $(1,1)$ and an absolute
maximum at $(3, 3 - \ln 3)$.

58. $g(x) = \dfrac{x}{\ln x}$ $g'(x) = \dfrac{\ln x - x\left(\frac{1}{x}\right)}{(\ln x)^2} = \dfrac{\ln x - 1}{(\ln x)^2}$.

Observe that $g'(x) = 0$ if $x = e$, a critical point of g.

x	2	e	5
$f(x)$	2.885	e	3.1067

From the table, we see that f has an absolute minimum at (e, e) and an absolute

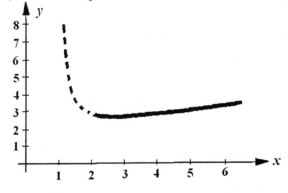

maximum at (5, 3 1067).

59. $f(x) = 7.2956 \ln(0.0645012 x^{0.95} + 1)$

$$f'(x) = 7.2956 \cdot \dfrac{\frac{d}{dx}(0.0645012 x^{0.95} + 1)}{0.0645012 x^{0.95} + 1} = \dfrac{7.2956(0.0645012)(0.95 x^{-0.05})}{0.0645012 x^{0.95} + 1}$$

$$= \dfrac{0.4470462}{x^{0.05}(0.0645012 x^{0.95} + 1)}$$

So $f'(100) = 0.05799$, or approximately 0.0580 percent/kg and

$f'(500) = 0.01329$, or approximately 0.0133 percent/kg.

60. $\ln W = \ln 2.4 + 1.84h$. Differentiating this equation implicitly with respect to h

yields $\dfrac{W'}{W} = 1.84$, or $W' = 1.84W$. Therefore, $\Delta W \approx dW = W'dh = 1.84Wdh$.

When $h = 1$, $\ln W = \ln 2.4 + 1.84(1) = 2.71546873735$, or $W = 15 \, 1116918264$.

So, with $dh = \Delta h = 0.1$, we have

$$\Delta W = (1.84)(15.1116918264)(0.1) = 2.78055,$$

and so the weight of the child increases by approximately 2.78 kg.

61. a. The projected number at the beginning of 2005 will be
$$N(1) = 34.68 + 23.88\ln(6.35) \approx 78.82 \text{ million}$$

   b. $N'(t) = 23.88\dfrac{1.05}{1.05t + 5.3} = \dfrac{25.074}{1.05t + 5.3}$

   The projected number will be changing at the rate of
   $$N'(1) = \frac{25.074}{1.05 + 5.3} \approx 3.95 \text{ (million/yr)}$$

62. a. The percent in 2001 is $P(1) = 28.5$. $P'(t) = \dfrac{14.42}{t}$ and so the percent in 2001 is

   changing at the rate of $P'(1) = 14.42\% / \text{yr}$.

   b. The percent in 2006 is expected to be $P(6) = 54.34$. The rate of change is

   expected to be $P'(6) = \dfrac{14.42}{6} \approx 2.4\% / \text{yr}$.

63. a. If $0 < r < 100$, then $c = 1 - \frac{r}{100}$ sastisfies $0 < c < 1$. It suffices to show that

   $A_1(n) = -(1 - \frac{r}{100})^n$ is increasing, (why?), or equivalently $A_2(n) = -A_1(n) = \left(1 - \frac{r}{100}\right)^n$

   is decreasing. Let $y = \left(1 - \frac{r}{100}\right)^n$. Then $\ln y = \ln\left(1 - \frac{r}{100}\right)^n = \ln c^n = n\ln c$.

   Differentiating both sides with respect to n, we find

   $\dfrac{y'}{y} = \ln c$ and so $y' = (\ln c)\left(1 - \frac{r}{100}\right)^n < 0$

   since $\ln c < 0$ and $\left(1 - \frac{r}{m}\right)^n > 0$ for $0 < r < 100$. Therefore, A is an increasing

   function of n on $(0, \infty)$.

   b.

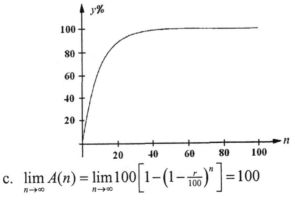

   c. $\displaystyle\lim_{n\to\infty} A(n) = \lim_{n\to\infty} 100\left[1 - \left(1 - \frac{r}{100}\right)^n\right] = 100$

64. a. $\ln I = \ln I_0 a^x = \ln I_0 + \ln a^x = \ln I_0 + x(\ln a)$.

Therefore, $\dfrac{I'}{I} = \dfrac{d}{dx}(\ln I_0 + x(\ln a)) = \dfrac{d}{dx}[x(\ln a)] = \ln a$

and $\qquad I' = (\ln a)I = (\ln a)I_0 a^x$.

b. Since $I' = (\ln a)I$, we conclude that I' is proportional to I with $\ln a$ as the constant of proportion.

65 a. $R = \log \dfrac{10^6 I_0}{I_0} = \log 10^6 = 6$.

b. $I = I_0 10^R$ by definition. Taking the natural logarithm on both sides, we find

$$\ln I = \ln I_0 10^R = \ln I_0 + \ln 10^R = \ln I_0 + R \ln 10.$$

Differentiating implicitly with respect to R, we obtain

$$\dfrac{I'}{I} = \ln 10 \ \text{ or } \ \dfrac{dI}{dR} = (\ln 10)I .$$

Therefore, $\Delta I \approx dI = \dfrac{dI}{dR} \Delta R = (\ln 10)I \Delta R$. With $|\Delta R| \le (0.02)(6) = 0.12$ and

$I = 1,000,000 I_0$, (see part a), we have

$$|\Delta I| \le (\ln 10)(1,000,000 I_0)(0.12) = 276310.21 I_o$$

So the error is at most 276,310 times the standard reference intensity.

66. a. $R(S_0) = k \ln \dfrac{S_0}{S_0} = k \ln 1 = 0 \quad (\ln 1 = 0)$

b. $\dfrac{dR}{dS} = \dfrac{d}{dS} k \ln \dfrac{S}{S_0} = k \dfrac{d}{ds}(\ln S - \ln S_0) = k \dfrac{d}{dS}(\ln S) = \dfrac{k}{S}$,

and so $\frac{dr}{dS}$ is inversely proportional to S, with k as the constant or proportion. Our result says that if the stimulus is small, then a small change in S is easily felt. But if the stimulus is larger, then a small change in S is not as discernible.

67. $f(x) = \ln (x - 1)$.

1. The domain of f is obtained by requiring that $x - 1 > 0$. We find the domain to be $(1, \infty)$.

2. Since $x \ne 0$, there are no y-intercepts. Next, setting $y = 0$ gives $x - 1 = 1$ or $x = 2$ as the x-intercept.

3. $\lim\limits_{x \to 1^+} \ln (x - 1) = -\infty$.

4. There are no horizontal asymptotes. Observe that $\lim\limits_{x\to 1^+} \ln(x-1) = -\infty$ so $x = 1$ is a vertical asymptote.

5. $f'(x) = \dfrac{1}{x-1}$

The sign diagram for f' is

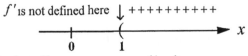

We conclude that f is increasing on $(1,\infty)$.

6. The results of (5) show that f is increasing on $(1,\infty)$.

7. $f''(x) = -\dfrac{1}{(x-1)^2}$. Since $f''(x) < 0$ for $x > 1$, we see that f is concave downward on $(1,\infty)$.

8. From the results of (7), we see that f has no inflection points.

The graph of f follows.

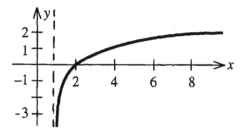

68. $f(x) = 2x - \ln x$.

We first gather the following information on f.

1. The domain of f is $(0,\infty)$.

2. There is no y-intercept.

3. $\lim\limits_{x\to\infty}(2x - \ln x) = \infty$ (Construct a table of values).

4. There are no asymptotes.

5. $f'(x) = 2 - \dfrac{1}{x} = \dfrac{2x-1}{x}$. Observe that $f'(x) = 0$ at $x = 1/2$, a critical point of f.

From the sign diagram of f'

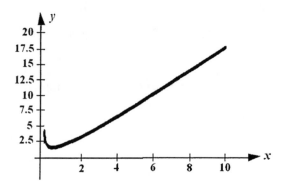

we conclude that f is decreasing on $(0, \frac{1}{2})$ and increasing on $(\frac{1}{2}, \infty)$.

6. The results of (5) show that $(\frac{1}{2}, 1 + \ln 2)$ is a relative minimum of f.

7. $f''(x) = \dfrac{1}{x^2}$ and is positive if $x > 0$. So the graph of f is concave upward on $(0, \infty)$.

8. The results of (7) show that f has no inflection points.
The graph of f follows.

69. False. $\ln 5$ is a constant function and $f'(x) = 0$.

70. True. $f(x) = \ln a^x = x \ln a.$ $f'(x) = \dfrac{d}{dx}[x \cdot \ln a] = \ln a.$

71. If $x \leq 0$, then $|x| = -x$. Therefore, $\ln |x| = \ln(-x)$. Writing $f(x) = \ln |x|$ we have $|x| = -x = e^{f(x)}$. Differentiating both sides with respect to x and using the Chain Rule, we have $\quad -1 = e^{f(x)} \cdot f'(x) \quad$ or $\quad f'(x) = -\dfrac{1}{e^{f(x)}} = -\dfrac{1}{-x} = \dfrac{1}{x}$

72. Let $f(x) = \ln x$. Then, by definition,
$$f'(1) = \lim_{h \to 0} \frac{f(1+h) - f(1)}{h} = \lim_{h \to 0} \frac{\ln(1+h) - \ln 1}{h} = \lim_{h \to 0} \frac{\ln(h+1)}{h}.$$
But $f'(x) = \dfrac{d}{dx} \ln x = \dfrac{1}{x}$ and so $f'(1) = 1 = \lim_{x \to 0} \dfrac{\ln(x+1)}{x}$. (Put $h = x$.).

5.6 CONCEPT QUESTIONS, page 386

1 $Q(t) = Q_0 e^{kt}$ where $k > 0$ is exponential growth and $k < 0$ is exponential decay The larger the magnitude of k the faster the former grows and the faster the latter decays.

2. The half-life of a radioactive substance is the time it takes for the substance to decay to half its original amount.

3. $Q(t) = \dfrac{A}{1 + Be^{-kt}}$, where A, B, and k are positive constants. Q increases rapidly for small values of t but the rate of increase slows down as Q (always increasing) approaches the number A.

EXERCISES 5.6 , page 386

1.   a. The growth constant is $k = 0.05$. b. Initially, the quantity present is 400 units.

   c.

t	0	10	20	100	1000
Q	400	660	1087	59365	2.07×10^{24}

2.   a. $k = -0.06$ b. $Q_0 = 2000$

   c.

t	0	5	10	20	100
Q	2000	1482	1098	602	5

3.   a. $Q(t) = Q_0 e^{kt}$. Here $Q_0 = 100$ and so $Q(t) = 100e^{kt}$. Since the number of cells doubles in 20 minutes, we have

$$Q(20) = 100e^{20k} = 200, \quad e^{20k} = 2, \quad 20k = \ln 2, \quad \text{or} \quad k = \tfrac{1}{20}\ln 2 \approx 0.03466.$$

$$Q(t) = 100e^{0.03466t}$$

   b. We solve the equation $100e^{0.03466t} = 1{,}000{,}000$. We obtain

$$e^{0.03466t} = 10000 \quad \text{or} \quad 0.03466t = \ln 10000,$$

$$t = \frac{\ln 10{,}000}{0.03466} \approx 266, \quad \text{or } 266 \text{ minutes.}$$

   c. $Q(t) = 1000e^{0.03466t}$.

4. $Q(t) = 5.3e^{kt}$. Since the population grows at the rate of 2% per year, we have
   $1.02(5.3) = 5.3e^{k}$, or $k = \ln 1.02 \approx 0.0198$. Therefore, $N(t) = 5.3e^{0.0198t}$ $(t = 0$

corresponds to the beginning of 1990).

a.

t	0	5	10	15	20	25	30	35
$Q(t)$	5.3	5.9	6.5	7.1	7.9	8.7	9.6	10.6

b. $Q'(t) = 5.3(0.0198)e^{0.0198t} = 0.10494e^{0.0198t}$. So the rate of growth in the year 2000 is $Q'(10) = 0.10494e^{0.198} \approx 0.1279$, or approximately 0.1 billion people per year.

5 a. We solve the equation
$$5.3e^{0.0198t} = 3(5.3) \text{ or } e^{0.0198t} = 3,$$
or $\qquad 0.0198t = \ln 3 \text{ and } t = \dfrac{\ln 3}{0.0198} \approx 55.5.$

So the world population will triple in approximately 55.5 years.
b. If the growth rate is 1.8 percent, then proceeding as before, we find
$1.018(5.3) = 5.3e^{k}$, and $\quad k = \ln 1.018 \approx 0.0178.$
So $N(t) = 5.3e^{0.0178t}$. If $t = 55.5$, the population would be
$$N(55.5) = 5.3e^{0.0178(55.5)} \approx 14.23, \text{ or approximately 14.23 billion.}$$

6. The resale value of the machinery at any time t is given by $V(t) = 500,000e^{-kt}$ ($t = 0$ three years ago). We have $V(3) = 320,000 = 500,000e^{-3k}$ which gives $e^{-3k} = \frac{320,000}{500,000} = 0.64$. Therefore, $-3k \ln e = \ln 0.64$ and $k = \dfrac{\ln 0.64}{-3} \approx 0.149$. Four years from now, the resale value of the machinery will be given by
$$V(7) = 500,000e^{-(0.149)(7)} \approx 176,198, \text{ or approximately } \$176,198.$$

7. $P(h) = p_0 e^{-kh}$, $P(0) = 15$, therefore, $p_0 = 15$.
$$P(4000) = 15e^{-4000k} = 12.5; \quad e^{-4000k} = \frac{12.5}{15},$$

$$-4000k = \ln\left(\frac{12.5}{15}\right) \quad \text{and } k = 0.00004558.$$

Therefore, $P(12{,}000) = 15e^{-0.00004558(12{,}000)} = 8.68$, or 8.7 lb/sq in.
The rate of change of the atmospheric pressure with respect to altitude is given by

$$P'(h) = \frac{d}{dh}(15e^{-0.00004558h}) = -0.0006837e^{-0.00004558h}.$$

So, the rate of change of the atmospheric pressure with respect to altitude when the altitude is 12,000 feet is $P'(12{,}000) = -0.0006837e^{-0.00004558(12{,}000)} \approx -0.00039566$.
That is, it is dropping at the rate of approximately 0.0004 lbs per square inch/foot.

8. We are given that $Q(280) = 20$. Using this condition, we have
$$Q(280) = Q_0 \cdot 2^{(-280/140)} = 20. \quad \text{So} \quad Q_0 \cdot 2^{-2} = 20 \text{ or } \frac{Q_0}{4} = \frac{20}{4} = 5. \text{ So the initial}$$
amount was 80 mg.

9 Suppose the amount of phosphorus 32 at time t is given by
$$Q(t) = Q_0 e^{-kt}$$
where Q_0 is the amount present initially and k is the decay constant. Since this element has a half–life of 14.2 days, we have

$$\tfrac{1}{2}Q_0 = Q_0 e^{-14.2k}, \quad e^{-14.2k} = \tfrac{1}{2}, \quad -14.2k = \ln\tfrac{1}{2}, \quad k = -\frac{\ln\tfrac{1}{2}}{14.2} \approx 0.0488.$$

Therefore, the amount of phosphorus 32 present at any time t is given by
$$Q(t) = 100e^{-0.0488t}$$
The amount left after 7.1 days is given by
$$Q(7.1) = 100e^{-0.0488(7.1)} = 100e^{-0.3465}$$
$$= 70.617, \text{ or } 70.617 \text{ grams.}$$
The rate at which the phosphorus 32 is decaying when $t = 7.1$ is given by

$$Q'(t) = \frac{d}{dt}[100e^{-0.0488t}] = 100(-0.0488)e^{-0.0488t} = -4.88e^{-0.0488t}$$

Therefore, $Q'(7.1) = -4.88e^{-0.0488(7.1)} \approx -3.451$; that is, it is changing at the rate of 3.451 gms/day.

10. Suppose the amount of strontium 90 present at time t is given by $Q(t) = Q_0 e^{-kt}$ where Q_0 is the amount present initially and k is the decay constant. Since this element has a half-life of 27 years, we find
$$\tfrac{1}{2}Q_0 = Q_0 e^{-27k}, \quad e^{-27k} = \tfrac{1}{2}, \quad -27k = \ln\tfrac{1}{2}, \quad k = -\tfrac{1}{27}\ln\tfrac{1}{2}.$$

Therefore, the amount of strontium 90 present at any time t is given by
$$Q(t) = Q_0 e^{((1/27)\ln 1/2)t} = Q_0 e^{\ln(1/2)(t/27)} = Q_0(1/2)^{t/27}.$$
We want to find t when $Q(t) = (1/4)Q_0$.

$$\frac{1}{4}Q_0 = Q_0\left(\frac{1}{2}\right)^{t/27}, \quad \left(\frac{1}{2}\right)^{t/27} = \frac{1}{4}, \quad \frac{t}{27}\ln\frac{1}{2} = \ln\frac{1}{4},$$

$$t = 27\frac{\ln\frac{1}{4}}{\ln\frac{1}{2}} = 27\left(\frac{-\ln 4}{-\ln 2}\right) \approx 54, \text{ or approximately 54 years.}$$

11. We solve the equation $0.2Q_0 = Q_0 e^{-0.00012t}$

    obtaining $\qquad t = \dfrac{\ln 0.2}{-0.00012} \approx 13{,}412$, or approximately 13,412 years.

12. We solve the equation $0.18Q_0 = Q_0 e^{-0.00012t}$ giving

$$t = \frac{\ln 0.18}{-0.00012} \approx 14{,}290, \quad \text{or approximately 14,290 years.}$$

13. The graph of $Q(t)$ follows.

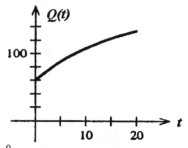

    a. $Q(0) = 120(1 - e^0) + 60 = 60$, or 60 w.p.m.
    b. $Q(10) = 120(1 - e^{-0.5}) + 60 = 107.22$, or approximately 107 w.p.m.
    c. $Q(20) = 120(1 - e^{-1}) + 60 = 135.65$, or approximately 136 w.p.m.

14. a. $S(t) = 50{,}000 + Ae^{-kt}$. Using the condition $S(1) = 83{,}515$ and $S(3) = 65{,}055$, we
    have $S(1) = 50{,}000 + Ae^{-k} = 83{,}515$ and $S(3) = 50{,}000 + Ae^{-3k} = 65{,}055$.
    The first equation gives $Ae^{-k} = 33{,}515$ and the second equation gives
    $Ae^{-3k} = 15055$ So

$$\frac{Ae^{-k}}{Ae^{-3k}} = \frac{33{,}515}{15{,}055}, \quad e^{2k} = \frac{33{,}515}{15{,}055}, \quad \text{or } k = \frac{1}{2}\ln\left(\frac{33{,}515}{15{,}055}\right) \approx 0.40014.$$

    b. $A = 33515e^{-k} = 33515e^{-0.40014} = 22463$. So $S(t) = 50{,}000 + 224633e^{-0.40014t}$.
    In particular, $S(4) = 50{,}000 + 22463e^{-0.40014(4)} \approx 54{,}533$,
    or approximately 54,533.

c. $S'(t) = \dfrac{d}{dt}[50,000 + 22463e^{-0.40014t}]$

$= 22,463(-0.40014)e^{-0.40014t} = -8988.34e^{-0.40014t}$

and so $S'(t) = -8988.34e^{-0.40014(4)} \approx -1813.7$

That is, the sales volume is dropping at the rate of approximately $1814/week.

15. The graph of $D(t)$ follows.

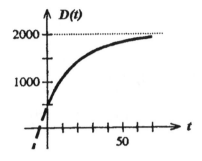

a. After one month, the demand is $D(1) = 2000 - 1500e^{-0.05} \approx 573$.
After twelve months, the demand is $D(12) = 2000 - 1500e^{-0.6} \approx 1177$.
After twenty-four months the demand is $D(24) = 2000 - 1500e^{-1.2} \approx 1548$.
After sixty months, the demand is $D(60) = 2000 - 1500e^{-3} \approx 1925$.
b. $\lim\limits_{t \to \infty} D(t) = \lim\limits_{t \to \infty} 2000 - 1500e^{-0.05t} = 2000$

and we conclude that the demand is expected to stabilize at 2000 computers per month.
c. $D'(t) = -1500e^{-0.05t}(-0.05) = 75e^{-0.05t}$. Therefore, the rate of growth after ten months is given by $D'(10) = 75e^{-0.5} \approx 45.49$, or approximately 46 computers per month.

16. a. The percent that will fail after 3 years is $P(3) = 100(1 - e^{-0.3}) \approx 25.92$.
Therefore, 74% will be usable.
b. $\lim\limits_{t \to \infty} P(t) = \lim\limits_{t \to \infty} 100(1 - e^{-0.1t}) = 100$. So all will fail eventually, as one might
expect.

17. a. The length is given by $f(5) = 200(1 - 0.956e^{-0.18(5)}) \approx 122.26$, or approximately
122.3 cm.
b. $f'(t) = 200(-0.956)e^{-0.18t}(-0.18) = 34.416e^{-0.18t}$. So, a 5-yr old is growing at the

rate of $f'(5) = 34.416e^{-0.18(5)} \approx 13.9925$, or approximately 14 cm/yr.

c. The maximum length is given by $\lim\limits_{t \to \infty} 200(1 - 0.956e^{-0.18t}) = 200$, or 200 cm.

18. a. $Q(1) = \dfrac{1000}{1 + 199e^{-0.8}} \approx 11.06$, or 11 children.

b. $Q(10) = \dfrac{1000}{1 + 199e^{-8}} \approx 937.4$, or 937 children.

c. $\lim\limits_{t \to \infty} \dfrac{1000}{1 + 199e^{-0.8t}} = 1000$, or 1000 children.

19. a. The percent of lay teachers is $f(3) = \dfrac{98}{1 + 2.77e^{-3}} \approx 86.1228$, or 86.12%.

b. $f'(t) = \dfrac{d}{dt}[98(1 + 2.77e^{-t})^{-1}] = 98(-1)(1 + 2.77e^{-t})^{-2}(2.77e^{-t})(-1)$

$$= \dfrac{271.46e^{-t}}{(1 + 2.77e^{-t})^2}$$

$$f'(3) = \dfrac{271.46e^{-3}}{(1 + 2.77e^{-3})^2} \approx 10.4377.$$

So it is increasing at the rate of 10.44%/yr.

c. $f''(t) = 271.46 \left[\dfrac{(1 + 2.77e^{-t})^2(-e^{-t}) - e^{-t} \cdot 2(1 + 2.77e^{-t})(-2.77e^{-t})}{(1 + 2.77e^{-t})^4} \right]$

$$= \dfrac{271.46[-(1 + 2.77e^{-t} + 5.54e^{-t}]}{e^t(1 + 2.77e^{-t})^3} = \dfrac{271.46(2.77e^{-t} - 1)}{e^t(1 + 2.77e^{-t})^3}.$$

Setting $f''(t) = 0$ gives $2.77e^{-t} = 1$

$$e^{-t} = \dfrac{1}{2.77}; \quad -t = \ln\left(\tfrac{1}{2.77}\right), \quad \text{and} \quad t = 1.0188.$$

The sign diagram of f'' shows that $t = 1.02$ gives an inflection point of P. So, the

percent of lay teachers was increasing most rapidly in 1970.

20. a. $N(0) = \dfrac{400}{1 + 39} = 10$ flies. b. $\lim\limits_{t \to \infty} \dfrac{400}{1 + 39e^{-0.16t}} = 400$ flies.

c. $N(20) = \dfrac{400}{1+39e^{-0.16(20)}} \approx 154.5$, or 154 flies.

d. $N'(t) = \dfrac{d}{dt}\left[400(1+39e^{-0.16t})^{-1}\right]$

$= -400(1+39e^{-0.16t})^{-2}\dfrac{d}{dt}(39e^{-0.16t})$

$= \dfrac{2496e^{-0.16t}}{(1+39e^{-0.16t})^2}$

$N'(20) = \dfrac{2496e^{-0.16(20)}}{(1+39e^{-0.16(20)})^2} \approx 15.17031574$, or approximately 15 fruit-flies per day.

21. The projected population of citizens 45-64 in 2010 is

$$P(20) = \frac{197.9}{1+3.274e^{-0.0361(20)}} \approx 76.3962$$

or 76.4 million.

22. The expected population of the U. S. in 2020 is $P(3) = \dfrac{616.5}{1+4.02e^{-0.5(3)}} \approx 324.99$,

or approximately 325 million people.

23. The first of the given conditions implies that $f(0) = 300$, that is,

$$300 = \frac{3000}{1+Be^0} = \frac{3000}{1+B}.$$

So $1+B = 10$, or $B = 9$. Therefore, $f(t) = \dfrac{3000}{1+9e^{-kt}}$ Next, the condition

$f(2) = 600$ gives the equation

$$600 = \frac{3000}{1+9e^{-2k}}, \quad 1+9e^{-2k} = 5, \ e^{-2k} = \frac{4}{9}, \quad \text{or } k = -\frac{1}{2}\ln\left(\frac{4}{9}\right).$$

Therefore, $f(t) = \dfrac{3000}{1+9e^{(1/2)t \cdot \ln(4/9)}} = \dfrac{3000}{1+9(\frac{4}{9})^{t/2}}$.

The number of students who had heard about the policy four hours later is given by

$$f(4) = \frac{3000}{1+9(\frac{4}{9})^2} = 1080, \quad \text{or } 1080 \text{ students.}$$

To find the rate at which the rumor was spreading at any time time, we compute

$$f'(t) = \frac{d}{dt}\left[3000(1+9e^{-0.405465t})^{-1}\right]$$

$$= (3000)(-1)(1+9e^{-0.405465})^{-2}\frac{d}{dt}(9e^{-0.405465t})$$

$$= -3000(9)(-0.405465)e^{-0.405465t}(1+9e^{-0.405465t})^{-2}$$

$$= \frac{10947.555\,e^{-0.405465t}}{(1+9e^{-0.405465t})^2}$$

In particular, the rate at which the rumor was spreading 4 hours after the ceremony

is given by $f'(4) = \dfrac{10947.555e^{-0.405465(4)}}{(1+9e^{-0.405465(4)})^2} \approx 280.25737.$

So , the rumor is spreading at the rate of 280 students per hour.

24. a. $f'(t) = -8e^{-2t} < 0$ for all t in $(0,\infty)$. So f is decreasing on $(0,\infty)$.

b. $f''(t) = 16e^{-2t} > 0$ for all t in $(0,\infty)$. So, f is concave upward on $(0,\infty)$.

c. $\lim\limits_{t\to\infty} f(t) = \lim\limits_{t\to\infty}(6+4e^{-2t}) = 6.$

d.

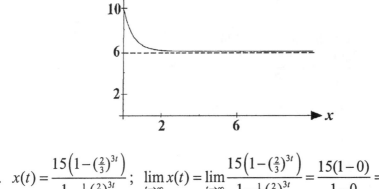

25. $x(t) = \dfrac{15\left(1-\left(\frac{2}{3}\right)^{3t}\right)}{1-\frac{1}{4}\left(\frac{2}{3}\right)^{3t}};\quad \lim\limits_{t\to\infty}x(t) = \lim\limits_{t\to\infty}\dfrac{15\left(1-\left(\frac{2}{3}\right)^{3t}\right)}{1-\frac{1}{4}\left(\frac{2}{3}\right)^{3t}} = \dfrac{15(1-0)}{1-0} = 15$

or 15 lbs.

26. a. $f'(t) = \dfrac{d}{dt}[a(1-be^{-kt})] = \dfrac{d}{dt}(a) - \dfrac{d}{dt}abe^{-kt} = 0 - be^{-kt}(-k) = bke^{-kt}.$

Since $f'(t) > 0$ for all $t \ge 0$, f is increasing on $(0,\infty)$.

b. $f''(t) = \dfrac{d}{dt}(bke^{-kt}) = -bk^2e^{-kt} < 0$ on $(0,\infty)$ and the conclusion follows.

c. $\lim\limits_{t\to\infty} f(t) = \lim\limits_{t\to\infty}[a(1-be^{-kt})] = \lim\limits_{t\to\infty}a - \lim\limits_{t\to\infty}abe^{-kt} = a - 0 = a.$

d.

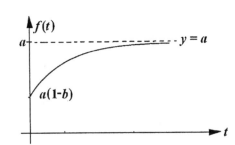

27. a. $C(t) = \dfrac{k}{b-a}\left(e^{-at} - e^{-bt}\right);$

$$C'(t) = \dfrac{k}{b-a}(-ae^{-at} + be^{-bt}) = \dfrac{kb}{b-a}\left[e^{-bt} - \left(\dfrac{a}{b}\right)e^{-at}\right]$$

$$= \dfrac{kb}{b-a}e^{-bt}\left[1 - \dfrac{a}{b}e^{(b-a)t}\right]$$

$C'(t) = 0$ implies that $1 = \dfrac{a}{b}e^{(b-a)t}$ or $t = \dfrac{\ln\left(\frac{b}{a}\right)}{b-a}$.

The sign diagram of C'

$$0 + + + + + - - - -$$

$$\begin{array}{c} \\ 0 \qquad\qquad \dfrac{\ln\left(\frac{b}{a}\right)}{b-a} \end{array} \longrightarrow t$$

shows that this value of t gives a minimum.

b. $\displaystyle\lim_{t\to\infty} C(t) = \dfrac{k}{b-a}.$

28. a. $\displaystyle\lim_{t\to\infty}\left\{\dfrac{r}{k} - \left[\left(\dfrac{r}{k}\right) - C_0\right]e^{-kt}\right\} = \dfrac{r}{k}$, and this shows that in the long run the

concentration of the glucose solution approaches r/k.

b. $C'(t) = -\left[\left(\frac{r}{k}\right) - C_0\right]e^{-kt}(-k) = k\left[\left(\frac{r}{k}\right) - C_0\right]e^{-kt} > 0 \qquad$ (since $\frac{r}{k} > C_0$)

for all $t > 0$. So, C is increasing on $(0, \infty)$.

c. $C''(t) = -k^2\left[\left(\frac{r}{k}\right) - C_0\right]e^{-kt} < 0 \qquad$ (since $\frac{r}{k} > C_0$)

for all $t > 0$. So, the graph of C is concave upward.

d.

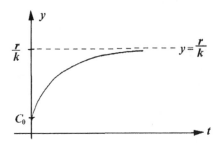

29. a. We solve $Q_0 e^{-kt} = \dfrac{1}{2}Q_0$ for t. Proceeding, we have

$$e^{-kt} = \frac{1}{2}, \quad \ln e^{-kt} = \ln\frac{1}{2} = \ln 1 = \ln 2 = -\ln 2;$$

$$-kt = -\ln 2;$$

So $\quad \bar{t} = \dfrac{\ln 2}{k}$

b. $\quad \bar{t} = \dfrac{\ln 2}{0.0001238} \approx 5598.927,$ or approximately 5599 years.

30. a. $Q'(t) = Ce^{-Ae^{-kt}}\dfrac{d}{dt}(-Ae^{-kt}) = -ACe^{-Ae^{-kt}} \cdot e^{-kt}(-k) = ACke^{(-Ae^{-kt}-kt)}$

b. $Q''(t) = ACke^{(-Ae^{-kt}-kt)} \cdot [-k - Ae^{-kt}(-k)] = 0$, if $Ae^{-kt} = 1$.

$$e^{-kt} = \frac{1}{A}, \quad -kt = \ln\frac{1}{A}, \quad \text{or } t = -\frac{1}{k}\ln\frac{1}{A} = \frac{1}{k}\ln A.$$

The sign diagram shows that $t = \frac{1}{k}\ln A$ is an inflection point and so the growth is most rapid at this time.

$$0\ +\ +\ +\ 0\ -\ -\ -\ -\ -\ -\ -\ -$$

$$\xrightarrow{\hspace{3cm}} t$$

$$\quad 0 \qquad \frac{1}{k}\ln A$$

c. $\lim\limits_{t\to\infty} Q(t) = C$.

1. a.

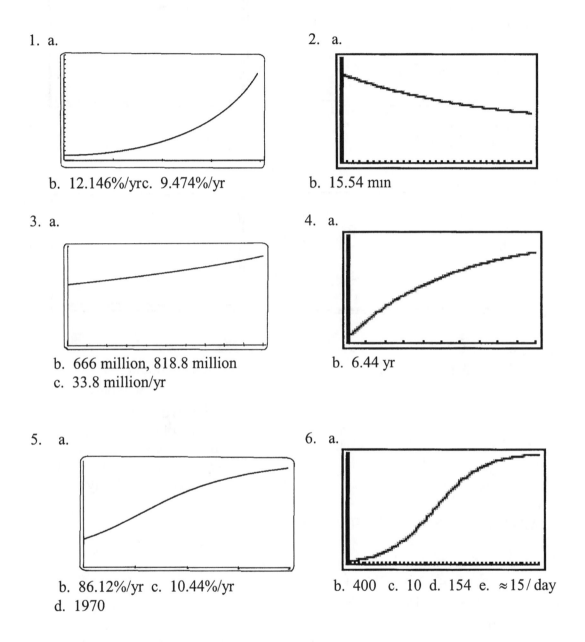

   b. 12.146%/yrc. 9.474%/yr

2. a.

   b. 15.54 min

3. a.

   b. 666 million, 818.8 million
   c. 33.8 million/yr

4. a.

   b. 6.44 yr

5. a.

   b. 86.12%/yr c. 10.44%/yr
   d. 1970

6. a.

   b. 400 c. 10 d. 154 e. ≈ 15/ day

7 a.
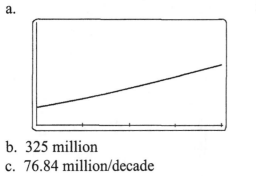
b. 325 million
c. 76.84 million/decade

8. a.
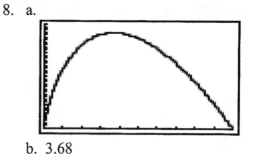
b. 3.68

9. a.
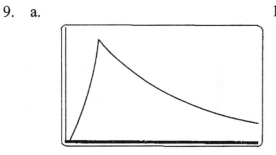
b. 0 c. 0.237 g/cm^3
d. 0.760 g/cm^3 e. 0

10. a.
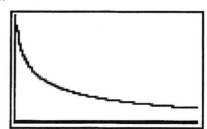
b. \$35,038.78/yr
c. ∞; If Christine withdraws
$25,000/yr she will only be
withdrawing the interest and so the
account will never be depleted.
d. 0; If Christine withdrew
everything in her account, it would
be depleted immediately!

CHAPTER 5 CONCEPT REVIEW, page 392

1. Power; 0; 1; exponential
2. a. $(-\infty,\infty)$; $(0,\infty)$ b. $(0, 1)$; $(-\infty,\infty)$
3. a. $(0,\infty)$; $(-\infty,\infty)$; $(1,0)$ b. < 1; >1
4. a. x b. x
5. Accumulated amount; principal; nominal interest rate; number of conversion
    periods; term
6. $\left(1+\dfrac{r}{m}\right)^{m}-1$ 7. Pe^{rt} 8. a. $e^{f(x)} \cdot f'(x)$ b. $\dfrac{f'(x)}{f(x)}$

9. a. Initially; growth   b. Decay   c. Time; one-half
10. a. Horizontal asymptote; C b. Horizontal asymptote; A; carrying capacity

CHAPTER 5 REVIEW EXERCISES, page 393

1. a-b

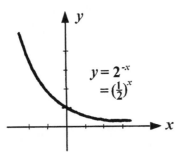

Since $y = \left(\dfrac{1}{2}\right)^x = \dfrac{1}{2^x} = 2^{-x}$, it has the same graph as that of $y = 2^{-x}$.

2. If $\left(\dfrac{2}{3}\right)^{-3} = \dfrac{27}{8}$, then $\log_{2/3}\left(\dfrac{27}{8}\right) = -3$.

3. $16^{-3/4} = 0.125$ is equivalent to $-\dfrac{3}{4} = \log_{16} 0.125$.

4. $\log_4(2x + 1) = 2$, $(2x + 1) = 4^2 = 16$, $2x = 15$, or $x = \frac{15}{2}$.

5.
$$\ln (x - 1) + \ln 4 = \ln (2x + 4) - \ln 2$$
$$\ln (x - 1) - \ln (2x + 4) = -\ln 2 - \ln 4 = -(\ln 2 + \ln 4)$$
$$\ln\left(\dfrac{x-1}{2x+4}\right) = -\ln 8 = \ln \tfrac{1}{8}.$$
$$\left(\dfrac{x-1}{2x+4}\right) = \dfrac{1}{8}$$
$$8x - 8 = 2x + 4$$
$$6x = 12, \text{ or } x = 2.$$

CHECK: l.h.s. $\ln (2 - 1) + \ln 4 = \ln 4$
r.h.s $\ln (4 + 4) - \ln 2 = \ln 8 - \ln 2 = \ln \tfrac{8}{2} = \ln 4.$

6. $\ln 30 = \ln 2 \times 3 \times 5 = \ln 2 + \ln 3 + \ln 5 = x + y + z.$

7. $\ln 3.6 = \ln \frac{36}{10} = \ln 36 - \ln 10 = \ln 6^2 - \ln 2 \cdot 5 = 2 \ln 6 - \ln 2 - \ln 5$
$= 2(\ln 2 + \ln 3) - \ln 2 - \ln 5 = 2(x + y) - x - z = x + 2y - z.$

8. $\ln 75 = \ln (3 \cdot 5^2) = \ln 3 + 2 \ln 5 = y + 2z.$

9   We first sketch the graph of $y = 2^{x-3}$. Then we take the reflection of this graph with respect to the line $y = x$.

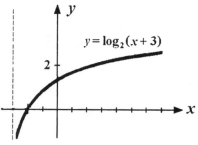

10. We first sketch the graph of $y = 3^{x-1}$. Then we take the reflection of this graph with respect to the line $y = x$.

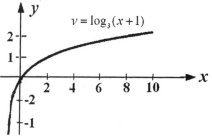

11. $f(x) = xe^{2x}; f'(x) = e^{2x} + xe^{2x}(2) = (1 + 2x)e^{2x}.$

12. $f(t) = \sqrt{t}e^t + t; \ f'(t) = \frac{1}{2}t^{-1/2}e^t + t^{1/2}e^t + 1 = \dfrac{e^t}{2\sqrt{t}} + \sqrt{t}e^t + 1.$

13   $g(t) = \sqrt{t}e^{-2t}; \ g'(t) = \frac{1}{2}t^{-1/2}e^{-2t} + \sqrt{t}e^{-2t}(-2) = \dfrac{1 - 4t}{2\sqrt{t}e^{2t}}.$

14. $g(x) = e^x(1 + x^2)^{1/2}.$

$g'(x) = e^x \dfrac{d}{dx}(1 + x^2)^{1/2} + (1 + x^2)^{1/2} \dfrac{d}{dx}e^x = e^x \frac{1}{2}(1 + x^2)^{-1/2}(2x) + (1 + x^2)^{1/2} e^x$

$$= e^x(1+x^2)^{-1/2}(x+1+x^2) = \frac{e^x(x^2+x+1)}{\sqrt{1+x^2}}.$$

15. $y = \dfrac{e^{2x}}{1+e^{-2x}}$; $y' = \dfrac{(1+e^{-2x})e^{2x}(2) - e^{2x} \cdot e^{-2x}(-2)}{(1+e^{-2x})^2} = \dfrac{2(e^{2x}+2)}{(1+e^{-2x})^2}$

16. $f(x) = e^{2x^2-1}$; $f'(x) = e^{2x^2-1}(4x) = 4xe^{2x^2-1}$.

17. $f(x) = xe^{-x^2}$; $f'(x) = e^{-x^2} + xe^{-x^2}(-2x) = (1 - 2x^2)e^{-x^2}$.

18. $g(x) = (1+e^{2x})^{3/2}$; $g'(x) = \frac{3}{2}(1+e^{2x})^{1/2} \cdot e^{2x}(2) = 3e^{2x}(1+e^{2x})^{1/2}$.

19. $f(x) = x^2e^x + e^x$;
$f'(x) = 2xe^x + x^2e^x + e^x = (x^2 + 2x + 1)e^x = (x+1)^2e^x$

20. $g(t) = t \ln t$; $g'(t) = \ln t + t(\frac{1}{t}) = \ln t + 1$

21. $f(x) = \ln(e^{x^2}+1)$; $f'(x) = \dfrac{e^{x^2}(2x)}{e^{x^2}+1} = \dfrac{2xe^{x^2}}{e^{x^2}+1}$.

22. $f(x) = \dfrac{x}{\ln x}$. $f'(x) = \dfrac{\ln x \frac{d}{dx}x - x\frac{d}{dx}\ln x}{(\ln x)^2} = \dfrac{\ln x - x \cdot \frac{1}{x}}{(\ln x)^2} = \dfrac{\ln x - 1}{(\ln x)^2}$.

23. $f(x) = \dfrac{\ln x}{x+1}$. $f'(x) = \dfrac{(x+1)\left(\frac{1}{x}\right) - \ln x}{(x+1)^2} = \dfrac{1 + \frac{1}{x} - \ln x}{(x+1)^2} = \dfrac{x - x\ln x + 1}{x(x+1)^2}$.

24. $y = (x+1)e^x$; $y' = e^x + (x+1)e^x = (x+2)e^x$.

25. $y = \ln(e^{4x}+3)$; $y' = \dfrac{e^{4x}(4)}{e^{4x}+3} = \dfrac{4e^{4x}}{e^{4x}+3}$.

26. $f(r) = \dfrac{re^r}{1+r^2}$; $f'(r) = \dfrac{(1+r^2)(e^r + re^r) - re^r(2r)}{(1+r^2)^2} = \dfrac{(r^3 - r^2 + r + 1)e^r}{(1+r^2)^2}$.

27 $f(x) = \dfrac{\ln x}{1 + e^x}$,

$$f'(x) = \frac{(1+e^x)\dfrac{d}{dx}\ln x - \ln x \dfrac{d}{dx}(1+e^x)}{(1+e^x)^2} = \frac{(1+e^x)\left(\dfrac{1}{x}\right) - (\ln x)e^x}{(1+e^x)^2}$$

$$= \frac{1 + e^x - xe^x \ln x}{x(1+e^x)^2} = \frac{1 + e^x(1 - x\ln x)}{x(1+e^x)^2}.$$

28. $g(x) = \dfrac{e^{x^2}}{1 + \ln x}$; $g'(x) = \dfrac{(1+\ln x)e^{x^2}(2x) - e^{x^2}\left(\dfrac{1}{x}\right)}{(1+\ln x)^2} = \dfrac{(2x^2 + 2x^2 \cdot \ln x - 1)e^{x^2}}{x(1+\ln x)^2}$

29 $y = \ln(3x + 1)$; $y' = \dfrac{3}{3x+1}$;

$$y'' = 3\frac{d}{dx}(3x+1)^{-1} = -3(3x+1)^{-2}(3) = -\frac{9}{(3x+1)^2}.$$

30. $y = x \ln x$; $y' = \ln x + x\left(\dfrac{1}{x}\right) = \ln x + 1$ and $y'' = \dfrac{1}{x}$.

31. $h'(x) = g'(f(x))f'(x)$. But $g'(x) = 1 - \dfrac{1}{x^2}$ and $f'(x) = e^x$.

So $f(0) = e^0 = 1$ and $f'(0) = e^0 = 1$. Therefore,

$$h'(0) = g'(f(0))f'(0) = g'(1)f'(0) = 0 \cdot 1 = 0.$$

32. $h'(1) = g'[f(1)]f'(1)$ by the Chain Rule. Now, $g'(x) = \dfrac{(x-1)-(x+1)}{(x-1)^2} = -\dfrac{2}{(x-1)^2}$;

$f'(x) = \dfrac{1}{x}$. Now, $f(1) = 0$. So $h'(1) = -\dfrac{2}{(-1)^2} \cdot 1 = -2$.

33. $y = (2x^3 + 1)(x^2 + 2)^3$. $\ln y = \ln(2x^3 + 1) + 3\ln(x^2 + 2)$.

$$\frac{y'}{y} = \frac{6x^2}{2x^3 + 1} + \frac{3(2x)}{x^2 + 2} = \frac{6x^2(x^2 + 2) + 6x(2x^3 + 1)}{(2x^3 + 1)(x^2 + 2)}$$

$$= \frac{6x^4 + 12x^2 + 12x^4 + 6x}{(2x^3 + 1)(x^2 + 2)} = \frac{18x^4 + 12x^2 + 6x}{(2x^3 + 1)(x^2 + 2)}.$$

Therefore, $y' = 6x(3x^3 + 2x + 1)(x^2 + 2)^2$.

34. $f(x) = \dfrac{x(x^2-2)^2}{x-1}$ $\ln f(x) = \ln x + 2\ln(x^2-2) - \ln(x-1)$. So

$$\frac{f'(x)}{f(x)} = \frac{1}{x} + \frac{2(2x)}{x^2-2} - \frac{1}{x-1} = \frac{(x^2-2)(x-1) + 4x^2(x-1) - x(x^2-2)}{x(x-1)(x^2-2)}$$

$$= \frac{4x^3 - 5x^2 + 2}{x(x-1)(x^2-2)}.$$

$$f'(x) = \frac{4x^3 - 5x^2 + 2}{x(x-1)(x^2-2)} \cdot \frac{x(x^2-2)^2}{x-1} = \frac{(4x^3 - 5x^2 + 2)(x^2-2)}{(x-1)^2}.$$

35. $y = e^{-2x}$. $y' = -2e^{-2x}$ and this gives the slope of the tangent line to the graph of $y = e^{-2x}$ at any point (x, y). In particular, the slope of the tangent line at $(1, e^{-2})$ is $y'(1) = -2e^{-2}$. The required equation is $y - e^{-2} = -2e^{-2}(x-1)$ or $y = \dfrac{1}{e^2}(-2x+3)$.

36. $y = xe^{-x}$; $y' = e^{-x} + xe^{-x}(-1) = (1-x)e^{-x}$. The slope of the tangent line at $(1, e^{-1})$, where $x = 1$, is 0. Therefore, a required equation is $y = 1/e$.

37. $f(x) = xe^{-2x}$.
We first gather the following information on f.
1. The domain of f is $(-\infty, \infty)$.
2. Setting $x = 0$ gives 0 as the y-intercept.
3. $\lim\limits_{x \to -\infty} xe^{-2x} = -\infty$ and $\lim\limits_{x \to \infty} xe^{-2x} = 0$.
4. The results of (3) show that $y = 0$ is a horizontal asymptote.
5. $f'(x) = e^{-2x} + xe^{-2x}(-2) = (1-2x)e^{-2x}$. Observe that $f'(x) = 0$ if $x = 1/2$, a critical point of f. The sign diagram of f'

$$+ + + + + + 0 - - - - - - - - - - - -$$

```
    +           +                           x
    0          1/2
```

shows that f is increasing on $(-\infty, \frac{1}{2})$ and decreasing on $(\frac{1}{2}, \infty)$.

6. The results of (5) show that $(\frac{1}{2}, \frac{1}{2}e^{-1})$ is a relative maximum.

7. $f''(x) = -2e^{-2x} + (1-2x)e^{-2x}(-2) = 4(x-1)e^{-2x}$ and is equal to zero if $x = 1$. The sign diagram of f''

$$- - - - - - 0 + + + + + + + + + +$$

```
    +           +                           x
    0           1
```

shows that the graph of f is concave downward on $(-\infty,1)$ and concave upward on $(1,\infty)$.

The graph of f follows.

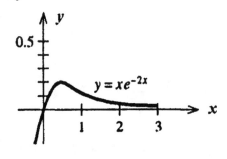

$y = xe^{-2x}$

38. $f(x) = x^2 - \ln x$.

We first gather the following information on f.
1. The domain of f is $(0,\infty)$.
2. There are no y-intercepts.
3. $\lim\limits_{x \to \infty} (x^2 - \ln x) = \infty$.
4. There are no asymptotes.
5. $f'(x) = 2x - \dfrac{1}{x} = \dfrac{2x^2 - 1}{x}$ Setting $f'(x) = 0$ gives $x = \pm \frac{\sqrt{2}}{2}$. We reject the

negative root. So $x = \frac{\sqrt{2}}{2}$ is a critical point of f. The sign diagram of f'

$$- - - - - - - - - - 0 + + + + + + + + + +$$

shows that f is decreasing on $(0, \frac{\sqrt{2}}{2})$ and increasing on $(\frac{\sqrt{2}}{2}, \infty)$.

6. The results of (5) show that $(\frac{\sqrt{2}}{2}, \frac{1}{2}(1 + \ln 2))$ is a relative minimum of f.

7. $f''(x) = 2 + \dfrac{1}{x^2}$. Observe that $f''(x) > 0$ for all x in $(0,\infty)$. So the graph of f

is concave upward on $(0,\infty)$.

8. The results of (7) show that f has no inflection points.

The graph of f follows.

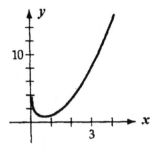

39. $f(t) = te^{-t}$. $f'(t) = e^{-t} + t(-e^{-t}) = e^{-t}(1 - t)$. Setting $f'(t) = 0$ gives $t = 1$ as the only critical point of f. From the sign diagram of f'

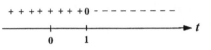

we see that $f(1) = e^{-1} = 1/e$ is the absolute maximum value of f.

40. $g(t) = \dfrac{\ln t}{t}$. $g'(t) = \dfrac{t\left(\frac{1}{t}\right) - \ln t}{t^2} = \dfrac{1 - \ln t}{t^2}$. Observe that $g'(t) = 0$ if $t = e$. But this point lies outside the interval $[1, 2]$.

t	1	2
$\frac{\ln t}{t}$	0	$\frac{\ln 2}{2}$

From the table, we see that g has an absolute minimum at $(1, 0)$ and an absolute maximum at $(2, \frac{\ln 2}{2})$.

41. We want to find r where r satisfies the equation $8.2 = 4.5 \, e^{r(5)}$ We have

$$e^{5r} = \frac{8.2}{4.5} \quad \text{or} \quad r = \frac{1}{5} \ln\left(\frac{8.2}{4.5}\right) \approx 0.12$$

and so the annual rate of return is 12 percent per year.

42. $P = 119346 e^{-(0.1)\,4} \approx 80{,}000$, or $\$80{,}000$.

43. We solve the equation $2 = 1(1 + 0.075)^t$ for t. Taking the logarithm on both sides,

we have $\ln 2 = \ln (1.075)^t \approx t \ln 1.075.$ So $t = \dfrac{\ln 2}{\ln 1.075} \approx 9.58,$ or 9.6 years.

44 a. $Q(t) = 2000e^{kt}.$ Now $Q(120) = 18{,}000$ gives $2000e^{120k} = 18{,}000,$ $e^{120k} = 9,$
   or $120k = \ln 9.$ So $k = \dfrac{1}{120} \ln 9 \approx 0.01831$ and $Q(t) = 2000e^{0.01831t}.$
   b. $Q(4) = 2000e^{0.01831(240)} \approx 161{,}992,$ or approximately $162{,}000.$

45 We have $Q(t) = Q_0 e^{-kt},$ where Q_0 is the amount of radium present initially. Since
   the half-life of radium is 1600 years, we have $\dfrac{1}{2} Q_0 = Q_0 e^{-1600k},$ $e^{-1600k} = \dfrac{1}{2},$
   $-1600k = \ln \dfrac{1}{2} = -\ln 2,$ and $k = \dfrac{\ln 2}{1600} \approx 0.0004332.$

46.

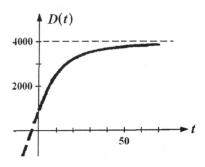

   a. $D(1) = 4000 - 3000\,e^{-0.06} = 1175,$ $D(12) = 4000 - 3000\,e^{-0.72} = 2540,$ and
      $D(24) = 4000 - 3000\,e^{-1.44} = 3289.$
   b. $\displaystyle\lim_{t\to\infty} D(t) = \lim_{t\to\infty} (4000 - 3000e^{-0.06t}) = 4000.$

47. We have $Q(10) = 90$ and this gives $\dfrac{3000}{1 + 499e^{-10k}} = 90,$ $1 + 499e^{-10k} = \dfrac{3000}{90},$

   $499e^{-10k} = \dfrac{2910}{90},$ $e^{-10k} = \dfrac{2910}{90(499)},$ and $k = -\dfrac{1}{10} \ln \dfrac{2910}{90(499)} \approx 0.2737.$

   So $N(t) = \dfrac{3000}{1 + 499e^{-0.2737t}}.$ The number of students who have contracted the flu

   by the 20th day is $N(20) = \dfrac{3000}{1 + 499e^{-0.2737(20)}} \approx 969.92,$ or approximately 970
   students.

48. a. The infant mortality rate in 1980 is given by
          $N(0) = 12.5e^{-0.0294(0)} = 12.5,$ or 12.5 per 1000 live births

The infant mortality rate in 1990 is given by
$$N(10) = 12.5e^{-0.0294(10)} = 9.3, \text{ or } 9.3 \text{ per } 1000 \text{ live births.}$$
The infant mortality rate in 2000 is given by
$$N(20) = 12.5e^{-0.0294(20)} = 6.9, \text{ or } 6.9 \text{ per } 1000 \text{ live births.}$$

b.

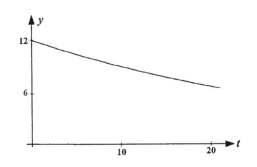

49 a. The concentration initially is given by $C(0) = 0.08(1 - e^{-0.02(0)}) = 0$, or 0 g/cm^3.

b. The concentration after 30 seconds is given by
$$C(30) = 0.08(1 - e^{-0.02(30)}) = 0.03609, \text{ or } 0.0361 \text{ g/cm}^3.$$

c. The concentration in the long run is given by
$$\lim_{t \to \infty} 0.08(1 - e^{-0.02t}) = 0.08 \text{ or } 0.08 \text{ g/cm}^3.$$

d.

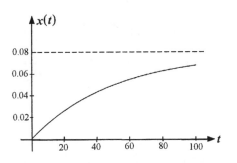

CHAPTER 5 BEFORE MOVING ON, page 394

1. $\dfrac{100}{1 + 2e^{0.3t}} = 40, \ 1 + 2e^{0.3t} = \dfrac{100}{40} = 2.5$;

$2e^{0.3t} = 1.5, \ e^{0.3t} = \dfrac{1.5}{2} = 0.75, \ 0.3t = \ln 0.75, \ t = \dfrac{\ln 0.75}{0.3} \approx -0.959$

2. $A = 3000 \left(1 + \dfrac{0.08}{52}\right)^{4(52)} = 4130.37$, or $\$4130.37$.

3. $f'(x) = \dfrac{d}{dx} e^{x^{1/2}} = e^{x^{1/2}} \dfrac{d}{dx}(x^{1/2}) = e^{x^{1/2}} (\tfrac{1}{2} x^{-1/2}) = \dfrac{e^{\sqrt{x}}}{2\sqrt{x}}$

4. $\dfrac{dy}{dx} = x \dfrac{d}{dx} \ln(x^2 + 1) + \ln(x^2 + 1) \cdot \dfrac{d}{dx}(x) = x \cdot \dfrac{2x}{x^2 + 1} + \ln(x^2 + 1) = \dfrac{2x^2}{x^2 + 1} + \ln(x^2 + 1)$

$\left. \dfrac{dy}{dx} \right|_{x=1} = \dfrac{1}{1+1} + \ln 2 = 1 + \ln 2$

5. $y' = e^{2x} \dfrac{d}{dx} \ln 3x + \ln 3x \cdot \dfrac{d}{dx} e^{2x} = \dfrac{e^{2x}}{x} + 2e^{2x} \ln 3x$

$y'' = \dfrac{d}{dx}(x^{-1} e^{2x}) + 2e^{2x} \dfrac{d}{dx} \ln 3x + (\ln 3x) \dfrac{d}{dx}(2e^{2x})$

$= -x^{-2} e^{2x} + 2x^{-1} e^{2x} + 2e^{2x} \left(\dfrac{1}{x}\right) + 4e^{2x} \cdot \ln 3x$

$= -\dfrac{1}{x^2} e^{2x} + \dfrac{4e^{2x}}{x} + 4(\ln 3x)e^{2x} = e^{2x} \left(\dfrac{4x^2 \ln 3x + 4x - 1}{x^2}\right)$

6. $T(0) = 200$ gives $70 + ce^0 = 70 + C = 200$, so $C = 130$. So $T(t) = 70 + 130e^{-kt}$.

$T(3) = 180$ implies $70 + 130e^{-3k} = 180$, $130e^{-3k} = 110$, $e^{-3k} = \dfrac{110}{130}$, $-3k = \ln \dfrac{11}{13}$,

$k = -\dfrac{1}{3} \ln \dfrac{11}{13} \approx 0.0557$. Therefore, $T(t) = 70 + 130e^{-0.0557t}$. So when $T(t) = 150$,

we have

$70 + 130e^{-0.0557t} = 150$; $130e^{-0.0557t} = 80$; $e^{-0.0557t} = \dfrac{80}{130} = \dfrac{8}{13}$; $-0.0557t = \ln \dfrac{8}{13}$

Thus, $t = -\dfrac{\ln \dfrac{8}{13}}{0.0557} \approx 8.716$, or approximately 8.7 minutes.

EXPLORE & DISCUSS

Page 344

1. Equating the two expressions for y, we obtain $y_0 b^{kx} = y_0 e^{px}$ or $b^x = e^{px}$. Taking the natural logarithms on both sides, we obtain
$$\ln b^{kx} = \ln e^{px}, \qquad kx \ln b = px \ln e = px,$$
and so $p = k \ln b$. Therefore, $y = y_0 e^{(k \ln b)x}$ as was to be shown.

Page 372

1.- 2. $f'(x) = \lim_{h \to 0} \dfrac{f(x+h) - f(x)}{h} = \lim_{h \to 0} \dfrac{\ln(x+h) - \ln x}{h} = \lim_{h \to 0} \left[\dfrac{1}{h} \ln \left(\dfrac{x+h}{x} \right) \right]$

$= \lim_{h \to 0} \ln \left(1 + \dfrac{h}{x} \right)^{1/h}.$

3 From (2), we have

$$f'(x) = \lim_{m \to \infty} \ln \left(1 + \frac{1}{m} \right)^{m/x} = \frac{1}{x} \lim_{m \to \infty} \ln \left(1 + \frac{1}{m} \right)^{m} = \frac{1}{x} \ln \left[\lim_{m \to \infty} \left(1 + \frac{1}{m} \right)^{m} \right]$$

$$= \frac{1}{x} \ln e = \frac{1}{x}.$$

EXPLORING WITH TECHNOLOGY QUESTIONS

Page 344

1. The graph of f in the viewing rectangle $[0, 500] \times [2,3]$ follows.

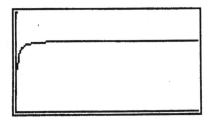

Using **ZOOM** and **TRACE**, we see that $f(x)$ approaches 2.71828..., as x gets larger and larger.

Page 354

1. The graphs of A_1 and A_2 follow.

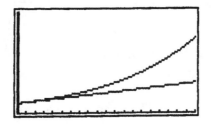

Page 355

1. The graphs of y_1 and y_2 are shown below.

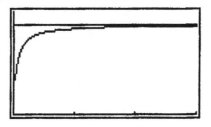

2. From the graph of (a), we see that the graph of y_1 approaches the line
    $y_2 = e^{0.1} - 1$ as x gets larger and larger. This shows that

    $$\lim_{m \to \infty} \left[\left(1 + \frac{0.1}{m} \right)^m - 1 \right] = e^{0.1} - 1.$$

Page 362

1. $f'(x) = \lim_{h \to 0} \dfrac{f(x+h) - f(x)}{h} = \lim_{h \to 0} \dfrac{b^{x+h} - b^x}{h} = \lim_{h \to 0} \dfrac{b^x(b^h - 1)}{h} = b^x \lim_{h \to 0} \dfrac{b^h - 1}{h},$

    because b^x is a constant with respect to the limiting process.

2. These results are immediately obvious if you replace b by 2 and 3, respectively.

3. Drawing the graph of $f(x) = \dfrac{2^x - 1}{x}$ using the viewing rectangle $[0,1] \times [0,1]$ and

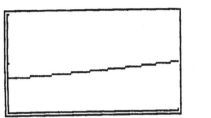 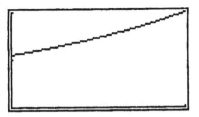

then using **ZOOM** and **TRACE** we see that $\displaystyle\lim_{h \to 0} \dfrac{2^h - 1}{h} = 0.69$. The other result is

obtained in a similar manner.

Page 374
The graphs of f, f', and f'' follow.

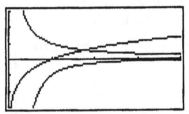

1. The graph of f' is always positive, but decreases to zero as $x \to \infty$. This tells us that the graph of f is increasing but more slowly as $x \to \infty$.

2. Since $f'' < 0$ for all values of $x > 0$, we see that f is concave downward for $x > 0$. But $f''(x) \to 0$ and this shows that the bend (concavity) of the graph of f is less pronounced as x gets larger.

Page 376
1. a. The graph of f is shown in the figure that follows.

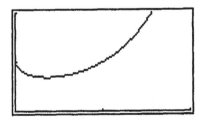

Using **ZOOM** and **TRACE**, we see that $\lim\limits_{x \to 0^+} x^x = 1.$

b. $\lim\limits_{x \to 0^+} f'(x) = \lim\limits_{x \to 0^+} x^x(1 + \ln x) = \lim\limits_{x \to 0^+} x^x, \ \lim\limits_{x \to 0^+}(1 + \ln x) = -\infty$, since $\lim\limits_{x \to 0^+}(1 + \ln x) = -\infty.$

Page 385

1 The graph of Q is shown below.

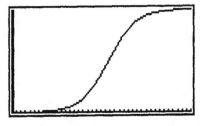

2. The point of intersection of the graphs is (17.405467118, 1000). Therefore, it takes approximately 17.4 days for the first 1000 soldiers to contract the flu.

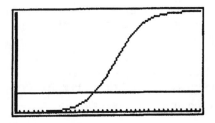

CHAPTER 6

6.1 CONCEPT QUESTIONS, page 404

1. An antiderivative of a continuous function f on an interval I is a function F such that $F'(x) = f(x)$ for every x in I. For example, an antiderivative of $f(x) = x^2$ on $(-\infty, \infty)$ is the function $F(x) = \frac{1}{3}x^3$ on $(-\infty, \infty)$.
2. If $f'(x) = g'(x)$ for all x in I, then $f(x) = g(x) + C$ for all x in I, where C is an arbitrary constant.
3. The indefinite integral of f is the family of functions $F(x) + C$, where F is an antiderivative of f, and C is an arbitrary constant.

EXERCISES 6.1, page 404

1. $F(x) = \frac{1}{3}x^3 + 2x^2 - x + 2$; $F'(x) = x^2 + 4x - 1 = f(x)$.

2. $F(x) = xe^x + \pi$; $F'(x) = xe^x + e^x = e^x(x+1) = f(x)$.

3. $F(x) = (2x^2 - 1)^{1/2}$; $F'(x) = \frac{1}{2}(2x^2 - 1)^{-1/2}(4x) = 2x(2x^2 - 1)^{-1/2} = f(x)$.

4. $F(x) = x\ln x - x$; $F'(x) = x(\frac{1}{x}) + \ln x - 1 = \ln x = f(x)$.

5. a. $G'(x) = \dfrac{d}{dx}(2x) = 2 = f(x)$

   b. $F(x) = G(x) + C = 2x + C$

   c.

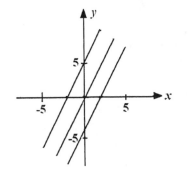

6. a. $G'(x) = 4x = f(x)$ and so G is an antiderivative of f.
    b. $H(x) = G(x) + C = 2x^2 + C$, where C is an arbitrary constant.
    c.

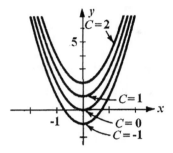

7   a. $G'(x) = \dfrac{d}{dx}(\tfrac{1}{3}x^3) = x^2 = f(x)$ b. $F(x) = G(x) + C = \tfrac{1}{3}x^3 + C$

    c.

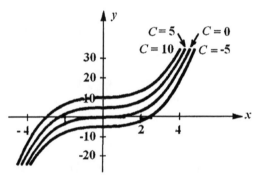

8. a. $G(x) = e^x$ and $G'(x) = e^x = f(x)$.   b. $F(x) = e^x + C$, C an arbitrary constant.
    c.

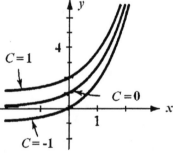

9. $\displaystyle\int 6\,dx = 6x + C.$

10. $\displaystyle\int \sqrt{2}\,dx = \sqrt{2}x + C$

11. $\displaystyle\int x^3\,dx = \tfrac{1}{4}x^4 + C$

12. $\displaystyle\int 2x^5\,dx = 2(\tfrac{1}{6}x^6) + C = \tfrac{1}{3}x^6 + C.$

6   Integration   500

13. $\displaystyle\int x^{-4}dx = -\tfrac{1}{3}x^{-3} + C$

14. $\displaystyle\int 3t^{-7}dt = 3(-\tfrac{1}{6}t^{-6}) + C = -\tfrac{1}{2}t^{-6} + C$

15. $\displaystyle\int x^{2/3}dx = \tfrac{3}{5}x^{5/3} + C$

16. $\displaystyle\int 2u^{3/4}du = 2(\tfrac{4}{7}u^{7/4}) + C = \tfrac{8}{7}u^{7/4} + C$

17. $\displaystyle\int x^{-5/4}dx = -4x^{-1/4} + C$

18. $\displaystyle\int 3x^{-2/3}dx = 3\left(\dfrac{x^{1/3}}{\tfrac{1}{3}}\right) + C = 9x^{1/3} + C$

19. $\displaystyle\int \dfrac{2}{x^2}\,dx = 2\int x^{-2}dx = 2(-1x^{-1}) + C = -\dfrac{2}{x} + C$

20. $\displaystyle\int \dfrac{1}{3x^5}\,dx = \tfrac{1}{3}\int x^{-5}dx = \tfrac{1}{3}(-\tfrac{1}{4}x^{-4}) + C = -\dfrac{1}{12x^4} + C$

21. $\displaystyle\int \pi\sqrt{t}\,dt = \pi\int t^{1/2}dt = \pi(\tfrac{2}{3}t^{3/2}) + C = \dfrac{2\pi}{3}t^{3/2} + C$

22. $\displaystyle\int \dfrac{3}{\sqrt{t}}\,dt = 3\int t^{-1/2}dt = 6t^{1/2} + C = 6\sqrt{t} + C$

23. $\displaystyle\int (3-2x)\,dx = \int 3\,dx - 2\int x\,dx = 3x - x^2 + C$

24. $\displaystyle\int (1+u+u^2)\,du = u + \tfrac{1}{2}u^2 + \tfrac{1}{3}u^3 + C$

25. $\displaystyle\int (x^2+x+x^{-3})\,dx = \int x^2\,dx + \int x\,dx + \int x^{-3}\,dx = \tfrac{1}{3}x^3 + \tfrac{1}{2}x^2 - \tfrac{1}{2}x^{-2} + C$

26. $\displaystyle\int (0.3t^2 + 0.02t + 2)\,dt = 0.3(\tfrac{1}{3}t^3) + 0.02(\tfrac{1}{2}t^2) + 2t + C = 0.1t^3 + 0.01t^2 + 2t + C$

27. $\displaystyle\int 4e^x\,dx = 4e^x + C$

28. $\displaystyle\int (1+e^x)\,dx = x + e^x + C$

29. $\displaystyle\int (1+x+e^x)\,dx = x + \tfrac{1}{2}x^2 + e^x + C$

30. $\displaystyle\int (2+x+2x^2+e^x)\,dx = 2x + \tfrac{1}{2}x^2 + \tfrac{2}{3}x^3 + e^x + C$

31. $\displaystyle\int \left(4x^3 - \dfrac{2}{x^2} - 1\right)dx = \int (4x^3 - 2x^{-2} - 1)\,dx = x^4 + 2x^{-1} - x + C = x^4 + \dfrac{2}{x} - x + C$

32. $\displaystyle\int (6x^3 + 3x^{-2} - x)\,dx = \dfrac{3}{2}x^4 - 3x^{-1} - \dfrac{1}{2}x^2 + C$

33. $\displaystyle\int (x^{5/2} + 2x^{3/2} - x)\,dx = \tfrac{2}{7}x^{7/2} + \tfrac{4}{5}x^{5/2} - \tfrac{1}{2}x^2 + C$

34. $\int (t^{3/2} + 2t^{1/2} - 4t^{-1/2})\,dt = \frac{2}{5}t^{5/2} + \frac{4}{3}t^{3/2} - 8t^{1/2} + C$

35. $\int (x^{1/2} + 3x^{-1/2})\,dx = \frac{2}{3}x^{3/2} + 6x^{1/2} + C$

36. $\int (x^{2/3} - x^{-2})\,dx = \frac{3}{5}x^{5/3} + \frac{1}{x} + C$

37. $\int \left(\frac{u^3 + 2u^2 - u}{3u}\right)du = \frac{1}{3}\int (u^2 + 2u - 1)\,du = \frac{1}{9}u^3 + \frac{1}{3}u^2 - \frac{1}{3}u + C$

38. $\int (x^2 - x^{-2})\,dx = \frac{1}{3}x^3 + x^{-1} = \frac{1}{3}x^3 + \frac{1}{x} + C$

39. $\int (2t+1)(t-2)\,dt = \int (2t^2 - 3t - 2)\,dt = \frac{2}{3}t^3 - \frac{3}{2}t^2 - 2t + C$

40. $\int u^{-2}(1 - u^2 + u^4)\,du = \int (u^{-2} - 1 + u^2)\,du = -u^{-1} - u + \frac{1}{3}u^3 + C$

41. $\int \frac{1}{x^2}(x^4 - 2x^2 + 1)\,dx = \int (x^2 - 2 + x^{-2})\,dx = \frac{1}{3}x^3 - 2x - x^{-1} + C$

$$= \frac{1}{3}x^3 - 2x - \frac{1}{x} + C$$

42. $\int t^{1/2}(t^2 + t - 1)\,dt = \int (t^{5/2} + t^{3/2} - t^{1/2})\,dt = \frac{2}{7}t^{7/2} + \frac{2}{5}t^{5/2} - \frac{2}{3}t^{3/2} + C$

43. $\int \frac{ds}{(s+1)^{-2}} = \int (s+1)^2\,ds = \int (s^2 + 2s + 1)\,ds = \frac{1}{3}s^3 + s^2 + s + C$

44. $\int (x^{1/2} + 3x^{-1} - 2e^x)\,dx = \frac{2}{3}x^{3/2} + 3\ln|x| - 2e^x + C$

45. $\int (e^t + t^e)\,dt = e^t + \frac{1}{e+1}t^{e+1} + C$

46. $\int \left(\frac{1}{x^2} - \frac{1}{\sqrt[3]{x^2}} + \frac{1}{\sqrt{x}}\right)dx = \int (x^{-2} - x^{-2/3} + x^{-1/2})\,dx$

$$= -x^{-1} - 3x^{1/3} + 2x^{1/2} + C = -\frac{1}{x} - 3x^{1/3} + 2\sqrt{x} + C$$

47. $\displaystyle\int\left(\frac{x^3+x^2-x+1}{x^2}\right)dx=\int\left(x+1-\frac{1}{x}+\frac{1}{x^2}\right)dx=\frac{1}{2}x^2+x-\ln|x|-x^{-1}+C$

48. $\displaystyle\int\left(\frac{t^3+\sqrt[3]{t}}{t^2}\right)dt=\int\,(t+t^{-5/3})\,dt=\frac{1}{2}t^2-\frac{3}{2}t^{-2/3}+C$

49. $\displaystyle\int\left(\frac{(x^{1/2}-1)^2}{x^2}\right)dx=\int\left(\frac{x-2x^{1/2}+1}{x^2}\right)dx=\int\,(x^{-1}-2x^{-3/2}+x^{-2})\,dx$

$$=\ln|x|+4x^{-1/2}-x^{-1}+C=\ln|x|+\frac{4}{\sqrt{x}}-\frac{1}{x}+C$$

50. $\displaystyle\int\,(x+1)^2\left(1-\frac{1}{x}\right)dx=\int\,(x^2+2x+1)\left(1-\frac{1}{x}\right)dx$

$$=\int\,(x^2+x-1-\frac{1}{x})\,dx=\frac{1}{3}x^3+\frac{1}{2}x^2-x-\ln|x|+C$$

51. $\displaystyle\int\,f'(x)\,dx=\int\,(2x+1)\,dx=x^2+x+C.$ The condition $f(1)=3$ gives

$f(1)=1+1+C=3,$ or $C=1.$ Therefore, $f(x)=x^2+x+1.$

52. $\displaystyle f(x)=\int\,f'(x)\,dx=\int\,(3x^2-6x)\,dx=x^3-3x^2+C.$ Using the given initial

condition, we have $f(2)=8-12+C=4,$ or $C=8.$ Therefore, $f(x)=x^3-3x^2+8.$

53. $f'(x)=3x^2+4x-1;\ f(x)=x^3+2x^2-x+C.$ Using the given initial condition,
we have $f(2)=8+2(4)-2+C=9,$ so $16-2+C=9,$ or $C=-5.$ Therefore,
$f(x)=x^3+2x^2-x-5.$

54. $\displaystyle f(x)=\int\,f'(x)\,dx=\int\,\frac{1}{\sqrt{x}}\,dx=\int\,x^{-1/2}\,dx=2x^{1/2}+C.$ Using the given condition,

we obtain $f(4)=2\sqrt{4}+C=4+C=2,$ or $C=-2.$ Therefore, $f(x)=2\sqrt{x}-2.$

55. $f(x) = \int f'(x)\,dx = \int \left(1 + \dfrac{1}{x^2}\right)dx = \int (1 + x^{-2})\,dx = x - \dfrac{1}{x} + C.$

Using the given initial condition, we have $f(1) = 1 - 1 + C = 2$, or $C = 2$.

Therefore, $f(x) = x - \dfrac{1}{x} + 2.$

56. $f(x) = \int (e^x - 2x)\,dx = e^x - x^2 + C.$

Using the initial condition, we have $f(0) = e^0 - 0 + C = 1 + C = 2,$
or $C = 1.$ So $f(x) = e^x - x^2 + 1.$

57. $f(x) = \int \dfrac{x+1}{x}\,dx = \int \left(1 + \dfrac{1}{x}\right)dx = x + \ln|x| + C.$ Using the initial condition, we

have $f(1) = 1 + \ln 1 + C = 1 + C = 1,$ or $C = 0.$ So $f(x) = x + \ln|x|.$

58. $f'(x) = 1 + e^x + \dfrac{1}{x}; \quad f(x) = xe^x + \ln|x| + C$

Using the initial condition, we have $f(1) = 1 + e + \ln 1 + C$ and so
$3 + e = 1 + e + C$ and $C = 2.$ Therefore, $f(x) = xe^x + \ln|x| + 2.$

59. $f(x) = \int f'(x)\,dx = \int \frac{1}{2}x^{-1/2}\,dx = \frac{1}{2}(2x^{1/2}) + C = x^{1/2} + C; \; f(2) = \sqrt{2} + C = \sqrt{2}$

implies $C = 0.$ So $f(x) = \sqrt{x}.$

60. $f(t) = \int f'(t)\,dt = \int (t^2 - 2t + 3)\,dt = \frac{1}{3}t^3 - t^2 + 3t + C$

$f(1) = \frac{1}{3} - 1 + 3 + C = 2$ implies $C = -\frac{1}{3}.$ So $f(t) = \frac{1}{3}t^3 - t^2 + 3t - \frac{1}{3}.$

61. $f'(x) = e^x + x; \; f(x) = e^x + \frac{1}{2}x^2 + C; \; f(0) = e^0 + \frac{1}{2}(0) + C = 1 + C$

So $3 = 1 + C$ or $2 = C.$ Therefore, $f(x) = e^x + \frac{1}{2}x^2 + 2.$

62. $f(x) = \int \left(\dfrac{2}{x} + 1\right)dx = 2\ln|x| + x + C.$ $f(1) = 2\ln 1 + 1 + C = 2.$ So

$f(x) = 2\ln|x| + x + 1.$

63. The net amount on deposit in Branch A is given by the area under the graph of f

from $t = 0$ to $t = 180$. On the other hand, the net amount on deposit in Branch B is given by the area under the graph of g over the same interval. Evidently the first area is larger than the second. Therefore, we see that Branch A has the larger net deposit.

64. Since $f(t) \geq g(t)$ for all t in $[0, T]$, we see that the velocity of car A is always greater than or equal to that of car B. We conclude accordingly that after t seconds, car a will be ahead of car B.

65. The position of the car is
$$s(t) = \int f(t)\,dt = \int 2\sqrt{t}\,dt = \int 2t^{1/2}\,dt = 2(\tfrac{2}{3}t^{3/2}) + C = \tfrac{4}{3}t^{3/2} + C.$$
$s(0) = 0$ implies $s(0) = C = 0$. So $s(t) = \tfrac{4}{3}t^{3/2}$

66. Let f be the position function of the maglev. Then $f'(t) = v(t)$. Therefore,
$$f(t) = \int f'(t)\,dt = \int v(t)\,dt = \int (0.2t + 3)\,dt = 0.1t^2 + 3t + C.$$

If we measure the position of the maglev from the station, then the required function is $f(t) = 0.1t^2 + 3t$.

67. $C(x) = \int C'(x)\,dx = \int (0.000009x^2 - 0.009x + 8)\,dx$

$\qquad = 0.000003x^3 - 0.0045x^2 + 8x + k.$

$C(0) = k = 120$ and so $C(x) = 0.000003x^3 - 0.0045x^2 + 8x + 120.$

$C(500) = 0.000003(500)^3 - 0.0045(500)^2 + 8(500) + 120,$ or $\$3370.$

68. a. $R(x) = \int R'(x)\,dx = \int (-0.009x + 12)\,dx = -0.0045x^2 + 12x + C$. But

$R(0) = C = 0$ and so $R(x) = -0.0045x^2 + 12x$
b. $R(x) = px$ and so $-0.0045x^2 + 12x = px$ or $p = -0.0045x + 12.$

69. $P'(x) = -0.004x + 20$, $P(x) = -0.002x^2 + 20x + C$. Since $C = -16,000$, we find that $P(x) = -0.002x^2 + 20x - 16,000.$ The company realizes a maximum profit when $P'(x) = 0$, that is, when $x = 5000$ units. Next,
$$P(5000) = -0.002(5000)^2 + 20(5000) - 16,000 = 34,000.$$
Thus, a maximum profit of $\$34,000$ is realized at a production level of 5000 units.

6 Integration

70. $C(x) = \int C'(x)\,dx = \int (0.002x + 100)\,dx = 0.001x^2 + 100x + k.$ But

$C(0) = k = 4000$ and so $C(x) = 0.001x^2 + 100x + 4000.$

71. a. $N(t) = \int N'(t)\,dt = \int (-3t^2 + 12t + 45)\,dt = -t^3 + 6t^2 + 45t + C$ But $N(0) = C = 0$

and so $N(t) = -t^3 + 6t^2 + 45t.$

b. The number is $N(4) = -4^3 + 6(4)^2 + 45(4) = 212.$

72. a. We have the initial-value problem: $T'(t) = 0.15t^2 - 3.6t + 14.4 \ ; \ T(0) = 24$

Integrating, we find

$$T(t) = \int T'(t)\,dt = \int (0.15t^2 - 3.6t + 14.4)\,dt = 0.05t^3 - 1.8t^2 + 14\ 4t + C$$

Using the initial condition, we find $T(0) = 24 = 0 + C$, so $C = 24.$

Therefore, $T(t) = 0.05t^3 - 1.8t^2 + 14.4t + 24.$

b. The temperature at 10 A.M. was

$$T(4) = 0.05(4^3) - 1.8(4^2) + 14.4(4) + 24 = 56 \ \text{ or } 56\,^\circ F.$$

73 a. The number of subscribers in year t is given by

$$N(t) = \int r(t)\,dt = \int (-0.375t^2 + 2.1t + 2.45)\,dt$$

$$= -0.125t^3 + 1.05t^2 + 2.45t + C$$

To find C, note that $N(0) = 1.5.$ This gives

$N(0) = C = 1.5.$

Therefore,

$N(t) = -0.125t^3 + 1.05t^2 + 2.45t + 1.5$

b. $N(5) = -0.125(5^3) + 1.05(5^2) + 2.45(5) + 1.5 = 24.375$, or 24.375 million

subscribers.

74. The total number of acres grown in year t is

$$N(t) = \int R(t)\,dt = \int (2.718t^2 - 19.86t + 50.18)\,dt$$

$$= 0.906t^3 - 9.93t^2 + 50.18t + C$$

Using the condition $N(0) = 27.2$, we find $N(0) = C = 27.2.$ Therefore,

$$N(t) = 0.906t^3 - 9.93t^2 + 50.18t + 27.2$$

The number of acres grown in 2003 is given by

$$N(6) = 0.906(6^3) - 9.93(6)^2 + 50.18(6) + 27.2 = 166.496$$
or approximately 166.5 acres.

75 a. The approximate average credit card debt per U.S. household in year t is
$$A(t) = \int D(t)\,dt = \int (-4.479t^2 + 69.8t + 279.5)\,dt$$
$$= -1.493t^3 + 34.9t^2 + 279.5t + C$$
Using the condition $A(0) = 2917$, we find
$$A(0) = C = 2917. \text{ Therefore,}$$
$$A(t) = -1.493t^3 + 34.9t^2 + 279.5t + 2917$$
b. The average credit card debt per U.S. household in 2003 was
$$A(13) = -1.493(13^3) + 34.9(13^2) + 279.5(13) + 2917 \approx 9168.479,$$
or approximately \$9168.

76. a. The total number of DVDs sold as of year t is
$$T(t) = \int R(t)\,dt = \int (-0.03t^2 + 0.218t - 0.032)\,dt$$
$$= -0.01t^3 + 0.109t^2 - 0.032t + C$$
Using the condition $T(0) = 0.1$, we find $T(0) = C = 0.1$. Therefore,
$$T(t) = -0.01t^3 + 0.109t^2 - 0.032t + 0.1$$
b. The total number of DVDs sold by 2003 is
$$T(4) = -0.01(4^3) + 0.109(4^2) - 0.032(4) + 0.1 = 1.076,$$
or 1.076 billion units.

77. a. The number of gastric bypass surgeries performed in year t is
$$N(t) = \int R(t)\,dt = \int (9.399t^2 - 13\ 4t + 14.07)\,dt$$
$$= 3.133t^3 - 6.7t^2 + 14.07t + C$$
Using the condition $N(0) = 36.7$, we find
$$N(0) = C = 36.7. \text{ Therefore, } N(t) = 3.133t^3 - 6.7t^2 + 14.07t + 36.7.$$
b. The number of bypass surgeries performed in 2003 was
$$N(3) = 3.133(3^3) - 6.7(3^2) + 14.07(3) + 36.7 = 103,201,$$
or approximately 103,201.

78. a. The proposed online ad market share at time t is

$$S(t) = \int R(t)\,dt = \int (-0.033t^2 + 0.3428t + 0.07)dt$$
$$= -0.011t^3 + 0.1714t^2 + 0.07t + C$$

Using the condition $S(0) = 2.9$, we find $S(0) = C = 2.9$. Therefore,
$$S(t) = -0.011t^3 + 0.1714t^2 + 0.07t + 2.9$$

b. The projected online ad market share at the beginning of 2005 will be
$$S(5) = -0.011(5)^3 + 0.1714(5)^2 + 0.07(5) + 2.9 = 6.16$$

or 6.16%.

79. a. We have the initial-value problem:
$$C'(t) = 12.288t^2 - 150.5594t + 695.23$$
$$C(0) = 3142$$

Integrating, we find
$$C(t) = \int C'(t)dt = \int (12.288t^2 - 150.5594t + 695.23)dt$$
$$= 4.096t^3 - 75.2797t^2 + 695.23t + k$$

Using the initial condition, we find
$$C(0) = 0 + k = 3142, \quad \text{and so } k = 3142.$$

Therefore, $C(t) = 4.096t^3 - 75.2797t^2 + 695.23t + 3142$.

b. The projected average out-of-pocket costs for beneficiaries is 2010 is
$$C(2) = 4.096(2^3) - 75.2797(2^2) + 695.23(2) + 3142 = 4264.1092$$

or $4264.11.

80. a. $h(t) = \int h'(t)dt = \int -32t\,dt = -16t^2 + C$. But $h(0) = C = 400$ and so

$h(t) = -16t^2 + 400$.

b. It strikes the ground when $h(t) = 0$; that is, when $-16t^2 + 400 = 0$, or $t = 5$.

c. Its velocity is $-32(5)$ or 160 ft/sec downwards.

81. The number of new subscribers at any time is
$$N(t) = \int (100 + 210t^{3/4})\,dt = 100t + 120t^{7/4} + C.$$

The given condition implies that $N(0) = 5000$. Using this condition, we find $C = 5000$. Therefore, $N(t) = 100t + 120t^{7/4} + 5000$. The number of subscribers 16 months from now is
$$N(16) = 100(16) + 120(16)^{7/4} + 5000, \text{ or } 21,960.$$

82. $C(t) = \int C'(t)\,dt = \int (0.003t^2 + 0.06t + 0.1)\,dt = 0.001t^3 + 0.03t^2 + 0.1t + k.$

But $C(0) = 2.$ So, $C(0) = k = 2.$ Therefore , $C(t) = 0.001t^3 + 0.03t^2 + 0.1t + 2.$
The pollution five years from now will be
$$C(5) = 0.001(5^3) + 0.03(5^2) + 0.1(5) + 2$$
$$= 3.375, \text{ or } 3.375 \text{ parts/million.}$$

83. $A(t) = \int A'(t)\,dt = \int (3.2922t^2 - 0.366t^3)\,dt = 1.0974t^3 - 0.0915t^4 + C$

Now, $A(0) = C = 0.$ So, $A(t) = 1.0974t^3 - 0.0915t^4.$

84. The rate of change of the population at any time t is $P'(t) = 4500t^{1/2} + 1000.$
Therefore, $P(t) = 3000t^{3/2} + 1000t + C.$ But $P(0) = 30,000$ and this implies that
$$P(t) = 3000t^{3/2} + 1000t + 30,000.$$
Finally, the projected population 9 years after the construction has begun is
$$P(9) = 3000(9)^{3/2} + 1000(9) + 30,000 = 120,000.$$

85. $h(t) = \int h'(t)\,dt = \int (-3t^2 + 192t + 120)\,dt = -t^3 + 96t^2 + 120t + C$

$$= -t^3 + 96t^2 + 120t + C.$$
$h(0) = C = 0$ implies $h(t) = -t^3 + 96t^2 + 120t.$
The altitude 30seconds after lift-off is
$$h(30) = -30^3 + 96(30)^2 + 120(30) = 63,000 \text{ ft.}$$

86. $S'(W) = 0.131773W^{-0.575};$ $S = \int 0.131773W^{-0.575}\,dW = 0.310054W^{0.425} + C$

$S(70) = 0.310054(70)^{0.425} + C = 1.8867 + C = 1.886277.$
Therefore $C = -0.000007 \approx 0.$ $S(75) = 0.310054(75)^{0.425} \approx 1.9424.$

87. a. The number of health-care agencies in year t is
$$N(t) = \int -0.186te^{-0.02t}\,dt = 9.3e^{-0.02t} + C$$
Using the condition $N(0) = 9.3,$ we find
$$N(0) = 9.3 + C = 9.3 \text{ or } C = 0.$$
Therefore,
$$N(t) = 9.3e^{-0.02t}$$
b. The number of health-care agencies in 2002 was

$N(14) = 9.3e^{-0.02(14)} \approx 7.03$, or 7.03 thousand units.

c. The number of health-care agencies in 2005 would be
$$N(17) = 9.3e^{-0.02(17)} \approx 6.62, \text{ or } 6.62 \text{ thousand units.}$$

88. a. Let y denote the height of a typical preschool child. Then
$$y = \int R(t)\,dt = -\tfrac{25.8931}{0.993} e^{-0.993t} + 6.39t + C$$
$$= -26.0756e^{-0.993t} + 6.39t + C$$
$$y(\tfrac{1}{4}) = -26.0756e^{-(0.993)(\frac{1}{4})} + 6.39(\tfrac{1}{4}) + C = 60.2952$$
Therefore, $C = 79.041$, and $y(t) = -26.0756e^{-0.993t} + 6.39t + 79.041$

b. $y(1) = -26.0756e^{-0.993} + 6.39 + 79.041 \approx 75.771$, or approximately 75.77 cm.

89. $v(r) = \int v'(r)\,dr = \int -kr\,dr = -\tfrac{1}{2}kr^2 + C.$

But $v(R) = 0$ and so $v(R) = -\tfrac{1}{2}kR^2 + C = 0$, or $C = \tfrac{1}{2}kR^2$ Therefore,
$v(R) = -\tfrac{1}{2}kr^2 + \tfrac{1}{2}kR^2 = \tfrac{1}{2}k(R^2 - r^2).$

90. Denote the constant acceleration by k (ft/sec^2). Then if $s = f(t)$ is the position function of the car, we have $f''(t) = k$. So $f'(t) = v(t) = \int k\,dt = kt + C_1$. We have $v(0) = 66$ and this gives $C_1 = 66$. Therefore, $f'(t) = v(t) = kt + 66$. So
$$s = f(t) = \int f'(t)\,dt = \int v(t)\,dt = (kt + 66)\,dt = \tfrac{1}{2}kt^2 + 66 + C_2.$$

Next we use the condition $s = 0$ when $t = 0$ to obtain $s = f(t) = \tfrac{1}{2}kt^2 + 66t$.
To find the time it takes for the car to go from 66 ft/sec to 88 ft/sec, we use the expression for $v(t)$ to write $88 = kt + 66$ giving $t = 22/k$. Finally using the expression for s and the condition that the car covered 440 ft during this period, we have
$$440 = \tfrac{1}{2}k\left(\tfrac{22}{k}\right)^2 + 66\left(\tfrac{22}{k}\right) = \tfrac{242}{k} + \tfrac{1452}{k} = \tfrac{1694}{k},$$
or $k = 3.85$. So the car was accelerating at the rate of 3.85 ft/sec^2.

91. Denote the constant deceleration by k (ft/sec^2). Then $f''(t) = -k$, so $f'(t) = v(t) = -kt + C_1$. Next, the given condition implies that $v(0) = 88$. This gives $C_1 = 88$, or $f'(t) = -kt + 88$.
$$s = f(t) = \int f'(t)\,dt = \int (-kt + 88)\,dt = -\tfrac{1}{2}kt^2 + 88t + C_2.$$

Also, $f(0) = 0$ gives $s = f(t) = -\frac{1}{2}kt^2 + 88t$. Since the car is brought to rest in 9 seconds, we have $v(9) = -9k + 88 = 0$, or $k = \frac{88}{9}$, or $9\frac{7}{9}$. So the deceleration is $9\frac{7}{9}$ ft/sec^2. The distance covered is

$$s = f(9) = -\frac{1}{2}\left(\frac{88}{9}\right)(81) + 88(9) = 396.$$

So the stopping distance is 396 ft.

92. The acceleration is $\dfrac{dv}{dt}$, where r is the velocity of the aircraft. So, suppose

$$\frac{dV}{dt} = c \quad (c, \text{ a constant})$$

$$v = \int \frac{dv}{dt}\,dt = cdt = dt + k \quad (k, \text{ constant of integration})$$

$$v(0) = 160(\text{mph}) = \frac{160}{60} \times 88 = \frac{704}{3}(\text{ft}/\sec).$$

This gives $v(0) = k = \dfrac{704}{3}$. Therefore, $v(t) = ct + \dfrac{704}{3}$. Since the aircraft was brought to rest in 1 second, we have $v(1) = 0$. Using this condition, we find

$$v(1) = c + \frac{704}{3} = 0, \quad \text{or} \quad c = -\frac{704}{3} \quad (\text{ft/sec}^2)$$

and the deceleration is equivalent to $\dfrac{704}{3} \times \dfrac{1}{32}$ gs, that is $\dfrac{22}{3}$ or $7\frac{1}{3}$ gs.

93. The time taken by runner A to cross the finish line is

$$t = \frac{200}{22} = \frac{100}{11} \text{ sec}$$

Let a be the constant acceleration of runner B as he begins to spurt. Then

$$\frac{dv}{dt} = a \text{ or } v = \int a\,dt = at + c,$$

the velocity of runner B as he runs towards the finish line. At $t = 0$, $v = 20$ and so $v = at = 20$. Now, $\dfrac{ds}{dt} = v = at + 20$, so $s = \int (at + 20)dt = \frac{1}{2}at^2 + 20t + k$

(k, constant of integration). Next, $s(0) = 0$ gives $s = \frac{1}{2}at^2 + 20t = (\frac{1}{2}at + 20)t$ In order for runner B to cover 220 ft in $\frac{100}{11}$ sec, we must have

$$[\tfrac{1}{2}a(\tfrac{100}{11})+20](\tfrac{100}{11})=220$$

$$\tfrac{50}{11}a+20=\tfrac{(220)(11)}{100}=\tfrac{121}{5};\ \tfrac{50}{11}a=\tfrac{121}{5}-20=\tfrac{21}{5}\ \text{or}\ a=\tfrac{21}{5}\cdot\tfrac{11}{50}=0.924\ (\text{ft}/\sec^2)$$

So B must have a minimum acceleration of 0.924 ft/sec^2.

94. $h(t)=\displaystyle\int h'(t)=\int -\frac{1}{25}\left(\sqrt{20}-\frac{t}{50}\right)dt=-\frac{1}{25}\left(\sqrt{20}t-\frac{t^2}{100}\right)+C.$

Next, we use the initial condition $h(0)=20$ to obtain $h(0)=C=20$.

Therefore, the required expression is $h(t)=-\dfrac{1}{25}\left(\sqrt{20}t-\dfrac{t^2}{100}\right)+20.$

95. a. We have the initial-value problem $R'(t)=\dfrac{8}{(t+4)^2}$ and $R(0)=0$.

Integrating, we find $R(t)=\displaystyle\int \frac{8}{(t+4)^2}\,dt=8\int(t+4)^{-2}\,dt=-\frac{8}{t+4}+C$

$R(0)=0$ implies $-\dfrac{8}{4}+C=0$ or $C=2$.

Therefore, $R(t)=-\dfrac{8}{t+4}+2=\dfrac{-8+2t+8}{t+4}=\dfrac{2t}{t+4}.$

b. After 1 hr, $R(1)=\dfrac{2}{5}=0.4$, or 0.0.4" had fallen. After 2 hr, $R(2)=\dfrac{4}{6}=\dfrac{2}{3}$, or

$\dfrac{2}{3}$" had fallen.

96. Suppose the acceleration is k ft/sec^2. The distance covered is $s=f(t)$ and satisfies

$f''(t)=k$. So $f'(t)=v(t)=\displaystyle\int k\,dt=kt+C_1$. Next, $v(0)=0$ gives $v(t)=kt$, and

$s=f(t)=\displaystyle\int kt\,dt=\tfrac{1}{2}kt^2+C_2$. Also, $f(0)=0$ gives $s=\tfrac{1}{2}kt^2$. If it traveled 800 ft,

we have $800=\dfrac{1}{2}kt^2$, or $t=\dfrac{40}{\sqrt{k}}$. Its speed at this time is

$$v(t)=kt=k\left(\frac{40}{\sqrt{k}}\right)=40\sqrt{k}.$$

We want the speed to be at least 240 ft/sec. So we require $40\sqrt{k}>240$, or $k>36$. In other words, the minimum acceleration must be 36 ft/sec^2.

97. True. See proof in Section 6.1 in the text.

98. False. $\int f(x)\,dx = F(x)+C,$ where C is an arbitrary constant.

99. True. Use the Sum Rule followed by the Constant Multiple Rule.

100. False. Take $f(x)=1$ and $g(x)=1.$ Then
$$\int f(x)g(x)\,dx = \int 1\,dx = x+C$$
$$\left[\int f(x)\,dx\right]\left[\int g(x)\,dx\right]=\left[\int 1\,dx\right]\left[\int 1\,dx\right]$$
$$= (x+C)(x+D) = x^2 +(C+D)x+CD$$
$$\int_{-1}^{2}[g(x)-f(x)]\,dx = \int_{-1}^{2} g(x)\,dx - \int_{-1}^{2} f(x)\,dx \quad = 3 - (\text{-}2) = 5$$

6.2 CONCEPT QUESTIONS, page 417

1. To find $I = \int f(g(x))g'(x)\,dx$ by the Method of Substitution, let $u = g(x)$, so that $du = g'(x)dx$ Making the substitution, we obtain $I = \int f(u)\,du$, which can be integrated with respect to u. Finally, replace u by $u = g(x)$ to obtain the integral.

2. For $I = xe^{-x^2}\,dx,$, we let $u = -x^2$ so that $du = -2x\,dx$ or $x\,dx = -\tfrac{1}{2}du.$ Then $I = -\tfrac{1}{2}\int e^{u}\,du$, which is easily integrated. But the substitution does not work for $J = \int e^{-x^2}\,dx$ because it does not reduce J to the form $f(u)\,du$, where f is easily Integrable.

EXERCISES 6.2, page 417

1. Put $u = 4x + 3$ so that $du = 4\,dx,$ or $dx = \tfrac{1}{4}du$. Then
$$\int 4(4x+3)^4\,dx = \int u^4\,du = \tfrac{1}{5}u^5 +C = \tfrac{1}{5}(4x+3)^5 +C.$$

2. Let $u = 2x^2 + 1$ so that $du = 4x\,dx.$ Then
$$\int 4x(2x^2 +1)^7\,dx = \int u^7\,du = \tfrac{1}{8}u^8 +C = \tfrac{1}{8}(2x^2 +1)^8 +C.$$

3. Let $u = x^3 - 2x$ so that $du = (3x^2 - 2)\, dx$. Then

$$\int (x^3 - 2x)^2 (3x^2 - 2)\, dx = \int u^2\, du = \tfrac{1}{3}u^3 + C = \tfrac{1}{3}(x^3 - 2x)^3 + C.$$

4. Put $u = x^3 - x^2 + x$ so that $du = (3x^2 - 2x + 1)\, dx$. Then,

$$\int (3x^2 - 2x + 1)(x^3 - x^2 + x)^4\, dx = \int u^4\, du = \tfrac{1}{5}u^5 + C = \tfrac{1}{5}(x^3 - x^2 + x)^5 + C$$

5. Let $u = 2x^2 + 3$ so that $du = 4x\, dx$. Then

$$\int \frac{4x}{(2x^2 + 3)^3}\, dx = \int \frac{1}{u^3}\, du = \int u^{-3}\, du = -\tfrac{1}{2}u^{-2} + C = -\frac{1}{2(2x^2 + 3)^2} + C.$$

6. Let $u = x^3 + 2x$ so that $du = (3x^2 + 2)\, dx$. Then

$$\int \frac{3x^2 + 2}{(x^3 + 2x)^2}\, dx = \int \frac{du}{u^2} = \int u^{-2}\, du = -u^{-1} + C = -\frac{1}{x^3 + 2x} + C.$$

7. Put $u = t^3 + 2$ so that $du = 3t^2\, dt$ or $t^2\, dt = \tfrac{1}{3}du$. Then

$$\int 3t^2 \sqrt{t^3 + 2}\, dt = \int u^{1/2}\, du = \tfrac{2}{3}u^{3/2} + C = \tfrac{2}{3}(t^3 + 2)^{3/2} + C$$

8. Let $u = t^3 + 2$ so that $du = 3t^2\, dt$. Then

$$\int 3t^2 (t^3 + 2)^{3/2}\, dt = \int u^{3/2}\, du = \tfrac{2}{5}u^{5/2} + C = \tfrac{2}{5}(t^3 + 2)^{5/2} + C.$$

9. Let $u = x^2 - 1$ so that $du = 2x\, dx$ and $x\, dx = \tfrac{1}{2}du$. Then,

$$\int (x^2 - 1)^9\, x\, dx = \int \tfrac{1}{2}u^9\, du = \tfrac{1}{20}u^{10} + C = \tfrac{1}{20}(x^2 - 1)^{10} + C.$$

10. Let $u = 2x^3 + 3$ so that $du = 6x^2\, dx$ or $x^2\, dx = \tfrac{1}{6}du$. Then

$$\int x^2 (2x^3 + 3)^4\, dx = \tfrac{1}{6}\int u^4\, du = \tfrac{1}{30}u^5 + C = \tfrac{1}{30}(2x^3 + 3)^5 + C.$$

11. Let $u = 1 - x^5$ so that $du = -5x^4\, dx$ or $x^4\, dx = -\tfrac{1}{5}du$. Then

$$\int \frac{x^4}{1 - x^5}\, dx = -\tfrac{1}{5}\int \frac{du}{u} = -\tfrac{1}{5}\ln|u| + C = -\tfrac{1}{5}\ln|1 - x^5| + C.$$

12. Let $u = x^3 - 1$ so that $du = 3x^2\,dx$ or $x^2\,dx = \frac{1}{3}du$. Then

$$\int \frac{x^2}{\sqrt{x^3-1}}\,dx = \frac{1}{3}\int \frac{du}{\sqrt{u}} = \frac{1}{3}\int u^{-1/2}\,du = \frac{2}{3}u^{1/2} + C = \frac{2}{3}\sqrt{x^3-1} + C.$$

13 Let $u = x - 2$ so that $du = dx$. Then

$$\int \frac{2}{x-2}\,dx = 2\int \frac{du}{u} = 2\ln|u| + C = \ln u^2 + C = \ln(x-2)^2 + C.$$

14 Let $u = x^3 - 3$, so that $du = 3x^2\,dx$, and $\frac{1}{3}du = x^2\,dx$.

$$\int \frac{x^2}{x^3-3}\,dx = \int \frac{du}{3u} = \frac{1}{3}\ln|u| + C = \frac{1}{3}\ln|x^3-3| + C.$$

15. Let $u = 0.3x^2 - 0.4x + 2$. Then $du = (0.6x - 0.4)\,dx = 2(0.3x - 0.2)\,dx$.

$$\int \frac{0.3x - 0.2}{0.3x^2 - 0.4x + 2}\,dx = \int \frac{1}{2u}\,du = \frac{1}{2}\ln|u| + C = \frac{1}{2}\ln(0.3x^2 - 0.4x + 2) + C.$$

16. Let $u = 0.2x^3 + 0.3x$. Then $du = (0.6x^2 + 0.3)dx = 0.3(2x^2 + 1)\,dx$.

$$\int \frac{2x^2 + 1}{0.2x^3 + 0.3x}\,dx = \int \frac{1}{0.3u}\,du = \frac{1}{0.3}\ln|u| + C = \frac{10}{3}\ln|0.2x^3 + 0.3x| + C.$$

17. Let $u = 3x^2 - 1$ so that $du = 6x\,dx$, or $x\,dx = \frac{1}{6}du$. Then

$$\int \frac{x}{3x^2-1}\,dx = \frac{1}{6}\int \frac{du}{u} = \frac{1}{6}\ln|u| + C = \frac{1}{6}\ln|3x^2-1| + C.$$

18. $I = \displaystyle\int \frac{x^2-1}{x^3-3x+1}\,dx$. Let $u = x^3 - 3x + 1$. Then, $du = (3x^2 - 3)\,dx = 3(x^2 - 1)\,dx$,

or $(x^2 - 1)\,dx = \frac{1}{3}\,du$. Therefore,

$$I = \int \frac{1}{3}u^{-1}\,du = \frac{1}{3}\ln|u| + C = \frac{1}{3}\ln|x^3 - 3x + 1| + C.$$

19. Let $u = -2x$ so that $du = -2\ dx$ or $dx = -\frac{1}{2} du$. Then

$$\int e^{-2x}\ dx = -\frac{1}{2}\int e^u\ du = -\frac{1}{2}e^u + C = -\frac{1}{2}e^{-2x} + C.$$

20. Let $u = -0.02x$ so that $du = -0.02\ dx$ or $dx = -\frac{1}{0.02}du = -50\ du$. Then

$$\int e^{-0.02x}\ dx = -50\int e^u\ du = -50e^{-0.02x} + C.$$

21. Let $u = 2 - x$ so that $du = -\ dx$ or $dx = -\ du$. Then

$$\int e^{2-x}dx = -\int e^u\ du = -e^u + C = -e^{2-x} + C.$$

22. Let $u = 2t + 3$ so that $du = 2\ dt$ or $dt = \frac{1}{2}du$.

$$\int e^{2t+3}\ dt = \frac{1}{2}\int e^u\ du = \frac{1}{2}e^u + C = \frac{1}{2}e^{2t+3} + C.$$

23. Let $u = -x^2$, then $du = -2x\ dx$ or $x\ dx = -\frac{1}{2}du$.

$$\int xe^{-x^2}\ dx = \int -\frac{1}{2}e^u\ du = -\frac{1}{2}e^u + C = -\frac{1}{2}e^{-x^2} + C.$$

24 Let $u = x^3 - 1$, so that $du = 3x^2\ dx$ and $x^2\ dx = \frac{1}{3}du$. Then

$$\int x^2 e^{x^3-1}\ dx = \int \frac{1}{3}e^u\ du = \frac{1}{3}e^u + C = \frac{1}{3}e^{x^3-1} + C.$$

25 $\int (e^x - e^{-x})\ dx = \int e^x\ dx - \int e^{-x}\ dx = e^x - \int e^{-x}\ dx.$

To evaluate the second integral on the right, let $u = -x$ so that $du = -dx$ or $dx = -du$. Therefore,

$$\int (e^x - e^{-x})\ dx = e^x + \int e^u\ du = e^x + e^u + C = e^x + e^{-x} + C.$$

26. $\int (e^{2x} + e^{-3x})\ dx = \int e^{2x}\ dx + \int e^{-3x}\ dx.$ To evaluate the first integral, let $u = 2x$, and to evaluate the second, let $u = -3x$. We find

$$\int (e^{2x} + e^{-3x})\ dx = \frac{1}{2}e^{2x} - \frac{1}{3}e^{-3x} + C.$$

27 Let $u = 1 + e^x$ so that $du = e^x \, dx$. Then

$$\int \frac{e^x}{1+e^x} dx = \int \frac{du}{u} = \ln |u| + C = \ln(1+e^x) + C.$$

28. Let $u = 1 + e^{2x}$ so that $du = 2e^{2x} \, dx$. Then $e^{2x} \, dx = \frac{1}{2} \, du$.

$$\int \frac{e^{2x}}{1+e^{2x}} dx = \frac{1}{2} \int \frac{du}{u} = \frac{1}{2} \ln |u| + C = \frac{1}{2} \ln(1+e^{2x}) + C.$$

29 Let $u = \sqrt{x} = x^{1/2}$. Then $du = \frac{1}{2} x^{-1/2} \, dx$ or $2 \, du = x^{-1/2} \, dx$.

$$\int \frac{e^{\sqrt{x}}}{\sqrt{x}} dx = \int 2e^u \, du = 2e^u + C = 2e^{\sqrt{x}} + C.$$

30. Let $u = e^{-1/x}$, then $du = -\frac{1}{x^2} e^{-1/2} \, dx$.

$$\int \frac{e^{-1/x}}{x^2} dx = \int -u \, du = -\frac{1}{2} u^2 + C = -\frac{1}{2} e^{-2/x} + C.$$

31. Let $u = e^{3x} + x^3$ so that $du = (3e^{3x} + 3x^2) \, dx = 3(e^{3x} + x^2) \, dx$ or $(e^{3x} + x^2) \, dx = \frac{1}{3} du$.
Then

$$\int \frac{e^{3x} + x^2}{(e^{3x} + x^3)^3} dx = \frac{1}{3} \int \frac{du}{u^3} = \frac{1}{3} \int u^{-3} \, du = -\frac{1}{6} u^{-2} + C = -\frac{1}{6(e^{3x} + x^3)^2} + C.$$

32. Let $u = e^x + e^{-x}$, so that $du = e^x - e^{-x} \, dx$.

$$\int \frac{e^x - e^{-x}}{(e^x + e^{-x})^{3/2}} dx = \int \frac{du}{u^{3/2}} = \int u^{-3/2} \, du = -2u^{-1/2} + C = -2(e^x + e^{-x})^{-1/2} + C.$$

33. Let $u = e^{2x} + 1$, so that $du = 2e^{2x} \, dx$, or $\frac{1}{2} du = e^{2x} \, dx$.

$$\int e^{2x} (e^{2x} + 1)^3 \, dx = \int \frac{1}{2} u^3 \, du = \frac{1}{8} u^4 + C = \frac{1}{8} (e^{2x} + 1)^4 + C.$$

34. Let $u = 1 + e^{-x} \, dx$ so that $du = -e^{-x} \, dx$.

$$\int e^{-x}(1+e^{-x})\,dx = \int -u\,du = -\tfrac{1}{2}u^2 + C = -\tfrac{1}{2}(1+e^{-x})^2 + C.$$

35 Let $u = \ln 5x$ so that $du = \dfrac{1}{x}\,dx$. Then

$$\int \frac{\ln 5x}{x}\,dx = \int u\,du = \tfrac{1}{2}u^2 + C = \tfrac{1}{2}(\ln 5x)^2 + C.$$

36. Let $v = \ln u$ so that $dv = \tfrac{1}{u}\,du$. Then

$$\int \frac{(\ln u)^3}{u}\,du = \int v^3\,dv = \tfrac{1}{4}v^4 + C = \tfrac{1}{4}(\ln u)^4 + C.$$

37. Let $u = \ln x$ so that $du = \tfrac{1}{x}\,dx$. Then

$$\int \frac{1}{x\,\ln x}\,dx = \int \frac{du}{u} = \ln|u| + C = \ln|\ln x| + C.$$

38. Let $u = \ln x$ so that $du = \tfrac{1}{x}\,dx$. Then

$$\int \frac{1}{x(\ln x)^2}\,dx = \int \frac{1}{u^2}\,du = \int u^{-2}\,du = -u^{-1} + C = -\frac{1}{\ln x} + C.$$

39. Let $u = \ln x$ so that $du = \tfrac{1}{x}\,dx$. Then

$$\int \frac{\sqrt{\ln x}}{x}\,dx = \int \sqrt{u}\,du = \tfrac{2}{3}u^{3/2} + C = \tfrac{2}{3}(\ln x)^{3/2} + C.$$

40. Let $u = \ln x$, so that $du = \tfrac{1}{x}\,dx$. Then

$$\int \frac{(\ln x)^{7/2}}{x}\,dx = \int u^{7/2}\,du = \tfrac{2}{9}u^{9/2} + C = \tfrac{2}{9}(\ln x)^{9/2} + C.$$

41. $$\int \left(xe^{x2} - \frac{x}{x^2+2} \right) dx = \int xe^{x^2}\,dx - \int \frac{x}{x^2+2}\,dx.$$

To evaluate the first integral, let $u = x^2$ so that $du = 2x\,dx$, or $x\,dx = \tfrac{1}{2}\,du$. Then

$$\int xe^{x^2}\,dx = \tfrac{1}{2}\int e^u\,du + C_1 = \tfrac{1}{2}e^u + C_1 = \tfrac{1}{2}e^{x^2} + C_1$$

To evaluate the second integral, let $u = x^2 + 2$ so that $du = 2x\,dx$, or $x\,dx = \frac{1}{2}\,du$. Then

$$\int \frac{x}{x^2+2}\,dx = \frac{1}{2}\int \frac{du}{u} = \frac{1}{2}\ln|u| + C_2 = \frac{1}{2}\ln(x^2+2) + C_2.$$

Therefore, $\displaystyle\int \left(xe^{x^2} - \frac{x}{x^2+2} \right) dx = \frac{1}{2}e^{x^2} - \frac{1}{2}\ln(x^2+2) + C.$

42. $\displaystyle\int \left(xe^{-x^2} + \frac{e^x}{e^x+3} \right) dx = \int xe^{-x^2}\,dx + \int \frac{e^x}{e^x+3}\,dx.$

To evaluate the first integral, let $u = -x^2$ so that $du = -2x\,dx$, or $x\,dx = -\frac{1}{2}\,du$. Then

$$\int xe^{-x^2}\,dx = -\frac{1}{2}\int e^u\,du = -\frac{1}{2}e^u + C_1 = -\frac{1}{2}e^{-x^2} + C_1$$

To evaluate the second integral, let $u = e^x + 3$ so that $du = e^x\,dx$. Then

$$\int \frac{e^x}{e^x+3}\,dx = \int \frac{du}{u} = \ln|u| + C_2 = \ln(e^x+3) + C_2.$$

Therefore, $\displaystyle\int \left(xe^{-x^2} - \frac{e^x}{e^x+3} \right) dx = -\frac{1}{2}e^{-x^2} + \ln(e^x+3) + C.$

43. Let $u = \sqrt{x} - 1$ so that $du = \frac{1}{2}x^{-1/2}\,dx = \frac{1}{2\sqrt{x}}\,dx$ or $dx = 2\sqrt{x}\,du$.

Also, we have $\sqrt{x} = u + 1$, so that $x = (u+1)^2 = u^2 + 2u + 1$ and $dx = 2(u+1)\,du$. So

$$\int \frac{x+1}{\sqrt{x}-1}\,dx = \int \frac{u^2+2u+2}{u} \cdot 2(u+1)\,du = 2\int \frac{(u^3+3u^2+4u+2)}{u}\,du$$

$$= 2\int \left(u^2 + 3u + 4 + \frac{2}{u} \right) du = 2\left(\frac{1}{3}u^3 + \frac{3}{2}u^2 + 4u + 2\ln|u| \right) + C$$

$$= 2\left[\frac{1}{3}(\sqrt{x}-1)^3 + \frac{3}{2}(\sqrt{x}-1)^2 + 4(\sqrt{x}-1) + 2\ln\left|\sqrt{x}-1\right| \right] + C.$$

44. Let $v = e^{-u} + u$. Then $dv = (-e^{-u} + 1)\,du$, or $-dv = (e^{-u} - 1)\,du$.

Therefore, $\displaystyle\int \frac{e^{-u}-1}{e^{-u}+u}du = \int -\frac{dv}{v} = -\ln|v| = -\ln\left|e^{-u}+u\right| + C.$

45 Let $u = x - 1$ so that $du = dx$. Also, $x = u + 1$ and so

$$\int x(x-1)^5\,dx = \int (u+1)u^5\,du = \int (u^6 + u^5)\,du$$

$$= \frac{1}{7}u^7 + \frac{1}{6}u^6 + C = \frac{1}{7}(x-1)^7 + \frac{1}{6}(x-1)^6 + C$$

$$= \frac{(6x+1)(x-1)^6}{42} + C.$$

46. $\displaystyle\int \frac{t}{t+1}dt = \int \left(1 - \frac{1}{t+1}\right)dt = \int dt - \int \frac{1}{t+1}dt = t - \ln|t+1| + C.$

47. Let $u = 1 + \sqrt{x}$ so that $du = \frac{1}{2}x^{-1/2}\,dx$ and $dx = 2\sqrt{x} = 2(u-1)\,du$

$$\int \frac{1-\sqrt{x}}{1+\sqrt{x}}dx = \int \left(\frac{1-(u-1)}{u}\right)\cdot 2(u-1)\,du = 2\int \frac{(2-u)(u-1)}{u}\,du$$

$$= 2\int \frac{-u^2+3u-2}{u}\,du = 2\int \left(-u+3-\frac{2}{u}\right)du = -u^2 + 6u - 4\ln|u| + C$$

$$= -(1+\sqrt{x})^2 + 6(1+\sqrt{x}) - 4\ln(1+\sqrt{x}) + C$$
$$= -1 - 2\sqrt{x} - x + 6 + 6\sqrt{x} - 4\ln(1+\sqrt{x}) + C$$
$$= -x + 4\sqrt{x} + 5 - 4\ln(1+\sqrt{x}) + C.$$

48. Let $u = 1 - \sqrt{x}$ so that $du = -\dfrac{1}{2\sqrt{x}}\,dx$ and $dx = -2\sqrt{x}\,du.$

Then $\sqrt{x} = 1 - u$ and $dx = -2(1-u)\,du.$ So

$$\int \frac{1+\sqrt{x}}{1-\sqrt{x}}dx = \int \left(\frac{2-u}{u}\right)(-2)(1-u)\,du = -2\int \frac{(u-2)(u-1)}{u}\,du$$

$$= -2\int \frac{u^2-3u+2}{u}\,du = -2\int \left(u-3+\frac{2}{u}\right)du$$

$$= -2\left(\frac{1}{2}u^2 - 3u + 2\ln|u|\right) + C = 6u - u^2 - 4\ln|u| + C$$

$$= 6(1-\sqrt{x}) - (1-\sqrt{x})^2 - 4\ln(1-\sqrt{x}) + C.$$

49. $I = \int v^2(1-v)^6 \, dv$. Let $u = 1 - v$, then $du = -dv$. Also, $1 - u = v$, and

$(1-u)^2 = v^2$. Therefore,

$$I = \int -(1-2u+u^2)u^6 \, du = \int -(u^6 - 2u^7 + u^8) \, du = -\left(\frac{u^7}{7} - \frac{2u^8}{8} + \frac{u^9}{9}\right) + C$$

$$= -u^7\left(\frac{1}{7} - \frac{1}{4}u + \frac{1}{9}u^2\right) + C = -\frac{1}{252}(1-v)^7[36 - 63(1-v) + 28(1-2v+v^2)]$$

$$= -\frac{1}{252}(1-v)^7[36 - 63 + 63v + 28 - 56v + 28v^2]$$

$$= -\frac{1}{252}(1-v)^7(28v^2 + 7v + 1) + C.$$

50. Let $u = x^2 + 1$ so that $du = 2x \, dx$ and $x \, dx = \frac{1}{2} du$. Then

$$\int x^3(x^2 + 1)^{3/2} \, dx = \int x^2(x^2 + 1)^{3/2} x \, dx$$

$$= \int (u-1)u^{3/2} \tfrac{1}{2} du \qquad\qquad (x^2 = u - 1)$$

$$= \frac{1}{2}\int (u^{5/2} - u^{3/2}) \, du = \frac{1}{2}(\frac{2}{7}u^{7/2} - \frac{2}{5}u^{5/2}) + C$$

$$= \frac{u^{5/2}}{35}(5u - 7) + C = \frac{1}{35}(x^2 + 1)^{5/2}(5x^2 - 2) + C.$$

51 $f(x) = \int f'(x) \, dx = 5\int (2x-1)^4 \, dx$. Let $u = 2x - 1$ so that $du = 2x-1$ so that

$du = 2 \, dx$, or $dx = \frac{1}{2} du$. Then

$$f(x) = \frac{5}{2}\int u^4 \, du = \frac{1}{2}u^5 + C = \frac{1}{2}(2x-1)^5 + C.$$

Next, $f(1) = 3$ implies $\frac{1}{2} + C = 3$ or $C = \frac{5}{2}$. Therefore,

$$f(x) = \frac{1}{2}(2x-1)^5 + \frac{5}{2}.$$

6 *Integration*

52. $f(x) = \int f'(x)\,dx = \int \dfrac{3x^2}{2\sqrt{x^3-1}}\,dx.$ Let $u = (x^3-1)$ so that $du = 3x^2\,dx.$

Then $f(x) = \int \dfrac{du}{2\sqrt{u}} = \dfrac{1}{2}\int u^{-1/2}\,du = \left(\dfrac{1}{2}\right)2u^{1/2} + C = u^{1/2} + C = (x^3-1)^{1/2} + C.$

Next, $f(1) = (0) + C = 1.$ Therefore, $C = 1.$ Hence $f(x) = \sqrt{x^3+1} + 1.$

53 $f(x) = \int -2xe^{-x^2+1}\,dx.$ Let $u = -x^2 + 1$ so that $du = -2x\,dx.$ Then

$f(x) = \int e^u\,du = e^u + C = e^{-x^2+1} + C.$ The condition $f(1) = 0$ implies

$f(1) = 1 + C = 0,$ or $C = -1.$ Therefore, $f(x) = e^{-x^2+1} - 1.$

54. $f(x) = \int f'(x)\,dx = \int \left(1 - \dfrac{2x}{x^2+1}\right)dx = \int dx - \int \dfrac{2x}{x^2+1}\,dx.$

Let us make the substitution $u = x^2 + 1$ for the second integral on the right. With $du = 2x\,dx,$ we find

$$f(x) = \int dx - \int \dfrac{du}{u} = x - \ln|u| + C = x - \ln(x^2+1) + C.$$

The condition that the graph of f passes through $(0, 2)$ translates into the condition $f(0) = 2.$ Using this condition, we find $f(0) = C = 2.$ Therefore, the required function is $f(x) = x - \ln(x^2 + 1) + 2.$

55. The number of subscribers at time t is

$$N(t) = \int R(t)\,dt = \int 3.36(t+1)^{0.05}\,dt$$

Let $u = t+1,$ so that $du = dt.$ Thus

$$N = 3.36\int u^{0.05}\,du = 3.2u^{1.05} + C = 3.2(t+1)^{1.05} + C$$

To find $C,$ use the condition $N(0) = 3.2$ giving

$$N(0) = 3.2 + C = 3.2,$$

so $C = 0.$ Therefore,

$$N(t) = 3.2(t+1)^{1.05}$$

If the projection holds true, then the number of subscribers at the beginning of 2008 will be

$N(4) = 3.2(4+1)^{1.05} \approx 17.341$, or 17.341 million.

56. The number of viewers in the tth year is given by $N(t) = \int 3(2 + \frac{1}{2}t)^{-1/3}\, dt$.

To evaluate this integral, let $u = 2 + \frac{1}{2}t$ so that $du = \frac{1}{2}\, dt$ and $dt = 2\, du$. Then

$$N(t) = 6\int u^{-1/3}\, du = 9u^{2/3} + C = 9(2 + \frac{1}{2}t)^{2/3} + C.$$

The given condition implies that $N(1) = 9(\frac{5}{2})^{2/3} + C$. Using this condition, we see that $N(1) = 9(\frac{5}{2})^{2/3} + C = 9(\frac{5}{2})^{2/3}$ so that $C = 0$. Therefore, $N(t) = 9(2 + \frac{1}{2}t)^{2/3}$. The number of viewers in the 2005 season is given by $N(5) = 9(5)^{2/3} \approx 26.32$, or approximately 26.3 million viewers.

57. $N'(t) = 2000(1 + 0.2t)^{-3/2}$. Let $u = 1 + 0.2t$. Then $du = 0.2\, dt$ and $5\, du = dt$.
Therefore, $N(t) = (5)(2000)$

$$\int u^{-3/2}\, du = -20{,}000u^{-1/2} + C = -20{,}000(1 + 0.2t)^{-1/2} + C.$$

Next, $N(0) = -20{,}000(1)^{-1/2} + C = 1000$. Therefore, $C = 21{,}000$ and

$N(t) = -\dfrac{20{,}000}{\sqrt{1 + 0.2t}} + 21{,}000$. In particular, $N(5) = -\dfrac{20{,}000}{\sqrt{2}} + 21{,}000 \approx 6{,}858$.

58. Let $u = (5 - x)$ so that $du = -x\, dx$. Then

$$p(x) = \int \frac{240}{(5-x)^2}\, dx = 240\int (5-x)^{-2}\, dx = 240\int -u^{-2}\, du = 240u^{-1} + C = \frac{240}{5-x} + C.$$

Next, the condition $p(2) = 50$ gives $\dfrac{240}{3} + C = 80 + C = 50$, or $C = 30$. Therefore,

$$p(x) = \frac{240}{5-x} + 30.$$

59. $p(x) = \displaystyle\int -\frac{250x}{(16+x^2)^{3/2}}\, dx = -250\int \frac{x}{(16+x^2)^{3/2}}\, dx.$

Let $u = 16 + x^2$ so that $du = 2x\, dx$ and $x\, dx = \frac{1}{2}\, du$.

Then $p(x) = -\frac{250}{2}\displaystyle\int u^{-3/2}\, du = (-125)(-2)u^{-1/2} + C = \dfrac{250}{\sqrt{16+x^2}} + C.$

$$p(3) = \frac{250}{\sqrt{16+9}} + C = 50 \text{ implies } C = 0 \text{ and } p(x) = \frac{250}{\sqrt{16+x^2}}$$

60. The population t years from now will be

$$P(t) = \int r(t)dt = \int 400\left(1 + \frac{2t}{24+t^2}\right)dt = \int 400dt + 800\int \frac{t}{24+t^2}dt$$

In order to evaluate the second integral on the right, let
$u = 24+t^2$, $du = 2t\,dt$, or $t\,dt = \frac{1}{2}du$

We obtain $P(t) = 400t + 800\int \frac{\frac{1}{2}du}{u} = 400t + 400|\ln u| + C$

$$= 400[t + \ln(24+t^2)] + C$$

To find C, use the condition $P(0) = 60,000$ giving

$$400[0 + \ln 24] + C = 60,000 \quad \text{or} \quad C = 58728.78$$

So $P(t) = 400[t + \ln(24+t^2)] + 58728.78$. Therefore, the population 5 years from now will be

$$400[5 + \ln(24+5^2)] + 58728.78 \approx 62,285.51, \text{ or approximately, } 62,286.$$

61. Let $u = 2t + 4$, so that $du = 2\,dt$. Then

$$r(t) = \int \frac{30}{\sqrt{2t+4}}dt = 30\int \frac{1}{2}u^{-1/2}\,du = 30u^{1/2} + C = 30\sqrt{2t+4} + C.$$

$r(0) = 60 + C = 0$, and $C = -60$. Therefore, $r(t) = 30\left(\sqrt{2t+4} - 2\right)$. Then

$r(16) = 30\left(\sqrt{36} - 2\right) = 120\,\text{ft}$. Therefore, the polluted area is

$$\pi r^2 = \pi(120)^2 = 14,400\pi, \text{ or } 14,400\pi \text{ sq ft.}$$

62. Let $u = 1 + 1.09t$, then $du = 1.09\,dt$. So

$$\int \frac{5.45218}{(1+1.09t)^{0.9}}dt = 5.45218\int (1+1.09t)^{-0.9}\,dt = \frac{5.45218}{1.09}\int u^{-0.9}\,du$$

$$= 50.02\,u^{0.1} + C = 50.02(1+1.09t)^{0.1} + C.$$

Then $g(0) = 50.02 + C = 50.02$ and $C = 0$. So $g(t) = 50.02(1 + 1.09t)^{0.1}$ and $g(100) = 50.02(110)^{0.1} \approx 80.04$.

63. Let $u = 1 + 2.449e^{-0.3277t}$ so that $du = -0.802537e^{-0.3277t}\,dt$ and $e^{-0.3277t}\,dt = -1.24605\,du$.

Then $h(t) = \displaystyle\int \frac{52.8706e^{-0.3277t}}{(1+2.449e^{-0.3277t})^2}\,dt = (52.8706)(-1.24605)\int \frac{du}{u^2}$

$\displaystyle = 65.8794u^{-1} + C = \frac{65.8794}{1+2.449e^{-0.3277t}} + C.$

$h(0) = \displaystyle\frac{65.8794}{1+2.449} + C = 19.4,\ \text{ and } \ C = 0.3.$

Therefore, $h(t) = \displaystyle\frac{65.8794}{1+2.449e^{-0.3277t}} + 0.3,$

and $h(8) = \displaystyle\frac{65.8794}{1+2.449e^{-0.3277(8)}} + 0.3 \approx 56.22$, or 56.22 inches.

64. $N(t) = \displaystyle\int N'(t)\,dt = 6\int e^{-0.05t}\,dt = \frac{6}{-0.05}e^{-0.05t}$ \qquad (Let u = -0.05t)

$\displaystyle = -120e^{-0.05t} + C.$

$N(0) = 60$ implies $-120 + C = 60$ or $C = 180$. Therefore, $N(t) = -120e^{-0.05t} + 180$.

65 $A(t) = \displaystyle\int A'(t)\,dt = r\int e^{-at}\,dt.$ Let $u = -at$ so that $du = -a\,dt,\ $ or $dt = -\frac{1}{a}\,du.$

$A(t) = r(-\frac{1}{a})\displaystyle\int e^u\,du = -\frac{r}{a}e^u + C = -\frac{r}{a}e^{-at} + C$

$A(0)$ implies $-\dfrac{r}{a} + C = 0,\ $ or $\ C = \dfrac{r}{a}$ \quad So, $A(t) = -\dfrac{r}{a}e^{-at} + \dfrac{r}{a} = \dfrac{r}{a}(1-e^{-at}).$

66. $x(t) = \displaystyle\int x'(t)\,dt = \int \frac{1}{V}(ac - bx_0)e^{-bt/V}\,dt = \frac{1}{V}(ac - bx_0)\int e^{-bt/V}\,dt$

Let $u = -bt/V$, so that $du = -b/V\,dt$ and $dt = -V/b\,du$. Then

$x(t) = \dfrac{1}{V}(ac - bx_0)\displaystyle\int -\frac{V}{b}e^u\,du = \left(-\frac{ac}{b} + x_0\right)e^u = \left(-\frac{ac}{b} + x_0\right)e^{-bt/V} + C.$

Since $x(0) = \left(-\dfrac{ac}{b} + x_0\right) + C = x_0,\ \ C = \dfrac{ac}{b},\ $ and $\ x(t) = \dfrac{ac}{b} + \left(x_0 - \dfrac{ac}{b}\right)e^{-bt/V}\ .$

6 Integration

6.3 CONCEPT QUESTIONS, page 427

1. See text page 424.
2. See text page 426.

EXERCISES 6.3, page 427

1. $\frac{1}{3}(1.9 + 1.5 + 1.8 + 2.4 + 2.7 + 2.5) = \frac{12.8}{3} \approx 4.27$.

2. $\frac{1}{4}(4.5 + 8.0 + 8.5 + 6.0 + 4.0 + 3.0 + 2.5 + 2.0) = \frac{38.5}{4} = 9.625$.

3.
a. $A = \frac{1}{2}(2)(6) = 6$ sq units.

b. $\Delta x = \frac{2}{4} = \frac{1}{2}$; $x_1 = 0$, $x_2 = \frac{1}{2}$, $x_3 = 1$, $x_4 = \frac{3}{2}$.

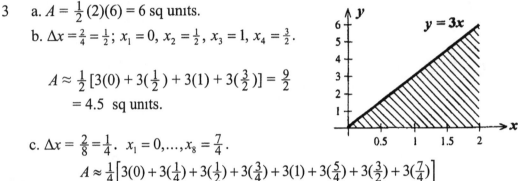

$$A \approx \frac{1}{2}[3(0) + 3(\tfrac{1}{2}) + 3(1) + 3(\tfrac{3}{2})] = \frac{9}{2}$$
$$= 4.5 \text{ sq units.}$$

c. $\Delta x = \frac{2}{8} = \frac{1}{4}$. $x_1 = 0, \dots, x_8 = \frac{7}{4}$.

$$A \approx \frac{1}{4}\left[3(0) + 3(\tfrac{1}{4}) + 3(\tfrac{1}{2}) + 3(\tfrac{3}{4}) + 3(1) + 3(\tfrac{5}{4}) + 3(\tfrac{3}{2}) + 3(\tfrac{7}{4})\right]$$
$$= \frac{21}{4} = 5.25 \text{ sq units.}$$

d. Yes.

4.
a. $A = 6$

b. $x_1 = \frac{1}{2}$, $x_2 = 1$, $x_3 = \frac{3}{2}$, $x_4 = 2$

$$A = \frac{1}{2}\left[3(\tfrac{1}{2}) + 3(1) + 3(\tfrac{3}{2}) + 3(2)\right] = 7.5.$$

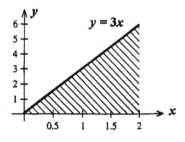

c. $x_1 = \frac{1}{4}$, $x_2 = \frac{1}{2}$, $x_3 = \frac{3}{4}$, ..., $x_8 = 2$.

$$A \approx \frac{1}{4}\left[3(\tfrac{1}{4}) + 3(\tfrac{1}{2}) + 3(\tfrac{3}{4}) + \cdots + 3(\tfrac{7}{4}) + 3(2)\right] = 6.75.$$

d. Yes.

5 a. $A = 4$

b. $\Delta x = \frac{2}{5} = 0.4$; $x_1 = 0$, $x_2 = 0.4$, $x_3 = 0.8$, $x_4 = 1.2$

$x_5 = 1.6$,

$A \approx 0.4\{[4 - 2(0)] + [4 - 2(0.4)] + [4 - 2(0.8)]$

$+ [4 - 2(1.2)] + [4 - 2(1.6)]\}$

$= 4.8$

c. $\Delta x = \frac{2}{10} = 0.2$, $x_1 = 0$, $x_2 = 0.2$, $x_3 = 0.4$, ..., $x_{10} = 1.8$.

$A \approx 0.2\{[4 - 2(0)] + [4 - 2(0.2)] + [4 - 2(0.4)]$

$+ \cdots + [4 - 2(1.8)]\} = 4.4$

d. Yes.

6. a. $A = 4$

b. $\Delta x = 0.4$, $x_1 = 0.4$, $x_2 = 0.8$, $x_3 = 1.2$, $x_4 = 1.6$, $x_5 = 2$

$A \approx 0.4\{[4 - 2(0.4)] + [4 - 2(0.8)] + \cdots + [4 - 2(2)]\} \approx 3.2$.

c. $\Delta x = 0.2$; $x_1 = 0.2$, $x_2 = 0.4$, $x_3 = 0.6$, ..., $x_{10} = 2$.

$A \approx 0.2\{[4 - 2(0.2)] + [4 - 2(0.4)] + \cdots + [4 - 2(2)]\} \approx 3.6$.

d. Yes.

7. a. $\Delta x = \dfrac{4 - 2}{2} = 1$; $x_1 = 2.5$, $x_2 = 3.5$;   The Riemann sum is $[(2.5)^2 + (3.5)^2] = 18.5$.

b. $\Delta x = \dfrac{4 - 2}{5} = 0.4$; $x_1 = 2.2$, $x_2 = 2.6$, $x_3 = 3.0$, $x_4 = 3.4$, $x_5 = 3.8$.

The Riemann sum is $0.4[2.2^2 + 2.6^2 + 3.0^2 + 3.4^2 + 3.8^2] = 18.64$.

c. $\Delta x = \dfrac{4 - 2}{10} = 0.2$; $x_1 = 2.1$, $x_2 = 2.3$, $x_2 = 2.5$, ..., $x_{10} = 3.9$

The Riemann sum is $0.2[2.1^2 + 2.3^2 + 2.5^2 + \cdots + 3.9^2] = 18.66$.

The area seems to be $18\frac{2}{3}$ sq units.

8. a. $\Delta x = \dfrac{4 - 2}{2} = 1$; $x_1 = 2$, $x_2 = 3$. The Riemann sum is $(1)[2^2 + 3^2] = 13$.

b. $\Delta x = \dfrac{4 - 2}{5} = 0.4$; $x_1 = 2$, $x_2 = 2.4$, $x_3 = 2.8$, $x_4 = 3.2$, $x_5 = 3.6$.

The Riemann sum is $0.4[2^2 + 2.4^2 + 2.8^2 + 3.2^2 + 3.6^2] = 16.32$.

c. $\Delta x = \dfrac{4 - 2}{10} = 0.2$; $x_1 = 2$, $x_2 = 2.2$, $x_3 = 2.4$, ..., $x_{10} = 3.8$

The Riemann sum is $0.2[2^2 + 2.2^2 + 2.4^2 + \cdots + 3.8^2] = 17.48$.

d. 17.5 sq units.

9 a. $\Delta x = \dfrac{4-2}{2} = 1$; $x_1 = 3$, $x_2 = 4$. The Riemann sum is $(1)[3^2 + 4^2] = 25$.

b. $\Delta x = \dfrac{4-2}{5} = 0.4$; $x_1 = 2.4$, $x_2 = 2.8$, $x_3 = 3.2$, $x_4 = 3.6$, $x_5 = 4$.

The Riemann sum is $0.4[2.4^2 + 2.8^2 + \cdots + 4^2] = 21.12$.

c. $\Delta x = \dfrac{4-2}{10} = 0.2$; $x_1 = 2.2$, $x_2 = 2.4$, $x_3 = 2.6$, ..., $x_{10} = 4$.

The Riemann sum is $0.2[2.2^2 + 2.4^2 + 2.6^2 + \cdots + 4^2] = 19.88$.

d. 19.9 sq units.

10. a. $\Delta x = \dfrac{1-0}{2} = \dfrac{1}{2}$; $x_1 = \dfrac{1}{4}$, $x_2 = \dfrac{3}{4}$. The Riemann sum is

$f(x_1)\Delta x + f(x_2)\Delta x = \left[(\tfrac{1}{4})^3 + (\tfrac{3}{4})^3\right]\tfrac{1}{2} = \left(\tfrac{1}{64} + \tfrac{27}{64}\right)\tfrac{1}{2} = \tfrac{7}{32} = 0.21875$.

b. $\Delta x = \dfrac{1-0}{5} = \dfrac{1}{5}$; $x_1 = \dfrac{1}{10}$, $x_2 = \dfrac{3}{10}$, $x_3 = \dfrac{5}{10}$, $x_4 = \dfrac{7}{10}$, $x_5 = \dfrac{9}{10}$.

The Riemann sum is

$f(x_1)\Delta x + f(x_2)\Delta x + \cdots f(x_5)\Delta x = \left[(\tfrac{1}{10})^3 + (\tfrac{3}{10})^3 + \cdots + (\tfrac{9}{10})^3\right]\tfrac{1}{5}$

$= \tfrac{1}{5000}(1 + 27 + \cdots + 729) = \tfrac{1225}{5000} = 0.245$.

c. $\Delta x = \dfrac{1-0}{10} = \dfrac{1}{10}$; $x_1 = \dfrac{1}{20}$, $x_2 = \dfrac{3}{20}$, $x_3 = \dfrac{5}{20}$, $\cdots$, $x_{10} = \dfrac{19}{20}$.

The Riemann sum is

$f(x_1)\Delta x + f(x_2)\Delta x + \cdots + f(x_{10})\Delta x = \left[(\tfrac{1}{20})^3 + (\tfrac{3}{20})^3 + \cdots + (\tfrac{19}{20})^3\right]\tfrac{1}{10}$

$= \tfrac{19,900}{80,000} \approx 0.24875$.

The Riemann sum seems to approach 1/4.

11. a. $\Delta x = \dfrac{1}{2}$, $x_1 = 0$, $x_2 = \dfrac{1}{2}$. The Riemann sum is

$f(x_1)\Delta x + f(x_2)\Delta x = \left[(0)^3 + (\tfrac{1}{2})^3\right]\tfrac{1}{2} = \tfrac{1}{16} = 0.0625$.

b. $\Delta x = \dfrac{1}{5}$, $x_1 = 0$, $x_2 = \dfrac{1}{5}$, $x_3 = \dfrac{2}{5}$, $x_4 = \dfrac{3}{5}$, $x_5 = \dfrac{4}{5}$. The Riemann sum is $f(x_1)\Delta x + f(x_2)\Delta x + \cdots + f(x_5)\Delta x = \left[(\tfrac{1}{5})^3 + (\tfrac{2}{5})^3 + \cdots + (\tfrac{4}{5})^3\right]\tfrac{1}{5} = \tfrac{100}{625} = 0.16.$

c. $\Delta x = \dfrac{1}{10}$; $x_1 = 0$, $x_2 = \dfrac{1}{10}$, $x_3 = \dfrac{2}{10}$, $\cdots$, $x_{10} = \dfrac{9}{10}$.

The Riemann sum is

$f(x_1)\Delta x + f(x_2)\Delta x + \cdots + f(x_{10})\Delta x = \left[(\tfrac{1}{10})^3 + (\tfrac{2}{10})^3 + \cdots + (\tfrac{9}{10})^3\right]\tfrac{1}{10}$
$$= \tfrac{2025}{10,000} = 0.2025 \approx 0.2 \text{ sq units.}$$

The Riemann sum seems to approach 0.2.

12. a. $\Delta x = \dfrac{1}{2}$; $x_1 = \dfrac{1}{2}$, $x_2 = 1$. The Riemann sum

is $f(x_1)\Delta x + f(x_2)\Delta x = \left[(\tfrac{1}{2})^3 + 1^3\right]\tfrac{1}{2} = 0.5625.$

b. $\Delta x = \dfrac{1}{5}$, $x_1 = \dfrac{1}{5}$, $x_2 = \dfrac{2}{5}$, $x_3 = \dfrac{3}{5}$, $x_4 = \dfrac{4}{5}$, $x_5 = 1$. The Riemann sum

$f(x_1)\Delta x + f(x_2)\Delta x + \cdots f(x_5)\Delta x = \left[(\tfrac{1}{5})^3 + (\tfrac{2}{5})^3 + \cdots + (\tfrac{4}{5})^3 + 1\right]\tfrac{1}{5}$
$$= \tfrac{225}{625} = 0.36.$$

c. $\Delta x = \dfrac{1}{10}$; $x_1 = \dfrac{1}{10}$, $x_2 = \dfrac{2}{10}$, $\cdots$, $x_{10} = 1$. The Riemann sum is

$f(x_1)\Delta x + f(x_2)\Delta x + \cdots + f(x_{10})\Delta x = \left[(\tfrac{1}{10})^3 + (\tfrac{2}{10})^3 + \cdots + 1\right]\tfrac{1}{10}$
$$= \tfrac{3025}{10,000} = 0.3025.$$

13. $\Delta x = \dfrac{2-0}{5} = \dfrac{2}{5}$; $x_1 = \dfrac{1}{5}$, $x_2 = \dfrac{3}{5}$, $x_3 = \dfrac{5}{5}$, $x_4 = \dfrac{7}{5}$, $x_5 = \dfrac{9}{5}$.

$A \approx \left\{\left[(\tfrac{1}{5})^2 + 1\right] + \left[(\tfrac{3}{5})^2 + 1\right] + \left[(\tfrac{5}{5})^2 + 1\right] + \left[(\tfrac{7}{5})^2 + 1\right] + \left[(\tfrac{9}{5})^2 + 1\right](\tfrac{2}{5})\right\}$
$= \tfrac{580}{125} = 4.64$ sq units.

14. $\Delta x = \dfrac{2-(-1)}{6} = \dfrac{1}{2}$; $x_1 = -1$, $x_2 = -\dfrac{1}{2}$, $x_3 = 0$, $x_4 = \dfrac{1}{2}$, $x_5 = 1$, $x_6 = \dfrac{3}{2}$

$A \approx \left\{\left[4-(-1)^2\right] + \left[4-(\tfrac{1}{2})^2\right] + \left[4-0^2\right] + \left[4-\tfrac{1}{2}^2\right] + \left[4-1^2\right] + \left[4-(\tfrac{3}{2})^2\right]\right\}(\tfrac{1}{2})$
$= \tfrac{77}{8} = 9.625$ sq units.

15. $\Delta x = \dfrac{3-1}{4} = \dfrac{1}{2}$; $x_1 = \dfrac{3}{2}, \; x_2 = \dfrac{4}{2}, \; x_3 = \dfrac{5}{2}, \; x_4 = 3$.

$A \approx \left[\dfrac{1}{\frac{3}{2}} + \dfrac{1}{\frac{4}{2}} + \dfrac{1}{\frac{5}{2}} + \dfrac{1}{3}\right]\dfrac{1}{2} \approx 0.95$ sq units.

16. $\Delta x = \dfrac{3-0}{5} = \dfrac{3}{5}$; $x_1 = \dfrac{3}{10}, \; x_2 = \dfrac{9}{10}, \; x_3 = \dfrac{15}{10}, \; x_4 = \dfrac{21}{10}, \; x_5 = \dfrac{27}{10}$

$A \approx [e^{3/10} + e^{9/10} + e^{15/10} + e^{21/10} + e^{27/10}]\left(\dfrac{3}{5}\right) \approx 18.8$ sq units.

17. $A = 20[f(10) + f(30) + f(50) + f(70) + f(90)]$
$= 20(80 + 100 + 110 + 100 + 80) = 9400$ sq ft.

18. $A = 20[f(10) + f(30) + f(50) + f(70)]$
$= 20(100 + 75 + 80 + 82.5) = 6750$ sq ft.

6.4 CONCEPT QUESTIONS, page 437

1. See the Fundamental of Calculus Theorem on page 429 in the text.
2. See page 433 in the text.
   a. It measures the total income generated over the $(b - a)$ days.
   b. $\displaystyle\int_a^b R(t)\,dt$

EXERCISES 6.4, page 437

1. $A = \displaystyle\int_1^4 2\,dx = 2x\Big|_1^4 = 2(4-1) = 6$, or 6

   square units. The region is a rectangle whose area is

   $3 \cdot 2$, or 6, square units.

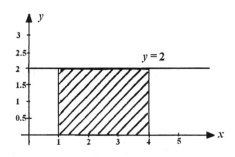

2. $A = \int_{-1}^{2} 4\,dx = 4x\big|_{-1}^{2} = 8 - (-4) = 12,$ or 12

    sq units. The region is a rectangle whose
    area is $4[2 - (-1)] = 12$ sq units.

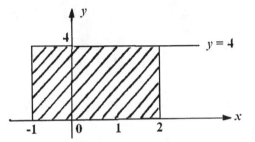

3. $A = \int_{1}^{3} 2x\,dx = x^2\big|_{1}^{3} = 9 - 1 = 8,$ or 8 sq units.

    The region is a parallelogram of area
    $(1/2)(3 - 1)(2 + 6) = 8$ sq units.

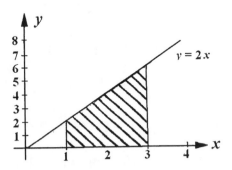

4. $A = \int_{1}^{4}\left(-\frac{1}{4}x + 1\right)dx = -\frac{1}{8}x^2 + x\big|_{1}^{4}$

    $= (-2 + 4) - (-\frac{1}{8} + 1) = \frac{9}{8},$

    or 9/8 sq units. The region is a triangle
    whose area is $(1/2)(3)(3/4) = 9/8$ sq units.

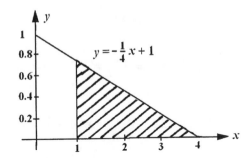

5. $A = \int_{-1}^{2}(2x + 3)\,dx = x^2 + 3x\big|_{-1}^{2} = (4 + 6) - (1 - 3) = 12$, or 12 sq units.

6. $A = \int_{2}^{4}(4x - 1)\,dx = 2x^2 - x\big|_{2}^{4} = (32 - 4) - (8 - 2) = 22$, or 22 sq units.

7. $A = \int_{-1}^{2}(-x^2+4)\,dx = -\dfrac{1}{3}x^3 + 4x \Big|_{-1}^{2} = \left(-\dfrac{8}{3}+8\right) - \left(\dfrac{1}{3}-4\right) = 9$, or 9 sq units.

8. $A = \int_{0}^{4}(4x-x^2)\,dx = 2x^2 - \dfrac{1}{3}x^3 \Big|_{0}^{4} = 32 - \dfrac{64}{3} = \dfrac{32}{3}$, or $\dfrac{32}{3}$ sq units.

9. $A = \int_{1}^{2}\dfrac{1}{x}\,dx = \ln|x| \Big|_{1}^{2} = \ln 2 - \ln 1 = \ln 2$, or $\ln 2$ sq units.

10. $A = \int_{2}^{4}\dfrac{1}{x^2}\,dx = \int_{2}^{4} x^{-2}\,dx = -\dfrac{1}{x} \Big|_{2}^{4} = -\dfrac{1}{4}+\dfrac{1}{2} = \dfrac{1}{4}$, or $\dfrac{1}{4}$ sq units.

11. $A = \int_{1}^{9}\sqrt{x}\,dx = \dfrac{2}{3}x^{3/2} \Big|_{1}^{9} = \dfrac{2}{3}(27-1) = \dfrac{52}{3}$, or $17\tfrac{1}{3}$ sq units.

12. $A = \int_{1}^{3} x^3\,dx = \tfrac{1}{4}x^4 \Big|_{1}^{3} = \tfrac{1}{4}(81-1) = 20$ sq units.

13. $A = \int_{-8}^{-1}(1-x^{1/3})\,dx = x - \tfrac{3}{4}x^{4/3} \Big|_{-8}^{-1} = (-1-\tfrac{3}{4})-(-8-12) = 18\tfrac{1}{4}$, or $18\tfrac{1}{4}$ sq units.

14. $A = \int_{1}^{9} x^{-1/2}\,dx = 2x^{1/2} \Big|_{1}^{9} = 2(3-1) = 4$, or 4 sq units.

15. $A = \int_{0}^{2} e^x\,dx = e^x \Big|_{0}^{2} = (e^2 - 1)$, or approximately 6.39 sq units.

16. $A = \int_{1}^{2}(e^x - x)\,dx = e^x - \tfrac{1}{2}x^2 \Big|_{1}^{2} = (e^2 - 2)-(e-\tfrac{1}{2}) = (e^2 - e - \tfrac{3}{2})$ or approximately
    3 17 sq units.

17. $\int_{2}^{4} 3\,dx = 3x \Big|_{2}^{4} = 3(4-2) = 6.$ 18. $\int_{-1}^{2} -2\,dx = -2x \Big|_{-1}^{2} = -4 - 2 = -6.$

19. $\int_{1}^{3}(2x+3)\,dx = x^2 + 3x \Big|_{1}^{3} = (9+9)-(1+3) = 14.$

20. $\int_{-1}^{0}(4-x)\,dx = 4x - \tfrac{1}{2}x^2 \Big|_{-1}^{0} = 0 - (-4 - \tfrac{1}{2}) = 4\tfrac{1}{2}.$

21. $\int_{-1}^{3} 2x^2\,dx = \tfrac{2}{3}x^3 \Big|_{-1}^{3} = \tfrac{2}{3}(27) - \tfrac{2}{3}(-1) = \tfrac{56}{3}.$

22. $\int_{0}^{2} 8x^3\,dx = 2x^4 \Big|_{0}^{2} = 32.$

23. $\int_{-2}^{2} (x^2 - 1)\, dx = \frac{1}{3}x^3 - x\Big|_{-2}^{2} = \left(\frac{8}{3} - 2\right) - \left(-\frac{8}{3} + 2\right) = \frac{4}{3}$

24. $\int_{1}^{4} \sqrt{u}\ du = \frac{2}{3}u^{3/2}\Big|_{1}^{4} = \frac{2}{3}(8) - \frac{2}{3}(1) = \frac{14}{3}.$

25. $\int_{1}^{8} 4x^{1/3}\, dx = (4)(\frac{3}{4})x^{4/3}\Big|_{1}^{8} = 3(16 - 1) = 45.$

26. $\int_{1}^{4} 2x^{-3/2}\, dx = (2)(-2)x^{-1/2}\Big|_{1}^{4} = -4(\frac{1}{2} - 1) - 2.$

27. $\int_{0}^{1} (x^3 - 2x^2 + 1)\, dx = \frac{1}{4}x^4 - \frac{2}{3}x^3 + x\Big|_{0}^{1} = \frac{1}{4} - \frac{2}{3} + 1 = \frac{7}{12}$

28. $\int_{1}^{2} (t^5 - t^3 + 1)\, dt = \frac{1}{6}t^6 - \frac{1}{4}t^4 + t\Big|_{1}^{2} = \left[\frac{1}{6}(64) - \frac{1}{4}(16) + 2\right] - \left[\frac{1}{6} - \frac{1}{4} + 1\right] = 7\frac{3}{4}.$

29. $\int_{2}^{4} \frac{1}{x}\, dx = \ln|x|\Big|_{2}^{4} = \ln 4 - \ln 2 = \ln(\frac{4}{2}) = \ln 2.$

30. $\int_{1}^{3} \frac{2}{x}\, dx = 2\ln|x|\Big|_{1}^{3} = 2\ln 3.$

31. $\int_{0}^{4} x(x^2 - 1)\, dx = \int_{0}^{4} (x^3 - x)\, dx = \frac{1}{4}x^4 - \frac{1}{2}x^2\Big|_{0}^{4} = 64 - 8 = 56.$

32. $\int_{0}^{2} (x - 4)(x - 1)\, dx = \int_{0}^{2} (x^2 - 5x + 4)\, dx = \frac{1}{3}x^3 - \frac{5}{2}x^2 + 4x\Big|_{0}^{2} = \frac{8}{3} - 10 + 8 = \frac{2}{3}$

33. $\int_{1}^{3} (t^2 - t)^2\, dt = \int_{1}^{3} t^4 - 2t^3 + t^2)\, dt = \frac{1}{5}t^5 - \frac{1}{2}t^4 + \frac{1}{3}t^3\Big|_{1}^{3}$

$$= \left(\frac{243}{5} - \frac{81}{2} + \frac{27}{3}\right) - \left(\frac{1}{5} - \frac{1}{2} + \frac{1}{3}\right) = \frac{512}{30} = \frac{256}{15}.$$

34. $\displaystyle\int_{-1}^{1}(x^2-1)^2\,dx = \int_{-1}^{1}(x^4-2x^2+1)\,dx = \frac{1}{5}x^5-\frac{2}{3}x^3+x\Big|_{-1}^{1}$

$$= \left(\frac{1}{5}-\frac{2}{3}+1\right)-\left(-\frac{1}{5}+\frac{2}{3}-1\right)=\frac{16}{15}$$

35 $\displaystyle\int_{-3}^{-1}x^{-2}\,dx = -\frac{1}{x}\Big|_{-3}^{-1} = 1-\frac{1}{3}=\frac{2}{3}.$ 36. $\displaystyle\int_{1}^{2}2x^{-3}\,dx = -\frac{1}{x^2}\Big|_{1}^{2} = -\frac{1}{4}+1=\frac{3}{4}$

37. $\displaystyle\int_{1}^{4}\left(\sqrt{x}-\frac{1}{\sqrt{x}}\right)dx = \int_{1}^{4}(x^{1/2}-x^{-1/2})\,dx = \frac{2}{3}x^{3/2}-2x^{1/2}\Big|_{1}^{4}$

$$= \left(\frac{16}{3}-4\right)-\left(\frac{2}{3}-2\right)=\frac{8}{3}$$

38. $\displaystyle\int_{0}^{1}\sqrt{2x}(\sqrt{x}+\sqrt{2})\,dx = \int_{0}^{1}(\sqrt{2}x+2\sqrt{x})\,dx = \frac{\sqrt{2}}{2}x^2+\frac{4}{3}x^{3/2}\Big|_{0}^{1} = \frac{\sqrt{2}}{2}+\frac{4}{3}.$

39. $\displaystyle\int_{1}^{4}\frac{3x^3-2x^{2\cdot}+4}{x^2}\,dx = \int_{1}^{4}(3x-2+4x^{-2})\,dx = \frac{3}{2}x^2-2x-\frac{4}{x}\Big|_{1}^{4}$

$$= (24-8-1)-(\tfrac{3}{2}-2-40 = \tfrac{39}{2}$$

40. $\displaystyle\int_{1}^{2}\left(1+\frac{1}{u}+\frac{1}{u^2}\right)du = u+\ln u-\frac{1}{u}\Big|_{1}^{2} = (2+\ln 2-\frac{1}{2})-(1+0-1)=\frac{3}{2}+\ln 2.$

41. a. $\displaystyle C(300)-C(0) = \int_{0}^{300}(0.0003x^2-0.12x+20)\,dx = 0.0001x^3-0.06x^2+20x\Big|_{0}^{300}$

$$= 0.0001(300)^3-0.06(300)^2+20(300) = 3300.$$

Therefore $C(300) = 3300 + C(0) = 3300 + 800 = 4100$, or $4100.

b. $\displaystyle\int_{200}^{300}C'(x)\,dx = (0.0001x^3-0.06x^2+20x)\Big|_{200}^{300}$

$$= [0.0001(300)^3-0.06(300)^2+20(300)]$$
$$-[0.0001(200)^3-0.06(200)^2+20(200)]$$
$$= 900 \text{ or } \$900.$$

42. a. $R(200) = \int_0^{200}(-0.1x + 40)\, dx = -0.05x^2 + 40x\Big|_0^{200} = 6000$ or \$6000.

   b. $R(300) - R(200) = \int_{200}^{300}(-0.1x + 40)\, dx = -0.05x^2 + 40x\Big|_{200}^{300}$
   $$= 7500 - 6000 = 1500, \text{ or } \$1500.$$

43. a. The profit is $\int_0^{200}(-0.0003x^2 + 0.02x + 20)\, dx + P(0)$
   $$= -0.0001x^3 + 0.01x^2 + 20x\Big|_0^{200} + P(0)$$
   $$= 3600 + P(0) = 3600 - 800, \text{ or } \$2800.$$

   b. $\int_{200}^{220} P'(x)\, dx = P(220) - P(200) = -0.0001x^3 + 0.01x^2 + 20x\Big|_{200}^{220}$
   $$= 219.20, \text{ or } \$219.20.$$

44. a. $N(4) - N(0) = \int_0^4 N'(t)\, dt = \int_0^4 \left(-\tfrac{3}{2}t^2 + 6t + 20\right) dt$
   $$= -\tfrac{1}{2}t^3 + 3t^2 + 20t\Big|_0^4 = -\tfrac{1}{2}(64) + 3(16) + 20(4) = 96.$$

   b. $N(1) - N(0) = -\tfrac{1}{2}t^3 + 3t^2 + 20t\Big|_0^1 = 22\tfrac{1}{2}.$
   $$N(2) - N(1) = -\tfrac{1}{2}t^3 + 3t^2 + 20t\Big|_1^2 = 25\tfrac{1}{2}$$

45. The distance is
   $$\int_0^{20} v(t)\, dt = \int_0^{20}(-t^2 + 20t + 440)\, dt = -\tfrac{1}{3}t^3 + 10t^2 + 440t\Big|_0^{20} \approx 10{,}133\tfrac{1}{3}\text{ ft.}$$

46. The number is given by
   $$\int_0^6 (0.18t^2 + 0.16t + 2.64)\, dt$$
   $$= 0.06t^3 + 0.08t^2 + 2.74t\Big|_0^6 = 0.06(216) + 0.08(36) + 2.64(6) = 31.68$$
   or approximately 31.68 million units.

47. a. The percent of these households in decade t is
   $$P(t) = \int R(t)\, dt = \int (0.8499t^2 - 3.872t + 5)\, dt$$
   $$= 0.2833t^3 - 1.936t^2 + 15t + C$$

The condition $P(0) = 5.6$ gives
$$P(0) = C = 5.6$$
Therefore,
$$P(t) = 0.2833t^3 - 1.936t^2 + 15t + 5.6$$
b. The percent of these households in 2010 will be
$$P(4) = 0.2833(4^3) - 1.936(4^2) + 5(4) + 5.6 = 12.7552$$
or approximately 12.8%.
c. The percent of these households in 2000 was
$$P(3) = 0.2833(3^3) - 1.936(3^2) + 5(3) + 5.6 = 10.8251.$$
Therefore, the net increase in the percent of these households from 1970 ($t = 0$) to 2000 ($t = 3$) is $P(3) - P(0) = 10.825 - 5.6 = 5.2$, or approximately 5.2%.

48. The amount of smoke left after 5 minutes is
$$100 - \int_0^5 R(t)\, dt = 100 - \int_0^5 (0.00032t^4 - 0.01872t^3 + 0.3948t^2 - 3.83t + 17.63)\, dt$$
$$= 100 - (0.000064t^5 - 0.00468t^4 + 0.1316t^3 - 1.915t^2$$
$$+ 17.63t)\Big|_0^5 = 46, \text{ or 46 percent.}$$

The amount of smoke left after 10 minutes is
$$100 - \int_0^{10} R(t)\, dt$$
$$= 100 - (0.000064t^5 - 0.00468t^4 + 0.1316t^3 - 1.915t^2 + 17.63\, t\Big|_0^{10}$$
$$= 24 \text{ percent.}$$

49. The average population over the period in question is
$$A = \tfrac{1}{3} \int \frac{85}{1 + 1.859e^{-0.66t}}\, dt$$
Multiplying the integrand by $e^{0.66t} / e^{0.66t}$ gives
$$A = \frac{85}{3} \int_0^3 \frac{e^{0.66t}}{e^{0.66t} + 1.859}\, dt$$
Let $u = 1.859 + e^{0.66t}$, $du = 0.66e^{0.66t}\, dt$, or $e^{0.66t}\, dt = \dfrac{du}{0.66}$.

If $t = 0$, then $u = 2.859$. If $t = 3$, then $u = 9.1017$
Substituting
$$A = \frac{85}{3} \int_{2.859}^{9.1017} \frac{du}{(0.66)u} = \frac{85}{3(0.66)} \ln u \Big|_{2.859}^{9.1017}$$

$$= \frac{85}{3(0.66)}(\ln 9.1017 - \ln 2.859) = \frac{85}{3(0.66)}\ln\frac{9.1017}{2.859} \approx 49.712,$$

or approximately 49.7 million people.

50. $V = \frac{k}{L}\int_0^R x(r^2 - x^2)dx.$ Use substitution with $u = R^2 - x^2$, so that $du = -2x\,dx$ or $x\,dx = -\frac{1}{2}du.$ Furthermore, if $x = 0$, then $u = R^2$, and if $x = R$, then $u = 0$. So

$$V = \frac{k}{L}\int_{R^2}^0 u(-\tfrac{1}{2}du) = -\frac{k}{2L}\int_{R^2}^0 u\,du = -\frac{k}{4L}u^2\Big|_{R^2}^0 = 0 - \left[-\frac{k}{4L}R^4\right] = \frac{kR^4}{4L}$$

51. $f(x) = x^4 - 2x^2 + 2.$ $f'(x) = 4x^3 - 4x = 4x(x^2 - 1) = 4x(x+1)(x-1)$
Setting $f'(x) = 0$ gives $x = -1, 0,$ and 1 as critical numbers.
$f''(x) = 12x^2 - 4 = 4(3x^2 - 1)$
Using the second derivative test, we find
$f''(-1) = 8 > 0$ and so $(-1, 1)$ is a relative minimum. $f''(0) = -4 < 0$ and so $(0, 2)$ is a relative maximum. $f''(1) = 8 > 0$ and so $(1, 1)$ is a relative minimum. The graph of f is symmetric with respect to the y-axis because
$$f(-x) = (-x)^4 - 2(-x)^2 + 2 = x^4 - 2x^2 + 2.$$
So, the required area is the area under the graph of f between $x = 0$ and $x = 1$. Thus,
$$A = \int_0^1 (x^4 - 2x^2 + 2)\,dx = \tfrac{1}{5}x^5 - \tfrac{2}{3}x^3 + 2x\Big|_0^1 = \tfrac{1}{5} - \tfrac{2}{3} + 2 = \tfrac{23}{15} \text{ sq units.}$$

52. $f(x) = \frac{x+1}{\sqrt{x}} = x^{1/2} + x^{-1/2},$ $f'(x) = \tfrac{1}{2}x^{-1/2} - \tfrac{1}{2}x^{-3/2} = \tfrac{1}{2}x^{-3/2}(x-1)$
Setting $f'(x) = 0$ gives $x = 1$ as the only critical number of f.
$f''(x) = -\tfrac{1}{4}x^{-3/2} + \tfrac{3}{4}x^{-5/2} = -\tfrac{1}{4}x^{-5/2}(x-3)$
Since $f''(1) = \tfrac{1}{2} > 0$, we see that $(1, 2)$ is a relative minimum of f. $f''(x) = 0$ gives $x = 3$. Since $f''(x) > 0$ if $x < 3$ and $f''(x) < 0$ if $x > 3$, we see that $(3, \tfrac{4}{\sqrt{3}})$ is an inflection point of f. The required area is

$$A = \int_1^3 (x^{1/2} + x^{-1/2})\,dx = \frac{2}{3}x^{3/2} + 2x^{1/2}\Big|_1^3 = \left[\frac{2}{3}(3^{3/2}) + 2(3^{1/2})\right] - \left[\frac{2}{3} + 2\right] = 4\sqrt{3} - \frac{8}{3}$$

$$= \frac{12\sqrt{3} - 8}{3} \text{ sq units.}$$

6   Integration

53. False. The integrand $f(x) = \dfrac{1}{x^3}$ is discontinuous at $x = 0$.

54. False. The integrand $f(x) = \dfrac{1}{x}$ is not defined at $x = 0$, which lies in the interval $[-1,1]$.

55 False. $f(x)$ is not nonnegative on $[0, 2]$.

56. True. It is given by $\displaystyle\int_0^{5000} R'(x)\,dx = R(5000) - R(0)$, where $R(x)$ is the total revenue.

USING TECHNOLOGY EXERCISES 6.4, page 440

1. 6.1787   2. 3.3279   3. 0.7873   4. 0.2024   5. −0.5888

6. 737,038.44   7 2.7044   8. 0.4251   9. 3.9973   10. 0.4182

11. 46 %; 24%   12. 49.7 million   13. 333,209   14. 60,156   15. 903,213

6.5 CONCEPT QUESTIONS, page 447

1. Approach I: We first find the indefinite integral. Let $u = x^3 + 1$ so that $du = 3x^2\,dx$ or $x^2 dx = \tfrac{1}{3}du$. Then
$$\int x^2(x^3 + 1)^2\,dx = \tfrac{1}{3}\int u^2\,du = \tfrac{1}{9}u^3 + C = \tfrac{1}{9}(x^3 + 1)^3 + C.$$
Therefore,
$$\int_0^1 x^2(x^3 + 1)^2\,dx = \tfrac{1}{9}(x^3 + 1)^3\Big|_0^1 = \tfrac{1}{9}(8 - 1) = \tfrac{7}{9}.$$
Approach II: Transform the definite integral in x into an integral in u: Let $u = x^3 + 1$, so that $du = 3x^2\,dx$ or $x^2\,dx = \tfrac{1}{3}du$. Next, find the limits of integration with respect to u: If $x = 0$, then $u = 0^3 + 1 = 1$ and if $x = 1$, then $u = 1^3 + 1 = 2$. Therefore,
$$\int_0^1 x^2(x^3 + 1)^2\,dx = \tfrac{1}{3}\int_1^2 u^2\,du = \tfrac{1}{9}u^3\Big|_1^2 = \tfrac{1}{9}(8 - 1) = \tfrac{7}{9}.$$

2. See the definition on page 445 of the text.

EXERCISES 6.5, page 449

1. Let $u = x^2 - 1$ so that $du = 2x\,dx$ or $x\,dx = \frac{1}{2}\,du$. Also, if $x = 0$,
    then $u = -1$ and if $x = 2$, then $u = 3$. So

    $$\int_0^2 x(x^2-1)^3\,dx = \frac{1}{2}\int_{-1}^3 u^3\,du = \frac{1}{8}u^4\Big|_{-1}^3 = \frac{1}{8}(81) - \frac{1}{8}(1) = 10.$$

2. Let $u = 2x^3 - 1$ so that $du = 6x^2\,dx$ or $x^2\,dx = \frac{1}{6}\,du$. Also, if $x = 0$,
    $u = -1$, and if $x = 1$, then $u = 1$. So

    $$\int_0^1 x^2(2x^3-1)^4\,dx = \frac{1}{6}\int_{-1}^1 u^4\,du = \frac{1}{30}u^5\Big|_{-1}^1 = \frac{1}{30} - \left(-\frac{1}{30}\right) = \frac{1}{15}$$

3. Let $u = 5x^2 + 4$ so that $du = 10x\,dx$ or $x\,dx = \frac{1}{10}\,du$. Also, if
    $x = 0$, then $u = 4$, and if $x = 1$, then $u = 9$. So

    $$\int_0^1 x\sqrt{5x^2+4}\,dx = \frac{1}{10}\int_4^9 u^{1/2}\,du = \frac{1}{15}u^{3/2}\Big|_4^9 = \frac{1}{15}(27) - \frac{1}{15}(8) = \frac{19}{15}.$$

4. Let $u = 3x^2 - 2$ so that $du = 6x\,dx$ or $x\,dx = \frac{1}{6}\,du$. Also, if $x = 1$,
    then $u = 1$, and if $x = 3$, then $u = 25$. So,

    $$\int_1^3 x\sqrt{3x^2-2}\,dx = \frac{1}{6}\int_1^{25} u^{1/2}\,du = \frac{1}{9}u^{3/2}\Big|_1^{25} = \frac{1}{9}(125) - \frac{1}{9}(1) = \frac{124}{9}.$$

5. Let $u = x^3 + 1$ so that $du = 3x^2\,dx$ or $x^2\,dx = \frac{1}{3}\,du$. Also, if $x = 0$,
    then $u = 1$, and if $x = 2$, then $u = 9$. So,

    $$\int_0^2 x^2(x^3+1)^{3/2}\,dx = \frac{1}{3}\int_1^9 u^{3/2}\,du = \frac{2}{15}u^{5/2}\Big|_1^9 = \frac{2}{15}(243) - \frac{2}{15}(1) = \frac{484}{15}.$$

6. Let $u = 2x - 1$ so that $du = 2\,dx$ or $dx = \frac{1}{2}\,du$. Also, if $x = 1$,
    then $u = 1$ and if $x = 5$ then $u = 9$. So

    $$\int_1^5 (2x-1)^{5/2}\,dx = \frac{1}{2}\int_1^9 u^{5/2}\,du = \frac{1}{7}u^{7/2}\Big|_1^9 = \frac{1}{7}(2187) - \frac{1}{7}(1) = \frac{2186}{7}.$$

7. Let $u = 2x + 1$ so that $du = 2\,dx$ or $dx = \frac{1}{2}\,du$. Also, if $x = 0$,
    then $u = 1$ and if $x = 1$ then $u = 3$. So

$$\int_0^1 \frac{1}{\sqrt{2x+1}}\,dx = \frac{1}{2}\int_1^3 \frac{1}{\sqrt{u}}\,du = \frac{1}{2}\int_1^3 u^{-1/2}\,du = u^{1/2}\Big|_1^3 = \sqrt{3}-1.$$

8. Let $u = x^2 + 5$ so that $du = 2x\,dx$ or $x\,dx = \frac{1}{2}\,du$. Also, if $x = 0$ then $u = 5$ and if $x = 2$ then $u = 9$. So

$$\int_0^2 \frac{x}{\sqrt{x^2+5}}\,dx = \frac{1}{2}\int_5^9 \frac{du}{\sqrt{u}} = u^{1/2}\Big|_5^9 = 3-\sqrt{5}.$$

9   $\int_1^2 (2x-1)^4\,dx$. Put $u = 2x-1$ so that $du = 2\,dx$ or $dx = \frac{1}{2}\,du$. Then if $x = 1$, $u = 1$ and if $x = 2$, then $u = 3$. Then

$$\int_1^2 (2x-1)^4\,dx = \frac{1}{2}\int_1^3 u^4\,du = \frac{1}{10}u^5\Big|_1^3 = \frac{1}{10}(243-1) = \frac{121}{5} = 24\tfrac{1}{5}$$

10. Let $u = x^2 + 4x - 8$ so that $du = (2x+4)\,dx$. Also, if $x = 1$ then $u = -3$ and if $x = 2$, then $u = 4$. So

$$\int_1^2 (2x+4)(x^2+4x-8)^3\,dx = \int_{-3}^4 u^3\,du = \frac{1}{4}u^4\Big|_{-3}^4 = \frac{1}{4}(256)-\frac{1}{4}(81) = \frac{175}{4}.$$

11. Let $u = x^3 + 1$ so that $du = 3x^2\,dx$ or $x^2\,dx = \frac{1}{3}\,du$. Also, if $x = -1$, then $u = 0$ and if $x = 1$, then $u = 2$. So

$$\int_{-1}^1 x^2(x^3+1)^4\,dx = \frac{1}{3}\int_0^2 u^4\,du = \frac{1}{15}u^5\Big|_0^2 = \frac{32}{15}.$$

12. Let $u = x^4 + 3x$ so that $du = (4x^3 + 3)\,dx = 4(x^3 + \frac{3}{4})\,dx$ or $dx = (x^3 + \frac{3}{4}) = \frac{1}{4}\,du$. Also, if $x = 1$, then $u = 4$ and if $x = 2$, then $u = 22$. So

$$\int_1^2 \left(x^3+\tfrac{3}{4}\right)(x^4+3x)^{-2}\,dx = \frac{1}{4}\int_4^{22} u^{-2}\,du = -\frac{1}{4u}\Big|_4^{22} = -\frac{1}{88}+\frac{1}{16} = \frac{-2+11}{176} = \frac{9}{176}.$$

13. Let $u = x - 1$ so that $du = dx$. Then if $x = 1$, $u = 0$, and if $x = 5$, then $u = 4$.

$$\int_1^5 x\sqrt{x-1}\,dx = \int_0^4 (u+1)u^{1/2}\,du = \int_0^4 (u^{3/2}+u^{1/2})\,du$$

$$= \frac{2}{5}u^{5/2}+\frac{2}{3}u^{3/2}\Big|_0^4 = \frac{2}{5}(32)+\frac{2}{3}(8) = 18\tfrac{2}{15}.$$

14. Let $u = x + 1$ so that $du = dx$ and also $x = u - 1$. If $x = 1$, then $u = 2$ and if $x = 4$, then $u = 5$. So

$$\int_1^4 x\sqrt{x+1}\,dx = \int_2^5 (u-1)\sqrt{u}\,du = \int_2^5 (u^{3/2} - u^{1/2})\,du$$

$$= \tfrac{2}{5}u^{5/2} - \tfrac{2}{3}u^{3/2}\Big|_2^5 = \tfrac{2}{15}u^{3/2}(3u-5)\Big|_2^5 = \tfrac{2}{15}(50\sqrt{5} - 2\sqrt{2}).$$

15. Let $u = x^2$ so that $du = 2x\,dx$ or $x\,dx = \tfrac{1}{2}du$. If $x = 0$, $u = 0$ and if $x = 2$, $u = 4$. So

$$\int_0^2 xe^{x^2}\,dx = \tfrac{1}{2}\int_0^4 e^u\,du = \tfrac{1}{2}e^u\Big|_0^4 = \tfrac{1}{2}(e^4 - 1).$$

16. Let $u = -x$ so that $du = -dx$ or $dx = -du$. If $x = 0$, $u = 0$ and if $x = 1$, $u = -1$. So

$$\int_0^1 e^{-x}\,dx = -\int_0^{-1} e^u\,du = -e^u\Big|_0^{-1} = -e^{-1} + 1 = 1 - \frac{1}{e}$$

17. $\int_0^1 (e^{2x} + x^2 + 1)\,dx = \tfrac{1}{2}e^{2x} + \tfrac{1}{3}x^3 + x\Big|_0^1 = (\tfrac{1}{2}e^2 + \tfrac{1}{3} + 1) - \tfrac{1}{2}$

$$= \tfrac{1}{2}e^2 + \tfrac{5}{6}.$$

18. $\int_0^2 (e^t - e^{-t})\,dt = e^t + e^{-t}\Big|_0^2 = (e^2 + e^{-2}) - (1+1) = e^2 + e^{-2} - 2.$

19. Put $u = x^2 + 1$ so that $du = 2x\,dx$ or $x\,dx = \tfrac{1}{2}du$. Then

$$\int_{-1}^1 xe^{x^2+1}\,dx = \frac{1}{2}\int_2^2 e^u\,du = \frac{1}{2}e^u\Big|_2^2 = 0$$

(Since the upper and lower limits are equal.)

20. Let $u = \sqrt{x}$, then $du = \dfrac{1}{2\sqrt{x}}dx$. If $x = 0$, $u = 0$, and if $x = 4$, $u = 2$.

$$\int_0^4 \frac{e^{\sqrt{x}}}{\sqrt{x}}\,dx = 2\int_0^2 e^u\,du = 2e^u\Big|_0^2 = 2(e^2 - 1).$$

21. Let $u = x - 2$ so that $du = dx$. If $x = 3$, $u = 1$ and if $x = 6$, $u = 4$. So

$$\int_3^6 \frac{2}{x-2}\,dx = 2\int_1^4 \frac{du}{u} = 2\ln|u|\Big|_1^4 = 2\ln 4.$$

22. Let $u = 1 + 2x^2$ so that $du = 4x\, dx$ or $x\, dx = \frac{1}{4}\, du$. If $x = 0$, $u = 1$ and if $x = 1$, $u = 3$. So

$$\int_0^1 \frac{x}{1+2x^2}\, dx = \frac{1}{4}\int_1^3 \frac{du}{u} = \frac{1}{4}\ln|u|\Big|_1^3 = \frac{1}{4}\ln 3.$$

23. Let $u = x^3 + 3x^2 - 1$ so that $du = (3x^2 + 6x)dx = 3(x^2 + 2x)dx$. If $x = 1$, $u = 3$, and if $x = 2$, $u = 19$. So

$$\int_1^2 \frac{x^2 + 2x}{x^3 + 3x^2 - 1}dx = \frac{1}{3}\int_3^{19} \frac{du}{u} = \frac{1}{3}\ln u\Big|_3^{19} = \frac{1}{3}(\ln 19 - \ln 3).$$

24. $\displaystyle\int_0^1 \frac{e^x}{1+e^x}\, dx = \ln(1+e^x)\Big|_0^1 = \ln(1+e) - \ln 2 = \ln\left(\frac{1+e}{2}\right).$

25. $\displaystyle\int_1^2 \left(4e^{2u} - \frac{1}{u}\right)du = 2e^{2u} - \ln u\Big|_1^2 = (2e^4 - \ln 2) - (2e^2 - 0) = 2e^4 - 2e^2 - \ln 2.$

26. $\displaystyle\int_1^2 \left(1 + \frac{1}{x} + e^x\right)dx = x + \ln x + e^x\Big|_1^2 = (2 + \ln 2 + e^2) - (1 + e)$

$$= 1 + \ln 2 + e^2 - e.$$

27. $\displaystyle\int_1^2 (2e^{-4x} - x^{-2})dx = -\frac{1}{2}e^{-4x} + \frac{1}{x}\Big|_1^2 = (-\frac{1}{2}e^{-8} + \frac{1}{2}) - (-\frac{1}{2}e^{-4} + 1)$

$$= -\frac{1}{2}e^{-8} + \frac{1}{2}e^{-4} - \frac{1}{2} = \frac{1}{2}(e^{-4} - e^{-8} - 1).$$

28. Let $u = \ln x$, $du = \frac{1}{x}dx$. If $x = 1$, $u = 0$ and if $x = 2$, $u = \ln 2$.

So $\displaystyle\int_1^2 \frac{\ln x}{x}\, dx = \int_0^{\ln 2} u\, du = \frac{1}{2}u^2\Big|_0^{\ln 2} = \frac{1}{2}(\ln 2)^2.$

29. $\text{AV} = \displaystyle\frac{1}{2}\int_0^2 (2x + 3)\, dx = \frac{1}{2}(x^2 + 3x)\Big|_0^2 = \frac{1}{2}(10) = 5.$

30. $AV = \dfrac{1}{b-a}\displaystyle\int_a^b f(x)\,dx = \dfrac{1}{4-1}\displaystyle\int_1^4 (8-x)\,dx = \dfrac{1}{3}\displaystyle\int_1^4 (8-x)\,dx$

$= \dfrac{1}{3}(8x - \tfrac{1}{2}x^2)\Big|_1^4 = \dfrac{1}{3}[(32-8)-(8-\tfrac{1}{2})] = 5\tfrac{1}{2}$

31. $AV = \dfrac{1}{2}\displaystyle\int_1^3 (2x^2-3)\,dx = \dfrac{1}{2}(\tfrac{2}{3}x^3 - 3x)\Big|_1^3 = \dfrac{1}{2}(9+\tfrac{7}{3}) = \dfrac{17}{3}$

32. $AV = \dfrac{1}{5}\displaystyle\int_{-2}^3 (4-x^2)\,dx = \dfrac{1}{5}(4x - \tfrac{1}{3}x^3)\Big|_{-2}^3 = \dfrac{1}{5}[(12-9)-(-8+\tfrac{8}{3})] = \dfrac{5}{3}$.

33. $AV = \dfrac{1}{3}\displaystyle\int_{-1}^2 (x^2+2x-3)\,dx = \dfrac{1}{3}(\tfrac{1}{3}x^3 + x^2 - 3x)\Big|_{-1}^2$

$= \dfrac{1}{3}[(\tfrac{8}{3}+4-6)-(-\tfrac{1}{3}+1+3)] = \dfrac{1}{3}(\tfrac{8}{3}-2+\tfrac{1}{3}-4) = -1.$

34. $AV = \dfrac{1}{2}\displaystyle\int_{-1}^1 x^3\,dx = \dfrac{1}{2}(\tfrac{1}{4}x^4)\Big|_{-1}^1 = \dfrac{1}{2}(\tfrac{1}{4}-\tfrac{1}{4}) = 0$

35. $AV = \dfrac{1}{4}\displaystyle\int_0^4 (2x+1)^{1/2}\,dx = (\tfrac{1}{4})(\tfrac{1}{2})(\tfrac{2}{3})(2x+1)^{3/2}\Big|_0^4 = \dfrac{1}{12}(27-1) = \dfrac{13}{6}$

36. $AV = \dfrac{1}{4-0}\displaystyle\int_0^4 e^{-x}\,dx = -\dfrac{1}{4}e^{-x}\Big|_0^4 = -\dfrac{1}{4}(e^{-4}-1) \approx 0.245.$

37. $AV = \dfrac{1}{2}\displaystyle\int_0^2 xe^{x^2}\,dx = \dfrac{1}{4}e^{x^2}\Big|_0^2 = \dfrac{1}{4}(e^4-1).$

38. $AV = \dfrac{1}{2}\displaystyle\int_0^2 \dfrac{dx}{x+1} = \dfrac{1}{2}\ln(x+1)\Big|_0^2 = \dfrac{1}{2}\ln 3.$

39. The amount produced was

$$\int_0^{20} 3.5e^{0.05t}\,dt = \dfrac{3.5}{0.05}e^u\Big|_0^{20} \qquad \text{(Use the substitution } u = 0.05t.)$$

$= 70(e-1) \approx 120.3, \quad \text{or } 120.3 \text{ billion metric tons.}$

40. The temperature will have dropped

$$\int_0^3 -18e^{-0.6t}\, dt = \frac{-18}{-0.6}e^{-0.6t}\Big|_0^3 \qquad \text{(Use the substitution } u = 0.05t.)$$

$$= 30e^{-0.6t}\Big|_0^3 = 30(e^{-1.8} - 1) = 25.04, \text{ or approximately 25 degrees.}$$

$f(t) = 30e^{-0.6t} + C; \ f(0) = 30 + C = 68, \text{ and } C = 38.$

The temperature of the wine at 7 P.M. is

$f(3) = 30e^{-1.8} + 38 \approx 42.96, \quad \text{or approximately } 43° F.$

41. The amount is $\int_1^2 t(\tfrac{1}{2}t^2 + 1)^{1/2}\, dt.$ Let $u = \tfrac{1}{2}t^2 + 1,$ so that $du = t\, dt.$ Therefore,

$$\int_1^2 t(\tfrac{1}{2}t^2 + 1)^{1/2}\, dt = \int_{3/2}^3 u^{1/2}\, du = \tfrac{2}{3}u^{3/2}\Big|_{3/2}^3 = \tfrac{2}{3}[(3)^{3/2} - (\tfrac{3}{2})^{3/2}]$$

$$\approx 2.24 \text{ million dollars.}$$

42. The amount of oil that the well can be expected to yield is

$$\int_0^5 \left(\frac{600t^2}{t^3 + 32} + 5\right) dt = 600\int_0^5 \frac{t^2}{t^3 + 32}\, dt + 5t\Big|_0^5 = 600\left(\frac{1}{3}\right) \ln(t^3 + 32)\Big|_0^5 + 25$$

$$= 200(\ln 157 - \ln 32) + 25 \approx 343$$

or 343 thousand barrels.

43. The tractor will depreciate

$$\int_0^5 13388.61e^{-0.22314t}\, dt = \frac{13388.61}{-0.22314}e^{-0.22314t}\Big|_0^5$$

$$= -60,000.94e^{-0.22314t}\Big|_0^5 = -60,000.94(-0.672314)$$

$$= 40,339\ 47, \quad \text{or } \$40,339$$

44. The distance traveled is $\int_0^4 3t\sqrt{16 - t^2}\, dt = 3(-\tfrac{1}{2})(\tfrac{2}{3})(16 - t^2)^{3/2}\Big|_0^4 = 64 \text{ ft.}$

45. $\bar{A} = \tfrac{1}{5}\int (\tfrac{1}{12}t^2 + 2t + 44)dt = \tfrac{1}{5}\left[\tfrac{1}{36}t^3 + t^2 + 44t\Big|_0^5\right]$

$= \tfrac{1}{5}\left[\tfrac{125}{36} + 25 + 220\right] = \frac{125 + 900 + 7920}{5(36)} \approx 49.69$, or 49.7 ft/sec.

46. The average rate of growth between $t = 0$ and $t = 9$ is

$$\frac{1}{9-0}\int_0^9 R(t)\,dt = \frac{1}{9}\int_0^9 (-0.0039t^2 + 0.0374t + 0.0046)\,dt$$

$$= \frac{1}{9}(-0.0013t^3 + 0.0187t^2 + 0.0046t)\big|_0^9$$

$$= \frac{1}{9}[-0.0013(9^3) + 0.0187(9^2) + 0.0046(9)]$$

$$= 0.0676$$

or 67,600/yr.

47. The average whale population will be

$$\frac{1}{10}\int_0^{10}(3t^3 + 2t^2 - 10t + 600)\,dt = \frac{1}{10}(\tfrac{3}{4}t^4 + \tfrac{2}{3}t^3 - 5t^2 + 600t)\big|_0^{10}$$

$$\approx \frac{1}{10}(7500 + 666.67 - 500 + 6000) \approx 1367 \text{ whales.}$$

48. The average rate of growth of these citizens between 2000 ($t = 10$) and 2050 ($t = 15$) is

$$\frac{1}{15-10}\int_{10}^{15} R(t)\,dt = \frac{1}{5}\int_{10}^{15}(0.063t^2 - 0.48t + 3.87)\,dt$$

$$= \frac{1}{5}(0.021t^3 - 0.24t^2 + 3.87t)\big|_{10}^{15}$$

$$= \frac{1}{5}\{[(0.021)(15^3) - 0.24(15^2) + 3.87(15)]$$

$$-[(0.021)(10^3) - 0.24(10^2) + 3.87(10)]\}$$

$$= 7.845, \text{ or } 7.845 \text{ million people/decade.}$$

The average rate between 1950 ($t = 5$) and 2000 ($t = 10$) is

$$\frac{1}{10-5}\int_5^{10} R(t)\,dt = \frac{1}{5}(0.021t^3 - 0.24t^2 + 3.87t)\big|_5^{10}$$

$$= \frac{1}{5}\{[0.021(10^3) - 0.24(10^2) + 3.87(10) -$$

$$[0.021(5^3) - 0.24(5^2) + 3.87(5)]\}$$

$$= 3.945, \text{ or } 3.945 \text{ million people/decade}$$

The conclusion follows.

49. The average yearly sales of the company over its first 5 years of operation is given

by $\qquad \frac{1}{5-0}\int_0^5 t(0.2t^2+4)^{1/2}\,dt = \frac{1}{5}[(\frac{5}{2})(\frac{2}{3})(0.2t^2+4)^{3/2}]\Big|_0^5$ $\qquad$ [Let $u = -0.2t^2+4$.]

$\qquad = \frac{1}{5}[\frac{5}{3}(5+4)^{3/2}-\frac{5}{3}(4)^{3/2}] = \frac{1}{3}(27-8) = \frac{19}{3}$, or $6\frac{1}{3}$ million dollars.

50. The average number is

$$\frac{1}{5}\int_0^5\left(-\frac{40{,}000}{\sqrt{1+0.2t}}+50{,}000\right)dt = -8000\int_0^5(1+0.2t)^{-1/2}\,dt + 10{,}000\int_0^5 dt$$

Integrating the first integral by substitution with $u = 1 + 0.2t$, so that $du = 0.2\,dt$ or $dt = 5\,du$, we find that the average value is

$$-8000\int_1^2 5u^{-1/2}\,du + \int_0^5 10{,}000\,dt = -40{,}000(2u^{1/2})\Big|_1^2 + 10{,}000t\Big|_0^5$$

$$= -40{,}000(2\sqrt{2}-2)+50{,}000 = 16{,}863$$

or 16,863 subscribers.

51. The average velocity is $\frac{1}{4}\int_0^4 3t\sqrt{16-t^2}\,dt = \frac{1}{4}(64) = 16$, or 16 ft/sec.

(Using the results of Exercise 44.)

52. The average concentration of the drug is

$$\frac{1}{4}\int_0^4\frac{0.2t}{t^2+1}\,dt = \frac{0.2}{4}\int_0^4\frac{t}{t^2+1}\,dt = \frac{0.2}{(4)(2)}\ln(t^2+1)\Big|_0^4$$

$$= 0.025\ln 17 \approx 0.071, \text{ or } 0.071 \text{ milligrams per cm}^3.$$

53 $\int_0^5 p\,dt = \int_0^5(18-3e^{-2t}-6e^{-t/3})\,dt = \frac{1}{5}\left[18t+\frac{3}{2}e^{-2t}+18e^{-t/3}\right]_0^5$

$\qquad = \frac{1}{5}\left[18(5)+\frac{3}{2}e^{-10}+18e^{-5/3}-\frac{3}{2}-18\right] = 14.78$, or $14.78.

54. The average velocity of the blood is

$$\frac{1}{R}\int_0^R k(R^2-r^2)\,dr = \frac{k}{R}\int_0^R(R^2-r^2)\,dr = \frac{k}{r}(R^2r-\frac{1}{3}r^3)\Big|_0^R$$

$$= \frac{k}{R}(R^3-\frac{1}{3}R^3) = \frac{k}{R}\cdot\frac{2}{3}R^3 = \frac{2k}{3}R^2 \text{ cm/sec.}$$

55. The average content of oxygen in the pond over the first 10 days is

$$\frac{1}{10-0}\int_0^{10}100\left(\frac{t^2+10t+100}{t^2+20t+100}\right)dt = \frac{100}{10}\int_0^{10}\left[1-\frac{10}{t+10}+\frac{100}{(t+10)^2}\right]dt$$

$$= 10 \int_0^{10} \left[1 - \frac{10}{t+10} + 100(t+10)^{-2} \right]$$

$$= 10 \left[t - 10\ln(t+10) - \frac{100}{t+10} \right]_0^{10} \quad \text{[Use the substitution } u = t + 10 \text{ for the}$$

third integral.]

$$= 10\{[10 - 10\ln 20 - \frac{100}{2p}] - [-10\ln 10 - 10]\}$$

$$= 10[10 - 10\ln 20 - 5 + 10\ln 10 + 10]$$

$$\approx 80.6853, \quad \text{or approximately } 80.7\%.$$

56. $\dfrac{1}{h}\displaystyle\int_0^h (2gx)^{1/2}\, dx = \dfrac{1}{3h}(2gx)^{3/2}\Big|_0^h = \dfrac{2}{3}\sqrt{2gh}$; that is, $\dfrac{2}{3}\sqrt{2gh}$ ft/sec.

57. $\displaystyle\int_a^a f(x)\, dx = F(x)\big|_a^a = F(a) - F(a) = 0,$ where $F'(x) = f(x).$

58. $\displaystyle\int_a^b f(x)\, dx = F(x)\big|_a^b = F(b) - F(a) = -[F(a) - F(b)]$

$$= -F(x)\big|_b^a = -\int_b^a f(x)\, dx$$

59. $\displaystyle\int_1^3 x^2\, dx = \frac{1}{3}x^3\Big|_1^3 = 9 - \frac{1}{3} = \frac{26}{3} = -\int_3^1 x^2\, dx = -\frac{1}{3}x^3\Big|_3^1 = -\frac{1}{3} + 9 = \frac{26}{3}.$

60. $\displaystyle\int_a^b cf(x)\, dx = xF(x)\big|_a^b = c[F(b) - F(a)] = c\int_a^b f(x)\, dx.$

61. $\displaystyle\int_1^9 2\sqrt{x}\, dx = \frac{4}{3}x^{3/2}\Big|_1^9 = \frac{4}{3}(27 - 1) = \frac{104}{3} = 2\int_1^9 \sqrt{x}\, dx = (2)(\frac{2}{3}x^{3/2})\Big|_1^9 = \frac{104}{3}.$

62. $\displaystyle\int_0^1 (1 + x - e^x)\, dx = x + \frac{1}{2}x^2 - e^x\Big|_0^1 = (1 + \frac{1}{2} - e) + 1 = \frac{5}{2} - e.$

$\displaystyle\int_0^1 dx + \int_0^1 x\, dx - \int_0^1 e^x\, dx = x\big|_0^1 + \frac{1}{2}x^2\big|_0^1 - e^x\big|_0^1 = (1 - 0) + (\frac{1}{2} - 0) - (e - 1) = \frac{5}{2} - e.$

63. $\int_0^3 (1+x^3)\,dx = (x+\tfrac{1}{4}x^4)\big|_0^3 = 3+\tfrac{81}{4} = \tfrac{93}{4}$.

$\int_0^1 (1+x^3)\,dx + \int_1^2 (1+x^3)\,dx + \int_2^3 (1+x^3)\,dx$

$= (x+\tfrac{1}{4}x^4)\big|_0^1 + (x+\tfrac{1}{4}x^4)\big|_1^2 + (x+\tfrac{1}{4}x^4)\big|_2^3$

$= (1+\tfrac{1}{4}) + (2+4) - (1+\tfrac{1}{4}) + (3+\tfrac{81}{4}) - (2+4) = \tfrac{93}{4}$.   [Property 5.]

64. $\int_0^3 (1+x^3)\,dx = x+\tfrac{1}{4}x^4\big|_0^3 = 3+\tfrac{81}{4} = \tfrac{93}{4}$.

$\int_0^1 (1+x^3)\,dx + \int_1^3 (1+x^3)\,dx$

$= (x+\tfrac{1}{4}x^4)\big|_0^1 + (x+\tfrac{1}{4}x^4)\big|_1^3$

$= (1+\tfrac{1}{4}) + (3+\dfrac{81}{4}) - (1+\tfrac{1}{4}) = \tfrac{93}{4}$.

65. $\int_3^3 (1+\sqrt{x})e^{-x}\,dx = 0$ by Property 1 of definite integrals.

66. $\int_3^0 f(x)\,dx = -\int_0^3 f(x)\,dx = -4$.   (Property 2)

67. a. $\int_{-1}^2 [2f(x)+g(x)]\,dx = 2\int_{-1}^2 f(x)\,dx + \int_{-1}^2 g(x)\,dx = 2(-2) + 3 = -1$.

b. $\int_{-1}^2 [g(x)-f(x)]\,dx = \int_{-1}^2 g(x)\,dx - \int_{-1}^2 f(x)\,dx = 3 - (-2) = 5$.

c. $\int_{-1}^2 [2f(x)-3g(x)]\,dx = 2\int_{-1}^2 f(x)\,dx - 3\int_{-1}^2 g(x)\,dx = 2(-2) - 3(3) = -13$.

68. a. $\int_{-1}^0 f(x)\,dx = \int_{-1}^2 f(x) - \int_0^2 f(x)\,dx = 2 - 3 = -1$.

b. $\int_0^2 f(x)\,dx - \int_{-1}^0 f(x)\,dx = 3 - (-1) = 4$.

69. True. This follows from Property 1 of the definite integral.

70. False. the integrand $f(x) = \dfrac{1}{x-2}$ is not defined at $x = 2$.

71. False. Only a constant can be "moved out" of the integral sign.

72. True. This follows from the Fundamental Theorem of Calculus.

73. True. This follows from Properties 3 and 4 of the definite integral.

74. True. We have

$$\int_a^b f(x)\,dx = \int_a^c f(x)\,dx + \int_c^b f(x)\,dx$$

and so

$$\int_c^b f(x)\,dx = \int_a^b f(x)\,dx - \int_a^c f(x)\,dx,$$

or

$$-\int_c^b f(x)\,dx = \int_c^b f(x)\,dx = \int_a^b f(x)\,dx - \int_a^c f(x)\,dx$$

and

$$\int_c^b f(x)\,dx = \int_a^c f(x)\,dx - \int_a^b f(x)\,dx.$$

1. 7.71667   2. 1.1531   3. 17.5649   4. -14$\frac{1}{3}$ 5 10,140

6. 159/bean stem   7. 60.5mg/day   8. 0.48 g/ cm^3 /day

6.6 CONCEPT QUESTIONS, page 458

1. $\int_a^b [f(x) - g(x)]\,dx$

2. $\int_a^b [f(x) - g(x)]\,dx + \int_b^c [g(x) - f(x)]\,dx + \int_c^d [f(x) - g(x)]\,dx$

EXERCISES 6.6, page 458

1. $-\int_0^6 (x^3 - 6x^2)\,dx = -\frac{1}{4}x^4 + 2x^3 \Big|_0^6 = -\frac{1}{4}(6^4) + 2(6^3) = 108$ sq units.

2. $-\int_0^2 (x^4 - 2x^3)\,dx = \frac{1}{2}x^4 - \frac{1}{5}x^5 \Big|_0^2 = 8 - \frac{32}{5} = \frac{8}{5}$ sq units.

3. $A = -\int_{-1}^0 x\sqrt{1-x^2}\,dx + \int_0^1 x\sqrt{1-x^2}\,dx = 2\int_0^1 x(1-x^2)^{1/2}\,dx$ (by symmetry). Let

$u = 1 - x^2$ so that $du = -2x\,dx$ or $x\,dx = -\frac{1}{2}\,du$. Also, if $x = 0$, then $u = 1$ and

if $x = 1$, $u = 0$. So $A = (2)(-\frac{1}{2})\int_1^0 u^{1/2}\,du = -\frac{2}{3}u^{3/2}\Big|_1^0 = \frac{2}{3}$, or $\frac{2}{3}$ sq unit.

4. $A = -\int_{-2}^0 \frac{2x}{x^2+4}\,dx + \int_0^2 \frac{2x}{x^2+4}\,dx = 2\int_0^2 \frac{2x}{x^2+4}\,dx = 2\ln(x^2+4)\Big|_0^2$
   $= (\ln 8 - \ln 4)2 = \ln 4$ sq units.

5. $A = -\int_0^4 (x - 2\sqrt{x})\,dx = \int_0^4 (-x + 2x^{1/2})\,dx = -\frac{1}{2}x^2 + \frac{4}{3}x^{3/2}\Big|_0^4$
   $= 8 + \frac{32}{3} = \frac{8}{3}$ sq units.

6. $A = \int_0^4 [\sqrt{x} - (x-2)]\,dx = \int_0^4 (x^{1/2} - x + 2)\,dx = (\frac{2}{3}x^{3/2} - \frac{1}{2}x^2 + 2x)\Big|_0^4$
   $= \frac{16}{3} - 8 + 8 = \frac{16}{3}$.

7. The required area is given by
$$\int_{-1}^0 (x^2 - x^{1/3})\,dx + \int_0^1 (x^{1/3} - x^2)\,dx = \frac{1}{3}x^3 - \frac{3}{4}x^{4/3}\Big|_{-1}^0 + \frac{3}{4}x^{4/3} - \frac{1}{3}x^3\Big|_0^1$$
$$= -(-\frac{1}{3} - \frac{3}{4}) + (\frac{3}{4} - \frac{1}{3}) = 1\frac{1}{2} \quad \text{sq units.}$$

8. $A = \int_{-4}^0 [(x+6) - (-\frac{1}{2}x)]\,dx + \int_0^2 [(x+6) - x^3]\,dx$
   $= \int_{-4}^0 (\frac{3}{2}x + 6)\,dx + \int_0^2 [(x+6) - x^3]\,dx$
   $= \frac{3}{4}x^2 + 6x\Big|_{-4}^0 + (\frac{1}{2}x^2 + 6x - \frac{1}{4}x^4)\Big|_0^2 = -(12 - 24) + (2 + 12 - 4) = 22$ sq units.

9. The required area is given by
   $-\int_{-1}^2 -x^2\,dx = \frac{1}{3}x^3\Big|_{-1}^2 = \frac{8}{3} + \frac{1}{3} = 3$ sq units.

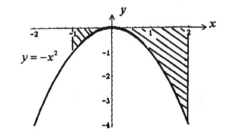

$y = -x^2$

10. $A = -\int_{-2}^{2} (x^2 - 4)\, dx = -2\int_{0}^{2} (x^2 - 4)\, dx$

$= 2(-\tfrac{1}{3}x^3 + 4x)\big|_0^2 = 2(-\tfrac{8}{3} + 8)$

$= \tfrac{32}{3}$ sq units.

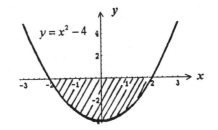

11. $y = x^2 - 5x + 4 = (x - 4)(x - 1) = 0$

if $x = 1$ or 4. These give the x-intercepts.

$A = -\int_{1}^{3} (x^2 - 5x + 4)\, dx = -\tfrac{1}{3}x^3 + \tfrac{5}{2}x^2 - 4x\Big|_1^3$

$= (-9 + \tfrac{45}{2} - 12) - (-\tfrac{1}{3} + \tfrac{5}{2} - 4) = \tfrac{10}{3} = 3\tfrac{1}{3}.$

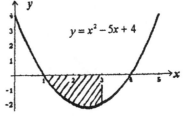

12. The required area is given by

$-\int_{-1}^{0} x^3\, dx = -\tfrac{1}{4}x^4\big|_{-1}^{0} = -\tfrac{1}{4}(0) + \tfrac{1}{4}(1) = \tfrac{1}{4}.$

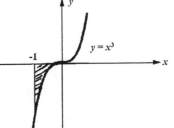

13. The required area is given by

$-\int_{0}^{9} -(1 + \sqrt{x})\, dx = x + \tfrac{2}{3}x^{3/2}\Big|_0^9 = 9 + 18 = 27.$

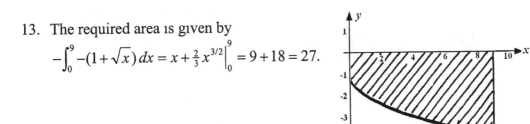

14. $A = -\int_0^4 (\tfrac{1}{2}x - x^{1/2}) \, dx = -\tfrac{1}{4}x^2 + \tfrac{2}{3}x^{3/2} \Big|_0^4$

$= (-4 + \tfrac{16}{3}) = \tfrac{4}{3}$ sq units.

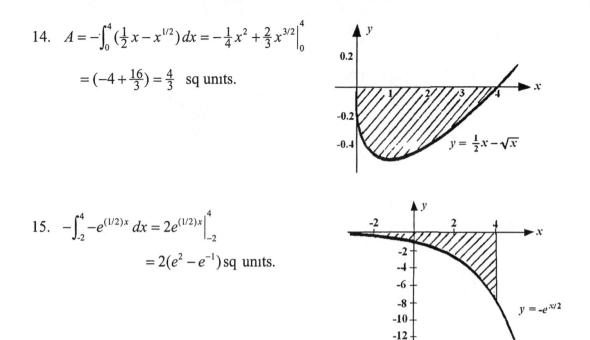

$y = \tfrac{1}{2}x - \sqrt{x}$

15. $-\int_{-2}^4 -e^{(1/2)x} \, dx = 2e^{(1/2)x} \Big|_{-2}^4$

$= 2(e^2 - e^{-1}) \, \text{sq units.}$

$y = -e^{x/2}$

16. $A = -\int_0^1 -xe^{-x^2} \, dx = \int_0^1 xe^{-x^2} \, dx$. Let $u = -x^2$ so that $du = -2x \, dx$

or $x \, dx = -\tfrac{1}{2} \, du$. Also, if $x = 0$, then $u = 0$
and if $x = 1$ then $u = -1$. So

$A = -\tfrac{1}{2}\int_0^{-1} e^u \, du = -\tfrac{1}{2} e^u \Big|_0^{-1}$

$= -\tfrac{1}{2}e^{-1} + \tfrac{1}{2} = \tfrac{1}{2}(1 - e^{-1})$ sq units.

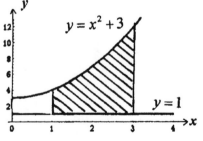

$y = -xe^{-x^2}$

17. $A = \int_1^3 [(x^2 + 3) - 1] \, dx$

$= \int_1^3 (x^2 + 2) \, dx = \tfrac{1}{3}x^3 + 2x \Big|_1^3$

$= (9 + 6) - (\tfrac{1}{3} + 2) = \tfrac{38}{3}.$

$y = x^2 + 3$

$y = 1$

18. $A = \int_{-1}^{2} [(x+2) - (x^2 - 4)] \, dx$

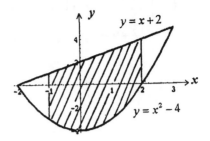

$$= \int_{-1}^{2} (-x^2 + x + 6) \, dx$$

$$= -\tfrac{1}{3}x^3 + \tfrac{1}{2}x^2 + 6x \Big|_{-1}^{2}$$

$$= (-\tfrac{8}{3} + 2 + 12) - (\tfrac{1}{3} + \tfrac{1}{2} - 6) = 16\tfrac{1}{2} \text{ sq units}$$

19. $A = \int_{0}^{2} (-x^2 + 2x + 3 + x - 3) \, dx$

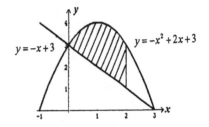

$$= \int_{0}^{2} (-x^2 + 3x) \, dx$$

$$= -\tfrac{1}{3}x^3 + \tfrac{3}{2}x^2 \Big|_{0}^{2} = -\tfrac{1}{3}(8) + \tfrac{3}{2}(4)$$

$$= 6 - \tfrac{8}{3} = \tfrac{10}{3} \text{ sq units}$$

20. The region is shown in the figure on the right.

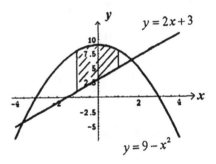

$$A = \int_{-1}^{1} [(9 - x^2) - (2x + 3)] \, dx$$

$$= \int_{-1}^{1} (-x^2 - 2x + 6) \, dx$$

$$= -\tfrac{1}{3}x^3 - x^2 + 6x \Big|_{-1}^{1}$$

$$= (-\tfrac{1}{3} - 1 + 6) - (\tfrac{1}{3} - 1 - 6) = \tfrac{34}{3} \text{ sq units.}$$

21. $A = \int_{-1}^{2} [(x^2 + 1) - \tfrac{1}{3}x^3] \, dx$

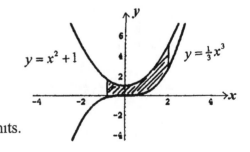

$$= \int_{-1}^{2} (-\tfrac{1}{3}x^3 + x^2 + 1) \, dx$$

$$= -\tfrac{1}{12}x^4 + \tfrac{1}{3}x^3 + x \Big|_{-1}^{2}$$

$$= (-\tfrac{4}{3} + \tfrac{8}{3} + 2) - (-\tfrac{1}{12} - \tfrac{1}{3} - 1) = 4\tfrac{3}{4} \text{ sq units.}$$

6   Integration

22. $A = \int_1^4 (x^{1/2} + \frac{1}{2}x + 1)\, dx = \frac{2}{3}x^{3/2} + \frac{1}{4}x^2 + x \Big|_1^4$

    $= (\frac{16}{3} + 4 + 4) - (\frac{2}{3} + \frac{1}{4} + 1) = \frac{137}{12}$ sq units.

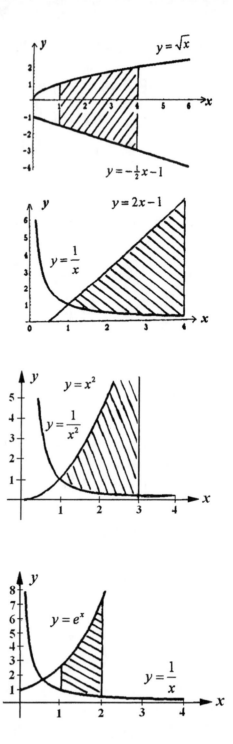

23   $A = \int_1^4 \left[(2x-1) - \frac{1}{x}\right] dx = \int_1^4 \left(2x - 1 - \frac{1}{x}\right) dx$

    $= (x^2 - x - \ln x) \Big|_1^4$

    $= (16 - 4 - \ln 4) - (1 - 1 - \ln 1)$

    $= 12 - \ln 4 \approx 10.6$ sq units.

24. $A = \int_1^3 \left[\left(x^2 - \frac{1}{x^2}\right) dx\right]$

    $= \int_1^3 (x^2 - x^{-2})\, dx = \left(\frac{1}{3}x^3 + \frac{1}{x}\right) \Big|_1^3$

    $= (9 + \frac{1}{3}) - (\frac{1}{3} + 1) = 8$ sq units.

25. $A = \int_1^2 \left(e^x - \frac{1}{x}\right) dx = e^x - \ln x \Big|_1^2$

    $= (e^2 - \ln 2) - e = (e^2 - e - \ln 2)$ sq units.

    $= \left(\frac{1}{2}e^6 - \frac{9}{2}\right) - \left(\frac{1}{2}e^2 - \frac{1}{2}\right)$

26. $A = \int_1^3 (e^{2x} - x) \, dx = \frac{1}{2}e^{2x} - \frac{1}{2}x^2 \Big|_1^3$

$\quad = \frac{1}{2}(e^6 - e^2 - 8) \approx 194$ sq units.

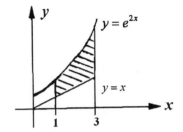

27. $A = -\int_{-1}^0 x \, dx + \int_0^2 x \, dx$

$\quad = -\frac{1}{2}x^2 \Big|_{-1}^0 + \frac{1}{2}x^2 \Big|_0^2$

$\quad = \frac{1}{2} + 2 = 2\frac{1}{2}$ sq units.

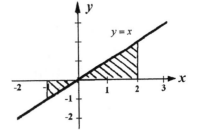

28. $A = \int_{-1}^0 (x^2 - 2x) \, dx - \int_0^1 (x^2 - 2x) \, dx$

$\quad = -(\frac{1}{3}x^3 - x^2) \Big|_{-1}^0 - (\frac{1}{3}x^3 - x^2) \Big|_0^1$

$\quad = -(-\frac{1}{3} - 1) - (\frac{1}{3} - 1) = 2.$

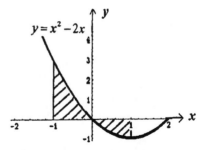

29. The x–intercepts are found by solving
$x^2 - 4x + 3 = (x - 3)(x - 1) = 0$ giving $x = 1$
or 3. The region is shown in the figure.

$A = -\int_{-1}^1 [(-x^2 + 4x - 3) \, dx + \int_1^2 (-x^2 + 4x - 3) \, dx$

$\quad = \frac{1}{3}x^3 - 2x^2 + 3x \Big|_{-1}^1 + (-\frac{1}{3}x^3 + 2x^2 - 3x) \Big|_1^2$

$\quad = (\frac{1}{3} - 2 + 3) - (-\frac{1}{3} - 2 - 3)$

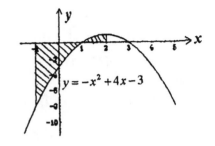

$$+(-\tfrac{8}{3}+8-6)-(-\tfrac{1}{3}+2-3) = \tfrac{22}{3} \text{ sq units.}$$

30. The region is shown in the figure at the right.

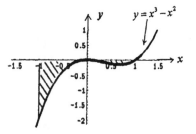

$$A = -\int_{-1}^{1}[(x^3 - x^2)\,dx = -\tfrac{1}{4}x^4 + \tfrac{1}{3}x^3\Big|_{-1}^{1}$$

$$= (-\tfrac{1}{4}+\tfrac{1}{3})-(-\tfrac{1}{4}-\tfrac{1}{3}) = \tfrac{2}{3}\text{ sq units}$$

31. The region is shown in the figure at the right.

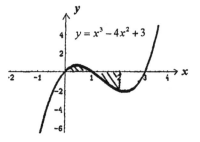

$$A = \int_{0}^{1}(x^3 - 4x^2 + 3x)\,dx - \int_{1}^{2}(x^3 - 4x^2 + 3x)\,dx$$

$$= (\tfrac{1}{4}x^4 - \tfrac{4}{3}x^3 + \tfrac{3}{2}x^2)\Big|_{0}^{1}$$

$$-(\tfrac{1}{4}x^4 - \tfrac{4}{3}x^3 + \tfrac{3}{2}x^2)\Big|_{1}^{2} = \tfrac{3}{2}\text{ sq units.}$$

32. The region is shown in the figure that follows at the right.

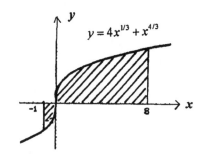

$$A = \int_{-1}^{0}(4x^{1/3} + x^{4/3})\,dx + \int_{0}^{8}(4x^{1/3} + x^{4/3})\,dx$$

$$= -3x^{4/3} - \tfrac{3}{7}x^{7/3}\Big|_{-1}^{0} + 3x^{4/3} + \tfrac{3}{7}x^{7/3}\Big|_{0}^{8}$$

$$= \tfrac{18}{7} + \tfrac{720}{7} = 105\tfrac{3}{7}\text{ sq units}$$

33. The region is shown in the figure at the right.

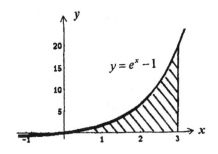

$$A = -\int_{-1}^{0}(e^x - 1)\,dx + \int_{0}^{3}(e^x - 1)\,dx$$

$$= (-e^x + x)\Big|_{-1}^{0} + (e^x - x)\Big|_{0}^{3}$$

$$= -1 - (-e^{-1} - 1) + (e^3 - 3) - 1$$

$$= e^3 - 4 + \tfrac{1}{e} \approx 16.5\text{ sq units.}$$

34. $A = \int_0^2 xe^{x^2}\, dx = \frac{1}{2}e^{x^2}\Big|_0^2 = \frac{1}{2}(e^4 - 1).$

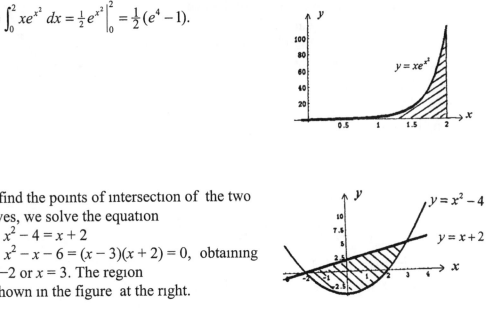

$y = xe^{x^2}$

35. To find the points of intersection of the two curves, we solve the equation
$$x^2 - 4 = x + 2$$
$$x^2 - x - 6 = (x - 3)(x + 2) = 0, \text{ obtaining}$$
$x = -2$ or $x = 3$. The region is shown in the figure at the right.

$y = x^2 - 4$

$y = x + 2$

$$A = \int_{-2}^{3} [(x+2) - (x^2 - 4)]\, dx = \int_{-2}^{3} (-x^2 + x + 6)\, dx = (-\tfrac{1}{3}x^3 + \tfrac{1}{2}x^2 + 6x)\Big|_{-2}^{3}$$
$$= (-9 + \tfrac{9}{2} + 18) - (\tfrac{8}{3} + 2 - 12) = \tfrac{125}{6} \text{ sq units.}$$

36. To find the intersection of the two curves, we solve $y = -x^2 + 4x$, $y = 2x - 3$ obtaining $-x^2 + 4x = 2x - 3$, $x^2 - 2x - 3 = 0$, $(x - 3)(x + 1) = 0$, or $x = -1, 3$. The required area is given by
$$A = \int_{-1}^{3} [(-x^2 + 4x) - (2x - 3)]\, dx$$
$$= \int_{-1}^{3} (-x^2 + 2x + 3)\, dx$$
$$= -\tfrac{1}{3}x^3 + x^2 + 3x\Big|_{-1}^{3}$$
$$= (-9 + 9 + 9) - (\tfrac{1}{3} + 1 - 3) = 10\tfrac{2}{3}.$$

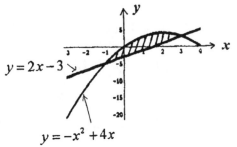

$y = 2x - 3$

$y = -x^2 + 4x$

6   Integration

37. To find the points of intersection of the two
curves, we solve the equation $x^3 = x^2$
or $x^3 - x^2 = x^2(x - 1) = 0$ giving $x = 0$ or 1
The region is shown in the figure.

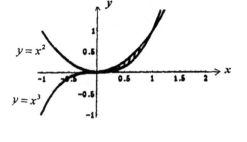

$$A = -\int_0^1 (x^2 - x^3)\,dx$$

$$= (\tfrac{1}{3}x^3 - \tfrac{1}{4}x^4)\Big|_0^1 \;=\; \tfrac{1}{3} - \tfrac{1}{4} = \tfrac{1}{12} \text{ sq units}$$

38. $A = \int_{-3}^0 (x^3 + 2x^2 - 3x) = \int_0^1 (x^3 + 2x^2 - 3x)\,dx$

$$= (\tfrac{1}{4}x^4 + \tfrac{2}{3}x^3 - \tfrac{3}{2}x^2)\Big|_{-3}^0 - (\tfrac{1}{4}x^4 + \tfrac{2}{3}x^3 - \tfrac{3}{2}x^2)\Big|_0^1$$

$$= 0 - [\tfrac{1}{4}(81) + \tfrac{2}{3}(-27) - \tfrac{3}{2}(9)] - (\tfrac{1}{4} + \tfrac{2}{3} - \tfrac{3}{2}) + 0$$

$$= -\tfrac{81}{4} + 18 + \tfrac{27}{2} - \tfrac{1}{4} - \tfrac{2}{3} + \tfrac{3}{2} = \tfrac{142}{12} = 11\tfrac{5}{16} \text{ sq}$$

units.

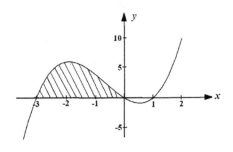

39. To find the points of intersection of the two
curves, we solve the equation
$$x^3 - 6x^2 + 9x = x^2 - 3x ,$$
or $x^3 - 7x^2 + 12x = x(x - 4)(x - 3) = 0$
obtaining $x = 0, 3,$ or 4.

$$A = \int_0^3 [(x^3 - 6x^2 + 9x) - (x^2 + 3x)]\,dx$$

$$+ \int_3^4 [(x^2 - 3x) - (x^3 - 6x^2 + 9x)]\,dx$$

$$= \int_0^3 (x^3 - 7x^2 + 12x)\,dx - \int_3^4 (x^3 - 7x^2 + 12x)\,dx$$

$$= (\tfrac{1}{4}x^4 - \tfrac{7}{3}x^3 + 6x^2)\Big|_0^3 - (\tfrac{1}{4}x^4 - \tfrac{7}{3}x^3 + 6x^2)\Big|_3^4$$

$$= (\tfrac{81}{4} - 63 + 54) - (64 - \tfrac{448}{3} + 96) + (\tfrac{81}{4} - 63 + 54) = \tfrac{71}{6} .$$

40. The graphs intersect at the points where $\sqrt{x} = x^2$ or $x = x^4$ and $x(x^3 - 1) = 0$; that
is, when $x = 0$ and $x = 1$. The required area is

$$A = \int_0^1 (x^{1/2} - x^2)\,dx = \tfrac{2}{3}x^{3/2} - \tfrac{1}{3}x^3 \Big|_0^1 = \tfrac{2}{3} - \tfrac{1}{3} = \tfrac{1}{3}.$$

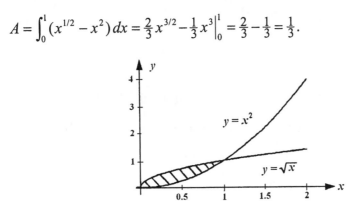

41. By symmetry, $A = 2\int_0^3 x(9 - x^2)^{1/2}\,dx$. We integrate by substitution with

$u = 9 - x^2$, $du = -2x\,dx$. If $x = 0$, $u = 9$, and if $x = 3, u = 0$. So

$$A = 2\int_9^0 -\tfrac{1}{2}u^{1/2}\,du = -\int_9^0 u^{1/2}\,du = -\tfrac{2}{3}u^{3/2}\Big|_9^0 = \tfrac{2}{3}(9)^{3/2} = 18 \text{ sq units.}$$

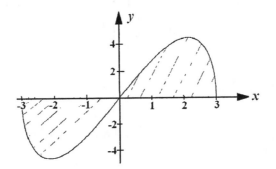

42. To find the points of intersection of the two graphs we solve
$x\sqrt{x+1} = 2x$, that is, when $x = 0$
and $x = 1$. Squaring, we obtain
$$x^2(x + 1) = 4x^2,$$
$x^3 - 3x^2 = x^2(x - 3) = 0$ giving
$x = 0$ or $x = 3$. The region is shown in
the figure at the right.

6   *Integration*

$$A = \int_0^3 (2x - x\sqrt{x-1})\,dx$$

$$= 2\int_0^3 x\,dx - \int_0^3 x\sqrt{x+1}\,dx.$$

Now $\quad 2\int_0^3 x\,dx = x^2\Big|_0^3 = 9.$ To evaluate the second integral, let $u = x+1$, so that so that $du = dx$ and $x = u - 1$. Also if $x = 0$, $u = 1$ and if $x = 3$, $u = 4$. So

$$\int_0^3 x\sqrt{x+1}\,dx = \int_1^4 (u-1)\sqrt{u}\,du = \int_1^4 (u^{3/2} - u^{1/2})\,du$$

$$= \tfrac{2}{5}u^{5/2} - \tfrac{2}{3}u^{3/2}\Big|_1^4 = (\tfrac{64}{5} - \tfrac{16}{3}) - (\tfrac{2}{5} - \tfrac{2}{3}) = \tfrac{116}{15}.$$

So, $A = 9 - \tfrac{116}{15} = \tfrac{19}{15}$ sq units.

43 S gives the additional revenue that the company would realize if it used a different advertising agency. $\quad S = \int_0^b [g(x) - f(x)]\,dx.$

44. S gives the difference between the total number of pulse beats between the present and that of six months ago. $S = \int_0^b [f(t) - g(t)]\,dt$.

45. Shortfall $= \int_{2010}^{2050} [f(t) - g(t)]\,dt$

46. a. S gives the difference in the amount of smoke removed by the two brands over the same time interval $[a, b]$.

   b. $\qquad S = \int_a^b [f(t) - g(t)]\,dt$

47. a. $\int_{T_1}^T [g(t) - f(t)]\,dt - \int_0^{T_1} [f(t) - g(t)]\,dt = A_2 - A_1.$

   b. The number $A_2 - A_1$ gives the distance car 2 is ahead of car 1 after t seconds.

48. $\int_{T_1}^T [g(t) - f(t)]\,dt - \int_0^{T_1} [f(t) - g(t)]\,dt$.

49 The turbo-charged model is moving at

$$A = \int_0^{10} [(4+1.2t+0.03t^2)-(4+0.8t)]\,dt$$

$$= \int_0^{10} (0.4t+0.03t^2)\,dt = (0.2t^2+0.1t^3)\Big|_0^{10}$$

$$= 20 + 10, \text{ or } 30 \text{ ft/sec faster than the standard model.}$$

50. The additional amount of coal that will be produced is

$$\int_0^{20} (3.5e^{0.05t}-3.5e^{0.01t})\,dt = 3.5\int_0^{20}(e^{0.05t}-e^{0.01t})\,dt$$

$$= 3.5(20e^{0.05t}-100e^{0.01t})\Big|_0^{20} = 3.5[20e-100e^{0.2})-(20-100)]$$

$$= 42.8 \text{ billion metric tons.}$$

51. The additional number of cars will be given by

$$\int_0^5 (5e^{0.3t}-5-0.5t^{3/2})\,dt = \frac{5}{0.3}e^{0.3t}-5t-0.2t^{5/2}\Big|_0^5$$

$$= \frac{5}{0.3}e^{1.5}-25-0.2(5)^{5/2}-\frac{5}{0.3} = 74.695-25-0.2(5)^{5/2}-\frac{50}{3}$$

$$\approx 21.85, \text{ or } 21,850 \text{ cars. (Remember } t \text{ is measured in thousands.)}$$

52. If the campaign is mounted, there will be

$$\int_0^5 (60e^{0.02t}+t^2-60)\,dt = 3000e^{0.02t}+\tfrac{t^3}{3}-60t\Big|_0^5$$

$$= 3315.5 + \frac{125}{3}-300-3000 \approx 57.179,$$

or 57,179 fewer people. (Remember t is measured in thousands.)

53. True. If $f(x) \geq g(x)$ on $[a, b]$, then the area of the said region is

$$\int_a^b [f(x)-g(x)]\,dx = \int_a^b |f(x)-g(x)|\,dx$$

If $f(x) \leq g(x)$ on $[a, b]$, then the area of the region is

$$\int_a^b [g(x)-f(x)]\,dx = \int_a^b -[f(x)-g(x)]\,dx = \int_a^b |f(x)-g(x)|\,dx$$

54. False. The area is given by $\int_0^2 [g(x)-f(x)]\,dx$ since $g(x) \geq f(x)$ on $[0, 2]$.

55. The area of R' is

$$A = \int_a^b \{[f(x)+C]-[g(x)+C]\}\,dx = \int_a^b [f(x)+C-g(x)-C]\,dx$$

6 Integration

$$= \int_a^b [f(x) - g(x)]dx$$

USING TECHNOLOGY EXERCISES 6.6, page 463

1. a.

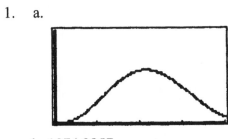

    b. 1074.2857 sq units

2. a.

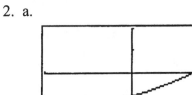

    b. 0.9566 sq units

3. a.

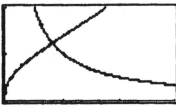

    b. 0.9961 sq units

4. a.

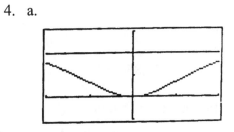

    b.   3.4721 sq units

5. a.

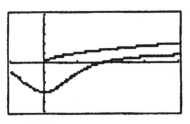

    b. 5.4603 sq units

6. a.

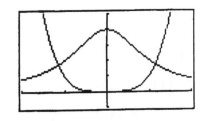

    b.   5.8832 sq units

7. a.

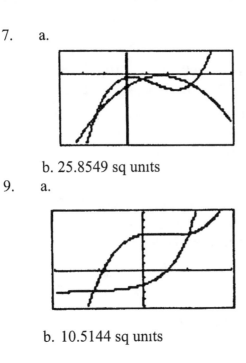

b. 25.8549 sq units

8. a.

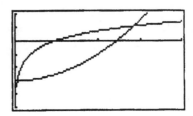

b. 3.8055 sq units

9. a.

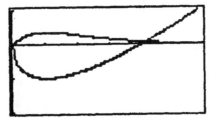

b. 10.5144 sq units

10. a.

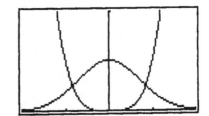

b. 4.8765 sq units

11. a.

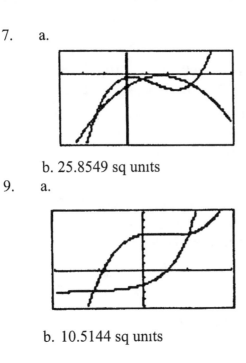

b. 3.5799 sq units

12. a.

b. 1.1889 sq units

13 207.43 sq units

6.7 CONCEPT QUESTIONS, page 474

1. a. See definition in text on page 465.   b. See definition in text on page 465.
2. a. See definition in text on page 468.   b. See definition in text on page 469.
3. See definition in text on page 470.
4. a. See definition in text on page 471-472. b. See definition in text on page 473.

EXERCISES 6.7, page 478

1. When $p = 4$, $-0.01x^2 - 0.1x + 6 = 4$ or $x^2 + 10x - 200 = 0$, $(x - 10)(x + 20) = 0$ and $x = 10$ or -20. We reject the root $x = -20$. The consumers' surplus is

$$CS = \int_0^{10} (-0.01x^2 - 0.1x + 6)\, dx - (4)(10)$$

$$= -\frac{0.01}{3}x^3 - 0.05x^2 + 6x\Big|_0^{10} - 40 \approx 11.667 \text{, or } \$11,667.$$

2. Setting $p = 5$, we find that the demand equation is $-0.01x^2 - 0.2x + 8 = 5$, or $-0.01x^2 - 0.2x + 3 = 0$, and $x^2 + 20x - 300 = (x + 30)(x - 10) = 0$, giving $x = -30$ or 10. So the equilibrium quantity is 10,000.

$$CS = \int_0^{10} (-0.01x^2 - 0.2x + 8)\, dx - 5(10) = -0.01(\tfrac{1}{3}x^3) - 0.1x^2 + 8x\Big|_0^{10} - 50$$

$$= -\tfrac{10}{3} - 10 + 80 - 50 = \tfrac{50}{3},$$

that is, the consumer's surplus is approximately \$16,667.

3. Setting $p = 10$, we have $\sqrt{225 - 5x} = 10$, $225 - 5x = 100$, or $x = 25$.

Then $CS = \int_0^{25} \sqrt{225 - 5x}\, dx - (10)(25) = \int_0^{25} (225 - 5x)^{1/2}\, dx - 250.$

To evaluate the integral, let $u = 225 - 5x$ so that $du = -5\, dx$ or $dx = -\tfrac{1}{5}\, du$. If $x = 0$, $u = 225$ and if $x = 25$, $u = 100$. So

$$CS = -\tfrac{1}{5}\int_{225}^{100} u^{1/2}\, du - 250 = -\tfrac{2}{15} u^{3/2}\Big|_{225}^{100} - 250$$

$$= -\tfrac{2}{15}(1000 - 3375) - 250 = 66.667 \text{, or } \$6,667.$$

4. When $p = 9$, $\sqrt{36 + 1.8x} = 9$ or $36 + 1.8x = 81$, or $1.8x = 45$, and $x = 25$. The producer's surplus is

$$PS = (9)(25) - \int_0^{25} (36 + 1.8x)^{1/2}\, dx = 225 - \frac{1}{1.8}\left(\frac{2}{3}\right)(36 + 1.8x)^{3/2}\Big|_0^{25}$$

$$= 225 - \frac{1}{2.7}[(36 + 45)^{3/2} - 36^{3/2}] = 35 \text{, or } \$3500.$$

5. To find the equilibrium point, we solve

$$0.01x^2 + 0.1x + 3 = -0.01x^2 - 0.2x + 8, \quad \text{or} \quad 0.02x^2 + 0.3x - 5 = 0,$$
$$2x^2 + 30x - 500 = (2x - 20)(x + 25) = 0$$

obtaining $x = -25$ or 10. So the equilibrium point is $(10,5)$. Then

$$PS = (5)(10) - \int_0^{10}(0.01x^2 + 0.1x + 3)\,dx$$

$$= 50 - (\frac{0.01}{3}x^3 + 0.05x^2 + 3x)\Big|_0^{10} = 50 - \frac{10}{3} - 5 - 30 = \frac{35}{3},$$

or approximately $11,667$.

6. To determine the market equilibrium, we solve $p = 144 - x^2$
and $p = 48 + \frac{1}{2}x^2$, simultaneously. We obtain
$\frac{1}{2}x^2 + 48 = 144 - x^2$, $\frac{3}{2}x^2 = 96$, and $x = \pm 8$. Since x must be nonnegative, we take
$x = 8$ and so $p = 80$. The consumers' surplus is

$$CS = \int_0^8 (144 - x^2)\,dx - (8)(80) = 144x - \frac{1}{3}x^3\Big|_0^8 - 640$$

$$= 144(8) - \frac{1}{3}(8)^3 - 640 \approx 341.333$$

or approximately $341,333$. The producers' surplus is

$$PS = 640 - (48x + \frac{1}{6}x^3)\Big|_0^8 = 640 - 48(8) - \frac{1}{6}(8)^3 \approx 170,667,$$

or approximately $170,667$.

7. To find the market equilibrium, we solve
$$-0.2x^2 + 80 = 0.1x^2 + x + 40, \quad 0.3x^2 + x - 40 = 0,$$
$$3x^2 + 10x - 400 = 0, \quad (3x + 40)(x - 10) = 0$$
giving $x = -\frac{40}{3}$ or $x = 10$. We reject the negative root. The corresponding
equilibrium price is 60. The consumers' surplus is

$$CS = \int_0^{10}(-0.2x^2 + 80)dx - (60)(10) = -\frac{0.2}{3}x^3 + 80x\Big|_0^{10} - 600 = 133\frac{1}{3},$$

or $13,333$. The producers' surplus is

$$PS = 600 - \int_0^{10}(0.1x^2 + x + 40)dx = 600 - [\frac{0.1}{3}x^3 + \frac{1}{2}x^2 + 40x]\Big|_0^{10}$$

$$= 116\frac{2}{3}, \text{ or } 11,667.$$

8. Let $u = -0.1t$ so that $du = -0.1\,dt$ or $dt = -\frac{1}{0.1}du = -10\,du$. Also, if $t = 0$, then
$u = 0$ and if $t = 3$, then $u = -0.3$. So

$$\int_0^3 580,000e^{-0.1t}dt - 180,000 = 580,000(-10)\int_0^{-0.3}e^u\,du - 180,000$$

$$= -5,800,000e^u\Big|_0^{-0.3} - 180,000 = -5,800,000(e^{-0.3} - 1) - 180,000 \approx 1,323,254.$$

9. Here $P = 200,000$, $r = 0.08$, and $T = 5$. So

$$PV = \int_0^5 200,000e^{-0.08t}\,dt = -\frac{200,000}{0.08}e^{-0.08t}\Big|_0^5 = -2,500,000(e^{-0.4} - 1)$$

$$\approx 824,199.85, \quad \text{or } \$824,200.$$

10. $PV = \int_0^{15} 400,000e^{-0.1t}\,dt = -\frac{400,000}{0.1}e^{-0.1t}\Big|_0^{15}$

$$= -4,000,000(e^{-1.5} - 1) \approx 3,107,479, \quad \text{or approximately } \$3,107,479.$$

11. Here $P = 250$, $m = 12$, $T = 20$, and $r = 0.08$. So

$$A = \frac{mP}{r}(e^{rT} - 1) = \frac{12(250)}{0.08}(e^{1.6} - 1) \approx 148,238.70$$

or approximately $148,239.

12. Here $P = 400$, $m = 12$, $T = 20$, and $r = 0.08$. So

$$A = \frac{12(400)}{0.08}(e^{1.6} - 1) \approx 237,181.90, \quad \text{or approximately } \$237,182.$$

13 Here $P = 150$, $m = 12$, $T = 15$, and $r = 0.08$. So

$$A = \frac{12(150)}{0.08}(e^{1.2} - 1) \approx 52,202.60, \quad \text{or approximately } \$52,203.$$

14. Here $P = 200$, $m = 12$, $T = 10$, and $r = 0.09$. So

$$A = \frac{12(200)}{0.09}(e^{0.9} - 1) \approx 38,922.7, \quad \text{or approximately } \$38,923.$$

15. Here $P = 2000$, $m = 1$, $T = 15\ 75$, and $r = 0.1$. So

$$A = \frac{1(2000)}{0.1}(e^{1.575} - 1) \approx 76,615, \quad \text{or approximately } \$76,615.$$

16. Here $P = 800$, $m = 12$, $T = 12$, and $r = 0.1$. So

$$PV = \frac{12(800)}{0.1}(1 - e^{-1.2}) \approx 67,085, \quad \text{or approximately } \$67,085.$$

17. Here $P = 1200$, $m = 12$, $T = 15$, and $r = 0.1$. So

$$PV = \frac{12(1200)}{0.1}(1 - e^{-1.5}) \approx 111,869, \quad \text{or approximately } \$111,869.$$

18. $PV = \dfrac{mP}{r}(1 - e^{-rT}) = \dfrac{1(50{,}000)}{0.08}(1 - e^{-0.08(20)})$

$\qquad = 625{,}000(1 - e^{-1.6}) = 498{,}814.68$, or approximately \$498,815.

19 We want the present value of an annuity with $P = 300$, $m = 12$,
$\qquad T = 10$, and $r = 0.12$. So

$\qquad PV = \dfrac{12(300)}{0.12}(1 - e^{-1.2}) \approx 20{,}964$, or approximately \$20,964.

20. We want the present value of an annuity with $P = 400$, $m = 12$,
$\qquad T = 15$, and $r = 0.09$. So

$\qquad PV = \dfrac{12(400)}{0.09}(1 - e^{-1.35}) \approx 39{,}507$, or approximately \$39,507.

21. a.

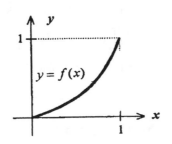

$\quad$ b.

$\quad f(0.4) = \tfrac{15}{16}(0.4)^2 + \tfrac{1}{16}(0.4) \approx 0.175$; $\; f(0.9) = \tfrac{15}{16}(0.9)^2 + \tfrac{1}{16}(0.9) \approx 0.816$

$\quad$ So, the lowest 40 percent of the people receive 17.5 percent of the total income
$\quad$ and the lowest 90 percent of the people receive 81.6 percent of the income.

22. $\quad$ a. $L_1 = 2\displaystyle\int_0^1 [x - f(x)]\,dx = 2\int_0^1 \left(x - \tfrac{13}{14}x^2 - \tfrac{1}{14}x\right)dx = 2\int_0^1\left(\tfrac{13}{14}x - \tfrac{13}{14}x^2\right)dx$

$\qquad = \dfrac{13}{7}\displaystyle\int_0^1 (x - x^2)\,dx = \tfrac{13}{7}\left[\tfrac{x^2}{2} - \tfrac{x^2}{3}\right]_0^1 = \tfrac{13}{7}(\tfrac{1}{2} - \tfrac{1}{3}) = \tfrac{13}{7}\cdot\tfrac{1}{6} = \tfrac{13}{42} = 0.3095.$

$\qquad L_2 = 2\displaystyle\int_0^1\left(x - \tfrac{9}{11}x^4 - \tfrac{2}{11}x\right)dx = 2\int_0^1\left(\tfrac{9}{11}x - \tfrac{9}{11}x^4\right)dx$

$\qquad = 2(\tfrac{9}{11})\displaystyle\int_0^1 (x - x^4)\,dx = \tfrac{18}{11}\left[\tfrac{x^2}{2} - \tfrac{x^5}{5}\right]_0^1 = \tfrac{18}{11}(\tfrac{1}{2} - \tfrac{1}{5}) = 0.4909.$

$\quad$ b. college teachers

23. a.

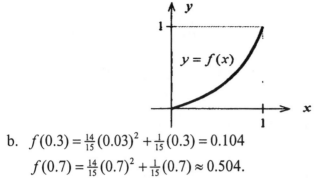

b. $f(0.3) = \frac{14}{15}(0.03)^2 + \frac{1}{15}(0.3) = 0.104$

$f(0.7) = \frac{14}{15}(0.7)^2 + \frac{1}{15}(0.7) \approx 0.504.$

24. a. The coefficient of inequality for stockbrokers is

$$2\int_0^1\left[x - \left(\tfrac{11}{12}x^2 + \tfrac{1}{12}x\right)\right]dx = 2\left(\tfrac{11}{12}\right)\int_0^1(x - x^2)\,dx = \tfrac{11}{6}\left(\tfrac{1}{2}x^2 - \tfrac{1}{3}x^3\right)\Big|_0^1 \approx 0.31.$$

The coefficient of inequality for high school teachers is

$$2\int_0^1[x - (\tfrac{5}{6}x^2 + \tfrac{1}{6}x)]dx = 2(\tfrac{5}{6})\int_0^1(x - x^2)\,dx = \tfrac{5}{3}(\tfrac{1}{2}x^2 - \tfrac{1}{3}x^3)\Big|_0^1 \approx 0.28.$$

b. The results of (a) suggest that the teaching profession has a more equitable income.

USING TECHNOLOGY EXERCISES 6.7, page 476

1. Consumer's surplus: $18,000,000; producer's surplus: $11,700,000.

2. Consumer's surplus: $13,333; producer's surplus: $11,667.

3 Consumer's surplus: $33,120; producer's surplus: $2,880.

4. Consumer's surplus: $55,104; producer's surplus: $141,669

5. Investment A   6. Investment B

CHAPTER 6, CONCEPT REVIEW, page 479

1. a. $F'(x) = f(x)$ b. $F(x) + C$

2. a. $c\int f(x)\,dx$ b. $\int f(x)\,dx \pm \int g(x)\,dx$

3. a. Unknown   b. Function

4. $g'(x)\,dx$; $\int f(u)\,du$

5 a. $\int_a^b f(x)\,dx$ b. Minus

6. a. $F(b) - F(a)$; antiderivative   b. $\int_a^b f'(x)\,dx$

7. a. $\dfrac{1}{b-a}\int_a^b f(x)\,dx$ b. Area; area

8. $\int_a^b [f(x) - g(x)]\,dx$

9 $\int_0^{\bar{x}} D(x)\,dx - \bar{p}\,\bar{x}$ b. $\bar{p}\,\bar{x} - \int_0^{\bar{x}} S(x)\,dx$

10. a. $e^{rT}\int_0^T R(t)e^{-rt}\,dt$ b. $\int_0^T R(t)e^{-rt}\,dt$

11. $\dfrac{mP}{r}(e^{rT} - 1)$ 12. $2\int_0^1 [x - f(x)]\,dx$

CHAPTER 6 REVIEW EXERCISES, page 479

1. $\int (x^3 + 2x^2 - x)\,dx = \tfrac{1}{4}x^4 + \tfrac{2}{3}x^3 - \tfrac{1}{2}x^2 + C$

2. $\int (\tfrac{1}{3}x^3 - 2x^2 + 8)\,dx = \tfrac{1}{12}x^4 - \tfrac{2}{3}x^3 + 8x + C$

3. $\int \left(x^4 - 2x^3 + \dfrac{1}{x^2}\right)dx = \dfrac{x^5}{5} - \dfrac{1}{2}x^4 - \dfrac{1}{x} + C$

4. $\int (x^{1/3} - x^{1/2} + 4)\,dx = \tfrac{3}{4}x^{4/3} - \tfrac{2}{3}x^{3/2} + 4x + C$

5 $\int x(2x^2 + x^{1/2})\,dx = \int (2x^3 + x^{3/2})\,dx = \tfrac{1}{2}x^4 + \tfrac{2}{5}x^{5/2} + C.$

6. $\int (x^2 + 1)(\sqrt{x} - 1)\,dx = \int (x^{5/2} - x^2 + x^{1/2} - 1)\,dx = \tfrac{2}{7}x^{7/2} - \tfrac{1}{3}x^3 + \tfrac{2}{3}x^{3/2} - x + C.$

7. $\int (x^2 - x + \frac{2}{x} + 5)\,dx = \int x^2\,dx - \int x\,dx + 2\int \frac{dx}{x} + 5\int dx$

$$= \tfrac{1}{3}x^3 - \tfrac{1}{2}x^2 + 2\ln|x| + 5x + C.$$

8. Let $u = 2x + 1$ so that $du = 2\,dx$ or $dx = \tfrac{1}{2}\,du$. So

$$\int \sqrt{2x+1}\,dx = \tfrac{1}{2}\int u^{1/2}\,du = \tfrac{1}{3}u^{3/2} = \tfrac{1}{3}(2x+1)^{3/2} + C.$$

9. Let $u = 3x^2 - 2x + 1$ so that $du = (6x - 2)\,dx = 2(3x - 1)\,dx$ or $(3x - 1)\,dx = \tfrac{1}{2}\,du$.

So $\int (3x-1)(3x^2 - 2x + 1)^{1/3}\,dx = \tfrac{1}{2}\int u^{1/3}\,du = \tfrac{3}{8}u^{4/3} + C = \tfrac{3}{8}(3x^2 - 2x + 1)^{4/3} + C.$

10. Put $u = x^3 + 2$ so that $du = 3x^2\,dx$ or $x^2\,dx = \tfrac{1}{3}\,du$. Then

$$\int x^2(x^3 + 2)^{10}\,dx = \tfrac{1}{3}\int u^{10}\,du = \tfrac{1}{33}u^{11} + C = \frac{(x^3 + 2)^{11}}{33} + C.$$

11. Let $u = x^2 - 2x + 5$ so that $du = 2(x - 1)\,dx$ or $(x - 1)\,dx = \tfrac{1}{2}\,du$.

$$\int \frac{x-1}{x^2 - 2x + 5}\,dx = \frac{1}{2}\int \frac{du}{u} = \frac{1}{2}\ln|u| + C = \frac{1}{2}\ln(x^2 - 2x + 5) + C.$$

12. Let $u = -2x$ so that $du = -2\,dx$. Then

$$\int 2e^{-2x}\,dx = -\int e^u\,du = -e^u + C = -e^{-2x} + C.$$

13. Put $u = x^2 + x + 1$ so that $du = (2x + 1)\,dx = 2(x + \tfrac{1}{2})\,dx$ and $(x + \tfrac{1}{2})\,dx = \tfrac{1}{2}\,du$.

$$\int (x + \tfrac{1}{2})e^{x^2 + x + 1}\,dx = \tfrac{1}{2}\int e^u\,du = \tfrac{1}{2}e^u + C = \tfrac{1}{2}e^{x^2 + x + 1} + C.$$

14. Let $u = e^{-x} + x$ so that $du = (-e^{-x} + 1)\,dx$ or $(e^{-x} - 1)\,dx = -du$. So

$$\int \frac{e^{-x} - 1}{(e^{-x} + x)^2}\,dx = -\int \frac{du}{u^2} = \frac{1}{u} + C = \frac{1}{e^{-x} + x} + C.$$

15 Let $u = \ln x$ so that $du = \tfrac{1}{x}\,dx$. Then

$$\int \frac{(\ln x)^5}{x}dx = \int u^5\,du = \frac{1}{6}u^6 + C = \frac{1}{6}(\ln x)^6 + C.$$

16. $\int \dfrac{\ln x^2}{x}dx = 2\int \dfrac{\ln x}{x}dx$. Now, put $u = \ln x$ so that $du = \frac{1}{x}\,dx$.

Then $\int \dfrac{\ln x^2}{x}dx = 2\int u\,du = u^2 + C = (\ln x)^2 + C.$

17. Let $u = x^2 + 1$ so that $du = 2x\,dx$ or $x\,dx = \frac{1}{2}\,du$. Then

$$\int x^3(x^2+1)^{10}\,dx = \frac{1}{2}\int (u-1)u^{10}\,du \qquad\qquad (x^2 = u - 1)$$

$$= \frac{1}{2}\int (u^{11} - u^{10})\,du = \frac{1}{2}(\tfrac{1}{12}u^{12} - \tfrac{1}{11}u^{11}) + C$$

$$= \frac{1}{264}u^{11}(11u - 12) + C = \frac{1}{264}(x^2+1)^{11}(11x^2 - 1) + C.$$

18. Let $u = x + 1$ so that $du = dx$. Then $x = u - 1$. So

$$\int x\sqrt{x+1}\,dx = \int (u-1)u^{1/2}\,du = \int (u^{3/2} - u^{1/2})\,du$$

$$= \frac{2}{5}u^{5/2} - \frac{2}{3}u^{3/2} + C = \frac{2}{15}u^{3/2}(3u - 5) + C$$

$$= \frac{2}{15}(3x - 2)(x+1)^{3/2} + C.$$

19. Put $u = x - 2$ so that $du = dx$. Then $x = u + 2$ and

$$\int \frac{x}{\sqrt{x-2}}\,dx = \int \frac{u+2}{\sqrt{u}}\,du = \int (u^{1/2} + 2u^{-1/2})\,du = \int u^{1/2}\,du + 2\int u^{-1/2}\,du$$

$$= \frac{2}{3}u^{3/2} + 4u^{1/2} + C = \frac{2}{3}u^{1/2}(u+6) + C = \frac{2}{3}\sqrt{x-2}(x-2+6) + C$$

$$= \frac{2}{3}(x+4)\sqrt{x-2} + C.$$

20. Let $u = x + 1$ so that $du = dx$. Furthermore, $x = u - 1$, so

$$\int \frac{3x}{\sqrt{x+1}}\,dx = 3\int \frac{u-1}{\sqrt{u}}\,du = 3\int (u^{1/2} - u^{-1/2})\,du = 3(\tfrac{2}{3}u^{3/2} - 2u^{1/2}) + C$$

$$= 2u^{1/2}(u - 3) + C = 2(x - 2)\sqrt{x+1} + C.$$

21. $\int_0^1 (2x^3 - 3x^2 + 1)\, dx = \frac{1}{2}x^4 - x^3 + x\Big|_0^1 = \frac{1}{2} - 1 + 1 = \frac{1}{2}.$

22. $\int_0^2 (4x^3 - 9x^2 + 2x - 1)\, dx = x^4 - 3x^3 + x^2 - x\Big|_0^2 = 16 - 24 + 4 - 2 = -6.$

23. $\int_1^4 (x^{1/2} + x^{-3/2})\, dx = \frac{2}{3}x^{3/2} - 2x^{-1/2}\Big|_1^4 = \frac{2}{3}x^{3/2} - \frac{2}{\sqrt{x}}\Big|_1^4 = (\frac{16}{3} - 1) - (\frac{2}{3} - 2) = \frac{17}{3}.$

24. Let $u = 2x^2 + 1$ so that $du = 4x\, dx$ or $x\, dx = \frac{1}{4} du$. Also, if $x = 0$,
    then $u = 1$ and if $x = 1$, then $u = 3$. So
    $$\int_0^1 20x(2x^2 + 1)^4\, dx = \frac{20}{4}\int_1^3 u^4\, du = u^5\Big|_1^3 = 243 - 1 = 242.$$

25. Put $u = x^3 - 3x^2 + 1$ so that $du = (3x^2 - 6x)\, dx = 3(x^2 - 2x)\, dx$ or
    $(x^2 - 2x)\, dx = \frac{1}{3} du$. Then if $x = -1$, $u = -3$, and if $x = 0$, $u = 1$,
    $$\int_{-1}^0 12(x^2 - 2x)(x^3 - 3x^2 + 1)^3\, dx = (12)(\tfrac{1}{3})\int_{-3}^1 u^3\, du = 4(\tfrac{1}{4})u^4\Big|_{-3}^1$$
    $$= 1 - 81 = -80.$$

26. Let $u = x - 3$ so that $du = dx$. If $x = 4$, then $u = 1$ and if $x = 7$, then $u = 4$. So
    $$\int_4^7 x\sqrt{x - 3}\, dx = \int_1^4 (u + 3)\sqrt{u}\, du = \int_1^4 (u^{3/2} + 3u^{1/2})\, du$$
    $$= \frac{2}{5}u^{5/2} + 2u^{3/2}\Big|_1^4 = (\frac{64}{5} + 16) - (\frac{2}{5} + 2) = \frac{132}{5}$$

27. Let $u = x^2 + 1$ so that $du = 2x\, dx$ or $x\, dx = \frac{1}{2} du$. Then, if $x = 0$,
    $u = 1$, and if $x = 2$, $u = 5$, so
    $$\int_0^2 \frac{x}{x^2 + 1}\, dx = \frac{1}{2}\int_1^5 \frac{du}{u} = \frac{1}{2}\ln u\Big|_1^5 = \frac{1}{2}\ln 5.$$

28. Let $u = 5 - 2x$ so that $du = -2\, dx$, or $dx = -\frac{1}{2} du$. If $x = 0$, then
    $u = 5$ and if $x = 1$, then $u = 3$. Therefore,

$$\int_0^1 (5-2x)^{-2} \, dx = \int_5^3 -\frac{1}{2} \cdot \frac{du}{u^2} = \frac{1}{2} u^{-1} \Big|_5^3 = \frac{1}{6} - \frac{1}{10} = \frac{1}{15}$$

29. Let $u = 1 + 2x^2$ so that $du = 4x \, dx$ or $x \, dx = \frac{1}{4} \, du$. If $x = 0$, then $u = 1$ and if $x = 2$, then $u = 9$.

$$\int_0^2 \frac{4x}{\sqrt{1+2x^2}} \, dx = \int_1^9 \frac{du}{u^{1/2}} = 2u^{1/2} \Big|_1^9 = 2(3-1) = 4.$$

30. Let $u = -\frac{1}{2} x^2$ so that $du = -x \, dx$ or $x \, dx = -\, du$. If $x = 0$, then $u = 0$ and if $x = 2$, then $u = -2$. So

$$\int_0^2 x e^{(-1/2)x^2} \, dx = -\int_0^{-2} e^u \, du = -e^u \Big|_0^{-2} = -e^{-2} + 1 = 1 - \frac{1}{e^2}$$

31. Let $u = 1 + e^{-x}$ so that $du = -e^{-x} \, dx$ and $e^{-x} \, dx = -\, du$. Then

$$\int_{-1}^0 \frac{e^{-x}}{(1+e^{-x})^2} \, dx = -\int_{1+e}^2 \frac{du}{u^2} = \frac{1}{u} \Big|_{1+e}^2 = \frac{1}{2} - \frac{1}{1+e} = \frac{e-1}{2(1+e)}$$

32. Let $u = \ln x$ so that $du = \frac{1}{x} \, dx$. If $x = 1$, then $u = 0$, and if $x = e$, then $u = \ln e = 1$. So

$$\int_1^e \frac{\ln x}{x} \, dx = \int_0^1 u \, du = \frac{1}{2} u^2 \Big|_0^1 = \frac{1}{2}.$$

33 $f(x) = \int f'(x) \, dx = \int (3x^2 - 4x + 1) \, dx = 3\int x^2 \, dx - 4\int x \, dx + \int dx$

$$= x^3 - 2x^2 + x + C.$$

The given condition implies that $f(1) = 1$ or $1 - 2 + 1 + C = 1$, and $C = 1$. Therefore, the required function is $f(x) = x^3 - 2x^2 + x + 1$.

34. $f(x) = \int f'(x) \, dx = \int \frac{x}{\sqrt{x^2+1}} \, dx$. Let $u = x^2 + 1$ so that

$du = 2x \, dx$ or $x \, dx = \frac{1}{2} \, du$. So $f(x) = \frac{1}{2} \int \frac{du}{\sqrt{u}} = \sqrt{u} + C = \sqrt{x^2+1} + C.$

6 Integration

Now $f(0) = 1$ implies $\sqrt{0+1} + C = 1$ or $C = 0$. So $f(x) = \sqrt{x^2 + 1}$.

35. $f(x) = \int f'(x)\,dx = \int (1 - e^{-x})\,dx = x + e^{-x} + C$, $f(0) = 2$ implies $0 + 1 + C = 2$
or $C = 1$. So $f(x) = x + e^{-x} + 1$.

36. $f(x) = \int f'(x)\,dx = \int \dfrac{\ln x}{x}\,dx$. Let $u = \ln x$ so that $du = \frac{1}{x}\,dx$. Then

$f(x) = \int u\,du = \frac{1}{2}u^2 + C = \frac{1}{2}(\ln x)^2 + C$. $f(1) = 0 + C = -2$ gives $C = -2$. So the

required function is $f(x) = \frac{1}{2}(\ln x)^2 - 2$.

37. $\Delta x = \frac{2-1}{5} = \frac{1}{5}$; $x_1 = \frac{6}{5}$, $x_2 = \frac{7}{5}$, $x_3 = \frac{8}{5}$, $x_4 = \frac{9}{5}$, $x_5 = \frac{10}{5}$. The Riemann sum is
$f(x_1)\Delta x + \cdots + f(x_5)\Delta x = \left\{ \left[-2(\frac{6}{5})^2 + 1 \right] + \left[-2(\frac{7}{5})^2 + 1 \right] + \cdots + \left[-2(\frac{10}{5})^2 + 1 \right] \right\}(\frac{1}{5})$
$= \frac{1}{5}(-1.88 - 2.92 - 4.12 - 5.48 - 7) = -4.28$.

38. $C(x) = \int C'(x)\,dx = \int (0.00003x^2 - 0.03x + 20)\,dx$

$= 0.00001x^3 - 0.015x^2 + 20x + k$.
$C(0) = k = 500$. So the required total cost function is
$C(x) = 0.00001x^3 - 0.015x^2 + 20x + 500$.
The total cost in producing the first 400 coffeemakers per day is
$C(400) = 0.00001(400)^3 - 0.015(400)^2 + 20(400) + 500 = 6740$, or \$6740.

39. a. $R(x) = \int R'(x)\,dx = \int (-0.03x + 60)\,dx = -0.015x^2 + 60x + C$.

$R(0) = 0$ implies that $C = 0$. So, $R(x) = -0.015x^2 + 60x$.
b. From $R(x) = px$, we have $-0.015x^2 + 60x = px$ or $p = -0.015x + 60$.

40. $V(t) = \int V'(t)\,dt = 3800\int (t - 10)\,dt = 1900(t - 10)^2 + C$. The initial condition

implies that $V(0) = 200,000$, that is, $190,000 + C = 200,000$ or $C = 10,000$.
Therefore, $V(t) = 1900(t - 10)^2 + 10,000$. The resale value of the computer after
6 years is given by
$V(6) = 1900(-4)^2 + 10,000 = 40,400$, or \$40,400.

41. The total number of systems that Vista may expect to sell t months from the time they are put on the market is given by $f(t) = 3000t - 50,000(1 - e^{-0.04t})$

The number is $\int_0^{12} (3000 - 2000e^{-0.04t})\,dt = \left(3000t - \dfrac{2000}{-0.04}e^{-0.04t}\right)\Big|_0^{12}$

$$= 3000(12) + 50,000e^{-0.48} - 50,000 = 16,939$$

42. The number will be

$$N(t) = \int 3000(1 + 0.4t)^{-1/2}\,dt = \frac{3000}{0.4}\cdot 2(1 + 0.4t)^{1/2} + C \quad \text{(Let } u = 1 + 0.4t.\text{)}$$

$= 15,000\sqrt{1 + 0.4t} + C.$
$N(0) = 100,000$ implies $15,000 + C = 100,000$, or $C = 85,000$. Therefore,
$N(t) = 15,000\sqrt{1 + 0.4t} + 85,000$. The number using the subway six months from now will be $N(6) = 15,000\sqrt{1 + 2.4} + 85,000 \approx 112,659$

43. The number of speakers sold at the end of 5 years is
$f(t) = \int f'(t)\,dt = \int_0^5 2000(3 - 2e^{-t})\,dt = 2000[3(5) - 2e^{-5}] - 2000[3 - 2(1)]$
$= 26,027.$

44. $C(x) = \int C'(x)\,dx = \int (0.00003x^2 - 0.03x + 10)\,dx$

$= 0.00001x^3 - 0.015x^2 + 10x + k.$
But $C(0) = 600$ and this implies that $k = 600$. Therefore,
$\quad C(x) = 0.00001x^3 - 0.015x^2 + 10x + 600.$
The total cost incurred in producing the first 500 corn poppers is
$\quad C(500) = 0.00001(500)^3 - 0.015(500)^2 + 10(500) + 600$
$\quad = 3,100,\ \text{or } \$3,100.$

45. The number will be
$\int (0.00933t^3 + 0.019t^2 - 0.10833t + 1.3467)\,dt$

$= 0.0023325t^4 + 0.0063333t^3 - 0.054165t^2 + 1.3467\,t\Big|_0^{10} = 377,$
or approximately 37.7 million Americans.

46. The amount of coal produced was

$$\int_0^5 3.5e^{0.04t}\,dt = \frac{3.5}{0.04}e^{0.04t}\Big|_0^5 = 87.5(e^{0.2}-1) \approx 19.4,$$

or approximately 19.4 billion metric tons.

47. $A = \int_{-1}^2 (3x^2 + 2x + 1)\,dx = x^3 + x^2 + x\big|_{-1}^2 = [2^3 + 2^2 + 2] - [(-1)^3 + 1 - 1]$
$= 14 - (-1) = 15.$

48. $A = \int_0^2 e^{2x}\,dx = \tfrac{1}{2}e^{2x}\big|_0^2 = \tfrac{1}{2}(e^4 - 1)$ sq units.

49 $A = \int_1^3 \frac{1}{x^2}\,dx = \int_1^3 x^{-2}\,dx = -\frac{1}{x}\Big|_1^3 = -\frac{1}{3} + 1 = \frac{2}{3}.$

50. $A = \int_{-2}^1 (-x^2 - x + 2)\,dx = -\frac{x^3}{3} - \frac{x^2}{2} + 2x\,\Big|_{-2}^1 = \left(-\frac{1}{3} - \frac{1}{2} + 2\right) - \left(\frac{8}{3} - \frac{4}{2} - 4\right)$

$= \frac{7}{6} + \frac{10}{3} = 4\frac{1}{2}$

51.

$A = \int_a^b [f(x) - g(x)]\,dx$

$= \int_0^2 (e^x - x)\,dx$

$= \left(e^x - \frac{1}{2}x^2\right)\Big|_0^2$

$= (e^2 - 2) - (1 - 0) = e^2 - 3.$

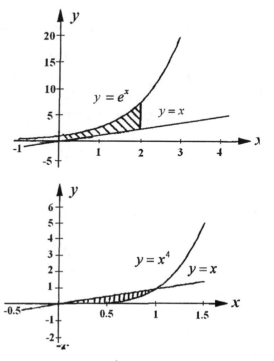

52. To find the points of intersection of the two curves, we solve $x^4 = x$, $x(x^3 - 1) = 0$ giving $x = 0$ or 1. The region is shown in the figure at the right.

$A = \int_0^1 (x - x^4)\,dx = \frac{1}{2}x^2 - \frac{1}{5}x^5\big|_0^1 = \frac{1}{2} - \frac{1}{5}$

$= \frac{3}{10}$ sq units.

53

$$A = \int_0^1 (x^3 - 3x^2 + 2x)\,dx - \int_1^2 (x^3 - 3x^2 + 2x)\,dx$$

$$= \tfrac{x^4}{4} - x^3 + x^2 \Big|_0^1 - \left(\tfrac{x^4}{4} - x^3 + x^2\right)\Big|_1^2$$

$$= \tfrac{1}{4} - 1 + 1 - [(4 - 8 + 4) - (\tfrac{1}{4} - 1 + 1)]$$

$$= \tfrac{1}{4} + \tfrac{1}{4} = \tfrac{1}{2}.$$

54. The additional oil that will be produced over the next ten years is given by

$$\int_0^{10} [R_2(t) - R_1(t)]\,dt = \int_0^{10} (100e^{0.08t} - 100e^{0.05t})\,dt = 100\int_0^{10} (e^{0.08t} - e^{0.05t})\,dt$$

$$= \frac{100}{0.08} e^{0.08t} - \frac{100}{0.05} e^{0.05t} \Big|_0^{10} = 1250e^{0.8} - 2000e^{0.5} - 1250 + 2000$$

$$= 2781.9 - 3297.4 - 1250 + 2000 = 234.5$$

or 234,500 barrels.   (*t* is expressed in thousands of barrels.)

55.

$$A = \frac{1}{3} \int_0^3 \frac{x}{\sqrt{x^2 + 16}}\,dx = \frac{1}{3} \cdot \frac{1}{2} \cdot 2(x^2 + 16)^{1/2} \Big|_0^3$$

$$= \frac{1}{3}(x^2 + 16)^{1/2} \Big|_0^3 = \frac{1}{3}(5 - 4) = \frac{1}{3} \text{ sq units.}$$

56. The average temperature is

$$\tfrac{1}{12} \int_0^{12} (-0.05t^3 + 0.4t^2 + 3.8t + 5.6)\,dt$$

$$= \tfrac{1}{12}\left(-\tfrac{0.05}{4}t^4 + \tfrac{0.4}{3}t^3 + 1.9t^2 + 5.6t\right)\Big|_0^{12} = 26°\,F.$$

57. Setting $p = 8$, we have $\quad -0.01x^2 - 0.2x + 23 = 8,\ -0.01x^2 - 0.2x + 15 = 0,$ or $x^2 + 20x - 1500 = (x - 30)(x + 50) = 0$, giving $x = -50$ or 30.

$$CS = \int_0^{30} (-0.01x^2 - 0.2x + 23)\,dx - 8(30) = -\frac{0.01}{3}x^3 - 0.1x^2 + 23x \Big|_0^{30} - 240$$

$$= -\frac{0.01(30)^3}{3} - 0.1(900) + 23(30) - 240 = 270, \text{ or } \$270,000.$$

58. To find the equilibrium point, we solve $0.1x^2 + 2x + 20 = -0.1x^2 - x + 40$

$0.2x^2 + 3x - 20 = 0,\ x^2 + 15x - 100 = 0,\ (x + 20)(x - 5) = 0,$ or $x = 5$

Therefore, $p = -0.1(25) - 5 + 40 = 32.5$.

$$CS = \int_0^5 (-0.1x^2 - x + 40)\, dx - (5)(32.5) = -\frac{0.1}{3}x^3 - \frac{1}{2}x^2 + 40x\Big|_0^5 - 162.5$$

$$= 20.833,\ \text{or } \$2083.$$

$$PS = (5)(32.5) - \int_0^5 (0.1x^2 + 2x + 20)\, dx = 162.5 - \tfrac{0.1}{3}x^3 + x^2 + 20x)\Big|_0^5$$

$$= 33.333,\ \text{or } \$3,333.$$

59. Use Equation (17) with $P = 4000,\ r = 0.08,\ T = 20,$ and $m = 1,$ obtaining

$$A = \frac{(1)(4000)}{0.08}(e^{1.6} - 1) \approx 197{,}651.62$$

that is, Chi-Tai will have approximately $197,652 in his account after 20 years.

60. Use Equation (18) with $P = 925,\ m = 12,\ T = 30,$ and $r = 0.12,$ obtaining

$$PV = \frac{mP}{r}(1 - e^{-rT}) = \frac{(12)(925)}{(0.12)}(1 - e^{-0.12(30)}) = 89{,}972.56,$$

and we conclude that the present value of the purchase price of the house is $89,972.56 + $9000 , or $98,972.56.

61. Here $P = 80{,}000,\ m = 1,\ T = 10,$ and $r = 0.1,$ so

$$PV = \frac{(1)(80{,}000)}{0.1}(1 - e^{-1}) \approx 505{,}696,\ \text{or approximately } \$505{,}696.$$

62. a.

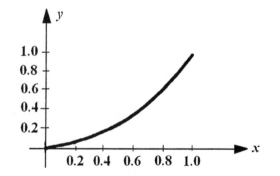

b. $f(0.3) = \frac{17}{18}(0.3)^2 + \frac{1}{18}(0.3) \approx 0.1$ so that 30 percent of the people receive 10 percent of the total income. $f(0.6) = \frac{17}{18}(0.6)^2 + \frac{1}{18}(0.6) \approx 0.37$ so that 60 percent of the people receive 37 percent of the total revenue.

c. The coefficient of inequality for this curve is

$$L = 2\int_0^1 [x - \tfrac{17}{18}x^2 - \tfrac{1}{18}x]\,dx = \tfrac{17}{9}\int_0^1 (x - x^2)\,dx = \tfrac{17}{9}\left(\tfrac{1}{2}x^2 - \tfrac{1}{3}x^3\right)\Big|_0^1$$

$$= \tfrac{17}{54} \approx 0.315$$

63.   The average population will be

$$\tfrac{1}{5}\int_0^5 80{,}000e^{-0.05t}\,dt = \frac{80{,}000}{5}\cdot\left(-\frac{1}{0.05}\right)e^{-0.05t}\Big|_0^5 = -320{,}000(e^{-0.25}-1) \approx 70{,}784.$$

CHAPTER 6, BEFORE MOVING ON, page 482

1. $\displaystyle \int (2x^3 + \sqrt{x} + \frac{2}{x} - \frac{2}{\sqrt{x}})\,dx = 2\int x^3\,dx + \int x^{1/2}\,dx + 2\int \frac{1}{x}\,dx - 2\int x^{-1/2}\,dx$

$$= \tfrac{1}{2}x^4 + \tfrac{2}{3}x^{3/2} + 2\ln|x| - 4x^{1/2} + C$$

2. $f(x) = \displaystyle\int f'(x)\,dx = \int (e^x + x)\,dx = e^x + \tfrac{1}{2}x^2 + C$

$f(0) = 2$ implies $f(0) = e^0 + 0 + C = 2$ or $C = 1$. Therefore, $f(x) = e^x + \tfrac{1}{2}x^2 + 1$

3. Let $u = x^2 + 1$ so that $du = 2x\,dx$ or $x\,dx = \tfrac{1}{2}du$. Then

$$\int \frac{x}{\sqrt{x^2+1}}\,dx = \frac{1}{2}\int \frac{du}{\sqrt{u}} = \frac{1}{2}\int u^{-1/2}\,du = \frac{1}{2}\left(2u^{1/2}\right) + C = \sqrt{u} + C = \sqrt{x^2+1} + C.$$

4. Let $u = 2 - x^2$. Then $du = -2x\,dx$ or $x\,dx = -\tfrac{1}{2}du$. If $x = 0$, then $u = 2$ and if $x = 1$, then $u = 1$. Therefore,

$$\int_0^1 x\sqrt{2-x^2}\,dx = -\tfrac{1}{2}\int_2^1 u^{1/2}\,du = -\tfrac{1}{2}\cdot\tfrac{2}{3}u^{3/2}\Big|_2^1 = -\tfrac{1}{3}u^{3/2}\Big|_2^1$$

$$= -\tfrac{1}{3}(1 - 2^{3/2}) = \tfrac{1}{3}(2\sqrt{2} - 1).$$

5. To find the points of intersection, we solve

$$x^2 - 1 = 1 - x,\ x^2 + x - 2 = 0,$$
$$(x+2)(x-1) = 0$$

Giving $x = -2$ or $x = 1$. The points of intersection are (-2,3) and (1,0). The required area is

$$A = \int_{-2}^{1}[(1-x)-(x^2-1)]dx = \int_{-2}^{1}(2-x-x^2)\,dx = (2x - \tfrac{1}{2}x^2 - \tfrac{1}{3}x^3)\big|_{-2}^{1}$$

$$= (2 - \tfrac{1}{2} - \tfrac{1}{3}) - (4 - 2 + \tfrac{8}{3}) = \tfrac{9}{2}, \text{ or } \tfrac{9}{2} \text{ sq units.}$$

EXPLORE & DISCUSS

Page 413

1. $F(2) = \tfrac{2}{15}(8+1)^{5/2} = \tfrac{162}{5} = 32\tfrac{2}{5}$.   To find $F(2)$ using the function G, we have to compute $G(u)$ where $u = 2^3 + 1 = 9$ obtaining $G(9) = \tfrac{2}{15}(9)^{5/2} = 32\tfrac{2}{5}$.
We use the value 9 for u because $u = x^3 + 1$ and when $x = 2$, $u = 2^3 + 1 = 9$.

Page 414

1. Let $u = ax + b$ so that $du = a\,dx$, or $dx = \tfrac{1}{a}\,du$. Therefore

$$\int f(ax+b)\,dx = \int f(u) \cdot \frac{1}{a}\,du = \frac{1}{a}\int f(u)\,du = \frac{1}{a}F(u) + C = \frac{1}{a}F(ax+b) + C.$$

2. In order to evaluate $\int (2x+3)^5\,dx$, we write $f(u) = u^5$, so that

$$F(u) = \int f(u)\,du = \int u^5\,du = \frac{1}{6}u^6 + C. \text{ Next, identifying } a = 2 \text{ and } b = 3, \text{ we obtain}$$

$$\int (2x+3)^5\,dx = \frac{1}{2}F(2x+3)^6 + C = \frac{1}{2}\cdot\frac{1}{6}(2x+3)^6 + C = \frac{1}{12}(2x+3)^6 + C$$

In order to evaluate $\int e^{3x-2}\,dx$, we let $f(x) = e^u$, $a = 3$, and $b = -2$. We find

$$\int e^{3x-2}\,dx = \frac{1}{3}e^{3x-2} + C.$$

Page 425

1. Consider the graph of f at the right. Observe that for each x in $[a, b]$, the point $(x_1 - f(x))$ is the mirror image of the point $(x, f(x))$ with respect to the x-axis. Therefore, the graph of the function

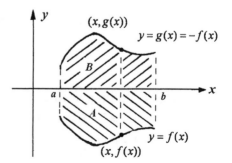

$g = -f$ is symmetric to that of f with respect to the x-axis. Therefore, the area of A is equal to the area of B. But $g(x) = -f(x) \geq 0$ for all x in $[a, b]$. Therefore,

$$\text{Area of } A = \text{Area of } B = \int g(x)\, dx = \int -f(x)\, dx = -\int f(x)\, dx$$

as was to be shown.

Page 432

1. A formal application of Equation (9) would seem to yield

$$\int_{-1}^{1} \frac{1}{x^2}\, dx = -\frac{1}{x}\Big|_{-1}^{1} = -1 - 1 = -2.$$

2. The indicated observation would appear to follow.

3. Because $f(x) = \dfrac{1}{x^2}$ is not continuous on the interval $[-1,1]$, the Fundamental Theorem of Calculus is not applicable. Thus, the result obtained in (1) is not valid. Furthermore, the fact that this result is suspect is suggested by the observation made in (2).

Page 435

1. The graph of the integrand $y = f(x) = \sqrt{9 - x^2}$ is the upper semi-circle with radius 3, centered at the origin (see figure). Therefore, interpreting the given integral as the area under the graph of f we find

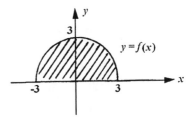

$$\int_{-3}^{3} \sqrt{9 - x^2}\, dx = \frac{1}{2}(\pi)(3)^2 = \frac{9\pi}{2}.$$

Page 444

1. The required area is $\displaystyle\int_{0}^{2} f(x)\, dx = \int_{0}^{1} f(x)\, dx + \int_{1}^{2} f(x)\, dx = \int_{0}^{1} x^{1/2}\, dx + \int_{1}^{2} \frac{1}{x}\, dx$

$$= \tfrac{2}{3} x^{3/2}\Big|_{0}^{1} + \ln x\Big|_{1}^{2} = \tfrac{2}{3} + (\ln 2 - \ln 1) = \tfrac{2}{3} + \ln 2.$$

Page 455

1. Suppose f is even so that $f(-x) = f(x)$. If $(x, f(x))$ is any point lying on the graph of f, then $(-x, f(-x)) = (-x, f(x))$ and thus the graph of f is symmetric with respect to the y-axis (see figure).

6 Integration

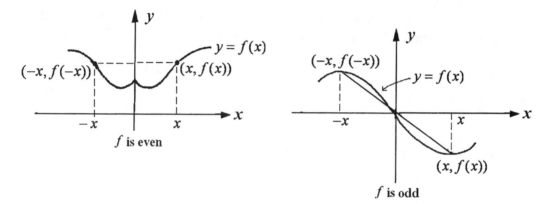

f is even

f is odd

If f is odd, then $f(-x) = -f(x)$ and so f is symmetric with respect to the x-axis. Finally, if f is even, then

$$\int_{-a}^{a} f(x)\,dx = \int_{-a}^{0} f(x)\,dx + \int_{0}^{a} f(x)\,dx.$$

Let $u = -x$ in the first integral on the right-hand side, then $du = -dx$. Furthermore, if $x = -a$, then $u = a$, and if $x = 0$, then $u = 0$. Using Property 2 of definite integrals, we have

$$\int_{-a}^{a} f(x)\,dx = \int_{a}^{0} f(-u)(-du) + \int_{0}^{a} f(x)\,dx = \int_{0}^{a} f(u)\,du + \int_{0}^{a} f(x)\,dx$$

[f is even.]

$$= 2\int_{0}^{a} f(x)\,dx \qquad \text{[}u \text{ is a "dummy variable".]}$$

If f is odd, a similar argument gives $\int_{-a}^{a} f(x)\,dx = \int_{a}^{0} f(x)\,dx + \int_{0}^{a} f(x)\,dx$

$$= -\int_{0}^{a} f(-u)(-du) + \int_{0}^{a} f(x)\,dx = -\int_{0}^{a} f(u)\,du + \int_{0}^{a} f(x)\,dx = 0. \qquad \text{[}f \text{ is odd.]}$$

EXPLORING WITH TECHNOLOGY QUESTIONS

Page 397

1. $F'(x) = \frac{1}{3}(3x^2) - 1 = x^2 - 1 = f(x)$ and so F is an antiderivative of f

2.

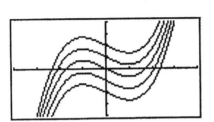

3.

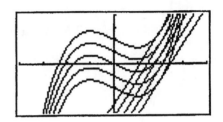

4. The slope of the tangent line is $f(2) = 4 - 1 = 3$.

Page 435

1.

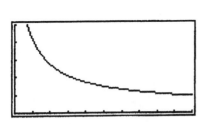

2.

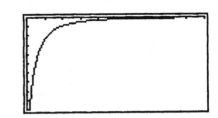

$C'(10) = -0.05664025$ $C'(10) = -0.056640625$

Since C' is the derivative of C, we can find $C'(10)$ by taking the derivative of C at $x = 10$, or by evaluating $C'(t)$ at $t = 10$.

Page 435

1. The graphs of y1 and y2 in the viewing rectangle $[-5,5] \times [0,10]$ follow.

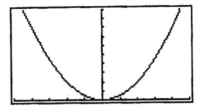

2. The two graphs are identical.

Page 443

1. $\displaystyle\int_0^4 x\sqrt{9+x^2}\,dx = 32.6666666667.$

2. $\displaystyle\frac{1}{2}\int_9^{25} \sqrt{u}\,du = \frac{1}{2}\cdot\frac{2}{3}u^{3/2}\Big|_9^{25} = \frac{1}{3}(25^{3/2}-9^{3/2}) = 32\frac{2}{3}$

Page 457

1. $\displaystyle F(x) = \int_0^x [R_1(t)-R(t)]dt = 20\left(\frac{e^{0.08t}}{0.08}-\frac{e^{0.05t}}{0.05}\right)\Big|_0^x = 250e^{0.08t}-400e^{0.05t}\Big|_0^x$

   $\displaystyle = 250e^{0.08x}-400e^{0.05x}+150.$

2.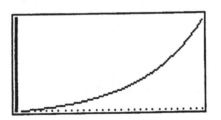

3. $F(5) = 250e^{0.08(5)} - 400e^{0.05(5)} + 150 = 9.346.$

4. The advantage of this model is that we can easily find the amount of oil saved by evaluating the function at the appropriate value of x.

Page 471

1. With $P = 2000$, $r = 0.1$, and $m = 1$ and $T = x$, we obtain

   $$A = f(x) = \frac{2000}{0.1}(e^{0.1x}-1) = 20{,}000(e^{0.1x}-1).$$

2.

3. The advantage of the model is that we can compute the amount that Marcus will have in his IRA at any time T, by simply evaluating the function f at $x = T$.

CHAPTER 7

7.1 CONCEPT QUESTIONS, page 488

1. $\int u\,dv = uv - \int v\,du$

2. See p 485. For the integral $\int x^2 e^{-x}\,dx$, we let $u = x^2$ and $dv = e^{-x}\,dx$ so that

   $du = 2x\,dx$ and $v = -e^{-x}$. This leads to $\int x^2 e^{-x}\,dx = -x^2 e^{-x} + 2\int xe^{-x}\,dx$.

   The integral on the right can be evaluated using integration by parts by letting $u = x$
   and $dv = e^{-x}\,dx$. If we had chosen the substitution $u = e^{-x}$ and $dv = x^2\,dx$, for
   example, then $du = -e^{-x}\,dx$ and $v = \frac{1}{3}x^3$. So

   $$\int x^2 e^{-x}\,dx = \frac{1}{3}x^3 e^{-x} + \frac{1}{3}\int x^3 e^{-x}\,dx$$

   The integral on the right is even harder to evaluate than the original.

EXERCISES 7.1, page 489

1. $I = \int xe^{2x}\,dx$. Let $u = x$ and $dv = e^{2x}\,dx$. Then $du = dx$ and $v = \frac{1}{2}e^{2x}$. Therefore,

   $I = uv - \int v\,du = \frac{1}{2}xe^{2x} - \int \frac{1}{2}e^{2x}\,dx = \frac{1}{2}xe^{2x} - \frac{1}{4}e^{2x} = \frac{1}{4}e^{2x}(2x-1) + C.$

2. $I = \int xe^{-x}\,dx$ Let $u = x$ and $dv = e^{-x}$ so that $du = dx$ and $v = -e^{-x}$ Then

   $$\int xe^{-x}\,dx = -xe^{-x} + \int e^{-x}\,dx = -xe^{-x} - e^{-x} + C = -(x+1)e^{-x} + C.$$

3. $I = \int xe^{x/4}\,dx$. Let $u = x$ and $dv = e^{x/4}\,dx$. Then $du = dx$ and $v = 4e^{x/4}$.

   $$\int xe^{x/4}\,dx = uv - \int v\,du = 4xe^{x/4} - 4\int e^{x/4}\,dx = 4xe^{x/4} - 16e^{x/4} + C$$
   $$= 4(x-4)e^{x/4} + C.$$

4. $I = \int 6xe^{3x}\,dx$. Let $u = 6x$ and $dv = e^{3x}\,dx$. Then $du = 6\,dx$ and $v = \frac{1}{3}e^{3x}$.

   Therefore, $I = 2xe^{3x} - \int 2e^{3x}\,dx = 2xe^{3x} - \frac{2}{3}e^{3x} + C = \frac{2}{3}e^{3x}(3x-1) + C.$

5. $\int (e^x - x)^2 \, dx = \int (e^{2x} - 2xe^x + x^2) \, dx = \int e^{2x} \, dx - 2\int xe^x \, dx + \int x^2 \, dx.$

Using the result $\int xe^x \, dx = (x-1)e^x + k,$ from Example 1, we see that

$\int (e^x - x)^2 \, dx = \tfrac{1}{2}e^{2x} - 2(x-1)e^x + \tfrac{1}{3}x^3 + C.$

6. $\int (e^{-x} + x)^2 \, dx = \int e^{-2x} \, dx + 2\int xe^{-x} \, dx + \int x^2 \, dx$

$= -\tfrac{1}{2}e^{-2x} + 2[-(x+1)e^{-x}] + \tfrac{1}{3}x^3 + C \quad \text{[See Example 1.]}$

$= -\tfrac{1}{2}e^{-2x} - 2(x+1)e^{-x} + \tfrac{1}{3}x^3 + C.$

7. $I = \int (x+1)e^x \, dx.$ Let $u = x + 1,$ $dv = e^x \, dx.$ Then $du = dx$ and $v = e^x.$ Therefore,

$I = (x+1)e^x - \int e^x \, dx = (x+1)e^x - e^x + C = xe^x + C.$

8. Let $u = x - 3$ and $dv = e^{3x} \, dx.$ Then $du = dx$ and $v = \tfrac{1}{3}e^{3x}.$

$\int (x-3)e^{3x} \, dx = uv - \int v \, du = \tfrac{1}{3}(x-3)e^{3x} - \tfrac{1}{3}\int e^{3x} \, dx$

$= \tfrac{1}{3}(x-3)e^{3x} - \tfrac{1}{9}e^{3x} + C.$

9. Let $u = x$ and $dv = (x + 1)^{-3/2} \, dx.$ Then $du = dx$ and $v = -2(x + 1)^{-1/2}.$

$\int x(x+1)^{-3/2} \, dx = uv - \int v \, du = -2x(x+1)^{-1/2} + 2\int (x+1)^{-1/2} \, dx$

$= -2x(x+1)^{-1/2} + 4(x+1)^{1/2} + C$

$= 2(x+1)^{-1/2}[-x + 2(x+1)] + C = \dfrac{2(x+2)}{\sqrt{x+1}} + C.$

10. Let $u = x$ and $dv = (x + 4)^{-2} \, dx.$ Then $du = dx$ and $v = -(x + 4)^{-1}$ and

$\int x(x+4)^{-2} \, dx = uv - \int v \, du = -x(x+4)^{-1} + \int \dfrac{1}{x+4} \, dx$

$= -\dfrac{x}{x+4} + \ln|x+4| + C.$

11. $I = \int x(x-5)^{1/2}\, dx.$ Let $u = x$ and $dv = (x-5)^{1/2}\, dx.$ Then $du = dx$ and

$v = \frac{2}{3}(x-5)^{3/2}.$ Therefore,

$$I = \frac{2}{3}x(x-5)^{3/2} - \int \frac{2}{3}(x-5)^{3/2}\, dx = \frac{2}{3}x(x-5)^{3/2} - \frac{2}{3}\cdot\frac{2}{5}(x-5)^{5/2} + C$$

$$= \frac{2}{3}(x-5)^{3/2}[x - \frac{2}{5}(x-5)] + C = \frac{2}{15}(x-5)^{3/2}(5x - 2x + 10) + C$$

$$= \frac{2}{15}(x-5)^{3/2}(3x + 10) + C.$$

12. $\int \frac{x}{\sqrt{2x+3}}\, dx = \int x(2x+3)^{-1/2}\, dx.$ Let $u = x$ and $dv = (2x+3)^{-1/2}\, dx.$

Then $du = dx$ and $v = \int (2x+3)^{-1/2}\, dx = (2x+3)^{1/2} + C.$

(Use the substitution $u = 2x + 3$.) Therefore,

$$\int \frac{x}{\sqrt{2x+3}}\, dx = x(2x+3)^{1/2} - \int (2x+3)^{1/2}\, dx$$

$$= x(2x+3)^{1/2} - \frac{1}{3}(2x+3)^{3/2} + C$$

(Use the substitution $u = 2x + 3$.)

$$= \frac{1}{3}(2x+3)^{1/2}[3x - (2x+3)] + C = \frac{1}{3}(x-3)\sqrt{2x+3} + C$$

13. $I = \int x \ln 2x\, dx.$ Let $u = \ln 2x$ and $dv = x\, dx.$ Then $du = \frac{1}{x}\, dx$ and $v = \frac{1}{2}x^2.$

Therefore, $I = \frac{1}{2}x^2 \ln 2x - \int \frac{1}{2}x\, dx = \frac{1}{2}x^2 \ln 2x - \frac{1}{4}x^2 + C = \frac{1}{4}x^2(2\ln 2x - 1) + C.$

14. Let $u = \ln 2x$ and $dv = x^2\, dx.$ Then $du = \frac{1}{x}\, dx$ and $v = \frac{1}{3}x^3,$ and

$$\int x^2 \ln 2x\, dx = \frac{1}{3}x^3 \ln 2x - \frac{1}{3}\int x^2\, dx = \frac{1}{3}x^3 \ln 2x - \frac{1}{9}x^3 + C.$$

15 Let $u = \ln x$ and $dv = x^3\, dx,$ then $du = \frac{1}{x}\, dx,$ and $v = \frac{1}{4}x^4.$

$$\int x^3 \ln x\, dx = \frac{1}{4}x^4 \ln x - \frac{1}{4}\int x^3\, dx = \frac{1}{4}x^4 \ln x - \frac{1}{16}x^4 + C$$

$$= \frac{1}{16}x^4(4\ln x - 1) + C.$$

16. $I = \int x^{1/2} \ln x\, dx$. Let $u = \ln x$ and $dv = x^{1/2}\, dx$. Then $du = \frac{1}{x}\, dx$

and $v = \frac{2}{3} x^{3/2}$. Therefore,

$$I = \frac{2}{3} x^{3/2} \ln x - \int \frac{2}{3} x^{1/2}\, dx = \frac{2}{3} x^{3/2} \ln x - \frac{4}{9} x^{3/2} + C$$

$$= \frac{2}{9} x^{3/2} (3 \ln x - 2) + C.$$

17. Let $u = \ln x^{1/2}$ and $dv = x^{1/2}\, dx$. Then $du = \frac{1}{2x}\, dx$ and $v = \frac{2}{3} x^{3/2}$,

and $\int \sqrt{x} \ln \sqrt{x}\, dx = uv - \int v\, du = \frac{2}{3} x^{3/2} \ln x^{1/2} - \frac{1}{3} \int x^{1/2}\, dx$

$$= \frac{2}{3} x^{3/2} \ln x^{1/2} - \frac{2}{9} x^{3/2} + C = \frac{2}{9} x \sqrt{x}(3 \ln \sqrt{x} - 1) + C.$$

18. $I = \int x^{-1/2} \ln x\, dx$. Let $u = \ln x$ and $dv = x^{-1/2}\, dx$ so that $du = \frac{1}{x}\, dx$ and $v = 2x^{1/2}$

Therefore, $I = 2x^{1/2} \ln x - \int 2x^{-1/2}\, dx = 2x^{1/2} \ln x - 4x^{1/2} + C$

$$= 2\sqrt{x}(\ln x - 2) + C.$$

19 Let $u = \ln x$ and $dv = x^{-2}\, dx$. Then $du = \frac{1}{x}\, dx$ and $v = -x^{-1}$,

$$\int \frac{\ln x}{x^2}\, dx = uv - \int v\, du = -\frac{\ln x}{x} + \int x^{-2}\, dx = -\frac{\ln x}{x} - \frac{1}{x} + C$$

$$= -\frac{1}{x}(\ln x + 1) + C.$$

20. Let $u = \ln x$ and $dv = x^{-3}\, dx$ so that $du = \frac{dx}{x}$ and $v = -\frac{1}{2} x^{-2}$.

Then $\int \frac{\ln x}{x^3}\, dx = -\frac{\ln x}{2x^2} + \frac{1}{2} \int x^{-3}\, dx = -\frac{\ln x}{2x^2} - \frac{1}{4} x^{-2} + C$

$$= -\frac{1}{4x^2}(2 \ln x + 1) + C.$$

21. Let $u = \ln x$ and $dv = dx$. Then $du = \frac{1}{x}\, dx$ and $v = x$ and

$$\int \ln x\, dx = uv - \int v\, du = x \ln x - \int dx = x \ln x - x + C = x(\ln x - 1) + C.$$

22. $I = \int \ln(x+1)\,dx$. Let $u = \ln(x+1)$ and $dv = dx$. Then $du = \dfrac{dx}{x+1}$

and $v = x$. Therefore, $I = x(\ln x + 1) - \displaystyle\int \frac{x}{x+1}\,dx$. Next, let

$J = \displaystyle\int \frac{x}{x+1}\,dx$. Let $u = x+1$ so that $du = dx$. Therefore,

$J = \displaystyle\int \frac{u-1}{u}\,du = \int \left(1 - \frac{1}{u}\right)du = u - \ln|u| + k$, k a constant

So, $I = x\ln(x+1) - (x+1) + \ln|x+1| + C = (x+1)[\ln|x+1| - 1] + C$.

23. Let $u = x^2$ and $dv = e^{-x}\,dx$. Then $du = 2x\,dx$ and $v = -e^{-x}$, and

$\displaystyle\int x^2 e^{-x}\,dx = uv - \int v\,du = -x^2 e^{-x} + 2\int xe^{-x}\,dx$.

We can integrate by parts again, or, using the result of Problem 2, we find

$\displaystyle\int x^2 e^{-x}\,dx = -x^2 e^{-x} + 2[-(x+1)e^{-x}] + C = -x^2 e^{-x} - 2(x+1)e^{-x} + C$

$\qquad\qquad = -(x^2 + 2x + 2)e^{-x} + C$.

24. Let $u = \sqrt{x} = x^{1/2}$, so that $du = \frac{1}{2}x^{-1/2}\,dx$ and $dx = 2\sqrt{x}\,dx = 2u\,du$. With this substitution

$$\int e^{-\sqrt{x}}\,dx = 2\int ue^{-u}\,du = -2(u+1)e^{-u} + C \quad \text{(Using the result of Exercise 2.)}$$

$$= -2(\sqrt{x}+1)e^{-\sqrt{x}} + C. \qquad \text{(Since } u = \sqrt{x}\text{)}$$

25. $I = \int x(\ln x)^2\,dx$. Let $u = (\ln x)^2$ and $dv = x\,dx$, so that

$du = 2(\ln x)\left(\dfrac{1}{x}\right) = \dfrac{2\ln x}{x}$ and $v = \frac{1}{2}x^2$. Then $I = \frac{1}{2}x^2(\ln x)^2 - \displaystyle\int x\ln x\,dx$.

Next, we evaluate $\displaystyle\int x\ln x\,dx$, by letting $u = \ln x$ and $dv = x\,dx$, so that $du = \frac{1}{x}\,dx$

and $v = \frac{1}{2}x^2$. Then $\displaystyle\int x\ln x\,dx = \frac{1}{2}x^2(\ln x) - \frac{1}{2}\int x\,dx = \frac{1}{2}x^2\ln x - \frac{1}{4}x^2 + C$.

Therefore, $\displaystyle\int x(\ln x)^2\,dx = \frac{1}{2}x^2(\ln x)^2 - \frac{1}{2}x^2\ln x + \frac{1}{4}x^2 + C$

$$= \tfrac{1}{4}x^2[2(\ln x)^2 - 2\ln x + 1] + C.$$

26. Let $u = x + 1$ so that $du = dx$. Then

$$\int x \ln(x+1)\,dx = \int (u-1)\ln u\,du = \int u \ln u\,du - \int \ln u\,du.$$

Integrating each integral by parts, or using the results of Example 2 and Problem 21, we obtain $\int u \ln u\,du - \int \ln u\,du = \tfrac{1}{4}u^2(2\ln u - 1) - u(\ln u - 1) + C$

So $\int x \ln(x+1)\,dx = \tfrac{1}{4}(x+1)^2[2\ln(x+1) - 1] - (x+1)[\ln(x+1) - 1] + C.$

27. $\displaystyle\int_0^{\ln 2} xe^x\,dx = (x-1)e^x\Big|_0^{\ln 2}$ (Using the results of Example 1.)

$$= (\ln 2 - 1)e^{\ln 2} - (-e^0) = 2(\ln 2 - 1) + 1 \ (\text{Recall } e^{\ln 2} = 2.) = 2\ln 2 - 1.$$

28. Using the results of Exercise 2, we have

$$\int_0^2 xe^{-x}\,dx = -(x+1)e^{-x}\Big|_0^2 = -3e^{-2} + 1.$$

29. We first integrate $I = \int \ln x\,dx$. Integrating by parts with $u = \ln x$ and $dv = dx$ so that $du = \tfrac{1}{x}\,dx$ and $v = x$, we find

$$I = x\ln x - \int dx = x\ln x - x + C = x(\ln x - 1) + C.$$

Therefore, $\displaystyle\int_1^4 \ln x\,dx = x(\ln x - 1)\Big|_1^4 = 4(\ln 4 - 1) - 1(\ln 1 - 1) = 4\ln 4 - 3.$

30. Using the result of Example 2, we find

$$\int_1^2 x\ln x\,dx = \tfrac{1}{4}x^2(2\ln x - 1)\Big|_1^2 = 2\ln 2 - 1 + \tfrac{1}{4} = \tfrac{1}{4}(8\ln 2 - 3).$$

31. Let $u = x$ and $dv = e^{2x}\,dx$. Then $u = dx$ and $v = \tfrac{1}{2}e^{2x}$ and

$$\int_0^2 xe^{2x}\,dx = \tfrac{1}{2}xe^{2x}\Big|_0^2 - \tfrac{1}{2}\int_0^2 e^{2x}\,dx = e^4 - \tfrac{1}{4}e^{2x}\Big|_0^2$$
$$= e^4 - \tfrac{1}{4}e^4 + \tfrac{1}{4} = \tfrac{1}{4}(3e^4 + 1).$$

32. We first integrate $I = \int x^2 e^{-x} \, dx$. Integrating by parts with $u = x^2$ and $dv = e^x \, dx$

so that $du = 2x \, dx$ and $v = -e^x$, we see that $I = -x^2 e^{-x} + 2 \int x e^{-x} \, dx$.

Let $J = \int x e^{-x} \, dx$. Integrating J by parts with $u = x$ and $dv = e^x \, dx$ so that

$du = dx$ and $v = e^x$, we have $J = \int x e^{-x} \, dx = -x e^{-x} + \int e^{-x} \, dx - x e^{-x} - e^{-x} + C$.

Therefore, $I = -x^2 e^{-x} - 2x e^{-x} - 2e^{-x} + C = (x^2 + 2x + 2)e^{-x} + C$

and so $\int_0^1 x^2 e^{-x} \, dx = -(x^2 + 2x + 2)e^{-x} \Big|_0^1 = -5e^{-1} + 2$.

33. Let $u = x$ and $dv = e^{-2x} \, dx$, so that $du = dx$ and $v = -\frac{1}{2}e^{-2x}$.

$f(x) = \int x e^{-2x} \, dx = -\frac{1}{2} x e^{-2x} - \frac{1}{4} e^{-2x} + C$; $f(0) = -\frac{1}{4} + C = 3$ and $C = \frac{13}{4}$.

Therefore, $y = -\frac{1}{2} x e^{-2x} - \frac{1}{4} e^{-2x} + \frac{13}{4}$.

34. Let $u = x$ and $dv = (x + 1)^{1/2}$, so that $du = dx$ and $v = \frac{2}{3}(x + 1)^{3/2}$.

$f(x) = \int x(x+1)^{1/2} \, dx = \frac{2x}{3}(x+1)^{3/2} - \frac{2}{3}\int (x+1)^{3/2} \, dx$

$= \frac{2x}{3}(x+1)^{3/2} - \frac{4}{15}(x+1)^{5/2} + C$.

$f(3) = 2(8) - \frac{4}{15}(32) + C = 6$ and $C = -\frac{22}{15}$.

Therefore, $f(x) = \frac{2x}{3}(x+1)^{3/2} - \frac{4}{15}(x+1)^{5/2} - \frac{22}{15}$.

35. The required area is given by $\int_1^5 \ln x \, dx$. We first find $\int \ln x \, dx$. Using the

technique of integration by parts with $u = \ln x$ and $dv = dx$ so that $du = \frac{1}{x} dx$ and

$v = x$, we have

$$\int \ln x \, dx = x \ln x - \int dx = x \ln x - x = x(\ln x - 1) + C.$$

Therefore, $\int_1^5 \ln x \, dx = x(\ln x - 1) \Big|_1^5 = 5(\ln 5 - 1) - 1(\ln 1 - 1) = 5 \ln 5 - 4$

and the required area is $(5 \ln 5 - 4)$ sq units.

36. $A = \int_0^3 xe^{-x}\, dx.$ Using the result of Exercise 2, we have

$A = -(x+1)e^{-x}\Big|_0^3 = -4e^{-3} +1 \approx 0.8$ sq units.

37. The distance covered is given by $\int_0^{10} 100te^{-0.2t}\, dt = 100\int_0^{10} te^{-0.2t}\, dt.$
We integrate by parts, letting $u = t$ and $dv = e^{-0.2t}\, dt$ so that $du = dt$ and

$v = -\dfrac{1}{0.2}e^{-0.2t} = -5e^{-0.2t}.$ Therefore,

$$100\int_0^{10} te^{-0.2t}\, dt = 100\left[-5te^{-0.2t}\Big|_0^{10}\right] + 5\int_0^{10} e^{-0.2t}\, dt$$

$$= 100[-5te^{-0.2t} - 25e^{-0.2t}]\Big|_0^{10} = -500e^{-0.2t}(t+5)\Big|_0^{10}$$

$$= -500e^{-2}(15) + 500(5) = 1485, \text{ or } 1485 \text{ feet.}$$

38. Let P denote the required function. Then $P'(t) = 2te^{-0.05t}.$ Next, we find that

$P(t) = 2\int te^{-0.05t}\, dt.$ Put $u = t$ and $dv = e^{-0.05t}\, dt$ so that $du = dt$ and

$v = -\dfrac{1}{0.05}e^{-0.05t} = -20e^{-0.05t}.$ Then

$P(t) = -40e^{-0.05t} + 40\int e^{-0.05t}\, dt = -40te^{-0.05t} - 800e^{-0.05t} + C$

$= -40(t+20)e^{-0.05t} + C.$

We now use the initial condition $P(0) = 20$ to obtain the equation
$-800 + C = 20,$ or $C = 820.$ Therefore, $P(t) = -40(t+20)e^{-0.05t} + 820.$
The amount of coal produced by the company in the next 20 years would be
$P(20) = -40(40)e^{-(0.05)(20)} + 820 \approx 231.39,$ or 231.39 million metric tons.

39. The average concentration is $C = \dfrac{1}{12}\int_0^{12} 3te^{-t/3}\, dt = \dfrac{1}{4}\int_0^{12} te^{-t/3}\, dt.$
Let $u = t$ and $dv = e^{-t/3}\, dt.$ So $du = dt$ and $v = -3e^{-t/3}.$ Then

$$C = \frac{1}{4}\left[-3te^{-t/3}\Big|_0^{12} + 3\int_0^{12} e^{-t/3}\, dt\right] = \frac{1}{4}\left\{-36e^{-4} - \left[9e^{-t/3}\Big|_0^{12}\right]\right\}$$

$$= \tfrac{1}{4}(-36e^{-4} - 9e^{-4} + 9) \approx 2.04 \text{ mg/ml.}$$

40. The number of accidents is expected to be

$$E = 982 + \int_0^{12} (-10 - te^{0.1t})\, dt = 982 - \int_0^{12} 10\, dt - \int_0^{12} te^{0.1t}\, dt$$

$$= 982 - 120 - \int_0^{12} te^{0.1t}\, dt = 862 - \int_0^{12} te^{0.1t}\, dt.$$

To evaluate the last integral, let $u = t$ and $dv = e^{0.1t}\, dt$ so that
$du = dt$ and $v = 10e^{0.1t}$. So

$$\int_0^{12} te^{0.1t}\, dt = 10te^{0.1t}\Big|_0^{12} - 10\int_0^{12} e^{0.1t}\, dt = 120e^{1.2} - 100e^{0.1t}\Big|_0^{12}$$

$$= 120e^{1.2} - 100e^{1.2} + 100 \approx 166.$$

Therefore, $E \approx 862 - 166 \approx 696$ or approximately 696 accidents.

41   $N = 2\int te^{-0.1t}\, dt$. Let $u = t$ and $dv = e^{-0.1t}$, so that $du = dt$ and $v = -10e^{-0.1t}$. Then

$v = -10e^{-0.1t}$. Then

$$N(t) = 2[-10te^{-0.1t} + 10\int e - 0.1t\, dt] = 2(-10te^{-0.1t} - 100e^{-0.1t}) + C$$

$$= -20e^{-0.1t}(t + 10) + 200. \qquad\qquad [N(0) = 0]$$

42. The average price is given by

$$\tfrac{1}{4}\int_0^4 (8 + 4e^{-2t} + te^{-2t})\, dt = \tfrac{1}{4}[8t - 2e^{-2t} - \tfrac{1}{4}e^{-2t}(1 + 2t)\Big|_0^4$$

(Integrate the last integral by parts)

$$= \tfrac{1}{4}[8t - 2e^{-2t} - \tfrac{1}{4}e^{-2t}(1 + 2t)\Big|_0^4$$

$$= \tfrac{1}{4}[8(4) - 2e^{-8} - \tfrac{1}{4}e^{-8}(1 + 8) + 2 + \tfrac{1}{4}(1)]$$

$$= \tfrac{1}{4}[32 - 2e^{-8} - \tfrac{9}{4}e^{-8} + \tfrac{9}{4}] = \tfrac{1}{4}[34\tfrac{1}{4} - \tfrac{17}{4}e^{-8}] \approx 8.56, \text{ or } \$8.56.$$

43. $$PV = \int_0^5 (30{,}000 + 800t)e^{-0.08t}\, dt = 30{,}000\int_0^5 e^{-0.08t}\, dt + 800\int_0^5 te^{-0.08t}\, dt.$$

Let $I = \int te^{-0.08t}\, dt$. To evaluate I by parts, let $u = t$, $dv = e^{-0.08t}\, dt$

and $du = dt$, $v = -\dfrac{1}{0.08}e^{-0.08t} = -12.5e^{-0.08t}$.

Therefore, $I = -12.5te^{-0.08t} + 12.5\int e^{-0.08t}\, dt = -12.5te^{-0.08t} - 156.25e^{-0.08t} + C.$

$$PV = \left[-\frac{30,000}{0.08}e^{-0.08t} - 800(12.5)te^{-0.08t} - 800(156.25)e^{-0.08t} \right]_0^5$$

$$= -375,000\, e^{-0.4} + 375,000 - 50,000e^{-0.4} - 125,000e^{-0.4} + 125,000$$

$$= 500,000 - 550,000e^{-0.4} = 131,323.97, \text{ or approximately } \$131,324.$$

44.   The present value of the franchise is

$$PV = \int_0^T P(t)e^{-rt}\, dt = \int_0^{15} (50,000 + 3000t)e^{-0.1t}\, dt$$

$$= 50,000\int_0^{15} e^{-0.1t}\, dt + 3000\int_0^{15} te^{-0.1t}\, dt.$$

The first integral is

$$50,000\int_0^{15} e^{-0.1t}\, dt = \frac{50,000}{-0.1}e^{-0.1t}\Big|_0^{15} = -500,000(e^{-1.5} - 1) \approx 388,435.$$

The second integral is evaluated by integration by parts . Let $u = t$ and $dv = e^{-0.1t}\, dt$ so that $du = dt$ and $v = -10e^{-0.1t}$.

$$3000\int_0^{15} te^{-0.1t}\, dt = 3000[-10te^{-0.1t}\Big|_0^{15} + 10\int_0^{15} e^{-0.1t}\, dt]$$

$$= 3000\left[-150e^{-1.5} - 100e^{-0.1t}\Big|_0^{15}\right]$$

$$= 3000(-150\, e^{-1.5} - 100e^{-1.5} + 100) \approx 132,652.$$

Therefore, $PV \approx 388,435 + 132,652 = 521,087$ or $\$521,087.$

45.   The membership will be

$$N(5) = N(0) + \int_0^5 9\sqrt{t+1}\ln\sqrt{t+1}\, dt = 50 + 9\int_0^5 \sqrt{t+1}\ \ln\sqrt{t+1}\, dt$$

To evaluate the integral, let $u = t + 1$ so that $du = dt$. Also, if $t = 0$, then $u = 1$ and if $t = 5$, then $u = 6$. So $9\int_0^5 \sqrt{t+1}\ \ln\sqrt{t+1}\, dt = 9\int_1^6 \sqrt{u}\ln\sqrt{u}\, du.$

Using the results of Problem 17, we find $9\int_1^6 \sqrt{u}\ln\sqrt{u}\, du = 2u\sqrt{u}(3\ln\sqrt{u} - 1)\Big|_1^6.$

Therefore, $N = 50 + 51.606 \approx 101.606$ or $101,606$ people.

46. a. $A(0) = 180(1 - e^0) - 6(0)e^0 = 0,$ or 0 lb.

   b. $A(180) = 180(1 - e^{-180/3}) - 6(180)e^{-180/3} = 176.877,$ or 176.9 lb.

   c.   The average amount of salt over the first 3 hr is

$$\overline{A} = \frac{1}{180} \int_0^{180} [180(1-e^{-t/30}) - 6te^{-t/30}]\,dt = \int_0^{180}(1-e^{-t/30})\,dt - \tfrac{1}{30}\int_0^{180} te^{-t/30}\,dt$$

Call the first integral I_1, and the second integral I_2. Then

$$I_1 = \int_0^{180}(1-e^{-t/30}) = (t+30e^{-t/30})\Big|_0^{180} \qquad \text{[Use substitution with } u=-t/30\text{]}$$

$$= (180+30e^{-6}) - (0+30e^0) \approx 150.074$$

To evaluate I_2, consider the corresponding indefinite integral $J = \int te^{-t/30}\,dt$.

Integrating by parts with $u=t$, $dv = e^{-t/30}\,dt$, so that $du=dt$, $v=-30e^{-t/30}$,

we find $J = -30te^{-t/30} - \int -30e^{-t/30}\,dt = -30te^{-t/30} - 900e^{-t/30} + C$

$$= -30(t+30)e^{-t/30} + C.$$

Therefore, $I_2 = \dfrac{1}{30} J\Big|_0^{180} = -(t+30)e^{-t/30}\Big|_0^{180} = -(180+30)e^{-6}+30e^0 \approx 29.479$

So $\overline{A} = I_1 - I_2 \approx 150.074 - 29.479 = 120.595$, or approximately 120.6 lb.

47. The average concentration from $r=r_1$ to $r=r_2$ is

$$A = \frac{1}{r^2 - r_1}\int_{r_1}^{r_2} c(r)\,dr = \frac{1}{r^2 - r_1}\int_{r_1}^{r_2}\left[\left(\frac{c_1 - c_2}{\ln r_1 - \ln r_2}\right)(\ln r - \ln r_2) + c_2\right]dr$$

$$= \frac{1}{r_2 - r_1}\left(\frac{c_1 - c_2}{\ln r_1 - \ln r_2}\right)\left[\int_{r_1}^{r_2}\ln r\,dr - \int_{r_1}^{r_2}\ln r_2\,dr\right] + \frac{1}{r_2 - r_1}\int_{r_1}^{r_2} c_2\,dr$$

We integrate $\int \ln r\,dr$ by parts, letting $u=\ln r$, $dv=dr$, or $du=\dfrac{dr}{r}$, and $v=r$, so

that $\int \ln r\,dr = r\ln r - \int r\dfrac{dr}{r} = r\ln r - r = r(\ln r - 1)$.

Therefore,

$$A = \frac{1}{r_2 - r_1}\left(\frac{c_1 - c_2}{\ln r_1 - \ln r_2}\right)\left[r(\ln r - 1)\Big|_{r_1}^{r_2} - (\ln r_2)\Big|_{r_1}^{r_2}\right] + c_2$$

$$= \frac{1}{r_2 - r_1}\left(\frac{c_1 - c_2}{\ln r_1 - \ln r_2}\right)\{r_2(\ln r_2 - 1) - r_1(\ln r_1 - 1) - (r_2 - r_1)\ln r_2] + c_2$$

$$= \frac{1}{r_2 - r_1}\left(\frac{c_1 - c_2}{\ln r_1 - \ln r_2} \right)\left[r_1(\ln r_2 - \ln r_1) - (r_2 - r_1) \right] + c_2 \right]$$

$$= (c_2 - c_1)\left[\frac{r_1}{r_2 - r_1} + \frac{1}{\ln r_1 - \ln r_2} \right] + c_2.$$

48. Let $u = x$ and $dv = f''(x)\,dx$ Then $du = dx$ and $v = f'(x)$. Then

$$\int xf''(x)\,dx = xf'(x) - \int f'(x)\,dx = xf'(x) - f(x) + C.$$

Therefore,

$$\int_1^3 xf''(x)\,dx = xf'(x) - f(x)\Big|_1^3 = [3f'(3) - f(x)] - [f'(x) - f(1)]$$
$$= [3(5) - (-1)] - [2 - 2] = 16$$

49.   True. This is just the integration by parts formula.

50.   True. Use the integration by parts formula with $u = e^x$ and $dv = g'(x)\,dx$. We
      find $du = e^x\,dx$ and $v = g(x)$. So
$$\int u\,dv = \int e^x g'(x)\,dx = uv - \int v\,du = e^x g(x) - \int e^x g(x)\,dx.$$

7.2 CONCEPT QUESTIONS, page 496

1. a. We would chose Formula 19.
    b. Put $a = \sqrt{2}$ and $x = u$. Then, using Formula 19, we find
$$\int \frac{\sqrt{2 - x^2}}{x}\,dx = \int \frac{\sqrt{(\sqrt{2})^2 - x^2}}{x}\,dx = \sqrt{2 - x^2} - \sqrt{2}\ln\left| \frac{\sqrt{a} + \sqrt{2 - x^2}}{x} \right| + C$$

2. a. We would choose Formula 16.
    b. First, we rewrite the indefinite integral
$$\int \frac{dx}{\sqrt{2x^2 - 5}} = \int \frac{dx}{\sqrt{2(x^2 - \frac{5}{2})}} = \frac{1}{\sqrt{2}}\int \frac{dx}{\sqrt{x^2 - (\sqrt{\frac{5}{2}})^2}}$$

So, let $u = x$ and $a = \dfrac{\sqrt{5}}{\sqrt{2}} = \dfrac{\sqrt{10}}{2}$. Then Formula 16 gives

$$\int \frac{dx}{\sqrt{2x^2 - 5}} = \frac{1}{\sqrt{2}}\ln\left| x + \sqrt{x^2 - \frac{5}{2}} \right| + C.$$

Therefore,

$$\int_2^3 \frac{dx}{\sqrt{2x^2-5}} = \frac{1}{\sqrt{2}}\left[\ln\left|3+\sqrt{9-\tfrac{5}{2}}\right|\right] - \ln\left|2+\sqrt{4-\tfrac{5}{2}}\right|$$

$$= \frac{1}{\sqrt{2}}\left[\ln\left|3+\sqrt{\tfrac{13}{2}}\right| - \ln\left|2+\sqrt{\tfrac{3}{2}}\right|\right] \approx 0.3839$$

EXERCISES 7.2, page 497

1. First we note that

$$\int \frac{2x}{2+3x}\,dx = 2\int \frac{x}{2+3x}\,dx.$$

Next, we use Formula 1 with $a = 2$, $b = 3$, and $u = x$. Then

$$\int \frac{2x}{2+3x}\,dx = \frac{2}{9}[2+3x-2\ln|2+3x|]+C.$$

2. Use Formula 3 with $a = 1$, $b = 2$, and $u = x$. Then

$$\int \frac{x}{(1+2x)^2}\,dx = \frac{1}{4}\left[\frac{1}{1+2x}+\ln|1+2x|\right]+C.$$

3. $\displaystyle\int \frac{3x^2}{2+4x}\,dx = \frac{3}{2}\int \frac{x^2}{1+2x}\,dx.$

Use Formula 2 with $a = 1$ and $b = 2$ obtaining

$$\int \frac{3x^2}{2+4x}\,dx = \frac{3}{32}[(1+2x)^2 - 4(1+2x) + 2\ln|1+2x|]+C.$$

4. $\displaystyle\int \frac{x^2}{3+x}\,dx = \frac{1}{2}[(3+x)^2 - 12(3+x) + 18\ln|3+x|]+C.$

Use Formula 2 with $a = 3$ and $b = 1$.)

5. $\displaystyle\int x^2\sqrt{9+4x^2}\,dx = \int x^2\sqrt{4(\tfrac{9}{4})+x^2)}\,dx = 2\int x^2\sqrt{(\tfrac{3}{2})^2+x^2}\,dx$.

Use Formula 8 with $a = 3/2$, we find that

$$\int x^2\sqrt{9+4x^2}\,dx == 2[\tfrac{x}{8}(\tfrac{9}{4}+2x^2)\sqrt{\tfrac{9}{4}+x^2} - \tfrac{81}{128}\ln\left|x+\sqrt{\tfrac{9}{4}+x^2}\right|]+C.$$

6. $\displaystyle\int x^2\sqrt{4+x^2}\,dx = \int x^2\sqrt{2^2+x^2}\,dx$

Use Formula 8 with $a = 2$, obtaining

$$\int x^2\sqrt{4+x^2}\,dx = \tfrac{x}{8}(4+2x^2)\sqrt{4+x^2} - 2\ln\left|x+\sqrt{4+x^2}\right| + C.$$

7 Use Formula 6 with $a = 1$, $b = 4$, and $u = x$, then

$$\int \frac{dx}{x\sqrt{1+4x}} = \ln\left|\frac{\sqrt{1+4x}-1}{\sqrt{1+4x}+1}\right| + C.$$

8. $\displaystyle\int_0^2 \frac{x+1}{\sqrt{2+3x}}\,dx = \int_0^2 \frac{x}{\sqrt{2+3x}}\,dx + \int_0^2 \frac{1}{\sqrt{2+3x}}\,dx$.

Use Formula 5 to evaluate the first integral and the method of substitution (let $u = 2 + 3x$) to evaluate the second integral. We obtain

$$\int_0^2 \frac{x+1}{\sqrt{2+3x}}\,dx = \tfrac{2}{27}(3x-4)\sqrt{2+3x}\,\Big|_0^2 + (\tfrac{1}{3})2\sqrt{2+3x}\,\Big|_0^2$$

$$= \tfrac{2}{27}(2\sqrt{8}+4\sqrt{2})+\tfrac{2}{3}(\sqrt{8}-\sqrt{2}) = \frac{34\sqrt{2}}{27}.$$

9. Use Formula 9 with $a = 3$ and $u = 2x$. Then $du = 2\,dx$ and

$$\int_0^2 \frac{dx}{\sqrt{9+4x^2}} = \frac{1}{2}\int_0^4 \frac{du}{\sqrt{3^2+u^2}} = \frac{1}{2}\ln\left|u+\sqrt{9+u^2}\right|\,\Big|_0^4$$

$$= \frac{1}{2}(\ln 9 - \ln 3) = \frac{1}{2}\ln 3.$$

Note that the limits of integration have been changed from $x = 0$ to $x = 2$ and from $u = 0$ to $u = 4$.

10. $\displaystyle\int \frac{dx}{x\sqrt{4+8x^2}} = \int \frac{dx}{2\sqrt{2}\,x\sqrt{(\tfrac{1}{\sqrt{2}})^2+x^2}}$.

Use Formula 10 with $a = \dfrac{1}{\sqrt{2}}$ and $u = x$, obtaining

$$\int \frac{dx}{x\sqrt{4+8x^2}} = -\sqrt{2}\ln\left|\frac{\sqrt{(\tfrac{1}{\sqrt{2}})^2+x^2}+\dfrac{1}{\sqrt{2}}}{x}\right| + C$$

11. Using Formula 22 with $a = 3$, we see that $\displaystyle\int \frac{dx}{(9-x^2)^{3/2}} = \frac{x}{9\sqrt{9-x^2}} + C.$

12. $\displaystyle\int \frac{dx}{(2-x^2)^{3/2}}.$ Use Formula 22 with $a = \sqrt{2}$ and $u = x$, obtaining

$$\int \frac{dx}{(2-x^2)^{3/2}} = \frac{x}{2\sqrt{2-x^2}} + C.$$

13. $\displaystyle\int x^2\sqrt{x^2-4}\, dx.$

Use Formula 14 with $a = 2$ and $u = x$, obtaining

$$\int x^2\sqrt{x^2-4}\, dx = \tfrac{x}{8}(2x^2-4)\sqrt{x^2-4} - 2\ln\left|x+\sqrt{x^2-4}\right| + C.$$

14 $\displaystyle\int_3^5 \frac{dx}{x^2\sqrt{x^2-9}}.$

Use Formula 17 with $u = x$ and $a = 3$, obtaining,

$$\int_3^5 \frac{dx}{x^2\sqrt{x^2-9}} = \left.\frac{\sqrt{x^2-9}}{9x}\right|_3^5 = \frac{1}{9}\left(\frac{\sqrt{16}}{5} - 0\right) = \frac{4}{45}.$$

15. Using Formula 19 with $a = 2$ and $u = x$, we have

$$\int \frac{\sqrt{4-x^2}}{x}\, dx = \sqrt{4-x^2} - 2\ln\left|\frac{2+\sqrt{4-x^2}}{x}\right| + C.$$

16. Using Formula 22 with $a = 2$ and $u = x$,

$$\int_0^1 \frac{dx}{(4-x^2)^{3/2}} = \left.\frac{x}{4\sqrt{4-x^2}}\right|_0^1 = \frac{1}{4\sqrt{3}} = \frac{\sqrt{3}}{12}.$$

17. $\displaystyle\int xe^{2x}\, dx.$

Use Formula 23 with $u = x$ and $a = 2$, obtaining

$$\int xe^{2x}\, dx = \frac{1}{4}(2x-1)e^{2x} + C.$$

18. Using Formula 25 with $a = -1$, $b = 1$, and $u = x$, we find

$$\int \frac{dx}{1+e^{-x}} = x + \ln(1+e^{-x}) + C$$

19. $\displaystyle \int \frac{dx}{(x+1)\ln(x+1)}.$

Let $u = x + 1$ so that $du = dx$. Then $\displaystyle \int \frac{dx}{(x+1)\ln(x+1)} = \int \frac{du}{u \ln u}.$

Use Formula 28 with $u = x$, obtaining $\displaystyle \int \frac{du}{u \ln u} = \ln|\ln u| + C$

Therefore, $\displaystyle \int \frac{dx}{(x+1)\ln(x+1)} = \ln|\ln(x+1)| + C$

20. First we make the substitution $u = x^2 + 1$, so that $du = 2x\,dx$ and $x\,dx = \frac{1}{2}du$.

Then $\displaystyle \int \frac{x\,dx}{(x^2+1)\ln(x^2+1)} = \frac{1}{2}\int \frac{du}{u \ln u}.$

Using Formula 28, we find $\displaystyle \frac{1}{2}\int \frac{du}{u \ln u} = \frac{1}{2}\ln|\ln u| + C$

Therefore, $\displaystyle \int \frac{x}{(x^2+1)\ln(x^2+1)}\,dx = \frac{1}{2}\ln[\ln(x^2+1)] + C.$

21. $\displaystyle \int \frac{e^{2x}}{(1+3e^x)^2}\,dx.$

Put $u = e^x$ then $du = e^x dx$. Then we use Formula 3 with $a = 1, b = 3$. Then

$$I = \int \frac{u}{(1+3u)^2}\,du = \frac{1}{9}\left[\frac{1}{1+3u} + \ln|1+3u|\right] + C = \frac{1}{9}\left[\frac{1}{1+3e^x} + \ln(1+3e^x)\right] + C$$

22. Let $u = e^x$ as in Problem 19. Then, using Formula 5

$$\int \frac{e^{2x}}{\sqrt{1+3e^x}}\,dx = \int \frac{e^x e^x}{(1+3e^x)^{1/2}}\,dx = \int \frac{u}{\sqrt{1+3u}}\,du$$

$$= \tfrac{2}{27}(3u-2)\sqrt{1+3u} = \tfrac{2}{27}(3e^x-2)\sqrt{1+3e^x} + C.$$

23. $\displaystyle\int \frac{3e^x}{1+e^{x/2}}\,dx = 3\int \frac{e^{x/2}}{e^{-x/2}+1}\,dx$.

Let $v = e^{x/2}$ so that $dv = \frac{1}{2}e^{x/2}dx$ or $e^{x/2}\,dx = 2\,dv$. Then

$$\int \frac{3e^x}{1+e^{x/2}}\,dx = 6\int \frac{dv}{\frac{1}{v}+1} = 6\int \frac{v}{v+1}\,dv.$$

Use Formula 1 with $a = 1$, $b = 1$, and $u = v$, obtaining

$$6\int \frac{v}{v+1}\,dv = 6[1+v-\ln|1+v|]+C. \text{ So } \int \frac{3e^x}{1+e^{x/2}}\,dx = 6[1+e^{x/2}-\ln(1+e^{x/2})]+C.$$

This answer may be written in the form $6[e^{x/2}-\ln(1+e^{x/2})]+C$ since C is an arbitrary constant.

24. $\displaystyle\int \frac{dx}{1-2e^{-x}}$ Use Formula 25 with $a = -1$ and $b = -2$, obtaining

$$\int \frac{dx}{1-2e^{-x}} = x+\ln(1-2e^{-x})+C.$$

25 $\displaystyle\int \frac{\ln x}{x(2+3\ln x)}\,dx$. Let $v = \ln x$ so that $dv = \frac{1}{x}\,dx$. Then

$$\int \frac{\ln x}{x(2+3\ln x)}\,dx = \int \frac{v}{2+3v}\,dv$$

Use Formula 1 with $a = 2$, $b = 3$, and $u = v$ to obtain

$$\int \frac{v}{2+3v}\,dv = \frac{1}{9}[2+3\ln x - 2\ln|2+3\ln x|]+C . \text{ So}$$

$$\int \frac{\ln x}{x(2+3\ln x)}\,dx = \frac{1}{9}[2+3\ln x-2\ln|2+3\ln x|]+C.$$

26. Using Formula 29 with $n = 2$ and $u = x$, we find

$$\int (\ln x)^2\,dx = x(\ln x)^2 - 2\int \ln x\,dx.$$

Then using Formula 29 again with $n = 1$ on the second integral on the right

$$\int (\ln x)^2\,dx = x(\ln x)^2 - 2\left[x\ln x - \int dx\right]$$

$$= x(\ln x)^2 - 2x\ln x + 2x + C = x[(\ln x)^2 - 2\ln x + 2]+C.$$

Therefore, $\int_1^e (\ln x)^2 \, dx = x[(\ln x)^2 - 2\ln x + 2]\Big|_1^e = e(1-2+2)-(2) = e-2.$

27. Using Formula 24 with $a = 1$, $n = 2$, and $u = x$. Then

$$\int_0^1 x^2 e^x \, dx = x^2 e^x \Big|_0^1 - 2\int_0^1 xe^x \, dx = x^2 e^x - 2(xe^x - e^x)\Big|_0^1$$

$$= x^2 e^x - 2xe^x + 2e^x \Big|_0^1 = e - 2e + 2e - 2 = e - 2.$$

28. Using Formula 24 with $a = 2$, $n = 3$, and $u = x$, we have

$$\int x^3 e^{2x} \, dx = \tfrac{1}{2} x^3 e^{2x} - \tfrac{3}{2}\int x^2 e^x \, dx = \tfrac{1}{2} x^3 e^{2x} - \tfrac{3}{2}\left[\tfrac{1}{2} x^2 e^{2x} - \int xe^x \, dx \right]$$

$$= \tfrac{1}{2} x^3 e^{2x} - \tfrac{3}{4} x^2 e^{2x} + \tfrac{3}{2}\int xe^{2x} \, dx.$$

(Use Formula 24 with $a = 2$, $n = 2$, and $u = x$.)

$$= \tfrac{1}{2} x^3 e^{2x} - \tfrac{3}{4} x^2 e^{2x} + \tfrac{3}{2}\left[\tfrac{1}{2} xe^{2x} - \tfrac{1}{2}\int e^{2x} \, dx \right]$$

(Use Formula 23 with $a = 2$, and $u = x$.)

$$= \tfrac{1}{2} x^3 e^{2x} - \tfrac{3}{4} x^2 e^{2x} + \tfrac{3}{4} xe^{2x} - \tfrac{3}{8} e^{2x} + C.$$

29. $\int x^2 \ln x \, dx.$ Use Formula 27 with $n = 2$ and $u = x$, obtaining

$$\int x^2 \ln x \, dx = \frac{x^3}{9}(3\ln x - 1) + C.$$

30. $\int x^3 \ln x \, dx.$ Use Formula 27 with $n = 3$ and $u = x$, obtaining

$$\int x^3 \ln x \, dx = \frac{x^4}{16}(4\ln x - 1) + C.$$

31. $\int (\ln x)^3 \, dx.$ Use Formula 29 with $n = 3$ to write

$$\int (\ln x)^3 \, dx = x(\ln x)^3 - 3\int (\ln x)^2 \, dx. \qquad \text{Using Formula 29 again with } n = 2, \text{ we}$$

obtain

$$\int (\ln x)^3 \, dx = x(\ln x)^3 - 3[x(\ln x)^2 - 2\int \ln x \, dx].$$

Using Formula 29 one more time with $n = 1$ gives

$$\int (\ln x)^3\, dx = x(\ln x)^3 - 3x(\ln x)^2 + 6(x \ln x - x) + C$$

$$= x(\ln x)^3 - 3x(\ln x)^2 + 6x \ln x - 6x + C.$$

32. Repeated use of Formula 29 yields

$$\int (\ln x)^4\, dx = x(\ln x)^4 - 4\int (\ln x)^3\, dx$$

$$= x(\ln x)^4 - 4[x(\ln x)^3 - 3\int (\ln x)^2\, dx$$

$$= x(\ln x)^4 - 4x(\ln x)^3 + 12\int (\ln x)^2\, dx$$

$$= x(\ln x)^4 - 2x(\ln x)^3 + 12[x(\ln x)^2 - 2\int \ln x\, dx]$$

$$= x(\ln x)^4 - 4x(\ln x)^3 + 12x(\ln x)^2 - 24(x \ln x - x) + C$$

$$= x[(\ln x)^4 - 4(\ln x)^3 + 12(\ln x)^2 - 24 \ln x + 24] + C.$$

33. Letting $p = 50$ gives $50 = \dfrac{250}{\sqrt{16 + x^2}}$, from which we deduce that

$\sqrt{16 + x^2} = 5$, $16 + x^2 = 25$, and $x = 3$. Using Formula 9 with $u = 3$, we see that

$$CS = \int_0^3 \frac{250}{\sqrt{16 + x^2}}\, dx = 50(3) = 250 \int_0^3 \frac{1}{\sqrt{16 + x^2}}\, dx - 150$$

$$= 250 \ln\left|x + \sqrt{16 + x^2}\right|\Big|_0^3 - 150 = 250[\ln 8 - \ln 4] - 150$$

$$= 23.286795, \text{ or approximately } \$2,329.$$

34. Letting $p = 50$ gives $50 = \dfrac{30x}{5 - x}$ or $5 = \dfrac{3x}{5 - x}$ or $25 - 5x = 3x$, and $x = \dfrac{25}{8} = 3.125$.

Using Formula 1 with $u = 5$ and $b = -1$, we have:

$$PS = (50)(3.125) - \int_0^{3.125} \frac{30x}{5 - x}\, dx = 156.25 - 30 \int_0^{3.125} \frac{x}{5 - x}\, dx$$

$$= 156.25 - 30\left[5 - x - 5 \ln|5 - x|\right]\Big|_0^{3.125}$$

$$= 156.25 - 30[(5 - 3.125 - 5 \ln 1.875) - 5 + 5 \ln 5] = 102.875,$$

or approximately $10,288.

35. The number of visitors admitted to the amusement park by noon is found by evaluating the integral

$$\int_0^3 \frac{60}{(2+t^2)^{3/2}}\,dt = 60\int_0^3 \frac{dt}{(2+t)^{3/2}}.$$

Using Formula 12 with $a = \sqrt{2}$ and $u = t$, we find

$$60\int_0^3 \frac{dt}{(2+t^2)^{3/2}} = 60\left[\frac{t}{2\sqrt{2+t^3}}\right]_0^3 = 60\left[\frac{3}{2\sqrt{11}-0}\right] = \frac{90}{\sqrt{11}} = 27.136, \text{ or } 27{,}136.$$

36. $N(5) - N(0) = \int_0^5 \frac{3000}{\sqrt{4+t^2}}\,dt = 3000\ln\left|t+\sqrt{4+t^2}\right|\Big|_0^5 = 3000[\ln(5+\sqrt{29})-\ln 2]$

$$= 4941.69.$$

Therefore, $N(5) = 4{,}942 + 20{,}000 = 24{,}942$

37. In the first 10 days

$$\frac{1}{10}\int_0^{10} \frac{1000}{1+24e^{-0.02t}}\,dt = 100\int_0^{10} \frac{1}{1+24e^{-0.02t}}\,dt = 100\left[t+\frac{1}{0.02}\ln(1+24e^{-0.02t})\right]_0^{10}$$

(Use Formula 25 with $a = 0.02$ and $b = 24$.)

$$= 100[10+50\ln 20.64953807 - 50\ln 25] = 44.0856,$$

or approximately 44 fruitflies. In the first 20 days:

$$\frac{1}{20}\int_0^{20} \frac{1000}{1+24e^{-0.02t}}\,dt = 50\int_0^{10} \frac{1}{1+24e^{-0.02t}}\,dt$$

$$= 500[t+\ln(1+24e^{-0.02t})]_0^{20}$$

$$= 50[20+50\ln 17.0876822 - 50\ln 25] = 48.71$$

or approximately 49 fruitflies.

38. The average percentage of households owning VCRs is given by

$$A = \frac{1}{12}\int_0^{12} \frac{68}{1+21.67e^{-0.62t}}\,dt = \frac{17}{3}\int_0^{12} \frac{dt}{1+21.67e^{-0.62t}}.$$

Using Formula 25 with $a = -0.62$, $b = 21.67$, and $u = x$, we find

$$A = \frac{17}{3}\left[t - \frac{1}{-0.62}\ln(1+21.67e^{-0.62t})\right]\Big|_0^{12}$$

$$= \frac{17}{3}\left\{\left[12 + \frac{1}{0.62}\ln(1+21.67e^{-7.44})\right] - \frac{1}{0.62}\ln(1+21.67)\right\}$$

$$= 39.59, \text{ or approximately 40 percent.}$$

39. $\displaystyle\frac{1}{5}\int_0^5 \frac{100,000}{2(1+1.5e^{-0.2t})}\,dt = 10,000\int_0^5 \frac{1}{1+1.5e^{-0.2t}}\,dt$

$$= 10,000[t + 5\ln(1+1.5e^{-0.2t})]\Big|_0^5$$

(Use Formula 25 with a = -0.2 and b = 1.5.)

$$= 10,000[5 + 5\ln 1.551819162 - 5\ln 2.5] \approx 26157,$$

or approximately 26,157 people.

40. $\displaystyle\int_0^{10}(250,000 + 2000t^2)e^{-0.1t}\,dt = -2,500,000e^{-0.1t}\Big|_0^{10} + 200\int_0^{10}t^2 e^{-0.1t}\,dt$

$$= 2,500,000(1-e^{-1}) + 2000\left[-10t^2 e^{-0.1t}\Big|_0^{10}\,\frac{2}{0.01}\int_0^{10}te^{-0.1t}\,dt\right]$$

(Using Formula 24 with a = -0.1 and n = 2 to evaluate the second integral.)

$$= 1580301.397 + 2000\{-1000e^{-1} + 200[100(-0.1t-1)e^{-0.1t}\Big|_0^{10}\}$$

$$= 1580301.397 + 2000\{-367.8794412 + (-200e^{-1} + 100)\} = \$1,901,510.$$

41. $\displaystyle\int_0^5 20,000te^{0.15t}\,dt = 20,000\int_0^5 te^{0.15t}\,dt = 20,000\left[\frac{1}{(0.15)^2}(0.15t-1)e^{0.15t}\right]\Big|_0^5$

(Use Formula 23 with a = 0.15.)

$$= 888,888.8889[-0.25e^{0.75} + 1] = \$418,444.$$

42. $\displaystyle L = 2\int_0^1 x - \frac{1}{3}x\sqrt{1+8x}\,dx = x^2\Big|_0^1 - \frac{2}{3}\int_0^1 x\sqrt{1+8x}\,dx$

$$= 1 - \frac{2}{3}\left(\frac{2}{15(64)}\right)(24x-2)(1+8x)^{3/2}\Big|_0^1$$

(Use Formula 4, with a = 1 and b = 8.)

$$= 1 - \frac{1}{720}[(22)(27) - (-2)] \approx 0.1722.$$

7.3 CONCEPT QUESTIONS, page 509

1. In the trapezoidal rule, each region under the graph of f (or over the graph of f) is approximated by the area of a trapezoid whose base consists of two consecutive points in the partition. Therefore, n can be odd or even. In Simpson's rule, the area of each subregion is approximated by part of a parabola passing through those points. Therefore, there are two subintervals involved in the approximations. This implies that n must be even.

2. In the trapezoidal rule, we are in effect approximating the function $f(x)$ on the interval $[x_0, x_1]$ by a *linear* function through the two points $(x_1, f(x_1))$ and $(x_2, f(x_2))$. If f is a linear function then there is no error because the approximation is exact. When we use Simpson's rule, we are in effect approximating the function $f(x)$ on the interval $[x_0, x_2]$ that passes through $(x_0, f(x_0)), (x_1, f(x_1))$, and $(x_2, f(x_2))$ by means of a quadratic function whose graph (a parabola) contains these three points. If the graph of $f(x)$ is a parabola, then the approximation is exact.

3. If we use the trapezoidal rule and f is a linear function, then $f''(x) = 0$, and therefore, $M = 0$, and consequently the maximum error is 0. If we use Simpson's rule, then $f^4(x) = 0$ and therefore, $M = 0$ and consequently the maximum error is 0.

EXERCISES 7.3, page 510

1. $\Delta x = \frac{2}{6} = \frac{1}{3}, x_0 = 0, x_1 = \frac{1}{3}, x_2 = \frac{2}{3}, x_3 = 1, x_4 = \frac{4}{3}, x_5 = \frac{5}{3}, x_6 = 2.$

   Trapezoidal Rule:

   $$\int_0^2 x^2 \, dx \approx \frac{1}{6}\left[0 + 2(\tfrac{1}{3})^2 + 2(\tfrac{2}{3})^2 + 2(1)^2 + 2(\tfrac{4}{3})^2 + 2(\tfrac{5}{3})^2 + 2^2\right]$$

   $\approx \frac{1}{6}$ (0.22222 + 0.88889 + 2 + 3.55556 + 5.55556 + 4) $\approx 2.7037.$

   Simpson's Rule:

   $$\int x^2 \, dx = \frac{1}{9}[0 + 4(\tfrac{1}{3})^2 + 2(\tfrac{2}{3})^2 + 4(1)^2 + 2(\tfrac{4}{3})^2 + 4(\tfrac{5}{3})^2 + 2^2]$$

   $\approx \frac{1}{9}$ (0.44444 + 0.88889 + 4 + 3.55556 + 11.11111 + 4) $\approx 2.6667.$

   Exact Value: $\int_0^2 x^2 \, dx = \frac{1}{3}x^3 \Big|_0^2 = \frac{8}{3} = 2\frac{2}{3}.$

2. $\Delta x = \frac{b-a}{n} = \frac{3-1}{4} = \frac{1}{2}; x_0 = 1, x_1 = \frac{3}{2}, x_2 = 2, x_3 = \frac{5}{2}, x_4 = 3.$

Trapezoidal Rule:

$$\int_1^3 (x^2 - 1)\, dx \approx \frac{1}{2} \cdot \frac{1}{2}\left\{\left[(1)^2 - 1\right] + 2\left[(\tfrac{3}{2})^2 - 1\right] + 2[2^2 - 1] + 2[(\tfrac{5}{2})^2 - 1] + [3^2 - 1]\right\} = 6.75.$$

Simpson's Rule:

$$\int_1^3 (x^2 - 1)\, dx \approx \frac{1}{2} \cdot \frac{1}{3}\left\{\left[(1)^2 - 1\right] + 4\left[(\tfrac{3}{2})^2 - 1\right] + 2[2^2 - 1] + 4[(\tfrac{5}{2})^2 - 1] + [3^2 - 1]\right\} = 6.67$$

The actual value is

$$\int_1^3 (x^2 - 1)\, dx = \tfrac{1}{3}x^3 - x\Big|_1^3 = (9 - 3) - (\tfrac{1}{3} - 1) = \tfrac{20}{3} = 6.66\ldots$$

3. $\Delta x = \frac{b-a}{n} = \frac{1-0}{4} = \frac{1}{4}; x_0 = 0, x_1 = \frac{1}{4}, x_2 = \frac{1}{2}, x_3 = \frac{3}{4}, x_4 = 1.$

Trapezoidal Rule:

$$\int_0^1 x^3\, dx \approx \frac{1}{4} \cdot \frac{1}{2}\left[0 + 2(\tfrac{1}{4})^3 + 2(\tfrac{1}{2})^3 + 2(\tfrac{3}{4})^3 + 1^3\right] \approx \frac{1}{8}(0 + 0.3125 + 0.25 + 0.8)$$

$$\approx 0.265625.$$

Simpson's Rule:

$$\int_0^1 x^3\, dx \approx \frac{1}{4} \cdot \frac{1}{3}\left[0 + 4(\tfrac{1}{4})^3 + 2(\tfrac{1}{2})^3 + 4(\tfrac{3}{4})^3 + 1\right] \approx \frac{1}{12}[0 + 0.625 + 0.25 + 1.6875 + 1]$$

$$\approx 0.25.$$

Exact Value: $\int_0^1 x^3\, dx = \frac{1}{4}x^4\Big|_0^1 = \frac{1}{4} - 0 = \frac{1}{4}$

4. $\Delta x = \frac{b-a}{n} = \frac{2-1}{6} = \frac{1}{6}; x_0 = 0, x_1 = \frac{7}{6}, x_2 = \frac{4}{3}, x_3 = \frac{3}{2}, x_4 = \frac{5}{3}, x_5 = \frac{11}{6}, x_6 = 2.$

Trapezoidal Rule:

$$\int_1^2 x^3\, dx \approx \frac{1}{6} \cdot \frac{1}{2}\left[1^3 + 2(\tfrac{7}{6})^3 + 2(\tfrac{4}{3})^3 + 2(\tfrac{3}{2})^3 + 2(\tfrac{5}{3})^3 + 2(\tfrac{11}{6})^3 + 2^3\right]$$

$$\approx \frac{1}{12}(1 + 3.17593 + 4.74074 + 6.75 + 9.25926 + 12.32407 + 8)$$

$$\approx 3.7708.$$

Simpson's Rule:

$$\int_1^2 x^3\, dx \approx \frac{1}{6} \cdot \frac{1}{3}\left[1^3 + 4(\tfrac{7}{6})^3 + 2(\tfrac{4}{3})^3 + 4(\tfrac{3}{2})^3 + 2(\tfrac{5}{3})^3 + 4(\tfrac{11}{6})^3 + 2^3\right]$$

$$\approx \frac{1}{18}(1 + 6.35185 + 4.74074 + 13.5 + 9.25926 + 24.64815 + 8)$$

$$\approx 3.7500.$$

Exact Value: $\int_1^2 x^3\, dx = \frac{1}{4}x^4\Big|_1^2 = \frac{1}{4}(16 - 1) = \frac{15}{4} = 3\tfrac{3}{4}.$

5   a. Here $a = 1$, $b = 2$, and $n = 4$; so $\Delta x = \frac{2-1}{4} = \frac{1}{4} = 0.25$, and $x_0 = 1$, $x_1 = 1.25$, $x_2 = 1.5$, $x_3 = 1.75$, $x_4 = 2$.

Trapezoidal Rule:

$$\int_1^2 \frac{1}{x}\,dx \approx \frac{0.25}{2}\left[1 + 2\left(\frac{1}{1.25}\right) + 2\left(\frac{1}{1.5}\right) + 2\left(\frac{1}{1.75}\right) + \frac{1}{2}\right] \approx 0.697.$$

Simpson's Rule:

$$\int_1^2 \frac{1}{x}\,dx \approx \frac{0.25}{3}\left[1 + 4\left(\frac{1}{1.25}\right) + 2\left(\frac{1}{1.5}\right) + 4\left(\frac{1}{1.75}\right) + \frac{1}{2}\right] \approx 0.6933.$$

$$\int_1^2 \frac{1}{x}\,dx = \ln x\Big|_1^2 = \ln 2 - \ln 1 \approx 0.6931.$$

6. $\Delta x = \frac{b-a}{n} = \frac{2-1}{8} = \frac{1}{8}; x_0 = 0, x_1 = \frac{9}{8}, x_2 = \frac{10}{8}, x_3 = \frac{11}{8}, \ldots, x_8 = \frac{16}{8}$.

Trapezoidal Rule:

$$\int_1^2 \frac{1}{x}\,dx \approx \frac{1}{2}\left[1 + 2(\tfrac{8}{9}) + 2(\tfrac{8}{10}) + 2(\tfrac{8}{11}) + \cdots + (\tfrac{8}{16})\right] \approx 0.69412.$$

Simpson's Rule:

$$\int_1^2 \frac{1}{x}\,dx \approx \frac{1}{3}\left[1 + 4(\tfrac{8}{9}) + 2(\tfrac{8}{10}) + 4(\tfrac{8}{11}) + \cdots + 4(\tfrac{8}{15}) + (\tfrac{8}{16})\right] \approx 0.69315.$$

The actual value is $\int_1^2 \frac{1}{x}\,dx = \ln x\Big|_1^2 = \ln 2 \approx 0.69315$.

7. $\Delta x = \frac{1}{4}$, $x_0 = 1$, $x_1 = \frac{5}{4}$, $x_2 = \frac{3}{2}$, $x_3 = \frac{7}{4}$, $x_4 = 2$.

Trapezoidal Rule:

$$\int_1^2 \frac{1}{x^2}\,dx \approx \frac{1}{8}\left[1 + 2(\tfrac{4}{5})^2 + 2(\tfrac{2}{3})^2 + 2(\tfrac{4}{7})^2 + (\tfrac{1}{2})^2\right] \approx 0.5090.$$

Simpson's Rule:

$$\int_1^2 \frac{1}{x^2}\,dx \approx \frac{1}{12}\left[1 + 4(\tfrac{4}{5})^2 + 2(\tfrac{2}{3})^2 + 4(\tfrac{4}{7})^2 + (\tfrac{1}{2})^2\right] \approx 0.5004.$$

Exact Value: $\int_1^2 \frac{1}{x^2}\,dx = -\frac{1}{x}\Big|_1^2 = -\frac{1}{2} + 1 = \frac{1}{2}$.

8. $\Delta x = \frac{b-a}{n} = \frac{1-0}{4} = \frac{1}{4}; x_0 = 0, x_1 = \frac{1}{4}, x_2 = \frac{2}{4}, x_3 = \frac{3}{4}, x_4 = \frac{4}{4}.$

Trapezoidal Rule:

$$\int_0^1 \frac{1}{1+x} dx \approx \frac{\frac{1}{4}}{2}\left[0 + 2\left(\frac{1}{1+\frac{1}{4}}\right) + 2\left(\frac{1}{1+\frac{1}{2}}\right) + 2\left(\frac{1}{1+\frac{3}{4}}\right) + \left(\frac{1}{1+1}\right)\right] \approx 0.57202.$$

Simpson's Rule:

$$\int_0^1 \frac{1}{1+x} dx \approx \frac{\frac{1}{4}}{3}\left[0 + 4\left(\frac{1}{1+\frac{1}{4}}\right) + 2\left(\frac{1}{1+\frac{1}{2}}\right) + 4\left(\frac{1}{1+\frac{3}{4}}\right) + \left(\frac{1}{1+1}\right)\right] \approx 0.60992.$$

The actual value is

$$\int_0^1 \frac{1}{1+x} dx = \ln(1+x)\Big|_0^1 = \ln 2 \approx 0.69315.$$

9. $\Delta x = \frac{b-a}{n} = \frac{4-0}{8} = \frac{1}{2}; x_0 = 0, x_1 = \frac{1}{2}, x_2 = \frac{2}{2}, x_3 = \frac{3}{2}, \ldots, x_8 = \frac{8}{2}.$

Trapezoidal Rule:

$$\int_0^4 \sqrt{x}\, dx \approx \frac{\frac{1}{2}}{2}\left[0 + 2\sqrt{0.5} + 2\sqrt{1} + 2\sqrt{1.5} + \cdots + 2\sqrt{3.5} + \sqrt{4}\right] \approx 5.26504.$$

Simpson's Rule:

$$\int_0^4 \sqrt{x}\, dx \approx \frac{\frac{1}{2}}{3}\left[0 + 4\sqrt{0.5} + 2\sqrt{1} + 4\sqrt{1.5} + \cdots + 4\sqrt{3.5} + \sqrt{4}\right] \approx 5.30463.$$

The actual value is $\int_0^4 \sqrt{x}\, dx \approx \frac{2}{3}x^{3/2}\Big|_0^4 = \frac{2}{3}(8) = \frac{16}{3} \approx 5.333333.$

10. $\Delta x = \frac{2}{6} = \frac{1}{3}; x_0 = 0, x_1 = \frac{1}{3}, x_2 = \frac{2}{3}, x_3 = 1, x_4 = \frac{4}{3}, x_5 = \frac{5}{3}, x_6 = 2.$

Trapezoidal Rule:

$$\int_0^2 x(2x^2+1)^{1/2}\, dx$$

$$\approx \frac{1}{6}\Big[0 + 2(\tfrac{1}{3})[2(\tfrac{1}{3})^2+1]^{1/2} + 2(\tfrac{2}{3})[2(\tfrac{2}{3})^2+1]^{1/2} + 2(1)[2(1)^2+1]^{1/2}$$

$$+ 2(\tfrac{4}{3})[2(\tfrac{4}{3})^2+1]^{1/2} + 2(\tfrac{5}{3})[2(\tfrac{5}{3})^2+1]^{1/2} + 2[2(2)^2+1]^{1/2}$$

$$\approx 4.3767.$$

Simpson's Rule:

$$\int_0^2 x(2x^2+1)^{1/2}\, dx$$

$$\approx \frac{1}{9}\Big[0 + 4(\tfrac{1}{3})[2(\tfrac{1}{3})^2+1]^{1/2} + 2(\tfrac{2}{3})[2(\tfrac{2}{3})^2+1]^{1/2}$$

$$+ 4(1)[2(1)^2+1]^{1/2} + 2(\tfrac{4}{3})[2(\tfrac{4}{3})^2+1]^{1/2} + 4(\tfrac{5}{3})[2(\tfrac{5}{3})^2+1]^{1/2} + 2[2(2)^2+1]^{1/2}$$

$$\approx 4.3329$$

7 Additional Topics in Integration

Exact Value:

$$\int_0^2 x(2x^2+1)^{1/2}\,dx = (\tfrac{1}{4})(\tfrac{2}{3})(2x^2+1)^{3/2}\Big|_0^2 = \tfrac{1}{6}(9^{3/2}-1) = \tfrac{26}{6} = \tfrac{13}{3} = 4\tfrac{1}{3}.$$

11. $\Delta x = \tfrac{1-0}{6} = \tfrac{1}{6}; x_0 = 0, x_1 = \tfrac{1}{6}, x_2 = \tfrac{2}{6}, \ldots, x_6 = \tfrac{6}{6}.$

Trapezoidal Rule:

$$\int_0^1 e^{-x}\,dx \approx \tfrac{1}{6}{}{}\Big[1+2e^{-1/6}+2e^{-2/6}+\cdots+2e^{-5/6}+e^{-1}\Big] \approx 0.633583.$$

Simpson's Rule:

$$\int_0^1 e^{-x}\,dx \approx \tfrac{1}{3}{}{}\Big[1+4e^{-1/6}+2e^{-2/6}+\cdots+4e^{-5/6}+e^{-1}\Big] \approx 0.632123.$$

The actual value is $\displaystyle\int_0^1 e^{-x}\,dx = -e^{-x}\Big|_0^1 = -e^{-1}+1 \approx 0.632121.$

12. $\Delta x = \tfrac{1-0}{6} = \tfrac{1}{6}; x_0 = 0, x_1 = \tfrac{1}{6}, x_2 = \tfrac{2}{6}, \ldots, x_6 = \tfrac{6}{6}.$

Trapezoidal Rule:

$$\int_0^1 xe^{-x^2}\,dx \approx \tfrac{\frac{1}{6}}{2}\Big[0+2\cdot\tfrac{1}{6}e^{-(1/6)^2}+2\cdot\tfrac{2}{6}e^{-(2/6)^2}+\cdots+2\cdot\tfrac{5}{6}e^{-(5/6)^2}+e^{-1}\Big] = 0.3129.$$

Simpson's Rule:

$$\int_0^1 xe^{-x^2}\,dx \approx \tfrac{\frac{1}{6}}{3}\Big[0+4\cdot\tfrac{1}{6}e^{-(1/6)^2}+2\cdot\tfrac{2}{6}e^{-(2/6)^2}+\cdots+4\cdot\tfrac{5}{6}e^{-(5/6)^2}+e^{-1}\Big] = 0.3161.$$

The actual value is

$$\int_0^1 xe^{-x^2}\,dx = -\tfrac{1}{2}e^{-x^2}\Big|_0^1 = -\tfrac{1}{2}(e^{-1}-1) \approx 0.316060.$$

13. $\Delta x = \tfrac{1}{4}; x_0 = 0, x_1 = \tfrac{5}{4}, x_2 = \tfrac{3}{2}, x_3 = \tfrac{7}{4}, x_4 = 2.$

Trapezoidal Rule:

$$\int_1^2 \ln x\,dx \approx \tfrac{1}{8}[\ln 1 + 2\ln\tfrac{5}{4} + 2\ln\tfrac{3}{2} + 2\ln\tfrac{7}{4} + \ln 2] \approx 0.38370.$$

Simpson's Rule:

$$\int_1^2 \ln x\,dx \approx \tfrac{1}{12}[\ln 1 + 4\ln\tfrac{5}{4} + 2\ln\tfrac{3}{2} + 4\ln\tfrac{7}{4} + \ln 2] \approx 0.38626.$$

Exact Value: $\displaystyle\int_1^2 \ln x\,dx \approx x(\ln x - 1)\Big|_1^2 = 2(\ln 2 - 1) + 1 = 2\ln 2 - 1 \approx 0.3863.$

14. $\Delta x = \tfrac{1-0}{8} = \tfrac{1}{8}; x_0 = 0, x_1 = \tfrac{1}{8}, x_2 = \tfrac{2}{8}, \ldots, x_8 = \tfrac{8}{8}.$

Trapezoidal Rule:

$$\int_0^1 x\ln(x^2+1)\,dx$$

$$\approx \tfrac{1}{2}\Big[0 + 2\cdot\tfrac{1}{8}\ln[(\tfrac{1}{8})^2 + 1] + 2\cdot\tfrac{2}{8}\ln[(\tfrac{2}{8})^2 + 1] + \cdots + 2\cdot\tfrac{7}{8}\ln[(\tfrac{7}{8})^2 + 1] + \ln 2\Big]$$

$$\approx 0.1954.$$

Simpson's Rule:

$$\int_0^1 x\ln(x^2 + 1)\,dx$$

$$\approx \tfrac{1}{3}\Big[0 + 4\cdot\tfrac{1}{8}\ln[(\tfrac{1}{8})^2 + 1] + 2\cdot\tfrac{2}{8}\ln[(\tfrac{2}{8})^2 + 1] + \cdots + 4\cdot\tfrac{7}{8}\ln[(\tfrac{7}{8})^2 + 1] + \ln 2\Big] \approx 0.1931.$$

To find the actual value, let $u = x^2 + 1$ so that $du = 2x\,dx$ or $x\,dx = \tfrac{1}{2}\,du$. Also, if $x = 0$, $u = 1$ and if $x = 1$, $u = 2$. So

$$\int_0^1 x\ln(x^2 + 1)\,dx = \tfrac{1}{2}\int_1^2 \ln u\,du = \tfrac{1}{2}u(\ln u - 1)\Big|_1^2 = \tfrac{1}{2}(2)(\ln 2 - 1) - \tfrac{1}{2}(-1) \approx 0.193147.$$

(See Problem 21, Exercises 7 1)

15. $\Delta x = \tfrac{1-0}{4} = \tfrac{1}{4}; x_0 = 0, x_1 = \tfrac{1}{4}, x_2 = \tfrac{2}{4}, x_3 = \tfrac{3}{4}, x_4 = \tfrac{4}{4}.$

Trapezoidal Rule:

$$\int_0^1 \sqrt{1+x^3}\,dx \approx \tfrac{1}{2}\cdot\tfrac{1}{4}\Big[\sqrt{1} + 2\sqrt{1+(\tfrac{1}{4})^3} + \cdots + 2\sqrt{1+(\tfrac{3}{4})^3} + \sqrt{2}\Big] \approx 1.1170.$$

Simpson's Rule:

$$\int_0^1 \sqrt{1+x^3}\,dx \approx \tfrac{1}{3}\cdot\tfrac{1}{4}\Big[\sqrt{1} + 4\sqrt{1+(\tfrac{1}{4})^3} + 2\sqrt{1+(\tfrac{2}{4})^3} \cdots + 4\sqrt{1+(\tfrac{3}{4})^3} + \sqrt{2}\Big] \approx 1.1114.$$

16. $\Delta x = \tfrac{2}{4} = \tfrac{1}{2}; x_0 = 0, x_1 = \tfrac{1}{2}, x_2 = 1, x_3 = \tfrac{3}{2}, x_4 = 2.$

Trapezoidal Rule:

$$\int_0^2 x(1+x^3)^{1/2}\,dx$$

$$\approx \tfrac{1}{4}\Big\{0 + 2(\tfrac{1}{2})[1+(\tfrac{1}{2})^3]^{1/2} + 2(1)(1+1^3)^{1/2} + 2(\tfrac{3}{2})[1+(\tfrac{3}{2})^3]^{1/2} + 2(1+2^3)^{1/2}\Big\}$$

$$\approx 4.0410.$$

Simpson's Rule:

$$\int_0^2 x(1+x^3)^{1/2}\,dx$$

$$\approx \tfrac{1}{6}\Big\{0 + 4(\tfrac{1}{2})[1+(\tfrac{1}{2})^3]^{1/2} + 2(1)(1+1^3)^{1/2} + 4(\tfrac{3}{2})[1+(\tfrac{3}{2})^3]^{1/2} + 2(1+2^3)^{1/2}\Big\}$$

$$\approx 3.9166.$$

17. $\Delta x = \tfrac{2-0}{4} = \tfrac{1}{2}; x_0 = 0, x_1 = \tfrac{1}{2}, x_2 = \tfrac{2}{2}, x_3 = \tfrac{3}{2}, x_4 = \tfrac{4}{2}.$

Trapezoidal Rule:

$$\int_0^2 \frac{1}{\sqrt{x^3+1}}\,dx = \frac{\frac{1}{2}}{2}\left[1 + \frac{2}{\sqrt{(\frac{1}{2})^3+1}} + \frac{2}{\sqrt{(1)^3+1}} + \frac{2}{\sqrt{(\frac{3}{2})^3+1}} + \frac{1}{\sqrt{(2)^3+1}}\right]$$

$$\approx 1.3973$$

Simpson's Rule:

$$\int_0^2 \frac{1}{\sqrt{x^3+1}}\,dx = \frac{\frac{1}{2}}{3}\left[1 + \frac{4}{\sqrt{(\frac{1}{2})^3+1}} + \frac{2}{\sqrt{(1)^3+1}} + \frac{4}{\sqrt{(\frac{3}{2})^3+1}} + \frac{1}{\sqrt{(2)^3+1}}\right]$$

$$\approx 1.4052$$

18.   a. Here $a = 0$, $b = 1$ and $n = 4$ so that
$$\Delta x = \frac{1}{4} = 0.25; x_0 = 0, x_1 = 0.25, x_2 = 0.5, x_3 = 0.75, x_4 = 1.$$
Trapezoidal Rule:
$$\int_0^1 (1-x^2)^{1/2}\,dx \approx \frac{0.25}{2}\left\{1 + 2[1-(0.25)^2]^{1/2} + 2(1-(0.5)^2]^{1/2} + 2[1-(0.75)^2]^{1/2} + 0\right\}$$
$$\approx 0.7489.$$
Simpson's Rule:
$$\int_0^1 (1-x^2)^{1/2}\,dx$$
$$\approx \frac{0.25}{2}\left\{1 + 4[1-(0.25)^2]^{1/2} + 2(1-(0.5)^2]^{1/2} + 4[1-(0.75)^2]^{1/2} + 0\right\} \approx 0.7709.$$

19. $\Delta x = \frac{2}{4} = \frac{1}{2}; x_0 = 0, x_1 = \frac{1}{2}, x_2 = 1, x_3 = \frac{3}{2}, x_4 = 2.$
Trapezoidal Rule:
$$\int_0^2 e^{-x^2}\,dx = \frac{1}{4}[e^{-0} + 2e^{-(1/2)^2} + 2e^{-1} + 2e^{-(3/2)^2} + e^{-4}] \approx 0.8806.$$
Simpson's Rule:
$$\int_0^2 e^{-x^2}\,dx = \frac{1}{6}[e^{-0} + 4e^{-(1/2)^2} + 2e^{-1} + 4e^{-(3/2)^2} + e^{-4}] \approx 0.8818.$$

20. $\Delta x = \frac{1-0}{6} = \frac{1}{6}; x_0 = 0, x_1 = \frac{1}{6}, x_2 = \frac{2}{6}, \ldots, x_6 = \frac{6}{6}$
Trapezoidal Rule:
$$\int_0^1 e^{x^2}\,dx = \frac{\frac{1}{6}}{2}\left[1 + 2e^{(1/6)^2} + 2e^{(2/6)^2} + \cdots + 2e^{(5/6)^2} + e^1\right] \approx 1.4752.$$

Simpson's Rule:

$$\int e^{x^2}\,dx = \tfrac{1}{3}[1+4e^{(1/6)^2}+2e^{(2/6)^2}+\cdots+4e^{(5/6)^2}+e^1] \approx 1.4629$$

21. $\Delta x = \frac{2-1}{4} = \frac{1}{4}; x_0 = 1,\ x_1 = \frac{5}{4},\ x_2 = \frac{6}{4},\ x_3 = \frac{7}{4},\ x_4 = \frac{8}{4}.$

Trapezoidal Rule:

$$\int_1^2 x^{-1/2}e^x\,dx = \tfrac{1}{2}\left[e + \frac{2e^{5/4}}{\sqrt{\frac{5}{4}}} + \cdots + \frac{2e^{7/4}}{\sqrt{\frac{7}{4}}} + \frac{e^2}{\sqrt{2}}\right] \approx 3.7757.$$

Simpson's Rule:

$$\int_1^2 x^{-1/2}e^x\,dx = \tfrac{1}{3}\left[e + \frac{4e^{5/4}}{\sqrt{\frac{5}{4}}} + \cdots + \frac{4e^{7/4}}{\sqrt{\frac{7}{4}}} + \frac{e^2}{\sqrt{2}}\right] \approx 3.7625.$$

22. $\Delta x = \frac{2}{6} = \frac{1}{3}; x_0 = 2,\ x_1 = \frac{7}{3},\ x_2 = \frac{8}{3},\ x_3 = 3,\ x_4 = \frac{10}{3},\ x_5 = \frac{11}{3},\ x_6 = 4.$

Trapezoidal Rule:

$$\int_2^4 \frac{dx}{\ln x} \approx \frac{1}{6}\left[\frac{1}{\ln 2} + \frac{2}{\ln \frac{7}{3}} + \frac{2}{\ln \frac{8}{3}} + \frac{2}{\ln 3} + \frac{2}{\ln \frac{10}{3}} + \frac{2}{\ln \frac{11}{3}} + \frac{1}{\ln 4}\right] \approx 1.9308.$$

Simpson's Rule:

$$\int_2^4 \frac{dx}{\ln x} \approx \frac{1}{9}\left[\frac{1}{\ln 2} + \frac{4}{\ln \frac{7}{3}} + \frac{2}{\ln \frac{8}{3}} + \frac{4}{\ln 3} + \frac{2}{\ln \frac{10}{3}} + \frac{4}{\ln \frac{11}{3}} + \frac{1}{\ln 4}\right] \approx 1.9228.$$

23 a. Here $a = -1$, $b = 2$, $n = 10$, and $f(x) = x^5$. $f'(x) = 5x^4$ and $f''(x) = 20x^3$. Because $f'''(x) = 60x^2 > 0$ on $(-1,0) \cup (0,2)$, we see that $f''(x)$ is increasing on $(-1,0) \cup (0,2)$. So, we take $M = f''(2) = 20(2^3) = 160$. Using (7), we see that the maximum error incurred is

$$\frac{M(b-a)^3}{12n^2} = \frac{160[2-(-1)]^3}{12(100)} = 3.6.$$

b. We compute $f''' = 60x^2$ and $f^{(iv)}(x) = 120x$. $f^{(iv)}(x)$ is clearly increasing on $(-1,2)$, so we can take $M = f^{(iv)}(2) = 240$. Therefore, using (8), we see that an

error bound is $\dfrac{M(b-a)^3}{180n^4} = \dfrac{240(3)^5}{180(10^4)} \approx 0.0324$.

24. a. Here $a = 0$, $b = 1$, $n = 8$, and $f(x) = e^{-x}$. We find $f'(x) = -e^{-x}$, $f''(x) = e^{-x}$.

Since f'' is positive and decreasing, the maximum of $f''(x)$ occurs at the left-end point of the interval $[0,1]$, so $|f''(x)| \leq 1$. Therefore the maximum error is

$$\frac{1(2-1)^3}{12(8)^2} = \frac{1}{768} = 0.0013021.$$

b. $f'''(x) = -e^{-x}, f^4(x) = e^{-x}$ The maximum error is

$$\frac{1(2-1)^5}{180(8)^4} = \frac{1}{737280} = 0.000001356.$$

25 a. Here $a = 1$, $b = 3$, $n = 10$, and $f(x) = \frac{1}{x}$ We find $f'(x) = -\frac{1}{x^2}$, $f'''(x) = \frac{2}{x^3}$.

Since $f'''(x) = -\frac{6}{x^4} < 0$ on $(1,3)$, we see that $f''(x)$ is decreasing there. We may take $M = f''(1) = 2$. Using (7), we find an error bound is

$$\frac{M(b-a)^3}{12n^2} = \frac{2(3-1)^3}{12(100)} \approx 0.013.$$

b. $f'''(x) = -\frac{6}{x^4}$ and $f^{(iv)}(x) = \frac{24}{x^5}$. $f^{(iv)}(x)$ is decreasing on $(1,3)$, so we can

take $M = f^{(iv)}(1) = 24$. Using (8), we find an error bound is $\frac{24(3-1)^5}{180(10^4)} \approx 0.00043$.

26. a. Here $a = 1$, $b = 3$, $n = 8$, and $f(x) = x^2$. We find $f'(x) = -2x^{-3}$ and $f''(x) = 6x^{-4}$. Since f'' is positive and decreasing on $(1,3)$, we have

$|f''(x)| \leq 6$. So the maximum error is $\frac{6(3-1)^3}{12(8)^2} = \frac{48}{768} = 0.0625.$

b. $f'''(x) = -24x^{-5}$ and $f^{(4)}(x) = 120x^{-6}$. Since $f^{(4)}$ is positive and decreasing on $(1,3)$, we have $|f^{(4)}(x)| \leq 120$. So, the maximum error is

$$\frac{120(3-1)^5}{180(8)^4} = \frac{3840}{737280} = 0.00521.$$

27 a. Here $a = 0$, $b = 2$, $n = 8$, and $f(x) = (1+x)^{-1/2}$. We find
$$f'(x) = -\frac{1}{2}(1+x)^{-3/2}, f''(x) = \frac{3}{4}(1+x)^{-5/2}.$$
Since f'' is positive and decreasing on $(0,2)$, we see that $|f''(x)| \leq \frac{3}{4}$.

So the maximum error is $\dfrac{\frac{3}{4}(2-0)^3}{12(8)^2} = 0.0078125.$

b. $f''' = -\frac{15x}{8}(1+x)^{-7/2}$ and $f^{(4)}(x) = \dfrac{105}{16}(1+x)^{-9/2}$. Since $f^{(4)}$ is positive

and decreasing on $(0,2)$, we find $\left|f^{(4)}(x)\right| \le \frac{105}{16}$

Therefore, the maximum error is $\dfrac{\frac{105}{16}(2-0)^5}{180(8)^4} = 0.000285.$

28. a. Here $a = 1$, $b = 3$, $n = 10$, and $f(x) = \ln x$. We find

$f'(x) = \dfrac{1}{x}$ and $f''(x) = -\dfrac{1}{x^2}$. Since f'' is negative and increasing on $(1,3)$, we

see that $\left|f''(x)\right| \le \left|-1\right| = 1$. So the maximum error is $\dfrac{1(3-1)^3}{12(10)^2} = 0.0067.$

b. $f'''(x) = 2x^{-3}$ and $f^{(4)}(x) = -6x^{-4}$. ince $f^{(4)}$ is negative and increasing on

$(1,3)$, we see that $\left|f^{(4)}(x)\right| \le 6$. So the maximum error is $\dfrac{6(3-1)^5}{180(10)^4} = 0.000107.$

29. The distance covered is given by

$d = \int_0^2 V(t)\,dt = \frac{\frac{1}{4}}{2}\left[V(0) + 2V(\frac{1}{4}) + \cdots + 2V(\frac{7}{4}) + V(2)\right]$

$= \frac{1}{8}[19.5 + 2(24.3) + 2(34.2) + 2(40.5) + 2(38.4) + 2(26.2)$

$+ 2(18) + 2(16) + 8] \approx 52.84$, or 52.84 miles.

30. $A = \dfrac{1000}{10} \cdot \dfrac{1}{3}[1000 + 4(900) + 2(1000) + 4(1000) + 2(1200) + 4(1400) + 2(1100)$

$+ 4(1100) + 2(1000) + 4(1200) + 1400]$

$= \frac{100}{3}(33,400) = 1,113,333\frac{1}{3}.$

31. $\dfrac{1}{13}\int_0^{13} f(t)\,dt = (\frac{1}{13})(\frac{1}{2})\{13.2 + 2[14.8 + 16.6 + 17.2 + 18.7 + 19.3 + 22.6 + 24.2 + 25$

$+ 24.6 + 25.6 + 26.4 + 26.6] + 26.6\} \approx 21.65$, or 21.65 mpg.

32. Trapezoidal Rule:

$A = \frac{1}{30}\int_0^{30} f(x)\,dx \approx (\frac{3}{2})(\frac{1}{30})[66 + 2(68 + 72 + 72 + 70 + 64 + 60 + 62 + 62 + 56) + 60]$

$\approx 64.9°\,F$

7   *Additional Topics in Integration*

Simpson's Rule:

$$AT = \tfrac{1}{30}\int_0^{30} f(t)\,dt \approx (\tfrac{1}{30})(\tfrac{3}{3})[66 + 4(68) + 2(72) + 4(72) + 2(70) + 4(64)$$
$$+ 2(60) + 4(62) + 2(62) + 4(56) + 60]$$

$$\approx 64.73\,^\circ F.$$

33 The average daily consumption of oil is

$$A = \frac{1}{b-1}\int_a^b f(t)\,dt$$

where $f(t)$ has the values shown in the table where $t = 0$ corresponds to 1980.
Using Simpson's Rule with $n = 10$ and $\Delta t = 2$

$$A = \frac{1}{20-0}\int_0^{20} f(t)\,dt \approx \frac{1}{20}\cdot\frac{2}{3}[f(0) + 4f(2) + 2f(4) + 4f(6) + \cdots + 4f(18) + f(20)]$$

$$= \frac{1}{30}[17\ 1 + 4(15.3) + 2(15.7) + 4(16.3) + 2(17.3) + 4(17) + 2(17) + 4(17.7)$$

$$+ 2(18.3) + 4(18.9) + 19.7]$$

$$= 17.14, \qquad \text{or 17.14 million barrels.}$$

34. The required area is

$$A \approx \frac{206}{3}[4(1030) + 291349) + 4(1498) + 2(1817) + 4(1910)$$

$$+ 2(1985) + 4(2304) + 2(2585) + 4(2323) + 1592]$$

$$= 3{,}661580, \text{ or approximately } 3{,}661{,}580 \text{ sq ft.}$$

35. The required rate of flow is

$$R = (\text{area of cross section of the river}) \times \text{rate of flow}$$
$$= (4)(\text{area of cross section})$$
$$= 4\int_0^{78} y(x)\,dx$$

Approximating the integral using the trapezoidal rule,

$$R \approx (4)(\tfrac{6}{2})[0.8 + 2(2.6) + 2(5.8) + 2(6.2) + 2(7.6) + 2(6.4) + 2(5.2) + 2(3.9)$$

$$+ 2(8.2) + 2(10.1) + 2(10.8) + 2(9.8) + 2(2.4) + 1.4]$$

$$= 1922.4$$

or 1922.4 cu ft/sec.

36. Solving the equation $25 = \dfrac{50}{0.01x^2 + 1}$, we see that $0.01x^2 + 1 = 2$, $0.01x^2 = 1$, and

$x = 10$. Therefore, $CS = \displaystyle\int_0^{10} \dfrac{50}{0.01x^2 + 1}\, dx - (25)(10)$ and $\Delta x = \dfrac{10}{8} = 1.25$, $x_0 = 0$,

$x_1 = 1.25$, $x_2 = 2.50$, ..., $x_8 = 10$.

a. $CS = \dfrac{1.25}{2}\left\{ 50 + 2\left[\dfrac{50}{0.01(1.25)^2 + 1}\right] + \cdots + \left[\dfrac{50}{0.01(10)^2 + 1}\right]\right\} - 250$

   $\approx 142{,}373.56$, or $\$142{,}373.56$.

b. $CS = \dfrac{1.25}{3}\left\{ 50 + 4\left[\dfrac{50}{0.01(1.25)^2 + 1}\right] + \cdots + \left[\dfrac{50}{0.01(10)^2 + 1}\right]\right\} - 250$

   $\approx 142{,}698.12$, or $\$142{,}698.12$.

37. We solve the equation $8 = \sqrt{0.01x^2 + 0.11x + 38}$.
$64 = 0.01x^2 + 0.11x + 38$, $0.01x^2 + 0.11x - 26 = 0$, $x^2 + 11x - 2600 = 0$,

and $x = \dfrac{-11 \pm \sqrt{121 + 10{,}400}}{2} \approx 45.786$. Therefore

$PS = (8)(45.786) - \displaystyle\int_0^{45.786} \sqrt{0.01x^2 + 0.11x + 38}\, dx.$

a. $\Delta x = \dfrac{45.786}{8} = 5.72$; $x_0 = 0$, $x_1 = 5.72$, $x_2 = 11.44$, ..., $x_8 = 45.79$

$PS = 366.288 - \dfrac{5.72}{2}\Big[\sqrt{38} + 2\sqrt{0.01(5.72)^2 + 0.11(5.72) + 38} + \cdots$

$+ \sqrt{0.01(45.79)^2 + 0.11(45.79) + 38}\,\Big] \qquad \approx 51{,}558$, or $\$51{,}558$.

$PS = 366.288 - \dfrac{5.72}{2}\Big[\sqrt{38} + 4\sqrt{0.01(5.72)^2 + 0.11(5.72) + 38} + \cdots$

$+ \sqrt{0.01(45.79)^2 + 0.11(45.79) + 38}\,\Big] \qquad \approx 51{,}708$, or $\$51{,}708$.

38. $\Delta t = \dfrac{5}{10} = 0.5$, $t_0 = 0$, $t_1 = 0.5$, $t_2 = 1$, ..., $t_{10} = 5$.

$PSI = \dfrac{1}{5}\displaystyle\int_0^5 \left[\dfrac{136}{1 + 0.25(t - 4.5)^2} + 28\right] dt = 27.2\displaystyle\int_0^5 \dfrac{1}{1 + 0.25(t - 4.5)^2}\, dt + \displaystyle\int_0^5 \dfrac{28}{5}\, dt$

$\approx \dfrac{(0.5)(27.2)}{2}\left[\dfrac{1}{1 + 0.25(-4.5)^2} + \dfrac{2}{1 + 0.25(0.5 - 4.5)^2} + \cdots + \dfrac{1}{1 + 0.25(5 - 4.5)^2}\right] + 28$

≈ 103.9

7 *Additional Topics in Integration*

39. The average petroleum reserves from 1981 through 1990 were
$$A = \frac{1}{9-0} \int_0^9 S(t)\,dt = \frac{1}{9} \int_0^9 \frac{613.7t^2 + 1449.1}{t^2 + 6.3}\,dt$$
Using the trapezoidal rule with $a = 0$, $b = 9$, and $n = 9$ so that $\Delta t = (9-0)/9 = 1$, we have $t_0 = 0$, $t = 1, ..., t_9 = 9$ so that
$$A = \frac{1}{9} \int_0^9 S(t)\,dt = \left(\frac{1}{9}\right)\left(\frac{1}{2}\right)[S(0) + 2S(1) + 2f(x) + 2f(x) + \cdots$$

$$\approx \frac{1}{18}[130.02 + 2(282.58) + 2(379.02) + 2(455.71) + 2(505.30) + 2(536.47)$$

$$+ 2(556.56) + 2(569.99) + 2(579.32) + 586.01]$$

$$\approx 474.77$$

or approximately 474.77 million barrels.

40. The percentage of the nonfarm work force in a certain country, will continue to grow at the rate of $A = 30 + \int_0^1 5e^{1/(t+1)}\,dt$ percent, t decades from now.
$$\Delta t = \tfrac{1}{10} = 0.1, \quad t_0 = 0, \ t_1 = 0.1, \ ..., \ t_{10} = 1.$$
Using Simpson's Rule we have
$$A = 30 + \tfrac{1}{3}(5e^1 + 4 \cdot 5e^{1/1.1} + 2 \cdot 5e^{1/1.2} + 4 \cdot 5e^{1/1.3} + \cdots + 4 \cdot 5e^{1/1.9} + 5e^{1/2})$$
$$= 40.1004, \quad \text{or approximately 40.1 percent.}$$

41. $\Delta x = \frac{40,000-30,000}{10} = 1000;$ $x_0 = 30,000$, $x_1 = 31,000$, $x_2, \ ..., \ x_{10} = 40,000$.
$$P = \frac{100}{2000\sqrt{2\pi}} \int_{30,000}^{40,000} e^{-0.5[x-40,000)/[2000]^2}\,dx$$
$$P = \frac{100(1000)}{2000\sqrt{2\pi}} \left[e^{-0.5[30,000-40,000)/[2000]^2} + 4e^{-0.5[(31,000-40,000)/2000]^2} + \cdots +1] \right]$$
$$\approx 50, \text{ or 50 percent.}$$

42. $\Delta x = \frac{21-19}{10} = 0.2;$ $x_0 = 19$, $x_1 = 19.2$ $x_2 = 19.4, \ ..., \ x_{10} = 21$
$$P = \frac{100}{2.6\sqrt{2\pi}} \int_{19}^{21} e^{-0.5[(x-20)/2.6]^2}\,dx$$
$$\approx \frac{100}{2.6\sqrt{2\pi}} \left(\frac{0.2}{3}\right)[e^{-0.5[(19-20)/2.6]^2} + 4e^{-0.5[19.2-20)/2.6]^2} + \cdots + e^{-0.5[(21-20)/2.6]^2}]$$
$$\approx 29.94, \text{ or 30 percent.}$$

43. $R = \dfrac{60D}{\displaystyle\int_0^T C(t)\,dt} = \dfrac{480}{\displaystyle\int_0^{24} C(t)\,dt}$. Now,

$\displaystyle\int_0^{24} C(t)\,dt \approx \tfrac{24}{12}\cdot\tfrac{1}{3}[0 + 4(0) + 2(2.8) + 4(6.1) + 2(9.7) + 4(7.6) + 2(4.8)$

$\qquad\qquad + 4(3.7) + 2(1.9) + 4(0.8) + 2(0.3) + 4(0.1) + 0] \approx 74.8$

and $R = \tfrac{480}{74.8} \approx 6.42$, or 6.42 liters/min.

44. The required rate of flow

$\quad R = (4.2)\,(\text{area of cross section})$

$\quad \approx (4.2)(\tfrac{6}{3})[0.8 + 4(1.2) + 2(3) + 4(4.1) + 2(5.8) + 4(6.6) + 2(6.8) + 4(7)$

$\qquad\qquad + 2(7.2) + 4(7.4) + 2(7.8) + 4(7.6) + 2(7.4) + 4(7) + 2(6.6)$

$\qquad\qquad + 4(6) + 2(5.1) + 4(4.3) + 2(3.2) + 4(2.2) + 1.1]$

$\quad = 2698.92 \;(\text{million gal/sec}).$

45. False. The number n can be odd or even.

46. False. The number n in Simpson's Rule must be even.

47. True.

48. True. Using Formula 8, we see that the error incurred in the approximation is zero since, in this situation $f^{(4)}(x) = 0$ for all x in $[a, b]$.

49 Taking the limit and recalling the definition of the Riemann sum, we find

$$\lim_{\Delta t \to 0}[c(t_1)R\Delta t + c(t_2)R\Delta t + \cdots + c(t_n)R\Delta t]/60 = D$$

$$\frac{R}{60}\lim_{\Delta t \to 0}[c(t_1)\Delta t + c(t_2)\Delta t + \cdots + c(t_n)\Delta t] = D$$

$$\frac{R}{60}\int_0^T c(t)\,dt = D, \text{ or } R = \frac{60D}{\displaystyle\int_0^T c(t)\,dt}$$

7.4 CONCEPT QUESTIONS, page 520

1. a. $\displaystyle\int_a^\infty f(x)\,dx = \lim_{b\to\infty}\int_a^b f(x)\,dx$

   b. $\displaystyle\int_{-\infty}^b f(x)\,dx = \lim_{a\to-\infty}\int_a^b f(x)\,dx$

   c. $\displaystyle\int_{-\infty}^\infty f(x)\,dx = \int_{-\infty}^c f(x)\,dx + \int_c^\infty f(x)\,dx$ where c is any real number.

2. A perpetuity is an annuity in which the payments continue indefinitely. The formula for computing the present value of a perpetuity is $PV = \dfrac{mP}{r}$.

EXERCISES 7.4, page 520

1. The required area is given by

$$\int_3^\infty \frac{2}{x^2}\,dx = \lim_{b\to\infty}\int_3^b \frac{2}{x^2}\,dx = \lim_{b\to\infty}\left(-\frac{2}{x}\right)\Big|_3^b = \lim_{b\to\infty}\left(-\frac{2}{b}+\frac{2}{3}\right) = \frac{2}{3} \text{ or } \frac{2}{3} \text{ sq units.}$$

2. $$A = \int_2^\infty \frac{2}{x^3}\,dx = \lim_{b\to\infty}\int_2^b 2x^{-3}\,dx = \lim_{b\to\infty}-\frac{1}{x^2}\Big|_2^b = \lim_{b\to\infty}\left(-\frac{1}{b^2}+\frac{1}{4}\right) = \frac{1}{4}\text{sq units.}$$

3. $$A = \int_3^\infty \frac{1}{(x-2)^2}\,dx = \lim_{b\to\infty}\int_3^b (x-2)^{-2}\,dx = \lim_{b\to\infty}-\frac{1}{x-2}\Big|_3^b = \lim_{b\to\infty}\left(-\frac{1}{b-2}+1\right)$$
$$= 1 \text{ sq unit.}$$

4. $$A = \int_0^\infty \frac{2}{(x+1)^3}\,dx = \lim_{b\to\infty}\int_0^b 2(x+1)^{-3}\,dx = \lim_{b\to\infty} -\frac{1}{(x+1)^2}\Big|_0^b = \lim_{b\to\infty}\left(-\frac{1}{(b+1)^2}+1\right)$$
$$= 1 \text{ sq unit.}$$

5. $$A = \int_1^\infty \frac{1}{x^{3/2}}\,dx = \lim_{b\to\infty}\int_1^b x^{-3/2}\,dx = \lim_{b\to\infty}-\frac{2}{\sqrt{x}}\Big|_1^b = \lim_{b\to\infty}\left(-\frac{2}{\sqrt{b}}+2\right) = 2 \text{ sq units.}$$

6. $$A = \int_4^\infty \frac{3}{x^{5/2}}\,dx = \lim_{b\to\infty}\int_4^\infty 3x^{-5/2}\,dx = \lim_{b\to\infty}-2x^{-3/2}\Big|_4^b = \lim_{b\to\infty}\left[-\frac{2}{b^{3/2}}+\frac{1}{4}\right] = \frac{1}{4}\text{sq units.}$$

7. $A = \displaystyle\int_0^\infty \frac{1}{(x+1)^{5/2}}\,dx = \lim_{b\to\infty}\int_1^b (x+1)^{-5/2}\,dx = \lim_{b\to\infty}-\frac{2}{3}(x+1)^{-3/2}\Big|_0^b$

$= \displaystyle\lim_{b\to\infty}\left[-\frac{2}{3(b+1)^{3/2}}+\frac{2}{3}\right] = \frac{2}{3}\,\text{sq units.}$

8. $A = \displaystyle\int_{-\infty}^0 \frac{1}{(1-x)^{3/2}}\,dx = \lim_{a\to-\infty}\int_a^0 (1-x)^{-3/2}\,dx = \lim_{a\to-\infty}(-1)(-2)(1-x)^{-1/2}\Big|_a^0$

$= \displaystyle\lim_{a\to-\infty}\left(2-\frac{2}{\sqrt{1-a}}\right) = 2\,\text{sq units.}$

9. $A = \displaystyle\int_{-\infty}^2 e^{2x}\,dx = \lim_{a\to-\infty}\int_a^2 e^{2x}\,dx = \lim_{a\to-\infty}\tfrac{1}{2}e^{2x}\Big|_a^2 = \lim_{a\to-\infty}\left(\tfrac{1}{2}e^4 - \tfrac{1}{2}e^{2a}\right) = \tfrac{1}{2}e^4 \,\text{sq units.}$

10. $A = \displaystyle\int_0^\infty xe^{-x^2}\,dx = \lim_{b\to\infty}\int_0^b xe^{-x^2}\,dx = \lim_{b\to\infty}-\tfrac{1}{2}e^{-x^2}\Big|_0^b = \lim_{b\to\infty}(-\tfrac{1}{2}e^{-b^2}+\tfrac{1}{2}) = \tfrac{1}{2}\,\text{sq units.}$

11. Using symmetry, the required area is given by

$2\displaystyle\int_0^\infty \frac{x}{(1+x^2)^2}\,dx = 2\lim_{b\to\infty}\int_0^\infty \frac{x}{(1+x^2)^2}\,dx.$

To evaluate the indefinite integral $\displaystyle\int \frac{x}{(1+x^2)^2}\,dx$, put $u = 1+x^2$ so that

$du = 2x\,dx$ or $x\,dx = \tfrac{1}{2}\,du$.

Then $\displaystyle\int \frac{x}{(1+x^2)^2}\,dx = \frac{1}{2}\int \frac{du}{u^2} = -\frac{1}{2u}+C = -\frac{1}{2(1+x^2)}+C.$

Therefore, $2\displaystyle\lim_{b\to\infty}\int_0^b \frac{x}{(1+x^2)}\,dx = \lim_{b\to\infty}-\frac{1}{(1+x^2)^2}\Big|_0^b = \lim_{b\to\infty}\left[-\frac{1}{(1+b^2)}+1\right] = 1,$

or 1 sq unit.

12. $A = \displaystyle\int_{-\infty}^\infty \frac{e^x}{(1+e^x)^2}\,dx = \int_{-\infty}^0 \frac{e^x}{(1+e^x)^2}\,dx + \int_0^\infty \frac{e^x}{(1+e^x)^2}\,dx$

$= \displaystyle\lim_{a\to-\infty}-\frac{1}{1+e^x}\Big|_a^0 + \lim_{b\to\infty}-\frac{1}{1+e^x}\Big|_0^b = \lim_{a\to-\infty}\left(-\frac{1}{2}+\frac{1}{1+e^a}\right)+\lim_{b\to\infty}\left(-\frac{1}{1+e^b}+\frac{1}{2}\right)$

$$= \frac{1}{2} + \frac{1}{2} = 1, \text{ or } 1 \text{ sq units.}$$

13 a. $I(b) = \int_0^b \sqrt{x} \, dx = \frac{2}{3} x^{3/2} \Big|_0^b = \frac{2}{3} b^{3/2}.$ b. $\lim_{b \to \infty} I(b) = \lim_{b \to \infty} \frac{2}{3} b^{3/2} = \infty.$

14. a. $I(b) = \int_1^b x^{-2/3} \, dx = 3x^{1/3} \Big|_0^b = 3\sqrt[3]{b} - 3(1) = 3(\sqrt[3]{b} - 1).$

   b. $\lim_{b \to \infty} I(b) = \lim_{b \to \infty} 3(\sqrt[3]{b} - 1) = \infty$ and so the improper integral diverges.

15 $\int_1^\infty \frac{3}{x^4} \, dx = \lim_{b \to \infty} \int_1^b 3x^{-4} \, dx = \lim_{b \to \infty} \left(-\frac{1}{x^3} \right) \Big|_1^b = \lim_{b \to \infty} \left(-\frac{1}{b^3} + 1 \right) = 1.$

16. $\int_1^\infty \frac{1}{x^3} \, dx = \lim_{b \to \infty} \int_1^\infty x^{-3} \, dx = \lim_{b \to \infty} \left(-\frac{1}{2x^2} \right) \Big|_1^b = \lim_{b \to \infty} \left(-\frac{1}{2b^2} + \frac{1}{2} \right) = \frac{1}{2}.$

17. $A = \int_4^\infty \frac{2}{x^{3/2}} \, dx = \lim_{b \to \infty} \int_4^b 2x^{-3/2} \, dx = \lim_{b \to \infty} -4x^{-1/2} \Big|_4^b = \lim_{b \to \infty} \left(-\frac{4}{\sqrt{b}} + 2 \right) = 2.$

18. $\int_1^\infty \frac{1}{\sqrt{x}} \, dx = \lim_{b \to \infty} 2\sqrt{x} \Big|_1^b = \lim_{b \to \infty} (2\sqrt{b} - 2) = \infty,$ so it is divergent.

19. $\int_1^\infty \frac{4}{x} \, dx = \lim_{b \to \infty} \int_1^b \frac{4}{x} \, dx = \lim_{b \to \infty} 4 \ln x \Big|_1^b = \lim_{b \to \infty} (4 \ln b) = \infty.$

20. $\int_2^\infty \frac{3}{x} \, dx = \lim_{b \to \infty} \int_2^b \frac{3}{x} \, dx = \lim_{b \to \infty} 3 \ln x \Big|_2^b = \lim_{b \to \infty} (3 \ln b) = \infty.$

21. $\int_{-\infty}^0 (x-2)^{-3} \, dx = \lim_{a \to -\infty} \int_a^0 (x-2)^{-3} \, dx = \lim_{a \to -\infty} -\frac{1}{2(x-2)^2} \Big|_a^0 = -\frac{1}{8}.$

22. $\int_2^\infty \frac{dx}{(x+1)^2} = \lim_{b \to \infty} \int_2^b (x+1)^{-2} \, dx = \lim_{b \to \infty} \left(-\frac{1}{x+1} \right) \Big|_2^b = \lim_{b \to \infty} \left(-\frac{1}{b+1} + \frac{1}{3} \right) = \frac{1}{3}.$

23. $\int_1^\infty \frac{1}{(2x-1)^{3/2}} \, dx = \lim_{b \to \infty} \int_1^b (2x-1)^{-3/2} \, dx = \lim_{b \to \infty} -\frac{1}{(2x-1)^{1/2}} \Big|_1^b$

$$= \lim_{b \to \infty} \left(-\frac{1}{\sqrt{2b-1}} + 1 \right) = 1.$$

24. $\int_{-\infty}^{0} (4-x)^{-3/2}\, dx = \lim_{a\to-\infty} \int_{a}^{0} (4-x)^{-3/2}\, dx = \lim_{a\to-\infty} 2(4-x)^{-1/2} \Big|_{a}^{0} = 1.$

25. $\int_{0}^{\infty} e^{-x}\, dx = \lim_{b\to\infty} \int_{0}^{b} e^{-x}\, dx = \lim_{b\to\infty} -e^{-x} \Big|_{0}^{b} = \lim_{b\to\infty}(-e^{-b}+1) = 1.$

26. $\int_{0}^{\infty} e^{-x/2}\, dx = \lim_{b\to\infty} \int_{0}^{b} e^{-x/2}\, dx = \lim_{b\to\infty} -2^{-e/2} \Big|_{0}^{b} = \lim_{b\to\infty}(-2e^{-b/2}+2) = 2.$

27. $\int_{-\infty}^{0} e^{2x}\, dx = \lim_{a\to-\infty} \tfrac{1}{2}e^{2x} \Big|_{a}^{0} = \lim_{a\to-\infty}\left(\tfrac{1}{2} - \tfrac{1}{2}e^{2a}\right) = \tfrac{1}{2}.$

28. $\int_{-\infty}^{0} e^{3x}\, dx = \lim_{a\to-\infty} \int_{a}^{0} e^{3x}\, dx = \lim_{a\to-\infty} \tfrac{1}{3}e^{3x} \Big|_{a}^{0} = \tfrac{1}{3}.$

29. $\int_{1}^{\infty} \frac{e^{\sqrt{x}}}{\sqrt{x}}\, dx = \lim_{b\to\infty} \int_{1}^{b} \frac{e^{\sqrt{x}}}{\sqrt{x}}\, dx = \lim_{b\to\infty} -2e^{\sqrt{x}} \Big|_{1}^{b}$ (Integrate by substitution: $u = \sqrt{x}$)

$= \lim_{b\to\infty}(2e^{\sqrt{b}} - 2e) = \infty,$ and so it diverges.

30. $\int_{1}^{\infty} \frac{e^{-\sqrt{x}}}{\sqrt{x}}\, dx = \lim_{b\to\infty} \int_{1}^{b} \frac{e^{-\sqrt{x}}}{\sqrt{x}}\, dx = \lim_{b\to\infty} -2e^{-\sqrt{x}} \Big|_{1}^{b}$ (Integrate by substitution: $u = -\sqrt{x}$.)

$= \lim_{b\to\infty}(-2e^{-\sqrt{b}.} + 2e^{-1}) = \dfrac{2}{e}$

31. $\int_{-\infty}^{0} xe^{x}\, dx = \lim_{a\to-\infty} \int_{a}^{0} xe^{x}\, dx = \lim_{a\to-\infty}(x-1)e^{x} \Big|_{a}^{0} = \lim_{a\to-\infty}[-1+(a-1)e^{a}] = -1.$
Note: We have used integration by parts to evaluate the integral.

32. $I = \int_{0}^{\infty} xe^{-2x}\, dx.$ Integrate by parts, letting $u = x$ and $dv = e^{-2x}$ so that $du = dx$ and $v = -\tfrac{1}{2}e^{-2x}$. Then

$$I = -\tfrac{1}{2}xe^{-2x} + \tfrac{1}{2}\int e^{-2x}\, dx = -\tfrac{1}{2}xe^{-2x} - \tfrac{1}{4}e^{-2x}$$

Next, $\lim_{b\to\infty} \int_{0}^{b} xe^{-2x}\, dx = \lim_{b\to\infty}\left[-\tfrac{1}{2}xe^{-2x} - \tfrac{1}{4}e^{-2x}\right]_{0}^{b} = \lim_{b\to\infty}\left[-\tfrac{1}{2}be^{-2b} - \tfrac{1}{4}e^{-2b} + \tfrac{1}{4}\right] = \tfrac{1}{4}.$

33. $\int_{-\infty}^{\infty} x\, dx = \lim_{a\to-\infty} \tfrac{1}{2}x^{2} \Big|_{a}^{0} + \lim_{b\to\infty} \tfrac{1}{2}x^{2} \Big|_{0}^{b}$ both of which diverge and so the integral diverges.

7 Additional Topics in Integration

34. $\int_{-\infty}^{\infty} x^3 \, dx = \lim_{a \to -\infty} \int_a^0 x^3 \, dx + \lim_{b \to \infty} \int_0^b x^3 \, dx$. But both integrals on the right do not exist.

For example, $\lim_{b \to \infty} \int_0^b x^3 \, dx = \lim_{b \to \infty} \frac{1}{4} x^4 \Big|_0^b = \lim_{b \to \infty} \frac{b^4}{4} = \infty$, and so the given integral diverges.

35 $\int_{-\infty}^{\infty} x^3 (1+x^4)^{-2} \, dx = \int_{-\infty}^0 x^3 (1+x^4)^{-2} \, dx + \int_0^{\infty} x^3 (1+x^4)^{-2} \, dx$

$$= \lim_{a \to -\infty} \int_a^0 x^3 (1+x^4)^{-2} \, dx + \lim_{b \to \infty} \int_0^b x^3 (1+x^4)^{-2} \, dx$$

$$= \lim_{a \to -\infty} \left[-\frac{1}{4}(1+x^4)^{-1} \Big|_a^0 \right] + \lim_{b \to \infty} \left[-\frac{1}{4}(1+x^4)^{-1} \Big|_0^b \right]$$

$$= \lim_{a \to -\infty} \left[-\frac{1}{4} + \frac{1}{4(1+a^4)} \right] + \lim_{b \to \infty} \left[-\frac{1}{4(1+b^4)} + \frac{1}{4} \right]$$

$$= -\frac{1}{4} + \frac{1}{4} = 0.$$

36. $\int_{-\infty}^{\infty} x(x^2+4)^{-3/2} \, dx = \lim_{a \to -\infty} \int_a^0 x(x^2+4)^{-3/2} \, dx + \lim_{b \to \infty} \int_0^b x(x^2+4)^{-3/2} \, dx$

$$= \lim_{a \to -\infty} -(x^2+4)^{-1/2} \Big|_a^0 + \lim_{b \to \infty} -(x^2+4)^{-1/2} \Big|_0^b$$

$$= \lim_{a \to -\infty} [-(4)^{-1/2} + (a^2+4)^{-1/2}] + \lim_{b \to \infty} [-(b^2+4)^{-1/2} + (4)^{-1/2}]$$

$$= -\frac{1}{2} + \frac{1}{2} = 0.$$

37 $\int_{-\infty}^{\infty} xe^{1-x^2} \, dx = \lim_{a \to -\infty} \int_a^0 xe^{1-x^2} \, dx + \lim_{b \to \infty} \int_0^b xe^{1-x^2} \, dx$

$$= \lim_{a \to -\infty} -\frac{1}{2} e^{1-x^2} \Big|_a^0 + \lim_{b \to \infty} -\frac{1}{2} e^{1-x^2} \Big|_0^b$$

$$= \lim_{a \to -\infty} \left(-\frac{1}{2} e + \frac{1}{2} e^{1-a^2} \right) + \lim_{b \to \infty} \left(-\frac{1}{2} e^{1-b^2} + \frac{1}{2} e \right) = 0.$$

38. $\int_{-\infty}^{\infty} (x - \frac{1}{2}) e^{-x^2+x-1} \, dx = \lim_{a \to \infty} \int_a^0 (x - \frac{1}{2}) e^{-x^2+x-1} \, dx + \lim_{b \to \infty} \int_0^b (x - \frac{1}{2}) e^{-x^2+x-1} \, dx$

$$= \lim_{a \to -\infty} -\frac{1}{2} e^{-x^2+x-1} \Big|_a^0 + \lim_{b \to \infty} -\frac{1}{2} e^{-x^2+x-1} \Big|_0^b = -\frac{1}{2} e^{-1} + \frac{1}{2} e^{-1} = 0.$$

39. $\displaystyle\int_{-\infty}^{\infty} \frac{e^{-x}}{1+e^{-x}}\,dx = \lim_{a\to-\infty} -\ln(1+e^{-x})\Big|_a^0 + \lim_{b\to\infty} -\ln(1+e^{-x})\Big|_0^b = \infty$, and it is divergent.

40. $\displaystyle\int_{-\infty}^{\infty} \frac{xe^{-x^2}}{1+e^{-x^2}}\,dx = \lim_{a\to-\infty} \int_a^0 \frac{xe^{-x^2}}{1+e^{-x^2}}\,dx + \lim_{b\to\infty} \int_0^b \frac{xe^{-x^2}}{1+e^{-x^2}}\,dx$

$\displaystyle\quad = \lim_{a\to-\infty} -\tfrac{1}{2}\ln(1+e^{-x^2})\Big|_a^0 + \lim_{b\to\infty} -\tfrac{1}{2}\ln(1+e^{-x^2})\Big|_0^b = -\tfrac{1}{2}\ln 2 + \tfrac{1}{2}\ln 2 = 0$

41. First, we find the indefinite integral $I = \displaystyle\int \frac{1}{x\ln^3 x}\,dx$. Let $u = \ln x$ so that

$du = \dfrac{1}{x}\,dx$. Therefore, $I = \displaystyle\int \frac{du}{u^3} = -\frac{1}{2u^2} + C = -\frac{1}{2\ln^2 x} + C$ So

$\displaystyle\int_e^{\infty} \frac{1}{x\ln^3 x}\,dx = \lim_{b\to\infty} \int_e^b \frac{1}{x\ln^3 x}\,dx$

$\displaystyle\quad = \lim_{b\to\infty} \left[-\frac{1}{2\ln^2 x}\Big|_e^b \right] = \lim_{b\to\infty}\left(-\frac{1}{2(\ln b)^2} + \frac{1}{2} \right) = \frac{1}{2}$

and so the given integral is convergent.

42. $\displaystyle\int_{e^2}^{\infty} \frac{1}{x\ln x}\,dx = \lim_{b\to\infty} \int_{e^2}^b \frac{1}{x\ln x}\,dx$

$\displaystyle\quad = \lim_{b\to\infty} \left[\frac{1}{2}\ln(\ln x)\Big|_{e^2}^b \right] = \lim_{b\to\infty}\left(\frac{1}{2}\ln(\ln b) - \frac{1}{2}\ln 2 \right) = \infty$

and so the given integral is divergent.

43. We want the present value PV of a perpetuity with $m = 1$, $P = 1500$, and $r = 0.08$.

We find $PV = \dfrac{(1)(1500)}{0.08} = 18{,}750$, or $\$18{,}750$.

44. We want the present value PV of a perpetuity with $m = 1$, $P = 50{,}000$, and

$r = 0.09$ We find $PV = \dfrac{(1)(50{,}000)}{0.09} \approx 555{,}556$, or approximately $\$555{,}556$.

45. $PV = \displaystyle\int_0^{\infty} (10{,}000 + 4000t)e^{-rt}\,dt = 10{,}000\int_0^{\infty} e^{-rt}\,dt + 4000\int_0^{\infty} te^{-rt}\,dt$

$$= \lim_{b \to \infty} \left(-\frac{10{,}000}{r} e^{-rt} \Big|_0^b \right) + 4000 \left(\frac{1}{r^2} \right) (-rt - 1) e^{-rt} \Big|_0^b)$$

(Integrating by parts.)

$$= \frac{10{,}000}{r} + \frac{4000}{r^2} = \frac{10{,}000r + 4000}{r^2} \text{ dollars.}$$

46. $PV = \int_0^\infty (20 + t) e^{-0.1t} dt = \lim_{b \to \infty} \int_0^b 20 e^{-0.1t} + \lim_{b \to \infty} \int_0^b t e^{-0.1t} \, dt$

$$= \lim_{b \to \infty} -200 e^{-0.1t} \Big|_0^b + \lim_{b \to \infty} 100(-0.1t - 1) e^{-0.1t} \Big|_0^b$$

(Integrating by parts)

$= 300$ or $300{,}000$.

47. True. $\int_a^\infty f(x) \, dx = \int_a^b f(x) \, dx + \int_b^\infty f(x) \, dx$. So if $\int_a^\infty f(x) \, dx$ exists then

$$\int_b^\infty f(x) \, dx = \int_a^\infty f(x) \, dx - \int_a^b f(x) \, dx.$$

48. False. Take $f(x) = x$. Then

$$\lim_{t \to \infty} \int_{-t}^t f(x) \, dx = \lim_{t \to \infty} \int_{-t}^t x \, dx = \lim_{t \to \infty} \left[\tfrac{1}{2} x^2 \Big|_{-t}^t \right]$$

$$= \lim_{t \to \infty} [\tfrac{1}{2} t^2 - \tfrac{1}{2} t^2] = \lim_{t \to \infty} (0) = 0$$

But $\int_{-\infty}^\infty f(x) \, dx$ does not exist because $\int_{-\infty}^\infty f(x) \, dx = \int_{-\infty}^0 f(x) \, dx + \int_0^\infty f(x) \, dx$

and $\int_0^\infty f(x) \, dx = \lim_{b \to \infty} \left[\int_0^b x \, dx \right] = \lim_{b \to \infty} \tfrac{1}{2} b^2 = \infty$, and so it does not exist.

49. False. Let $f(x) = \begin{cases} e^{2x} & \text{if } -\infty < x \le 0 \\ e^{-x} & \text{if } \quad 0 < x < \infty \end{cases}$. Then

$$\int_{-\infty}^\infty f(x) \, dx = \int_{-\infty}^0 e^{2x} \, dx + \int_0^\infty e^{-x} \, dx = \frac{1}{2} + 1 = \frac{3}{2}. \text{ But } 2 \int_0^\infty f(x) \, dx = 2 \int_0^\infty e^{-x} \, dx = 2.$$

50. False. Take $f(x) = e^{-x}$ and $a = 0$. then $\int_0^\infty e^{-x} \, dx$ exists, but $\int_{-\infty}^0 e^{-x} \, dx$ does not exist.

51. a. $CV \approx \int_0^\infty Re^{-it}\, dt = \lim_{b\to\infty} \int_0^b Re^{-it}\, dt = \lim_{b\to\infty} -\frac{R}{i}e^{-it}\Big|_0^b = \lim_{b\to\infty}\left(-\frac{R}{i}e^{-ib} + \frac{R}{i}\right) = \frac{R}{i}$

   b. $CV \approx \dfrac{10,000}{0.12} \approx 83,333$, or \$83,333.

52. $\displaystyle\int_0^\infty e^{-px}\, dx = \lim_{b\to\infty}\int_a^b e^{-px}\, dx = \lim_{b\to\infty}\left[-\frac{1}{p}e^{-px}\right]_a^b = \lim_{b\to\infty}\left(-\frac{1}{p}e^{-pb} + \frac{1}{p}e^{-pa}\right)$

   $= \dfrac{1}{pe^{pa}}$ if $p > 0$ and is divergent if $p < 0$.

53. $\displaystyle\int_{-\infty}^b e^{px}\, dx = \lim_{a\to-\infty}\int_a^b e^{px}\, dx = \lim_{a\to-\infty}\left[\frac{1}{p}e^{px}\right]_a^b = \lim_{a\to-\infty}\left(\frac{1}{p}e^{pb} - \frac{1}{p}e^{pa}\right)$

   $= -\dfrac{1}{p}e^{pa}$ if $p > 0$ and is divergent if $p < 0$.

54. If $p < 0$, then $1/x^p$ is unbounded and the improper integral diverges. If $p > 0$, $p \neq -1$, and so

$$\int_1^\infty \frac{1}{x^p\, dx} = \lim_{b\to\infty}\int_1^b x^{-p}\, dx = \lim_{b\to\infty}\left[\frac{x^{1-p}}{1-p}\right]_1^b$$

$$= \lim_{b\to\infty}\left[\frac{b^{1-p}}{1-p} - \frac{1}{1-p}\right]$$

$$= \frac{1}{p-1} \text{ if } p > 1,$$

and diverges (to infinity) if $p < 1$. If $p = 1$, then

$$\int_1^\infty \frac{1}{x}\, dx = \lim_{b\to\infty}\int_1^b \frac{dx}{x} = \lim_{b\to\infty}\ln b = \infty.$$

So the integral converges if $p > 1$.

7.5 CONCEPT QUESTIONS, page 530

1. See the definition given on page 523 of the test. For example, $f(x) = \dfrac{3x^2}{125}$ on the interval $[0, 5]$.

2. a. See the definition given on page 528 of the text.

b. $E(x) = \dfrac{1}{k}$

EXERCISES 7.5, page 530

1. $f(x) \geq 0$ on $[2,6]$. Next $\displaystyle\int_2^6 \frac{2}{32} x\, dx = \frac{1}{32} x^2\Big|_2^6 = \frac{1}{32}(36-4) = 1$,

and so f is a probability density function on $[2,6]$.

2. $f(x) = \frac{2}{9}(3x - x^2)$ is nonnegative on $[0,3]$ since both the factors x
and $3 - x$ are nonnegative there. Next, we compute

$$\int_0^3 \frac{2}{9}(3x - x^2)\,dx = \frac{2}{9}\left(\frac{3}{2}x^2 - \frac{1}{3}x^3\right)\Big|_0^3 = \frac{2}{9}\left(\frac{27}{2} - 9\right) = 1,$$

and so f is a probability density function.

3. $f(x) = \frac{3}{8}x^2$ is nonnegative on $[0,2]$. Next, we compute

$$\int_0^2 \frac{3}{8}x^2\,dx = \frac{1}{8}x^3\Big|_0^2 = 1$$

and so f is a probability density function.

4.   Since $(x - 1) \geq 0$ and $(5 - x) \geq 0$ on $[1,5]$, we see that $f(x) \geq 0$ on $[1,5]$. Next,

$$\int_1^5 f(x)\,dx = \frac{3}{32}\int_1^5 (x-1)(5-x)\,dx = \frac{3}{32}\int_1^5 (-x^2 + 6x - 5)\,dx$$

$$= \frac{3}{32}\left(-\frac{1}{3}x^3 + 3x^2 - 5x\right)\Big|_1^5 = \frac{3}{32}\left[\left(-\frac{125}{3} + 75 - 25\right) - \left(-\frac{1}{3} + 3 - 5\right)\right] = 1,$$

and so f is a probability density function on $[1,5]$.

5. $\displaystyle\int_0^1 20(x^3 - x^4)\,dx = 20\left(\frac{1}{4}x^4 - \frac{1}{5}x^5\right)\Big|_0^1 = 20\left(\frac{1}{4} - \frac{1}{5}\right) = 20\left(\frac{1}{20}\right) = 1$.

Furthermore, $f(x) = 20(x^3 - x^4) = 20x^3(1 - x) \geq 0$ on $[0,1]$.

Therefore, f is a density function on $[0,1]$ as asserted.

6. $f(x) = \dfrac{8}{7x^2}$ is nonnegative on $[1,8]$. Next, we compute

$$\int_1^8 \frac{8}{7x^2}\,dx = -\frac{8}{7x}\Big|_1^8 = -\frac{8}{7}\left(\frac{1}{8} - 1\right) = 1,$$

and so f is a probability density function.

7. Clearly $f(x) \geq 0$ on $[1,4]$. Next,
$$\int_1^4 f(x)\,dx = \tfrac{3}{14}\int_1^4 x^{1/2}\,dx = (\tfrac{3}{14})(\tfrac{2}{3})x^{3/2}\big|_1^4 = \tfrac{1}{7}(8-1) = 1,$$
and so f is a probability density function on $[1,4]$.

8. $f(x) = \dfrac{12-x}{72}$ is nonnegative on $[0,12]$. Next, we see that
$$\int_0^{12} \tfrac{12-x}{72}\,dx = \int_0^{12}\left(\tfrac{1}{6} - \tfrac{x}{72}\right)dx = \tfrac{1}{6}x - \tfrac{1}{144}x^2\Big|_0^{12} = 2 - 1 = 1,$$
and conclude that f is a probability function.

9. First, $f(x) \geq 0$ on $[0,\infty)$. Next, we compute
$$I = \int_0^\infty \frac{x}{(x^2+1)^{3/2}}\,dx = \lim_{b\to\infty}\int_0^b x(x^2+1)^{-3/2}\,dx.$$
Letting $u = x^2 + 1$, so that $du = 2x\,dx$, we find
$$I = \lim_{b\to\infty}\int_1^{b^2+1} u^{-3/2}\,du = \tfrac{1}{2}\lim_{b\to\infty} -2u^{-1/2}\Big|_1^{b^2+1} = \lim_{b\to\infty}\left(-\frac{1}{\sqrt{b^2+1}} + 1\right) = 1.$$
So the given function is a probability density function on $[0,\infty)$.

10. First, $f(x) \geq 0$ on $[0,\infty)$. Next, we compute
$$I = \int_0^\infty 4xe^{-2x^2}\,dx = \lim_{b\to\infty}\int_0^b 4xe^{-2x^2}\,dx$$
Letting $u = -2x^2$, so that $du = -4x\,dx$, we find
$$I = \lim_{b\to\infty}\int_0^{-2b^2} -e^u\,du = \lim_{b\to\infty} -e^u\Big|_0^{-2b^2} = \lim_{b\to\infty}(-e^{-2b^2} + 1) = 1$$
So the given function is a probability density function on $[0,\infty)$.

11. a. $\int_0^4 k(4-x)\,dx = k\int_0^4 (4-x)\,dx = k(4x - \tfrac{1}{2}x^2)\big|_0^4 = k(16-8) = 8k = 1$
implies that $k = 1/8$.

b. $P(1 \leq x \leq 3) = \tfrac{1}{8}\int_1^3 (4-x)\,dx = \tfrac{1}{8}(4x - \tfrac{1}{2}x^2)\big|_1^3 = \tfrac{1}{8}[(12 - \tfrac{9}{2}) - (4 - \tfrac{1}{2})] = \tfrac{1}{2}.$

12. a. $\int_1^{10} \dfrac{k}{x^2}\,dx = k\int_1^{10} x^{-2}\,dx = -\dfrac{k}{x}\Big|_1^{10} = -k\left(\dfrac{1}{10} - 1\right) = \dfrac{9}{10}k = 1.$

Thus, $k = 10/9$.

b. The required probability is
$$\frac{10}{9}\int_2^6 x^{-2}\,dx = -\frac{10}{9x}\Big|_2^6 = -\frac{10}{9}\left(\frac{1}{6} - \frac{1}{2}\right) = -\frac{10}{9}\left(-\frac{1}{3}\right) = \frac{10}{27}.$$

13 a. $\displaystyle\int_0^4 f(x)\,dx = \int_0^4 2ke^{-kx}\,dx = (2k)\left(-\frac{1}{k}\right)e^{-kx}\Big|_0^4$

$$= -2e^{-kx}\Big|_0^4 = -2e^{-4k} + 2 = 2(1 - e^{-4k}) = 1$$

gives
$$1 - e^{-4k} = \frac{1}{2}$$

$$e^{-4k} = \frac{1}{2}$$

$$-4k = \ln\frac{1}{2} = \ln 1 - \ln 2 = -\ln 2$$

So
$$k = \frac{\ln 2}{4}$$

b. $\displaystyle P(1 \le x \le 2) = \frac{2\ln 2}{4}\int_1^2 e^{-\left(\frac{\ln 2}{4}\right)x}\,dx = \frac{2\ln 2}{4}\cdot\left(-\frac{4}{\ln 2}\right)e^{-\left(\frac{\ln 2}{4}\right)x}\Big|_1^2$

$$= -2e^{-\left(\frac{\ln 4}{2}\right)2} + 2e^{-\frac{\ln 4}{2}} \approx 0.2676.$$

14. a. We compute
$$\int_0^\infty kxe^{-2x^2}\,dx = k\lim_{b\to\infty}\int_0^b xe^{-2x^2}\,dx = k\lim_{b\to\infty}\left[-\frac{1}{4}e^{-2x^2}\Big|_0^b\right]dx$$

[Use the method of substitution with $u = -2x^2$]
$$= k\lim_{b\to\infty}\left(-\frac{1}{4}e^{-2b^2} + \frac{1}{4}\right) = \frac{1}{4}k.$$

Since this value must be equal to 1, we see that $k = 4$.

b. The required probability is given by
$$P(x > 1) = \int_1^\infty f(x)\,dx = \lim_{b\to\infty}\int_1^b 4xe^{-2x^2}\,dx$$

$$= \lim_{b\to\infty}\left[-e^{-2x^2}\Big|_1^b\right] = \lim_{b\to\infty}(-e^{-2b^2} + e^{-2(1)}) = e^{-2} \approx 0.1353.$$

15.   a. Here $k = \frac{1}{15}$ and so $f(x) = \frac{1}{15}e^{(-1/15)x}$

b. The probability is

$$\int_{10}^{12} \frac{1}{15} e^{(-1/15)x} \, dx = -e^{(-1/15)x} \Big|_{10}^{12} = -e^{-12/15} + e^{-10/15} \approx 0.06.$$

c. The probability is

$$\int_{15}^{\infty} \frac{1}{15} e^{(-1/15)x} \, dx = \lim_{b \to \infty} \int_{15}^{b} \frac{1}{15} e^{(-1/15)x} \, dx$$

$$= \lim_{b \to \infty} -e^{(-1/15)x} \Big|_{15}^{b} = \lim_{b \to \infty} -e^{(-1/15)b} + e^{-1} \approx 0.37$$

16. a. $P(x \le 100) = \dfrac{1}{100} \displaystyle\int_0^{100} e^{-x/100} \, dx = -e^{-x/100} \Big|_0^{100} = -e^{-1} + 1 \approx 0.63.$

  b. $P(x \ge 120) = \dfrac{1}{100} \displaystyle\int_{120}^{\infty} e^{-x/100} \, dx = \lim_{b \to \infty}(-e^{-b/100} + e^{-1.2}) = e^{-1.2} \approx 0.30.$

  c. $P(60 \le x \le 140) = \dfrac{1}{100} \displaystyle\int_{60}^{140} e^{-x/100} dx = -e^{-x/100} \Big|_{60}^{140} = (-e^{-1.4} + e^{-0.6})$

$$\approx 0.30.$$

17. $\mu = \displaystyle\int_0^5 t \cdot \frac{2}{25} t \, dt = \frac{2}{25} \int_0^5 t^2 \, dt = \frac{2}{75} t^3 \Big|_0^5 = \frac{2}{75}(125) = 3\frac{1}{3}$

So a shopper is expected to spend $3\frac{1}{3}$ minutes in the magazine section.

18. $\mu = \displaystyle\int_1^3 t \cdot \frac{9}{4t^3} \, dt = \frac{9}{4} \int_1^3 t^{-2} \, dt = -\frac{9}{4t} \Big|_1^3 = -\frac{9}{4}\left(-\frac{1}{3} + 1\right) = \frac{3}{2}.$

So the expected reaction time is 1.5 seconds.

19 $\mu = \displaystyle\int_0^5 x \cdot \frac{6}{125} x(5 - x) \, dx = \frac{6}{125} \int_0^5 (5x^2 - x^3) dx = \frac{6}{125}\left(\frac{5}{3}x^3 - \frac{1}{4}x^4\right)\Big|_0^5$

$$= \frac{6}{125}\left(\frac{625}{3} - \frac{625}{4}\right) = 2.5.$$

So the expected demand is 2500 lb.

20. $\mu = \displaystyle\int_0^3 x \cdot \frac{2}{9} x(3 - x) \, dx = \frac{2}{9} \int_0^3 (3x^2 - x^3) dx = \frac{2}{9}\left(x^3 - \frac{1}{4}x^4\right)\Big|_0^3$

$$= \frac{2}{9}\left(27 - \frac{81}{4}\right) = 1.5.$$

So the expected amount of snowfall is 1.5 ft.

21. The required probability is given by

$$P(0 \le x \le \tfrac{1}{2}) = \int_0^{1/2} 12x^2(1-x)\,dx = 12\int_0^{1/2}(x^2 - x^3)\,dx$$

$$= 12\left(\tfrac{1}{3}x^3 - \tfrac{1}{4}x^4\right)\Big|_0^{1/2} = 12x^3\left[\tfrac{1}{3} - \tfrac{1}{4}(x)\right]\Big|_0^{1/2}$$

$$= 12\left(\tfrac{1}{2}\right)^3\left[\tfrac{1}{3} - \tfrac{1}{4}\left(\tfrac{1}{2}\right)\right] - 0 = \tfrac{5}{16}.$$

22. $\mu = \int_2^3 x \cdot 4(x-2)^3\,dx = 4\int_2^3 (x^4 - 6x^3 + 12x^2 - 8x)\,dx = 4\left(\tfrac{1}{5}x^5 - \tfrac{3}{2}x^4 + 4x^3 - 4x^2\right)\Big|_2^3$

$$= 4\left[\left(\tfrac{243}{5} - \tfrac{243}{2} + 108 - 36\right) - \left(\tfrac{32}{5} - 24 + 32 - 16\right)\right] \approx 0.7$$

So the station can expect to sell 700 gallons of gas on each Monday

23. $\mu = \int_0^\infty t \cdot 9(9 + t^2)^{-3/2}\,dt = \lim_{b\to\infty}\int_0^b 9t(9 + t^2)^{-3/2}\,dt$

$$= \lim_{b\to\infty}\left[(9)(\tfrac{1}{2})(-2)(9 + t^2)^{-1/2}\right]\Big|_0^b = \lim_{b\to\infty}\left[-\frac{9}{\sqrt{9 + t^2}} + 3\right] = 3.$$

So the tubes are expected to last 3 years.

24. a. The probability function is $0.001e^{-0.001x}$. The required probability is

$$P(600 \le x \le 800) = 0.001\int_{600}^{800} e^{-0.001x}\,dx = -e^{-0.001x}\Big|_{600}^{1200} = -e^{-0.8} + e^{-0.6} \approx 0.099$$

b. The probability is

$$P(x \ge 1200) = 0.001\int_{1200}^\infty e^{-0.001k}\,dx = \lim_{b\to\infty}\int_{1200}^b e^{-0.001x} = \lim_{b\to\infty} -e^{-0.001x}\Big|_{1200}^b$$

$$= \lim_{b\to\infty} -e^{-0.001b} + e^{-1.2} \approx 30.$$

25. The probability function is $f(x) = \tfrac{1}{8}e^{-x/8}$. The required probability is

$$P(x \ge 8) = \tfrac{1}{8}\int_8^\infty e^{-x/8}\,dx = \lim_{b\to\infty} -e^{-x/8}\Big|_8^b = \lim_{b\to\infty}(-e^{-b/8} + e^{-1}) = e^{-1} \approx 0.37$$

26. Here $f(x) = \tfrac{1}{30}e^{-x/30}$. $P(x \ge 120) = \tfrac{1}{30}\int_{120}^\infty e^{-x/30}\,dx = \lim_{b\to\infty} -e^{-x/30}\Big|_{120}^b = e^{-120/30} \approx 0.02.$

27. The probability function is $f(x) = 0.00001e^{-0.00001x}$. The required probability is

$$P(x \le 20,000) = 0.00001\int_0^{20,000} e^{-0.00001x}\,dx = -e^{-0.00001x}\Big|_0^{20,000} = -e^{0.2} + 1 \approx 0.18.$$

28. True. Observe that $P(x < a) = \int_{-\infty}^{a} f(x)\,dx$ and $P(x > b) = \int_{b}^{\infty} f(x)\,dx$. So

$$P(x < a) + P(a < x < b) + P(x > b)$$

$$= \int_{-\infty}^{a} f(x)\,dx + \int_{a}^{b} f(x)\,dx + \int_{b}^{\infty} f(x)\,dx = \int_{-\infty}^{\infty} f(x)\,dx = 1$$

and so $P(x < a) + P(x > b) = 1 - \int_{a}^{b} f(x)\,dx$

29. False. f must be nonnegative on $[a, b]$ as well.

30. False. The expected value of x is $\int_{a}^{b} x f(x)\,dx$.

31. False. Let $f(x) = 1$ for all x in the interval $[0, 1]$. Then f is a probability density function on $[0, 1]$, but f is not a probability density function on $\left[\frac{1}{2}, \frac{3}{4}\right]$ since

$$\int_{1/2}^{3/4} 1\,dx = \frac{1}{4} \neq 1.$$

CHAPTER 7 CONCEPT REVIEW, page 533

1. Product; $uv - \int v\,du$; u; easy to integrate

2. $x^2 + 1$; $2x\,dx$; (27)

3. $\dfrac{\Delta x}{2}[f(x_0) + 2f(x_1) + 2f(x_2) + \cdots 2f(x_{n-1}) + f(x_n)]$; even; $\dfrac{M(b-a)^3}{12n^2}$

4. $\dfrac{\Delta x}{3}[f(x_0) + 4f(x_1) + 2f(x_2) + 4f(x_3) + 2f(x_4) + \cdots + 4f(x_{n-1}) + f(x_n)]$, even;

$\dfrac{M(b-a)^5}{180n^4}$

5. $\displaystyle\lim_{a \to -\infty} \int_{a}^{b} f(x)\,dx$; $\displaystyle\lim_{b \to \infty} \int_{a}^{b} f(x)\,dx$; $\displaystyle\int_{-\infty}^{c} f(x)\,dx + \int_{c}^{\infty} f(x)\,dx$

CHAPTER 7 REVIEW EXERCISES, page 534

1. Let $u = 2x$ and $dv = e^{-x}\,dx$ so that $du = 2\,dx$ and $v = -e^{-x}$. Then

$$\int 2xe^{-x}\,dx = uv - \int v\,du = -2xe^{-x} + 2\int e^{-x}\,dx$$

$$= -2xe^{-x} - 2e^{-x} + C = -2(1+x)e^{-x} + C.$$

2. Let $u = x$ and $dv = e^{4x}\, dx$, so that $du = dx$ and $v = \frac{1}{4}e^{4x}$ Then

$$\int xe^{4x}\, dx = \frac{1}{4}xe^{4x} - \frac{1}{4}\int e^{4x}\, dx = \frac{1}{4}xe^{4x} - \frac{1}{16}e^{4x} + C = \frac{1}{16}(4x-1)e^{4x} + C.$$

3. Let $u = \ln 5x$ and $dv = dx$, so that $du = \frac{1}{x}\, dx$ and $v = x$. Then

$$\int \ln 5x\, dx = x \ln 5x\, dx - \int dx = x \ln 5x - x + C = x(\ln 5x - 1) + C.$$

4. Let $u = \ln 2x$ and $dv = dx$, so that $du = \frac{1}{x}\, dx$ and $v = x$. Then

$$\int_1^4 \ln 2x\, dx = x \ln 2x \Big|_1^4 - \int_1^4 dx = 4\ln 8 - \ln 2 - \left[x\big|_1^4\right] = 4\ln 8 - \ln 2 - 3.$$

5. Let $u = x$ and $dv = e^{-2x}\, dx$ so that $du = dx$ and $v = -\frac{1}{2}e^{-2x}$ Then

$$\int_0^1 xe^{-2x}\, dx = -\frac{1}{2}xe^{-2x}\Big|_0^1 + \frac{1}{2}\int_0^1 e^{-2x}\, dx = -\frac{1}{2}e^{-2} - \frac{1}{4}e^{-2x}\Big|_0^1$$
$$= -\frac{1}{2}e^{-2} - \frac{1}{4}e^{-2} + \frac{1}{4} = \frac{1}{4}(1 - 3e^{-2}).$$

6. Let $u = x$ and $dv = e^{2x}\, dx$ so that $du = dx$ and $v = \frac{1}{2}e^{2x}$

$$\int_0^2 xe^{2x}\, dx = \frac{1}{2}xe^{2x}\Big|_0^2 - \frac{1}{2}\int_0^2 e^{2x}\, dx = e^4 - \frac{1}{4}e^{2x}\Big|_0^2 = e^4 - \frac{1}{4}e^4 + \frac{1}{4} = \frac{1}{4}(1 + 3e^4).$$

7. $f(x) = \int f'(x)\, dx = \int \dfrac{\ln x}{\sqrt{x}}\, dx.$ To evaluate the integral, we integrate by parts

with $u = \ln x$, $dv = x^{-1/2}\, dx$, $du = \frac{1}{x}\, dx$ and $v = 2x^{1/2}\, dx$. Then

$$\int \frac{\ln x}{x^{1/2}}\, dx = 2x^{1/2}\ln x - \int 2x^{-1/2}\, dx = 2x^{1/2}\ln x - 4x^{1/2} + C$$

$$= 2x^{1/2}(\ln x - 2) + C = 2\sqrt{x}(\ln x - 2) + C.$$

But $f(1) = -2$ and this gives $2\sqrt{1}(\ln 1 - 2) + C = -2$, or $C = 2$. Therefore,
$f(x) = 2\sqrt{x}(\ln x - 2) + 2.$

8. $f'(x) = xe^{-3x}$; Let $u = x$, $dv = e^{-3x}\, dx$, $du = dx$, $v = -\dfrac{1}{3}e^{-3x}$. Then

$$f(x) = uv - \int v\,du = -\frac{1}{3}xe^{-3x} + \frac{1}{3}\int e^{-3x}\,dx = -\frac{1}{3}xe^{-3x} - \frac{1}{9}e^{-3x} + C$$

Since $f(0) = 0$, $\quad -\frac{1}{9} + C = 0$ and $C = \frac{1}{9}$ Therefore,

$$f(x) = -\frac{1}{3}xe^{-3x} - \frac{1}{9}e^{-3x} + \frac{1}{9}.$$

9. Using Formula 4 with $a = 3$ and $b = 2$, we obtain

$$\int \frac{x^2}{(3+2x)^2}\,dx = \frac{1}{8}\left[3 + 2x - \frac{9}{3+2x} - 6\ln|3+2x|\right] + C.$$

10. Using Formula 5 with $a = 3$ and $b = 2$, we have

$$\int \frac{2x}{\sqrt{2x+3}}\,dx = 2\int \frac{x}{\sqrt{2x+3}}\,dx = 2 \cdot \frac{2}{3(4)}(2x-6)\sqrt{2x+3} + C$$

$$= \frac{2}{3}(x-3)\sqrt{2x+3} + C.$$

11. Use Formula 24 with $a = 4$ and $n = 2$, obtaining $\int x^2 e^{4x}\,dx = \frac{1}{4}x^2 e^{4x} - \frac{1}{2}\int xe^{4x}\,dx.$

Use Formula 23 to obtain

$$\int x^2 e^{4x}\,dx = \frac{1}{4}x^2 e^{4x} - \frac{1}{2}\left[\frac{1}{16}(4x-1)e^{4x}\right] + C$$

$$= \frac{1}{32}(8x^2 - 4x + 1)e^{4x} + C.$$

12. Use Formula 18 with $a = 5$. We obtain $\int \frac{dx}{(x^2-25)^{3/2}} = -\frac{x}{25\sqrt{x^2-25}} + C.$

13. Use Formula 17 with $a = 2$ obtaining $\int \frac{dx}{x^2\sqrt{x^2-4}} = \frac{\sqrt{x^2-4}}{4x} + C.$

14. First, we make the subtitution $u = 2x$ so that $du = 2\,dx$, or $dx = \frac{1}{2}du$.

Then with $x = \frac{1}{2}u$, we have $\int 8x^3 \ln 2x\,dx = \int 8(\frac{u}{2})^3 \ln u(\frac{1}{2}du) = \frac{1}{2}\int u^3 \ln u\,du.$

Then use Formula 27 with $n = 3$, obtaining

$$\int u^3 \ln u\,du = \frac{u^4}{16}(4\ln u - 1) + C.$$

Therefore, $\int 8x^3 \ln 2x\, dx = \frac{1}{2} \cdot \frac{(2x)^4}{16}(4\ln 2x - 1) + C = \frac{1}{2}x^4(4\ln 2x - 1) + C.$

15. $\int_0^\infty e^{-2x}\, dx = \lim_{b\to\infty}\int_0^b e^{-2x}\, dx = \lim_{b\to\infty}(-\frac{1}{2}e^{-2x})\Big|_0^b = \lim_{b\to\infty}(-\frac{1}{2}e^{-2b} + \frac{1}{2}) = \frac{1}{2}.$

16. $\int_{-\infty}^0 e^{3x}\, dx = \lim_{a\to-\infty}\int_a^0 e^{3x}\, dx = \lim_{a\to-\infty}(\frac{1}{3}e^{3x})\Big|_a^0 = \lim_{a\to-\infty}(\frac{1}{3} - \frac{1}{3}e^{3a}) = \frac{1}{3}.$

17. $\int_3^\infty \frac{2}{x}\, dx = \lim_{b\to\infty}\int_3^b \frac{2}{x}\, dx = \lim_{b\to\infty} 2\ln x\Big|_3^b = \lim_{b\to\infty}(2\ln b - 2\ln 3) = \infty.$

18. $\int_2^\infty \frac{1}{(x+2)^{3/2}}\, dx = \lim_{b\to\infty}\int_2^b (x+2)^{-3/2}\, dx = \lim_{b\to\infty} -2(x+2)^{-1/2}\Big|_2^b$

$$= \lim_{b\to\infty}\left[-\frac{2}{(b+2)^{1/2}} + 1\right] = 1.$$

19. $\int_2^\infty \frac{dx}{(1+2x)^2} = \lim_{b\to\infty}\int_2^b (1+2x)^{-2}\, dx = \lim_{b\to\infty}(\frac{1}{2})(-1)(1+2x)^{-1}\Big|_2^b$

$$= \lim_{b\to\infty}\left(-\frac{1}{2(1+2b)} + \frac{1}{2(5)}\right) = \frac{1}{10}.$$

20. $\int_1^\infty 3e^{1-x}\, dx = \lim_{b\to\infty}\int_1^b 3e^{1-x}\, dx = \lim_{b\to\infty} -3e^{1-x}\Big|_1^b = \lim_{b\to\infty}(-3e^{1-b} + 3) = 3.$

21.. $\Delta x = \frac{b-a}{n} = \frac{3-1}{4} = \frac{1}{2}; x_0 = 1, x_1 = \frac{3}{2}, x_2 = 2, x_3 = \frac{5}{2}, x_4 = 3.$

Trapezoidal Rule:

$$\int_1^3 \frac{dx}{1+\sqrt{x}} \approx \frac{\frac{1}{2}}{2}\left[\frac{1}{2} + \frac{2}{1+\sqrt{1.5}} + \frac{2}{1+\sqrt{2}} + \frac{2}{1+\sqrt{2.5}} + \frac{1}{1+\sqrt{3}}\right] \approx 0.8421.$$

Simpson's Rule

$$\int_1^3 \frac{dx}{1+\sqrt{x}} \approx \frac{\frac{1}{2}}{3}\left[\frac{1}{2} + \frac{4}{1+\sqrt{1.5}} + \frac{2}{1+\sqrt{2}} + \frac{4}{1+\sqrt{2.5}} + \frac{1}{1+\sqrt{3}}\right] \approx 0.8404.$$

22. $\Delta x = \frac{b-a}{n} = \frac{1-0}{4} = \frac{1}{4}; x_0 = 0, x_1 = \frac{1}{4}, x_2 = \frac{2}{4}, x_3 = \frac{3}{4}, x_4 = \frac{4}{4}.$

Trapezoidal Rule:

$$\int_0^1 e^{x^2} dx \approx \frac{\frac{1}{4}}{2}\left[1 + 2e^{(0.25)^2} + 2e^{(0.5)^2} + 2e^{(0.75)^2} + e\right] \approx 1.491$$

Simpson's Rule:

$$\int_0^1 e^{x^2} dx \approx \frac{\frac{1}{4}}{3}\left[1 + 4e^{(0.25)^2} + 2e^{(0.5)^2} + 4e^{(0.75)^2} + e\right] \approx 1.464$$

23 $\Delta x = \frac{1-(-1)}{4} = \frac{1}{2}$; $x_0 = -1$, $x_1 = -\frac{1}{2}$, $x_2 = 0$, $x_3 = \frac{1}{2}$, $x_4 = 1$.

Trapezoidal Rule:

$$\int_{-1}^1 \sqrt{1+x^4}\, dx \approx \frac{0.5}{2}\left[\sqrt{2} + 2\sqrt{1+(-0.5)^4} + 2 + 2\sqrt{1+(0.5)^4} + \sqrt{2}\right]$$
$$\approx 2.2379.$$

Simpson's Rule:

$$\int_{-1}^1 \sqrt{1+x^4}\, dx \approx \frac{0.5}{3}\left[\sqrt{2} + 4\sqrt{1+(-0.5)^4} + 2 + 4\sqrt{1+(0.5)^4} + \sqrt{2}\right]$$
$$\approx 2.1791.$$

24. Here $a = 1$, $b = 3$, $n = 4$ and $\Delta x = 0.5$, $x_0 = 1$, $x_1 = 1.5$, $x_2 = 2$, $x_3 = 2.5$, and $x_4 = 3$

Trapezoidal Rule:

$$\int_1^3 \frac{e^x}{x}\, dx \approx \frac{0.5}{2}\left(e^1 + \frac{2e^{1.5}}{1.5} + \frac{2e^2}{2} + \frac{2e^{2.5}}{2.5} + \frac{e^3}{3}\right)$$
$$\approx 0.25(2.7182818 + 5.9755854 + 7.389056 + 9.7459952 + 6.695179)$$
$$\approx 8.1310.$$

Simpson's Rule:

$$\int_1^3 \frac{e^x}{x}\, dx \approx \frac{0.5}{3}\left(e^1 + \frac{4e^{1.5}}{1.5} + \frac{2e^2}{2} + \frac{4e^{2.5}}{2.5} + \frac{e^3}{3}\right)$$
$$\approx 0.1666667(2.7182818 + 11.951171 + 7.389056 + 19\,49199$$
$$+ 6.695179) \approx 8.041.$$

25. a. Here $a = 0, b = 1$, and $f(x) = \dfrac{1}{x+1}$. We have

$$f'(x) = -\frac{1}{(x+1)^2} \quad \text{and} \quad f''(x) = \frac{2}{(x+1)^3}$$

Since f'' is positive and decreasing on $(0,1)$, it attains its maximum value of 2 at $x = 0$. So we take $M = 2$. Using (7), we see that the maximum error incurred is

$$\frac{M(b-a)^3}{12n^2} = \frac{2(1^3)}{12(8^2)} = \frac{1}{384} \approx 0.002604$$

b. We compute
$$f'''(x) = -\frac{6}{(x+1)^4} \quad \text{and} \quad f^{(iv)}(x) = \frac{24}{(x+1)^5}$$

Since $f^{(4)}(x)$ is positive and decreasing on $(0,1)$, we take $M = 24$. The maximum

error is $\quad \dfrac{24(1^5)}{180(8^4)} = \dfrac{1}{30720} \approx 0.000033$

26. $\frac{3}{128} \int_0^4 (16 - x^2)\, dx = \frac{3}{128} (16x - \frac{1}{3}x^3)\big|_0^4 = \frac{3}{128}(64 - \frac{64}{3}) = \frac{3}{128}(\frac{192-64}{3}) = 1.$

Also, $f(x) \geq 0$ on $[0,4]$.

27. $f(x) \geq 0$ on $[0,3]$. Next,

$$\frac{1}{9} \int_0^3 x\sqrt{9-x^2}\, dx = \frac{1}{9} \int_0^3 x(9-x^2)^{1/2}\, dx = (\frac{1}{9})(-\frac{1}{2})(\frac{2}{3})(9-x^2)^{3/2}\big|_0^3$$
$$= -\frac{1}{27}(9-x^2)^{3/2}\big|_0^3 = 0 + \frac{1}{27}(9)^{3/2} = 1.$$

28. a. $\int_0^2 kx\sqrt{4-x^2}\, dx = k\int_0^2 x(4-x^2)^{1/2}\, dx = k(-\frac{1}{2})(\frac{2}{3})(4-x^2)^{3/2}\big|_0^2$
    $$= (-\frac{k}{3})(0 - 4^{3/2}) = \frac{k}{3}(8) = 1, \text{ or } k = 3/8.$$

    b. $\int_1^2 \frac{3}{8}x\sqrt{4-x^2}\, dx = \frac{3}{8}(-\frac{1}{3})(4-x^2)^{3/2}\big|_1^2 = -\frac{1}{8}(0 - 3^{3/2}) = 0.6495.$

29. a. $\int_1^4 \frac{k}{\sqrt{x}}\, dx = k\int_1^4 x^{-1/2}\, dx = 2k\sqrt{x}\big|_1^4 = 2k(2-1) = 2k = 1, \text{ or } k = 1/2.$

    b. $\int_2^3 \frac{\frac{1}{2}}{\sqrt{x}}\, dx = \frac{1}{2}\int_2^3 x^{-1/2}\, dx = 2\left(\frac{1}{2}\right)\sqrt{x}\big|_2^3 = \sqrt{3} - \sqrt{2} = 0.3178,$

30. a. $\int_0^3 kx^2(3-x)\, dx = k\int_0^3 (3x^2 - x^3)\, dx = k(x^3 - \frac{1}{4}x^4)\big|_0^3$
    $$= k(27 - \frac{81}{4}) = k(\frac{108-81}{4}) = k(\frac{27}{4}) = 1, \text{ or } k = \frac{4}{27}$$

    b. $\int_1^2 \frac{4}{27}x^2(3-x)\, dx = \frac{4}{27}\int_1^2 (3x^2 - x^3)\, dx = \frac{4}{27}(x^3 - \frac{1}{4}x^4)\big|_1^2$
    $$= \frac{4}{27}(8-4) - (1-\frac{1}{4}) = \frac{13}{27} \approx 0.4815.$$

31. a. The probability that a woman entering the maternity wing stays in the hospital more than 6 days is given by

$$\int_6^\infty \tfrac{1}{4}e^{-0.25t}\,dt = \lim_{b\to\infty}\int_6^b \tfrac{1}{4}e^{-0.25t}\,dt = \lim_{b\to\infty}-e^{-0.25t}\Big|_6^b = \lim_{b\to\infty}(-e^{-0.25b}+e^{-1.5}) = 0.22$$

b. The probability that a woman entering the maternity wing at the hospital stays there less than 2 days is given by $\int_0^2 \tfrac{1}{4}e^{-0.25t}\,dt = -e^{-0.25t}\Big|_0^2 = -e^{-0.5}+1 = 0.39$

c. $E = \dfrac{1}{k} = \dfrac{1}{\frac{1}{4}} = 4$, or 4 days.

32. The producer's surplus is given by $PS = \bar{p}\bar{x} - \int_0^{\bar{x}} s(x)\,dx$, where $\bar{x}$ is found by

solving the equation $2\sqrt{25+x^2} = 13$. Then $\sqrt{25+x^2} = 13$, $25+x^2 = 169$, and

$x = \pm 12$. So $\bar{x} = 12$. Therefore, $PS = (26)(12) - 2\int_0^{12}(25+x^2)^{1/2}\,dx$.

Using Formula 7 with $a = 5$, we obtain

$$PS = (26)(12) - 2\int_0^{12}(25+x^2)^{1/2}\,dx$$

$$= 312 - 2\left(\tfrac{x}{2}(25+x^2)^{1/2} + \tfrac{25}{2}\ln\left|x+(25+x^2)^{1/2}\right|\right)\Big|_0^{12}$$

$$= 312 - 2[6(13) + \tfrac{25}{2}\ln(12+13) - \tfrac{25}{2}\ln 5] \approx 115.76405,$$

or $1,157,641.

33. Let $u = t$ and $dv = e^{-0.05t}$ so that $du = 1$ and $v = -20e^{-0.05t}$, and integrate by parts obtaining $S(t) = -20te^{-0.05t} + \int 20e^{-0.05t}\,dt = -20te^{-0.05t} - 400e^{-0.05t} + C$

$$= -20te^{-0.05t} - 400e^{-0.05t} + C = -20e^{-0.05t}(t+20) + C.$$

The initial condition implies $S(0) = 0$ giving $-20(20) + C = 0$, or $C = 400$. Therefore, $S(t) = -20e^{-0.05t}(t+20) + 400$. By the end of the first year, the number of units sold is given by $S(12) = -20e^{-0.6}(32) + 400 = 48.761$, or 48,761 cartridges.

34. If $p = 30$, we have $2\sqrt{325-x^2} = 30$, $\sqrt{325-x^2} = 15$, or $325 - x^2 = 225$, $x^2 = 100$, or $x = \pm 10$. So the equilibrium point is $(10, 30)$.

$$CS = \int_0^{10} 2\sqrt{325-x^2}\,dx - (30)(10).$$

To evaluate the integral using Simpson's Rule with $n = 10$, we have

$\Delta x = \dfrac{10-0}{10} = 1$; $x_0 = 0, x_1 = 1, x_2 = 2, \ldots, x_{10} = 10$.

$$2\int_0^{10}\sqrt{325-x^2}\,dx$$

$$\approx \tfrac{2}{3}\left[\sqrt{325}+4\sqrt{325-1}+2\sqrt{325-4}+\cdots+4\sqrt{325-81}+\sqrt{325-100}\right]$$

Therefore, $CS \approx 341.0 - 300 \approx 41.1$, or \$41,100.

35. Trapezoidal Rule:

$A = \tfrac{100}{2}\,[0 + 480 + 520 + 600 + 680 + 680 + 800 + 680 + 600 + 440 + 0]$

$= 274{,}000$, or 274,000 sq ft.

Simpson's Rule:

$A = \tfrac{100}{3}\,[0 + 960 + 520 + 1200 + 680 + 1360 + 800 + 1360 + 600 + 880 + 0]$

$= 278{,}667$, or 278,667 sq ft.

36. Think of the "upper" curve as the graph of f and the lower curve as the graph of g Then the required area is given by

$$A = \int_0^{150}[f(x)-g(x)]dx = \int_0^{150} h(x)dx$$

where $h = f - g$. Using Simpson's rule,

$A \approx \tfrac{15}{3}[h(0)+4h(1)+2f(2)+4f(3)+2f(4)+\cdots 4f(9)+f(10)]$

$= 5[0+4(25)+2(40)+4(70)+2(80)+4(90)+$

$\quad 2(65)+4(50)+2(60)+4(35)+0]$

$= 7850 \ $ or $ \ 7850$ sq ft.

37. We want the present value of a perpetuity with $m = 1$, $P = 10{,}000$, and $r = 0.09$

We find $PV = \dfrac{(1)(10{,}000)}{0.09} \approx 111{,}111$ or approximately \$111,111.

CHAPTER 7 BEFORE MOVING ON, page 535

1. Let $u = \ln x$ and $dv = x^2\,dx$. Then $du = \dfrac{1}{x}dx$ and $v = \dfrac{1}{3}x^3$

$\displaystyle\int x^2 \ln x\,dx = \frac{1}{3}x^3 \ln x - \int \frac{1}{3}x^2\,dx = \frac{1}{3}x^3 \ln x - \frac{1}{9}x^3 + C$

$\displaystyle = \frac{1}{9}x^3(3\ln x - 1) + C$

2. $I = \displaystyle\int \frac{du}{x^2\sqrt{x+2x^2}}$. Let $u = \sqrt{2}x$. Then $du = \sqrt{2}\,dx$ or $dx = \dfrac{du}{\sqrt{2}} = \dfrac{\sqrt{2}}{2}du$.

$$I = \frac{\sqrt{2}}{2} \int \frac{du}{\frac{u^2}{2}\sqrt{8+u^2}} = \sqrt{2} \int \frac{du}{u^2\sqrt{(2\sqrt{2})^2+u^2}}$$

With $a = 2\sqrt{2}$ and $x = u$,

$$I = \sqrt{2} \int \frac{du}{u^2\sqrt{(2\sqrt{2})^2+u^2}} = \sqrt{2}\left[-\frac{\sqrt{8+u^2}}{8u}\right]+C = -\frac{\sqrt{8+2x^2}}{8x}+C$$

3. $n = 5$, $\Delta x = \dfrac{4-2}{5} = 0.4$; $x_0 = 2$, $x_1 = 2.4$, $x_2 = 2.8$, $x_3 = 3.2$, $x_4 = 3.6$, $x_5 = 4$

$$\int_2^4 \sqrt{x^2+1}\, dx \approx \frac{0.4}{2}[f(2)+2f(2.4)+2f(2.8)+2f(3.2)+2f(3.2)+2f(3.6)+f(4)]$$

$$= 0.2[2.23607+2(2.6)+2(2.97321)+2(3.35261)+2(3\ 73631)+4.12311]$$

$$\approx 6.3367$$

4. $n = 6$, $\Delta x = \dfrac{3-1}{6} = \dfrac{1}{3}$; $x_0 = 1$, $x_1 = \frac{4}{3}$, $x_2 = \frac{5}{3}$, $x_3 = 2$, $x_4 = \frac{7}{3}$, $x_5 = \frac{8}{3}$, $x_6 = 3$

$$\int_1^3 e^{0.2x}\, dx \approx \frac{\frac{1}{3}}{3}[f(1)+4f(\tfrac{4}{3})+2f(\tfrac{5}{3})+4f(2)+2f(\tfrac{7}{3})+4f(\tfrac{8}{3})+f(3)]$$

$$\approx \frac{1}{9}[1.2214+4(1.30561)+2(1.39561)+4(1\ 49182)+2(1.59467)$$

$$+4(1.7046)+1.82212]$$

$$\approx 3.0036$$

5. $\displaystyle\int_1^\infty e^{-2x}\, dx = \lim_{b\to\infty}\int_1^b e^{-2x}\, dx = \lim_{b\to\infty}\left[-\tfrac{1}{2}e^{-2x}\Big|_1^b\right] = \lim_{b\to\infty}\left(-\frac{1}{2}e^{-2b}+\frac{1}{2}e^{-2}\right) = \frac{1}{2}e^{-2} = \frac{1}{2e^2}$

6. a. $f(x) \geq 0$ on $[0,8]$ and $\displaystyle\int_0^8 \frac{5}{96}x^{2/3}\, dx = \frac{5}{96}\left[\frac{3}{5}x^{5/3}\Big|_0^8\right] = \frac{5}{96}(\frac{3}{5})(8^{5/3}) = 1$

Therefore f is a probability density function on $[0, 8]$.

b. $P(1 \leq x \leq 8) = \displaystyle\int_1^8 \frac{5}{96}x^{2/3}\, dx = \frac{5}{96}(\frac{3}{5})x^{5/3}\Big|_1^8 = \frac{1}{32}(32-1) = \frac{31}{32}$.

EXPLORE & DISCUSS

Page 487

1. Let $u = x^n$ and $dv = e^{ax}dx$. Then $du = nx^{n-1}dx$ and $v = \dfrac{1}{a}e^{ax}$.

7 Additional Topics in Integration

Therefore, $\int x^n e^{ax}\, dx = x^n \cdot \dfrac{1}{a} e^{ax} - \dfrac{1}{a}\int e^{ax}nx^{n-1}\, dx = \dfrac{1}{a}x^n e^{ax} - \dfrac{n}{a}\int x^{n-1}e^{ax}\, dx.$

2. Let $n = 3$ and $a = 1$. Then $\int x^3 e^x\, dx = x^3 e^x - 3\int x^2 e^x\, dx.$

Using the results of Example 4, we have

$$\int x^3 e^x\, dx = x^3 e^x - 3[e^x(x^2 - 2x + 2)] + C = e^x(x^3 - 3x^2 + 6x - 6) + C.$$

Page 493

1. Differentiate the antiderivative (the expression on the right of the formula) and show that it is equal to the integrand. For example, we can verify Formula 16 as follows.

$$\frac{d}{du}\left[\ln\left|u + \sqrt{u^2 + a^2}\right| + C\right] = \frac{\frac{d}{du}\left[u + (u^2 - a^2)^{1/2}\right]}{u + (u^2 - a^2)^{1/2}} = \frac{1 + \frac{1}{2}(u^2 - a^2)^{-1/2}(2u)}{u + (u^2 - a^2)^{1/2}}$$

$$= \frac{(u^2 - a^2)^{-1/2}[(u^2 - a^2)^{1/2} + u]}{u + (u^2 - a^2)^{1/2}} = \frac{1}{\sqrt{u^2 - a^2}}.$$

Page 495

1. Let $v = a + bu$ so that $dv = b\, du$ or $du = \frac{1}{b}dv$. Furthermore, from the first equation,

we find $u = \dfrac{1}{b}(v - a)$. Substituting, we have

$$\int \frac{u\, du}{a + bu} = \int \frac{\frac{1}{b}(v - a)}{v}\cdot \frac{1}{b}dv$$

$$= \frac{1}{b^2}\int\left(1 - \frac{a}{v}\right)dv = \frac{1}{b^2}(v - a\ln|v|) = \frac{1}{b^2}\left[a + bu - a\ln|a + bu| + C\right].$$

Page 503

1. Here $a = 0$, $b = 2$, and $n = 10$, so $\Delta x = \frac{b-a}{n} = \frac{2}{10} = 0.2$

and $x_0 = 0$, $x_1 = 0.2$, $x_2 = 0.4$, ..., $x_{10} = 2$. The Trapezoidal Rule yields

$$\int_0^2 f(x)\, dx = \frac{0.2}{2}\left[1 + 2\sqrt{1 + (0.2)^2} + 2\sqrt{1 + (0.4)^2} + \cdots + 2\sqrt{1 + (1)^2}\right.$$

$$\left. + 2\cdot\frac{2}{\sqrt{1 + (1.2)^2}} + 2\cdot\frac{2}{\sqrt{1 + (1.4)^2}} + \cdots + \frac{2}{\sqrt{1 + (2)^2}}\right]$$

$$\approx 0.1(1 + 2.0396 + 2.1541 + 2.3324 + 2.5612 + 2.8284 +$$

$$2.5607 + 2.3250 + 2.1200 + 1.9426 + 0.8944) \approx 2.276.$$

Page 508

1. Here $a = 0$, $b = 2$, and $n = 10$, so $\Delta x = \frac{b-a}{n} = \frac{2}{10} = 0.2$ and

$x_0 = 0$, $x_1 = 0.2$, $x_2 = 0.4$, ..., $x_{10} = 2$. Simpson's Rule yields

$$\int f(x)\,dx = \frac{0.2}{3}\left[1 + 4\sqrt{1+(0.2)^2} + 2\sqrt{1+(0.4)^2} + \cdots + 4\sqrt{1+(1)^2}\right.$$

$$\left. +2\cdot\frac{2}{\sqrt{1+(1.2)^2}} + 4\cdot\frac{2}{\sqrt{1+(1.4)^2}} + \cdots + \frac{2}{\sqrt{1+(2)^2}}\right]$$

$$\approx \frac{0.2}{3}\,[1 + 4.0792 + 2.1541 + 4.6648 + 2.5612 + 5.6569$$

$$+ 2.5607 + 4.6499 + 2.1200 + 3.8851 + 0.8944] \approx 2.282.$$

Page 509

1. To find the maximum error in using the Trapezoidal Rule to approximate
$\int_0^2 f(x)\,dx$ with $n = 10$, we find M_1, such that $|f''(x)| < M_1$ where $f(x) = \sqrt{1+x^2}$

   in [0, 1], and M_2, such that $|f''(x)| < M_2$ where $f(x) = \dfrac{2}{\sqrt{1+x^2}}$ on [1,2]. Take M

   to be the larger of M_1 and M_2. Then use formula (7).
2. This is similar to (1) except we use $f^{(4)}(x)$ in lieu of $f''(x)$ and we use formula (8).

Page 515

1. Since $L > 0$, the number $L/2 > 0$. Next, because $\lim\limits_{x\to\infty} f(x) = L$, there is some

   number $a \geq 0$ such that $f(x) > \dfrac{L}{2}$ whenever $x \geq a$. Therefore,

$$\int_0^\infty f(x)\,dx = \int_0^a f(x)\,dx + \int_a^\infty f(x)\,dx \geq \int_0^a f(x)\,dx + \int_a^\infty \frac{L}{2}\,dx$$

$$= \int_0^a f(x)\,dx + \lim_{b\to\infty}\int_a^b \frac{L}{2}\,dx = \int_0^a f(x)\,dx + \lim_{b\to\infty}\frac{L}{2}(b-a) = \infty.$$

So we see that $\int_0^\infty f(x)\,dx$ is divergent.

2. In this case, $\int_0^\infty f(x)\,dx$ may converge or diverge. For example, if $f(x) = \dfrac{1}{x+1}$

on $[0,\infty)$, then clearly $\lim\limits_{x\to\infty} f(x) = \lim\limits_{x\to\infty}\dfrac{1}{x+1} = 0$, but you can verify that

$\int_0^\infty \dfrac{1}{x+1}\,dx = \infty$. Next, if $f(x) = \dfrac{1}{(x+1)^2}$ on $[0,\ \infty)$, then $\lim\limits_{x\to\infty}\dfrac{1}{(x+1)^2} = 0$ but

$\int_0^\infty \dfrac{1}{(x+1)^2}\,dx = 1$, as you can verify.

Page 516

1 - 2.

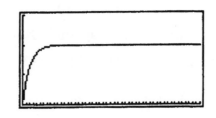

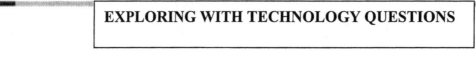

EXPLORING WITH TECHNOLOGY QUESTIONS

Page 487

1.

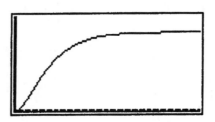

2. $\lim\limits_{t\to\infty} T(t) = \lim\limits_{t\to\infty}[-1000e^{-0.1t}(t+10)+10{,}000]$

$$= -\lim\limits_{t\to\infty}\frac{1000(t+10)}{e^{0.1t}} + 10{,}000 = 10{,}000$$

CHAPTER 8

8.1 CONCEPT QUESTIONS, page 544

1. A function of two variables is a rule that assigns to each point (x, y) in a subset of the plane, a unique number $f(x, y)$. For example, $f(x, y) = x^2 + 2y^2$ has the whole xy-plane as its domain.

2. By the uniqueness property in the definition of a function, we must have $f(a,b) = f(c,d)$.

3. a. The graph of $f(x, y)$ is the set $S = \{(x, y, z)| z = f(x, y), (x, y) \in \text{Domain of } f \}$

   b. The level curve of f is the projection onto the xy-plane of the trace of $f(x, y)$ in the plane $z = k$, where k is a constant in the range of f.

EXERCISES 8.1, page 544

1. $f(0, 0) = 2(0) + 3(0) - 4 = -4.$ $f(1, 0) = 2(1) + 3(0) - 4 = -2.$
   $f(0, 1) = 2(0) + 3(1) - 4 = -1.$ $f(1, 2) = 2(1) + 3(2) - 4 = 4.$
   $f(2,-1) = 2(2) + 3(-1) - 4 = -3.$

2. $g(1, 2) = 2 - 4 = -2;$ $g(2, 1) = 8 - 1 = 7;$ $g(1, 1) = 2 - 1 = 1;$
   $g(-1, 1) = 2 - 1 = 1; g(2, -1) = 8 - 1 = 7.$

3. $f(1, 2) = 1^2 + 2(1)(2) - 1 + 3 = 7; f(2, 1) = 2^2 + 2(2)(1) - 2 + 3 = 9$
   $f(-1, 2) = (-1)^2 + 2(-1)(2) - (-1) + 3 = 1; f(2, -1) = 2^2 + 2(2)(-1) - 2 + 3 = 1.$

4. $h(x, y) = \dfrac{x + y}{x - y}.$ $h(0,1) = \dfrac{0+1}{0-1} = -1, h(-1,1) = \dfrac{-1+1}{-1-1} = 0, h(2,1) = \dfrac{2+1}{2-1} = 3,$

   $h(\pi,-\pi) = \dfrac{\pi - \pi}{\pi - (-\pi)} = 0.$

5. $g(s,t) = 3s\sqrt{t} + t\sqrt{s} + 2; \ g(1,2) = 3(1)\sqrt{2} + 2\sqrt{1} + 2 = 4 + 3\sqrt{2}$
   $g(2, 1) = 3(2)\sqrt{1} + \sqrt{2} + 2 = 8 + \sqrt{2};$
   $g(0, 4) = 0 + 0 + 2 = 2, \ g(4,9) = 3(4)\sqrt{9} + 9\sqrt{4} + 2 = 56.$

6. $f(x,y)=xye^{x^2+y^2}$; $f(0,0)=0, f(0,1)=0, f(1,1)=e^2, f(-1,-1)=e^{1+1}=e^2.$

7. $h(1,e)=\ln e-e\ln 1=\ln e=1$; $h(e,1)=e\ln 1-\ln e=-1$;
   $h(e,e)=e\ln e-e\ln e=0.$

8. $f(0,1)=e^0=1, f(-1,-1)=(1+1)e^{-1}=2e^{-1}$; $f(a,b)=(a^2+b^2)e^{ab^2}$,
   $f(b,a)=(a^2+b^2)e^{a^2b}.$

9. $g(r,s,t)=re^{s/t}$; $g(1,1,1)=e, g(1,0,1)=1, g(-1,-1,-1)=-e^{-1/(-1)}=-e.$

10. $g(u,v,w)=\dfrac{ue^{vw}+ve^{uw}+we^{uv}}{u^2+v^2+w^2}$; $g(1,2,3)=\dfrac{e^6+2e^3+3e^2}{1+4+9}=\dfrac{e^2(3+2e+e^4)}{14}$

    $g(3,2,1)=\dfrac{3e^2+2e^3+e^6}{9+4+1}=\dfrac{e^2(3+2e+e^4)}{14}.$

11. The domain of f is the set of all ordered pairs (x, y) where x and y are real numbers.

12. The domain of g is the set of all ordered triplets (x,y,z) where x, y, and z are real numbers.

13. All real values of u and v except those satisfying the equation $u = v$.

14. Since $s^2 + t^2 \geq 0$ for all values of s and t, the domain of f is the set of all values of s and t.

15. The domain of g is the set of all ordered pairs (r,s) satisfying $rs \geq 0$, that is the set of all ordered pairs where both $r \geq 0$ and $s \geq 0$, or in which both $r \leq 0$ and $s \leq 0$.

16. The domain of f is the set of all ordered pairs (x, y) where x and y are real numbers.

17. The domain of h is the set of all ordered pairs (x, y) such that $x + y > 5$.

18. All real values of u and v satisfying $u^2 + v^2 \leq 4$.

19. The level curves of
$z = f(x, y) = 2x + 3y$
for $z = -2, -1, 0, 1, 2$, follow.

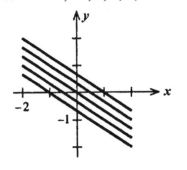

20. The level curves of
$f(x, y) = -x^2 + y$;
for $z = -2, -1, 0, 1, 2$, follow.

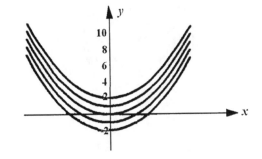

21. The level curves of
$f(x,y) = 2x^2 + y$ for
$z = -2, -1, 0, 1, 2$, are shown below.

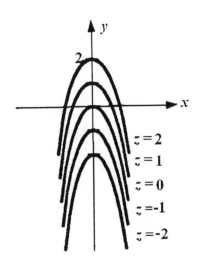

22. $f(x,y) = xy$;
$z = -4, -2, 2, 4$

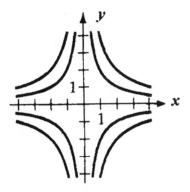

23. The level curves of
$f(x, y) = \sqrt{16 - x^2 - y^2}$
for $z = 0, 1, 2, 3, 4$

24. The level curves of
$e^x - y$;
for $z = -2, -1, 0, 1, 2$

8 Calculus of Several Variables

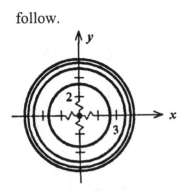 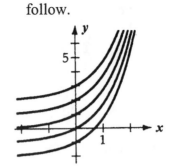

25. $V = f(1.5,4) = \pi(1.5)^2(4) = 9\pi$, or 9π cu ft

26. $f(13.5,9) = \dfrac{100(13.5)}{9} = 150.$

27. a. $M = \dfrac{80}{(1.8)^2} = 24.69$.

   b. $\dfrac{w}{(1.8)^2} < 25;$ that is, $w < 25(1.8)^2 = 81$, that is less than 81 kg.

28. $R(4,0.1) = \dfrac{4k}{(0.1)^4} = 40{,}000\,k$ dynes.

29   a. $R(x,y) = xp + yq = x(200 - \tfrac{1}{5}x - \tfrac{1}{10}y) + y(160 - \tfrac{1}{10}x - \tfrac{1}{4}y)$
$$= -\tfrac{1}{5}x^2 - \tfrac{1}{4}y^2 - \tfrac{1}{5}xy + 200x + 160y.$$
   b. The domain of R is the set of all points (x,y) satisfying
$$200 - \tfrac{1}{5}x - \tfrac{1}{10}y \ge 0,\ 160 - \tfrac{1}{10}x - \tfrac{1}{4}y \ge 0$$

30. $R(x,y) = xp + yq = x(200 - \tfrac{1}{5}x - \tfrac{1}{10}y) + y(160 - \tfrac{1}{10}x - \tfrac{1}{4}y)$
$$= -\tfrac{1}{5}x^2 - \tfrac{1}{4}y^2 - \tfrac{1}{5}xy + 200x + 160y.$$
$R(100,60) = -\tfrac{1}{5}(10{,}000) - \tfrac{1}{4}(3600) - \tfrac{1}{5}(6000) + 200(100) + 160(60) = 25{,}500,$
and this says that the revenue from the sales of 100 units of the finished and 60 units of the unfinished furniture per week is $25,500,
$R(60,100) = -\tfrac{1}{5}(3600) - \tfrac{1}{4}(10{,}000) - \tfrac{1}{5}(6000) + 200(60) + 160(100) = 23{,}580,$
and this says that the revenue from the sales of 60 units of the finished and 100

units of the unfinished furniture per week is $23,580.

31.   a. $R(x, y) = xp + yq = 20x - 0.005x^2 - 0.001xy + 15y - 0.001xy - 0.003y^2$
$$= -0.005x^2 - 0.003y^2 - 0.002xy + 20x + 15y$$
b. Since p and q must both be nonnegative, the domain of R is the set of all ordered pairs (x, y) for which
$$20 - 0.005x - 0.001y \geq 0$$
and $\qquad 15 - 0.001x - 0.003y \geq 0.$

32. $R(300, 200) = -0.005(90000) - 0.003(40000) - 0.002(60000) + 20(300)$
$$+ 15(200)$$
$$= 8310, \text{ or } \$8310.$$
$R(200, 300) = -0.005(40000) - 0.003(90000) - 0.002(60000) + 20(200)$
$$+ 15(300)$$
$$= 7910, \text{ or } \$7910.$$

33.   a. The domain of V is the set of all ordered pairs (P,T) where P and T are positive real numbers.
b. $V = \dfrac{30.9(273)}{760} = 11.10$ liters.

34.   a. The domain of S is the set of all ordered pairs (W,H) such that W and H are nonnegative real numbers.
b. $S = 0.007184(70)^{0.425}(178)^{0.725} \approx 1.87$ sq meters.

35. The output is $f(32, 243) = 100(32^{3/5})(243)^{2/5} = 100(8)(9) = 7200$ or $\$7,200$ billlion.

36. a. $f(px, py) = a(px)^b(py)^{1-b} = ap^b x^b p^{1-b} y^{1-b} = apx^b y^{1-b} = pf(x, y)$
b.   Increasing the amount of money expended for labor by $r\%$ gives $x + 0.01rx = (1.01r)x$ as the new amount spent on labor. Similarly, the new amount spent on capital is $(1 + 0.01r)y$. Using the result of part (a) with $p = 1.01r$, we see that the resultant output is
$$f[(1 + 0.01r)x, (1 + 0.01r)y] = (1.01r)f(x, y) = f(x, y) + (0.01r)f(x, y)$$
that is; the output is increased by $(0.01r) f(x, y)$ or $r\%$.

37.   The number of suspicious fires is

$$N(100,20) = \frac{100[1000 + 0.03(100^2)(20)]^{1/2}}{[5 + 0.2(20)]^2} = 103.29, \text{ or approximately } 103$$

38. $A = f(10,000, 0.1, 3) = 10,000e^{(0.1)(3)} = 10,000e^{0.3}$, or $13,498.59.

39. a. $P = f(100,000, 0.08, 30) = \dfrac{100,000(0.08)}{12\left[1 - \left(1 + \dfrac{0.08}{12}\right)^{-360}\right]} \approx 733.76,$ or $733.76.

$P = f(100,000, 0.1, 30) = \dfrac{100,000(0.1)}{12\left[1 - \left(1 + \dfrac{0.1}{12}\right)^{-360}\right]} \approx 877.57,$ or $877.57.

b. $P = f(100,000, 0.08, 20) = \dfrac{100,000(0,08)}{12\left[1 - \left(1 + \dfrac{0.08}{12}\right)^{-240}\right]} \approx 836.44,$ or $836.44.

40. $B = f(280,000, 0.06, 30, 60) = 280,000\left[\dfrac{\left(1 + \dfrac{0.06}{12}\right)^{60} - 1}{\left(1 + \dfrac{0.06}{12}\right)^{360} - 1}\right] \approx 19,447.80.$

Therefore, they owe $280,000 - 19,447.80$, or $260,552.20.

$$B = f(280,000, 0.06, 30, 240) = 280,000\left[\dfrac{\left(1 + \dfrac{0.06}{12}\right)^{240} - 1}{\left(1 + \dfrac{0.06}{12}\right)^{360} - 1}\right] = 128,789.96.$$

Therefore, they owe $280,000 - 128,789.96$, or $151,210.04.

41. $f(M, 600, 10) = \dfrac{\pi^2(360,000)M(10)}{900} \approx 39,478.42\,M$

or $\dfrac{39,478.42}{980} \approx 40.28$ times gravity.

42. $f(20, 40, 5) = \sqrt{\dfrac{2(20)(40)}{5}} = \sqrt{320} \approx 17.9$, or 18 bicycles.

43. False. Let $h(x, y) = xy$. Then there are no functions f and g such that
$h(x, y) = f(x) + g(y)$.

44. False. Let $f(x, y) = xy$. Then
$$f(ax, ay) = (ax)(ay) = a^2 xy \neq axy = a f(x, y).$$

45. False. Since $x^2 - y^2 = (x + y)(x - y)$, we see that $x^2 - y^2 = 0$ if $y = \pm x$.
Therefore, the domain of f is $\{(x, y) \mid y \neq \pm x\}$.

46. True. If $c > 0$, then $z = f(x, y) = c$ and the point (x, y, c) on the graph of f is c units above the xy-plane. Similarly, if $c < 0$, then $z = f(x, y) = c$ and the point (x, y, c) on the graph of f lies $|c|$ units below the xy-plane.

8.2 CONCEPT QUESTIONS, page 556

1 a. $\dfrac{\partial f}{\partial x}(a, b) = \dfrac{\partial f}{\partial x}(x, y)\bigg|_{(a,b)} = \left[\lim_{h \to 0} \dfrac{f(x+h, y) - f(x, y)}{h}\right]_{(a,b)}$

b. See page 547-548 of the text.

2. a. Two commodities are substitute commodities if a decrease in the demand for one results in an increase in the demand for the other. Examples are coffee and tea. Two commodities are complementary commodities if a decrease in the demand for one results in a decrease in the demand for the other as well. Examples are cameras (non-digital) and film.

b. If the demand equation relating the quantities x and y to the unit prices are $x = f(p, q)$ and $y = g(p, q)$, then the commodities are substitute commodities if

$\dfrac{\partial f}{\partial q} > 0$ and $\dfrac{\partial g}{\partial p} > 0$ and are complementary commodities if $\dfrac{\partial f}{\partial q} < 0$ and $\dfrac{\partial g}{\partial p} < 0$

3. $f_x, f_y, f_{xx}, f_{xy},$ and f_{yy}.

EXERCISES 8.2, page 557

1. $f_x = 2, f_y = 3$

2. $f_x = 2y, f_y = 2x$

3. $g_x = 4x, g_y = 4$

4. $f_x = 2x$ and $f_y = 2y$

5. $f_x = -\dfrac{4y}{x^3}; f_y = \dfrac{2}{x^2}.$

6. $f_x = \dfrac{1}{1+y}, f_y = -\dfrac{x}{(1+y)^2}$

7. $g(u,v) = \dfrac{u-v}{u+v}; \dfrac{\partial g}{\partial u} = \dfrac{(u+v)(1)-(u-v)(1)}{(u+v)^2} = \dfrac{2v}{(u+v)^2}$

$\dfrac{\partial g}{\partial v} = \dfrac{(u+v)(-1)-(u-v)(1)}{(u+v)^2} = -\dfrac{2u}{(u+v)^2}$

8. $f(x,y) = \dfrac{x^2-y^2}{x^2+y^2}; f_x = \dfrac{(x^2+y^2)(2x)-(x^2-y^2)(2x)}{(x^2+y^2)^2} = \dfrac{4xy^2}{(x^2+y^2)^2}$

$f_y = \dfrac{(x^2+y^2)(-2y)-(x^2-y^2)(2y)}{(x^2+y^2)^2} = -\dfrac{4x^2y}{(x^2+y^2)^2}.$

9. $f(s,t) = (s^2 - st + t^2)^3; f_s = 3(s^2 - st + t^2)^2(2s - t)$ and $f_t = 3(s^2 - st + t^2)^2(2t -s)$

10. $g(s,t) = s^2t + st^{-3}; g_s = 2st + t^{-3}$ and $g_t = s^2 - 3st^{-4}.$

11. $f(x,y) = (x^2 + y^2)^{2/3}; f_x = \tfrac{2}{3}(x^2 + y^2)^{-1/3}(2x) = \tfrac{4}{3}x(x^2 + y^2)^{-1/3}$ Similarly, $f_y = \tfrac{4}{3}y(x^2 + y^2)^{-1/3}.$

12. $f(x,y) = x(1+y^2)^{1/2}; f_x = \sqrt{1+y^2}$ and $f_y = x(\tfrac{1}{2})(1+y^2)^{-1/2}(2y) = \dfrac{xy}{\sqrt{1+y^2}}.$

13. $f(x,y) = e^{xy+1}; f_x = ye^{xy+1}, f_y = xe^{xy+1}.$

14. $f(x,y) = (e^x + e^y)^5; f_x = 5e^x(e^x + e^y)^4, f_y = 5e^y(e^x + e^y)^4.$

15. $f(x,y) = x \ln y + y \ln x; f_x = \ln y + \dfrac{y}{x}, f_y = \dfrac{x}{y} + \ln x.$

16. $f(x,y) = x^2e^{y^2} . \dfrac{\partial f}{\partial x} = 2xe^{y^2}, \dfrac{\partial f}{\partial y} = x^2e^{y^2}(2y) = 2x^2ye^{y^2}.$

17. $g(u,v) = e^u \ln v. g_u = e^u \ln v, g_v = \dfrac{e^u}{v}.$

18. $f(x) = \dfrac{e^{xy}}{x+y}$; $f_x = \dfrac{(x+y)e^{xy}(y) - e^{xy}(1)}{(x+y)^2} = \dfrac{(xy+y^2-1)e^{xy}}{(x+y)^2}$. Similarly,

$f_y = \dfrac{(x^2+xy-1)e^{xy}}{(x+y)^2}$.

19 $f(x,y,z) = xyz + xy^2 + yz^2 + zx^2$; $f_x = yz + y^2 + 2xz$,

$f_y = xz + 2xy + z^2, f_z = xy + 2yz + x^2$.

20. $g(u,v,w) = \dfrac{2uvw}{u^2+v^2+w^2}$;

$g_u = \dfrac{(u^2+v^2+w^2)(2vw) - 2uvw(2u)}{(u^2+v^2+w^2)^2} = \dfrac{2vw(v^2+w^2-u^2)}{(u^2+v^2+w^2)^2}$. Similarly,

$g_v = \dfrac{2uw(u^2+w^2-v^2)}{(u^2+v^2+w^2)^2}$, $g_w = \dfrac{2uv(u^2+v^2-w^2)}{(u^2+v^2+w^2)^2}$.

21. $h(r,s,t) = e^{rst}$; $h_r = ste^{rst}$, $h_s = rte^{rst}$, $h_t = rse^{rst}$.

22. $f(x,y,z) = xe^{y/z}$; $\dfrac{\partial f}{\partial x} = e^{y/z}, \dfrac{\partial f}{\partial y} = xe^{y/z}\left(\dfrac{1}{z}\right) = \dfrac{x}{z}e^{yz}$;

$\dfrac{\partial f}{\partial z} = xe^{y/z}\left(-\dfrac{y}{z^2}\right) = -\dfrac{xy}{z^2}e^{y/z}$

23 $f(x,y) = x^2y + xy^2$; $f_x(1,2) = 2xy + y^2\big|_{(1,2)} = 8$; $f_y(1,2) = x^2 + 2xy\big|_{(1,2)} = 5$.

24. $f(x,y) = x^2 + xy + y^2 + 2x - y$; $f_x(-1,2) = 2x + y + 2\big|_{(-1,2)} = 2(-1) + 2 + 2 = 2$.

$f_y(-1,2) = x + 2y - 1\big|_{(-1,2)} = -1 + 2(2) - 1 = 2$.

25. $f(x,y) = x\sqrt{y} + y^2 = xy^{1/2} + y^2$; $f_x(2,1) = \sqrt{y}\big|_{(2,1)} = 1$,

$f_y(2,1) = \dfrac{x}{2\sqrt{y}} + 2y\big|_{(2,1)} = 3$.

26. $g(x,y) = \sqrt{x^2+y^2} = (x^2+y^2)^{1/2}$;

$$g_x(3,4) = \dfrac{x}{\sqrt{x^2+y^2}}\bigg|_{(3,4)} = \dfrac{3}{5}; \quad g_y(3,4) = \dfrac{y}{\sqrt{x^2+y^2}}\bigg|_{(3,4)} = \dfrac{4}{5}.$$

27. $f(x,y) = \dfrac{x}{y}; \quad f_x(1,2) = \dfrac{1}{y}\bigg|_{(1,2)} = \dfrac{1}{2}, \quad f_y(1,2) = -\dfrac{x}{y^2}\bigg|_{(1,2)} = -\dfrac{1}{4}.$

28. $f(x,y) = \dfrac{x+y}{x-y};$

$$f_x(1,-2) = \dfrac{(x-y)(1)-(x+y)(1)}{(x-y)^2}\bigg|_{(1,-2)} = -\dfrac{2y}{(x-y)^2}\bigg|_{(1,-2)} = \dfrac{4}{9}.$$

$$f_y(1,-2) = \dfrac{(x-y)(1)-(x+y)(-1)}{(x-y)^2}\bigg|_{(1,-2)} = \dfrac{2x}{(x-y)^2}\bigg|_{(1,-2)} = \dfrac{2}{9}.$$

29 $f(x,y) = e^{xy}. \quad f_x(1,1) = ye^{xy}\big|_{(1,1)} = e, \quad f_y(1,1) = xe^{xy}\big|_{(1,1)} = e.$

30. $f(x,y) = e^x \ln y. \quad f_x(0,e) = e^x \ln y\big|_{(0,e)} = \ln e - 1, \quad f_y(0,e) = \dfrac{e^x}{y}\bigg|_{(0,e)} = \dfrac{1}{e}.$

31. $f(x,y,z) = x^2yz^3; \quad f_x(1,0,2) = 2xyz^3\big|_{(1,0,2)} = 0; \quad f_y(1,0,2) = x^2z^3\big|_{(1,0,2)} = 8.$

$f_z(1,0,2) = 3x^2yz^2\big|_{(1,0,2)} = 0.$

32. $f(x,y,z) = x^2y^2 + z^2; \quad f_x(1,1,2) = 2xy^2\big|_{(1,1,2)} = 2, \quad f_y(1,1,2) = 2x^2y\big|_{(1,1,2)} = 2,$

$f_z(1,1,2) = 2z\big|_{(1,1,2)} = 4.$

33. $f(x,y) = x^2y + xy^3; \quad f_x = 2xy + y^3, \quad f_y = x^2 + 3xy^2.$

Therefore, $f_{xx} = 2y, \quad f_{xy} = 2x + 3y^2 = f_{yx}, \quad f_{yy} = 6xy.$

34. $f(x,y) = x^3 + x^2y + x + 4; \quad f_x = 3x^2 + 2xy + 1, \quad f_y = x^2; \quad f_{xx} = 6x + 2y,$

$f_{xy} = 2x = f_{yx}, \quad f_{yy} = 0.$

35. $f(x,y) = x^2 - 2xy + 2y^2 + x - 2y$; $f_x = 2x - 2y + 1$, $f_y = -2x + 4y - 2$; $f_{xx} = 2$, $f_{xy} = -2$, $f_{yx} = -2$, $f_{yy} = 4$.

36. $f(x,y) = x^3 + x^2 y^2 + y^3 + x + y$; $f_x = 3x^2 + 2xy^2 + 1$, $f_y = 2x^2 y + 3y^2 + 1$; $f_{xx} = 6x + 2y^2$, $f_{yy} = 2x^2 + 6y$, $f_{xy} = 4xy = f_{yx}$.

37. $f(x,y) = (x^2 + y^2)^{1/2}$; $f_x = \frac{1}{2}(x^2 + y^2)^{-1/2}(2x) = x(x^2 + y^2)^{-1/2}$;

    $f_y = y(x^2 + y^2)^{-1/2}$.

$$f_{xx} = (x^2 + y^2)^{-1/2} + x(-\tfrac{1}{2})(x^2 + y^2)^{-3/2}(2x) = (x^2 + y^2)^{-1/2} - x^2(x^2 + y^2)^{-3/2}$$

$$= (x^2 + y^2)^{-3/2}(x^2 + y^2 - x^2) = \frac{y^2}{(x^2 + y^2)^{3/2}}.$$

$$f_{xy} = x(-\tfrac{1}{2})(x^2 + y^2)^{-3/2}(2y) = -\frac{xy}{(x^2 + y^2)^{3/2}} = f_{yx}.$$

$$f_{yy} = (x^2 + y^2)^{-1/2} + y(-\tfrac{1}{2})(x^2 + y^2)^{-3/2}(2y) = (x^2 + y^2)^{-1/2} - y^2(x^2 + y^2)^{-3/2}$$

$$= (x^2 + y^2)^{-3/2}(x^2 + y^2 - y^2) = \frac{x^2}{(x^2 + y^2)^{3/2}}.$$

38. $f(x,y) = xy^{1/2} + yx^{1/2}$; $f_x = y^{1/2} + \frac{1}{2}yx^{-1/2}$, $f_y = \frac{1}{2}xy^{-1/2} + x^{1/2}$;

    $f_{xx} = -\frac{1}{4}yx^{-3/2}$, $f_{yy} = -\frac{1}{4}xy^{-3/2}$, $f_{xy} = \frac{1}{2}y^{-1/2} + \frac{1}{2}x^{-1/2} = f_{yx}$.

39. $f(x,y) = e^{-x/y}$; $f_x = -\frac{1}{y}e^{-x/y}$; $f_y = \frac{x}{y^2}e^{-x/y}$; $f_{xx} = \frac{1}{y^2}e^{-x/y}$;

$$f_{xy} = -\frac{x}{y^3}e^{-x/y} + \frac{1}{y^2}e^{-x/y} = \left(\frac{-x+y}{y^3}\right)e^{-x/y} = f_{yx}.$$

$$f_{yy} = -\frac{2x}{y^3}e^{-x/y} + \frac{x^2}{y^4}e^{-x/y} = \frac{x}{y^3}\left(\frac{x}{y} - 2\right)e^{-x/y}.$$

40. $f(x,y) = \ln(1 + x^2 y^2)$; $f_x = \frac{2xy^2}{1 + x^2 y^2}$, $f_y = \frac{2x^2 y}{1 + x^2 y}$.

$$f_{xx} = \frac{(1 + x^2 y^2)(2y^2) - 2xy^2(2xy^2)}{(1 + x^2 y^2)^2} = \frac{2y^2(1 - x^2 y^2)}{(1 + x^2 y^2)^2}$$

8 *Calculus of Several Variables*

$$f_{yy} = \frac{(1+x^2y^2)(2x^2) - (2x^2y)(2x^2y)}{(1+x^2y^2)^2} = \frac{2x^2(1-x^2y^2)}{(1+x^2y^2)^2}.$$

$$f_{xy} = \frac{(1+x^2y^2)(4xy) - 2xy^2(2x^2y)}{(1+x^2y^2)^2} = \frac{4xy}{(1+x^2y^2)^2} = f_{yx}.$$

41. a. $f(x,y) = 20x^{3/4}y^{1/4}$. $f_x(256,16) = 15\left(\dfrac{y}{x}\right)^{1/4}\Bigg|_{(256,16)}$

$$= 15\left(\frac{16}{256}\right)^{1/4} = 15\left(\frac{2}{4}\right) = 7.5.$$

$$f_y(256,16) = 5\left(\frac{x}{y}\right)^{3/4}\Bigg|_{(256,16)} = 5\left(\frac{256}{16}\right)^{3/4} = 5(80) = 40.$$

b. Yes.

42. a. $f(x,y) = 40x^{4/5}y^{1/5}$. $f_x = 32x^{-1/5}y^{1/5}$, $f_x(32,243) = 32(32)^{-1/5}(243)^{1/5} = 48$
or 48 units/unit change in labor.
$f_y = 8x^{4/5}y^{-4/5}$, $f_y(32,243) = \frac{8(16)}{81} = \frac{128}{81}$, or $\frac{128}{81}$ units/unit change in capital
b. No

43. $p(x,y) = 200 - 10(x-\frac{1}{2})^2 - 15(y-1)^2$. $\dfrac{\partial p}{\partial x}(0,1) = -20(x-\frac{1}{2})\big|_{(0,1)} = 10$;

At the location $(0,1)$ in the figure, the price of land is changing at the rate of \$10 per sq ft per mile change to the right.

$$\frac{\partial p}{\partial y}(0,1) = -30(y-1)\big|_{(0,1)} = 0;$$

At the location $(0,1)$ in the figure, the price of land is constant per mile change upwards.

44. $f(p,q) = 10{,}000 - 10p + 0.2q^2$; $g(p,q) = 5000 + 0.8p^2 - 20q$.

$\dfrac{\partial f}{\partial q} = 0.4q > 0$ and $\dfrac{\partial g}{\partial p} = 1.6p > 0$ and so the two products are substitute commodities.

45. $f(p,q) = 10{,}000 - 10p - e^{0.5q}$; $g(p,q) = 50{,}000 - 4000q - 10p$.

$$\frac{\partial f}{\partial q} = -0.5e^{0.5q} < 0 \text{ and } \frac{\partial g}{\partial p} = -10 < 0$$

and so the two commodities are complementary commodities.

46. We have $\frac{1}{5}x + \frac{1}{10}y = 200 - p$ and $x + \frac{1}{2}y = 1000 - 5p$

or $\frac{1}{10}x + \frac{1}{4}y = 160 - q$, $x + \frac{5}{2}y = 1600 - 10q$.

Then $2y = 600 + 5p - 10q$ or $y = \frac{1}{2}(600 + 5p - 10q) = g(p,q)$.

Also, $x = 1000 - 5p - (\frac{1}{2})(\frac{1}{2})(600 + 5p - 10q) = 1000 - 5p - 150 - \frac{5}{4}p + \frac{5}{2}q$

$= 850 - \frac{25}{4}p + \frac{5}{2}q = f(p,q)$.

Next, we compute $\dfrac{\partial f}{\partial q} = \dfrac{5}{2} > 0$ and $\dfrac{\partial g}{\partial p} = \dfrac{5}{2} > 0$ and so they are substitute

commodities.

47. $R(x,y) = -0.2x^2 - 0.25y^2 - 0.2xy + 200x + 160y$.

$$\frac{\partial R}{\partial x}(300,250) = -0.4x - 0.2y + 200\big|_{(300,250)}$$

$$= -0.4(300) - 0.2(250) + 200 = 30$$

and this says that at a sales level of 300 finished and 250 unfinished units the revenue is increasing at the rate of $30 per week per unit increase in the finished units.

$$\frac{\partial R}{\partial y}(300,250) = -0.5y - 0.2x + 160\big|_{(300,250)}$$

$$= -0.5(250) - 0.2(300) + 160 = -25$$

and this says that at a level of 300 finished and 250 unfinished units the revenue is decreasing at the rate of $25 per week per increase in the unfinished units.

48. $P(x,y) = -0.02x^2 - 15y^2 + xy + 39x + 25y - 20,000$.

$$\frac{\partial P}{\partial x}(4000,150) = -0.04x + y + 39\big|_{(4000,150)} = -0.04(4000) + 150 + 39 = 29,$$

and this says that when the inventory is $4,000,000 and the floor space is 150,000 sq ft, the monthly profit is increasing at the rate of $29 per thousand dollars increase in the inventory. A similar interpretation holds for

$$\frac{\partial P}{\partial y}(4000,150) = x - 30y + 25\big|_{(4000,150)} = -475.$$

Next, $\dfrac{\partial P}{\partial x}(5000,150) = -0.04x + y + 395\big|_{(5000,150)} = -0.04(5000) + 150 + 39 = -11,$

$\dfrac{\partial P}{\partial y}(5000,150) = -30y + x + 25\big|_{(5000,150)} = -30(150) + 5000 + 25 = 5.$

49. a. $T = f(32,20) = 35.74 + 0.6215(32) - 35.75(20^{0.16}) + 0.4275(32)(20^{0.16})$
      $\approx 19.99,$ or approximately $20°\,F.$

   b. $\dfrac{\partial T}{\partial s} = -35.75(0.16S^{-0.84}) + 0.4275t(0.16S^{-0.84})$

      $= 0.16(-35.75 + 0.4275t)s^{-0.84}$

      $\dfrac{\partial T}{\partial s}\bigg|_{(32,20)} = 0.16[-35.75 + 0.4275(32)]20^{-0.84} \approx -0.285,$

      that is, the wind chill will drop by 0.3 degrees for each 1 mph increase in wind speed.

50. a. $\dfrac{\partial E}{\partial V} = 0.4\left(1 - \dfrac{v}{V}\right)^{-0.6}\dfrac{\partial}{\partial V}\left(-\dfrac{v}{V}\right) = 0.4\left(1 - \dfrac{v}{V}\right)^{-0.6}\left(\dfrac{v}{V^2}\right)$

      $= \dfrac{0.4v}{V^2\left(1 - \dfrac{v}{V}\right)^{0.6}} > 0$

      and this says that with v held constant, an increase in V increases the engine efficiency, which is to be expected.

   b. $\dfrac{\partial E}{\partial v} = 0.4\left(1 - \dfrac{v}{V}\right)^{-0.6}\dfrac{\partial}{\partial v}\left(-\dfrac{v}{V}\right) = -\dfrac{0.4v}{V\left(1 - \dfrac{v}{V}\right)^{0.6}} < 0$

      and this says that with V held fixed, an increase in v decreases the engine efficiency.

51. $V = \dfrac{30.9T}{P}$ $\dfrac{\partial V}{\partial T} = \dfrac{30.9}{P}$ and $\dfrac{\partial V}{\partial P} = -\dfrac{30.9T}{P^2}.$

      Therefore, $\dfrac{\partial V}{\partial T}\bigg|_{T=300,\,P=800} = \dfrac{30.9}{800} = 0.039,$ or 0.039 liters/degree.

$$\frac{\partial V}{\partial P}\bigg|_{T=300,P=800} = -\frac{(30.9)(300)}{800^2} = -0.015$$

or -0.015 liters/mm of mercury.

52. $\dfrac{\partial S}{\partial W}(70,180) = 0.007184(0.425)W^{-0.575}H^{0.725}\bigg|_{(70,180)}$

$$= 0.0030532(70)^{-0.575}(180)^{0.725} = 0.01145$$

and this says that the surface area is increasing at the rate of 0.01145 square meters per increase of 1 kg weight, the weight and height being fixed at 70 kg and 180 cm.

$\dfrac{\partial S}{\partial H}(70,180) = 0.007184(0.725)W^{0.425}H^{-0.275}\bigg|_{(70,180)}$

$$= 0.0052084(70)^{0.425}(180)^{-0.275} = 0.00760,$$

and this says that the surface area is increasing at the rate of 0.0076 square meters per increase of 1 cm in height, the weight and height being fixed at 70 kg and 180 cm.

53. $V = \dfrac{kT}{P}$ and $\dfrac{\partial V}{\partial T} = \dfrac{k}{P}$; $T = \dfrac{VP}{k}$ and $\dfrac{\partial T}{\partial P} = \dfrac{V}{k} = \dfrac{T}{P}$; and

$P = \dfrac{kT}{V}$ and $\dfrac{\partial P}{\partial V} = -\dfrac{kT}{V^2} = -kT \cdot \dfrac{P^2}{(kT)^2} = -\dfrac{P^2}{kT}$

Therefore $\dfrac{\partial V}{\partial T} \cdot \dfrac{\partial T}{\partial P} \cdot \dfrac{\partial P}{\partial V} = \dfrac{k}{P} \cdot \dfrac{T}{P} \cdot -\dfrac{P^2}{kT} = -1.$

54. $\dfrac{\partial K}{\partial m} = \dfrac{1}{2}v^2$, $\dfrac{\partial K}{\partial v} = mv$ and $\dfrac{\partial^2 K}{\partial v^2} = m$. Therefore

$\dfrac{\partial K}{\partial m} \cdot \dfrac{\partial^2 K}{\partial v^2} = \left(\dfrac{1}{2}v^2\right)(m) = \dfrac{1}{2}mv^2 = K$ as was to be shown.

55. False. Let $f(x,y) = xy^{1/2}$. Then $f_x = y^{1/2}$ is defined at $(0, 0)$. But

$f_y = \dfrac{1}{2}xy^{-1/2} = \dfrac{x}{2y^{1/2}}$ is not defined at $(0, 0)$.

56. True. This is a consequence of the definition of $f_x(a,b)$ as the rate of change of

8 *Calculus of Several Variables*

f in the x-direction at (a,b) with y held fixed.

57. True. See Section 8.2.

58. False. Let $f(x,y) = xy^{5/3}$. Then $f_{xy} = \dfrac{5}{3}y^{2/3} = f_{yx}$. So both f_{xy} and f_{yx} exist

   at $(0,0)$. But $f_{yy} = \dfrac{10x}{9y^{1/3}}$ is not defined at $(0,0)$.

USING TECHNOLOGY EXERCISES 8.2, page 560

1. 1.3124; 0.4038
2. 9.4548; 2.3637
3. −1.8889; 0.7778

4. 0.0370; 0.7407
5. −0.3863; −0.8497
6. −0.0255; −0.0316

8.3 CONCEPT QUESTIONS, page 569

1. a. A function $f(x,y)$ has a relative maximum at (a,b) if $f(a,b)$ is the largest number compared to $f(x,y)$ for all (x,y) near (a,b).
   b. $f(a,y)$ has an absolute maximum at (a,b) if $f(a,b)$ is the largest number compared to $f(x,y)$ for all (x,y) in the domain of f.
2. a. See the definition in the text on page 563.
   b. If f has a relative extremum at (a,b), then (a,b) must be a critical point of f The converse is false.
3. See the procedure given in the text on page 564.

EXERCISES 8.3, page 570

1. $f(x,y) = 1 - 2x^2 - 3y^2$. To find the critical point(s) of f, we solve the system
$$\begin{cases} f_x = -4x = 0 \\ f_y = -6y = 0 \end{cases}$$
obtaining $(0,0)$ as the only critical point of f. Next,
   $f_{xx} = -4, f_{xy} = 0$, and $f_{yy} = -6$.
In particular, $f_{xx}(0,0) = -4, f_{xy}(0,0) = 0$, and $f_{yy}(0,0) = -6$, giving
   $D(0,0) = (-4)(-6) - 0^2 = 24 > 0$.
Since $f_{xx}(0,0) < 0$, the Second Derivative Test implies that $(0,0)$ gives rise to a relative maximum of f. Finally, the relative maximum of f is $f(0,0) = 1$.

2. To find the critical points of f, we solve the system
$$\begin{cases} f_x = 2x - y = 0 \\ f_y = -x + 2y = 0 \end{cases}$$
obtaining $x = 0$ and $y = 0$ and so $(0,0)$ is the only critical point. Next, $f_{xx} = 2$, $f_{xy} = -1$, and $f_{yy} = 2$. So $D(x,y) = f_{xx}f_{yy} - f_{xy}^2 = 3$. In particular, since $D(0,0) = 3 > 0$ and $f_{xx}(0,0) = 2 > 0$, we see that $(0,0)$ gives rise to a relative minimum.

3. To find the critical points of f, we solve the system
$$\begin{cases} f_x = 2x - 2 = 0 \\ f_y = -2y + 4 = 0 \end{cases}$$
obtaining $x = 1$ and $y = 2$ so that $(1,2)$ is the only critical point.
$$f_{xx} = 2, f_{xy} = 0, \text{ and } f_{yy} = -2.$$
So $D(x,y) = f_{xx}f_{yy} - f_{xy}^2 = -4$. In particular, $D(1,2) = -4 < 0$ and so $(1,2)$ affords a saddle point of f and $f(1,2) = 4$.

4. $f(x,y) = 2x^2 + y^2 - 4x + 6y + 3$. To find the critical points of f, we solve the system
$$\begin{cases} f_x = 4x - 4 = 0 \\ f_y = 2y + 6 = 0 \end{cases}$$
obtaining $(1,-3)$ as the only critical point of f. Next, $f_{xx} = 4, f_{xy} = 0$, and $f_{yy} = 2$. Therefore,
$$D(1,-3) = f_{xx}(1,-3)f_{yy}(1,-3) - f_{xy}^2(1,-3) = (4)(2) - 0 = 8 > 0.$$
Since $f_{xx}(1,-3) > 0$, $(1,-3)$ gives rise to a relative minimum of f Finally,
$$f(1,-3) = 2 + 9 - 4 + 6(-3) + 3 = -8$$
is the relative minimum value.

5. $f(x,y) = x^2 + 2xy + 2y^2 - 4x + 8y - 1$. To find the critical point(s) of f, we solve the system
$$\begin{cases} f_x = 2x + 2y - 4 = 0 \\ f_y = 2x + 4y + 8 = 0 \end{cases}$$
obtaining $(8,-6)$ as the critical point of f. Next, $f_{xx} = 2, f_{xy} = 2, f_{yy} = 4$. In particular, $f_{xx}(8,-6) = 2, f_{xy}(8,-6) = 2, f_{yy}(8,-6) = 4$, giving $D = 2(4) - 4 = 4 > 0$. Since $f_{xx}(8,-6) > 0$, $(8,-6)$ gives rise to a relative minimum of f. Finally, the relative minimum value of f is $f(8,-6) = -41$.

6. To find the critical points of f, we solve the system
$$\begin{cases} f_x = 2x - 4y + 4 = 0 \\ f_y = -4x + 4y + 8 = 0, \end{cases}$$
obtaining $x = 6$ and $y = 4$ so that $(6,4)$ is the only critical point. Next, $f_{xx} = 2, f_{xy} = -4$, and $f_{yy} = 4$. So $D(x,y) = f_{xx}f_{yy} - f_{xy}^2 = 8 - (16) = -8$. In particular, $D(6,4) = -8 < 0$ and so $(6,4)$ gives a saddle point of f.

7. $f(x,y) = 2x^3 + y^2 - 9x^2 - 4y + 12x - 2..$ To find the critical points of f, we solve the system
$$\begin{cases} f_x = 6x^2 - 18x + 12 = 0 \\ f_y = 2y - 4 = 0 \end{cases}$$
The first equation is equivalent to $x^2 - 3x + 2 = 0$, or $(x-2)(x-1) = 0$ which gives $x = 1$ or 2. The second equation of the system gives $y = 2$. Therefore, there are two critical points, $(1,2)$ and $(2,2)$. Next, we compute
$$f_{xx} = 12x - 18 = 6(2x - 3), f_{xy} = 0, f_{yy} = 2.$$
At the point $(1,2)$:
$$f_{xx}(1,2) = 6(2-3) = -6, f_{xy}(1,2) = 0, \text{ and } f_{yy}(1,2) = 2.$$
Therefore, $D = (-6)(2) - 0 = -12 < 0$ and we conclude that $(1,2)$ gives rise to a saddle point of f. At the point $(2,2)$:
$$f_{xx}(2,2) = 6(4-3) = 6, f_{xy}(2,2) = 0, \text{ and } f_{yy}(2,2) = 2.$$
Therefore, $D = (6)(2) - 0 = 12 > 0$. Since $f_{xx}(2,2) > 0$, we see that $(2,2)$ gives rise to a relative minimum with value $f(2,2) = -2$.

8. To find the critical points of f, we solve the system
$$\begin{cases} f_x = 6x^2 - 12x + 12 = 0 \\ f_y = 2y - 4 = 0 \end{cases}$$
The first equation is equivalent to $x^2 - 2x + 2 = 0$. Using the quadratic formula, we find that the equation has no real solutions. Therefore, there are no critical points.

9. To find the critical points of f, we solve the system
$$\begin{cases} f_x = 3x^2 - 2y + 7 = 0 \\ f_y = 2y - 2x - 8 = 0 \end{cases}$$
Adding the two equations gives $3x^2 - 2x - 1 = 0$, or $(3x + 1)(x - 1) = 0$. Therefore, $x = -1/3$ or 1. Substituting each of these values of x into the second

equation gives $y = 8/3$ and $y = 5$, respectively. Therefore, $(-\frac{1}{3}, \frac{11}{3})$ and $(1,5)$ are critical points of f.

Next, $f_{xx} = 6x$, $f_{xy} = -2$, and $f_{yy} = 2$. So $D(x,y) = 12x - 4 = 4(3x - 1)$. Then

$$D(-\tfrac{1}{3}, \tfrac{11}{3}) = 4(-1-1) = -8 < 0$$

and so $(-\frac{1}{3}, \frac{11}{3})$ gives a saddle point. Next, $D(1,5) = 4(3 - 1) = 8 > 0$ and since $f_{xx}(1,5) = 6 > 0$, we see that $(1,5)$ gives rise to a relative minimum.

10. $f(x,y) = 2y^3 - 3y^2 - 12y + 2x^2 - 6x + 2$. To find the critical points of f, we solve the system

$$\begin{cases} f_x = 4x - 6 = 0 \\ f_y = 6y^2 - 6y - 12 = 0 \end{cases}$$

we find $x = 3/2$ and $y = -1$ or 2. Therefore, $(\frac{3}{2}, -1)$ and $(\frac{3}{2}, 2)$ are critical points of f Next, we find $f_{xx} = 4$, $f_{xy} = 0$ and $f_{yy} = 12y - 6 = 6(2y - 1)$.

At the point $(\frac{3}{2}, -1)$:

$$f_{xx}(\tfrac{3}{2}, -1) = 4,\ f_{xy}(\tfrac{3}{2}, -1) = 0,\ \text{and } f_{yy}(\tfrac{3}{2}, -1) = 6(-2 - 1) = -18.$$

Therefore, $D = (4)(-18) - 0 = -72 < 0$ and $(\frac{3}{2}, -1)$ gives rise to a saddle point of f.

At the point $(\frac{3}{2}, 2)$:

$$f_{xx}(\tfrac{3}{2}, 2) = 4,\ f_{xy}(\tfrac{3}{2}, 2) = 0,\ \text{and } f_{yy}(\tfrac{3}{2}, 2) = 6(4 - 1) = 18.$$

Since $D > 0$ and $f_{xx}(\frac{3}{2}, 0) > 0$, we conclude that $(\frac{3}{2}, 2)$ gives rise to a relative minimum of f. Also $f(\frac{3}{2}, 2) = 2(2)^3 - 3(2)^2 - 12(2) + 2(\frac{3}{2})^2 - 6(\frac{3}{2}) + 2 = -\frac{45}{2}$.

So the relative minimum is $f(\frac{3}{2}, 2) = -\frac{45}{2}$.

11. To find the critical points of f, we solve the system

$$\begin{cases} f_x = 3x^2 - 3y = 0 \\ f_y = -3x + 3y^2 = 0 \end{cases}$$

The first equation gives $y = x^2$ which when substituted into the second equation gives $-3x + 3x^4 = 3x(x^3 - 1) = 0$. Therefore, $x = 0$ or 1. Substituting these values of x into the first equation gives $y = 0$ and $y = 1$, respectively Therefore, $(0,0)$ and $(1,1)$ are critical points of f. Next, we find $f_{xx} = 6x$, $f_{xy} = -3$, and $f_{yy} = 6y$. So $D = f_{xx}f_{yy} - f_{xy}^2 = 36xy - 9$. Since $D(0,0) = -9 < 0$, we see that $(0,0)$ gives a saddle point of f. Next, $D(1,1) = 36 - 9 = 27 > 0$ and since $f_{xx}(1,1) = 6 > 0$, we see that $f(1,1) = -3$ is a relative minimum value of f.

12. $f_x = 3x^2 - 2y = 0$ and $f_y = -2x + 2y = 0 \Rightarrow 3x^2 - 2x = x(3x - 2) = 0 \Rightarrow x = 0$,

or $x = 2/3$. Therefore, $y = 0$, or $y = 2/3$. So the critical points of f are $(0,0)$, and $(\frac{2}{3}, \frac{2}{3})$. Next, $f_{xx} = 6x, f_{xy} = -2, f_{yy} = 2$, and therefore, $D = 12x - 4 = 4(3x - 1)$. At the point $(0,0)$: $D(0,0) = -4 < 0$, so $(0,0)$ gives a saddle point with value $f(0,0) = 5$
At the point $(\frac{2}{3}, \frac{2}{3})$: $D(\frac{2}{3}, \frac{2}{3}) = 4 > 0$ and $f_{xx}(\frac{2}{3}, \frac{2}{3}) > 0$, so

$f(\frac{2}{3}, \frac{2}{3}) = \frac{8}{27} - \frac{8}{9} + \frac{4}{9} + 5 = \frac{131}{27}$ is a relative minimum value.

13. Solving the system of equations
$$\begin{cases} f_x = y - \frac{4}{x^2} = 0 \\ f_y = x - \frac{2}{y^2} = 0 \end{cases}$$

we obtain $y = \frac{4}{x^2}$. Therefore, $x - 2(\frac{x^4}{16}) = 0$ and $8x - x^4 = x(8 - x^3) = 0$, and $x = 0$, or $x = 2$. Since $x = 0$ is not in the domain of f, $(2,1)$ is the only critical point of f Next, $f_{xx} = \frac{8}{x^3}, f_{xy} = 1$, and $f_{yy} = \frac{4}{y^3}$ Therefore,

$D(2,1) = \left.\frac{32}{x^3 y^3} - 1\right|_{(2,1)} = 4 - 1 = 3 > 0$ and $f_{xx}(2,1) = 1 > 0$. Therefore, the relative minimum value of f is $f(2,1) = 2 + 4/2 + 2/1 = 6$.

14. $f_x = \frac{1}{y^2} + y = 0; f_y = -\frac{2x}{y^3} + x = 0$. Therefore, $1 + y^3 = 0$ and $y = -1$.

So $\frac{2x}{1} + x = 0$ and $x = 0$ and $(0,-1)$ is a critical point. Next,

$f_{xx} = 0, f_{xy} = -\frac{2}{y^3} + 1, f_{yy} = \frac{6x}{y^4}$.

Therefore, $D(0,-1) = 0 - 9 < 0$ and $f(0,-1)$ gives rise to a saddle point.

15. Solving the system of equations $f_x = 2x = 0$ and $f_y = -2ye^{y^2} = 0$, we obtain $x = 0$ and $y = 0$. Therefore, $(0,0)$ is the only critical point of f. Next,
$f_{xx} = 2, f_{xy} = 0, f_{yy} = -2e^{y^2} - 4y^2 e^{y^2}$.
Therefore, $D(0,0) = \left.-4e^{y^2}(1 + 2y^2)\right|_{(0,0)} = -4(1) < 0$, and we conclude that $(0,0)$ gives rise to a saddle point.

16. To find the critical points of f, we solve the system
$$\begin{cases} f_x = 2xe^{x^2 - y^2} = 0 \\ f_y = -2ye^{x^2 - y^2} \end{cases}$$

obtaining $x = 0$ and $y = 0$. Therefore, $(0,0)$ is the only critical point of f.

$$f_{xx} = 2e^{x^2-y^2} + 4x^2e^{x^2-y^2} = 2(1+2x^2)e^{x^2-y^2}$$

$$f_{xy} = -4xye^{x^2-y^2}$$

$$f_{yy} = -2e^{x^2-y^2} + 4y^2e^{x^2-y^2} = -2(1-2y^2)e^{x^2-y^2}.$$

At $(0,0)$, we see that $f_{xx}(0,0) = 2$, $f_{xy}(0,0) = 0$, $f_{yy}(0,0) = -2$. Since $D(0,0) = f_{xx}(0,0)f_{yy}(0,0) - f_{xy}^2(0,0) = -4 < 0$, we see that $(0,0)$ gives a saddle point of f.

17. $f(x,y) = e^{x^2+y^2}$

Solving the system

$$\begin{cases} f_x = 2xe^{x^2+y^2} = 0 \\ f_y = 2ye^{x^2+y^2} = 0 \end{cases}$$

we see that $x = 0$ and $y = 0$ (recall that $e^{x^2+y^2} \neq 0$). Therefore, $(0,0)$ is the only critical point of f. Next, we compute

$$f_{xx} = 2e^{x^2+y^2} + 2x(2x)e^{x^2+y^2} = 2(1+2x^2)e^{x^2+y^2}$$

$$f_{xy} = 2x(2y)e^{x^2+y^2} = 4xye^{x^2+y^2}$$

$$f_{yy} = 2(1+2y^2)e^{x^2+y^2}$$

In particular, at the point $(0,0)$, $f_{xx}(0,0) = 2$, $f_{xy}(0,0) = 0$, and $f_{yy}(0,0) = 2$. Therefore, $D = (2)(2) - 0 = 4 > 0$. Furthermore, since $f_{xx}(0,0) > 0$, we conclude that $(0,0)$ gives rise to a relative minimum of f. The relative minimum value of f is $f(0,0) = 1$.

18. To find the critical points of f, we solve the system

$$\begin{cases} f_x = ye^{xy} = 0 \\ f_y = xe^{xy} = 0 \end{cases}$$

obtaining $y = 0$ and $x = 0$. So $(0,0)$ is a critical point of f. Next,

$$f_{xx} = y^2e^{xy}, \quad f_{xy} = e^{xy} + xye^{xy} = (1+xy)e^{xy}, \quad f_{yy} = x^2e^{xy}.$$

So $D(x,y) = x^2y^2e^{2xy} - (1+xy)^2e^{2xy}$. In particular, $D(0,0) = -1 < 0$ and so $(0,0)$ gives rise to a saddle point of f.

19. $f(x,y) = \ln(1+x^2+y^2)$. We solve the system of equations

$$f_x = \frac{2x}{1+x^2+y^2} = 0 \text{ and } f_y = \frac{2y}{1+x^2+y^2} = 0,$$

obtaining $x = 0$ and $y = 0$. Therefore, $(0,0)$ is the only critical point of f. Next,

$$f_{xx} = \frac{(1+x^2+y^2)2-(2x)(2x)}{(1+x^2+y^2)^2} = \frac{2+2y^2-2x^2}{(1+x^2+y^2)^2}$$

$$f_{yy} = \frac{(1+x^2+y^2)2-(2y)(2y)}{(1+x^2+y^2)^2} = \frac{2+2x^2-2y^2}{(1+x^2+y^2)^2}$$

$$f_{xy} = -2x(1+x^2+y^2)^{-2}(2y) = -\frac{4xy}{(1+x^2+y^2)^2}.$$

Therefore, $D(x,y) = \dfrac{(2+2y^2-2x^2)(2+2x^2-2y^2)}{(1+x^2+y^2)^4} - \dfrac{16x^2y^2}{(1+x^2+y^2)^4}$

Since $D(0,0) = \frac{4}{1} > 0$ and $f_{xx}(0,0) = 2 > 0$, $f(0,0) = 0$ is a relative minimum value.

20. $f(x,y) = xy + \ln x + 2y^2$.

$f_x = y + \dfrac{1}{x} = 0$ and $f_y = x + 4y = 0$. Therefore, $y = -\dfrac{1}{x}$, $x + 4\left(-\dfrac{1}{x}\right) = 0$,

or $x^2 - 4 = 0$, or $x = 2$. (Remember x must be positive.) Therefore, $y = -1/2$ and $(2,-\frac{1}{2})$ is a critical point. Next,

$f_{xx} = -\dfrac{1}{x^2}$, $f_{xy} = 1$, $f_{yy} = 4$ and $D(2,-\frac{1}{2}) = (-\frac{1}{4})(4) - 1 < 0$.

Therefore, $(2,-\frac{1}{2})$ gives rise to a saddle point.

21. $P(x) = -0.2x^2 - 0.25y^2 - 0.2xy + 200x + 160y - 100x - 70y - 4000$
    $= -0.2x^2 - 0.25y^2 - 0.2xy + 100x + 90y - 4000$.

Then $\begin{cases} P_x = -0.4x - 0.2y + 100 = 0 \\ P_y = -0.5y - 0.2x + 90 = 0 \end{cases}$

implies that $\begin{cases} 4x + 2y = 1000 \\ 2x + 5y = 900 \end{cases}$. Solving, we find $x = 200$ and $y = 100$.

Next, $P_{xx} = -0.4$, $P_{yy} = -0.5$, $P_{xy} = -0.2$, and

$D(200,100) = (-0.4)(-0.5) - (-0.2)^2 > 0$. Since $P_{xx}(200, 100) < 0$, we conclude that $(200,100)$ is a relative maximum of P. Thus, the company should manufacture 200 finished and 100 unfinished units per week. The maximum

profit is
$$P(200,100) = -0.2(200)^2 - 0.25(100)^2 - 0.2(100)(200) + 100(200) + 90(100) - 4000$$
$$= 10,500, \text{ or } \$10,500.$$

22. $P(x, y) = -0.005x^2 - 0.003y^2 - 0.002xy + 20x + 15y - 6x - 3y - 200$
$$= -0.005x^2 - 0.003y^2 - 0.002xy + 14x + 12y - 200.$$

Next,
$$\begin{cases} P_x = -0.01x - 0.002y + 14 = 0 \\ P_y = -0.006y - 0.002x + 12 = 0 \end{cases}$$

Therefore, $\begin{cases} 10x + 2y = 14,000 \\ 2x + 6y = 12,000 \end{cases}$.

Solving, we find $x \approx 1071$ and $y \approx 1643$. Next, $P_{xx} = -0.01$, $P_{xy} = -0.002$, $P_{yy} = -0.006$. Therefore,
$$D(1071, 1643) = (-0.01)(-0.006) - (-0.002)^2 = 0.000056 > 0.$$
Since $P_{xx}(1071, 1643) < 0$, we conclude that $(1071, 1643)$ is a relative maximum of P. Thus, the company should publish 1071 deluxe and 1643 standard copies. The maximum profit is
$$P(1071, 1643) = -0.005(1071)^2 - 0.003(1643)^2 - 0.002(1071)(1643)$$
$$+ 14(1071) + 12(1643) - 200$$
$$= 17,157.14, \text{ or } \$17,157.14.$$

23. $p(x, y) = 200 - 10(x - \frac{1}{2})^2 - 15(y - 1)^2$. Solving the system of equations
$$\begin{cases} p_x = -20(x - \frac{1}{2}) = 0 \\ p_y = -30(y - 1) = 0 \end{cases}$$
we obtain $x = 1/2$, $y = 1$. We conclude that the only critical point of f is $(\frac{1}{2}, 1)$.
Next, $p_{xx} = -20$, $p_{xy} = 0$, $p_{yy} = -30$
so $D(\frac{1}{2}, 1) = (-20)(-30) = 600 > 0.$
Since $p_{xx} = -20 < 0$, we conclude that $f(\frac{1}{2}, 1)$ gives a relative maximum. So we conclude that the price of land is highest at $(\frac{1}{2}, 1)$.

24. We wish to maximize the function
$$P(x) = R(x) - C(x) = (2000 - 150p + 100q)p + (1000 + 80p - 120q)q$$
$$- 4(2000 - 150p + 100q) - 3(1000 + 80p - 120q)$$
$$= 2360p - 150p^2 + 180pq + 960q - 120q^2 - 11,000.$$

$$\text{Then } \begin{cases} P_p = 2360 - 300p + 180q \\ P_q = 180p + 960 - 240q \end{cases}. \text{ Solving the system } \begin{cases} 300p - 180q = 2360 \\ -180p + 240q = 960 \end{cases}$$

we find that $(\frac{56}{3}, 18)$ is a critical point. Next,

$$P_{pp} = -300, P_{qq} = -240, \text{ and } P_{pq} = 180.$$

Therefore, $D(\frac{56}{3}, 18) = (-300)(-240) - (180)^2 = 39600 > 0$. Since $P_{pp} < 0$, we conclude that P is maximized at $(\frac{56}{3}, 18)$ and the company should therefore sell the German wine at \$18.67 per bottle and the Italian wine at \$18 per bottle.

25   We want to minimize

$$f(x,y) = D^2 = (x-5)^2 + (y-2)^2 + (x+4)^2 + (y-4)^2 + (x+1)^2 + (y+3)^2.$$

$$\text{Next, } \begin{cases} f_x = 2(x-5) + 2(x+4) + 2(x+1) = 6x = 0, \\ f_y = 2(y-2) + 2(y-4) + 2(y+3) = 6y - 6 = 0 \end{cases}$$

and we conclude that $x = 0$ and $y = 1$. Also,

$$f_{xx} = 6, f_{xy} = 0, f_{yy} = 6 \text{ and } D(x,y) = (6)(6) = 36 > 0.$$

Since $f_{xx} > 0$, we conclude that the function is minimized at $(0,1)$ and so $(0,1)$ gives the desired location.

26.   Solving the equation $xyz = 108$ for x, we have $z = 108/xy$. Substituting this value of z into the expression for S, we obtain

$$S = f(x,y) = xy + 2y\left(\frac{108}{xy}\right) + 2x\left(\frac{108}{xy}\right) = xy + \frac{216}{x} + \frac{216}{y}$$

To minimize f, we first find the critical points of f. To do this, we solve the system

$$\begin{cases} f_x = y - \frac{216}{x^2} = 0 \\ f_y = x - \frac{216}{y^2} = 0. \end{cases}$$

Solving the first equation for y, we obtain $y = 216/x^2$. Substituting this value into the second equation then yields

$$x - 216\left(\frac{x^2}{216}\right)^2 = 0$$

$$x - \frac{x^4}{216} = 0, \text{ or } x(216 - x^3) = 0,$$

from which we deduce that $x = 0$, or $x = 6$. We reject the root $x = 0$, since it is not in the domain of the function f. Next, substituting $x = 6$ into the expression for y obtained earlier, we find $y = 6$. Thus, the point $(6,6)$ is the only critical point of f. Next, we compute

$$f_{xx} = \frac{432}{x^3}, \; f_{xy} = 1, \; f_{yy} = \frac{432}{y^3}.$$

In particular, $f_{xx}(6,6) = 2, f_{xy}(6,6) = 1$, and $f_{yy}(6,6) = 2$. Thus, $D = (2)(2) - 1 = 3 > 0$. Since $f_{xx}(6,6) > 0$, we conclude that $(6,6)$ gives rise to a relative minimum of f. Substituting these values of x and y into the expression for z yields $z = 108/(6)(6) = 3$. Therefore, the required dimensions of the box are 6 inches by 6 inches by 3 inches.

27. Refer to the figure in the text.

$$xy + 2xz + 2yz = 300; \quad z(2x + 2y) = 300 - xy; \quad \text{and} \quad z = \frac{300 - xy}{2(x + y)}.$$

Then the volume is given by

$$V = xyz = xy \left[\frac{300 - xy}{2(x + y)} \right] = \frac{300xy - x^2 y^2}{2(x + y)}.$$

We find

$$\frac{\partial V}{\partial x} = \frac{1}{2} \frac{(x + y)(300y - 2xy^2) - (300xy - x^2 y^2)}{(x + y)^2}$$

$$= \frac{300xy - 2x^2 y^2 + 300y^2 - 2xy^3 - 300xy + x^2 y^2}{2(x + y)^2}$$

$$= \frac{300y^2 - 2xy^3 - x^2 y^2}{2(x + y)^2} = \frac{y^2 (300 - 2xy - x^2)}{2(x + y)^2}.$$

Similarly, $\dfrac{\partial V}{\partial y} = \dfrac{x^2 (300 - 2xy - y^2)}{2(x + y)^2}$. Setting both $\partial V / \partial x$ and $\partial V / \partial y$ equal to zero and observing that both $x > 0$ and $y > 0$, we have the system

$$\begin{cases} 2yx + x^2 = 300 \\ 2yx + y^2 = 300 \end{cases}.$$ Subtracting, we find $y^2 - x^2 = 0$; that is $(y - x)(y + x) = 0$. So $y = x$ or $y = -x$. The latter is not possible since $x, y > 0$. Therefore, $y = x$. Substituting this value into the first equation in the system gives

$$2x^2 + x^2 = 300; \quad x^2 = 100; \quad \text{and} \quad x = 10.$$

Therefore, $y = 10$. Substituting this value into the expression for z gives $z = \dfrac{300 - 10^2}{2(10 + 10)} = 5$. So the dimensions are $10" \times 10" \times 5"$. The volume is 500 cu in.

28. The volume is given by $V = xyz = xz(108 - 2x - 2z) = 108xz - 2x^2z - 2xz^2$.
Solving the system of equations, $V_x = 108z - 4xz - 2z^2 = 0$ and
$$V_z = 108x - 2x^2 - 4xz = 0, \text{ we obtain}$$
$$(108 - 4x - 2z)z = 0, \text{ or } 108 - 4x - 2z = 0$$
and $(108 - 4z - 2x)x = 0$, or $108 - 2x - 4z = 0$. Thus
$$\begin{cases} 108 - 4x - 2z = 0 \\ 216 - 4x - 8z = 0 \end{cases}$$
gives $-108 + 6z = 0$, or $z = 18$. So $x = \frac{1}{4}(108 - 36) = 18$ and
$y = 108 - 2x - 2z = 108 - 72 = 36$, and $(18,18)$ is the critical point of V. Next,
$$V_{xx} = -4z, \ V_{zz} = -4x, \ V_{xz} = 108 - 4x - 4z, \text{ and}$$
$$D(18,18) = -4(18)(-4)(18) - [108 - 4(18) - 4(18)]^2 > 0$$
and $V_{xx}(18,18) < 0$. We conclude that the dimensions yielding the maximum volume are $18'' \times 36'' \times 18''$.

29. The heating cost is $C = 2xy + 8xz + 6yz$. But $xyz = 12{,}000$ or $z = 12{,}000/xy$.
Therefore,
$$C = f(x,y) = 2xy + 8x\left(\frac{12{,}000}{xy}\right) + 6y\left(\frac{12{,}000}{xy}\right) = 2xy + \frac{96{,}000}{y} + \frac{72{,}000}{x}$$
To find the minimum of f, we find the critical point of f by solving the system
$$\begin{cases} f_x = 2y - \dfrac{72{,}000}{x^2} = 0 \\ f_y = 2x - \dfrac{96{,}000}{y^2} = 0 \end{cases}.$$
The first equation gives $y = 36000/x^2$, which when substituted into the second equation yields
$$2x - 96{,}000\left(\frac{x^2}{36{,}000}\right)^2 = 0, \ (36{,}000)^2 x - 48{,}000x^4 = 0$$
$$x(27{,}000 - x^3) = 0.$$
Solving this equation, we have $x = 0$, or $x = 30$. We reject the first root because $x \neq 0$. With $x = 30$, we find $y = 40$ and
$$f_{xx} = \frac{144{,}000}{x^3}, \ f_{xy} = 2, \text{ and } f_{yy} = \frac{192{,}000}{y^3}.$$
In particular, $f_{xx}(30,40) = 5.33, f_{xy} = (30,40) = 2$, and $f_{yy}(30,40) = 3$. So
$$D(30,40) = (5.33)(3) - 4 = 11.99 > 0$$

and since $f_{xx}(30,40) > 0$, we see that (30,40) gives a relative minimum. Physical considerations tell us that this is an absolute minimum. The minimal annual heating cost is

$$f(30,40) = 2(30)(40) + \frac{96,000}{40} + \frac{72,000}{30} = 7200, \text{ or } \$7,200.$$

30. Since $V = xyz$, $z = \frac{48}{xy}$. Then the amount of material used in the box is given by

$$S = xy + 2xz + 3yz = xy + \frac{48}{xy}(2x + 3y) = xy + \frac{96}{y} + \frac{144}{x}.$$

Solving the system of equations $\begin{cases} S_x = y - \frac{144}{x^2} = 0 \\ S_y = x - \frac{96}{y^2} = 0 \end{cases}$, we have $y = \frac{144}{x^2}$.

Therefore $x - \frac{96x^4}{144^2} = 0$, $144^2 x - 96x^4 = 0$, $96x(216 - x^3) = 0$, and $x = 0$ or $x = 6$.

Then $y = \frac{144}{36} = 4$. Next, $S_{xx} = \frac{288}{x^3}$, $S_{yy} = \frac{192}{y^3}$, and $S_{xy} = 1$.

At the point (6,4): $D(x,y) = \frac{(288)(192)}{x^3 y^3} - 1 \bigg|_{(6,4)} = \frac{288(192)}{216(64)} - 1 = 3 > 0$,

and $S_{xx} > 0$. Therefore, we conclude that the function is minimized when its dimensions are 6" × 4" × 2".

31. False. Let $f(x,y) = xy$. Then $f_x(0,0) = 0$ and $f_y(0,0) = 0$. But (0,0) does not afford a relative extremum of (0,0). In fact, $f_{xx} = 0$, $f_{yy} = 0$, and $f_{xy} = 1$. Therefore, $D(x,y) = f_{xx}f_{yy} - f_{xy}^2 = -1$ and so $D(0,0) = -1$ which shows that (0, 0, 0) is a saddle point.

32. False. Let $f(x,y) = -x^2 - y^2 + 4xy$. Then setting
$$f_x(x,y) = -2x + 4y = 0$$
$$f_y(x,y) = -2y + 4x = 0$$
we find that (0,0) is the only critical point of f. Next,
$$f_{xx} = -2, \quad f_{xy} = 4, \quad \text{and} \quad f_{yy} = -2.$$
Since $D(x,y) = f_{xx}f_{yy} - f_{xy}^2 = (-2)(-2) - 4^2 = -12 < 0$,
we see that (0, 0, 0) is a saddle point.

8.4 CONCEPT QUESTIONS, page 544

1. a. A scatter diagram is a graph showing the data points that describe the relationship between the two variables x and y.

   b. The least squares line is the straight line that best fits a set of data points when the points are scattered about a straight line.

EXERCISES 8.4, page 578

1. a. We first summarize the data:

x	y	x^2	xy
1	4	1	4
2	6	4	12
3	8	9	24
4	11	16	44
10	29	30	84

The normal equations are $4b + 10m = 29$
$$10b + 30m = 84.$$
Solving this system of equations, we obtain $m = 2.3$ and $b = 1.5$. So an equation is $y = 2.3x + 1.5$.

   b. The scatter diagram and the least squares line for this data follow:

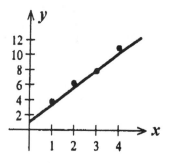

2. a. We first summarize the data:

x	y	x^2	xy
1	9	1	9
3	8	9	24
5	6	25	30
7	3	49	21
9	2	81	18
25	28	165	102

The normal equations are $165m + 25b = 102$
$$25m + 5b = 28.$$
Solving, we find $m = -0.95$ and $b = 10.35$. The required equation is
$y = -0.95x + 10.35$.
b. The scatter diagram and the least-squares line for these data follow·

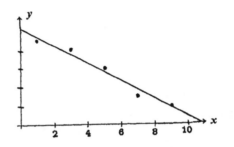

3. a. We first summarize the data:

x	y	x^2	xy
1	4.5	1	4.5
2	5	4	10
3	3	9	9
4	2	16	8
4	3.5	16	14
6	1	36	6
20	19	82	51.5

The normal equations are $6b + 20m = 19$
$$20b + 82m = 51.5.$$

The solutions are $m \approx -0.7717$ and $b \approx 5.7391$ and so a required equation is
$y = -0.772x + 5.739$.

8 Calculus of Several Variables

b. The scatter diagram and the least-squares line for these data follow.

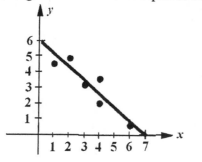

4. a. We first summarize the data:

x	y	x^2	xy
1	2	1	2
1	3	1	3
2	3	4	6
3	3.5	9	10.5
4	3.5	16	14.0
4	4	16	16
5	5	25	25
20	24	72	76.5

The normal equations are $72m + 20b = 76.5$
$$20m + 7b = 24.$$

Solving, we find $m = 0.53$ and $b = 1.91$. The required equation is $y = 0.53x + 1.91$.
b. The scatter diagram and the least squares line for the given data are shown in the following figure.

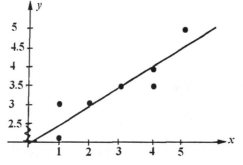

5. a. We first summarize the data:

x	y	x^2	xy
1	3	1	3
2	5	4	10
3	5	9	15
4	7	16	28
5	8	25	40
15	28	55	96

The normal equations are $55m + 15b = 96$
$$15m + 5b = 28.$$
Solving, we find $m = 1.2$ and $b = 2$, so that the required equation is $y = 1.2x + 2$.

b. The scatter diagram and the least-squares line for the given data follow

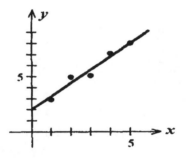

6. a. We first summarize the data:

x	y	x^2	xy
1	8	1	8
2	6	4	12
5	6	25	30
7	4	49	28
10	1	100	10
25	25	179	88

The normal equations are $5b + 25m = 25$
$$25b + 179m = 88.$$
The solutions are $m = -0.68519$ and $b = 8.4259$ and so a required equation is

$y = -0.685x + 8.426.$

b. The scatter diagram and least-squares line for the given data follow.

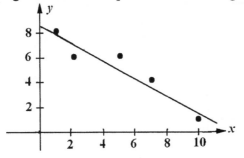

7   a. We first summarize the data:

x	y	x^2	xy
4	0.5	16	2
4.5	0.6	20.25	2.7
5	0.8	25	4
5.5	0.9	30.25	4.95
6	1.2	36	7.2
25	4	127.5	20.85

The normal equations are
$$5b + 25m = 4$$
$$25b + 127.5m = 20.85.$$

The solutions are $m = 0.34$ and $b = -0.9$, and so a required equation is
$y = 0.34x - 0.9.$

b. The scatter diagram and the least-squares line for these data follow.

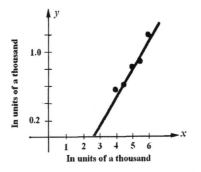

c. If $x = 6.4$, then $y = 0.34(6.4) - 0.9 = 1.276$ and so 1276 completed applications might be expected.

8. a. We first summarize the data:

x	y	x^2	xy
0	929	0	0
1	1270	1	1270
2	1622	4	3244
3	2038	9	6114
4	2446	16	9784
10	8305	30	20412

The normal equations are

$$5b + 10m = 8305$$
$$10b + 30m = 20412$$

The solutions are $b = 900.6$ and $m = 380.2$. Therefore, the required least-squares line   is given by $y = 380x + 901$

b. The required rate is given by the slope of the least-squares line, namely, 380/yr.

9. a. We first summarize the data:

x	y	x^2	xy
1	436	1	436
2	438	4	876
3	428	9	1284
4	430	16	1720
5	426	25	2130
15	2158	55	6446

The normal equations are $5b + 15m = 2158$
$$15b + 55m = 6446.$$
Solving this system, we find $m = -2.8$ and $b = 440$.
Thus, the equation of the least-squares line is $y = -2.8x + 440$.

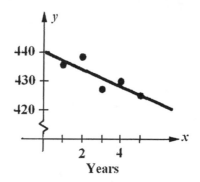

Years

b. The scatter diagram and the least-squares line for this data are shown in the figure that follows.

c. Two years from now, the average SAT verbal score in that area will be $y = -2.8(7) + 440 = 420.4$.

10. a. We first summarize the data:

x	y	x^2	xy
1	426	1	426
2	437	4	874
3	460	9	1380
4	473	16	1892
5	477	25	2385
15	2273	55	6957

The normal equations are $55m + 15b = 6957$
$$15m + 5b = 2273.$$
Solving, we find $m = 13.8$ and $b = 413.2$, so that a required equation is $y = 13.8x + 413.2$.

b.

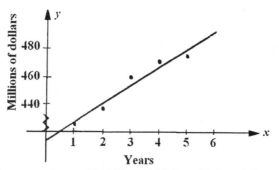

Years

c. When $x = 6$, $y = 13.8(6) + 413.2 = 496$ and the predicted net sales for the upcoming year are $496 million.

11. a. We first summarize the data:

x	y	x^2	xy
1	20	1	20
2	24	4	48
3	26	9	78
4	28	16	112
5	32	25	160
15	130	55	418

The normal equations are $5b + 15m = 130$
$$15b + 55m = 418.$$
The solutions are $m = 2.8$ and $b = 17.6$, and so an equation of the line is
$$y = 2.8x + 17.6.$$
b. When $x = 8$, $y = 2.8(8) + 17.6 = 40$. Hence, the state subsidy is expected to be $40 million for the eighth year.

12. a.

t	y	t^2	ty
0	6.8	0	0
1	8.3	1	8.3
2	9.8	4	19.6
3	11.3	9	33.9
4	12.8	16	51.2
5	14.9	25	74.5
15	63.9	55	187.5

The normal equations are
$$6b + 15m = 63.9$$

$$15b + 55m = 187.5$$
The solutions are $m \approx 1.5857$ and $b \approx 6.6857$. Therefore, the required equation is
$$y = 1.5857t + 6.6857$$
b. $y = 1.5857(6) + 6.6857 \approx 16.2$, or $16.2 billion.

13. a.

t	y	t^2	ty
0	126	1	0
1	144	4	144
2	171	9	343
3	191	16	573
4	216	25	864
10	848	30	1923

The normal equations are
$$5b + 10m = 848$$
$$10b + 30m = 1923$$
The solutions are $m \approx 22.7$ and $b \approx 124.2$. Therefore, the required equation is $y = 22.7t + 124.2$.

b. $y = 22.7(6) + 124.2 = 260.4$, or $260.4 billion.

14. a.

x	y	x^2	xy
0	501	0	0
1	540	1	540
2	585	4	1170
3	631	9	1893
4	680	16	2720
5	728	25	3640
6	779	36	4674
21	4444	91	14637

The normal equations are
$$7b + 21m = 444$$
$$21b + 91m = 14637$$
The solutions are $m \approx 46.6071$ and $b \approx 495.0357$. Therefore, the required equation is $y = 46.6071x + 495.0357$.

b. The rate of change is given by the slope of the least-squares line; that is, approximately $46.6/buyer/year.

15 a.

x	y	x^2	xy
0	3.7	0	0
1	4.0	1	4
2	4.4	4	8.8
3	4.8	9	14.4
4	5.2	16	20.8
5	5.8	25	29.0
6	6.3	36	37.8
21	34.2	91	114.8

The normal equations are
$$7b+21m = 34.2$$

$$21b+91m = 114.8$$
The solutions are $m \approx 0.4357$ and $b \approx 3.5786$. Therefore, the required equation is
$y = 0.4357x + 3.5786$.

b. The rate of change is given by the slope of the least-squares line, that is,
approximately $0.4357 billion/yr.

16. a.

x	y	x^2	xy
1	21.2	1	21.2
2	26.7	4	53.4
3	32.2	9	96.6
4	37.7	16	150.8
5	43.2	25	216
6	48.7	36	292.2
7	54.2	49	379.4
28	263.9	140	1209.6

The normal equations are
$$7b+ 28m = 263.9$$

$$28b+140m = 1209.6$$
The solutions are $m = 5.5$ and $b = 15.7$. Therefore, the required equation is
$$y = 5.5x + 15.7$$

b. $y = 5.5(8) + 15.7 = 59.7$ or 59.7%,

17. a.

x	y	x^2	xy
0	7.9	0	0
1	9.6	1	9.6
2	11.5	4	23
3	13.3	9	39.9
4	15.2	16	60.8
5	16	25	80
6	18.8	36	112.8
21	92.3	30	326.1

The normal equations are
$$7b + 21m = 92.3$$
$$21b + 91m = 326.1$$
The solutions are $m \approx 1.7571$ and $b \approx 7.9143$. Therefore, the required equation is
$$y = 1.7571x + 7.9143$$

b. $y = 1.7571(5) + 7.9143 \approx 16.7$ or $16.7 billion.

18.

x	y	x^2	xy
0	1	0	0
1	1.4	1	1.4
2	2.2	4	4.4
3	2.8	9	8.4
4	3.6	16	14.4
5	4.2	25	21
6	5.0	36	30
7	5.8	49	40.6
28	26	140	120.2

The normal equations are
$$8b + 28m = 26$$
$$28b + 140m = 120.2$$
The solutions are $m \approx 0.6952$ and $b \approx 0.8167$. Therefore, the required equation is
$$y = 0.6952x + 0.8167$$

b. $y = 0.6952(8) + 0.8167 = 6.3783$, or approximately $6.4 million.

19 a.

x	y	x^2	xy
1	72.6	1	72.6
2	76.2	4	152.4
3	80.4	9	241.2
4	84.9	16	339.6
5	87	25	435
6	87.9	36	527.6
21	489	91	1768.2

The normal equations are
$$6b + 21m = 489$$
$$21b + 91m = 1768.2$$
The solutions are $m \approx 3.24$ and $b \approx 70.16$. Therefore the required equation is
$$y = 3.24x + 70.16$$
b. Then the FICA wage base for the year 2006 is given by
$$y = 3.24(8) + 70.16 = 96.08, \text{ or } \$96,080.$$

20. a.

x	y	x^2	xy
1	21.2	1	21.2
2	26.7	4	53.4
3	32.2	9	96.6
4	37.7	16	150.8
5	43.2	25	216
6	48.7	36	292.2
7	54.2	49	379.4
28	263.9	140	1209.6

The normal equations are
$$7b + 28m = 263.9$$
$$28b + 140m = 1209.6$$

The solutions are $m = 5.5$ and $b = 15.7$. Therefore, the required equation is
$$y = 5.5x + 15.7$$
b. $y = 5.5(8) + 15.7 = 59.7$ or 59.7%,

21 a. We first summarize the given data:

x	y	x^2	xy
0	15.9	0	0
10	16.8	100	168
20	17.6	400	352
30	18.5	900	555
40	19.3	1600	772
50	20.3	2500	1015
150	108.4	5500	2862

The normal equations are
$$6b + 150m = 108.4$$
$$150b + 5500m = 2862$$
The solutions are $b = 15.90$ and $m = 0.09$. Therefore, $y = 0.09x + 15.9$
b. The life expectancy at 65 of a male in 2040 is
$$y = 0.9(40) + 15.9 = 19.50 \quad \text{or} \quad 19.50 \text{ years}$$
The datum gives a life expectancy of 19.5 years.
c. The life expectancy at 65 of a male in 2030 is
$$y = 0.09(30) + 15.9 = 18.6 \quad \text{or} \quad 18.6 \text{ years.}$$

22. a. We first summarize the given data:

x	y	x^2	xy
0	2.4	0	0
1	2.9	1	2.9
2	3.7	4	7.4
3	4.5	9	13.5
4	5.2	16	20.8
5	6.1	25	30.5
15	24.8	55	75.1

The normal equations are
$$6b + 15m = 24.8$$
$$15b + 55m = 75.1$$
The solutions are $m = 0.75$ and $b = 2.26$. Therefore $y = 0.75x + 2.26$.

b. In 2007, $x = 8$ and $y = 0.75(8) + 2.26 = 8.26$, or $8.3 billion.

23. a. We first summarize the given data:

x	y	x^2	xy
0	90.4	0	0
1	100.0	1	100
2	110.4	4	220.8
3	120.4	9	361.2
4	130.8	16	523.2
5	140.4	25	702
6	150	36	900
21	842.4	91	2807.2

The normal equations are $\begin{cases} 7b + 21m = 842.4 \\ 21b + 91m = 2807.2 \end{cases}$.

The solutions are $m = 10$ and $b = 90.34$. Therefore, the required equation is
$y = 10x + 90.34$.
b. If $x = 6$, then $y = 10(6) + 90.34 = 150.34$, or 150,340,000. This compares well
with the actual data for that year-- 150,000,000 subscribers.

24. a. We first summarize the data:

x	y	x^2	xy
4.25	178	18.0625	756.5
10	667	100	6670
14	1194	196	16716
15.5	1500	240.25	23250
17.8	1388	316.84	24706.4
19.5	1640	380.25	31980
81.05	6567	1251.4025	104,078.9

The normal equations are $6b + \qquad 81.05m = 6567$
$\qquad\qquad\qquad\qquad 81.05b + \quad 1251.4025m = 104,078.9$.
The solutions are $m = 98.1761$ and $b = -231.696$ and so a required equation is
$y = 98.176x - 231.7$.
b. If $x = 20$, then $y = 98.176(20) - 231.7 = 1731.82$. Hence, if the health-spending
in the U.S. were in line with OECD countries, it should only have been $1732 per

capita.

25 False. See Example 1, page 575.

26. True. The error involves the sum of the squares of the form $[f(x_i) - y_i]^2$ where f is the least-squares function and y_i is a data point. Thus, the error is zero if and only if $f(x_i) = y_i$ for each $1 \le i \le n$.

27. True   28. True

USING TECHNOLOGY EXERCISES 8.4, page 582

1 $y = 2.3596x + 3.8639$ 2. $y = 1.4068x - 2.1241$ 3. $y = -1.1948x + 3.5525$

4. $y = -2.07715x + 5.23847$ 5. a. $y = 0.5471x + 1.1671$ b. $5.54 billion

6. a. $y = 74x + 384$ b. $902 million   7. a. $y = 13.321x + 72.57$ b. 192 million tons

8. a. $4.1t + 16.7$ b. $29 billion   9. a. $1.95x + 12.19$; $23.89 billion

10. a. $423x + 7068$
     b.   c. $423/yr

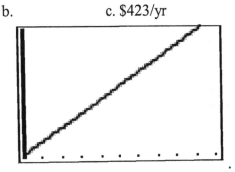

8.5 CONCEPT QUESTIONS, page 592

1. A constrained relative extremem of f is an extremum of f subject to a constraint of the form $g(x, y) = 0$.
2. See the procedure given on pages 585-586 of the text.

EXERCISES 8.5, page 592

1. We form the Lagrangian function $F(x,y,\lambda) = x^2 + 3y^2 + \lambda(x + y - 1)$. We solve the system

$$\begin{cases} F_x = 2x + \lambda = 0 \\ F_y = 6y + \lambda = 0 \\ F_\lambda = x + y - 1 = 0. \end{cases}$$

Solving the first and the second equations for x and y in terms of λ we obtain $x = -\frac{\lambda}{2}$ and $y = -\frac{\lambda}{6}$ which, upon substitution into the third equation, yields $-\frac{\lambda}{2} - \frac{\lambda}{6} - 1 = 0$ or $\lambda = -\frac{3}{2}$. Therefore, $x = \frac{3}{4}$ and $y = \frac{1}{4}$ which gives the point $(\frac{3}{4}, \frac{1}{4})$ as the sole critical point of F. Therefore, $(\frac{3}{4}, \frac{1}{4}) = \frac{3}{4}$ is a minimum of F.

2. We form the Lagrangian function $F(x,y,\lambda) = x^2 + y^2 - xy + \lambda(x + 2y - 14)$. We solve the system

$$\begin{cases} F_x = 2x - y + \lambda = 0 \\ F_y = 2y - x + 2\lambda = 0 \\ F_\lambda = x + 2y - 14 = 0 \end{cases}$$

Then $\begin{cases} 4x - 2y + 2\lambda = 0 \\ -x + 2y + 2\lambda = 0 \end{cases}$ and $\begin{cases} 5x - 4y = 0 \\ 5x + 10y = 70 \end{cases}$.

Thus, $14y = 70$. Therefore, $y = 5$ and $x = 4$ and the minimum value is $F(4,5) = 21$.

3. We form the Lagrangian function $F(x,y,\lambda) = 2x + 3y - x^2 - y^2 + \lambda(x + 2y - 9)$. We then solve the system

$$\begin{cases} F_x = 2 - 2x + \lambda = 0 \\ F_y = 3 - 2y + 2\lambda = 0. \\ F_\lambda = x + 2y - 9 = 0 \end{cases}$$

Solving the first equation λ, we obtain $\lambda = 2x - 2$. Substituting into the second equation, we have $3 - 2y + 4x - 4 = 0$, or $4x - 2y - 1 = 0$. Adding this equation to the third equation in the system, we have $5x - 10 = 0$, or $x = 2$. Therefore, $y = 7/2$ and $f(2, \frac{7}{2}) = -\frac{7}{4}$ is the maximum value of f

4.   We form the Lagrangian function $F(x,y,\lambda) = 16 - x^2 - y^2 + \lambda(x + y - 6)$. We then solve the system

$$\begin{cases} F_x = -2x + \lambda = 0 \\ F_y = -2y + \lambda = 0 \\ F_\lambda = x + y - 6 = 0. \end{cases}$$

The first two equations imply that $x = y$. Substituting into the third equation, we have $2x - 6 = 0$, or $x = 3$. So $y = 3$ and $f(3,3) = -2$ is the maximum value of f

5   Form the Lagrangian function $F(x,y,\lambda) = x^2 + 4y^2 + \lambda(xy - 1)$. We then solve the system

$$\begin{cases} F_x = 2x + \lambda y = 0 \\ F_y = 8y + \lambda x = 0. \\ F_\lambda = xy - 1 = 0 \end{cases}$$

Multiplying the first and second equations by x and y, respectively, and subtracting the resulting equations, we obtain $2x^2 - 8y^2 = 0$, or $x = \pm 2y$. Substituting this into the third equation gives $2y^2 - 1 = 0$ or $y = \pm\frac{\sqrt{2}}{2}$. We conclude that $f(-\sqrt{2},-\frac{\sqrt{2}}{2}) = f(\sqrt{2},\frac{\sqrt{2}}{2}) = 4$ is the minimum value of f.

6.   Form the Lagrangian function $F(x,y,\lambda) = xy - \lambda(x^2 + 4y^2 - 4) = 0$. We solve

$$\begin{cases} F_x = y - 2\lambda x = 0 \\ F_y = x - 8\lambda y = 0 \\ F_\lambda = x^2 + 4y^2 - 4 = 0 \end{cases}$$

Multiplying the first and second equations by $4y$ and x, respectively, and subtracting the resulting equations, we obtain $4y^2 - x^2 = 0$ and so $x = \pm 2y$. Substituting this into the third equation, we find $4y^2 + 4y^2 - 4 = 0$, $8y^2 = 4$, or $y = \pm 2\sqrt{2}/2$. Therefore, $f(-\sqrt{2},\frac{\sqrt{2}}{2}) = f(\sqrt{2},-\frac{\sqrt{2}}{2}) = -1$ is the minimum value of f

7.   We form the Lagrangian function
$$F(x,y,\lambda) = x + 5y - 2xy - x^2 - 2y^2 + \lambda(2x + y - 4).$$
Next, we solve the system

$$\begin{cases} F_x = 1 - 2y - 2x + 2\lambda = 0 \\ F_y = 5 - 2x - 4y + \lambda = 0 \\ F_\lambda = 2x + y - 4 = 0 \end{cases}$$

Solving the last two equations for x and y in terms of λ, we obtain
$$y = \tfrac{1}{3}(1+\lambda) \text{ and } x = \tfrac{1}{6}(11-\lambda)$$
which, upon substitution into the first equation, yields
$$1-\tfrac{2}{3}(1+\lambda)-\tfrac{1}{3}(11-\lambda)+2\lambda = 0$$
$$\text{or } 1-\tfrac{2}{3}-\tfrac{2}{3}\lambda-\tfrac{11}{3}+\tfrac{\lambda}{3}+2\lambda = 0$$
or $\lambda = 2$. Therefore, $x = 3/2$ and $y = 1$. The maximum of f is
$$f(\tfrac{3}{2},1) = \tfrac{3}{2}+5-2(\tfrac{3}{2})-(\tfrac{3}{2})^2 -2 = -\tfrac{3}{4}$$

8. We form the Lagrangian function $F(x,y,\lambda) = xy + \lambda(2x + 3y - 6)$. We solve the
    system
    $$\begin{cases} F_x = y+2\lambda = 0 \\ F_y = x+3\lambda = 0 \\ F_\lambda = 2x+3y-6 = 0. \end{cases}$$
    Then $\begin{cases} 3y+6\lambda = 0 \\ 2x+6\lambda = 0 \end{cases}$ and $2x + 3y = 6$. So $x = \tfrac{3}{2}$ and $y = 1$. Thus, the relative
    maximum of F is $F(\tfrac{3}{2},1) = \tfrac{3}{2}$.

9. Form the Lagrangian $F(x,y,\lambda) = xy^2 + \lambda(9x^2 + y^2 - 9)$. We then solve
    $$\begin{cases} F_x = y^2 +18\lambda x = 0 \\ F_y = 2xy+2\lambda y = 0 \\ F_\lambda = 9x^2 + y^2 -9 = 0. \end{cases}$$
    The first equation gives $\lambda = -\dfrac{y^2}{18x}$. Substituting into the second gives
    $$2xy +2y\left(-\frac{y^2}{18x}\right) = 0, \text{ or } 18x^2 y - y^3 = y(18x^2 - y^2) = 0,$$
    giving $y = 0$ or $y = \pm 3\sqrt{2}x$. If $y = 0$, then the third equation gives $9x^2 - 9 = 0$ or
    $x = \pm 1$. If $y = \pm 3\sqrt{3}/3$. Therefore, the points $(-1,0),(-\sqrt{3}/3,-\sqrt{6})$,
    $(-\sqrt{3}/3,\sqrt{6})$, $(\sqrt{3}/3,-\sqrt{6})$ and $(\sqrt{3}/3,\sqrt{6})$ give rise to extreme values of f
    subject to the given constraint. Evaluating $f(x,y)$ at each of these points, we see
    that $f(\sqrt{3}/3,-\sqrt{6}) = (\sqrt{3}/3,\sqrt{6}) = 2\sqrt{3}$ is the maximum value of f.

10. We form the Lagrangian function $F(x,y,\lambda) = \sqrt{y^2 - x^2} + \lambda(x+2y-5)$.
    We then solve the system

8 *Calculus of Several Variables*

$$\begin{cases} F_x = -\dfrac{x}{\sqrt{y^2 - x^2}} + \lambda = 0 \\[4mm] F_y = \dfrac{x}{\sqrt{y^2 - x^2}} + 2\lambda = 0 \\[4mm] F_\lambda = x + 2y - 5 = 0. \end{cases}$$

Then $-\dfrac{2x}{\sqrt{y^2 - x^2}} + 2\lambda = 0,\ \dfrac{y}{\sqrt{y^2 - x^2}} + 2\lambda = 0, -2x - y = 0$, and

$2x + 4y = 10$. So, $y = \frac{10}{3}$, and $x = -\frac{5}{3}$. Therefore, the relative minimum of F is

$F(-\frac{5}{3}, \frac{10}{3}) = \frac{5\sqrt{3}}{3}$.

11. We form the Lagrangian function $F(x,y,\lambda) = xy + \lambda(x^2 + y^2 - 16)$. To find the critical points of F, we solve the system

$$\begin{cases} F_x = y + 2\lambda x = 0 \\ F_y = x + 2\lambda y = 0 \\ F_\lambda = x^2 + y^2 - 16 = 0 \end{cases}$$

Solving the first equation for λ and substituting this value into the second

equation yields $x - 2\left(\dfrac{y}{2x}\right)y = 0,$ or $x^2 = y^2$. Substituting the last equation into

the third equation in the system, yields $x^2 + x^2 - 16 = 0$, or $x^2 = 8$, that is,
$x = \pm 2\sqrt{2}$. The corresponding values of y are $y = \pm 2\sqrt{2}$. Therefore the critical
points of F are $(-2\sqrt{2}, -2\sqrt{2}), (-2\sqrt{2}, 2\sqrt{2}), (2\sqrt{2}, -2\sqrt{2})(2\sqrt{2}, 2\sqrt{2})$.
Evaluating f at each of these values, we find that $f(-2\sqrt{2}, 2\sqrt{2}) = -8$ and
$f(2\sqrt{2}, -2\sqrt{2}) = -8$ are relative minimum values and $f(-2\sqrt{2}, -2\sqrt{2}) = 8$ and
$f(2\sqrt{2}, 2\sqrt{2}) = 8$, are relative maximum values.

12. Form the Lagrangian function $F(x,y,\lambda) = e^{xy} + \lambda(x^2 + y^2 - 8)$ and solve the system

$$\begin{cases} F_x = ye^{xy} - 2\lambda x = 0 \\ F_y = xe^{xy} - 2\lambda y = 0 \\ F_\lambda = x^2 + y^2 - 8 = 0. \end{cases}$$

Multiplying the first and second equations by x and y, respectively, and
subtracting the resulting equations, we obtain $2\lambda(x^2 - y^2) = 0$. This gives $\lambda = 0$, or

$y = \pm x$. But $\lambda \ne 0$, otherwise $x = y = 0$ and the third equation is not satisfied. If $y = \pm x$, then $x^2 + x^2 - 8 = 0$ or $x = \pm 2$. Therefore, the points $(-2,2)$, $(-2,-2)$, $(2,-2)$, and $(2,2)$ give rise to extrema of f. The maximum of f is e^4 and the minimum is e^{-4}.

13. We form the Lagrangian function $F(x,y,\lambda) = xy^2 + \lambda(x^2 + y^2 - 1)$. Next, we solve the system

$$\begin{cases} F_x = \quad y^2 + 2x\lambda = 0 \\ F_y = 2xy + 2y\lambda = 0 \\ F_\lambda = x^2 + y^2 - 1 = 0 \end{cases}.$$

We find that $x = \pm\sqrt{3}/3$ and $y = \pm\sqrt{6}/3$ and $x = \pm 1$, $y = 0$ Evaluating f at each of the critical points $(-\frac{\sqrt{3}}{3}, -\frac{\sqrt{6}}{3})$, $(-\frac{\sqrt{3}}{3}, \frac{\sqrt{6}}{3})(\frac{\sqrt{3}}{3}, -\frac{\sqrt{6}}{3})(\frac{\sqrt{3}}{3}, \frac{\sqrt{6}}{3})$,$(-1,0)$, and $(1,0)$, we find that $f(-\frac{\sqrt{3}}{3}, -\frac{\sqrt{6}}{3}) = -\frac{2\sqrt{3}}{9}$ and $f(-\frac{\sqrt{3}}{3}, \frac{\sqrt{6}}{3}) = -\frac{2\sqrt{3}}{9}$ are relative minimum values and $f(\frac{\sqrt{3}}{3}, -\frac{\sqrt{6}}{3}) = \frac{2\sqrt{3}}{9}$ and $f(\frac{\sqrt{3}}{3}, \frac{\sqrt{6}}{3}) = \frac{2\sqrt{3}}{9}$ are relative maximum values.

14. We form the Lagrangian function $F(x,y,z,\lambda) = xyz + \lambda(2x + 2y + z - 84)$. Then, we solve the system

$$\begin{cases} F_x = yz + 2\lambda = 0 \\ F_y = xz + 2\lambda = 0 \\ F_z = xy + \lambda \quad = 0 \\ F_\lambda = 2x + 2y + z - 84 = 0. \end{cases}$$

From the third equation, we find that $\lambda = -xy$. Then

$$\begin{cases} yz - 2xy = 0 \\ xz - 2xy = 0 \\ yz - \quad xz = 0 \end{cases}$$

which implies that $z = 0$ or $y = x$. If $x = 0$, $\lambda = 0$ and $xy = 0$, then $x = 0$ or $y = 0$. If $z = 0$ and $x = 0$, then $y = 42$. If $x = 0$, $y = 0$, then $x = 42$. Thus, the relative minimum values of F are $F(0, 42, 0)$ and $F(42, 0, 0)$. Next, if $y = x$ then $x^2 = -\lambda$ and $xz - 2x^2 = 0$, $x(z - 2x) = 0$, which implies that $z = 2x$ or $x = 0$. But, if $x = 0$, then $y = 42$ and $z = 0$ as above. Therefore, $z = 2x$ and $2x + 2x + 2x = 84$, or $x = \frac{84}{6} = 14 = y$. Therefore, the required maximum of F is

$$F(14, 14, 28) = 5488.$$

15 Form the Lagrangian function $F(x,y,z,\lambda) = x^2 + y^2 + z^2 + \lambda(3x + 2y + z - 6)$. We solve the system

$$\begin{cases} F_x = 2x + 3\lambda = 0 \\ F_y = 2y + 2\lambda = 0 \\ F_z = 2x + \lambda = 0 \\ F_\lambda = 3x + 2y + z - 6 = 0. \end{cases}$$

The third equation give $\lambda = -2z$. Substituting into the first two equations gives

$$\begin{cases} 2x - 6z = 0 \\ 2y - 4z = 0. \end{cases}$$

So $x = 3z$ and $y = 2z$. Substituting into the third equation yields $9z + 4z + z - 6 = 0$, or $z = 3/7$. Therefore, $x = 9/7$ and $y = 6/7$. Therefore, $f(\frac{9}{7}, \frac{6}{7}, \frac{3}{7}) = \frac{18}{7}$ is the minimum value of F.

16. Form the Lagrangian $F(x,y,z,\lambda) = x + 2y - 3z + \lambda(4x^2 + y^2 - z)$. Next, we solve the system

$$\begin{cases} F_x = 1 + 8\lambda x = 0 \\ F_y = 2 + 2\lambda y = 0 \\ F_z = -3 - \lambda = 0 \\ F_\lambda = 4x^2 + y^2 - z = 0 \end{cases}$$

From the third equation, we find $\lambda = -3$. Substituting into the first two equations, we obtain $1 - 24x = 0$ or $x = 1/24$ and $2 - 6y = 0$ or $y = 1/3$. Substituting into the third equation gives $4(\frac{1}{24})^2 + \frac{1}{9} - z = 0$, or $z \approx 0.118$. So $f(\frac{1}{24}, \frac{1}{3}, \frac{17}{144}) = \frac{17}{48} \approx 0.35$ is the maximum value of F.

17. We want to maximize P subject to the constraint $x + y = 200$. The Lagrangian function is

$$F(x, y, \lambda) = -0.2x^2 - 0.25y^2 - 0.2xy + 100x + 90y - 4000 + \lambda(x + y - 200).$$

Next, we solve

$$\begin{cases} F_x = -0.4x - 0.2y + 100 + \lambda = 0 \\ F_y = -0.5y - 0.2x + 90 + \lambda = 0 \\ F_\lambda = x + y - 200 = 0. \end{cases}$$

Subtracting the first equation from the second yields
$$0.2x - 0.3y - 10 = 0, \text{ or } 2x - 3y - 100 = 0.$$

Multiplying the third equation in the system by 2 and subtracting the resulting equation from the last equation, we find $-5y + 300 = 0$ or $y = 60$. So $x = 140$ and the company should make 140 finished and 60 unfinished units.

18. We want to maximize the function $P(x,y)$ subject to the constraint $x + y = 400$.
We form the Lagrangian function
$F(x,y,\lambda) = -0.005x^2 - 0.003y^2 - 0.002xy + 14x + 12y - 200 + \lambda(x + y - 400)$.
To find the critical points of F, we solve the system
$$\begin{cases} F_x = -0.01x - 0.002y + 14 + \lambda = 0 \\ F_y = -.006y - 0.002x + 12 + \lambda = 0 \\ F_\lambda = x + y - 400 = 0 \end{cases}$$
Solving the first equation for λ, we obtain $\lambda = 0.01x + 0.02y - 14$ which, upon substitution into the second equation, yields
$$-0.006y - 0.002x + 12 + 0.01x + 0.002y - 14 = 0$$
$$0.008x - 0.004y - 2 = 0$$
or $$y = 2x - 500.$$
Substituting this value of y into the third equation in the system gives
$$x + 2x - 500 - 400 = 0 \text{ or } x = 300 \text{ and so } y = 100.$$
Thus, the company should publish 100 deluxe and 300 standard editions.

19. Suppose each of the sides made of pine board is x feet long and those of steel are y feet long. Then $xy = 800$. The cost is $C = 12x + 3y$ and is to be minimized subject to the condition $xy = 800$. We form the Lagrangian function
$$F(x,y,\lambda) = 12x + 3y + \lambda(xy - 800).$$
We solve the system
$$\begin{cases} F_x = 12 + \lambda y = 0 \\ F_y = 3 + \lambda x = 0 \\ F_\lambda = xy - 800 = 0. \end{cases}$$
Multiplying the first equation by x and the second equation by y and subtracting the resulting equations, we obtain $12x - 3y = 0$, or $y = 4x$. Substituting this into the third equation of the system, we obtain
$$4x^2 - 800 = 0, \text{ or } x = \pm\sqrt{200} = \pm 10\sqrt{2}.$$
Since x must be positive, we take $x = 10\sqrt{2}$. So $y = 40\sqrt{2}$ So the dimensions are approximately 14 14ft by 56.56 ft.

20. $V = \pi r^2 \ell$. The constraint is $2\pi r + \ell = 108$ so $g(r, \ell) = 2\pi r + \ell - 108$.
The Lagrange function is $F(r, \ell, \lambda) = \pi r^2 \ell + \lambda(2\pi + \ell - 108)$. Set
$$F_r = 2\pi r \ell + 2\pi \lambda = 0$$
$$F_\ell = \pi r^2 + \lambda = 0$$
$$F_\lambda = 2\pi r + \ell - 108 = 0$$
The second equation gives $\lambda = -\pi r^2$. Substituting into the first equation gives
$$2\pi r \ell + 2\pi(-\pi r^2) = 0; \quad 2\pi r(\ell - \pi r) = 0;$$
Since $r \neq 0$, we have $\ell = \pi r$, which when substituted into the third equation
gives $2\pi r + \pi r - 108 = 0$; $3\pi r = 108$; $r = \frac{108}{3\pi} = \frac{36}{\pi}$. Therefore, $\ell = \pi\left(\frac{36}{\pi}\right) = 36$, or
36" The volume is $\pi r^2 \ell = \pi \left(\frac{36}{\pi}\right)^2 (36) = \frac{46{,}656}{\pi}$, or $\frac{46{,}656}{\pi}$ in^3

21. We want to minimize the function $C(r,h)$ subject to the constraint $\pi r^2 h - 64 = 0$.
We form the Lagrangian function $F(r,h,\lambda) = 8\pi rh + 6\pi r^2 - \lambda(\pi r^2 h - 64)$. Then we
solve the system
$$\begin{cases} F_r = 8\pi h + 12\pi r - 2\lambda \pi rh = 0 \\ F_h = 8\pi r - \lambda r^2 = 0 \\ F_\lambda = \pi r^2 h - 64 = 0 \end{cases}$$
Solving the second equation for λ yields $\lambda = 8/r$, which when substituted into
the first equation yields
$$8\pi h + 12\pi r - 2\pi rh\left(\tfrac{8}{r}\right) = 0$$
$$12\pi r = 8\pi h$$
$$h = \tfrac{3r}{2}.$$
Substituting this value of h into the third equation of the system, we find
$$3r^2\left(\tfrac{3r}{2}\right) = 64, \quad r^3 = \frac{128}{3\pi}, \text{ or } r = \frac{4}{3}\sqrt[3]{\frac{18}{\pi}} \text{ and } h = 2\sqrt[3]{\frac{18}{\pi}}.$$

22. Refer to the following figure.

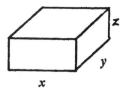

We form the Lagrangian function $F(x,y,\lambda) = xyz + \lambda(3xy + 2xz + 2yz - 36)$. Then,
we solve the system

$$\begin{cases} F_x = yz + 3\lambda y + 2\lambda z = 0 \\ F_y = xz + 3\lambda x + 2\lambda z = 0 \\ F_z = xy + 2\lambda x + 2\lambda y = 0 \\ F_\lambda = 3xy + 2xz + 2yz - 36 = 0 \end{cases}$$

Multiplying the first, second, and third equation by x, y, and z, respectively, we obtain

$$\begin{cases} xyz + 3\lambda xy + 2\lambda xz = 0 \\ xyz + 3\lambda xy + 2\lambda yz = 0 \\ xyz + 2\lambda xz + 2\lambda yz = 0. \end{cases}$$

Subtracting the second equation from the first and the third equation from the second, yields

$$\begin{cases} 2\lambda(x-y)z = 0 \\ \lambda x(3y - 2z) = 0. \end{cases}$$

Solving this system, we find that $x = y$ and $x = 3/2y$. Substituting these values into the third equation, we find that

$$3y^2 + 2y(\tfrac{3}{2})y + 2y(\tfrac{3}{2}) - 36 = 0$$

and $y = \pm 2$. We reject the negative root, and find that $x = 2$, $y = 2$, and $z = 3$ provides the desired relative maximum and the dimensions are 2' $\times$ 2' $\times$ 3'.

23. Let the box have dimensions x' by y' by z'. Then $xyz = 4$. We want to minimize
$$C = 2xz + 2yz + \tfrac{3}{2}(2xy) = 2xz + 2yz + 3xy.$$

Form the Lagrangian function
$$F(x,y,z,\lambda) = 2xz + 2yz + 3xy + \lambda(xyz - 4).$$

Next, we solve the system

$$\begin{cases} F_x = 2z + 3y + \lambda yz = 0 \\ F_y = 2z + 3x + \lambda xz = 0 \\ F_z = 2x + 2y + \lambda xy = 0 \\ F_\lambda = xyz - 4 = 0. \end{cases}$$

Multiplying the first, second, and third equations by x, y, and z, respectively, we have

$$\begin{cases} 2xz + 3xy + \lambda xyz = 0 \\ 2yz + 3xy + \lambda xyz = 0 \\ 2xz + 2yz + \lambda xyz = 0. \end{cases}$$

8 Calculus of Several Variables

The first two equations imply that $2z(x - y) = 0$. Since $z \neq 0$, we see that $x = y$.
The second and third equations imply that $x(3y - 2z) = 0$ or $x = (3/2)y$.
Substituting these values into the fourth equation in the system, we find

$$y^2(\tfrac{3}{2}y) = 4 \quad \text{or} \quad y^3 = \tfrac{8}{3} \quad \text{Therefore,} \quad y = \frac{2}{3^{1/3}} = \frac{2}{3}\sqrt[3]{9} \quad \text{and} \quad x = \frac{2}{3}\sqrt[3]{9}, \quad \text{and} \quad z = \sqrt[3]{9}$$

So the dimensions are $\dfrac{2}{3}\sqrt[3]{9} \times \dfrac{2}{3}\sqrt[3]{9} \times \sqrt[3]{9}$.

24. We want to maximize $f(x,y) = 90x^{1/4}y^{3/4}$ subject to $x + y = 60{,}000$. We form the
Lagrangian function $F(x,y,\lambda) = 90x^{1/4}y^{3/4} + \lambda(x + y - 60{,}000)$. Now set

$$\begin{cases} F_x = \tfrac{45}{2}x^{-3/4}y^{3/4} + \lambda = 0 \\ F_y = \tfrac{135}{2}x^{1/4}y^{-1/4} + \lambda = 0 \\ F_\lambda = x + y - 60{,}000 = 0. \end{cases}$$

Eliminating λ in the first two equations gives

$$\frac{45}{2}\left(\frac{y}{x}\right)^{3/4} - \frac{135}{2}\left(\frac{x}{y}\right)^{1/4} = 0$$

$$\frac{y}{x} - 3 = 0, \quad \text{or} \quad y = 3x.$$

Substituting this value into the third equation in the system, we find
$x + 3x = 60{,}000$ and $x = 15{,}000$ and $y = 45{,}000$. So the company should spend
$\$15{,}000$ on newspaper advertisements and $\$45{,}000$ on television advertisements.

25. We want to maximize $f(x,y) = 100x^{3/4}y^{1/4}$ subject to $100x + 200y = 200{,}000$.
Form the Lagrangian function
$$F(x,y,\lambda) = 100x^{3/4}y^{1/4} + \lambda(100x + 200y - 200{,}000).$$
We solve the system

$$\begin{cases} F_x = 75x^{-1/4}y^{1/4} + 100\lambda = 0 \\ F_y = 25x^{3/4}y^{-3/4} + 200\lambda = 0 \\ F_\lambda = 100x + 200y - 200{,}000 = 0. \end{cases}$$

The first two equations imply that $150x^{-1/4}y^{1/4} - 25x^{3/4}y^{-3/4} = 0$ or upon
multiplying by $x^{1/4}y^{3/4}$, $150y - 25x = 0$, which implies that $x = 6y$. Substituting
this value of x into the third equation of the system, we have
$$600y + 200y - 200{,}000 = 0$$
giving $y = 250$ and therefore $x = 1500$. So to maximize production, he should

spend 1500 units on labor and 250 units of capital.

26. We want to minimize $C = 2xy + 8xz + 6yz$ subject to $xyz = 12000$. Form the Lagrangian function $F(x,y,z,\lambda) = 2xy + 8xz + 6yz + \lambda(xyz - 12000)$. Next, we

solve the system
$$\begin{cases} F_x = 2y + 8z + \lambda yz = 0 \\ F_y = 2x + 6z + \lambda xz = 0 \\ F_z = 8x + 6y + 3xy = 0 \\ F_\lambda = xyz - 12,000 = 0. \end{cases}$$

Multiplying the first, second, and third equations by x, y, and z, we obtain
$$\begin{cases} 2xy + 8yz + 3xyz = 0 \\ 2xy + 6yz + \lambda xyz = 0 \\ 8xz + 6yz + \lambda xyz = 0. \end{cases}$$

The first two equations imply that $z(8x - 6y) = 0$ or since $z \neq 0$, we have $x = (3/4)y$. The second and third equations imply that $x(8z - 2y) = 0$ or $x = (1/4)y$. Substituting these values into the third equation of the system, we have $(\frac{3}{4}y)(y)(\frac{1}{4}y) = 12,000$ or $y^3 = 64,000$, or $y = 40$. Therefore, $x = 30$ and $z = 10$. So the heating cost is $C = 2(30)(40) + 8(30)(10) + 6(40)(10) = 7200$, or $7200 as obtained earlier.

27. False. See Example 1, Section 8.5. 28. False. See Example 1, Section 8.5.

8.6 CONCEPT QUESTIONS, page 604

1. It gives the volume of the solid region bounded above by the graph of f and below by the region R.

2. An iterated integral is a single integral such as $\displaystyle\int_a^b f(x,y)\,dx$, where we think of y as a constant.
$$\iint\limits_R f(x,y)\,dA = \int_c^d \left[\int_a^b f(x,y)\,dx \right] dy$$

3. $\displaystyle\iint\limits_R f(x,y)\,dA = \int_a^b \left[\int_{g_1(x)}^{g_2(x)} f(x,y)\,dy \right] dx$

4. $\displaystyle\iint\limits_R f(x,y)\,dA = \int_c^d \left[\int_{h_1(y)}^{h_2(y)} f(x,y)\,dx \right] dy$

5. The average value is $\dfrac{\displaystyle\iint_R f(x,y)\,dA}{\displaystyle\iint_R dA}$

EXERCISES 8.6, page 604

1. $\displaystyle\int_1^2\int_0^1 (y+2x)\,dy\,dx = \int_1^2 \tfrac{1}{2}y^2 + 2xy\Big|_{y=0}^{y=1}\,dx = \int_1^2 (\tfrac{1}{2}+2x)\,dx = \tfrac{1}{2}x + x^2\Big|_1^2 = 5 - \tfrac{3}{2} = \tfrac{7}{2}$

2. $\displaystyle\int_0^2\int_{-1}^2 (x+2y)\,dx\,dy = \int_0^2 \tfrac{1}{2}x^2 + 2xy\Big|_{-1}^2\,dy = \int_0^2 [(2+4y)-(\tfrac{1}{2}-2y)]\,dy = \int_0^2 (\tfrac{3}{2}+6y)\,dy$

$$= (\tfrac{3}{2}y + 3y^2)\Big|_0^2 = 3 + 12 = 15.$$

3. $\displaystyle\int_{-1}^1\int_0^1 xy^2\,dy\,dx = \int_{-1}^1 \tfrac{1}{3}xy^3\Big|_0^1\,dx = \int_{-1}^1 \tfrac{1}{3}x\,dx = \tfrac{x^2}{6}\Big|_{-1}^1 = \tfrac{1}{6} - (\tfrac{1}{6}) = 0.$

4. $\displaystyle\int_0^1\int_0^2 (12xy^2 + 8y^3)\,dy\,dx = \int_0^1 4xy^3 + 2y^4\Big|_0^2\,dx = \int_0^1 (32x+32)\,dx = 16x^2 + 32x\Big|_0^1 = 48.$

5. $\displaystyle\int_{-1}^2\int_1^{e^3} \frac{x}{y}\,dy\,dx = \int_{-1}^2 x\ln y\Big|_1^{e^3}\,dx = \int_{-1}^2 x\ln e^3\,dx = \int_{-1}^2 3x\,dx = \tfrac{3}{2}x^2\Big|_{-1}^2$

$$= \tfrac{3}{2}(4) - \tfrac{3}{2}(1) = \tfrac{9}{2}.$$

6. $\displaystyle\int_0^1\int_{-2}^2 \frac{xy}{1+y^2}\,dx\,dy = \int_0^1 \frac{1}{2}\left(\frac{y}{1+y^2}\right)x^2\Big|_{x=-2}^{x=2}\,dy = \int_0^1 0\ dy = 0.$

7. $\displaystyle\int_{-2}^0\int_0^1 4xe^{2x^2+y}\,dx\,dy = \int_{-2}^0 e^{2x^2+y}\Big|_{x=0}^{x=1}\,dy = \int_{-2}^0 (e^{2+y}-e^y)\,dy = (e^{2+y}-e^y)\Big|_{-2}^0$

$$= [(e^2-1)-(e^0-e^{-2}) = e^2 - 2 + e^{-2} = (e^2-1)(1-e^{-2}).$$

8. $\displaystyle\int_0^1\int_1^2 \frac{y}{x^2}e^{y/x}\,dx\,dy = \int_0^1 -e^{y/x}\Big|_{x=1}^{x=2}\,dy = \int_0^1 (-e^{y/2}+e^y)\,dy = (-2e^{y/2}+e^y)\Big|_0^1$

$$= (-2e^{1/2}+e)-(-2+1) = -2e^{1/2}+e+1.$$

9. $\displaystyle\int_0^1\int_1^e \ln y\,dy\,dx = \int_0^1 y\ln y - y\Big|_{y=1}^{y=e}\,dx = \int_0^1 dx = 1.$

10. $\int_1^e \int_1^{e^2} \frac{\ln y}{x}\,dx\,dy = \int_1^e (\ln y)(\ln x)\Big|_{x=1}^{x=e^2}\,dy = \int_1^e 2\ln y\,dy = 2(y\ln y - y)\Big|_1^e$

$\qquad = 2[(e-e)-(-1)] = 2.$

11. $\int_0^1 \int_0^x (x+2y)\,dy\,dx = \int_0^1 (xy+y^2)\Big|_{y=0}^{y=x}\,dx = \int_0^1 2x^2\,dx = \tfrac{2}{3}x^3\Big|_0^1 = \tfrac{2}{3}.$

12. $\int_0^1 \int_0^x xy\,dy\,dx = \int_0^1 \tfrac{1}{2}xy^2\Big|_{y=0}^{y=x}\,dx = \int_0^1 \tfrac{1}{2}x^3\,dx = \tfrac{1}{8}x^4\Big|_0^1 = \tfrac{1}{8}.$

13. $\int_1^3 \int_0^{x+1} (2x+4y)\,dy\,dx = \int_1^3 2xy+2y^2\Big|_{y=0}^{y=x+1}\,dx = \int_1^3 [2x(x+1)+2(x+1)^2]\,dx$

$\qquad = \int_1^3 (4x^2+6x+2)\,dx = (\tfrac{4}{3}x^3+3x^2+2x)\Big|_1^3$

$\qquad = (36+27+6)-(\tfrac{4}{3}+3+2) = \tfrac{188}{3}.$

14. $\int_0^2 \int_{-1}^{1-y} (2-y)\,dx\,dy = \int_0^2 2x-yx\Big|_{x=-1}^{x=1-y}\,dy = \int_0^2 [2(1-y)-y(1-y)-(-2+y)]\,dy$

$\qquad = \int_0^2 4-4y+y^2\,dy = 4y-2y^2+\tfrac{1}{3}y^3\Big|_0^2 = 8-2(4)+\tfrac{1}{3}(8) = \tfrac{8}{3}.$

15. $\int_0^4 \int_0^{\sqrt{y}} (x+y)\,dx\,dy = \int_0^4 \tfrac{1}{2}x^2+xy\Big|_{x=0}^{x=\sqrt{y}}\,dy = \int_0^4 (\tfrac{1}{2}y+y^{3/2})\,dy$

$\qquad = (\tfrac{1}{4}y^2+\tfrac{2}{5}y^{5/2})\Big|_0^4 = 4+\tfrac{64}{5} = \tfrac{84}{5}.$

16. $\int_0^1 \int_{x^3}^{x^2} x^2y^2\,dy\,dx = \int_0^1 \tfrac{1}{3}x^2y^3\Big|_{y=x^3}^{y=x^2}\,dx = \int_0^1 \tfrac{1}{3}(x^8-x^{11})\,dx = \tfrac{1}{3}(\tfrac{1}{9}x^9-\tfrac{1}{12}x^{12})\Big|_0^1$

$\qquad = \tfrac{1}{3}(\tfrac{1}{9}-\tfrac{1}{12}) = \tfrac{1}{108}.$

17. $\int_0^2 \int_0^{\sqrt{4-y^2}} y\,dx\,dy = \int_0^2 xy\Big|_0^{\sqrt{4-y^2}}\,dy = \int_0^2 y\sqrt{4-y^2}\,dy = -\tfrac{1}{2}(\tfrac{2}{3})(4-y^2)^{3/2}\Big|_0^2$

$\qquad = \tfrac{1}{3}(4^{3/2}) = \tfrac{8}{3}$

18. $\int_0^1 \int_0^x \frac{y}{x^3+2}\,dy\,dx = \int_0^1 \frac{1}{2}\left(\frac{y^2}{x^3+2}\right)\Big|_0^x\,dx = \frac{1}{2}\int_0^1 \frac{x^2}{x^3+2}\,dx = \frac{1}{6}\ln(x^3+2)\Big|_0^1$

699

8 Calculus of Several Variables

$$= \tfrac{1}{6}(\ln 3 - \ln 2) = \tfrac{1}{6}\ln\tfrac{3}{2}.$$

19. $\displaystyle\int_0^1\int_0^x 2xe^y\,dy\,dx = \int_0^1 2xe^y\Big|_{y=0}^{y=x}dx = \int_0^1 (2xe^x - 2x)\,dx = 2(x-1)e^x - x^2\Big|_0^1 = (-1) + 2 = 1.$

20. $\displaystyle\int_0^1\int_y^{e^{2y}} 2x\,dx\,dy = \int_0^1 x^2\Big|_{x=y}^{x=e^{2y}}dy = \int_0^1 (e^{4y} - y^2)\,dy = (\tfrac{1}{4}e^{4y} - \tfrac{1}{3}y^3)\Big|_0^1$

$$= \tfrac{1}{4}e^4 - \tfrac{1}{3} - \tfrac{1}{4} = \tfrac{1}{12}(3e^4 - 7).$$

21. $\displaystyle\int_0^1\int_x^{\sqrt{x}} ye^x\,dy\,dx = -\int_0^1\int_{\sqrt{x}}^{x} ye^x\,dy\,dx = \int_0^1 -\tfrac{1}{2}y^2 e^x\Big|_{y=\sqrt{x}}^{y=x}dx = -\tfrac{1}{2}\int_0^1 (x^2 e^x - xe^x)\,dx$

$$= -\tfrac{1}{2}[x^2 e^x\Big|_0^1 - 2\int_0^1 xe^x\,dx - \int_0^1 xe^x\,dx] = -\tfrac{1}{2}[x^2 e^x\Big|_0^1 - 3\int_0^1 xe^x\,dx]$$

$$= -\tfrac{1}{2}[x^2 e^x - 3xe^x + 3e^x]\Big|_0^1 = -\tfrac{1}{2}[e - 3e + 3e - 3] = \tfrac{1}{2}(3 - e).$$

22. $\displaystyle\int_0^4\int_0^{\sqrt{y}} xe^{-y^2}\,dx\,dy = \int_0^4 \tfrac{1}{2}x^2 e^{-y^2}\Big|_0^{\sqrt{y}}dy = \tfrac{1}{2}\int_0^4 ye^{-y^2}\,dy = -\tfrac{1}{4}e^{-y^2}\Big|_0^4$

$$= -\tfrac{1}{4}(e^{-16} - 1) = \tfrac{1}{4}(1 - e^{-16}).$$

23. $\displaystyle\int_0^1\int_{2x}^2 e^{y^2}\,dy\,dx = \int_0^2\int_0^{y/2} e^{y^2}\,dx\,dy = \int_0^2 xe^{y^2}\Big|_{x=0}^{x=y/2}dy = \int_0^2 \tfrac{1}{2}ye^{y^2}\,dy$

$$= \tfrac{1}{4}e^{y^2}\Big|_0^2 = \tfrac{1}{4}(e^4 - 1).$$

24. $\displaystyle\int_0^{\ln x}\int_1^e y\,dx\,dy = \int_0^{\ln x} yx\Big|_1^e\,dy = \int_0^{\ln x}(e-1)y\,dy = (e-1)\tfrac{1}{2}y^2\Big|_0^{\ln x} = \tfrac{1}{2}(e-1)(\ln x)^2.$

25 $\displaystyle\int_0^2\int_{y/2}^1 ye^{x^3}\,dx\,dy = \int_0^1\int_0^{2x} ye^{x^3}\,dy\,dx = \int_0^1 \tfrac{1}{2}y^2 e^{x^3}\Big|_{y=0}^{y=2x}dx = \int_0^1 2x^2 e^{x^3}\,dx$

$$= \tfrac{2}{3}e^{x^3}\Big|_0^1 = \tfrac{2}{3}(e-1).$$

26. $\displaystyle V = \int_0^4\int_0^3 (4 - x + \tfrac{1}{2}y)\,dx\,dy = \int_0^4 (4x - \tfrac{1}{2}x^2 + \tfrac{1}{2}xy)\Big|_{x=0}^{x=3}dy$

$$= \int_0^4 (\tfrac{15}{2} + \tfrac{3}{2}y)\,dy = \tfrac{15}{2}y + \tfrac{3}{4}y^2\Big|_0^4 = 42, \quad \text{or 42 cu units.}$$

27. $V = \int_0^4 \int_0^3 (6-x)\, dy\, dx = \int_0^4 (6-x)y\Big|_{y=0}^{y=3}\, dx = 3\int_0^4 (6-x)\, dx$

$\qquad = 3(6x - \tfrac{1}{2}x^2)\Big|_0^4 = 3(24-8) = 48$, or 48 cu units.

28. $V = \int_0^2 \int_x^{4-x} 5\, dy\, dx = \int_0^2 5y\Big|_{y=x}^{y=4-x}\, dx = 5\int_0^2 (4-2x)\, dx = 5(4x - x^2)\Big|_0^2 = 20$

or 20 cu units.

29. $V = \int_0^2 \int_0^{3-(3/2)z} (6-2y-3z)\, dy\, dz = \int_0^2 6y - y^2 - 3yz\Big|_{y=0}^{y=3-(3/2)z}\, dz$

$\qquad = \int_0^2 [(6(3-\tfrac{3}{2}z) - (3-\tfrac{3}{2}z)^2 - 3(3-\tfrac{3}{2}z)z]\, dz$

$\qquad = -2(3-\tfrac{3}{2}z)^2 - \tfrac{2}{9}(3-\tfrac{3}{2}z)^3 - \tfrac{3}{2}z^2 + \tfrac{3}{2}z^3\Big|_0^2$

$\qquad = (-18+12) - (-18+6) = 6$, or 6 cu units.

30. $V = \int_0^2 \int_0^{4-x^2} 4\, dy\, dx = \int_0^2 4y\Big|_{y=0}^{y=4-x^2}\, dx = \int_0^2 4(4-x^2)\, dx = 4\int_0^2 (4-x^2)\, dx$

$\qquad = 4(4x - \tfrac{1}{3}x^3)\Big|_0^2 = \tfrac{64}{3}$, or $21\tfrac{1}{3}$ cu units.

31. $V = \int_0^1 \int_0^{-2x+2} (4-x^2-y^2)\, dy\, dx = \int_0^1 (4y - x^2 y - \tfrac{1}{3}y^3)\Big|_{y=0}^{y=2(1-x)}\, dx$

$\qquad = \int_0^1 [8(1-x) - 2x^2 + 2x^3 - \tfrac{8}{3}(1-x)^3]\, dx$

$\qquad = [(8x - 4x^2 - \tfrac{2}{3}x^3 + \tfrac{1}{2}x^4) + \tfrac{2}{3}(1-x)^4]\Big|_0^1$

$\qquad = (8 - 4 - \tfrac{2}{3} + \tfrac{1}{2}) - \tfrac{2}{3} = \tfrac{19}{6}$, or $\tfrac{19}{6}$ cu units.

32. $V = \int_0^1 \int_0^y \sqrt{1-y^2}\, dx\, dy = \int_0^1 x\sqrt{1-y^2}\Big|_{x=0}^{x=y}\, dy = \int_0^1 y\sqrt{1-y^2}\, dy$

$\qquad = (-\tfrac{1}{2})(\tfrac{2}{3})(1-y^2)^{3/2}\Big|_0^1 = \tfrac{1}{3}$, or $\tfrac{1}{3}$ cu units.

33. $V = \int_0^2 \int_0^2 5e^{-x-y}\, dx\, dy = \int_0^2 -5e^{-x-y}\Big|_{x=0}^{x=2}\, dy = \int_0^2 -5(e^{-2-y} - e^{-y})\, dy$

$\qquad = -5(-e^{-2-y} + e^{-y})\Big|_0^2 = -5(-e^{-4} + e^{-2}) + 5(-e^{-2} + 1) = 5(1 - 2e^{-2} + e^{-4})$ cu units.

34. $V = \int_0^1 \int_0^2 (4 - 2x - y) \, dy \, dx = \int_0^1 [4y - 2xy - \tfrac{1}{2} y^2]\Big|_{y=0}^{y=2} dx$

$= \int_0^1 (8 - 4x - 2) \, dx = \int_0^1 (6 - 4x) \, dx = 6x - 2x^2 \Big|_0^1 = 6 - 2 = 4$ cu units.

35 $V = \int_0^2 \int_0^{2x} (2x + y) \, dy \, dx = \int_0^2 2xy + \tfrac{1}{2} y^2 \Big|_0^{2x} dx = \int_0^2 (4x^2 + 2x^2) \, dx$

$= \int_0^2 6x^2 \, dx = 2x^3 \Big|_0^2 = 16$, or 16 cu units.

36. $V = \int_0^1 \int_0^2 (x^2 + y^2) \, dy \, dx = \int_0^1 x^2 y + \tfrac{1}{3} y^3 \Big|_{y=0}^{y=2} dx = \int_0^1 (2x^2 + \tfrac{8}{3}) \, dx$

$= \int_0^1 (\tfrac{2}{3} x^2 + \tfrac{8}{3}) \, dx = (\tfrac{2}{3} x^3 + \tfrac{8}{3} x)\Big|_0^1 = \tfrac{2}{3} + \tfrac{8}{3} = \tfrac{10}{3}$ cu units.

37 $V = \int_0^1 \int_0^{-x+1} e^{x+2y} \, dy \, dx = \int_0^1 \tfrac{1}{2} e^{x+2y} \Big|_{y=0}^{y=-x+1} dx = \tfrac{1}{2} \int_0^1 (e^{-x+2} - e^x) \, dx$

$= \tfrac{1}{2} (-e^{-x+2} - e^x)\Big|_0^1 = \tfrac{1}{2} (-e - e + e^2 + 1) = \tfrac{1}{2} (e^2 - 2e + 1) = \tfrac{1}{2} (e - 1)^2$ cu units.

38. $V = \int_0^2 \int_x^2 2xe^y \, dy \, dx = \int_0^2 2xe^y \Big|_{y=x}^{y=2} dx = \int_0^2 (2xe^2 - 2xe^x) \, dx$

$= e^2 x^2 - 2(x-1)e^x \Big|_0^2$ (Integrating by parts.)

$= 4e^2 - 2e^2 - 2 = 2(e^2 - 1)$ cu units.

39. $V = \int_0^4 \int_0^{\sqrt{x}} \frac{2y}{1+x^2} \, dy \, dx = \int_0^4 \frac{y^2}{1+x^2} \Big|_0^{\sqrt{x}} dx = \int_0^4 \frac{x}{1+x^2} \, dx$

$= \tfrac{1}{2} \ln(1 + x^2)\Big|_0^4 = \tfrac{1}{2} (\ln 17 - \ln 1) = \tfrac{1}{2} \ln 17$ cu units.

40. $V = \int_0^1 \int_{x^2}^x 2x^2 y \, dy \, dx = \int_0^1 x^2 y^2 \Big|_{y=x^2}^{y=x} dx = \int_0^1 (x^4 - x^6) \, dx = \tfrac{1}{5} - \tfrac{1}{7} = \tfrac{2}{35}$, or $\tfrac{2}{35}$ cu units.

41. $V = \int_0^4 \int_0^{\sqrt{16-x^2}} x \, dy \, dx = \int_0^4 xy \Big|_{y=0}^{y=\sqrt{16-x^2}} dx = \int_0^4 x(16 - x^2)^{1/2} \, dx$

$$= (-\tfrac{1}{2})(\tfrac{2}{3})(16-x^2)^{3/2}\Big|_0^4 = \tfrac{1}{3}(16)^{3/2} = \tfrac{64}{3}.$$

42. $A = \tfrac{1}{6}\int_0^3\int_0^2 6x^2 y^3\, dx\, dy = \int_0^3 \tfrac{1}{3}x^3 y^3\Big|_0^2 dy = \tfrac{8}{3}\int_0^3 y^3\, dy = \tfrac{2}{3}y^4\Big|_0^3 = 54.$

43 $A = \dfrac{1}{\tfrac{1}{2}}\int_0^1\int_0^x (x+2y)\,dy\,dx = 2\int_0^1 xy+y^2\Big|_0^x dx = 2\int_0^1 (x^2+x^2)\,dx = 4\int_0^1 x^2\,dx$

$\qquad = \tfrac{4x^3}{3}\Big|_0^1 = \tfrac{4}{3}.$

44. The area of R is $\tfrac{1}{2}(2)(1) = 1.$ Therefore, the average value of f is

$$\int_0^1\int_y^{2-y} xy\,dx\,dy = \int_0^1 \tfrac{1}{2}x^2 y\Big|_{x=y}^{x=2-y} dy = \int_0^1 \tfrac{1}{2}(2-y)^2 y - \tfrac{1}{2}y^3]\,dy$$

$$= \int_0^1 (2y-2y^2)\,dy = (y^2 - \tfrac{2}{3}y^3)\Big|_0^1 = \tfrac{1}{3}.$$

45. The area of R is $1/2$. The average value of f is

$$\frac{1}{1/2}\int_0^1\int_0^x e^{-x^2}\,dy\,dx = 2\int_0^1 e^{-x^2} y\Big|_{y=0}^{y=x} dx = 2\int_0^1 xe^{-x^2}\,dx = -e^{-x^2}\Big|_0^1 = -e^{-1}+1 = 1-\frac{1}{e}$$

46. The area of R is $1/2$. Therefore, the average value of f is

$$2\int_0^1\int_0^x xe^y\,dy\,dx = 2\int_0^1 xe^y\Big|_0^x dx = 2\int_0^1 (xe^x - x)\,dx = 2(xe^x - e^x - \tfrac{1}{2}x^2)\Big|_0^1$$

$$= 2(e-e-\tfrac{1}{2}+1) = 1.$$

47. The area of the region is, by elementary geometry, $[4 + \tfrac{1}{2}(2)(4)]$, or 8 sq units. Therefore, the required average value is

$$A = \tfrac{1}{8}\int_1^3\int_0^{2x} \ln x\,dy\,dx = \tfrac{1}{8}\int_1^3 (\ln x)y\Big|_0^{2x} dx = \tfrac{1}{4}\int_1^3 x\ln x\,dx$$

$$= \tfrac{1}{4}(\tfrac{x^2}{4})(2\ln x - 1)\Big|_1^3 \quad \text{(Integrating by parts)}$$

$$= \tfrac{9}{16}(2\ln 3 - 1) - \tfrac{1}{16}(-1) = \tfrac{1}{8}(9\ln 3 - 4).$$

48. The population is

$$2\int_0^5\int_{-2}^0 \frac{10{,}000e^y}{1+0.5x}\,dy\,dx = 20{,}000\int_0^5 \frac{e^y}{1+0.5x}\Big|_{y=-2}^{y=0} dx$$

$$= 20,000(1-e^{-2})\int_0^5 \frac{1}{1+0.5x}\,dx = 20,000(1-e^{-2})2\,\ln(1+0.5x)\Big|_0^5$$

$$= 40,000(1 - e^{-2})\,\ln 3.5 \approx 43,329.$$

49. The average population density inside R is $\dfrac{43,329}{20} \approx 2166$ people/sq mile.

50. By symmetry, it suffices to compute the population in the first quadrant. In the first quadrant, $f(x,y) = \dfrac{50,000xy}{(x^2+20)(y^2+36)}$. Therefore, the population in R is given by

$$\iint\limits_R f(x,y)\,dA = 4\int_0^{15}\left[\int_0^{20}\frac{50,000xy}{(x^2+20)(y^2+36)}\,dy\right]dx$$

$$= 4\int_0^{15}\left[\frac{50,000(x)(\frac{1}{2})\ln(y^2+36)}{(x^2+20)}\Bigg|_0^{20}\right]dx$$

$$= 100,000(\ln 436 - \ln 36)\int_0^{15}\frac{x}{x^2+20}\,dx$$

$$= 100,000(\ln 436 - \ln 36)(\tfrac{1}{2})\ln(x^2+20)\Big|_0^{15}$$

$$= 50,000(\ln 436 - \ln 36)(\ln 245 - \ln 20) \approx 312,439.08$$

or approximately 312,439 people.

51. The average weekly profit is

$$\frac{1}{(20)(20)}\int_{100}^{120}\int_{180}^{200}(-0.2x^2 - 0.25y^2 - 0.2xy + 100x + 90y - 4000)\,dx\,dy$$

$$= \frac{1}{400}\int_{100}^{120} -\tfrac{1}{15}x^3 - 0.25y^2x - 0.1x^2y + 50x^2 + 90xy - 4000x\Big|_{x=180}^{x=200}\,dy$$

$$= \frac{1}{400}\int_{100}^{120}(-144,533.33 - 5y^2 - 760y + 380,000 + 1800y - 80,000)\,dy$$

$$= \frac{1}{400}\int_{100}^{120}(155,466.67 - 5y^2 + 1040y)\,dy$$

$$= \frac{1}{400}(155,466.67y - \tfrac{5}{3}y^3 + 520y^2)\Big|_{100}^{120}$$

$$= \frac{1}{400}(3,109,333.40 - 1,213,333.30 + 2,288,000)$$

$$\approx 10,460 \text{, or } \$10,460/\text{wk.}$$

52. The average price is

$$\frac{1}{2}\int_0^1\int_0^2[200-10(x-\tfrac{1}{2})^2-15(y-1)^2]\,dy\,dx$$

$$=\frac{1}{2}\int_0^1[200y-10(x-\tfrac{1}{2})^2y-5(y-1)^3]\Big|_0^2\,dx$$

$$=\frac{1}{2}\int_0^1[400-20(x-\tfrac{1}{2})^2-5-5]\,dx$$

$$=\frac{1}{2}\int_0^1[390-20(x-\tfrac{1}{2})^2]\,dx=\frac{1}{2}[390x-\tfrac{20}{3}(x-\tfrac{1}{2})^3]\Big|_0^1$$

$$=\frac{1}{2}[390-\tfrac{20}{3}(\tfrac{1}{8})-\tfrac{20}{3}(\tfrac{1}{8})]\approx 194.17 \text{ or approximately } \$194 \text{ per sq ft.}$$

53. True. This result follows from the definition.

54. False. Let $f(x,y)=\dfrac{x}{y-2}$, $a=0$, $b=3$, $c=0$, and $d=1$. Then

$\displaystyle\iint_{R_1} f(x,y)\,dA$ is defined on $R_1=\{(x,y)\mid 0\le x\le 3, 0\le y\le 1\}$. But

$\displaystyle\iint_{R_2} f(x,y)\,dA$ is not defined on $R_2=\{(x,y)\mid 0\le x\le 1, 0\le y\le 3\}$, because

f is discontinuous on R_2 (where $y=2$).

55. True. $\displaystyle\iint_R g(x,y)\,dA$ gives the volume of the solid bounded above by the surface

$z=g(x,y)$. $\displaystyle\iint_R f(x,y)\,dA$ gives the volume of the solid bounded above by the

surface $z=f(x,y)$. Therefore,

$$\iint_R g(x,y)\,dA - \iint_R f(x,y)\,dA = \iint_R [g(x,y)-f(x,y)]\,dA$$

gives the volume of the solid bounded above by $z=g(x,y)$ and below by
$z=f(x,y)$.

56. True. The average value (AV) is given by

$$AV=\frac{\displaystyle\iint_R f(x,y)\,dA}{\displaystyle\iint_R dA} \quad\text{and so } AV\iint_R dA = \iint_R f(x,y)\,dA.$$

The quantity on the left-hand side is the volume of such a cylinder.

CHAPTER 8 CONCEPT REVIEW, page 608

1. xy; ordered pair; real number; $f(x,y)$
2. Independent; dependent; value   3. $z = f(x,y)$; f; surface
4. $f(x,y) = c$; level curve; level curves; c
5. Fixed number; x
6. Slope; $(a,b,f(a,b))$; x; b
7. $\leq$; (a,b); $\leq$; domain
8. Domain; $f_x(a,b) = 0$ and $f_y(a,b) = 0$; exist; candidate
9. Scatter; minimizing; least-squares; normal
10. $g(x,y) = 0$; $f(x,y) + \lambda g(x,y)$; $F_x = 0$, $F_y = 0$, $F_\lambda = 0$; extrema
11. Volume; solid
12. Iterated; $\int_3^5 \int_0^1 (2x + y^2)\, dx\, dy$

CHAPTER 8 REVIEW EXERCISES, page 609

1. $f(0,1) = 0$; $f(1,0) = 0$; $f(1,1) = \dfrac{1}{1+1} = \dfrac{1}{2}$.

    $f(0,0)$ does not exist because the point $(0,0)$ does not lie in the domain of f.

2. $f(1,1) = \dfrac{e}{1 + \ln 1} = e$; $f(1,2) = \dfrac{e^2}{1 + \ln 2}$; $f(2,1) = \dfrac{2e}{1 + \ln 2}$; .

    $f(1,0)$ does not exist because the point $(0,0)$ does not lie in the domain of f.

3. $h(1,1,0) = 1 + 1 = 2$; $h(-1,1,1) = -e - 1 = -(e + 1)$;
    $h(1,-1,1) = -e - 1 = -(e + 1)$.

4. The domain of f is the set of all ordered pairs (u,v) of real numbers such that
    $u \geq 0$ and $u \neq v$.

5. $D = \{(x,y) | y \neq -x\}$ 6. $D = \{(x,y) | x \leq 1, y \geq 0\}$

7. The domain of f is the set of all ordered triplets (x,y,z) of real numbers such that
    $z \geq 0$ and $x \neq 1$, $y \neq 1$, and $z \neq 1$.

8. $2x + 3y = z$

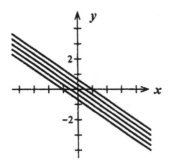

9. $z = y - x^2$

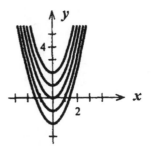

10. $z = \sqrt{x^2 + y^2}$

11. $z = e^{xy}$

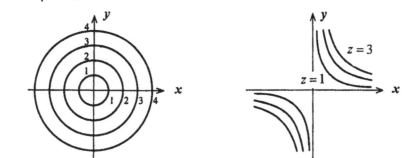

12. $f(x,y) = x^2 y^3 + 3xy^2 + \dfrac{x}{y}$; $f_x = 2xy^3 + 3y^2 + \dfrac{1}{y}$; $f_y = 3x^2 y^2 + 6xy - \dfrac{x}{y^2}$.

13. $f(x,y) = x\sqrt{y} + y\sqrt{x}$; $f_x = \sqrt{y} + \dfrac{y}{2\sqrt{x}}$; $f_y = \dfrac{x}{2\sqrt{y}} + \sqrt{x}$

14. $f(u,v) = \sqrt{uv^2 - 2u}$; $f_u = \tfrac{1}{2}(uv^2 - 2u)^{1/2}(v^2 - 2) = \dfrac{v^2 - 2}{2\sqrt{uv^2 - 2u}}$.

$f_v = \tfrac{1}{2}(uv^2 - 2u)^{-1/2}(2uv) = \dfrac{uv}{\sqrt{uv^2 - 2u}}$.

15. $f(x,y) = \dfrac{x-y}{y+2x}$. $f_x = \dfrac{(y+2x) - (x-y)(2)}{(y+2x)^2} = \dfrac{3y}{(y+2x)^2}$.

$f_y = \dfrac{(y+2x)(-1) - (x-y)}{(y+2x)^2} = \dfrac{-3x}{(y+2x)^2}$.

16. $g(x,y) = \dfrac{xy}{x^2+y^2}$;

$$g_x = \frac{(x^2+y^2)y - xy(2x)}{(x^2+y^2)^2} = \frac{y^3 - x^2 y}{(x^2+y^2)^2} = \frac{y(y^2 - x^2)}{(x^2+y^2)^2} = \frac{y(y-x)(y+x)}{(x^2+y^2)^2};$$

$$g_y = \frac{(x^2+y^2)x - xy(2y)}{(x^2+y^2)^2} = \frac{x(x^2 - y^2)}{(x^2+y^2)^2} = \frac{x(x-y)(x+y)}{(x^2+y^2)^2};$$

17. $h(x,y) = (2xy + 3y^2)^5; h_x = 10y(2xy + 3y^2)^4; h_y = 10(x+3y)(2xy + 3y^2)^4.$

18. $f(x,y) = (xe^y + 1)^{1/2}; f_x = \frac{1}{2}(xe^y + 1)^{-1/2} e^y = \dfrac{e^y}{2(xe^y + 1)^{1/2}};$

$$f_y = \tfrac{1}{2}(xe^y + 1)^{-1/2} xe^y = \frac{xe^y}{2(xe^y + 1)^{1/2}}$$

19. $f(x,y) = (x^2 + y^2)e^{x^2+y^2},$

$$f_x = 2xe^{x^2+y^2} + (x^2 + y^2)(2x)e^{x^2+y^2} = 2x(x^2 + y^2 + 1)e^{x^2+y^2}.$$

$$f_y = 2ye^{x^2+y^2} + (x^2 + y^2)(2y)e^{x^2+y^2} = 2y(x^2 + y^2 + 1)e^{x^2+y^2}.$$

20. $f(x,y) = \ln(1 + 2x^2 + 4y^4); \quad f_x = \dfrac{4x}{1 + 2x^2 + 4y^4}; \quad f_y = \dfrac{16y^3}{1 + 2x^2 + 4y^4}.$

21. $f(x,y) = \ln\left(1 + \dfrac{x^2}{y^2}\right). \quad f_x = \dfrac{\frac{2x}{y^2}}{1 + \frac{x^2}{y^2}} = \dfrac{2x}{x^2+y^2}; \quad f_y = \dfrac{-\frac{2x^2}{y^3}}{1 + \frac{x^2}{y^2}} = -\dfrac{2x^2}{y(x^2+y^2)}.$

22. $f(x,y) = x^3 - 2x^2 y + y^2 + x - 2y; \quad f_x = 3x^2 - 4xy + 1; \quad f_y = -2x^2 + 2y - 2;$
Therefore, $f_{xx} = 6x - 4y, \quad f_{xy} = f_{yx} = -4x, \quad f_{yy} = 2.$

23. $f(x,y) = x^4 + 2x^2 y^2 - y^4; \quad f_x = 4x^3 + 4xy^2; \quad f_y = 4x^2 y - 4y^3;$
$f_{xx} = 12x^2 + 4y^2, \quad f_{xy} = 8xy = f_{yx}, \quad f_{yy} = 4x^2 - 12y^2.$

24. $f_x = 3(2x^2 + 3y^2)^2(4x) = 12x(2x^2 + 3y^2)^2;$
$f_y = 3(2x^2 + 3y^2)^2(6y) = 18y(2x^2 + 3y^2)^2;$
$f_{xx} = 12(2x^2 + 3y^2)^2 + 12x(2)(2x^2 + 3y^2)(4x)$

$$= 12(2x^2 + 3y^2)^2[(2x^2 + 3y^2) + 8x^2] = 12(2x^2 + 3y^2)(10x^2 + 3y^2)$$

$$f_{xy} = 12x(2)(2x^2 + 3y^2)(6y) = 144xy(2x^2 + 3y^2)$$

$$f_{yy} = 18(2x^2 + 3y^2)^2 + 18y(2)(2x^2 + 3y^2)(6y)$$

$$= 18(2x^2 + 3y^2)[(2x^2 + 3y^2) + 12y^2] = 18(2x^2 + 3y^2)(2x^2 + 15y^2)$$

25. $\quad g(x,y) = \dfrac{x}{x+y^2}; \; g_x = \dfrac{(x+y^2)-x}{(x+y^2)^2} = \dfrac{y^2}{(x+y^2)^2}, \; g_y = \dfrac{-2xy}{(x+y^2)^2}$

Therefore, $g_{xx} = -2y^2(x+y^2)^{-3} = -\dfrac{2y^2}{(x+y^2)^3}$,

$$g_{yy} = \dfrac{(x+y^2)^2(-2x) + 2xy(2)(x+y^2)2y}{(x+y^2)^4} = \dfrac{2x(x^2+y^2)[-x-y^2+4y^2]}{(x+y^2)^4}$$

$$= \dfrac{2x(3y^2-x)}{(x+y^2)^3}.$$

and $\quad g_{xy} = \dfrac{(x+y^2)2y - y^2(2)(x+y^2)2y}{(x+y^2)^4} = \dfrac{2(x+y^2)[xy+y^3-2y^3]}{(x+y^2)^4}$

$$= \dfrac{2y(x-y^2)}{(x+y^2)^3} = g_{yx}.$$

26. $\quad g(x,y) = e^{x^2+y^2}; \; g_x = 2xe^{x^2+y^2}, \; g_y = 2ye^{x^2+y^2};$

$$g_{xx} = 2e^{x^2+y^2} + (2x)^2 e^{x^2+y^2} = 2(1+2x^2)e^{x^2+y^2}$$

$$g_{xy} = 4xye^{x^2+y^2} = g_{yx}; \; g_{yy} = 2e^{x^2+y^2} + (2y)^2 e^{x^2+y^2} = 2(1+2y^2)e^{x^2+y^2}$$

27 $\quad h(s,t) = \ln\left(\dfrac{s}{t}\right).$ Write $h(s,t) = \ln s - \ln t.$ Then $h_s = \dfrac{1}{s}, \; h_t = -\dfrac{1}{t}.$

Therefore, $h_{ss} = -\dfrac{1}{s^2}, \; h_{st} = h_{ts} = 0, \; h_{tt} = \dfrac{1}{t^2}.$

28. $\quad f(x,y,z) = x^3y^2z + xy^2z + 3xy - 4z; \; f_x(1,1,0) = 3x^2yz + y^2z + 3y\big|_{(1,1,0)} = 3;$

$\quad f_y(1,1,0) = 2x^3yz + 2xyz + 3x\big|_{(1,1,0)} = 3; \; f_z(1,1,0) = x^3y^2 + xy^2 - 4\big|_{(1,1,0)} = -2.$

29. $\quad f(x,y) = 2x^2 + y^2 - 8x - 6y + 4;$ To find the critical points of f, we solve the

system $\begin{cases} f_x = 4x - 8 = 0 \\ f_y = 2y - 6 = 0 \end{cases}$ obtaining $x = 2$ and $y = 3$. Therefore, the sole critical

point of f is $(2,3)$. Next, $f_{xx} = 4, f_{xy} = 0, f_{yy} = 2$. Therefore,
$$D = f_{xx}(2,3)f_{yy}(2,3) - f_{xy}(2,3)^2 = 8 > 0.$$
Since $f_{xx}(2,3) > 0$, we see that $f(2,3) = -13$ is a relative minimum.

30. $f(x,y) = x^2 + 3xy + y^2 - 10x - 20y + 12$. We solve the system
$$\begin{cases} f_x = 2x + 3y - 10 = 0 \\ f_y = 3x + 2y - 20 = 0 \end{cases} \quad \text{or} \quad \begin{cases} 2x + 3y = 10 \\ 3x + 2y = 20 \end{cases}$$
obtaining $x = 8$ and $y = -2$ so that $(8,-2)$ is the only critical point of f. Next, we compute $f_{xx} = 2, f_{xy} = 3$, and $f_{yy} = 2$.
Therefore, $D = f_{xx}(8,-2)f_{yy}(8,-2) - f_{xy}^2(8,-2) = (2)(2) - 3^2 = -5 < 0$.
Since $D < 0$, we see that $(8,-2)$ gives rise to a saddle point of f.

31. $f(x,y) = x^3 - 3xy + y^2$. We solve the system of equations $\begin{cases} f_x = 3x^2 - 3y = 0 \\ f_y = -3x + 2y = 0 \end{cases}$

obtaining $x^2 - y = 0$, or $y = x^2$. Then $-3x + 2x^2 = 0$, and $x(2x - 3) = 0$, and $x = 0$, or $x = 3/2$ and $y = 0$, or $y = 9/4$. Therefore, the critical points are $(0,0)$ and $(\frac{3}{2}, \frac{9}{4})$.
Next, $f_{xx} = 6x, f_{xy} = -3$, and $f_{yy} = 2$ and $D(x,y) = 12x - 9 = 3(4x - 3)$. Therefore, $D(0,0) = -9$ so $(0,0)$ is a saddle point. $D(\frac{3}{2}, \frac{9}{4}) = 3(6-3) = 9 > 0$, and

$f_{xx}(\frac{3}{2}, \frac{9}{4}) > 0$ and therefore, $f(\frac{3}{2}, \frac{9}{4}) = \frac{27}{8} - \frac{81}{8} + \frac{81}{16} = -\frac{27}{16}$ is the relative minimum value.

32. $f(x,y) = x^3 + y^2 - 4xy + 17x - 10y + 8$. To find the critical points of f, we solve the system
$$\begin{cases} f_x = 3x^2 - 4y + 17 = 0 \\ f_y = 2y - 4x - 10 = 0 \end{cases}$$
From the second equation, we have $y = 2x + 5$ which, when substituted into the first equation gives
$$3x^2 - 8x - 20 + 17 = 0$$
or $\quad 3x^2 - 8x - 3 = (3x + 1)(x - 3) = 0$.
The solutions are $x = -1/3$ or 3. Therefore, the critical points of f are $(-\frac{1}{3}, \frac{13}{3})$ and $(3,11)$. Next, we compute $f_{xx} = 6x, f_{xy} = -4, f_{yy} = 2$ and so

$$D(x,y) = f_{xx}f_{yy} - f_{xy}^2 = 12x - 16.$$

Since $D(-\tfrac{1}{3}, \tfrac{13}{3}) = -20 < 0$, we see that $(-\tfrac{1}{3}, \tfrac{13}{3})$ gives a saddle point. Since $D(3,11) = 20 > 0$ and $f_{xx}(3,11) = 18 > 0$, we see that $(3,11)$ affords a relative minimum of f.

33. $f(x,y) = f(x,y) = e^{2x^2+y^2}$. To find the critical points of f, we solve the system

$$\begin{cases} f_x = 4xe^{2x^2+y^2} = 0 \\ f_y = 2ye^{2x^2+y^2} = 0 \end{cases}$$

giving $(0,0)$ as the only critical point of f. Next,

$$f_{xx} = 4(e^{2x^2+y^2} + 4x^2 e^{2x^2+y^2}) = 4(1+4x^2)e^{2x^2+y^2}$$
$$f_{xy} = 8xye^{2x^2+y^2}$$
$$f_{yy} = 2(1+2y^2)e^{2x^2+y^2}.$$

Therefore, $D = f_{xx}(0,0)f_{yy}(0,0) - f_{xy}^2(0,0) = (4)(2) - 0 = 8 > 0$

and so $(0,0)$ gives a relative minimum of f since $f_{xx}(0,0) > 0$. The minimum value of f is $f(0,0) = e^0 = 1$.

34. We solve the system

$$\begin{cases} f_x = \dfrac{2x-2}{x^2+y^2-2x-2y+4} = 0 \\ f_y = \dfrac{2y-2}{x^2+y^2-2x-2y+4} = 0 \end{cases}$$

obtaining $x = 1$ and $y = 1$ and giving $(1,1)$ as the only critical point of f. Next, we compute

$$f_{xx} = \frac{(x^2+y^2-2x-2y+4)(2)-(2x-2)^2}{(x^2+y^2-2x-2y+4)^2}$$

$$f_{xy} = \frac{(x^2+y^2-2x-2y+4)(0)-(2x-2)(2y-2)}{(x^2+y^2-2x-2y+4)^2}$$

$$= \frac{-4(x-1)(y-1)}{(x^2+y^2-2x-2y+4)^2}$$

$$f_{yy} = \frac{(x^2+y^2-2x-2y+4)(2)-(2y-2)^2}{(x^2+y^2-2x-2y+4)^2}.$$

In particular, $f_{xx}(1,1) = \dfrac{2}{2^2} = \dfrac{1}{2}$, $f_{xy}(1,1) = 0$, and $f_{yy}(1,1) = 1$. Therefore,

8 Calculus of Several Variables

$D = f_{xx}(1,1)f_{yy}(1,1) - f_{xy}(1,1) = \frac{1}{2} > 0$ and since $f_{xx}(1,1) = 1 > 0$, we conclude that $(1,1)$ gives rise to a relative minimum of f. The relative minimum of f is $f(1,1) = \ln 2$.

35. We form the Lagrangian function $F(x,y,\lambda) = -3x^2 - y^2 + 2xy + \lambda(2x + y - 4)$.
Next, we solve the system
$$\begin{cases} F_x = 6x + 2y + 2\lambda = 0 \\ F_y = -2y + 2x + \lambda = 0. \\ F_\lambda = 2x + y - 4 = 0 \end{cases}$$
Multiplying the second equation by 2 and subtracting the resultant equation from the first equation yields $6y - 10x = 0$ so $y = 5x/3$. Substituting this value of y into the third equation of the system gives $2x + \frac{5}{3}x - 4 = 0$. So $x = \frac{12}{11}$ and consequently $y = \frac{20}{11}$. So $(\frac{12}{11}, \frac{20}{11})$ gives the maximum value for f subject to the given constraint.

36. We form the Lagrangian function
$$F(x,y,\lambda) = 2x^2 + 3y^2 - 6xy + 4x - 9y + 10 + \lambda(x + y - 1).$$
Next, we solve the system
$$\begin{cases} F_x = 4x - 6y + 4 + \lambda = 0 \\ F_y = 6y - 6x - 9 + \lambda = 0 \\ F_\lambda = x + y - 1 = 0. \end{cases}$$
Subtracting the second equation from the first, we obtain $10x - 12y + 13 = 0$. Adding this equation to the equation obtained by multiplying the third equation in the system by 12, we obtain $22x - 1 = 0$ or $x = \frac{1}{22}$. Therefore $y = \frac{21}{22}$ and so the point $(\frac{1}{22}, \frac{21}{22})$ gives the minimum value of f subject to the given constraint.

37. The Lagrangian function is $F(x,y,\lambda) = 2x - 3y + 1 + \lambda(2x^2 + 3y^2 - 125)$. Next, we solve the system of equations
$$\begin{cases} F_x = 2 + 4\lambda x = 0 \\ F_y = -3 + 6\lambda y = 0 \\ F_\lambda = 2x^2 + 3y^2 - 125 = 0. \end{cases}$$
Solving the first equation for x gives $x = -1/2\lambda$. The second equation gives $y = 1/2\lambda$. Substituting these values of x and y into the third equation gives

$$2\left(-\frac{1}{2\lambda}\right)^2 + 3\left(\frac{1}{2\lambda}\right)^2 - 125 = 0$$

$$\frac{1}{2\lambda^2} + \frac{3}{4\lambda^2} - 125 = 0$$

$$2 + 3 - 500\lambda^2 = 0, \text{ or } \lambda = \pm\frac{1}{10}.$$

Therefore, $x = \pm 5$ and $y = \pm 5$ and so the critical points of f are $(-5,5)$ and $(5,-5)$.
Next, we compute

$$f(-5,5) = 2(-5) - 3(5) + 1 = -24.$$
$$f(5,-5) = 2(5) - 3(-5) + 1 = 26.$$

So f has a maximum value of 26 at $(5,-5)$ and a minimum value of -24 at $(-5,5)$.

38. Form the Lagrangian function $F(x,y,\lambda) = e^{x-y} + \lambda(x^2 + y^2 - 1)$. Next, we solve the system

$$\begin{cases} F_x = e^{x-y} + 2\lambda x = 0 \\ F_y = -e^{x-y} + 2\lambda y = 0. \\ F_\lambda = x^2 + y^2 - 1 = 0 \end{cases}$$

Adding the first two equations, we obtain $2\lambda(x + y) = 0$. Since $\lambda \neq 0$, (otherwise we have $e^{x-y} = 0$ which is impossible), we find $y = -x$. Substituting this value of y into the third equation of the system gives $2x^2 - 1 = 0$, or $x = \pm \sqrt{2}/2$. The corresponding values of y are $\pm \sqrt{2}/2$. We see that $(-\sqrt{2}/2, \sqrt{2}/2)$ gives rise to a minimum of f with value $e^{-\sqrt{2}}$, whereas $(\sqrt{2}/2, -\sqrt{2}/2)$ gives rise to a maximum of f with value $e^{\sqrt{2}}$.

39. $\displaystyle\int_{-1}^{2}\int_{2}^{4}(3x - 2y)dx\,dy = \int_{-1}^{2}\frac{3}{2}x^2 - 2xy\Big|_{x=2}^{x=4}dy = \int_{-1}^{2}[(24 - 8y) - (6 - 4y)]dy$

$$= \int_{-1}^{2}(18 - 4y)\,dy = (18y - 2y^2)\Big|_{-1}^{2} = (36 - 8) - (-18 - 2) = 48.$$

40. $\displaystyle\int_{0}^{1}\int_{0}^{2}e^{-x-2y}\,dx\,dy = \int_{0}^{1}-e^{-x-2y}\Big|_{x=0}^{x=2}dy = \int_{0}^{1}(-e^{-2-2y} + e^{-2y})\,dy$

$$= \frac{1}{2}e^{-2-2y} - \frac{1}{2}e^{-2y}\Big|_{0}^{1} = (\tfrac{1}{2}e^{-4} - \tfrac{1}{2}e^{-2}) - (\tfrac{1}{2}e^{-2} - \tfrac{1}{2})$$

$$= \frac{1}{2}(e^{-4} - 2e^{-2} + 1) = \frac{1}{2}(e^{-2} - 1)^2.$$

41. $\int_0^1 \int_{x^3}^{x^2} 2x^2 y \, dy \, dx = \int_0^1 x^2 y^2 \Big|_{y=x^3}^{y=x^2} dx = \int_0^1 x^2 (x^4 - x^6) dx$

$$= \int_0^1 (x^6 - x^8) dx = \frac{x^7}{7} - \frac{x^9}{9} \Big|_0^1 = \frac{1}{7} - \frac{1}{9} = \frac{2}{63}.$$

42. $\int_1^2 \int_1^x \frac{y}{x} dy \, dx = \int_1^2 \frac{1}{x} \left(\frac{y^2}{2} \right) \Big|_{y=1}^{y=x} dx = \int_1^2 \left(\frac{1}{2} x - \frac{1}{2x} \right) dx = \left(\frac{1}{4} x^2 - \frac{1}{2} \ln x \right) \Big|_1^2$

$$= (1 - \tfrac{1}{2} \ln 2) - (\tfrac{1}{4}) = \tfrac{3}{4} - \tfrac{1}{2} \ln 2 = \tfrac{1}{4} (3 - 2 \ln 2).$$

43. $\int_0^2 \int_0^1 (4x^2 + y^2) dy \, dx = \int_0^2 4x^2 y + \tfrac{1}{3} y^3 \Big|_{y=0}^{y=1} dx = \int_0^2 (4x^2 + \tfrac{1}{3}) dx$

$$= (\tfrac{4}{3} x^3 + \tfrac{1}{3} x) \Big|_0^2 = \tfrac{32}{3} + \tfrac{2}{3} = \tfrac{34}{3}.$$

44. $V = \int_0^4 \int_{y/4}^{\sqrt{y}} (x + y) dx \, dy = \int_0^4 (\tfrac{1}{2} x^2 + xy) \Big|_{x=y/4}^{x=\sqrt{y}} = \int_0^4 (\tfrac{1}{2} y - y^{3/2} - \tfrac{1}{32} y^2 - \tfrac{1}{4} y^2) dy$

$$= (\tfrac{1}{4} y^2 + \tfrac{2}{5} y^{5/2} - \tfrac{3}{32} y^3) \Big|_0^4 = 4 + \tfrac{64}{5} - 6 = \tfrac{54}{5} = 10 \tfrac{4}{5} \text{ cu units.}$$

45. The area of R is

$$\int_0^2 \int_{x^2}^{2x} dy \, dx = \int_0^2 y \Big|_{y=x^2}^{y=2x} dx = \int_0^2 (2x - x^2) dx = (x^2 - \tfrac{1}{3} x^3) \Big|_0^2 = \tfrac{4}{3}.$$

Then

$$AV = \frac{1}{4/3} \int_0^2 \int_{x^2}^{2x} (xy + 1) dy \, dx = \frac{3}{4} \int_0^2 \frac{xy^2}{2} + y \Big|_{x^2}^{2x} dx$$

$$= \tfrac{3}{4} \int_0^2 (-\tfrac{1}{2} x^5 + 2x^3 - x^2 + 2x) dx = \tfrac{3}{4} (-\tfrac{1}{12} x^6 + \tfrac{1}{2} x^4 - \tfrac{1}{3} x^3 + x^2) \Big|_0^2$$

$$= \tfrac{3}{4} (-\tfrac{16}{3} + 8 - \tfrac{8}{3} + 4) = 3.$$

46. a. $R(x,y) = px + qy = -0.02x^2 - 0.2xy - 0.05y^2 + 80x + 60y.$

b. The domain of R is the set of all points satisfying

$$0.02x + 0.1y \le 80$$
$$0.1x + 0.05y \le 60$$
$$x \ge 0, y \ge 0$$

c. $R(100, 300) = -0.02(100)^2 - 0.2(100)(300) - 0.05(300)^2 + 80(100)^2 + 60(300)$
$= 15,300$
giving the revenue of \$15,300 realized from the sale of 100 and 300 units, respectively, of 16-speed and 10-speed electric blenders.

47. $f(p,q) = 900 - 9p - e^{0.4q}$; $g(p,q) = 20,000 - 3000q - 4p$.

We compute $\dfrac{\partial f}{\partial q} = -0.4e^{0.4q}$ and $\dfrac{\partial g}{\partial p} = -4$. Since $\dfrac{\partial f}{\partial q} < 0$ and $\dfrac{\partial g}{\partial p} < 0$

for all $p > 0$ and $q > 0$, we conclude that compact disc players and audio discs are complementary commodities.

48. We first summarize the data:

x	y	x^2	xy
1	369	1	369
3	390	9	1170
5	396	25	1980
7	420	49	2940
9	436	81	3924
25	2011	165	10383

The normal equations are
$$5b + 25m = 2011$$
$$25b + 165m = 10383$$
The solutions are $b = 361.2$ and $m = 8.2$. Therefore, the least-square line has equation $y = 8.2x + 361.2$.

b. The average daily viewing time in 2002 ($x = 11$) will be
$y = 8.2(11) + 361.2 = 451.4 = 7.52$, or 7 hr 31 min.

49. a. We first summarize the data.

x	y	x^2	xy
0	19.5	0	0
10	20	100	200
20	20.6	400	412
30	21.2	900	636
40	21.8	1600	872
50	22.4	2500	1120
150	125.5	5500	3240

The normal equations are
$$6b + 150m = 125.5$$
$$150b + 5500m = 3240$$
The solutions are $b = 19.45$ and $m = 0.0586$. Therefore, $y = 0.059x + 19.5$.
b. The life expectancy at 65 of a female in 2040 is
$$y = 0.059(40) + 19.5 = 21.86 \quad \text{or } 21.9 \text{ years.}$$
The datum gives a life expectancy of 21.8 years.
c. The life expectancy at 65 of a female in 2030 is
$$y = 0.059(30) + 19.5 = 21.27 \quad \text{or } 21.3 \text{ years.}$$
The data give a life expectancy of 21.2 years.

50. We want to maximize the function $R(x,y) = -x^2 - 0.5y^2 + xy + 8x + 3y + 20$.
To find the critical point of R, we solve the system
$$R_x = -2x + y + 8 = 0$$
$$R_y = -y + x + 3 = 0.$$

Adding the two equations, we obtain $-x + 11 = 0$, or $x = 11$. So $y = 14$.
Therefore, $(11,14)$ is a critical point of R. Next, we compute
$$R_{xx} = -2, \ R_{xy} = 1, \ R_{yy} = -1.$$
So $D(x,y) = R_{xx}R_{yy} - R_{xy}^2 = 2 - 1 = 1.$

In particular $D(11,14) = 1 > 0$. Since $R_{xx}(11,14) = -2 < 0$, we see that $(11,14)$ gives a relative maximum of R. The nature of the problem suggests that this in fact an absolute maximum. So the company should spend $11,000 on advertising and employ 14 agents in order to maximize its revenue.

51. Refer to the following diagram.

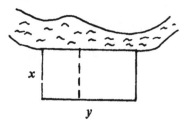

We want to minimize $C(x,y) = 3(2x) + 2(x) + 3y = 8x + 3y$ subject to $xy = 303{,}750$. The Lagrangian function is
$$F(x,y,\lambda) = 8x + 3y + \lambda(xy - 303{,}750).$$
Next, we solve the system
$$\begin{cases} F_x = 8 + \lambda y = 0 \\ F_y = 3 + \lambda x = 0 \\ F_\lambda = xy - 303{,}750 = 0 \end{cases}$$
Solving the first equation for y gives $y = -8/\lambda$. The second equation gives $x = -3/\lambda$. Substituting this value into the third equation gives
$$\left(-\frac{3}{\lambda}\right)\left(-\frac{8}{\lambda}\right) = 303{,}750 \quad \text{or} \quad \lambda^2 = \frac{24}{303{,}750} = \frac{4}{50{,}625},$$
or $\lambda = \pm\frac{2}{225}$. Therefore, $x = 337.5$ and $y = 900$ and so the required dimensions of the pasture are 337.5 yd by 900 yd.

52. We want to maximize the function Q subject to the constraint $x + y = 100$. We form the Lagrangian function $f(x,y,\lambda) = x^{3/4}y^{1/4} + \lambda(x + y - 100)$. To find the critical points of F, we solve
$$\begin{cases} F_x = \frac{3}{4}\left(\frac{y}{x}\right)^{1/4} + \lambda = 0 \\ F_y = \frac{1}{4}\left(\frac{x}{y}\right)^{3/4} + \lambda = 0 \\ F_\lambda = x + y - 100 = 0. \end{cases}$$

Solving the first equation for λ and substituting this value into the second equation yields $\frac{1}{4}\left(\frac{x}{y}\right)^{3/4} - \frac{3}{4}\left(\frac{y}{x}\right)^{1/4} = 0$, $\left(\frac{x}{y}\right)^{3/4} = 3\left(\frac{y}{x}\right)^{1/4}$, or $x = 3y$. Substituting this value of x into the third equation, we have $4y = 100$ or $y = 25$, and $x = 75$. Therefore, 75 units should be spent on labor and 25 units on capital.

CHAPTER 8 BEFORE MOVING ON, page 610

1. We have the constraints $x \geq 0$, $y \geq 0$, $x \neq 1$ and $y \neq 2$. Therefore the domain of f is
   $D = \{(x, y) | x \geq 0, \ y \geq 0; \ x \neq 1 \text{ and } y \neq 2\}$.

2. $f_x = 2xy + ye^{xy}$, $f_y = x^2 + xe^{xy}$, $f_{xx} = 2y + y^2e^{xy}$, $f_{xy} = 2x + (1 + xy)e^{xy} = f_{yx}$
   $f_{yy} = x \cdot xe^{xy} = x^2e^{xy}$

3.
$$\left. \begin{array}{l} f_x = 6x^2 + 6y = 6(x^2 - y^2) = 0 \\ f_y = 6y^2 - 6x = 6(y^2 - x) = 0 \end{array} \right\} \text{ gives } y = x^2 \text{ and } x = y^2 \quad \text{Therefore,}$$

$x = x^4$, $x^4 - x = x(x^3 - 1) = 0$ giving $x = 0$ or 1. The critical points of f are $(0, .0)$
and $(1,1)$. $f_{xx} = 12x$, $f_{xy} = -6$, $f_{yy} = 12y$.
$D(x, y) = 144x^2 + 144y^2 - 36$; $D(0,0) = -36 < 0$; and so $(0,0,-5)$ is a relative
minimum.
$f(x, y) = 2x^3 + 2y^3 - 6xy - 5$ and $f(1,1) = 2(1)^3 + 2(1)^3 - 6(1)(1) - 5 = -7$

4.

x	y	x^2	xy
0	2.9	0	0
1	5.1	1	5.1
2	6.8	4	13.6
3	8.8	9	26.4
5	13.2	25	66
11	36.8	39	113.1

The normal equations are
$$5b + 11m = 36.8$$
$$11b + 39m = 111.1$$
Solving, we find $m = 2.036$ and $b = 2.8797$. The least-squares equation is
$$y = 2.036x + 2.8797.$$

5. $F(x, y, \lambda) = 3x^2 + 3y^2 + 1 + \lambda(x + y - 1)$

$$F_x = 6x + \lambda = 0$$
$$F_y = 6y + \lambda = 0$$
$$F_\lambda = x + y - 1 = 0$$

Gives $\lambda = -6x - 6y$ so $y = x$. Substituting into the third equation gives $2x = 1$ or $x = \frac{1}{2}$ and $y = \frac{1}{2}$. Therefore, $(\frac{1}{2}, \frac{1}{2}, \frac{5}{2})$ is the required minimum.

6. $\displaystyle\iint\limits_{R}(1-xy)\,dA = \int_0^1 \int_{x^2}^x (1-xy)\,dy\,dx$

$$= \int_0^1 [(y - \tfrac{1}{2}xy^2)\big|_{x^2}^x]\,dx$$

$$= \int_0^1 [x - \tfrac{1}{2}x^3 - x^2 + \tfrac{1}{2}x^5]\,dx$$

$$= \tfrac{1}{2}x^2 - \tfrac{1}{8}x^4 - \tfrac{1}{3}x^3 + \tfrac{1}{12}x^6\big|_0^1$$

$$= \tfrac{1}{2} - \tfrac{1}{8} - \tfrac{1}{3} + \tfrac{1}{12} = \tfrac{1}{8}$$

EXPLORE & DISCUSS

Page 540

1. $f(y) = P(a,y)$ gives the total profit realized by the company through the sales of y units of the second product with the sales of the first product held fixed at a units. Next, $g(x) = P(x,b)$ gives the total profit realized by the company through the sales of x units of the first product when the sales of the second product are held fixed at b units.

Page 549

1. Since the sales of the first product are fixed at a units, the profit is just a function of y, the number of units of the second product produced and sold. This function is $f(y) = P(a,y)$. In order to determine the number of units of the second product to be produced and sold so as to maximize the profit, we should determine the value of y that maximizes the function f. In the second case, we maximize the function g with respect to x.

1. $$f_x(a,b) = \lim_{h \to 0} \frac{f(a+h,b) - f(a,b)}{h} = \lim_{h \to 0} \frac{g(a+h) - g(a)}{h} = g'(a)$$ and this justifies the

said procedure for calculating $f_x(a,b)$. Similarly, we let $h(y) = f(a,y)$ and compute

$$f_y(a,b) = \lim_{k \to 0} \frac{f(a,b+k) - f(a,b)}{k} = \lim_{k \to 0} \frac{h(b+k) - h(b)}{k} = h'(b),$$

and this suggests that we can compute $f_y(a,b)$ by finding the derivative $h'(b)$.
We give a geometric interpretation of the first process:
For the value of y fixed at b, the graph of $g(x) = f(x,b)$ is a curve C passing through the point $(a,b,f(a,b))$. The derivative $g'(a)$ gives the slope of the tangent line to C at this point and is precisely the value of $f_x(a,b)$.

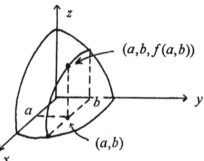

2. First, we let $b = 2$ and put $g(x) = f(x,2) = x^2(2^3) - 3x^2(2) + 2 = 2x^2 + 2$. Therefore, $g'(x) = 4x$ and $g'(1) = 4$. This give $f_x(1,2) = 4$. Next, letting $a = 1$ and
$$h(y) = f(1, y) = (1)y^3 - 3(1)y + 2 = y^3 - 3y + 2,$$
we find $h'(y) = 3y^2 - 3$ and $h'(2) = 3(4) - 3 = 9$.

Page 566

1. If f has a relative extremum at (a,b) and f is differentiable, then $f_x(a,b) = 0$ and $f_y(a,b) = 0$. But
$$f_x(a,b) = g'(x)\big|_{x=a} = g'(a) \quad \text{and} \quad f_y(a,b) = h'(y)\big|_{y=b} = h'(b).$$
Therefore, $g'(a) = 0$ and $h'(b) = 0$.

Page 566

1. Yes. The condition $f_{xx}(a,b) < 0$ in 2(a) can be replaced by the condition $f_{yy}(a,b) < 0$. This is because at a relative maximum the surface is "locally" concave downward.

This is true in the x–direction ($f_{xx}(a,b) < 0$) and must be true in the y–direction as well; that is, $f_{yy}(a,b) < 0$.

2. a. $f_x = 4x^3$ and $f_y = 4y^3$ so that $(0,0)$ is a critical point of f. Next, $f_{xx} = 12x^2$, $f_{xy} = 0$ and $f_{yy} = 12y^2$. Therefore,
$$D(x,y) = f_{xx} f_{yy} - f_{xy}^2 = 144x^2 y^2 - 0$$
and $\quad D(0,0) = 0$.

b. f has an absolute minimum at $(0,0)$ because $f(x,y) = x^4 + y^4 > 0$ for all $(x,y) \ne (0,0)$. This does not contradict the Second Derivative Test because the Second Derivative Test states that if $D(a,b) > 0$ at a critical point (a,b), then f has a relative extremum. It does not say that if f has a relative extremum at a critical point

Page 595

If we write $z = \sqrt{4 - x^2 - y^2} = f(x,y)$ we see that this equation is equivalent to
$$\left. \begin{array}{r} x^2 + y^2 + z^2 = 4 \\ z \ge 0 \end{array} \right\}$$
and so the integrand is the upper hemisphere with radius 2 , centered at $(0,0,0)$. therefore, the integral gives the volume of the hemisphere, and
$$\iint\limits_R \sqrt{4 - x^2 - y^2}\, dA = \tfrac{1}{2}\left[\tfrac{4}{3}\pi(2)^3\right] = \tfrac{16\pi}{3}$$
cubic units. [Note the volume of a sphere is $\tfrac{4}{3}\pi r^3$]

Page 599

1. $h_1(y) = y$ and $h_2(y) = \sqrt{y}$. Also, $c = 0$ and $d = 1$.

2. $\displaystyle \iint\limits_R f(x,y)\, dA = \int_0^1 \left[\int_y^{\sqrt{y}} xe^y\, dx \right] dy$

3. $\displaystyle \int_0^1 \left[\int_y^{\sqrt{y}} xe^y\, dx \right] dy = \int_0^1 \left[\tfrac{1}{2}x^2 e^y \Big|_y^{\sqrt{y}} \right] dy = \int_0^1 (\tfrac{1}{2} ye^y - \tfrac{1}{2} y^2 e^y)\, dy.$

    Then
$$\iint\limits_R f(x,y)\, dA = \tfrac{1}{2}\int_0^1 ye^y\, dy - \tfrac{1}{2} y^2 e^y\Big|_0^1 + \tfrac{1}{2}(2)\int_0^1 ye^y\, dy = \tfrac{3}{2}\int_0^1 ye^y\, dy - \tfrac{1}{2}e.$$

    Next $\displaystyle \iint\limits_R f(x,y)\, dA = \tfrac{3}{2}(y-1)e^y\Big|_0^1 - \tfrac{1}{2}e = \tfrac{3}{2} - \tfrac{1}{2}e = \tfrac{1}{2}(3-e)$

    as obtained in Example 3.

721   8 *Calculus of Several Variables*

4.   Clearly, viewing the region R as in Example 3, leads to an integral that is much easier to evaluate.

Page 600

1.   It certainly makes sense to define

$$\iint_R f(x,y)\,dA = \int_0^\infty \left[\int_0^\infty f(x,y)\,dx\right]dy = \int_0^\infty \left[\int_0^\infty f(x,y)\,dy\right]dx.$$

Then, using the definition of improper integrals of functions of one variable, we might define

$$\int_0^\infty \int_0^\infty f(x,y)\,dA = \lim_{N\to\infty}\int_0^N \left[\lim_{M\to\infty}\int_0^M f(x,y)\,dx\right]dy$$

$$= \lim_{m\to\infty}\int_0^M \left[\lim_{N\to\infty}\int_0^N f(x,y)\,dy\right]dx$$

provided the limits exist.

2.   Let D^c denote the plane region in the first quadrant outside the region R. Then the population outside the rectangular region is

$$4\iint_D f(x,y)\,dA - 4\iint_R f(x,y)\,dA$$

$$= 4\int_0^\infty \left[\int_0^\infty 10,000e^{-0.2x-0.1y}\,dx\right]dy - 680,438$$

$$= 4\int_0^\infty \left[\lim_{M\to\infty} 10,000e^{-0.2x-0.1y}\,dx\right]dy - 680,438$$

$$= 4\int_0^\infty \left[\lim_{M\to\infty} -\frac{10,000}{0.2}(e^{-0.2M-0.1y}\Big|_0^M\right]dy - 680,438$$

$$= 4\int_0^\infty \left[\lim_{M\to\infty} -50,000(e^{-0.2M-0.1y} - e^{-0.1y})\right]dy - 680,438$$

$$= 200,000\int_0^\infty e^{-0.1y}\,dy - 680,438 = \lim_{N\to\infty}\frac{200,000}{-0.1}e^{-0.1y}\Big|_0^N - 680,438$$

$$= \lim_{N\to\infty}(-2,000,000e^{-0.1N} + 2,000,000) - 680,438$$

$$= 2,000,000 - 680,438 = 1,319,562 \quad \text{or} \quad \$1,319,562.$$

Page 551

1. $g(x) = f(x,1) = \dfrac{e^{\sqrt{x}}}{(1+x)^{3/2}}$. The graph of g follows.

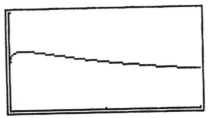

2 . $g'(1) = f_x(1,1) = -0.2402644393$

3. $h(y) = f(1,y) = \dfrac{e^{\sqrt{y}}}{(1+y^2)^{3/2}}$.

lThe graph of h follows.

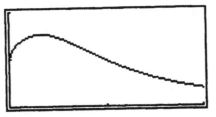

4. $h'(1) = f_y(1,1) = -0.961057757$. 41.
    $P(x,y) = -0.0005x^2 - 0.003y^2 - 0.002xy + 14x + 12y - 200$.
    $\Delta P \approx dP = (-0.001x - 0.002y + 14)dx + (-0.006y - 0.002x + 12)dy$
    With $x = 100$, $y = 1700$, $dx = 50$, and $dy = $ -50, we have
    $\Delta P \approx (-1 - 3.4 + 14)(50) + (-10.2 - 2 + 12)(-50) = 490$, or \$490.